Outlines of
Tudor and Stuart Plays

tectum

porticus

mimorum
ædes

orchestra

ingressus

proscænium

planities siue arena.

um tum fed ispari et structura, bestiarum conrectatio
ni destinatum, in quo multi vrsi, tauri, et stupenda
iar multudinis canes, districtib canti e septis aluntur; qui
ad

An Elizabethan Theatre

From a contemporary drawing of The Swan, c. 1595.

ABOUT THE AUTHOR

The late Professor Holzknecht received his doctorate from the University of Pennsylvania. For over thirty-one years he taught at the Universities of Louisville, Southern California, Iowa, and New York. At the time of his death he was Head of the Department of English at the Graduate School of New York University. Professor Holzknecht was a member of the Shakespeare Association, The Modern Language Association, and was Chairman of the College Conference on English in the Central Atlantic States. In addition to contributions to various scholarly journals in his field, Professor Holzknecht wrote and edited many books, including *Selected Plays of Shakespeare, Backgrounds of Shakespeare's Plays, Sixteenth-Century Prose,* and *Outlines of Shakespeare's Plays.*

A COMPOSITE OF FAVORITE CHARACTERS, 1662

Frontispiece to Kirkman's *The Wits*, a collection of abridged plays performed surreptitiously during the Commonwealth Period. Represented are: Falstaff and the Hostess from "The Bouncing Knight" (*1 King Henry IV*); Claus from "The Lame Commonwealth" (*Beggars' Bush*); M. Gaillard from the Duke of Newcastle's *The Variety*; Young Simpleton from *Simpleton the Smith*; Bartholomew Bubble from Cooke's *Greene's Tu Quoque*; and either Antonio or Dr. Alibius from *The Changeling*.

UNIVERSITY PAPERBACKS

Outlines of
TUDOR AND
STUART PLAYS
1497–1642

KARL J. HOLZKNECHT

Late Chairman, Department of English
Graduate School of Arts and Sciences
New York University

The Roaring Girl

New York

BARNES & NOBLE, INC.
PUBLISHERS BOOKSELLERS SINCE 1873

PREFACE

"Why, Sir," said Dr. Johnson, "if you were to read Richardson for the story, your impatience would be so much fretted that you would hang yourself. But you must read him for the sentiment, and consider the story as only giving occasion to the sentiment. . . . There is more knowledge of the heart in one letter of Richardson's, than in all *Tom Jones."*

Whatever may be the relative merits of the major novelists, it is apparent that a half-truth similar to this about Richardson has fairly general currency regarding the Elizabethan dramatists. Not even excluding Shakespeare, they are popularly supposed to have been careless of their plots or to have considered them as little more than a complicated necessary framework for their poetry, their philosophies of life, or their observations of human nature. Compared with what is generally believed to be the real flesh and blood of their plays, the skeletons are sometimes thought to be of secondary importance. Certainly the modern reader often has difficulty in following an Elizabethan story and is inclined to dismiss what he does not understand as of little import or significance.

Hence, this little volume of play synopses has three main purposes: (*a*) to demonstrate that far from being mean and insignificant, Elizabethan drama-plots on the whole are not impossibly or purposely intricate or poorly constructed; (*b*) to make clear that an ability to follow the plot is essential to an understanding of the play; and (*c*) to point out that with the plot clearly in mind the reader is better able to appreciate the beauty and the wit, the wisdom and the whimsey, the humor and the pathos—in short, that understanding of the great constants of human nature in both joy and sorrow which has made the best Elizabethan drama a lastingly relevant commentary on human life.

In no sense is this book a substitute for the dramas themselves, however; it is merely a device—like a collection of opera librettos—which will prove convenient, it is hoped, in familiarizing the reader beforehand with the stories of great plays he expects to read and so whet his interest in them; in clarifying what at first seems complex; and in reviewing for him the plots of plays he has previously read. Fully to appreciate and understand these dramas, he must read them himself in full; it is not likely that he will have an opportunity of seeing many of them come to life in the theatre.

In preparing these outlines the author has kept before him several definite principles and objectives. He has tried:

(*a*) To make the volume as representative as possible of the various types of drama from the time of the earliest secular play to the closing of the theatres. The first criterion of selection has been dramatic excellence, then historical or other significance. As far as possible the choice has been made independently; the plays here summarized represent no mere anthology canon. This book outlines nearly twice as many plays as are included in the most comprehensive anthology now obtainable, and it includes many plays which are seldom or never so reprinted.

(*b*) To tell, completely and smoothly, the story of each play, act by act. No episode essential to an understanding of the whole plot has been omitted and care has been taken that there shall be no broken story threads. In the interests of continuity and coherence, however, no effort has been made to preserve the order of events within an act for its own sake alone; scene divisions in Elizabethan plays seldom have any narrative significance. In the cases of plays which are divisible only into scenes the same principle of coherence has been followed. The warp and the woof of the narrative have been kept intact, and everything else made secondary to telling a good story.

(*c*) To reflect, as far as possible in a limited space, the dramatic art of the playwright by indicating his use of physical, social, and intellectual character-contrasts; of conflicts between individuals, groups, or ideologies; of parallel or contrasting story elements; of the relation of plot and sub-plot—in short, of all important dramatic patterns and devices. Elizabethans did not always construct their plays as do the moderns, but they are not, therefore, to be thought careless of their effects.

(*d*) To suggest—even in a brief synopsis—something of the flavor of the original. Hence, quotations from the plays have frequently been woven into the narrative, especially passages of beauty, vigor, or exceptional significance for which a particular drama is famous.

(*e*) To describe each major figure in the *dramatis personae*—and to a lesser extent the minor ones as well—largely by quoting the actual language of the play. Elizabethan authors seldom leave any doubt about the essential qualities of their personages; and a single vivid, colorful phrase from the dialogue often reveals more than would pages of more subjective character analysis. Care, of course, has been taken to select for these brief sketches only such passages as are really applicable to the persons and the play and to exclude remarks which are discolored by rage, hate, or similar bias. No character in any of these plays, no matter how insignificant he may be, has been named without some indication of his part in the action. Thus, the meaningless catalogues of mere names have been avoided, and whatever descriptions there were of the *dramatis personae* in the original have been supplemented from the author's own words.

(*f*) To rearrange the *dramatis personae* according to their dramatic significance without distinction of social rank or sex. Thus, characters whose destinies are bound up together are placed side by side; those which are obviously *foils,* or contrasts, or are otherwise related, are grouped together. Only tradition can justify the character listings in the average Elizabethan play without regard to dramatic importance but in strict accordance with social precedence, male and female.

(*g*) To supply short biographical sketches of the playwrights, brief critical estimates of their work, notes on sources, and bibliographical information about the earliest printings of these plays, the best editions not only of single dramas but also of the complete works of authors as well, and a list of the leading recent collections of Elizabethan plays in which individual works have been reprinted. In short, this volume should serve as a guide to the reader, who, having familiarized himself with the plots, wishes to go to the plays themselves. For such firsthand reading—to repeat—this book is no substitute.

Care has been taken to make the outlines themselves, the critical apparatus, and the bibliographical guide as accurate as possible. For biographical details the author has relied chiefly upon the *Dictionary of National Biography* and Sir Edmund Chambers' *The Elizabethan Stage* (1923), particularly Volume IV. For bibliographical matters he has consulted W. W. Greg's *A Bibliography of the English Printed Drama* (1939), only Part I of which, to 1616, has appeared; *A Short Title Catalogue of English Books* (1926); and *The Cambridge Bibliography of English Literature* (1941). For the dates of composition of individual plays—most of which are largely conjectural—he has depended upon Alfred Harbage's *Annals of English Drama* (1940), and upon Chambers.

The following collections are those referred to in the bibliographical notes, briefly by editors' names, unless otherwise indicated:

The Mermaid Series, London, 1887–1909.
  (Many volumes of selected plays by various editors; includes the work of Beaumont and Fletcher, Chapman, Dekker, Ford, Greene, Thomas Heywood, Jonson, Marlowe, Massinger, Middleton, Shirley, Tourneur, and Webster.)

The Temple Dramatists, London, Series I, 1896–1906; Series II, 1933— [Cited as TD].
  (Many volumes of single plays by various editors.)

The Belles Lettres Series, Boston, 1902–15.

(Many volumes of selected plays by various editors.)

Tudor Facsimile Texts, edited by J. S. Farmer, London, 1907–14.
[Cited as TFT].

(143 volumes of photolithographic facsimiles.)

The Malone Society Reprints, edited by W. W. Greg and others, London,
1907—   [Cited as MSR].

(Many volumes of facsimile reprints of single plays, with textual
introductions.)

TABLE OF CONTENTS

TABULATED BIBLIOGRAPHY OF STANDARD ANTHOLOGIES OF TUDOR AND STUART PLAYS

(See next four pages.)

The following list provides a key to the anthologies of Tudor and Stuart plays which are referred to by number on the four succeeding pages. Those available in paperbound editions are so indicated.

1. Adams, Joseph Quincy (ed.). *Chief Pre-Shakespearean Dramas.* Houghton Mifflin, 1924.

2. Baskervill, C. R., V. B. Heltzel, and A. H. Nethercot (eds.). *Elizabethan & Stuart Plays.* Holt, 1949.

3. Boas, Fred S. (ed.). *Five Pre-Shakespearean Comedies: Early Tudor Period.* Oxford, World's Classics, 1952.

4. Brooke, C. F. Tucker and N. B. Paradise (eds.). *English Drama, 1580–1642.* Heath, 1933.

5. Dunn, Esther Cloudman (introd. by), *Eight Famous Elizabethan Plays.* Random House, Modern Library College Editions, 1950. (Paperbound)

6. Ellis, Havelock (ed.). *John Ford (Five Plays).* Hill and Wang, Dramabooks, 1957. (Paperbound)

7. Gassner, John (introd. by). *Four Great Elizabethan Plays.* Bantam, 1960. (Paperbound)

8. Heilman, Robert B. (ed.). *An Anthology of English Drama Before Shakespeare.* (Holt,) Rinehart (& Winston), 1958. (Paperbound)

9. McIlwraith, A. K. (ed.). *Five Elizabethan Comedies.* Oxford, World's Classics, 1934.

10. ——— (ed.). *Five Elizabethan Tragedies.* Oxford, World's Classics, 1959.

11. ——— (ed.). *Five Stuart Tragedies.* Oxford, World's Classics, 1959.

12. Neilson, William A. (ed.). *The Chief Elizabethan Dramatists, Excluding Shakespeare.* Houghton Mifflin, 1939.

13. Parks, Edd. W. and R. C. Beatty (eds.). *The English Drama, An Anthology 900–1642.* Norton, 1935.

14. Spencer, Hazleton (ed.). *Elizabethan Plays.* Heath, 1933.

15. Thorndike, Ashley H. (ed.). *The Minor Elizabethan Drama,* Vol. I, *Pre-Shakespearean Tragedies.* Dutton, Everyman's Library, 1949.

16. ——— (ed.). *The Minor Elizabethan Drama,* Vol. II, *Pre-Shakespearean Comedies.* Dutton, Everyman's Library, 1949.

17. Wheeler, C. B. (ed.). *Six Plays by Contemporaries of Shakespeare.* Oxford, World's Classics, 1915.

QUICK REFERENCE TABLE TO STANDARD ANTHOLOGIES

Column numbers refer to key on preceding page.

TITLE OF PLAY	1	2	3	4	5	6	7	8	9	10	11	12	13	14	15	16	17
Fulgens and Lucrece			X														
The Pardoner and the Friar																	
The Four P's	X		X														
John John, Tyb, and Sir John	X												X				
The Play of the Weather	X																
Thersites																	
Ralph Roister Doister	X	X											X			X	
Gammer Gurton's Needle	X	X	X					X									
Jack Juggler																	
Gorboduc	X	X								X					X		
Supposes	X	X	X														
Cambises	X	X													X		
Alexander and Campaspe	X								X								
Endymion		X		X								X		X		X	
The Arraignment of Paris		X		X								X	X	X			
The Old Wives' Tale		X		X					X				X			X	
Mucedorus		X															
The Spanish Tragedy		X		X				X		X		X	X	X	X		
Tamburlaine (I)		X		X								X		X			

TITLE OF PLAY	1	2	3	4	5	6	7	8	9	10	11	12	13	14	15	16	17
Tamburlaine (II)	X																
Doctor Faustus		X		X	X		X	X				X	X	X			
The Jew of Malta				X								X	X	X			
Edward the Second		X		X								X	X	X			
George a Greene	X	X															
Friar Bacon and Friar Bungay		X		X				X	X			X	X	X		X	
James the Fourth																X	
Arden of Feversham		X								X					X		
Two Angry Women of Abington																	
The Parnassus Trilogy																	
The Merry Devil of Edmonton									X								
Old Fortunatus									X	X							
The Shoemakers' Holiday				X	X		X		X			X	X	X			X
The Honest Whore (I)		X										X		X			
The Honest Whore (II)												X		X			
Every Man in His Humor		X		X								X	X	X			
Sejanus, His Fall		X										X	X				
Volpone, or the Fox		X		X	X		X					X	X	X			
Epicoene				X													
The Alchemist		X		X								X		X			

Column numbers refer to key on preceding page.

TITLE OF PLAY	1	2	3	4	5	6	7	8	9	10	11	12	13	14	15	16	17
Bartholomew Fair														X			
The Staple of News																	
A Woman Killed with Kindness		X		X	X					X		X	X	X			
The Fair Maid of the West																	
The Dutch Courtesan																	
The Malcontent		X		X								X		X			
All Fools																	
Bussy D'Ambois		X		X							X	X		X			
The Revenge of Bussy D'Ambois																	
Eastward Hol				X										X			
Miseries of Enforced Marriage																	
A Yorkshire Tragedy																	
A Trick to Catch the Old One		X										X		X			
Michaelmas Term																	
The Roaring Girl																	
The Changeling		X		X								X		X			
The Revenger's Tragedy																	
The Atheist's Tragedy																	
The White Devil					X		X						X	X			X
The Duchess of Malfi		X		X	X						X	X					X

TITLE OF PLAY	1	2	3	4	5	6	7	8	9	10	11	12	13	14	15	16	17
Knight of the Burning Pestle		X		X								X		X			X
The Maid's Tragedy		X		X	X						X	X		X			
Philaster		X		X								X	X	X			X
The Faithful Shepherdess		X										X					
The Wild-Goose Chase												X		X			
The Island Princess				X													
Rule a Wife and Have a Wife																	
The Two Noble Kinsmen													X				
Beggars' Bush				X													
The Fatal Dowry																	
The Maid of Honor		X															
A New Way to Pay Old Debts		X		X	X							X	X	X			X
The Witch of Edmonton		X															
'Tis Pity She's a Whore					X	X					X		X				
The Broken Heart		X		X		X						X		X			
Perkin Warbeck		X				X											
The Lady of Pleasure		X		X								X	X	X			
The Cardinal		X										X	X				
Love and Honor																	
A Jovial Crew																	

¶Here is côteyned a godely interlude of Fulgens
Cenatoure of Rome. Lucres his doughter. Gayus
flaminius. & Publi⁹. Corneli⁹. of the disputacyon of
noblenes. & is deuyded in two ptyes/to be played at
ii.tymes. Cōppled by mayster Henry medwall. late
chapelayne to þ ryght reuerent fader in god Johan
Morton cardynall & Archebysshop of Caūterbury.

PD

Title page of *Fulgens and Lucrece*, c. 1512–16

HENRY MEDWALL

(fl. 1490–1500)

BIOGRAPHY. Until 1919 when a unique copy of *Fulgens and Lucrece* came into the auction room, the first English secular play was known only from a fragment of printed text. The fame of its author, Henry Medwall, rested only upon a morality called *Nature,* which also exists in a single copy, and upon an uncomplimentary allusion, probably forged. A lost play of his called *The Finding of Truth* was said to have proved too long on a double bill at court, at least for the king, who departed for bed before it was over. Consequently, the discovery of a complete copy of *Fulgens and Lucrece,* which is a sprightly play, has done much to rehabilitate its author's reputation.

Of Henry Medwall little is known except that he was a chaplain in the household of Cardinal John Morton, Archbishop of Canterbury under Henry VII. His play appears to have been written for performance at Christmas time 1497, between the courses of a banquet at which Morton entertained ambassadors from Flanders and from Spain. The occasion was one of considerable political and diplomatic interest: trade relations with Flanders were established, a seven years' truce between Henry VII of England and James IV of Scotland was negotiated, and the marriage of Katherine of Aragon and Arthur, Prince of Wales, was discussed (see *Perkin Warbeck,* below).

SOURCE. *Fulgens and Lucrece* is based upon a long-winded, inconclusive, Ciceronian declamation on true noblesse—*De Vera Nobilitate* (1428)—written in Latin by Bonus Accursius, or Bonaccorso, of Pistoja. By way of a French version made by Jean Mielot, secretary to Philip the Good of Burgundy, Bonaccorso's book was translated into English by John Tiptoft, Earl of Worcester, and printed by William Caxton in 1481 along with Tiptoft's renderings of Cicero's *De Amicitia* and *De Senectute.* It is Tiptoft's version which served as Medwall's source, and the connection of this early play with the development of English Humanism is therefore important.

CRITICAL COMMENT. Medwall's treatment of his source, however, is free, and in some ways highly original. In both the treatise and the play Lucrece has two contrasting suitors, the rich aristocrat Publius Cornelius and the plain, humble Gaius Flaminius. But in the treatise she leaves the choice to her father and to the Roman Senate, before whom the long speeches of the suitors are delivered, and from whom no decision is announced. In the play, however, the young men dramatically plead their cause before the lady herself, and with admirable resolution Lucrece makes her own choice of the poor but virtuous wooer. Aside from this improvement, however, the main plot of *Fulgens and*

Lucrece is still largely conventional; the play is little more than a medieval *debat,* or disputation, on what makes a gentleman, and it is didactic in purpose. But it is in the underplot that Medwall reveals the hand of a master and antici- pates the comic technique of a later generation. The competition for the maid Jone by the servingmen of the rival suitors is a parody below stairs of the dignified serious wooing which takes place in a better social circle.

BIBLIOGRAPHY

Early edition: n.d. [probably 1512–16].

Modern editions: Facs. Seymour de Ricci (1920); ed. F. S. Boas and A. W. Reed (1926).

A Goodly Interlude of

FULGENS . . . [AND] LUCRECE . . .

[and] The Disputation of Nobleness

(1497)

DRAMATIS PERSONAE

FULGENS, a noble and well-to-do senator of Rome.

LUCRECE, his daughter and "chief jewel and riches . . . [his] comfort against all care and heaviness, . . . a woman of inestimable prudence, . . . [whose] noble virtue did her fame exceed. . . . She is so discreet and sad in all demeaning and thereto full of honest and virtuous counsel of her own mind, that wonder is to tell the gifts of Nature and of especial grace. . . . Great labor was made her favor to attain in the way of marriage."

GAIUS FLAMINIUS, a plebeian; "his ancestors were of full poor degree," and he is "of small possession and great scarceness, . . . but for all that many a fair day through his great wisdom and virtuous behavior he ruled the commonweal to his great honor, . . . [and] for the victories that [he has] done . . . [he has returned] to this noble city twice or thrice crowned with laurel as it is the guise,"

PUBLIUS CORNELIUS, a patrician; "there is not within all this city a man born of a better blood, . . . [whose] progenitors and ancestors have been the chief aid and defense of this noble city," and to him have they "left many a castle and tower which in their triumphs they right- fully won . . . [and] all their treasure." His life, however, "is so voluptuous and so bestial . . . [that] he weeneth . . . by his proud countenance, . . . his great oaths, . . . his riotous disports and play, his sloth, . . . and other excess . . . by these things only [to] have noblesse. . . . Why should he those goods spare sith he labored never therefor?"

}her suitors.

A, youths who become the servants respectively of Gaius Flaminius and Publius
A, Cornelius. These fellows "be masterless and live most part in idleness; therefore
B, some manner of business would become [them] both well. . . . There is not in
    this hundred mile a feater bawd than [B]."

JONE, maid (ancilla) to Lucrece, "a trull of trust, . . . a little pretty mouset. . . .
    But the worst that grieveth me, she hath no leisure nor liberty for an hour or twain
    to be out of her mistress' sight."

Setting: Rome, "when the Empire . . . was in such flower that all the world was
    subject to the same."

> "There is no difference that I can tell
> Which maketh one man another to excel
> So much as doth virtue and goodly manner."

Part I

In a hall in which a banquet is being served, A and B emerge from
the crowd of guests and serve as Prologue by discussing the subject of a
play about to be produced. In Rome there lives a noble senator named
Fulgens who has a matchless daughter, Lucrece, much sought after in
marriage. Two suitors, however, are in especial favor with father and
daughter: Publius Cornelius, a wealthy patrician born of noble blood,
and Gaius Flaminius, a plebeian of poor stock but great virtue in himself.
Although Fulgens has his daughter's welfare always in mind, he has
such confidence in her judgment that he has given her free choice and
liberty in the selection of a husband. Each suitor comes a-wooing;
Cornelius solicits Fulgens to be his advocate, and Flaminius speaks to
Lucrece herself. After some coquetry, Lucrece promises to marry the one
who is judged the most noble and to give both young men a definite
answer on the morrow. Meanwhile, to assist in their wooing, B takes
service with Cornelius and A with Flaminius. But they are little help,
and the sole result is that there develops below stairs a burlesque version
of the main theme of the play as these unprofitable servants become
rivals for the favors of Jone, the handmaid of Lucrece and the comic
counterpart of her mistress. Promising to accept that suitor who can
show most mastery whether in cookery or in deeds of chivalry, Jone
encourages the men to vie with each other by showing off their abilities
in singing, wrestling, and jousting. But she is as hard to win as her
mistress, and all A and B get for their efforts is a thrashing from Jone
and a sound scolding from their masters for idling when sent on
errands.

Part II

The time comes when Lucrece should make her choice between her rival suitors, and after some farcical message-bearing by the two servants, the wealthy Cornelius takes advantage by whiling away the time until Flaminius arrives in entertaining Lucrece with a mumming and minstrelsy. Both men reject her suggestion that some neutral be appointed to decide this question of true noblesse, and, on condition that her opinion never be cited as a general precedent, Lucrece herself agrees to act as judge. Accordingly each pleads his cause before her. Cornelius stresses his ancestry and noble family, with whose deeds the histories of Rome are filled; he describes his ancestral possessions and inheritance, his riches, and the pleasures of hawking, hunting, minstrelsy, and dancing which shall be hers when Lucrece is his wife. But in the course of his remarks he alludes slightingly to his rival Flaminius, and earns a rebuke from the lady. In his speech Flaminius stresses the principle that it is worth and not birth which makes one man excel another and that noblesse grows out of long continued virtue; all men have common ancestry in Adam and Eve. Cornelius' forebears, it is true, were noble in deed but Cornelius, he feels justified in pointing out, has been able to say little of his own merits because his life is too voluptuous, riotous, and full of excess. On the other hand, his own life, Flaminius says modestly, has been devoted to God, to charity toward his neighbors, to purity of life, and to the defense and service of his country. To eschew idleness, the causer of sin, he has devoted his time to study. If his heirs will but follow his example they will attain to nobility through him, whereas, it is to be feared that in Cornelius the noblesse of his ancestors will utterly die. He has little wealth, it is true, says Flaminius in conclusion, but such small possessions as he has he offers the lady, assuring her not of luxury but of moderate riches, sufficient for them both.

Because of the heat with which this debate has been carried on, Lucrece still hesitates immediately to prefer one suitor before the other, but she promises with all speed to inquire what common opinion is upon the subject and to let her suitors know her decision by letter. To the audience, however, she announces her unequivocal choice of Flaminius

> As the more noble man sith he this wise
> By mean of his virtue to honor doth arise. . . .
> Although he be of a poor stock bore
> Yet I will honor and commend him more
> Than one that is descended of right noble kin
> Whose life is all dissolute and rotted in sin.

A and B are left, choruslike, to argue about her decision.

JOHN HEYWOOD

(c. 1497–after 1578)

BIOGRAPHY. The author usually credited with freeing English comedy completely from didacticism as well as allegory is John Heywood, one of Henry VIII's "singing men," and master of the royal choir school. Little is known of his life. He was born about 1497, perhaps at Stock, near Chelmsford, educated at Oxford, and from 1519 to 1528 employed as a musician at court. In 1523 he married Joan, the daughter of John Rastell the printer and of Elizabeth the sister of Sir Thomas More. After 1528 Heywood earned his living as a teacher of music and a writer of lively dialogues. At the Reformation, despite his apparent dislike for pardoners and friars, Heywood, like his uncle, remained a staunch Catholic, and in 1544 narrowly escaped hanging for his complicity in a plot against Archbishop Cranmer. In 1564 he left England forever, was befriended by the Jesuits at Malines, and died at Louvain, sometime after 1578. In addition to his plays, Heywood wrote *A Dialogue containing . . . All the Proverbs in the English Tongue* (1546); *Epigrams* (1550 ff.); and *The Spider and the Fly* (1556), a parable in verse. His son Jasper was one of the translators of the plays of Seneca (1581), and his daughter Elizabeth became the mother of the poet John Donne.

CRITICAL COMMENT. In all of Heywood's plays plot is of less consequence than dialogue and situation. All are short, one-act affairs, and several are hardly dramatic at all; they are little more than medieval *debats*, though they are more crisp and lively than the average. But, unlike the *debat*, in none is there an obtrusive moral purpose; Heywood's interludes are intended for pure entertainment, realistic and rowdy, without any ulterior ends.

SOURCES. John Heywood's plays are either original or derived from French fabliaux or farces; *The Four P's*, for example, is based upon the farce *D'un pardonneur, d'un triacleur, et d'une tavernière*, and *John John* upon that *De Pernet qui va au vin* and the *Farce du Pasté*. For *The Pardoner and the Friar* or *The Play of the Weather* no sources have been found.

BIBLIOGRAPHY

Collected Works: *The Dramatic Writings of John Heywood*, edited by J. S. Farmer (Early English Drama Society, 1905).

Monographs: R. W. Bolwell, *The Life and Works of John Heywood*, 1922. R. de la Bere, *John Heywood, Entertainer*, 1937.

The Pardoner and the Friar:

Early edition: 1533.
Modern editions: Facs. J. S. Farmer (TFT, 1907); ed. J. S. Farmer (1906).

The Four P's:

Early editions: n.d. [1544?]; n.d. [1555?]; 1569.
Modern edition: Facs. J. S. Farmer (TFT, 1908).

John John, Tyb, and Sir John:
    Early edition: 1533.
    Modern edition: Facs. J. S. Farmer (TFT, 1907).

The Play of the Weather:
    Early editions: 1533; n.d. [1544?]; n.d. [before 1560]; n.d. [1565?].
    Modern edition: Facs. J. S. Farmer (TFT, 1908, 1909).

A MERRY PLAY BETWEEN

THE PARDONER AND THE FRIAR

THE CURATE AND NEIGHBOR PRATT

(1513–1521)

DRAMATIS PERSONAE

A PARDONER, from Rome with holy relics and indulgences, which "will edify more with the sight . . . than all the prating of Holy Writ."

A FRIAR, vowed to poverty, who has "come hither to preach the word of God, . . . [and] turn the people and make them to repent."

THE CURATE, a parson who has let his church to both the Pardoner and the Friar and repents it.

NEIGHBOR PRATT, friend of the curate and appointed constable *pro tem.*

Setting: An English village, once upon a time.

"I shrew your hearts both for this lurch!"

A poor Friar, having heard of an assembly of people who are glad to hear the Word of God, hastens hither to edify souls and to preach the gospel. While he prepares for his sermon by praying apart, a Pardoner, seeking the same audience, begins to spread out his relics and to describe the powers and virtues of each: a holy hipbone which will cure swellings and scab in cattle and jealousy in human beings; a holy mitten which will produce increase in grain; the blessed arm of St. Sunday which protects travellers on sea or land; the great toe of Holy Trinity, good for toothache and cancer; the bongrace and French hood of Our Lady, beneficial to women with child; the jawbone of Allhallows, affording protection against poison; and St. Michael's brainpan, good for headache. All of these wonders the Pardoner bids the crowd come to see, but first to make an offering to them or there will be no benefit from them. Then he holds up the Pope's bull of indulgence and begins his sales talk, just as the Friar begins his sermon against covetousness and avarice.

For some while the two compete by talking at once; then they turn upon each other, the Friar maintaining that his purpose is to bring people to Heaven's gate by teaching them the Word of God, the Pardoner that his is to bring them there by their purse strings. Taking advantage, the exasperated Pardoner openly curses the Friar, excommunicates his rival by the Pope's authority, and bids the audience listen only to true doctrine. Again the two compete for a hearing; again they quarrel; and again they resume their sermons, the ends of which are identical—a collection of alms. The Pardoner rebukes the Friar, who is vowed to poverty, for preaching against avarice and yet begging for alms all day, and they wrangle violently, each justifying his right to charity. At last they fight, pulling hair, scratching, and biting.

Punishment seems about to descend upon them. The Curate of the church hastens in to separate the combatants, calls Neighbor Pratt to assist him, and declares that it would be a good deed to punish such rascals as an example to others and to make them repent they ever met in this church. Neighbor Pratt seizes the Pardoner to carry him off to the stocks, and the Curate takes on the Friar. But both of the knaves resist; each fights with his captor, and the representatives of law and order find that they "have more tow on [their] distaffs than [they] can well spin." In the end the rogues overthrow the honest men. Master Parson and Neighbor Pratt get broken heads and are glad to let these rascals depart—"and mischief go with you twain."

The Play Called

THE FOUR P'S

A New and Very Merry Interlude

(1520–1522)

DRAMATIS PERSONAE

A Palmer,
A Pardoner, } representatives of four callings with bad reputations for veracity, all
A Potecary, } quacks.
A Peddler,

Setting: An English road somewhere, once upon a time.

> *"For hard it is, as I have heard say,*
> *To begin virtue where none is pretended."*

Having met by chance on the road, a Palmer, a Pardoner, and a Potecary [i.e., apothecary or quack doctor] engage in a dispute concerning the merits of their respective callings. For the salvation of his soul, says the Palmer, he has travelled diligently on pilgrimage to all of the great shrines of Christendom. The Pardoner argues that such wandering is utterly useless and labor lost, because for a few pence invested in pardons, a man can achieve salvation readily at home. The Potecary, however, points out that men of his profession are of superlative importance because they have helped thousands on their road to Heaven, and he asks quaintly how anybody was ever saved without dying, and

> *Whom have ye known die honestly*
> *Without the help of a potecary?*

These three quacks are soon joined by another, who is a peddler of knickknacks, and after some discussion of why women take so long to dress and especially of the accomplishments of peddlers—drinking, sleeping, and singing—they refer to the Peddler their original argument.

Reluctant to be a judge in such a weighty matter, the Peddler soon perceives that the accomplishment which these rascals have in common is not buying or selling or any other art than lying, for they can all three "lie as well as can the falsest devil in Hell." Because he too has some skill in falsehood, the Peddler agrees to settle the differences between them in a contest as to which one can tell the biggest lie. At first the Palmer is a modestly reluctant participant in this trial of skill. The Pardoner, however, is more of an exhibitionist, and he digresses enthusiastically in a sales talk descriptive of the properties of his relics, which he offers his audience to kiss: the blessed jawbone of Allhallows, the great toe of the Trinity, the buttock-bone of Pentecost, a slipper of one of the Seven Sleepers, the eyetooth of the Great Turk, the bumblebees that stung Eve as she ate the forbidden fruit, and even the holy yeast from which was brewed the wedding drink of Adam and Eve. Warmed by such competition, the Potecary also exercises his talents by describing his cures: a medicine which will preserve a man from hanging; ointments, syrups, and drugs which deliver men from all pain and give them everlasting rest; a cure for a mangy dog—indeed, remedies so universally effective that they do him as much good when he sells them as they do those who buy.

After another false start and further exercise and argument, the contest at last gets under way, and the Peddler asks each of the participants to tell a tale. The Potecary describes his cure of a young woman patient by means of a tampion, which, released with explosive violence, destroyed two castles ten miles away and so disposed of the debris as to bridge a river near-by. In his turn the Pardoner describes the spiritual cure of the shrew Margery Coorson, who died without benefit of the sacraments, and whom he had to seek in both Purgatory and Hell before his influence obtained her release. He found her at last in Hell's kitchen, and led her out to the joyful roaring of all the devils, for she had such a tongue and such a temper that she made Hell hotter with them.

Throughout this recital the Palmer listens quietly. When his time comes, he does not begin a tale himself; instead, he solemnly expresses doubt about a portion of the Pardoner's tale which has been told as truth. He marvels how there should be any shrews in Hell when, as far as he can perceive, women are so gentle here on earth. On his conscience, he swears, in all of his travels he has never seen or known a woman out of patience! "That is the greatest lie of all!" exclaim his admiring rivals, and with one voice they declare him the winner and curtsey to him. In his turn the Palmer graciously absolves them both of the losers' penalty of becoming his servants.

The farce closes somewhat anticlimactically with the naive admission of the characters that no one here has pretended to virtue, and by their revoking anything said by negligence:

> To pass the time in this without offense
> Was the cause why the maker did make it.

A MERRY PLAY BETWEEN

JOHN JOHN, THE HUSBAND; TYB, HIS WIFE; AND SIR JOHN, THE PRIEST

(1520–1522)

DRAMATIS PERSONAE

JOHN JOHN, a stupid henpecked husband who "knew of married men the pain that they have, and yet dared not complain." ("He must needs go that the Devil driveth.")

TYB, his shrewish, gadding wife, "always chiding and brawling, . . . which doth nothing but go and come."

SIR JOHN, her gossip, the "peel'd [i.e., tonsured] parish priest; . . . he is a whoremonger, a haunter of the stews, an hypocrite, a wretch, a maker of strife."

Setting: An English village somewhere, once upon a time.

> "Now by my troth, it is a pretty jape
> For a wife to make her husband her ape."

John John is the long-suffering husband of a gadding wife named Tyb. More than a little John suspects Tyb of misconduct with Sir John the village priest, and he enjoys contemplating the thorough beating he will give his gadding spouse when she returns home. But when the shrewish Tyb appears, he very meekly and carefully avoids a brawl. So reasonable is he, also, about Sir John that Tyb tells him of a pie which she, her gossip Margery, their neighbor's daughter Anne, and Sir John have cooked up between them, the priest paying for the stuff and Dame Margery paying for the baking. Tyb has the pie in her possession and proposes, since John John is such a good fellow, that they eat it for supper. But because Sir John is so honest a man too, it seems a pity that he should be cheated out of his part. Hence, Tyb sends her unwilling husband to invite Master Parson to supper. Before John John can leave, however, Tyb calls him back to do numerous household chores—get out the trestles, set the table, put on candlesticks, bring in a stool, wash two cups, see that there is ale in the pot, bring in the bread. Meanwhile, the pie is warming by the fire.

When at last John carries his invitation, he finds Sir John reluctant to accept. The priest protests that he does not wish to stir up trouble, and Tyb, he admits, is just a little vexed with her confessor for suggesting that she do penance because she is continually nagging her husband. Anyway, he has a previous engagement with some friends to eat a pie that they have baked and had delivered to Tyb. Hence, he is easily persuaded to reconsider.

When the two men arrive home, Tyb prevents her stupid husband from sitting down at table with their guest by sending him first to fetch water to wash their hands, and then setting him to mend a leaky pail with wax which must be softened by the fire. While Sir John and Tyb enjoy their supper of good drink and a good pie, the poor husband labors vainly—his fingers crack, smoke gets in his eyes, he burns his face, and he soils his clothes. "Is not this a very purgatory to see folks eat and may not eat a bit?" Supper is finished, but the pail is still unmended. For pastime, therefore, Sir John tells three edifying miracles— of a seaman who was absent for seven years and returned home to find himself the father of seven children, born in the interval; of a barren woman who offered a live pig at the shrine of St. Modwin and within a month of her return from her pilgrimage bore a child; and of a woman who gave birth to a daughter, perfect in every limb, after being but five months married.

At last John is ready for his share of the pie, but he finds it all eaten. His complaints, however, produce only surprise and astonishment on the parts of his wife and the guest that he had not been served with both meat and drink while he worked. Awake at last, John John rebels, throws down the dilapidated old pail, and smashes it. Tyb reaches for her distaff, which serves as her husband tamer; John counters with a shovel full of hot coals, and "they fight by the ears a while." Finally John succeeds in driving out both wife and priest, but no sooner are they gone than he hastens after them, lest they cuckold him in revenge.

THE PLAY OF THE WEATHER

A NEW AND VERY MERRY INTERLUDE OF ALL MANNER OF WEATHERS

(1533)

DRAMATIS PERSONAE

JUPITER, a god of "high renown, [and] since [his] father's fall, . . . above all gods, . . . ever principal."

MERRY REPORT, the Vice, appointed court crier and "squire for God's precious body."

The GENTLEMAN, "of noble and ancient stock." ("A goodly occupation, by Saint Anne, . . . your ma[ster]ship hath a merry life.")

The MERCHANT. "who should afore . . . merchants accounted be?"

The RANGER, or gamekeeper of a royal park.

The WATER-MILLER.

The WIND-MILLER.

The GENTLEWOMAN, "a goodly dame, an idle thing, iwis."

The LAUNDER [i.e., laundress], no longer young, who has to work for a living.

A BOY, "the least that can play."

Setting: An anteroom to the Court of Heaven, once upon a time.

"Blessed was the time wherein we were born!"

Because of the complaints and dissatisfaction which arose in the days when Saturn, Phoebus, Eolus, and Phoebe had charge of the weather, a parliament of the gods has substituted centralization for bureaucracy and given Jupiter full control. The new executive has straightway issued a proclamation calling upon all persons who have complaints to declare them, so that he may "shape remedy for their relief." Merry Report, the Vice, applies for the office of crier to the court, and though too light both in behavior and in array, is appointed because at least he is impartial. This officious rascal then sets out to publish the proclamation.

Soon petitioners begin to come into court and are heard, Merry Report promising each to be his advocate with Jupiter, or general "well-willer." The first to appear is a Gentleman whose principal recreation is hunting and who asks for warm pleasant weather, dry and not misty, with little wind, so that he can stalk game. Next, is a Merchant who professes to speak for traders throughout the world. Merchants bring wealth to all the rest by exporting that of which there is a surplus and by importing goods that are scarce. Because of their importance merchants ask for clear weather, neither stormy nor misty and with moderate winds which do not blow in one direction too long and so cause a loss of market by too long a voyage. Next comes a Ranger, speaking for the keepers of forests, parks, purlieus, and chases stocked with game. His principal fees are extras which come from clearing up the wood after a windfall, and he asks for a "good rage of blustering and blowing" to tear trees to pieces and uproot them. Next come two Millers, one dependent upon water, the other upon wind to grind his grain. If there is too much wind the mill dams are as dry as flint and the water-millers grind nothing at all. On the other hand, if it rains all the time, there is no wind and the wind-millers suffer. The two engage in a heated debate about their crafts and the relative merits of their two kinds of mill, until they are interrupted by Merry Report and the entrance of another suppliant, a Gentlewoman. She is young and beautiful, and she wants to stay that way. But there is the sun in summer, the cold in winter, the wind and the rain at all times—all equally hard on the complexion—and she does not know where to turn. The lady asks, therefore, for nothing but close fair weather so that she can jet abroad on the streets and save her beauty. But a Laundress, who overhears her, protests that she should be quite undone if the sun did not shine; she wants weather that is hot and clear. It is better, in her opinion, that faces be sunburnt and clothes clean, than that women's cheeks be fair and their smocks foul. Finally, a small Boy, sent as a spokesman for a hundred of his fellows, protests that his pleasure is in catching birds and in throwing snowballs; hence, he wants frost for his pitfalls and plenty of snow.

In the face of all these contradictory wishes Merry Report is puzzled, but Jupiter needs no counsel. He has the solution to the problem. To the assembled petitioners he announces that under his administration they shall all have even better than they asked for. The Gentleman will often have fair weather for hunting; the Merchant shall often have fair breezes on the sea when there are none on land; at night when there is no hunting, winds shall rise and tear down trees to benefit the Ranger; rains will replenish the streams in the valleys for the Water-miller; and there will be fair, windy weather on the hills for the Wind-miller; the Gentlewoman will have sufficient fair time in which to gad about; the sun will often be hot enough to dry the Laundress' clothes; and the small Boy will have both frost and snow. No kind of weather is suitable for all, and the petitioners depart praising the prudence of Jupiter and full of thanks for his consideration of them and his satisfactory and peaceful solution to the problem. It is Merry Report who perceives what this sagacity amounts to:

> Lo, how this is brought to pass!
> Sirs, now shall ye have the weather even as it was!

····•————◀◈▶————•····

THERSITES

SOURCE AND CRITICAL COMMENT. *Thersites,* this vivacious little lesson against unseemly boasting, written about 1537 and sometimes assigned to Nicholas Udall, is based upon a Latin dialogue by J. Ravisius Textor (Jean Textier), a professor of rhetoric at the Collège de Navarre, who from 1520 to 1524 was rector of the University of Paris. Ultimately it derives from the plays of Plautus; Thersites is the earliest example of the braggart soldier (*miles gloriosus*) on the English stage. But even so, neither the dialogue nor the play based on it is wholly classical; the combat of a man-at-arms with a snail is an old medieval joke, usually at the expense of the Lombards.

In adapting Textor's dialogue to English schoolboys, the anonymous author handled his materials freely. For example, there is no counterpart in the Latin original of the episode of Telemachus coming to Thersites' mother to be cured of worms.

BIBLIOGRAPHY

Early edition: n.d. [c. 1561–63].

Modern editions: Facs. E. W. Ashbee (1876), and J. S. Farmer (TFT, 1912); ed. J. S. Farmer (*Six Anonymous Plays,* 1905).

A NEW INTERLUDE CALLED

THERSITES

(1537)

DRAMATIS PERSONAE

THERSITES, a boaster, with "great strength . . . in [his] body so lusty, which for lack of exercise is now almost rusty. . . . [He] verily think[s] that none in Christendie with [him] to meddle dare be so bold. Now have at the lions on Cotswold!"

MATER, Thersites' mother and chief protector.

MULCIBER [Vulcan], a smith and armor-maker, "whom the poets doth call the god of fire."

MILES, a knight, "a poor soldier come of late from Calais."

A Snail with a "horned brow."

TELEMACHUS, young son of Ulysses, and his father's "chief treasure. . . . Ywis, it is a proper child and in behavior nothing wild; ye may see what is good education." ("What, little Telemachus, what makest thou here among us?")

Setting: The legendary past.

"This interlude following doth declare how that the greatest boasters are not the greatest doers."

Having lost all of his weapons except a club at the siege of Troy, the unheroic boaster Thersites calls at the shop of Mulciber the smith to obtain new equipment. He purchases successively a sallet [i.e., a helmet], a habergeon [i.e., a coat of mail], "briggen irons" [i.e., a brigandine], and a sword, and then challenges all comers—the monster Cacus, Hercules, King Arthur and his knights, Robin Hood—or anyone at all, to come and fight with him. His mother tries to dissuade him from this comprehensive defiance, lest he be killed—but in vain. At last a snail appears and frightens Thersites nearly to death. But the doughty warrior throws aside his club and draws sword, succeeding after some effort in making the snail draw in its horns. In a fight with Miles, a broken-down soldier from Calais, Thersites is completely put to rout and obliged to hide behind his mother's skirts until his enemy has retired. For her pains the poor mother must endure her ungrateful son's scurrilous tongue-lashing.

Meanwhile, there arrives Telemachus, the son of Ulysses. On a previous occasion this great warrior had discomfited Thersites. But bygones are forgotten, and the boy has now been sent to Thersites' mother to be cured of the worms. The woman speaks an elaborate charm over the child, and he is restored to health. But Thersites continues to rail and is at last driven from the stage by Miles, who, even if he is no great soldier himself, knows that cowards talk more than they will make good.

NICHOLAS UDALL

(1505-1556)

BIOGRAPHY. Born in Hampshire in 1505, Nicholas Udall was educated at Winchester College and Corpus Christi, Oxford, where he was fellow in 1524 and received the M.A. degree in 1534. In the same year he became a flogging headmaster of Eton College, a position which he held until 1541 when charges against him and a confession of misconduct caused his dismissal. Guilty or not, Udall subsequently held various positions in the church, and at the close of his life became headmaster of Westminster School (1555). He died in 1556.

Udall's literary work was various. In 1533 he published *Flowers for Latin Speaking,* selections with translations from Terence. In the same year he and John Leland the antiquary prepared for the coronation of Anne Bullen a classical pageant in English and Latin verse in which Paris bestowed the golden apple upon the queen instead of upon Venus (cf. Peele's *The Arraignment of Paris* below, where the same compliment is paid to Elizabeth, Queen Anne's daughter). In 1542 he translated Erasmus' *Apophthegms,* and in 1548 one book of the same author's paraphrase of the New Testament. Besides these, Udall wrote a number of religious and controversial works.

CRITICAL COMMENT. Even if *Thersites* did anticipate it by something more than a decade, *Ralph Roister Doister* is the first English comedy to illustrate the modification of native humor by imitation of the classics. In structure, character, and incident, this comedy suggests a Roman model, but the setting and sentiment are wholly English. As in the classical drama the simple scene is a village street, and the unities of time, place, and action are reasonably well adhered to. But the whole has a wholesome English rather than a Roman atmosphere. The hero, Roister Doister, may be like the *miles gloriosus* of Plautus and the Thraso of Terence, but he is really an English braggart. His companion Merrygreek also partakes of both the classical parasite-intriguer and the native English mischief-making Vice of the old morality tradition. But the courtesan of Latin comedy has been replaced by a virtuous English widow with a household of lively gossiping maids, and her suitor, instead of being a young rake, is a substantial, honest English merchant, the master of a trading ship. What happens, however, is as much a part of the rough and tumble of the native English morality and interlude as it is of Latin farce.

BIBLIOGRAPHY

Collected Works: *The Dramatic Writings of Nicholas Udall,* edited by J. S. Farmer (Early English Drama Society, 1906).

Early edition: c. 1566 (the unique copy surviving at Eton lacks both title page and colophon).

Modern editions: ed. W. H. Williams and P. A. Robins (TD, 1901); W. W. Greg (MSR, 1935).

RALPH ROISTER DOISTER
(1550–1553)

DRAMATIS PERSONAE

DAME CHRISTIAN CUSTANCE, a widow of "sober life" and "the pearl of perfect honesty . . . [as] maid, widow, and wife." ("I hear she is worth a thousand pound or more.")

Tom Truepenny, a boy, servant to Dame Christian.

Margery, or Madge, Mumblecrust, her gullible nurse, "a girl . . . scarce yet three-score year old."

Tibet Talkapace, } her maids.
Annot Alyface, }

Gawyn Goodluck, a merchant, absent on voyage, and affianced to Dame Christian, "whom he tendereth no less than his life."

Tristram Trusty, the "true and faithful friend" of Gawyn and Dame Christian; "no alderman can go, I dare say, a sadder pace than [he] can."

Sym Suresby, trusted servant to Gawyn Goodluck.

Ralph Roister Doister, a vainglorious "brainsick fool," suitor of Dame Christian's who "vaunteth himself for a man of prowess great, whereas a good gander, I dare say, may him beat. . . . All the day long is he facing and cracking of his great acts in fighting and fray-making." Yet, he looks "as fierce as a Cotswold lion" [i.e., a sheep]; "he thinketh each woman to be brought in dotage with the only sight of his goodly personage. . . . Oft is he wooer, but never doth he speed." Dame Christian "hath called him fool and [ad]dressed him like a fool, mocked him like a fool, used him like a fool." But, in spite of all, as he himself knows, "no man, woman, nor child can hate [him] long."

Matthew Merrygreek, "Roister Doister's champion," a carefree, intriguing parasite and witty opportunist who supports his master in his folly. ("He doth it for a jest; I know him out of doubt.")

Dobinet Doughty, a boy, } servants to Roister Doister.
Harpax, }

A Scrivener, or public letter writer, who composes a love letter for Roister Doister.

A Parish Clerk.

Musicians and Servants.

Setting: A village street outside the house of Dame Christian Custance, somewhere in England at some unspecified time.

> *"What creature is in health, either young or old,*
> *But some mirth with modesty will be glad to use?"*

Act I

After having sponged on various masters, Matthew Merrygreek, a carefree, clever parasite, has become the hanger-on of a vainglorious blusterer named Ralph Roister Doister. Roister Doister has wooed many women, and is once again in love, this time with the rich and virtuous widow Dame Christian Custance, the betrothed of Gawyn Goodluck, a merchant who is away on voyage. All women, thinks Roister Doister, are enamored of him as they would be of another Launcelot, Guy of Warwick, Alexander, or at least a tenth Worthy, and he sees no reason to doubt of his success with Dame Christian. With the aid of Matthew Merrygreek he plans his campaign, ordering his musicians to serenade his beloved. With flattery, boasting, vain promises of future finery, and kisses even, he ingratiates himself with Dame Christian's servants, Madge Mumblecrust, Tibet Talkapace, and Annot Alyface, and seeks their good will in his suit. Especially does he cultivate old Madge, who carries a love letter from Roister Doister to her mistress. Dame Christian does not even open the missive and bids Madge bring her no more of them.

Act II

Having been scolded by Dame Christian for taking Roister Doister's part, Madge refuses to deliver the ring and the love token which Dobinet Doughty brings from his master, and the lad must find other means of placing the missives in Dame Christian's hands. Accordingly, the clever page cultivates the acquaintance of the other servants. To Tom Truepenny he represents himself merely as the servant of Dame Christian's husband to be, and is heartily welcomed. Through Truepenny Dobinet is introduced to Tibet and Annot, who are still beside themselves because of the rich promises Roister Doister has made to them. The four quickly become fast friends, and, aided by the impressionable houseboy and the maids, Dobinet delivers the ring and the token. For their pains, however, these meddlesome servants merely receive a good scolding from their mistress and strict injunctions never to accept messages or gifts from strangers.

Act III

Sent by Roister Doister to learn how his letter and love tokens are likely to succeed, Matthew Merrygreek overhears Tibet Talkapace vow vengeance upon the unknown suitor who has been the cause of their scolding. Tibet has learned her lesson and will bear no more messages, but she does help Merrygreek to speak with Dame Christian herself. But, although Merrygreek paints out the suitor in the best colors, the good widow utterly spurns Roister Doister's proposal that they be married on Sunday next. So easily is Roister Doister discouraged, that when he hears of his lack of success with the widow, he vows that he will go home and die. As he lies in a feigned swoon, Merrygreek amuses himself by reciting over him a parody of the church service for the dead. He then rouses Roister Doister to woo the lady face to face himself, and fetches Roister Doister's musicians to assist him. But Dame Christian is annoyed by the caterwauling in front of her house, and repeats to the presumptuous suitor himself the contempt she had previously expressed to his proxy. Reminded that she has received tokens and a fine letter from her lover, she produces the latter and condescends to let Merrygreek read it. The letter is well phrased, but the mischievous Merrygreek so alters the punctuation that it says the opposite of what it means. Roister Doister threatens to avenge himself upon the scrivener who wrote the letter for him, and Merrygreek goes to fetch him only on condition that the braggart will not kill him. The scrivener, however, is capable of taking care of himself and easily proves that Roister Doister merely copied a good letter wrong. At last Merrygreek confesses that he read the letter amiss and promises to atone by explaining to Dame Christian.

Act IV

Sent by his master, Gawyn Goodluck, Sym Suresby returns home from his voyage and calls on Dame Christian to know how she fares. Their interview is interrupted by Roister Doister and Merrygreek come to explain about the letter, and Sym hears enough to have his suspicions aroused that all is not well. He refuses to bear a token from the lady to her beloved Gawyn and hurries away to report to his master. Vexed at this undeserved shadow on her good name and enraged at the persistent and confident wooing of Roister Doister and Merrygreek, Dame Christian bids them go packing. In reply Roister Doister threatens to burn her house and to destroy her and all of her possessions. Merely as a precaution and not from fear, Dame Christian sends Truepenny to her friend Tristram Trusty and arms her maids with spits and fire-forks for protection. To Tristram, when he at last arrives, she explains everything, and is assured that she need fear neither Roister Doister, who is a braggart, nor Merrygreek, who is a practical joker. When Merrygreek arrives with more threats, they convert him into an ally, and together the three plot the downfall of Roister Doister. Still swaggering, Roister Doister learns from Merrygreek that his threats have been ineffectual and is advised, if he would win the lady, to play the man. Together they rehearse blows in anticipation of the coming combat. Encouraged by Merrygreek, Roister Doister sets out; as agreed, Dame Christian runs away pretending to be afraid, but even so Roister Doister advocates strategic retreat as the best offensive, has forgotten his helmet and must send back for it, and invents excuses for not going on. In a parley with Tristram, Roister Doister even insists that he fights a defensive war because Dame Christian forces him against his will and is almost persuaded to take the law on her. At last, even with drums beating and ensigns waving, the whole fracas would have come to nothing had not Merrygreek for his "heart's ease" discharged first a harquebus and then a popgun at Dame Christian's house. This brings forth the lady and her maids. Tibet, seeking revenge on Dobinet for his deception about the tokens, takes on the braggart's boy; Dame Christian makes for

Roister Doister himself; while Merrygreek, as agreed, seems to protect his master by striking at Dame Christian, but actually hitting Roister Doister. The attackers are routed by women, and the braggart declares the Widow Custance an Amazon, expresses the belief that she probably slew her first husband, and swears that "slay else whom she will, by Gog, she shall not slay me!"

Act V

Meanwhile, Sym Suresby dutifully reports what he has seen and heard to Gawyn Goodluck, who has returned home. Mindful of the dangers of judging by hasty surmise, they interview Dame Christian, who calls on Gawyn's true and faithful friend Tristram to clear her, and Gawyn and the widow are reconciled. To celebrate, Gawyn invites his friends to a supper, and not only accepts Merrygreek's apologies for Roister Doister, but includes both the braggart and his parasite among the guests. The play closes with a song by the whole company in praise of the Queen.

"MR. S., MASTER OF ART"

BIOGRAPHY. Since the sixteenth century, identifications of "Mr. S." have been various, but scholars today are generally agreed that William Stevenson is the most likely author of *Gammer Gurton's Needle*. Stevenson was fellow of Christ's College, Cambridge, where the play is said to have been produced, and he is known to have written a play acted at the college in 1553–54. Born at Hunswick, Durham, about 1521, he was educated at Cambridge, served as fellow of his college from 1551 to 1554 and from 1559 to 1561, was ordained a deacon in London in 1552, and made prebendary of Durham in 1561. He died in 1575.

CRITICAL COMMENT. Like *Ralph Roister Doister, Gammer Gurton's Needle* reveals the influence of Latin comedy, but it is even more truly English in its realism. There are the classical five acts with subdivision into scenes, the simple stage setting of the intersection of two streets, the action which takes place outside the doors of opposite houses, the narrow limitation of time and place. But the theme is much ado about nothing, and the life which inspired it is the English village with its miry roads and its cozy but badly kept houses, and its absurd character types. Even Diccon, as manipulator of the action, may be related to both the intriguing slave of Latin comedy and the practical-joking Vice of the morality plays; but he is nevertheless essentially a native type, the Bedlam beggar of the English roads. The dialogue, too, is racy and realistic:

> *A man I think might make a play*
> *And need no word to this they say*
> *Being but half a clerk.*

Here, then, is a good earthy bit of English life, as for comic purposes it was enjoyed by an academic playwright who loved a rustic row and transcribed it for the delectation of his fellow gownsmen at the college and for all others who like rollicking fun and approve of a draught of ale and a game of trump by the fire.

No literary source is known.

BIBLIOGRAPHY

Early editions: 1575; 1661.

Modern editions: Facs. J. S. Farmer (TFT, 1910); ed. H. F. Brett-Smith (Percy Reprints, 1920).

A RIGHT PITHY, PLEASANT, AND MERRY COMEDY ENTITLED

GAMMER GURTON'S NEEDLE (1552–1563)

DRAMATIS PERSONAE

DICCON, a Bedlam beggar, "a vengeable knave . . . [and] a bonable whoreson," the mischievous, merry liar, given to practical jokes and roguish misrepresentations. "A false knave, by God's pity; ye were but a fool to trow him." He is the expositor or chorus, the commentator on the action as well as the controller of it.

GAMMER GURTON, a gullible, suspicious old village goody.

HODGE, a simple ditcher, her stupid man of all work.

TYB, her maid.

COCK, her boy.

DAME CHAT, "a subtle quean as any in this town, . . . that false vixen . . . that counts herself so honest," a contentious alewife, neighbor to Gammer Gurton.

DOLL, her maid.

DR. RAT, the curate, a red-nosed, interfering hedge-priest, "a man esteemed wise."

MASTER BAILEY, officer of the law.

SCAPETHRIFT, his tattered servant.

Setting: A village in England before the houses of Gammer Gurton and Dame Chat, at some unspecified time.

> *"Sighing and sobbing, they weep and they wail,*
> *I marvel in my mind, what the Devil they ail."*

Act I

Diccon the Bedlam beggar, a carefree rogue in search of amusing adventure, discovers the house of old Gammer Gurton in the utmost confusion and takes advantage of the fact to steal a slip of bacon which he hopes will come in handy as the "shoeing horn to draw on two pots of ale" at some roadside tavern. Inquiry of Hodge, Gammer Gurton's man, whose breeches are even more sadly torn than usual, elicits only the conviction that the weeping and wailing are not unusual in that house, but that, if old signs are to be believed, strange events will take place there in the near future. It is Tyb, the maid, who brings Hodge the dire tidings that as Gammer sat mending a pair of Hodge's breeches she was interrupted by Gib the cat's stealing some milk set aside for Hodge's supper and in the ensuing turmoil lost her "goodly tossing spurrier's needle," that was her only treasure! Diligent search within doors and out, however, is wholly fruitless and leads only to further vexation and wringing of hands.

Act II

Meanwhile, from Dame Chat's alehouse across the way the strains of a drinking song are heard, as Diccon feasts and carouses, while poor Hodge can only grumble that he must go supperless as well as ragged. From Hodge the solicitous Diccon learns why whole breeches are so important to the ditcher—tomorrow Kirstian Clack, Tom Simson's maid, is coming hither. She smiled at Hodge on Sunday last, and who knows what may come to pass between them? A matter of weight, agrees Diccon, and swearing Hodge to secrecy, he draws a magic circle preparatory to conjuring up the Devil—the great Devil—to assist them in finding the needle. This hocus-pocus is too much for the simple Hodge, who, losing all restraint, befouls himself, and flees in terror. Deprived of his sport, Diccon now calls Dame Chat from a card game with her gossips and tells her that Gammer Gurton's yellow-legged red cock has been stolen and that he had heard Tyb the maid accuse Dame Chat to Gammer Gurton of the theft. Of course he swears the grateful alewife to secrecy "that Diccon bear no blame." To Hodge, who has returned in fresh breeches, Diccon reports the success of his interview with the Devil, from whose gibbering of "cat," "rat," and "Chat," it is evident—Diccon says—either that Gib the cat ate the needle, that Dr. Rat the curate found it, or that Dame Chat stole it. Hopeless of recovering the needle, Hodge hies to Sim Glover's shop to seek a leather thong to patch up his damaged garment as best he may in the emergency. Going in turn to the disconsolate Gammer Gurton, Diccon reports that not twenty hours be-

fore Dame Chat picked up something at the gate, and there can be no
doubt that it was the lost needle. While Gammer hurries in to get on a
clean apron, Diccon awaits the fray between the suspicious neighbors.

Act III

When he returns with the thong, Hodge meets an excited and hopeful
Gammer, girding for a fight. Urged on by Hodge, who only gets in the
way, the two women exchange barnyard billingsgate and engage in a
rowdy squabble which decides nothing and certainly does not recover
the needle. Dame Chat has knocked Gammer down and retired to safety,
when Gammer decides to send Cock, her boy, on a round of the ale-
houses to seek Dr. Rat the curate, a decision which seems wise to Hodge
in the light of the Devil's utterances. Meanwhile, Tyb reports that Gib
the cat has been gasping behind the door as if something were caught
in its throat, and Hodge, who is no believer in half measures, excitedly
prepares to rake the unhappy beast.

Act IV

Grumbling at being disturbed while boozing at Hob Filcher's, Dr. Rat
listens as Gammer, Hodge, and Diccon each tells his version of the
needle's loss. At Diccon's advice all retire lest Dame Chat see them and
become suspicious, and he promises to reconnoiter and bring them news
shortly. Instead, he calls Dame Chat and warns her of a plot by Hodge
to rob her hen-roost. To Dr. Rat Diccon then reports that with his own
eyes he has seen Dame Chat sewing with Gammer's needle and that, if
he will but put off his gown and creep through a hole in the wall, the
good doctor can see it for himself. For his pains, in the dark Dr. Rat
promptly has his head broken with a stout oaken door bar, and sends
for the village bailiff to punish these murderers and all their accomplices.

Act V

Master Bailey listens patiently to all complaints. Circumstances certainly are against Dr. Rat's innocence; Dame Chat stoutly denies that
she broke his head; Hodge the suspect is sent for and found whole;
Gammer Gurton accuses Dame Chat of theft, which the alewife as vigorously denies; and at last Diccon the author of all these mix-ups is called
for. Everyone turns upon him, but he confesses readily and is so unre-
pentant that Master Bailey assures him of a fair punishment to which
the others agree. To set an example of good humor, the bailiff waives his

usual fee in assault cases and decrees that Diccon kneel down and take a
riddling oath on Hodge's leather breeches: first, never on pain of the
cleric's curse, to offer to pay for drinks when Dr. Rat is willing, always
to give the curate the first pull at an alepot, but never to offer the cup to
him unless it is full; second, if Dame Chat refuse money never to offer it
twice, and never to decline should he have an opportunity at her house
to drink free; third, to help Gammer Gurton recover her needle if possible, and always to be kind to Gib her cat; and, finally, never to mistake
Hodge for a fine gentleman. A prankster to the end, Diccon seals the
oath by giving Hodge a sharp whack on the buttocks, and the screaming
ditcher discovers the lost needle where Gammer had left it in her mending. General rejoicing concludes this much ado about nothing; hard
feelings are put aside, and all heap thanks upon Diccon as they retire
to the alehouse for a drink.

JACK JUGGLER

CRITICAL COMMENT. *Jack Juggler,* written sometime between 1553 and
1558, also represents a graft of conventional Roman comedy upon English
village life, and its author makes specific acknowledgment of his debt to the
classics: "in this manner of making Plautus did excel." But it is more than
manner which the writer of *Jack Juggler* derived from Plautus; his little play
is a development of an episode in *Amphitruo,* in which a servant is barred
out of his master's house by another in disguise. Yet, like *Thersites* and *Roister
Doister, Jack Juggler* reveals only a partial assimilation of Roman material and
only the use of such situations and characters as are suitable "for children to
play." The subject is borrowed, but the spirit in which it is treated is thoroughly and wholesomely English.

BIBLIOGRAPHY

Early editions: n.d. [1562?]; n.d. [1565?]; n.d. [?].

Modern editions: Facs. E. W. Ashbee (1876), and J. S. Farmer (TFT, 1912);
ed. W. H. Williams (1914); E. L. Smart and W. W. Greg (1st edn.,
MSR, 1933); B. I. Evans and W. W. Greg (3rd edn., MSR, 1937).

A New Interlude for Children to Play, Named

JACK JUGGLER

Both Witty, and Very Pleasant

(c. 1553–1558)

DRAMATIS PERSONAE

JENKIN CAREAWAY, a lackey, page to Master Bongrace, "as cursed a lad and as ungracious as ever man had, an unhappy wag and as foolish a knave withal as any is now within London Wall. . . . If you command him to go speak with some one, it is an hour ere he would be gone. Then will he run forth and play in the street and come again and say that he cannot with him meet. . . . Is that the guise of a trusty page to play when he is sent on his master's message?"

JACK JUGGLER, the Vice, who plays a practical joke on Jenkin Careaway and becomes his victim's "other I. . . . Many here smell strong, but none so rank as he."

MASTER BONGRACE, a gallant. ("Of all unkind and churlish husbands this is the cast, to let their wives sit at home and fast while they be forth and make good cheer, pastime, and sport.")

DAME COY, a gentlewoman, his wife, "a very cursed shrew, by the blessed Trinity, and a very devil. She is an angry piece of flesh, and soon displeased, quickly moved, but not lightly appeased."

ALICE TRIP-AND-GO, her maid. "She simpereth, she pranketh, . . . she minceth, she brideleth, she swimmeth to and fro; she treadeth not one hair awry, she trippeth like a doe abroad in the street. . . . She quavereth and wardeleth, like one in a galliard, every joint in her body and every part. O, it is a jolly wench!"

Setting: Once upon a time, and in a certain place.

> *"Such is the fashion of the world nowadays*
> *That the simple innocents are deluded."*

In search of mirth and of revenge for an old argument, Jack Juggler, a mischievous old rascal, resolves to settle scores with Jenkin Careaway, the irresponsible page of Master Bongrace, who lives near-by. Jack knows that Jenkin has been sent to fetch his mistress, Dame Coy, to join her husband at dinner, and he knows also that Jenkin has played on the way, got into an altercation with a fruit-wife, and gathered up a sleeve full of apples. So stupid is Jenkin withal that the rogue Jack believes, with such inside information as he has been able to pick up, he can persuade Jenkin that the page is not himself, but another man altogether.

Hence, when Jenkin seeks admission to his master's house, Jack Juggler in disguise bars his way, and by arguments and blows forces the hapless page to believe that he, Jack, is the real Jenkin Careaway, and that the message has already been delivered. As a result poor Jenkin is beside himself, and when he tells his tale of confused identity, he is upbraided and beaten by both his master and his quick-tempered mistress, who has had to go supperless because of the lackey's derelictions:

> *Why thou naughty villain darest thou affirm to me*
> *That which was never seen nor hereafter shall be,*
> *That one man may have two bodies and two faces,*
> *And that one man at one time may be in two places!*

Jenkin's further explanations only make matters worse, and his master and mistress bequeath him "with a hot vengeance to the Devil of Hell."

THOMAS NORTON AND THOMAS SACKVILLE
(1532–1584)   (1536–1608)

BIOGRAPHIES. The first English tragedy was the work of two gentlemen who were statesmen primarily rather than authors. Both were outstanding politicians, and both were prominent members of Elizabeth's first Parliament. The elder, Thomas Norton, was born in London in 1532, was educated at Cambridge and the Inner Temple, and had a distinguished career as a lawyer and a diplomat. In addition he devoted much time to literature, writing Latin and English verse, translating the Psalms and Calvin's *Institution of Christian Religion* (1561), and penning pamphlets of religious controversy. In spite of his historical importance to the English drama, Norton was opposed to the stage in his later years. He died in 1584.

Thomas Sackville was even more distinguished. The son of Sir Richard Sackville, cousin of Anne Bullen, Thomas was probably educated at one of the Universities and certainly at the Inner Temple. He too was a man of affairs and a diplomat, serving as ambassador to various countries; commissioner of state trials, in which capacity he announced to Mary Queen of Scots the sentence of death; and Lord Treasurer from 1599 on. He was also elected Chancellor of Oxford University (1591) and created Earl of Dorset (1604). He died at the council table in 1608. In addition to his part authorship of *Gorboduc*, Sackville contributed the celebrated Induction (1563) to *The Mirror for Magistrates*, a collection of tragic narratives in verse about the falls of English nobles designed as a continuation of Lydgate's *Falls of Princes*.

CRITICAL COMMENT. Hence, with such authors, it is not surprising that *Gorboduc* probably had more significance for its first audiences as politics than as literature. It is a story from legendary British history, but its theme is succession to the crown, a subject which was uppermost in the minds of thinking Englishmen in 1562 when this play was first produced before the Queen. The drama is a kind of mirror for magistrates and the vehicle for special warning of the chaos, dissension, and civil war which might result should Elizabeth die without an heir.

But whatever its original import, *Gorboduc* is an important literary landmark. It stems from both a native and a foreign tradition: *The Mirror for Magistrates,* which is narrative, and the works of the Latin philosopher Seneca the Younger (4 B.C.–65 A.D.), which are dramatic. Both draw their themes from legend, preferably sensational legends of murder, revenge, adultery, and incest. Both are didactic; the characters are of high estate and individually responsible for their falls; their stories all illustrate what is the "salary of sin." Both are psychological analyses of passions and sentiments; both are rhetorical and filled with talk rather than action, interminable soliloquies, set speeches, reports of happenings, sententious moralizing, and declamation. This double model sufficed for much Elizabethan tragedy, early and late. But whereas the *Mirror* could only relate deeds of violence, and classical decorum excluded such scenes from representation on a stage—as also in *Gorboduc*—later Elizabethan dramatists modelling on the *Mirror* and the plays of Seneca did not deny themselves such important tragic aides. They presented such scenes on the boards.

Furthermore, the very form in which *Gorboduc* was written set a pattern for the future. The play was couched in blank verse rather than the rhymed doggerel which had served in earlier popular drama, and from that time on blank verse was customary for dignified drama. *Gorboduc,* however, did disregard the classical unities of time and place, but native English drama had always done so and was to continue doing so.

SOURCE. The source of *Gorboduc* is Grafton's *Chronicle* (1556), but the story springs ultimately from Geoffrey of Monmouth's *Historia Regum Britanniae.*

BIBLIOGRAPHY

Early editions: 1565 [unauthorized]; n.d. [c. 1570–71]; 1590.

Modern editions: Facs. J. S. Farmer (TFT, 1908); ed. H. A. Watt, Madison, Wisconsin, 1910; J. W. Cunliffe (*Early Classical Tragedies,* 1912).

THE TRAGEDY OF

GORBODUC

OR FERREX AND PORREX

(1562)

DRAMATIS PERSONAE

GORBODUC, aged King of Britain, renowned for his just, peaceful, and prosperous reign.

AROSTUS, a faithful old councilor to the king.

EUBULUS, confidential secretary to the king.

VIDENA, queen of Gorboduc and mother of Ferrex and Porrex. She loves her eldest son "more dearly than herself," and hates the younger. ("O queen of adamant! O marble breast!")

MARCELLA, a lady of the queen's privy chamber.

FERREX, elder son to King Gorboduc and Queen Videna; his mother's favorite.

HERMON, his parasite, and the foolish adviser of his youth.

DORDAN, a wise councilor assigned by the king to Ferrex.

PORREX, younger son of King Gorboduc and Queen Videna, "traitor to kin and kind . . . to [his] own flesh, and traitor to [himself]."

TYNDAR, his parasite and foolish adviser.

PHILANDER, a sage councilor assigned by the king to Porrex.

FERGUS, Duke of Albany, a proud, dissembling, willful traitor who takes advantage of unhappy times.

CLOTYN, Duke of Cornwall,
MANDUD, Duke of Logris, } loyal nobles of the kingdom.
GWENARD, Duke of Cumberland,

Nuntius, a messenger who announces the elder brother's death.

Nuntius, a messenger who announces Duke Fergus' rising in arms.

Chorus, four ancient and sage men of Britain.

Characters in the Dumb Shows:

Act I: Six wild men, clothed in leaves.
Act II: A king; a grave and aged councilor; a brave and lusty, but false, young councilor; various nobles and gentlemen.
Act III: A company of mourners.
Act IV: Three furies from Hell—Alecto, Megaera, and Tisiphone—clad in black garments sprinkled with blood and flame, their heads covered with serpents instead of hair; Tantalus, Medea, Athamas, Ino, Cambises, and Althea, kings and queens who have murdered their own children.
Act V: Companies of harquebusiers and other armed men.

Setting: Legendary Britain.

*"Within one land one single rule is best;
Divided reigns do make divided hearts,
But peace preserves the country and the prince."*

Act I

Dumb show: Six wild men, clothed in leaves, enact the fable of the faggot and the sticks; each in turn tries to break a strong bundle of sticks but fails, whereas each easily breaks a single stick.

Gorboduc, King of Britain, and direct descendant from Brute, founder of the kingdom, plans to divide his realm between his two sons, Ferrex and Porrex, and retire from rule. He calls his councilors together to explain his purpose and to get their opinion of the plan as beneficial for him, his sons, his subjects, and the country as a whole. Arostus, his senior adviser, expresses his full approval of the scheme as the best way to ensure continued peace and prosperity in the kingdom. Philander approves of the division of the territory, but cautions against putting the plan into effect during the king's lifetime, arguing that the princes in their youth can learn to rule by the example of their father. Eubulus, the king's secretary, disapproves of the plan altogether, primarily because he believes that centralized power is best for a commonwealth and that divided rule makes divided hearts. Moreover, he fears that should the elder brother be deprived of the full heritage which custom might rightfully lead him to expect, he may think himself wronged by his younger brother; or, on the other hand, should the younger son be so upraised in state, he may become proud and envious of the elder. In either case civil war might result, and to avoid so dire a possibility the king might better keep the young princes at home where he can control their advisers and set an example for them of both good governance and obedience. None of these arguments seems weighty to the king, however, and he announces his decision to award the realm south of the Humber to his elder son, Ferrex, and that north of this boundary to the younger, Porrex. As assurance against the calamities Eubulus has warned him of, he will appoint for each of the princes a sage and tried adviser.

The Chorus interprets these events in the light of the fable of the faggot and the sticks; in unity there is strength, in division weakness.

Act II

Dumb show: A king, seated on his throne and surrounded by his nobles, is offered wine in a clear glass by a grave and aged courtier, but refuses it. Instead he accepts from a flashy young gentleman a golden cup filled with poison, drinks of it, and immediately falls down dead.

In their respective courts the two young kings consult their councilors. Ferrex, the elder, begins to marvel that without deserving it he should have been deprived by his father of half of his kingdom. His wicked parasite, Hermon, encourages these rebellious thoughts, and, in spite of all that the sage Dordan can do, he stirs up in Ferrex a mortal distrust and hate of his brother Porrex. For the time being, however, Ferrex puts aside Hermon's foul suggestion that he kill his brother and seize his kingdom, but thinks it wise nevertheless to arm against any possible emergency. The virtuous Dordan resolves in haste to inform old King Gorboduc of the mischief that is brewing. In the north Porrex, too, has a foolish and a wise councilor. Tyndar, his parasite, fans the latent fire of his treacherous ambition by reporting the secret preparations of Ferrex and the spread of ugly rumors through both kingdoms. In vain does Philander, his wise friend, urge the king before acting rashly to send to Ferrex and to Gorboduc for explanations. Porrex, instead, resolves to invade his brother's realm and kill the prince at his own court. Philander hurries off to Gorboduc's court, hopeful of averting grave disaster.

The Chorus interprets this twofold preference of flattery and deceit to wholesome counsel in the light of the parable of the two cups:

> *Lo, thus it is, poison in gold to take,*
> *And wholesome drink in homely cup forsake.*

Act III

Dumb show: Mourners clad in black march about the stage betokening death and sorrow to ensue upon the ill-advised misgovernment and dissension of the brothers.

Gorboduc is in council over a letter received from Dordan and containing the grievous news of Ferrex's preparations against his brother, when Philander arrives with even worse tidings from the north. Before the woe-stricken king can act, however, a messenger brings word that Porrex has invaded the southern kingdom, slain his brother Ferrex with his own hand, and taken possession of his realm.

The Chorus again interprets the action and the symbolism of the dumb show which opened the act.

Act IV

Dumb show: Three snaky-haired furies out of Hell—Alecto, Megaera, and Tisiphone—clad in black garments sprinkled with blood and flame, the first wielding in her hand a serpent, the second a whip, and the third a burning firebrand, drive before them Tantalus, Medea, Athamas, Ino, Cambises, and Althea, all kings or queens who unnaturally have slain their children.

In soliloquy Queen Videna, with uncontrollable grief for her favorite son Ferrex, renounces the younger brother as a false and caitiff wight and swears vengeance upon him for his crime. Meanwhile, Gorboduc has sent Eubulus to bring Porrex to court for judgment. The prince justifies himself as best he can and is temporarily banished from the royal presence. Before Gorboduc can decide upon a proper punishment, however, Marcella, one of the queen's women-in-waiting, brings the dire news that as he slept Porrex has been stabbed to death by his mother.

Once more the Chorus interprets the symbolism of the dumb show.

Act V

Dumb show: To the martial music of drums and flutes companies of harque-busiers and other armed men, in battle array, march tumultuously about the stage, firing their weapons.

Deeply moved by these crimes and forgetful of both law and loyalty, the people have arisen in rebellion and slain both Gorboduc and his guilty queen, leaving the kingdom without an accepted head and the open prey to any ambitious noble or foreign prince who cares to under-take the conquest. A council, attended by Clotyn, Duke of Cornwall; Mandud, Duke of Logris; Gwenard, Duke of Cumberland; Fergus, Duke of Albany; and the ever-sagacious Eubulus, discusses how best to quiet the common people's minds and save the kingdom from utter ruin. Fergus of Albany, however, sees in the tumult and confusion his op-portunity for power. While the other nobles are arresting the leaders of the rebellion, hanging or putting to the sword those who refuse to lay down their arms, and disbanding the more reasonable of the in-surgents, Fergus represents himself to the country as the only savior of the people and the land and raises an army of twenty thousand men. Around the faithful Arostus and Eubulus the remaining nobles rally, fully realizing the danger that Britain will be torn by civil strife, murder, and rapine, and that there is little hope that Parliament, should it as-semble, could agree upon an heir to the throne. Only God at last can restore the crown to the proper lawful authority:

> *These mischiefs spring when rebels will arise*
> *To work revenge and judge their prince's fact.*
> *This, this ensues, when noble men do fail*
> *In loyal truth, and subjects will be kings.*

GEORGE GASCOIGNE
(c. 1542–1578)

BIOGRAPHY. As courtier, soldier, member of Parliament, dilettante, poet, satirist, playwright, and general literary pioneer, George Gascoigne was a typi-cal Elizabethan in his versatility. Born in Bedfordshire about 1542 or earlier, he was a descendant of that Sir William Gascoigne, Henry IV's Chief Justice, who is said to have committed Prince Hal to prison for insubordination (see Elyot's *The Governor,* 1531). However apocryphal this story may be, it is certain that the Elizabethan Gascoigne emulated the Plantagenet prince rather than the distinguished jurist. George Gascoigne was educated at Trinity College, Cambridge, and Gray's Inn; became a dissipated hanger-on at court; was disinherited by his father for his notorious escapades; was prevented from sitting in Parliament because of charges; recouped his fortunes in 1566 by marrying Elizabeth Breton, a wealthy widow and the mother of Nicholas Breton the poet; joined the army of William of Orange in the Low Countries to avoid his debtors at home; was captured by the Spaniards; returned to England and wrote two books about his adventures; and contributed to *The Princely Pleasures* at Kenilworth (1575)—all before he was thirty-three. He died in 1577 or 1578.

Gascoigne's literary output was as varied as his life; in addition to plays he wrote lyrics, satires, criticism, fiction, devotional treatises, penitential pamphlets, and translations.

CRITICAL COMMENT. A remarkably successful play in its time, *Supposes* was first produced at Gray's Inn in 1566, and restaged at Oxford in 1582. For the student of the English drama the work has four main significances: (*a*) it is the earliest comedy written in prose throughout, and brilliant dramatic prose at that; (*b*) it is the first English translation of an Italian adaptation of Roman comedy; (*c*) it set the fashion for Italian settings in plays until the time of Ben Jonson and beyond; and (*d*) it is the source of the Bianca-Lucentio subplot for Shakespeare's *The Taming of the Shrew*. But like other early English comedies, *Supposes* is really a blend of the classic and the romantic. Whereas in Latin and Italian comedy love is treated cynically, in English drama it is a healthy source of mirth or a sentiment of beauty. *Supposes* is not wholly pure, but it is not abnormal.

SOURCE. *Suppose* is just what it claims to be, a free translation of Ludovico Ariosto's *I Suppositi* (The Substitutes) (1509), which in turn borrows several devices from Latin comedy, notably the *Captivi* of Plautus, where a master exchanges roles with his servant, and the *Eunuchus* of Terence, in which a lover adopts disguise to enter the house of a girl. Other character types and devices also common in Roman comedy are the parasite and the rich wooer, the substitute for the father, the love intrigue, the mistaken identity, and the discovery of the long-lost son.

BIBLIOGRAPHY

Collected Works: *The Complete Works of George Gascoigne,* edited by J. W. Cunliffe, 2 volumes, Cambridge, 1907-10.

Early editions: 1573 [with *A Hundred Sundry Flowers*]; 1575 (2) [with *Posies*]; 1587 [in *The Whole Works*].

Modern editions: ed. J. W. Cunliffe (Belles Lettres Series, 1906); R. Warwick Bond (*Early Plays from the Italian,* 1911).

SUPPOSES

A COMEDY

(1566)

DRAMATIS PERSONAE

DAMON, a widower of Ferrara, possessed of one fair daughter, Polynesta. "He is a wise man and desirous to place his daughter well. He will not be too rash in his determination; he will think well of the matter." ("O poor dolorous Damon, more miserable than misery itself!")

POLYNESTA, his daughter; wooed by three suitors, she loves only the feigned Dulippo. "A costly jewel may [Damon] well account her, that hath been [his] chief comfort in youth, and now is become the corrosive of [his] age! . . . Five years are past since [he] might have married her, when by continual excuses [he has] prolonged it to [his] own perdition. Alas, [he] should have considered she is a collop of [his] own flesh. . . . O God, how men may be deceived in a woman! Who would have believed the contrary but that she had been a virgin? . . . Mark her behaviors, and you would have judged her very maidenly—seldom seen abroad but in place of prayer and there very devout, and no gazer at outward sights, no blazer of her beauty above in the windows, no stale at the door for the by-passers. You would have thought her a holy young woman."

BALIA, her nurse, "the broker of all this bargain. . . . Indeed, [she has] thought it always a deed of charity to help the miserable young men whose tender youth consumeth with the furious flames of love."

DULIPPO, feigned servant in Damon's household; really Erostrato, gentleman and student from Sicilia, and Polynesta's lover, who "to follow this amorous enterprise [has] set aside all study, all remembrance of [his] duty, and all dread of shame." [Called Dulippo throughout the play.]

EROSTRATO, feigned master, who presents himself as "an earnest suitor to [Polynesta] and requireth [her] of [her] father in marriage." He is really Dulippo, a servant, "who took upon him the name of Erostrato, his master, his habit, the credit, books, and all things needful to a student, and in short space profited very much. . . . Indeed, he is very much commended of all men, and specially of the best reputed students." [Called Erostrato throughout the play.]

DALIO, the cook,

CRAPINO, the lackey, a "whoreson boy. . . . He fighteth ⎫ servants to the feigned with the dogs, beateth the bears; at everything in the ⎬ Erostrato. street he findeth occasion to tarry," ⎭

CLEANDER, doctor of law, "Doctor Dotipole, . . . the doting [old] fool that dare presume to become a suitor to such a peerless paragon" as Polynesta; "an excellent good bibbler, especially in a bottle." ("What a lusky yonker is this?")

CARION, his servingman, "greedy gut."

PASIPHILO, a parasite, "now with one, and then with the other, according as [he] sees their caters provide good cheer at the market; . . . thus [he] becomes a broker on both sides. . . . He is not to trust unto—a very flattering and a lying knave."

PHILOGANO, a Sicilian gentleman, "the right father of the right Erostrato, . . . one of the worthiest men in all Cathanea."

LITIO, his worldly-wise servant.

A Sienese Merchant, stranger in Ferrara. ("By my troth, he looks even like a good soul! He that fisheth for him might be sure to catch a cod's head!")

PAQUETTO, ⎫
PETRUCHIO,⎭ his servants.

A Ferrarese Innkeeper.

PSITERIA, an old trot in Damon's household. ("You old callet, you tattling huswife!")

NEVOLA, and two other Servants of Damon's.

Setting: Ferrara at some unspecified time.

> "*The strangest case that ever you heard! A man might make a comedy of it.*"

Act I

Damon, a well-to-do widower of Ferrara, has a beautiful daughter named Polynesta, who is of marriageable age, and around her or the amorous intrigues of which she is the object all of the *supposes* (i.e., substitutions or mix-ups) occur. "More desirous of the dower than mindful of his gentle and gallant daughter," Damon is a deliberate man, and now for five years on one pretext or another he has postponed a decision about a proper marriage for her. As the play opens Polynesta is being bid for by two suitors—Cleander, an old doting doctor of law—"this buzzard, this bribing villain, . . . this old mumpsimus"—who is nearly sixty, and Erostrato, a young Sicilian gentleman who came to Ferrara as a student. The latter's suit, however, is but a strategic scheme to provide competition for the doctor and to place obstacles in his way, for Polynesta has already provided herself with a lover. He is Dulippo, who for two years now has been a servant in Damon's household and "under color of Damon's service . . . [has] been a sworn servant to Cupid." But the wily wench has bestowed her love more worthily than at first appears. Dulippo is really the noble-born Erostrato, who, meeting Polynesta in the street, became enamored of her, cast aside gown and books, and changed name, clothes, and credit with his servant. So, with the turning of a hand, Erostrato the gentleman became Dulippo the servingman employed by Damon, and the real Dulippo strutted it bravely as a student and in short space, as a blind for his master's amour, became before Damon an earnest competitor with the doctor for Polynesta's hand.

Act II

Informed by Pasiphilo, the parasite, whom he had taken home to supper, the feigned Erostrato learns that Damon is inclined to accept the handsome dowry offered by Cleander. Through Pasiphilo, the feigned Erostrato offers a like sum and requests Damon to reserve his decision for a fortnight until Philogano, his father, shall arrive in Ferrara to confirm the offer. Then, under necessity of producing his father and meeting a gullible old gentleman from Siena, the rascal tells him of the sudden enmity that has arisen between the Ferrarese and the Sienese and the danger that will ensue if he is known in Ferrara to be from the enemy town. He so frightens the stranger that for protection the old man is willing to go home with the feigned Erostrato and permit himself to be passed off as Philogano of Cathanea. At the same time, the feigned Dulippo, informed of the feigned Erostrato's arrangements, does what he can to discredit Pasiphilo with Cleander, by secretly accusing him of double-dealing and slandering the doctor to Damon.

Act III

By overhearing a servants' quarrel, Damon discovers the truth about his daughter. Deeply grieved at his dishonor, desirous of revenge, but even more fearful that the disgrace be published to the world, Damon has his offending servant, the feigned Dulippo, apprehended and thrown into a dungeon, his agents supposing merely that Dulippo, who always has gone bravely apparelled, is guilty of embezzling his master's money. Unfortunately, however, Pasiphilo had been eavesdropping in the stable when Damon wrung the secret out of his old servant Psiteria, and the parasite expects to find this spicy information useful.

Act IV

To Ferrara now comes the real Philogano, a doting father on a visit to a son who has been so "studious" that he has seldom written home and has never permitted any of his father's friends to interrupt his academic meditations when they have come to call on him. Through an accommodating Ferrarese innkeeper, Philogano finds his son's house, is confronted by the feigned Philogano and outfaced by him, recognizes the feigned Erostrato as the servant Dulippo, but at last is barred out of the house by armed servants. Philogano the father naturally suspects foul play, but he is accompanied by a keen-witted and cynical servant named Litio who sees in all these events nothing but "the falsehood of Ferrara." Partly for the honor of the town and partly to vindicate himself of complicity, the innkeeper offers to help the old man to the police that he may have redress for his wrongs. Philogano takes eagerly to the suggestion so that he may "disclose a pack of the greatest knavery, a fardel of the foulest falsehood, that ever was heard of." Litio, however, is more practical or more experienced in the ways of the world. He who would go to law, he reminds his master, "must be sure of four things: first, a right and a just cause; then a righteous advocate to plead; next favor *coram judice* [i.e., before the judge]; and, above all, a good purse to procure it." The innkeeper knows just the lawyer for them, a learned doctor who hates Erostrato and will do whatever he can to spite him; they are rivals for the hand of the same girl. His name is Cleander.

Act V

Both characters and situations become more mixed up before there are any clarifying explanations. The feigned Erostrato is smitten with remorse because of his necessary deception of the old man who has been more of a father than a master to him. Pasiphilo reveals to him that the affair of Polynesta and Dulippo has been discovered and that the feigned servant is in prison. Believing that under the circumstances the feigned Erostrato will never marry the girl now, the parasite resolves to assist Cleander in the match, but he is railed at by the doctor who believes him a knave and a villain. And the grief-stricken Damon discovers that Pasiphilo knows his disgrace and will spread it throughout the city. "He that will have a thing kept secret, let him tell it to Pasiphilo! The people shall know it, and as many as have ears, and no mo."

Gradually the "supposes" are cleared up. It is discovered that the servant Dulippo (i.e., the feigned Erostrato) is really Doctor Cleander's long-lost son, captured when the Turks took Otranto, and sold into slavery. This revelation is small comfort to the litigants, however, for the lawyer chosen as an especially favorable advocate will now become an adversary. Philogano is proved to be the real father of Erostrato and in no way the social inferior of Damon; Damon graciously accepts his feigned servant as a son-in-law; the old Sienese merchant resolves in the future not to trust at first sight every man he meets; and even Cleander— who no longer wishes a wife so that he may have children—apologizes for believing tales of the parasite Pasiphilo and invites him to sup at his house every night for a week.

THOMAS PRESTON
(Dates unknown)

BIOGRAPHY. Of Thomas Preston, the author of *Cambises,* this crude mixture of morality and tragedy, nothing is known, and his very identity is in dispute. Historians of the drama were once inclined to identify him with the

Thomas Preston who entered King's College, Cambridge, from Eton in 1553, became a fellow in 1556, was appointed Master of Trinity Hall in 1584, and proceeded to the vice-chancellorship of the University in 1589. More recently, however, Sir Edmund Chambers has expressed doubt that an academic admired for his Latinity would write a play so clearly designed for production by a professional troupe of actors with limited resources as to personnel. He suggests, therefore, another Thomas Preston, who about 1570 was a popular author of broadside ballads, some of which, like *Cambises,* are subscribed: "Finis, Quod Thomas Preston."

CRITICAL COMMENT. Whoever its author, *Cambises* is an important example of the transition from the old morality to historical tragedy on the popular stage. In technique the play offers a sharp contrast to *Gorboduc;* the story is carried on or explained largely by abstract characters, and the action is manipulated by Ambidexter, who is derived directly from the Vice of the morality plays. Its loose structure; its mixture of history, farce, and allegory; and its representations of crude horror are illustrative of popular Elizabethan tragedy at its worst. Moreover, its bombast became proverbial. Burlesquing Prince Hal's royal father, Falstaff reproves the playboy prince in a parody of this old melodrama: "for I must speak in passion, and I will do it in King Cambises' vein" (*1 Henry IV,* II, iv, 425). The very title is parodied in *A Midsummer Night's Dream:* "The Most Lamentable Comedy, and Most Cruel Death of Pyramus and Thisby"—very tragical mirth.

SOURCE. The story of Cambises, King of Persia, derives originally from Herodotus and found its way into those collections of tragic narrative popular in the Middle Ages and the Renaissance, like Boccaccio's *De Casibus Virorum Illustrium,* Lydgate's *Falls of Princes,* and *The Mirror for Magistrates,* which told of the fall of an eminent personage at the height of his arrogance.

BIBLIOGRAPHY

Early editions: n.d. [c. 1569]; n.d. [1585?]; n.d. [1585–88?].
Modern edition: Facs. J. S. Farmer (TFT, 1910).

A LAMENTABLE TRAGEDY, MIXED FULL OF PLEASANT MIRTH, CONTAINING

THE LIFE OF CAMBISES KING OF PERSIA

(c. 1558–1570)

DRAMATIS PERSONAE

AMBIDEXTER, the Vice, "one that with both hands finely can play," a double-dealing mischief-maker who serves both as tempter and as commentator upon the action.

CAMBISES, cruel King of Persia, son of Cyrus the Great. "The king himself was godly uptrained; he professed virtue—but I think it was feigned. . . . All piety and virtuous life he doth it clean refuse; lechery and drunkenness he doth it much frequent; . . . he naught esteems his counsel grave ne virtuous bringing up."

SMIRDIS, his brother and next heir to the throne, "of youth and manly might." Victim of Cambises' treachery.

SISAMNES, "a judge . . . of prudent skill, . . . learned in the law, having the gift of wit, . . . [but] a man that to himself is nigh [i.e., self-seeking], . . . [and] one that favoreth much the world and sets too much thereby." Condemnation of his grafting ways is King Cambises' one good deed.

OTIAN, Sisamnes' son and successor.

PRAXASPES, a virtuous courtier who courageously condemns the king's intemperance.

His Wife.

Their Young Son, another victim of Cambises' tyranny.

A Lady, later Queen, "cousin-german [to the king], nigh by birth, by mother's side come in. . . . For beauty she most worthy is to sit in prince's chair," were she not so closely akin to the king. Still another victim of Cambises' cruelty.

A Waiting Maid, attending her.

Lords, Knights, and Councilors of Cambises' court.

HUF,
RUF, }ruffianly soldiers.
SNUF,

MERETRIX, a courtesan and a common camp follower.

HOB, }clownish countrymen.
LOB,

MARIAN-MAY-BE-GOOD, Hob's shrewish wife.

SMALL ABILITY, SHAME, COMMONS' CRY, COMMONS' COMPLAINT, TRIAL, PROOF, EXECUTION, ATTENDANCE, DILIGENCE, PREPARATION, CRUELTY, MURDER, VENUS, CUPID.

Setting: Persia in the sixth century B.C.

"The odious facts and shameless deeds that Cambises king doth use."

Act I

Upon succeeding to the throne, Cambises, son of Cyrus the Great, King of Persia, resolves to emulate his warlike father by conducting a campaign against the Egyptians. He is supported in his purpose by his council, his nobility, and his knights, but they all admonish him, once he has set out upon a noble course, to put aside vice and devote himself wholly to martial feats, kingly sports, and virtue. Because war is fraught with danger, his council advises him also to appoint a deputy to rule the kingdom during his absence. Cambises selects Sisamnes, a learned judge, but one, it is rumored, who is nevertheless somewhat worldly and self-seeking. Sisamnes in soliloquy reviews his opportunities for gaining wealth and power, but virtuously resolves to keep the king's laws and not overstep his authority.

Act II

War gives opportunity to viciousness of all kinds, and Ambidexter the Vice demonstrates how he can adapt himself passably to either war or peace. With a pot for a helmet and a rake for a spear, he engages in some knock-about horseplay with the ruffianly soldiers, Huf, Ruf, and Snuf, who hope for plenty of plunder from the war, and with them he competes for the favors of Mistress Meretrix, the courtesan. Meretrix drives them all away because they have too little money, and Ambidexter now turns his attention to corrupting Sisamnes. The judge readily forsakes his high principles and follows the custom of the time by taking bribes. Small Ability, a poor simple man, appeals to him for justice, but is denied fair treatment because he cannot pay. Meanwhile, Shame is trumpeting forth the odious crimes of King Cambises himself, who is given to drunkenness and lechery and will suffer no restraints. Returning home from his battles, the king hears Commons' Cry denouncing his deputy for his corrupt practices, and righteously sits in judgment on him with Commons' Complaint, Proof, and Trial as accusers. Convinced of his guilt, Cambises condemns Sisamnes to death. Praxaspes, a courtier, suggests that since in the course of events Otian, Sisamnes' son, will succeed his father to the judgeship, it might be a salutary lesson to the young man if he were to witness his father's execution. Otian's pleas of mercy for his father are vain, and Sisamnes is cruelly put to the sword and afterwards flayed.

Act III

But this one commendable deed on Cambises' part in condemning a dishonest judge, is soon completely eclipsed by renewed acts of cruelty. Because Praxaspes continues to rebuke the king for drunkenness, even in the presence of his flatterers, Cambises becomes revengeful and angrily proposes a proof of his sobriety. Praxaspes has a young son; if, in his cups, the king can shoot an arrow through the boy's heart, it will prove that he is no drunkard. Unmoved by Praxaspes' pleading, Cambises drinks deep and shoots the child. Then, not content with its death, he has its cleft heart cut out and presented to the horror-stricken father as proof of his marksmanship.

Act IV

Ambidexter now tries to corrupt Smirdis, brother of the king and next heir to the throne, but without notable success, although the prince grieves for his brother's crimes. The Vice then suggests to Cambises that Smirdis prays for the king's death and lives virtuously only that by contrast he may attain more fame and honor than his brother. Cambises resolves that Smirdis shall die. Accordingly, as the prince walks alone, he is seized by Cruelty and Murder and brutally slain. The double-dealing Ambidexter alternately pretends to weep and to laugh at the crimes he has caused; and, meeting Goodman Hob and Goodman Lob, two countrymen on their way to market, he at first encourages their criticism of the king's cruelty and then roundly accuses them of treason. In their fright the two clowns begin to quarrel among themselves, urged on by Ambidexter, until Marian-May-Be-Good, Hob's shrewish wife, parts them and effects a reconciliation. Then she belabors the Vice with her broom until he runs away.

Act V

To infect the wicked king with unholy love for a kinswoman who lives at his court, Venus bids her son Cupid loose his golden arrow at Cambises' heart. The king is smitten by the shaft as he sees the lady out walking with her maid-in-waiting and a lord, and forthwith makes love to her. At first she refuses him, but at length, against her better judgment, he persuades her to marriage. Preparation, aided by Ambidexter, makes ready an elaborate marriage feast. At the banquet Cambises tells a tale which reminds the queen of the king's treatment of his brother, and she rebukes him for his unnatural crime. Angered beyond control, Cambises swears to have her life, and in spite of the intercession of his courtiers, he orders his executioners, Cruelty and Murder, to take her out and kill her. Alternately, Ambidexter weeps for the queen and rehearses the king's murders, prophesying that a monarch who has shed so much blood will die a violent death. Accordingly, Cambises soon makes his appearance with a sword in his side. As the king leapt upon horseback his weapon accidentally shot from its scabbard and wounded him mortally—in just reward for his misdeeds. Ambidexter fears lest, being at the scene of the accident, he be charged with murder.

JOHN LYLY
(1554?–1606)

BIOGRAPHY. John Lyly, born c. 1554, came of a Hampshire family and was the grandson of William Lyly, Colet's first headmaster of Paul's School.

His father, Peter Lyly, was a diocesan official at Canterbury, and the dramatist, therefore, was probably born in the cathedral city. He was educated at Magdalen College, Oxford (B.A., 1573; M.A., 1575), and also studied at Cambridge (M.A., 1579). In 1579 Lyly achieved fame by his *Euphues, the Anatomy of Wit,* which depicted the well-bred man of Elizabethan standards, and popularized in elegant circles a precious style of writing and speaking. "Our nation are in his debt for a new English which he taught them," wrote Edward Blount, who edited *Six Court Plays* in 1632. "All our ladies were then his scholars, . . . [and] that beauty in court which could not parley Euphuism was as little regarded, as she which now there speaks not French." During the 1580's Lyly wrote dramas for Paul's boys for presentation at court. All but one is in the same self-conscious prose employed in *Euphues.* From 1589 to 1601 Lyly was a member of Parliament, and he seems to have been involved on the episcopal side in the Marprelate Controversy.

In literature everything which Lyly did was calculated to advance him at court. About 1585 he seems to have had some promise of favor from the Queen, and later a hint to "aim his courses at the Revels." But if so, he was disappointed; in 1597 the Mastership had been definitely promised to George Buc, and there exist several letters in which Lyly complains bitterly of the wrong done him. "Thirteen years your Highness' servant, but yet nothing. Twenty friends that though they say they will be sure, I find them sure to be slow. A thousand hopes, but all nothing; a hundred promises but yet nothing. Thus casting up the inventory of my friends, hopes, promises, and times, the *summa totalis* amounteth to just nothing." He died in November, 1606.

CRITICAL COMMENT. To modern tastes the dramas of John Lyly seem precious, anemic, and overliterary when compared with the more robust writing of some of his contemporaries. The stories he chose from mythology and ancient history and his themes of courtly unemotional love are academic and unexciting. His characters are wooden and too easily referable to stock types— the lover, the coy mistress, the faithful friend, the intriguer, the eccentric, the witty little page. His wit, too, seems thin and outmoded, and his dialogue utterly unlifelike. But it must be remembered that Lyly was striving to please a limited audience of the court, not that of the public theatres, and that to that cultivated group he was "the only rare poet of that time, the witty, comical, facetiously quick and unparalleled John Lyly, Master of Arts." Also as he explains in the Prologue to *Sapho and Phao,* his purpose is merely "to breed . . . soft smiling, not loud laughing; knowing it to the wise to be as great pleasure to hear counsel mix'd with wit, as to the foolish to have sport mingled with rudeness." Prattled by little boys, Lyly's lines were probably amusing enough.

John Lyly may not have been a great dramatist, but he was an influential one. In the 1580's the fare at the public theatres was too crude, too formless, too flamboyant. By the force of his courtly example, Lyly raised the drama to the level of art and gave it dignity, finish, and discipline. Shakespeare and his fellows learned much from Lyly.

It is not surprising, either, to learn that from the beginning Lyly's plays have been suspected of allegory. This is especially true of *Endymion;* the Prologue simply protests too much for an Elizabethan audience or a modern reader not to suspect that there is more here than meets the eye. Various explanations have been suggested by modern scholars, that the play treats of (*a*) the relations of the Queen and either the Earl of Leicester or the Earl of Oxford; (*b*) the rivalry of Elizabeth with Mary Queen of Scots (Tellus); or (*c*) the hopes of James VI of Scotland (Endymion) of the throne. Others have even identified the minor characters: Geron as the Earl of Shrewsbury; Dipsas as his countess; Eumenides the good counselor as Sir Philip Sidney or the Earl of Sussex or Lord Burleigh; Semele as Penelope Rich or Frances Sidney; Sir Tophas as Stephen Gosson or Gabriel Harvey. But without denying the presence of topical allusions in the play, more recent opinion is sceptical of these allegorical interpretations. The play may be no more than a study in Platonic love in which Endymion passes from love of Tellus or Earthly Beauty to the adoration of Cynthia or Heavenly Beauty. See the articles by Professor P. W. Long, "The Purport of Lyly's *Endymion,*" *PMLA*, XXIV (1909) and *MP*, VII (1911). Sir Edmund Chambers is probably right: "if Lyly had meant half of what [the critics] suggest, he would have ruined his career . . . at the outset."

SOURCES. The story of Alexander's renunciation of Campaspe in favor of Apelles is told in Pliny's *Natural History* (XXV, 36); Alexander's conquest of Thebes, and his relations with Hephestion, Timoclea, and Diogenes are mentioned in Plutarch's *Life of Alexander* (tr. by Sir Thomas North, 1579). But there is no mention here of either Apelles or Campaspe. Diogenes' story is found in Diogenes Laertius' *Vitae Philosophorum.* It is Lyly who brought the material all together.

The classic myth of Endymion's sleep and Cynthia's kiss is found in Lucian's *Dialogues of the Gods* (No. 11), and in Ovid's *Metamorphoses.*

BIBLIOGRAPHY

Collected Works: *The Works of John Lyly,* edited by R. Warwick Bond, 3 volumes, Oxford, 1902.

Monographs:

J. Dover Wilson, *John Lyly,* 1905.

Albert Feuillerat, *John Lyly: Contribution à l'histoire de la renaissance en Angleterre,* 1910.

V. M. Jeffrey, *John Lyly and the Italian Renaissance,* 1929.

Alexander and Campaspe:

Early editions: 1584 (3); 1591; 1632 [*Six Court Comedies*].
Modern edition: ed. W. W. Greg (MSR, 1933).

Endymion:

Early editions: 1591; 1632 [*Six Court Comedies*].
Modern edition: ed. G. P. Baker, 1894

A Most Excellent Comedy of

ALEXANDER, CAMPASPE, AND DIOGENES

(1580–1584)

DRAMATIS PERSONAE

CAMPASPE, a Theban captive girl, "born of a mean parentage, but to extreme fortune, . . . whose eyes are framed by art to enamor, and whose heart was made by nature to enchant, . . . a hair curling by nature, not art; sweet alluring eyes; . . . a wit apt to conceive and quick to answer; a skin as soft as silk. . . . What of this? Though she have heavenly gifts, virtue, and beauty, is she not earthly metal, flesh and blood?"

ALEXANDER THE GREAT, King of Macedon, who falls in love with his captive. "He drinketh not blood, but thirsteth after honor; he is greedy of victory, but never satisfied with mercy; in fight terrible, as becometh a captain; in conquest mild, as beseemeth a king; in all things than which nothing can be greater he is Alexander." ("Will you handle the spindle with Hercules when you should shake the spear with Achilles?")

APELLES, a painter. ("O Apelles, thy love cometh from the heart, but Alexander's from the mouth!")

DIOGENES THE CYNIC, an independent, churlish philosopher, who lives frugally in a tub and "keeps but cold cheer. . . . He is dogged, but discreet; I cannot tell how sharp, with a kind of sweetness; full of wit, yet too-too wayward."

ARISTOTLE,
PLATO,
CHRYSIPPUS,
CRATES,   }philosophers summoned to Athens by Alexander.
CLEANTHES,
ANAXARCHUS,
CRYSUS,

MELIPPUS, chamberlain to Alexander, who summons the philosophers to the king's presence.

HEPHESTION, Alexander's general, "who thirsteth for honor, not ease."

CLYTUS,   }officers in Alexander's armies.
PARMENIO,

TIMOCLEA, a Theban captive girl of "stout courage."

LAIS, a courtesan.

MILECTUS, }soldiers accompanying Lais the courtesan.
PHRYGIUS,

SYLVIUS, citizen of Athens, who brings his sons to Diogenes to school.

PERIM, who dances,
MILO, who tumbles, }young sons of Sylvius.
TRICO, who sings,

SOLINUS, citizen of Athens, who comes to see Diogenes fly.

GRANICHUS, servant to Plato.

MANES, hungry servant to Diogenes, who "had rather fill [his] guts than [his] brains. . . . Could [he] see but a cook's shop painted, [it] would make [his] eyes fat as butter."

PSYLLUS, servant to Apelles; he "shall be hanged for tarrying so long."

Page to Alexander.

Citizens of Athens, Soldiers, Populace.

Setting: Athens in the fourth century B.C.

"Thou shalt see that Alexander maketh but a toy of love and leadeth affection in fetters, using fancy as a fool to make him sport, or a minstrel to make him merry."

Act I

After a successful campaign against Thebes, which, as is usual with this honorable young prince, has been concluded with a mild peace, Alexander the Great has returned to Athens. With him are many captives, among them two beautiful girls, Timoclea, who bears herself proudly and defiantly as befits the sister of a warrior who lost his life fighting Alexander's father; and Campaspe, who is dejected and terror-stricken, and who comes of humble parentage. Assuring his captives that they will be honorably treated, not as abjects of war, but as subjects of Alexander, the young conqueror turns his attention to the opportunities of peacetime. He realizes that nothing becomes a king better than knowledge; hence, he summons to his court as many philosophers and bookish men as possible—his own teacher Aristotle, Plato, Chrysippus, Crates, Cleanthes, Anaxarchus, and Crysus—that they may "instruct the young with rules and confirm the old with reasons." All have come willingly, except Diogenes, who lives in a tub and is as "crooked in his shape as crabbed in his sayings." The scenes in which this old philosopher appears are filled with familiar anecdotes about him or his barbed remarks about all sorts of men and happenings, often reported by his disgruntled and hungry boy-servant, the quick-witted Manes, who is friends with Granichus, the servant of Plato, and Psyllus, the apprentice of Apelles.

Act II

For instance, in daylight, Diogenes comes out of his tub with a lighted lantern, "seeking either for bones for his dinner or pins for his sleeves," —or so Psyllus says,—and engaging in a snarling wit-combat with these servingmen. He is visited by Alexander, whom he bids stand out of his light and who remarks of his independence, "Were I not Alexander, I would wish to be Diogenes."

Meanwhile, Hephestion admires the stout courage of Timoclea, but is too much the soldier to fall in love with her. Alexander, however, confesses to his general that he is in love with the other captive, Campaspe —that he, the conqueror of the world, has become the subject of the captive of Thebes. Disregarding Hephestion's reminder that he has a camp to govern, Alexander sends his page for the artist Apelles that he may show him "that finished by nature that [the painter has] been trifling about by art."

Act III

In his studio Apelles flatters his subject for both her beauty and her wit, while he paints her portrait, saying that "it is not possible that a face so fair and a wit so sharp, both without comparison, should not be apt to love." Meanwhile, two of Alexander's officers comment upon the conqueror's occasional melancholy and his general impatience, and cannot decide whether it is love or an unquenchable thirst for conquering that makes him unquiet. To Hephestion, however, Alexander admits that though he is smitten, he is "not so far in love with Campaspe as with Bucephalus [his war horse], if occasion serve either of conflict or conquest." He visits Apelles' studio during a sitting, tries to sketch, because sketching looks so easy, and is once more struck by the "chaste disdain, . . . [the] curst, yielding modesty" of the Theban captive. Apelles, however, has also fallen completely in love with the girl and realizes that he is the rival of the "monarch of the earth." When the portrait is finished he knows that he will no longer see his subject, and he resolves, therefore, to blemish the picture a little each day as a means of getting Campaspe to come again to his studio. As an expression of his infatuation for the beautiful, modest maiden he sings the famous lyric, "Cupid and my Campaspe played at cards for kisses."

Act IV

Diogenes has announced that he will attempt to fly; and when the Athenian populace assemble to see him do so, he not only disappoints them but also rails at their manners and their dissolute lives.

About the same time Campaspe, in soliloquy, confesses her preference for the poor painter instead of the powerful prince, and wonders if Apelles feels a like affection. Alexander's officers continue to worry over the softness that has crept into the army and indeed into every man's mind because of the pleasing peace. They are especially concerned over the change that has come about in Alexander himself. At last, Apelles declares his love to Campaspe and finds that it is returned. Alexander also grows impatient, and perhaps a little suspicious, for he demands that the painter send him the picture of the Theban girl immediately— "the king thinketh that, now you have painted it, you play with it."

Act V

Diogenes continues to rail at the lax Athenians, especially at a father who brings his three sons to be educated by the philosopher, and at two soldiers and the courtesan with whom they have been enjoying the piping times of peace. Even Hephestion is out of tune. There is such a rust crept into his bones, he says, that he fears he shall not scour it out with infinite labor. Alexander knows that he must undertake more conquests. Suspecting that the painter Apelles is in love, he sends for him, and by a stratagem makes him reveal himself. While the king and the artist are in conversation, by arrangement a page rushes in to say that Apelles' studio is on fire, and the artist tries to run out to save his portrait of Campaspe. The Theban captive is also sent for, and by another stratagem Alexander discovers that she returns the painter's love. For the good qualities he knows in Apelles and the virtue he sees in the girl, Alexander orders them to marry, and perceives that Campaspe has no objections to the enforced marriage. The lovers are united; though he conquer the world, Alexander cannot subdue the affections of men. For himself, he will make a toy of love. Let the drum sound; he is off to Persia! To Hephestion's remark that Alexander's conquest of Thebes was not so honorable as Alexander's conquest of himself, the young prince has this simple reply: "It were a shame Alexander should desire to command the world, if he could not command himself. . . . When all the world is won, . . . either find me out another to subdue, or . . . I will fall in love."

ENDYMION

THE MAN IN THE MOON

(1588)

DRAMATIS PERSONAE

CYNTHIA, goddess of the moon, "the miracle of nature, of time, of fortune," beloved of Endymion. "Nothing pleaseth her but the fairness of virginity. All things must be not only without lust but without suspicion of lightness."

SEMELE, a beautiful lady of Cynthia's court, beloved of Eumenides, "the very wasp of all women, whose tongue stingeth as much as an adder's tooth. . . . [but]

whose golden locks [to Eumenides] seem most curious when they seem most care-less; whose sweet looks seem most alluring when they are most chaste; and whose words the more virtuous they are, the more amorous they be accounted."

TELLUS, another beautiful lady of Cynthia's court, "too fair to be true, . . . too false for one so fair, . . . [and] as suspicious as Juno"; in love with Endymion. She is an earth goddess, the rival of Cynthia, but dependent upon her, one "whose body is decked with fair flowers, and veins are vines, yielding sweet liquor to the dullest spirits; whose ears are corn, to bring strength; and whose hairs are grass, to bring abundance."

ENDYMION, "the flower of [Cynthia's] court, and the hope of succeeding time, . . . whose ripe years foretell rare virtues, and whose unmellowed conceits promise ripe counsel. . . . [His] thoughts . . . are stitched to the stars, . . . [and he is] settled either to die or possess the moon herself."

EUMENIDES, the friend of Endymion who loves Semele, one whose "fortunes . . . creep on the earth, . . . [and] who for [his friend is] careless of his own content."

"Didst thou ever hear such a sighing, the one for Cynthia, the other for Semele, and both for moonshine in the water?"

CORSITES, a captain, in love with Tellus. ("It agreeth not with your calling to use words so soft as that of love.")

FLOSCULA, friend of Tellus and of Endymion, in love, not with his person, but with his virtue.

DIPSAS, an old enchantress, whose "years are not so many as [her] vices. . . . Why, she is a fool, a scold, fat, without fashion, and quite without favor!"

GERON, an old man, "who this fifty years hath had her to wife [and is] so familiar . . . with misery that [he] esteem[s] sorrow [his] chiefest solace, and welcomes . . . that guest . . . that can rehearse the saddest tale of the bloodiest tragedy."

SIR TOPHAS, at first a martialist, who "thinks himself the valiantest man in the world if he kill a wren; so warlike a thing he accompteth to take away life, though it be from a lark. . . . Custom hath made [his] words bloody and [his] heart barbar-ous." But he falls in love with Dipsas, and love "hath justled [his] liberty from the wall and taken the upper hand of [his] reason. . . . In [his] love [he has] worn the nap of [his] wit quite off and made it threadbare." ("Not mad, . . . no, but a little vainglorious. . . . Nothing hath made [him] a fool but flat scholarship.")

DARES; "it will be a forward cock that croweth in the shell,"

SAMIAS,

EPITON, "an absolute microcosmos, a petty world of [himself],"

three wags, the witty, mischievous pages respec-tively to Endymion, Eumenides, and Sir Tophas, "in knavery to the crowns."

FAVILLA; "though she be but a spark, yet is she fire,"

SCINTILLA, "not much more than a spark, though [she] would be esteemed a flame,"

friends of the pages, "girls, who coming but yesterday from making of babies [i.e., dressing dolls], would before tomorrow be accounted matrons."

BAGOA, servant to Dipsas.

PANELION,
ZONTES, } lords of Cynthia's court.

PYTHAGORAS, a Greek philosopher,
GYPTES, an Egyptian soothsayer, } consulted by Cynthia.

MASTER CONSTABLE,⎱"they smell all of drink, like a beggar's beard, . . . their wits
Two of the Watch, ⎰ are all as rusty as their bills."

Fairies, guarding the sleeping Endymion, "so fair fiends that cause my hairs to stand
upright and spirits to fall down."

Dumb Show:—Three Ladies and an Ancient Man.

Setting: The Gardens of Cynthia's Palace and the vicinity in the mythical past.

"I account more strength in a true heart than in a walled city."

Act I

Because of his hopeless passion for Cynthia, goddess of the moon,
Endymion is urged by his friend Eumenides to overcome his vain
dotage and to cease to feed upon fancies which he cannot attain: "Sleep
would do thee more good than speech; the moon heareth thee not, or if
she do regardeth thee not." Eumenides himself is secretly in love with
Semele, a lady of Cynthia's court, and for her he sighs as much as
Endymion does for Cynthia. Unfortunately, in his love for the moon
Endymion has slighted Tellus, an earth goddess and a dependent upon
Cynthia, and the scorned beauty resolves that he shall know the malice
of a woman deluded in love. Loath that he should die, because she
really loves him well, and equally loath that he should live and love
Cynthia, Tellus determines to entangle Endymion in a net from which
he shall neither find the means to escape, nor desire it. Accordingly,
Tellus seeks out Dipsas, an old and cunning enchantress, in the hope
that by herbs, stones, spells, incantations, exorcisms, planets, or any other
trickery, love can be planted where it is not, or supplanted where it is.
Unlike the gods, however, Dipsas cannot rule hearts, but she can breed
slackness in love or create jealousy and distrust.

Meanwhile, dwelling near these infatuated amorists, there is an absurd
martialist, Sir Tophas, who is completely free of the idle humor of love
and devoted only to war. He is clothed with artillery; commonly he
kills by the dozen, and his very words not only wound, but also confound. For every adversary he has a particular weapon—a bird bolt for
that ugly beast, the blackbird; a musket for the untamed wild mallard;
a spear and shield to subdue the terrible trout. He has a handful of
wit named Epiton, who serves as his page, and who is friends with
Dares, page to Endymion, and Samias, page to Eumenides.

Act II

Seeking out Endymion in the solitary cell to which he has retired from
the bravery of courts, the amiableness of ladies, and the company of men,
Tellus hears from the young man himself, despite his dissembling, that

he is wholly devoted to Cynthia. With the aid of her servant Bagoa, Dipsas casts a spell upon Endymion which will cause him to sleep out his "youth and flowering time, and become dry hay before [he knows himself] green grass, . . . ready by age to step into the grave when [he awakes]." As the spell operates, Endymion sees a vision in dumb show: three ladies appear; one, with a knife and a looking glass, at the instigation of one of the others is about to stab him. But the third wrings her hands in lamentation and seems to wish to prevent the deed, but dares not. At last, the first lady, looking in the glass, throws down her knife. Immediately after, an old man appears, holding a book with only three leaves. He offers it to Endymion, who refuses it. Then the old man tears up one of the leaves and offers the book a second time. But Endymion again refuses, and the old man tears up a second leaf. Finally, he offers the book with only one leaf, and Endymion accepts it. So the vision ends and Endymion falls into a deep sleep.

Meanwhile, Epiton the page has shown off the phenomenon who is his master to two maids of the court, but Sir Tophas' "tough heart receiveth no impression with sweet words. Mars may pierce it, Venus shall not paint on it."

Act III

Eumenides reports to Cynthia that Endymion has fallen into such a dead sleep that nothing can waken him. Suspecting Tellus, who has angered her by her slighting remarks, Cynthia orders Corsites to carry her prisoner to his castle in the desert where she may weave tapestries of the stories in poetry and history dealing with those who were punished for their tattling tongues. Then Cynthia assures Eumenides that if the soothsayers of Egypt, the enchanters of Thessaly, the philosophers of Greece, or all the sages of the world can find a remedy, she will procure it for Endymion. Accordingly, she dispatches messengers with all speed —Eumenides to Thessaly, Zontes to Greece, and Panelion to Egypt.

But while this is going on, *mirabile dictu,* Sir Tophas has fallen in love with the old enchantress Dipsas. He trims his beard, he writes love sonnets; love has made him so eloquent that he can speak nothing but verses: "O what a fine, thin hair hath Dipsas! What a pretty low forehead! . . . What little hollow eyes! What great and goodly lips! How harmless she is, being toothless! . . . What a low stature she is, and yet what a great foot she carrieth! . . . How virtuous is she like to be, over whom no man can be jealous!" Moreover, love has made him sleepy.

At the same time, while on his way to Thessaly Eumenides meets Geron, an old hermit soured on the world, and from him he learns that it is unnecessary to travel for a cure for Endymion's disease, for whoever can clearly see the bottom of a fountain near-by shall have remedy for anything. However, only a man who can shed the tears of a faithful lover can obtain his wish. Eumenides thinks of Semele and through his tears sees engraved on the marble bottom of the well: *Ask one for all, and but one thing at all.* Torn between love and friendship, Eumenides at first does not know what to ask. But when Geron reassures him that "love is but an eye worm, which only tickleth the head with hopes and wishes; [whereas] friendship [is] the image of eternity," the faithful friend asks the remedy for Endymion's dead sleep. In the well he sees these words: *When she whose figure of all is the perfectest, . . . always one, yet never the same—still inconstant, yet never wavering— shall come and kiss Endymion in his sleep, he shall then rise, else never.* Geron demonstrates that it is Cynthia the Moon who is meant—a circle is the most perfect of all figures; the moon is seldom of the same size, but is always waxing and waning, yet never moved from her course in the heavens. Twenty years have elapsed since Endymion fell asleep.

Act IV

In her prison Tellus has spent her time embroidering, not stories of tattling tongues, but rather pictures of Endymion and devices of love. Corsites, her jailer, has fallen in love with her, and by promising him favors of love, Tellus persuades him to go to the lunary bank where Endymion sleeps and remove him to some secret and obscure cave where she may see him again. Yet she knows the task impossible to perform.

Meanwhile, hearing of Endymion's sleep, Sir Tophas has sent his page Epiton to get him a lodging with Endymion; he too would like to take a nap for forty or fifty years. He also would like to know the location of the fountain of the faithful lovers so that he can weep into it some three or four pailfuls of the tears of love. But the place is guarded by a watch set by Cynthia.

At great risk of incurring the displeasure of Cynthia, Corsites reaches the sleeping lover, but he finds him too heavy to move. For his audacity he is pinched black and blue by the fairy guardians and also cast into a sleep. There he is found by Cynthia, who has brought thither the Greek philosopher Pythagoras and the Egyptian soothsayer Gyptes in the hope that their wits can revive Endymion. But they fail, though, of course, they have no difficulty in reviving Corsites. At the same time, for her spiteful remarks Semele is threatened by Cynthia with the forfeit of her tongue if she speaks within a twelvemonth. [Actually Semele speaks little throughout the play, spitefully or otherwise.]

Act V

At last, after being given up for lost, Eumenides returns, and Cynthia tries the experiment he suggests. She kisses the sleeping Endymion, who is promptly aroused. But his beard is gray, his eyes hollow, and his body withered. Gyptes is appointed to interpret the vision of the three ladies which Endymion had seen as he fell asleep. But Endymion himself explains that the remaining leaf of the book offered by the old man contained pictures of many wolves—including Ingratitude, Treachery, and Envy—howling at Cynthia, and drones or beetles creeping under the wings of a princely eagle and seeking to suck the blood from its veins. Cynthia suggests her willingness to hear a fuller report of it later. Bagoa, Dipsas' assistant, confesses the secret of Endymion's sleep, and is turned into an aspen tree as punishment; Tellus confesses and reveals Endymion's love for Cynthia, who, far from discouraging him, bids him persevere, and restores him to youth again. Eumenides confesses his love for Semele, and that lady, permitted to speak, rejects the young man as no faithful lover because when he had the opportunity at the fountain he did not ask for his mistress. Geron reminds everyone that if Eumenides had not been true he could never have seen the bottom of the magic well, and Eumenides himself proves his fidelity by imploring Cynthia to cut out his tongue to ransom Semele's. Because Endymion is vowed to a service which will last forever, Cynthia rewards Corsites with the beautiful Tellus; Dipsas reforms and is reunited to Geron, who had been her husband years before he became a hermit; and Sir Tophas finds consolation in Bagoa, who at his request is transformed into herself again—"turn her to a true love or false, so she be a wench I care not." Pythagoras and Gyptes accept Cynthia's invitation "to fall from vain follies of philosophers to such virtues as are . . . practiced" at her court, preferring the sight of Cynthia to all that Greece or Egypt possessed.

GEORGE PEELE

(1556–1596)

BIOGRAPHY. Born about 1556, George Peele was the son of a clerk in Christ's Hospital and was educated there, at Broadgates Hall (now Pembroke College), and Christchurch, Oxford, where he proceeded B.A., 1577, and M.A., 1579. While at Oxford Peele participated in amateur theatricals. A roisterer and a spendthrift, upon his return to London Peele led so riotous an existence that the governors of Christ's Hospital requested their clerk in 1579 to "discharge his house of his son, George Peele." But the young man did acquire a reputation as a wit, and *The Merry Conceited Jests of George Peele,* a chapbook published a decade after his death, depicts him as a taverner, a wencher, and a cheat. About 1583 he married a woman of some means; sometime after 1596, burned out by dissipation, he died.

CRITICAL COMMENT. In his own day George Peele enjoyed a reputation as one of the "University Wits" who made plays and as "the chief supporter of pleasance now living, the Atlas of poetry, and *primus verborum artifex;* . . . his pregnant dexterity of wit and manifold variety of invention . . . goeth a step beyond all that write" (Nashe, Preface to Greene's *Menaphon,* 1589). Today, however, Peele is significant because he experimented with various types of drama in vogue between 1585 and 1595—chronicle history (*Edward I*), drama of conquest (*The Battle of Alcazar*), Biblical drama (*The Love of King David and Fair Bethsabe*), as well as court play (*The Arraignment of Paris*), and burlesque (*The Old Wives' Tale*)—and because he had an important part in transforming the crude popular drama of the London stage into literary drama. He familiarized audiences with classical myth and legend by combining such material with homely and familiar English life.

SOURCES. *The Arraignment of Paris,* Peele's first and best play, combines mythological and pastoral elements and was originally written for the boy actors of the Chapel Royal for performance before the Queen. Its theme— Paris' judgment among the three goddesses—is a commonplace one derived from Homer and occasionally employed before Peele's time to flatter a living sovereign (see Thornton S. Graves, *"The Arraignment of Paris* and Sixteenth Century Flattery," *MLN,* 1913). Peele's originality consisted in his transformation of the story into a masque-like pastoral drama and his arraignment of Paris before the gods for his judgment.

The Old Wives' Tale, written for the public stage, is a melange of folk tales and romance, mildly burlesquing the drama of chivalric adventure. The general idea seems to have been suggested by Greene's *Perimedes the Blacksmith* (1588), which deals with a blacksmith, his wife Delia, and the motif of storytelling. Within this framework the play is a mixture of folk themes: (*a*) the rescue of a heroine from a conjurer, a modified form of the story of Childe Roland; (*b*) the life-index, or flame which the conjurer must keep alive if he is to succeed or survive; (*c*) the story of the grateful dead, i.e., a ghost helper who exacts a promise of half the hero's gains and tests his loyalty; (*d*) the tale of the Three Heads in the Well, with its contrasting sisters, here linked to the main plot. The result is ingenious. *The Old Wives' Tale* influenced Milton's *Comus,* which is a treatment of the same theme.

BIBLIOGRAPHY

Collected Works:

The Works of George Peele, edited by A. H. Bullen, 2 volumes, 1888.
The Plays and Poems of George Peele, edited by Henry Morley, 1887.

Monograph: P. H. Cheffaud, *Étude sur George Peele,* Paris, 1913.

The Arraignment of Paris:

    Early edition: 1584.

    Modern editions: ed. Oliphant Smeaton (TD, 1905); H. H. Child (MSR, 1910).

The Old Wives' Tale:

    Early edition: 1595.

    Modern edition: ed. W. W. Greg (MSR, 1908).

THE ARRAIGNMENT OF PARIS

A Pastoral

(c. 1581–1584)

DRAMATIS PERSONAE

ATE, Prologue of the drama and goddess of discord, "condemned soul . . . from lowest Hell," who tosses among the goddesses "a ball of gold, a fair and worthy prize," which is, however, the "bane of Troy, . . . the fatal fruit raught from the golden tree of Proserpine."

JUNO; her "face is fair; but yet the majesty that all the gods in Heaven have seen in [her] have made them choose [her] of the planets seven to be the wife of Jove and Queen of Heaven," }

PALLAS; her "beauty is the beauty of the mind; this fairness Virtue hight in general, that many branches hath in special," } "not earthly, but divine, and goddesses all three."

VENUS, "Sovereign of Love, . . . so fair and bright, and lovely and so trim, . . . whose sweetness doth both gods and creatures move," }

RHANIS, "the conductor of the train."

PAN, "the god of shepherds," FAUNUS, "high ranger in Diana's chase," SILVANUS, god of the woods, } "country gods" who welcome the goddesses to Ida.

POMONA, goddess of fruits, FLORA, goddess of flowers, } harbingers of the three goddesses, who "enrich this gaudy, gallant soil."

PARIS, Priam's younger son, the shepherd swain, . . . [Oenone's] heart's contentment and [her] choice. . . . The Queen of Love hath made him false his troth; . . . his double deed will hurt a many shepherds else that might go nigh to speed." ("Ye gods, alas, what can a mortal man discern betwixt the sacred gifts of Heaven?")

OENONE, "the lovely nymph, that in these Ida vales plays with Amyntas' lusty boy [Paris] and coys him in the dales." Deserted by Paris, "beguiled, disdained, and out of love, . . . her cheer is changed; her mirthful looks are laid." ("Thy hope consumed, poor nymph, thy hap is worse than all the rest.")

HELEN OF TROY, "the fairest face, the flower of gallant Greece, . . . a gallant girl, a lusty minion trull," of whom Paris has only a glimpse.

SATURN, god of time,
JUPITER, chief of the gods,
NEPTUNE, god of the sea,
PLUTO, "Prince of Hell,"
APOLLO, god of the sun, with knowledge of the future, } council before whom Paris is arraigned.
MARS, "a lusty buck," god of war,
BACCHUS, "god of wine,"
VULCAN, god of fire, and husband of Venus,
MERCURY, "the messenger of Heaven,"

DIANA, or "PHOEBE, sweet mistress of this sylvan } to whom the case is submitted for chase," } final decision.

COLIN, "yon thriveless swain," an enamored shepherd. "Woeful man, [he is] denied his young and lovely choice," Thestylis.

THESTYLIS, "a fair lass, . . . the scorpion . . . that breaks his sweet assault."

A "rusty Churl, . . . [of] ill-favored face, . . . the organ of [Venus'] wrath," against Thestylis for her cruelty to Colin. Wooed by Thestylis, "he crabbedly refuseth her." ("Ah, poor unhappy Thestylis, . . . there is no pain to foul disdain in hardy suits of love.")

HOBBINOL,
DIGGON, } shepherds, friends of Colin.
THENOT,

The Muses, to sing a song.

CLOTHO,
LACHESIS, } the Fates, "unpartial daughters of Necessity."
ATROPOS,

A "dainty Nymph" of Diana, wooed as a diversion by Bacchus and Vulcan. ("A harlotry, I warrant her! A peevish, elvish shrew!")

Cyclops, Vulcan's "chimney sweepers," who assist Mercury to seek out Paris.

Cupids, Shepherds, and Knights.

Setting: Mount Olympus and a vale in Ida in the mythical past.

"Ye gods, alas, what can a mortal man
Discern betwixt the sacred gifts of Heaven?"

Act I

The "country gods," Pan, Faunus, and Silvanus, each bearing an appropriate gift, are making their way to the Vale of Ida "to bid Queen Juno and her feres [Pallas and Venus] most humbly welcome hither" on progress. They are soon joined by other harbingers, Pomona and Flora, who have been decorating the fields and groves and bowers and preparing a second spring in anticipation of this celestial visit. For stately Juno there are yellow oxslips bright as burnished gold—a rare device, says Pomona, with yellow to symbolize the goddess' jealousy. For Pallas there are July flowers of red to set forth her warlike tendencies. And for Venus there are sweet violets of blue, the color commonly betokening fidelity, as well as other flowers "infixed for change of hue." Soon, conducted by Rhanis, and greeted by the piping of Pan, a chorus of bird song, and a song of the Muses, the goddesses arrive and are made formally welcome for the honor which they do to Ida.

Meanwhile, in another part of the vale, Paris and Oenone make love, exchange vows, and between them pipe and sing a pretty sonnet called "Cupid's Curse," the refrain of which is:

> *They that do change old love for new,*
> *Pray gods they change for worse.*

Act II

Gossiping about current scandals on Olympus, the three goddesses are overtaken by a summer storm and retire for shelter to Diana's Bower. There, to the accompaniment of thunder and lightning, and with the cry of "Fatum Trojae," Ate, goddess of discord, tosses in their midst a golden apple inscribed *Detur pulcherrimae*—"Let this unto the fairest given be." Each of the goddesses claims the prize, none is disposed to yield to the others, and all three are prepared to maintain their claims by angry words. To avoid a long controversy, however, they agree to submit the matter to a judge, and spy Paris, a shepherd swain, tending his flocks near by. Paris is chosen "daysman . . . by full consent" of the three goddesses and tries to award the prize as impartially as possible. Each of the goddesses, however, does her best to influence his choice, and each puts on a show to support her promises. Juno offers Paris empires, kingdoms, heaps of massy gold, rich robes, and untold wealth, even offering to turn the fleece of his sheep to gold and showing him a tree of gold, laden with diadems and crowns. Pallas offers him wisdom, the honors of chivalry, and victories in war, showing him a warlike dance in which nine knights in armor take part, accompanied by fifes and drums. Venus, however, with surer psychology, bids Paris turn away from these calls to arms and look on her, promising him Cupid's aid wherever he may love, kisses should he come to her on Ida,

> *And, if thou wilt a face that hath no peer,*
> *A gallant girl, a lusty minion trull, . . .*
> *To ravish all thy beating veins with joy,*
> *Here is a lass of Venus' court, my boy.*

Then she shows him Helen of Troy "in her bravery, with four Cupids attending on her." The dazzled shepherd promptly gives the prize to the Queen of Love, much to the chagrin of Juno and Pallas.

Act III

In the vale of Ida, poor Colin, an enamored shepherd, "like to the stricken deer," is dying of true love for a disdainful little shepherdess named Thestylis. At the same time, Oenone, deserted now by the false Paris, complains (in song) of his duplicity. As she walks about the vale with Paris, Venus sees Colin's hearse and decrees upon Thestylis a strange, but an appropriate revenge. Telling her fickle companion of the foresworn lovers in Hell who must with open hearts sleep daily under a tree which drips fiery phlegiton into their breasts because they made a jest of love, Venus causes Thestylis, who is a pretty lass, to dote upon a "rusty churl, . . . [of] ill-favored face," who only disdains her—a fortune not unlike that which she had caused Colin and which Paris is causing poor Oenone. As messenger of the gods, Mercury is seeking Paris—whom he finds with Oenone's assistance—to summon him to the court of Heaven "at Juno's suit, Pallas assisting her," and to arraign him "of sentence partial and unjust, for that without indifferency, beyond desert or merit fair," he gave the golden apple to the goddess of love.

Act IV

Before the court, assembled in Diana's Bower, Paris ably and eloquently defends himself. He lays the blame upon human fallibility and imperfect human eyesight when confronted by the dazzling beauty of all three goddesses, explains the preference of a man of simple shepherd's tastes "tempted more than ever creature was with wealth, with beauty, and with chivalry," and points out that, after all, the apple was inscribed "To the Fairest," not the most majestic or the most wise. Knowing already that in his bosom Paris carries fire to Troy, the gods are content to free the shepherd boy, but they are wholly unable and reluctant to decide how to dispose of the golden ball. Since the prize is to go to the fairest, most are willing to vote for Venus and sustain the judgment of Paris. But that would hardly settle the dispute or rid the gods of blame and trouble. At last, however, Apollo suggests that they refer the whole question to Diana, in whose territory, after all, the affair occurred. Rightly considered, the senate of the gods does not have jurisdiction in the case. Besides, he argues, the question requires impartial judgment, and who could be more impartial in a matter of this kind than "a woman to be judge among her feres"?

Act V

Before the chaste goddess of the hunt, Juno, Pallas, and Venus appear and swear that they will be satisfied by the impartial decision of the new arbiter. But Diana also neatly evades a delicate choice. Instead of awarding the prize, she first describes a nymph Eliza, also called Zabeta, who is one of her votaries, and who governs a kingdom very much like hers:

> *An ancient seat of kings, a second Troy,*
> *Ycompassed round with a commodious sea,*
> *Her people are yclepéd Angeli.*

She it is

> *In honor of whose name the Muses sing—*
> *In state Queen Juno's peer, for power in arms*
> *And virtues of the mind Minerva's mate,*
> *As fair and lovely as the Queen of Love,*
> *As chaste as Dian in her chaste desires.*

To "this peerless nymph, whom Heaven and earth beloves, this paragon," all the goddesses agree, the golden ball belongs. And while the Fates sing a song and Clotho lays down her distaff, Lachesis her spindle and reel, and Atropos her shears, Diana delivers the golden apple to Queen Elizabeth, who is present at the performance, and the other goddesses make obeisance:

> *Live long the noble phoenix of our age,*
> *Our fair Eliza, our Zabeta fair.*

THE OLD WIVES' TALE

A Pleasant, Conceited Comedy

(c. 1588–1594)

DRAMATIS PERSONAE

ANTIC, FROLIC, FANTASTIC, "three merry men" who have lost their "way in the wood, without either fire or candle,"

CLUNCH, the SMITH, who finds them and who "leads a life as merry as a king with Madge, his wife,"

MADGE, an OLD WOMAN, his wife, "content to drive away the time with an old wives' winter's tale,"

BALL, Clunch's dog,

characters of the Induction or Frame-story.

SACRAPANT, "that cursed sorcerer, . . . whom Heaven hath in hate. . . . By enchanting spells [he] do[es] deceive those that behold and look upon [his] face . . . [and] change and alter shapes of mortal men." It is he who "turned himself into a great dragon and carried the king's daughter away in his mouth to a castle that he made of stone."

DELIA, "mistress of [his] heart," daughter of Thenores, King of Thessaly, and the "fairest flower of these western parts." She was stolen away by the magician who had turned himself into a dragon. "This vile enchanter hath ravished Delia of her senses clean, and she forgets that she is Delia."

ERESTUS, SENEX or OLD MAN, who "keeps by a cross that parts three several ways." Although "in April of [his] age, . . . [and] a proper young man," he is at night turned by the enchanter into "the white bear of England's wood," and in the day into "a miserable, old, and crooked man."

VENELIA, "neither maid, wife, nor widow," but Erestus' "dearest love, [his] true betrothed wife," who was coveted by the sorcerer and now "runs madding, all enraged, about the woods, all by his curséd and enchanting spells."

LAMPRISCUS, Erestus' "discontented neighbor. . . . Never was one so cumbered as is poor Lampriscus."

ZANTIPPA, Lampriscus' daughter by his first wife, a handsome girl, but "one that afflicts [him] with her continual clamors, and hangs on [him] like a bur. . . . As curst as a wasp and as froward as a child new-taken from the mother's teat; she is to [his] age as smoke to the eyes or as vinegar to the teeth. . . . I think this be the curstest quean in the world. You see what she is, a little fair, but as proud as the Devil, and the veriest vixen that lives upon God's earth." . . . Her "father says [she] must rule [her] tongue. Why, alas, what [is she] then? A woman without a tongue is as a soldier without his weapon."

CELANTA, Lampriscus' daughter by his second wife, "so foul and ill-faced, that I think a grove full of golden trees, and the leaves of rubies and diamonds, would not be a dowry answerable to her deformity." ("Though [she is] black, [at least she is] not the Devil.")

CALYPHA, the FIRST BROTHER, ⎱ "Thenores' sons of Thessaly," who seek their sister.
THELEA, the SECOND BROTHER, ⎰

EUMENIDES, the Wandering Knight, "still unfortunate, envied by Fortune and forlorn by Fate," lover of Delia who is at last successful in rescuing her. ("Thou well deservest to have our favors.")

HUANEBANGO, a braggart, armed with a two-handed sword, who has "abandoned the court and honorable company to do [his] devoir against this sore sorcerer and mighty magician. . . . Here is he that commandeth ingress and egress with his weapon, . . . he that can monsters tame, labors achieve, riddles resolve, loose enchantments, murther magic, and kill conjuring"—or so *he* thinks. ("What a prating ass is this!")

COREBUS, or BOOBY the clown, his attendant.

The GHOST OF JACK, "the frolic'st franion amongst you; . . . as good a fellow as ever trod upon neat's-leather, . . . [he was] a marvellous fellow! He was but a poor man, but very well beloved."

WIGGIN, a parish unthrift, "his sweet sworn brother. . . . This fellow does but the part of a friend, to seek to bury his friend."

STEVEN LOACH, the CHURCHWARDEN.

A Sexton, a "whoreson, sodden-headed sheep's-face."

A Friar, "the veriest knave in all Spain," servant to Sacrapant.

Two Furies, assistants to Sacrapant.

A Hostess of an Inn where Eumenides stops.

Harvestmen, Harvestwomen, and Fiddlers.

Setting: England in some mythical time.

> *"So I am content to drive away the time with an old wives'*
> *winter's tale."*

INDUCTION OR FRAME-STORY

While assisting their young master on amorous adventure, Antic, Frolic, and Fantastic are lost at night in a wood. They are soon found, however, by Clunch the Smith, who takes them to his cottage, where he can offer them houseroom and a good fire to sit by, if no bedding to sleep on. Here Madge, Clunch's wife, makes the wayfarers welcome with food, drink, song, and "an old wives' winter's tale" to pass the time. She begins her story—"Once upon a time there was a king . . . that had . . . the fairest [daughter] that ever was . . . [who] was stolen away [by a] conjurer [who] turned himself into a great dragon, and carried the king's daughter away in his mouth to a castle that he made of stone, and there he kept her . . . till at last all the king's men went . . . to seek her"— And at the entrance of Calypha and Thelea, newly arrived in England from Thessaly to seek their sister Delia, there begins

THE PLAY PROPER

The Princess Delia is sought by three separate pairs of knights-errant: her brothers Calypha and Thelea; an absurd braggart named Huanebango and his man, Booby the clown (also called Corebus); and Eumenides, the girl's faithful suitor, who acquires a helper on the way and is successful where the others have failed. Each of these pairs of searchers meets the Old Man (Erestus) who dwells at a cross that parts three several ways, and, in return for alms, each receives from the Old Man a riddling prophecy which is fulfilled. The two young princes are bid to

> *Be not afraid of every stranger;*
> *Start not aside at every danger;*
> *Things that seem are not the same;*
> *Blow a blast at every flame;*
> *For, when one flame of fire goes out,*
> *Then comes your wishes well about.*

The braggart Huanebango disdainfully refuses to give alms to the Old Man, but his boy Corebus offers a piece of cake and hears this saw:

> *He shall be deaf when thou shalt not see.*
> *Farewell, my son. Things may so hit*
> *Thou mayst have wealth to mend thy wit.*

To Eumenides, the Wandering Knight, the Old Man of the Cross reveals the fact that his fortune is good if he have but the wit to govern it, and bids him:

> *Bestow thy alms, give more than all,*
> *Till dead men's bones come at thy call.*

Erestus, it happens, has also suffered mishap at the hands of the sorcerer named Sacrapant, who coveted Venelia, the beautiful betrothed of Erestus and drove her mad. Seeking means to deprive Erestus of his life, Sacrapant transformed him into an ugly bear at night and into an old and miserable man by day, permitted to speak only in riddles.

Erestus also has as neighbor a discontented beggar named Lampriscus, who brings a pot of honey for the bear. Never was man so encumbered as is poor Lampriscus. Although now unmarried, Lampriscus has once lived so unquietly with the two wives he has had that every year he keeps holiday the anniversaries of their burials. Worse still, he has two daughters—Zantippa, who is handsome enough but proud and shrewish of tongue, and Celanta, who is so ugly and hard-favored that it is altogether unlikely that any man will marry her without a very handsome dowry. The advice of the Old Man is therefore worth heeding: "Send them to the well for the Water of Life; there shall they find their fortunes unlooked for."

Everything happens as the Old Man of the Cross has riddlingly foretold. Calypha and Thelea, the two brothers, remember the first part of Erestus' spell—to fear no danger because things are not what they seem—they advance courageously until in thunder and lightning they are confronted by the magician's furies. Then they are carried off to slave labor, goaded on by their enchanted sister who has been given a potion of forgetfulness and a new name. At the same time Sacrapant, who has taken the form of a handsome young man, reveals his "life-index," a flame enclosed in glass that not only prolongs his life, but is also the source of his magic power. As long as it burns, his skill will endure, and none shall ever break the glass "but she that's neither wife, widow, nor maid." Moreover, he boasts, it is his destiny never to die, except by a dead man's hand.

The second pair of adventurers is no more successful than the first. In his encounter with the sorcerer, Huanebango, for all his huffing, is quickly overthrown; there is a flash of fire, Huanebango is knocked down, deafened by the noise, and carried out by furies. When he tries to replace his master in the fight, Corebus is stricken blind. But there is more in store for both.

Coming to the Well of Life for water and in hope of a husband, Lampriscus' elder daughter dips her pitcher in and hears a head speak:

Gently dip, but not too deep
For fear you make the golden beard to weep,
Fair maiden, white and red,
Stroke me smooth, and comb my head;
And thou shalt have some cockle-bread.

In anger Zantippa breaks her crock over the head; once more it lightens and thunders, and the noise awakens Huanebango, who has been laid near the well by Sacrapant's furies. He is Zantippa's fortune, his destiny that of a henpecked Elizabethan husband, in spite of his promise to his wife to "royalize [her] progeny with [his] pedigree." Luckily, he is still deaf.

In her turn the younger sister also comes to the well, but she brings with her her husband, Corebus the clown. He is still blind and is easily assured that Celanta is the fairest wife alive. Nevertheless, the girl dips her pitcher in the well; she hears the same request and sees the same head as her sister. But being more gentle than Zantippa, Celanta combs ears of corn into her lap from the head. The first head is followed by a second, covered with gold, and so through his ill-favored but patient wife Corebus has at last got wealth to mend his wit.

To the princess' suitor Eumenides, Fortune is at last kind. On the road he falls asleep, but is promptly awakened by an altercation between a sexton and a churchwarden on the one hand, and some villagers on the other, over the burial at parish expense of one Jack, who seems to have been a good enough fellow, but about whose claims to charity there is some difference of opinion. Learning that it will cost some fifteen or sixteen shillings to bestow Jack honestly, Eumenides gives the money freely, and finds that he has only three halfpence left in his purse. But he remembers the Old Man's prophecy and goes his way, leaving the villagers to stop at the church-stile alehouse for a pot to celebrate their agreement. Discouraged and ready to die, Eumenides is overtaken at last by the Ghost of the grateful Jack, who has come to serve the man who has paid for his funeral, and the knight accepts the dead man as his copartner. Together they seek the conjurer. Jack, who seems to know everything, stops his master's ears with wool to protect him from hearing enchanting speeches, takes away Sacrapant's wreath and sword, and kills the sorcerer. Giving Eumenides the sword, Jack instructs him where to dig to find the magic light. Then, winding a horn, the Ghost calls Venelia—who is neither maid, wife, nor widow, but the betrothed love of the keeper of the cross, and she extinguishes the flame. All enchantments are broken. The Old Man at the Cross is restored to youth and united to Venelia. The brothers are released from bondage. Eumenides is betrothed to Delia.

But before he parts from his master Jack demands a partner's share of the gains, and orders Eumenides to divide Delia in half. Rather than be false to his word, the knight offers Jack the whole girl. But he refuses anything more or less than half, and Eumenides prepares to cut his beloved in two. But Jack is merely testing the constancy of a man who has once before given his all for a friend, and, reminding the knight to thank that good deed for a good turn, he disappears into the ground. The happy lovers return to Thessaly, and the Old Wife, who has been telling the tale, is awakened and makes ready for breakfast.

MUCEDORUS

CRITICAL COMMENT. To judge from the number of times *Mucedorus* was printed—seventeen, from 1598 to 1668—this simple old thriller was one of the most popular plays ever written. Attributed to Shakespeare (*mirabile dictu!*) on the title pages of 1610 and later, the piece was in the repertory of the Globe Company until the closing of the theatres, and its life on the boards, at least among strolling players, was certainly longer. The reason is clear; *Mucedorus* has everything—several kinds of love, adventure, romance, melodrama, villainy, pathos, a little droll clownery. One cannot imagine greater audience appeal.

SOURCE. No satisfactory source for *Mucedorus* has been discovered, but the bare outline of the action—considerably simplified—springs ultimately from Sir Philip Sidney's *Arcadia*—the hero's name, his disguise as a shepherd, his rescue of the heroine from a bear, their elopement, capture, and final happy union. From other pastoral stories the author added a wild man of the woods, more fierce than usual in such tales, and a stupid clown as a concession to popular theatrical taste. In short, with its absurd mixture of pastoralism, chivalric romance, and horseplay, *Mucedorus* is just the sort of drama Sir Philip Sidney would have disapproved (cf. his *Defense of Poesie*).

Sometime early in the seventeenth century the play was reduced to a ballad which differs from the play in some particulars and may be based upon a version of the story now lost.

BIBLIOGRAPHY

Early editions: 1598; 1606; 1610 [with additions]; 1611; 1613; 1615; 1618; 1619; 1621; 1626; n.d. [1629?]; 1631; 1634; 1639; n.d. [1656?]; 1663; 1668.

Modern editions: Facs. J. S. Farmer (TFT, 1910); ed. C. F. Tucker Brooke (*Shakespeare Apocrypha,* 1908).

A Most Pleasant Comedy of

MUCEDORUS

The King's Son of Valencia, and Amadine, the King's Daughter of Aragon, with the Merry Conceits of Mouse, . . . Very Delectable and Full of Conceited Mirth

(1588–1598)

DRAMATIS PERSONAE

COMEDY, a "mild, gentle [girl], willing for to please, . . . [seeking] to ⎫ contenders
gain the love of all estates, . . . [and] delighting in mirth, mixed all ⎪ in the
with lovely tales," ⎬ Induction
ENVY, a "monstrous ugly hag, . . . besmeared with gory blood, . . . ⎪ and the
delight[ing] in nothing but in spoil and death," ⎭ Epilogue.

AMADINE, "rich Aragon's bright jewel," the only daughter of King Adrostus, sole heir to his crown, and "the comfort of [his] life."

MUCEDORUS, Prince of Valencia, "a prince both wise, virtuous, and valiant." ("Ah, what a thing is firm, unfeignéd love!")

SEGASTO, cowardly, unworthy courtier of Aragon, betrothed to Amadine, "one whose wealth through father's former usury is known to be no less than wonderful. . . . The more [he] seek[s] to shun the worst, the more by proof [he] find[s himself] accursed."

BREMO, a wild man of the woods, the "bloody butcher" who kidnaps Amadine.

MOUSE, the clown—"Ay, plain Mouse without either welt or guard. . . . Goodman Rat's son of the next parish over the hill"—servant to Segasto. He "can keep [his] tongue from picking and stealing, and [his] hands from lying and slandering, I warrant you, as well as ever you had man in all your life."

The KING OF VALENCIA, father of Mucedorus.

ADROSTUS, King of Aragon, father of Amadine.

ANSELMO, courtier of Valencia, friend of Mucedorus, "an upright, loyal man."

COLLEN, of "truth and valor proved," counselor to the king of Aragon.

TREMELIO, an Aragonian captain.

RUMBELO, courtier of Aragon, friend of Segasto.

RODERIGO, ⎱ courtiers of Valencia.
BORACHIUS, ⎰

A Catalonian Prince, prisoner of the king of Aragon.

MOTHER NIP, an old woman, keeper of an alehouse.

ARIENA, Amadine's maid.

A Boy.

A Messenger.

A Bear. ("Nay, sure, it cannot be a bear, but some devil in a bear's doublet, for a bear could never have had that agility.")

Setting: Valencia and Aragon once upon a time.

"Let's live and love together faithfully."

INDUCTION

"With a garland of bays on her head," Comedy engages in a controversy with Envy, that "disdainer of men's joys," for precedence on the stage, insists that death not be mixed in comedies, and bids the ugly monster begone. But Envy threatens to cross Comedy's actors from the first, turn her mirth into a deadly dole, and drench the plot of her play in a sea of blood. "Do thy worst," says Comedy. "I'll grace it so thyself shall it confess from tragic stuff to be a pleasant comedy."

Act I

At the court of Valencia, Prince Mucedorus has heard accounts of the beauty of the Princess Amadine, "Aragon's bright jewel," and, "lest report . . . mangle verity," he determines to see for himself whether what he has heard "gilded a worthless trunk or Amadine deserved her high extolment." With the assistance of his friend Anselmo, he procures a shepherd's disguise and sets out, telling no one else where he has gone: "Better than kings have not disdained that state, and much inferior to obtain their mate." Mucedorus arrives in Aragon just in time to rescue the princess from a bear. Walking in the forest, Amadine and Segasto, her betrothed, are attacked by the beast; cowardlike, Segasto flees, leaving Amadine to shift for herself; the shepherd kills the monster, presents the lady with the animal's head, and earns the gratitude of the princess.

Act II

When he returns from his Catalonian wars, King Adrostus of Aragon confirms the betrothal of his daughter to Lord Segasto. The latter has taken into his service a clown named Mouse, and, chagrined at the reputation which the shepherd Mucedorus enjoys at court because of his prowess, Segasto engages Captain Tremelio to find some means of compassing the shepherd's death. Tremelio on no pretext at all attacks Mucedorus, who defends himself valiantly and promptly kills his assailant. Thereupon, Segasto, who had been both the instigator and the witness of the fray, accuses Mucedorus of murder, and the disguised prince is condemned to death by the king. But the princess has the bear's head brought into court and tells her father how the shepherd saved her life. Perceiving by Segasto's silence that the story of his cowardice is true, the king spares Mucedorus' life and joins with his daughter in rewarding the shepherd's valor.

Act III

Nothing daunted, Segasto contrives to have Mucedorus banished, but Amadine seeks the shepherd out before he can depart, and to his plea that she honor him by making him her servant, she replies that she will rather honor him as sovereign of her heart. If he can return her love, she will follow him to exile and share his misfortune with him. Mucedorus accepts the proposal, and in three hours' time, after the princess has gathered a few necessaries for the journey, they agree to meet again at a broad-branched beech that grows in the valley where the bear was slain, and flee. Amadine arrives first, and is surprised by Bremo, a brutal wild man of the woods, who, deaf to her pleading, tries to kill her, but cannot because he is bewitched by her beauty. Instead, he carries her away to live with him in the forest. When Mucedorus arrives he waits for his lady as long as he dares, but hears the hue and cry which is seeking the runaway princess and the shepherd, and hides until the pursuit of the fugitives is over. Segasto sends Mouse to the constable to make diligent search for the shepherd who has run away with the king's daughter or the king's daughter who has run away with the shepherd, he does not quite know which.

Act IV

Meanwhile, in Valencia, the King grieves so for his son Mucedorus that Anselmo feels justified in breaking his vow of secrecy and tells his sovereign where the prince has gone and why. Rejoicing, the King sets out for Aragon.

Unable to find his lost lady, and unsafe in the vicinity of the Aragonian court, Mucedorus adopts a new disguise—the white gown, white hat, and staff of a hermit leading a solitary life within the wood. Here, one day, he meets Amadine and her savage captor, who, in the nearest thing to poetry in the play, is making golden promises of what he could give the lady if she would forget her shepherd lover and be his love instead:

> *If thou wilt love me, thou shalt be my queen:*
> *I will crown thee with a chaplet made of ivory,*
> *And make the rose and lily wait on thee. . . .*

Thou shalt be fed with quails and partridges,
With blackbirds, larks, thrushes, and nightingales.
Thy drink shall be goat's milk and crystal water,
Distilled from the fountains and the clearest springs. . . .
The day I'll spend to recreate my love
With all the pleasures that I can devise. . . .
The satyrs and the wood nymphs shall attend on thee
And lull thee asleep with music's sound,
And in the morning when thou dost awake,
The lark shall sing good morrow to my queen,
And, whilst he sings, I'll kiss my Amadine. . . .
When thou art up, the wood lanes shall be strowed,
With violets, cowslips, and sweet marigolds
For thee to trample and to trace upon.

Unfortunately, hermits go unarmed; the cutthroat Bremo "spareth none, and none doth him escape." But he is dissuaded from murder, bloodshed, and the like cruelty, not by a lecture on chivalry which Mucedorus gives him, but by the lady's acceptance of his offer to be his queen, if he will spare the holy hermit's life. Amadine, of course, has been unable to penetrate her lover's new disguise.

Act V

Serving the bloody Bremo, and in daily proximity of the Lady Amadine, Mucedorus one day asks her to tell him her story. She begins, but they are interrupted by the suspicious Bremo, who demands to hear their secrets. They pretend that their talk has been about the hazards the wild man must run each day in wandering through the woods, and about their lack of skill in handling weapons. Satisfied that he is not being deceived, Bremo offers to teach them both to fight. Amadine is a poor pupil, but the hermit is apt, and with a knotty crab-tree staff he strikes the wild man dead. Only then does Mucedorus reveal himself to the lady. Mouse the clown finds the dead Bremo; Segasto discovers the lovers and asserts his claim to Amadine; the lady chooses Mucedorus, and the rival graciously steps aside. The lovers return to court to beg the King of Aragon's pardon, and the Valencian King arrives in time to identify his son and to contribute to the general rejoicing.

EPILOGUE

Envy refuses to acknowledge defeat, but threatens instead to raise up "a lean and hungry neger cannibal" as poet, whet him on to write a comedy full of "dark sentences pleasing to factious brains; and every other where place me a jest, whose high abuse shall more torment than blows." Then, Envy says, she will fly to the nearest magistrate, repeat these quips with some additions, and thus get the company of players who put on the play into trouble. Comedy laughs at the threat, but, seeing the weary sun about to set, they both kneel and ask pardon for any unwilling error they may have made from the "glorious and wise Arch-Caesar on this earth," King James, before whom one performance of this play was given.

----•----◆----•----

THOMAS KYD
(1558–1594)

BIOGRAPHY. Thomas Kyd was born in London in 1558, the son of a scrivener; he attended the Merchant Tailors' School, where he had Richard Mulcaster as Headmaster, but he probably did not go to the university. For a time he followed his father's calling, then joined the coterie around the Countess of Pembroke interested in developing a literary tragedy on Senecan models. For this group he translated the *Cornelia* of Robert Garnier, a French Senecan, and this drama is the only one of Kyd's to bear his name. For a time, too, Kyd was associated with Marlowe and wrote in the same chamber with him (1591). His friendship with Marlowe got him into trouble on charges of atheism, and in 1593 he was arrested on suspicion of having written certain "lewd and mutinous libels" against foreigners on a wall of the Dutch churchyard in London. He was tortured, explained away the charge of atheism, and was released. Meanwhile, Marlowe had been killed. In 1594 Kyd died intestate, and his parents renounced the administration of his effects.

CRITICAL COMMENT. Thomas Kyd's reputation rests solely upon *The Spanish Tragedy,* which is known to be his only from a chance reference in Thomas Heywood's *Apology for Actors* (1612). Unlike Marlowe, Kyd was not a poet; he was gifted with little imagination, but he had a real flair for the stage and a gift for plot-construction which was unusual. It was Kyd who adapted the academic Senecan tragedy to the popular theatre. He is the first great English master of melodrama. The devices he borrowed from Seneca or invented to supplement what he appropriated were tremendously influential —the careful articulation of plot and subplot, the ghost superintending the action, the Machiavellian villain, the suffering heroine, the revenge theme, the hesitating avenger, the madness real and feigned, the murders and physical horrors, the dumb shows, the play within the play, the declamatory and sententious speeches—all this Kyd articulated, breathed into life, and transmitted alive to his successors on the public stage. *The Spanish Tragedy* held the boards for a generation and was kept up to date; in 1601–2 Ben Jonson received payment from Philip Henslowe, business manager of the Admiral's Men, for

Scene from *The Spanish Tragedy*

From the title page of the edition of 1615.

Scene from *The Merry Devil of Edmonton*

From the title page of the edition of 1655.

Dr. Faustus Conjuring

From the title page of the edition of 1620.

Friar Bacon and Friar Bungay

From the title page of the edition of 1630.

"additions to *Jeronimo*." Kyd may also have been the author of the original *Hamlet*, now lost, but known to have been in existence in 1592.

The Spanish Tragedy differs from most Elizabethan plays in having only four acts; but so originally had one or two of Seneca's.

SOURCE. No source has been found for *The Spanish Tragedy;* but it is not unlikely, if Kyd did not invent the plot himself, that he took the story from some romantic tale that has not survived. The political and military background is unhistorical, but there was war between Spain and Portugal in 1580.

BIBLIOGRAPHY

Collected Works: *The Works of Thomas Kyd,* edited by F. S. Boas, Oxford, 1901.

Monograph: Fredson T. Bowers, *Elizabethan Revenge Tragedy, 1587-1642,* Princeton, 1940.

Early editions: First edition lost; n.d. [1592?]; 1594; 1599; 1602 [enlarged]; 1603; 1611; 1615; 1618; 1623; 1633.

Modern editions: ed. J. Schick (TD, 1898); W. W. Greg (1602 edn., MSR, 1925).

THE SPANISH TRAGEDY

CONTAINING THE LAMENTABLE END OF DON HORATIO AND BEL-IMPERIA WITH THE PITIFUL DEATH OF OLD HIERONIMO

(c. 1584–1589)

DRAMATIS PERSONAE

GHOST OF DON ANDREA, once "a courtier in the Spanish court, . . . [a] brave man-at-arms," the friend of Don Horatio, and the beloved of the lady Bel-imperia. "This knight both lived and died in love, . . . and by war's fortune lost both love and life," } Induction and Chorus
REVENGE, his companion and conductor,

HIERONIMO, Marshal of Spain, "the hopeless father of a hapless son," who has won "common love and kindness . . . by his deserts within the court of Spain. . . . [He] rest[s him] in unrest, dissembling quiet in unquietness, not seeming that [he] know[s] their villainies."

DON HORATIO, his son, "the very arm that did hold up our house, . . . a mirror in our days," friend of Don Andrea and "the hinderer of [Balthazar's] love. . . . Had he not loved Andrea as he did, he could not sit in Bel-imperia's thoughts." ("Sweet lovely rose, ill-pluck'd before thy time; fair, worthy son, not conquered, but betrayed.")

BEL-IMPERIA, "daughter and half-heir" to Don Cyprian, "on whom [Don Andrea] doted more than all the world"; she loves Horatio, her "Andrea's friend, the more to spite the prince that wrought his end. . . . [But] dangerous suspicion waits on [their] delight."

The KING OF SPAIN.

DON CYPRIAN, Duke of Castile, his brother.

LORENZO, Don Cyprian's "proud and politic" son, brother of Bel-imperia, and custodian of Don Balthazar. "Had he lived, he might ha' come to wear the crown of Spain."

The VICEROY OF PORTUGAL; his "years are mellow."

DON BALTHAZAR, his son, "the warlike prince of Portingale, . . . [and] the author of [Don Andrea's] death." A captive, he lives in Spain with Lorenzo, in "pleasing servitude," and is a suitor for the hand of Bel-imperia.

ISABELLA, Hieronimo's wife, mother of Don Horatio.

Maid to Isabella.

PEDRINGANO, traitorous servant to Bel-imperia, "full of merry conceits. . . . I have not seen a wretch so impudent."

SERBERINE, Balthazar's servingman.

PEDRO,
JAQUES,} Hieronimo's servants.

DON PEDRO, brother to the Viceroy of Portugal.

ALEXANDRO, a loyal Portuguese nobleman.

VILLUPPO, his envious, lying enemy, a "false, unkind, unthankful, traitorous beast."

The Portuguese Ambassador to Spain.

BAZARDO, a painter, whose son has been murdered.

DON BAZULTO, also called SENEX, another "grieved man, and not a ghost, that came for justice for [his] murdered son."

The Spanish Lord General.

The Deputy to Hieronimo as Justicer.

CHRISTOPHIL, custodian of Bel-imperia.

Page to Lorenzo.

A Hangman.

A Messenger.

Three Watchmen.

THREE KINGS, }characters in a masque in dumb show presented by Hieronimo at
THREE KNIGHTS,} the king's banquet (I, iv).

HYMEN,
TWO TORCHBEARERS,} characters in a dumb show in the Chorus to Act III.

PERSEDA, "blissful lamp of excellence, . . . an Italian dame whose beauty ravished all that her beheld" .... taken by Bel-imperia,

SOLIMAN, the Turkish Emperor; "ignoble prince, . . . by sundry means [he] sought to win the love of Perseda," .... taken by Balthazar,

ERASTO, Knight of Rhodes, beloved of Perseda, ... taken by Lorenzo,

PASHA and traitorous friend of Soliman. .... taken by Hieronimo,

} characters in Hieronimo's tragedy of *Soliman and Perseda* presented in Act IV, scene iii.

Army, Royal Suites, Noblemen, Portuguese Gentlemen, Citizens, Officers, Halberdiers, Servants, and Attendants.

Setting: Spain and Portugal once upon a time.

> *"They did what Heaven unpunished would not leave."*

INDUCTION

The Ghost of Don Andrea, late courtier of Spain and secret lover of the beautiful Bel-imperia, daughter of the Duke of Castile, discusses with Revenge, a companion assigned to him by Proserpine, goddess of Hell, the events which have occurred since his death in the Portuguese wars and the uncertainties attendant upon them. For three days, until his rites of burial were performed by his friend Don Horatio, Andrea's shade was not even permitted to sit in Charon's boat or cross the stream of Acheron. Then, having eluded Cerberus, the Ghost sought a passport from Minos, Aeacus, and Rhadamanth, the gods of Hell, but, because Andrea was both a lover and a soldier, they could not rightly decide where to place him. Hence, at last, he was sent for judgment to Pluto's court itself, past more hellish sights than a thousand tongues can tell, and now at Proserpine's request delivered over to Revenge. Andrea's companion then reveals the purpose of this wandering—the two have come to see Don Balthazar, the prince who slew Don Andrea in battle, be deprived of life by Bel-imperia, and to serve as Chorus to this tragedy.

Act I

After a fierce battle with the Portuguese, the Spanish army has achieved the victory and forced the vanquished host to promise tribute and customary homage. In the fight, however, both sides have sustained casualties—among the Spaniards brave Don Andrea, the leader of a troop of lancers, has been slain by Don Balthazar, son of the Portuguese Viceroy, and in turn Balthazar has been taken prisoner in single combat with Horatio, the valiant friend of Andrea and son of Hieronimo, the Spanish knight marshal. When the army arrives in Spain with the royal prisoner, however, he is claimed by two captors: Don Horatio, whom report has credited with the victory, and Don Lorenzo, nephew of the King. Lorenzo claims to have seized Balthazar's horse and disarmed the prince, Horatio to have unhorsed him and forced him to yield. Without investigating either claim the King settles the dispute by granting Horatio the ransom for the prince's person, dividing the spoils between the two captors, and decreeing that while negotiations with Portugal are pending, Balthazar be the guest rather than the prisoner of Lorenzo. The captive prince expresses his admiration of Don Horatio's chivalry, and his wish that this valiant young man also bear them company.

In Portugal a less chivalrous dispute between two courtiers has more immediate results in woe. Rumors rather than authentic news about the battle are current, and the Viceroy, only too conscious of his guilt in starting the war, nurses his sorrows by trusting in his nightly dreams of disaster, and taking a pessimistic view of all he hears, especially about his son. He is an easy victim, therefore, when a quarrel breaks out between two of his courtiers, the loyal Alexandro, who sensibly believes that Prince Balthazar is a prisoner of war, and the villain Villuppo, who accuses Alexandro of shooting the prince in the back during the combat. Without an opportunity to defend himself, Alexandro is hurried off to prison by the King to await execution.

Meanwhile, in Spain, Don Horatio reports to Bel-imperia how her lover Don Andrea met his death and brings her as a memento the scarf of hers which Andrea wore upon his sleeve. She bids Andrea's friend now wear it for them both, and while Horatio goes to seek the prince, Bel-imperia in soliloquy expresses her grief for the loss of her lover, her desire for revenge of his death, and her choice of Horatio as Andrea's successor to further that revenge. Moreover, she reveals the fact that Don Balthazar, Andrea's slayer and her brother's guest, has already begun to make love to her. Accordingly, when Lorenzo and Balthazar appear and the prince begins to make complimentary speeches, Bel-imperia indignantly leaves. But, as she does so, she contrives to drop her glove so that it is Horatio, returning, and not Balthazar, who picks it up and receives it as a favor for his pains. Lorenzo smooths over the incident as best he can, and the three men hasten to a banquet where the Portuguese ambassador is being entertained. Here Marshal Hieronimo, who has some skill at court theatricals, presents a masque importing comfort and consolation to the Portuguese in their defeat, by reminding them that Portugal, and Spain too, had before been conquered by little England.

CHORUS

Somewhat impatiently, the Ghost of Andrea asks Revenge if they have come all the way from Hell just to see Balthazar feast and to witness nothing but spectacles of friendship, love, and banqueting. Revenge assures him that ere they go this friendship will be turned to fell despite, this love to mortal hate, and this bliss to misery.

Act II

Finding Balthazar depressed because of his lack of success with Bel-imperia, Lorenzo encourages his guest and assures him that there must be a cause why Bel-imperia shows him no favor and swearing that that obstacle to the prince's suit shall be removed. From Pedringano, his sister's servant, Lorenzo at dagger's point, wrings the name of Bel-imperia's new lover, and, binding the servant to secrecy, he promises him a substantial reward for information when the lovers meet. To Balthazar the news is intolerable that his rival in arms is also his rival in love, and that the man who has overthrown him in battle is also preferred before him in love. Balthazar vows revenge, and, concealed by Pedringano, he and Lorenzo witness a meeting between the lovers and hear them agree upon a rendezvous at night in Hieronimo's pleasant bower.

Meanwhile, at court, plans are going forward for cementing the amity between Spain and Portugal by means of a marriage between Balthazar and Bel-imperia. Don Cyprian, her father, sends assurances to the Viceroy of his approval of the match and of the girl's good will, while the Spanish King, her uncle, promises a handsome dowry, release of the tribute, and succession to the Spanish crown, should Balthazar and Bel-imperia have a son.

At night Balthazar settles his score with Don Horatio. Disguised, and accompanied by the servants Serberine and Pedringano, he and Lorenzo surprise Horatio and Bel-imperia at their love-making, hang Horatio in the arbor, and stab him with swords as he hangs. The lady recognizes the assailants, however, and cries for help, but her mouth is stopped and she is carried off. It is Hieronimo, aroused from bed, who discovers the murder and cuts down Horatio's body. He is joined by his wife Isabella, and the aged parents, almost beside themselves with grief, lament their son. Hieronimo dips his handkerchief in the blood, vowing never to part with the memento nor to bury Horatio's body until he has discovered his murderers and avenged his death.

CHORUS

Again the Ghost of Andrea objects. Was he brought hither from Hell only to increase his pain? He had hoped to witness Balthazar's death; but it is his friend Horatio who is slain and his sweetheart Bel-imperia who is abused! Revenge bids him wait for the harvest till the corn is ripe.

Act III

In Portugal, only the return of the ambassador from Spain with word that Prince Balthazar is really alive saves the life of the loyal Alexandro, who is already tied to a stake for burning. Confronted by his villainy, Villuppo admits that his only reason for treachery was hope of preferment from the Viceroy, and then is justly sent off to execution.

In Spain, however, where court rivalry and ambition have already cost an innocent life, the case is more complex. Intrigue is followed by counterintrigue, as the avengers seek their victims, and the murderers try to conceal their crime. One day as the sorrowing Hieronimo is passing the Duke of Castile's house, a letter, written in blood and purporting to come from Bel-imperia, is dropped from a window to his feet. The letter accuses Don Balthazar and Don Lorenzo of Horatio's murder and urges him to avenge his son's death. Instantly suspicious, however, Hieronimo thinks it a trap and determines not to risk any accusations without first by indirections confirming the revelations made by the letter. His first impulse is to seek out Bel-imperia, but, meeting Pedringano and asking for her, the old man is confronted by Lorenzo—one of those the letter accused—and he replies simply that the girl is in disgrace with her father and has been sent away for a while. Hieronimo quickly evades any further question as to why he wished to see the missing young woman.

But the request alone is enough to arouse the suspicions of Lorenzo. Whether or not Hieronimo knows the secret he is not sure, but he does know that the fewer who know his and Balthazar's guilt, the safer they are. Accordingly, on the suggestion that Serberine has been talking, he agrees with Pedringano that Balthazar's man be killed at night in St. Luigi's Park. But at the same time Lorenzo warns the watch, and though Pedringano succeeds in his murder, he is taken prisoner by the guard of which old Hieronimo is marshal. To prevent Pedringano from talking and to effect his speedy liquidation is a simple matter. Lorenzo urges Balthazar to avenge his man's death by appealing for justice directly to the King, and he encourages Pedringano in the hope of a speedy pardon. Hence, the prisoner conducts himself impudently at his trial before Hieronimo and makes no revelations, but at the end is disappointed of reprieve and executed. Yet, somehow, through the hangman, a letter which Pedringano had written to Lorenzo falls into Hieronimo's hands, and in it the old man finds confirmation of the suspected letter written by Bel-imperia. He determines to go directly to the King and cry aloud for justice through the court.

Meanwhile, however, several events occur which make this simple course extremely difficult to follow. Hieronimo's wife Isabella goes mad with grief for her son. Bel-imperia is released by Lorenzo after Pedringano's execution, but is as inaccessible as before, for Lorenzo and Balthazar explain that what they have done is to preserve her honor and to save her from the wrath of her father. At the very time when she was in Horatio's arms, Lorenzo and Balthazar say, the King and her father were on the way to Hieronimo's to confer on matters of state. Unexpectedly finding the girl with Horatio, and remembering the old disgrace which Bel-imperia had endured because of Andrea, the pair say they got Horatio out of the way and had Bel-imperia carried off lest she be found there. Old Cyprian had noticed his daughter's melancholy after Andrea's death and was angry about it, but Lorenzo had excused her absence to their father. The two schemers propose, therefore, that Bel-imperia accept Balthazar as a lover and go into retirement with the prince as keeper. But they do not convince Bel-imperia. Worse still, grief and his own ineffectiveness at revenge have caused Hieronimo to rave, and all who come into contact with him are convinced that he is mad. The old man even contemplates suicide and provides the means, but decides against this desperate act because it will prevent his avenging Horatio.

It is while he is in this melancholy state of mind that Hieronimo has his first opportunity to accuse the murderers to the King. But the circumstances are most inopportune. His Majesty is just receiving from the Portuguese ambassador the news of the acceptance of the marriage plans, and Lorenzo takes care that he shall not be interrupted. The ambassador also brings Balthazar's ransom to Horatio, and, apparently never having missed the murdered man, the King orders the sum paid to him. At the mention of his son's name, Hieronimo cries out for justice, digs in the ground with his dagger, and is generally so unrestrained in word and action, that the King readily accepts Lorenzo's explanation that Hieronimo covets for himself the ransom due his son and so is lunatic. Such frustration and the caution he must exercise soon lead to other outbursts; Hieronimo's servants believe him to be insane, and when as judge he receives petitions for justice, he sees in the petitioners the lively image of his own grief, loses restraint, and even publicly addresses his son Horatio as if he saw his ghost come to seek justice and avenge his death.

At last the Portuguese Viceroy arrives in Spain, the betrothal is arranged, and the marriage date set. But the Duke of Castile has heard reports of how his son Lorenzo has interfered with Hieronimo's suits to the King, and he speaks to Lorenzo about the matter. The son, however, easily convinces his father that Hieronimo is "a silly man, distract of mind," whose interruptions of His Majesty were unseemly, and whose talk about a murdered son merely a figment of the imagination. Nevertheless, the duke, at Lorenzo's suggestion, effects a reconciliation between the two, assuring Hieronimo that he has no need to suspect his son of interference, and receiving in turn ironical assurances of perfect amity for one who loved his son well. Apparently old grudges are forgot.

CHORUS

At this seeming reconciliation, the Ghost of Andrea passionately calls upon Revenge and all the forces of Hell to awake and rouse themselves to action. But Revenge again patiently reassures him and interprets for him a dumb show in which two nuptial torchbearers are followed by Hymen clad in sable and a saffron robe, who blows out their bright torches and quenches them in blood. The Ghost understands and settles himself quietly to watch the rest.

Act IV

Impatient at his delay, Bel-imperia rebukes and shames Hieronimo, vowing to undertake Horatio's revenge herself. But the old man apologizes for suspecting her letter, bids her bear with him a little longer, and receives her assurance of full co-operation. His opportunity comes almost immediately. To grace the wedding celebrations and to entertain the Portuguese Viceroy, the King requests one of Hieronimo's theatrical entertainments, and, as suitable for the occasion, the old marshal suggests "a stately written tragedy, . . . fitting kings, containing matter, and not common things," which he wrote while a student at Toledo. It is called *Soliman and Perseda,* and for variety each part was written in a different language. This he suggests that Balthazar, Lorenzo, Bel-imperia, and himself enact, and to humor him the three accept their parts.

Meanwhile, there occurs another woeful incentive to Hieronimo's revenge. Distraught by the delay of justice and her husband's vengeance for his son, Isabella herself cuts down the arbor where her son was slain and stabs herself.

In the palace at the appointed time, *Soliman and Perseda* is presented before the royal audience. The tragedy concerns a beautiful Italian lady named Perseda (taken by Bel-imperia), who is married to a knight of Rhodes named Erasto (taken by Lorenzo), but wooed by the Turkish emperor Soliman (taken by Balthazar). To one of his pashas (taken by Hieronimo), Soliman reveals his passion. The Pasha, too, has long loved Perseda, and, knowing that she cannot otherwise be won, he advises the murder of her husband Erasto, whom treacherously he slays. Perseda then slays Soliman, and, finally, to avoid the Pasha, stabs herself. In Hieronimo's production, instead of killing in sport, the actors of this tragedy kill in earnest; in a long curtain speech Hieronimo draws the parallel between his play and his real tragedy, reveals the body of his murdered son, and retails the whole course of his revenge. At the end he tries to hang himself, but is prevented; bites out his tongue when he is questioned; and at last, pretending to be ready to write a full confession, calls for a knife with which to mend a pen and stabs both Lorenzo's father and himself.

Satisfied at last, the Ghost of Andrea summarizes the whole unhappy spectacle, anticipates the pleasant reunion he expects to have with his friends, asks that his enemies replace the victims on Hell's famous torture engines, and hurries down with Revenge to meet these friends and foes,

> To place [his] friends in ease, the rest in woes.
> For here, though death doth end their misery,
> I'll there begin their endless tragedy.

....•————◄◆►————•...

CHRISTOPHER MARLOWE
(1564–1593)

BIOGRAPHY. Christopher Marlowe, "the Muses' darling," was the most brilliant of all of the "University Wits" and the earliest first-rate artist to write plays. The son of a shoemaker and a clergyman's daughter, Marlowe was born in Canterbury, educated at King's School in his native city, and at Corpus Christi College, Cambridge. There he enjoyed a scholarship provided by Archbishop Parker, and there he received his B.A. degree in 1584 and his M.A. in 1587, the latter only by direct intervention of Her Majesty's Privy Council as a reward "for his faithful dealing." Probably while still an undergraduate, Marlowe was already in government service as a confidential agent. Certainly he was in bad odor with the University authorities.

Marlowe's career in the theatre begins in the same year, 1587, and is over in May of 1593. A hot-tempered rebel and a man of ungoverned life, Marlowe could be charming when he wanted to be; but his personal reputation even for Elizabethan London was not high. He was more than suspected of atheism, and he had enemies. On May 30, 1593, Marlowe was killed in a tavern brawl at Deptford by one Ingram Frizer. He was only twenty-nine.

CRITICAL COMMENT. Marlowe's great significances for the Elizabethan drama are that he was a poet who cast his lot with the theatre, and that he created on the stage energetic, individualistic characters who are true children of the Renaissance. In each of his great dramas there is one figure who dwarfs all the rest, a kind of superman about whom all the action centers. In *Tamburlaine* this figure is a conqueror with an "undeviating pursuit of a vision," who personifies and voices the boundless aspiration of the Renaissance in a great ten-act epic drama. In *Doctor Faustus* he is the idealist in pride of life seeking knowledge infinite and selling his soul to attain his aspirations and the lusts of the flesh. In technique this play is a blend of the old and the new; the Good and the Bad Angels and the Seven Deadly Sins derive from the medieval moralities, but the central figure belongs to the Renaissance.

The Jew of Malta depicts a consummate crafty, self-centered, intriguing villain who at last overreaches himself. *Edward II* transforms the old loose-jointed chronicle play into a tragedy of character. The theme is the conflict between a wavering, pathetic king and his barons; against a background of hard ruthless men, the figure of the sentimental, misguided monarch makes an effective picture. But Edward's fate is not bound up with any capricious turning of Fortune's Wheel; it is the result of his own personality. So is Mortimer's. Only one of the peers at first, Mortimer grows in power as his ambition grows, until he is unmasked as a Machiavellian without conscience. Technically, *Edward II* is Marlowe's most mature play. He has a masterly control over his material; his characterization for the first time extends to other persons besides the central figures; and, without in the least extenuating the faults of the king, at the right moment the author contrives to transfer the sympathy of the audience to him. Shakespeare was to learn a great deal from Marlowe when he wrote *Richard II*.

SOURCES. For the story of Tamburlaine Marlowe had recourse to the Spaniard Pedro Mexia's *Silva de Varia Leccion,* a book already translated into English by Thomas Fortescue as *The Forest* (1571 and 1576), and to Petrus Perodinus' *Magni Tamerlanis Scytharum Imperatoris Vita* (1553), as well as numerous other volumes. For *Faustus* his immediate source was *The History of the Damnable Life and Deserved Death of Dr. J. Faustus* (1592, but known to have been in existence earlier). It is a translation from the German *Historia von D. Johann Fausten* (1587), and has the moral application of the story. The morality elements, like the Good and the Bad Angels, are Marlowe's additions from earlier drama. For *The Jew of Malta* no source has been discovered, and the plot therefore may be Marlowe's own invention. The main source of *Edward II,* which covers twenty-three years of history (1307-30), was Holinshed's *Chronicles* (1577 and 1587), with some reference to Fabyan's and Stow's.

BIBLIOGRAPHY

Collected Works:

> *The Works and Life of Christopher Marlowe,* edited by R. H. Case and others, 6 volumes, 1930–33.
> *The Works of Christopher Marlowe,* edited by C. F. Tucker Brooke, Oxford, 1910.
> *The Best Plays of Christopher Marlowe,* edited by Havelock Ellis, Mermaid Series, 1887.

Monographs:

> John Bakeless, *Christopher Marlowe: the Man in His Time,* 1937.
> John Bakeless, *The Tragical History of Christopher Marlowe,* 2 volumes, 1942.

Tamburlaine:

> Early editions: Both parts: 1590; 1593; 1597; Part I alone: 1606; Part II alone: 1605.

Doctor Faustus:
 Early editions (two radically different textual traditions):
  a) that of 1604, 1609, 1611—a bad text, shorter than later editions; and
  b) that of 1616 [enlarged and altered]; 1619 [with new additions]; 1620;
   1624; 1628; 1631; 1663—a new text about 550 lines longer than (*a*),
   much rewritten and modified by theatrical conditions.
 Modern editions: Facs. (1604 edn.) J. S. Farmer (TFT, 1914); ed. I. Gollancz (TD, 1897).

The Jew of Malta:
 Early edition: 1633 [a corrupt text].

Edward II:
 Early editions: 1594; 1598; 1612; 1622.
 Modern editions: ed. W. D. Briggs (1914); A. W. Verity (TD, 1896); W. W. Greg (MSR, 1925).

TAMBURLAINE THE GREAT

WHO, FROM A SCYTHIAN SHEPHERD, BY HIS RARE AND WONDERFUL CONQUESTS, BECAME A MOST PUISSANT AND MIGHTY MONARCH . . .

DIVIDED INTO TWO TRAGICAL DISCOURSES

(1587–1588)

Part I

DRAMATIS PERSONAE

TAMBURLAINE, a ruthless conqueror and "fiery thirster after sovereignty, . . . the Scourge and Wrath of God, . . . threatening the world with high astounding terms, and scourging kingdoms with his conquering sword." He is "a lord, for so [his] deeds shall prove, and yet a [Scythian] shepherd by [his] parentage; . . . so embellished with Nature's pride and richest furniture, . . . [he] hold[s] the Fates bound fast in iron chains, and with [his] hand turn[s] Fortune's Wheel about." Herein, "as in a mirror, may be seen his honor, that consists in shedding blood when men presume to manage arms with him."

THERIDAMAS, "the chiefest captain of Mycetes' host, the hope of Persia, and the very legs whereon [the] state doth lean," a deserter to Tamburlaine, and later King of Argier,

TECHELLES, follower of Tamburlaine, and later King of Fez,

USUMCASANE, follower of Tamburlaine, and later King of Morocco,

"the strangest men that ever Nature made; I know not how to take their tyrannies,"

Tamburlaine's "contributory kings."

ZENOCRATE, daughter to the Sultan of Egypt, the captive and the "dearest love" of Tamburlaine, "she that hath calm'd the fury of his sword, [but] whose fortunes never mastered her griefs." She is "the loveliest maid alive, fairer than rocks of pearl and precious stone, the only paragon of Tamburlaine, whose eyes are brighter than the lamps of heaven, and speech more pleasant than sweet harmony, that with [her] looks [can] clear the darkened sky and calm the rage of thund'ring Jupiter."

ANIPPE, her maid.

AGYDAS, } Median lords, attendants upon Zenocrate.
MAGNETES,

MYCETES, weak and witless King of Persia, "one that knew not what a king should do."

COSROE, his rebellious brother, "monster of Nature, shame unto [his] stock." Later he becomes "Monarch of the East, Emperor of Asia, and of Persia, Great Lord of Medea and Armenia, Duke of Africa and Albania, Mesopotamia, and of Parthia, East India, and the late discovered Isles, Chief Lord of all the wide vast Euxine Sea and of the ever-raging Caspian Lake." All of these honors he holds from Tamburlaine, "that only made him king to make us sport."

MEANDER, "faithful councilor" to the King of Persia.

ORTYGIUS, }
CENEUS,   } Persian lords and "trusty friends of Cosroe."
MENAPHON, }

BAJAZETH, "the Turkish Emperor, dread Lord of Afric, Europe, and Asia; great King and conqueror of Grecia, the Ocean, Terrene, and the Coal-black Sea, the high and highest Monarch of the World, . . . for all flesh quakes at [his] magnificence . . . and trembles at [his] looks, . . . and all the trees are blasted with [his] breaths,"
who prefer death to dishonor.

ZABINA, his wife, the "Turkess, . . . queen of fifteen contributory queens, . . . [and] mother of three braver boys than Hercules, . . . who, when they come unto their father's age, will batter turrets with their manly fists,"

EBEA, her maid.

The KING OF FEZ,
The KING OF MOROCCO,   } "great kings of Barbary," Bajazeth's "stout contrib-
The KING OF ARGIER [Algiers], } utory kings."

The SULTAN OF EGYPT, a mighty opponent of Tamburlaine, and father of Zenocrate.

CAPOLIN, an Egyptian lord, attendant upon the Sultan.

The KING OF ARABIA, "the first affecter of [Zenocrate's] excellence," and her "first betrothed love."

The GOVERNOR OF DAMASCUS.

PHILEMUS, a messenger.

A Persian Spy.

Four Virgins of Damascus.

Pashas, Lords, Citizens, Moors, Messengers, Soldiers, and Attendants.

Setting: Western Asia and the Near East in the fourteenth century.

*"Nature doth strive with Fortune and his stars
To make him famous in accomplisht worth."*

Act I

In Persia the weakling King Mycetes dispatches his great general Theridamas with a force of cavalry to suppress

> . . . Tamburlaine, that sturdy Scythian thief
> That robs [his] merchants of Persepolis, . . .
> And in [his] confines with his lawless train
> Daily commits incivil outrages.

At the same time a palace revolution, led by Ortygius, Ceneus, and other Persian noblemen and captains of the Medean garrisons, replaces Mycetes on the Persian throne by his intriguing brother Cosroe. To his Scythian camp Tamburlaine has brought as captive Zenocrate, daughter of the mighty Sultan of Egyptia and the betrothed of the King of Arabia, whom he has apprehended as she traveled with a Medean guard toward Memphis after a visit to her uncle. Experiencing tender emotions for the first time, the rough bandit, who aspires to be the conqueror of Asia and the terror of the world, clumsily makes love to the proud beauty. At the approach of the Persian army, which outnumbers him two to one, Tamburlaine, with unerring psychology, opens up his looted treasure for the Persians to see and, without striking a blow, wins over Theridamas and his men to join his band.

Act II

Impressed by the irresistible power of Tamburlaine, who seems "his Fortune's master and the king of men," the new, but unsure, Persian emperor Cosroe decides to follow a policy of co-operation with the conqueror by "joining with the man, ordain'd by Heaven to further every action to the best." "With duty and with amity," Tamburlaine readily agrees to serve Cosroe and make him Emperor of Asia; he defeats in battle a small force which the cowardly Mycetes has raised against him; and, as reward, he accepts from Cosroe the title of "Regent of Persia and General Leftenant of the Armies." But the simple Scythian shepherd is much impressed by the pomp attending King Cosroe, and he too longs for a crown:

> Is it not passing brave to be a king? . . .
> A god is not so glorious as a king. . . .
> To wear a crown enchas'd with pearl and gold,
> Whose virtues carry with it life and death;
> To ask and have; command and be obeyed;
> When looks breed love, with looks to gain the prize—
> Such power attractive shines in princes' eyes. . . .

Nature that fram'd us of four elements,
Warring within our breasts for regiment,
Doth teach us all to have aspiring minds.
Our souls, whose faculties can comprehend
The wondrous architecture of the world, . . .
Still climbing after knowledge infinite, . . .
Wills us to wear ourselves and never rest,
Until we reach the ripest fruit of all,
That perfect bliss and sole felicity,
The sweet fruition of an earthly crown.

The "thirst of reign" is too much for Tamburlaine; accordingly he treacherously challenges the new monarch for his crown and defeats him. "Who think you now is King of Persia?"

Act III

Tamburlaine's unbounded ambition and ruthless cruelty carry everything before him; he even succeeds in love. In spite of the advice of Agydas, to whom Tamburlaine is only a vile barbarian, Zenocrate confesses her love for the Scythian. Tamburlaine overhears her and leads her away lovingly by the hand, expressing his displeasure toward Agydas in the only language he knows by sending the princess' adviser a naked dagger. Being both wise and honorable, Agydas takes the hint and stabs himself. Meanwhile, Bajazeth, Emperor of the Turks, has been menaced by the advance of Tamburlaine. Taking counsel with his "contributory kings" of Barbary, he offers Tamburlaine a truce, lest they be diverted from their siege of Constantinople. Tamburlaine, of course, defies the Turk, and while Zabina, the "Turkess," and Tamburlaine's Zenocrate hold the emperors' crowns, the two armies fight off stage, and the women sit watching the battle and taunting each other. The fight is short; Bajazeth is overcome; and Tamburlaine bids his Zenocrate take the Turkish diadem away from the indignant empress, and crown him Emperor of Africa. Refusing to set a ransom for his prisoners, Tamburlaine orders them bound and led away. Then he celebrates his triumph with a martial feast.

Act IV

At length the Sultan of Egypt arouses the men of Memphis to save his daughter Zenocrate, and, though unprepared for war, he joins with the King of Arabia at Damascus to oppose the increasing tide of Tamburlaine's armies. By the time he lays siege to Damascus, Tamburlaine's ingenious custom of terrifying a beleaguered city is fully established. On successive days he flaunts before the town varying-colored equipment to symbolize his intentions toward the inhabitants:

> *The first day when he pitcheth down his tents,*
> *White is their hue, and on his silver crest*
> *A snowy feather spangled white he bears,*
> *To signify the mildness of his mind. . . .*
> *But, when Aurora mounts the second time,*
> *As red as scarlet is his furniture.*
> *Then must his kindled wrath be quenched with blood. . . .*
> *But, if these threats move not submission,*
> *Black are his colors, black pavilion;*
> *His spear, his shield, his horse. his armor, plumes,*
> *And jetty feathers menace death ana hell.*

While he waits for Damascus to fall and as he feasts and makes merry, "the rogue of Volga" accords the Emperor Bajazeth the most inhuman treatment. He leads him about in a cage, uses him as a footstool to mount his throne, brings him in at banquets to taunt him unmercifully, and alternately starves him or throws him food as to a captive beast. As a further insult, Tamburlaine usurps the titles and crowns his generals Theridamas, Techelles, and Usumcasane respectively kings of Argier, Fez, and Morocco, calling them his "contributory kings" as Bajazeth had done their predecessors. His ferocity is softened only to the extent that he promises Zenocrate that the lives of her father and her friends shall be spared when Damascus falls, provided, of course, that they yield and recognize the conqueror's claim to be emperor.

Act V

When Damascus can hold out no longer, and Tamburlaine is displaying his black colors, the citizens send out a deputation of four young girls to plead for mercy. But Tamburlaine, unmoved, orders his cavalry to charge them and to hoist their slaughtered bodies up on Damascus' walls. The next moment, by an astonishing contrast, he is seen at his tenderest, soliloquizing lyrically about his love for Zenocrate and apostrophizing Beauty:

> *If all the pens that ever poets held*
> *Had fed the feeling of their masters' thoughts,*
> *And every sweetness that inspir'd their hearts,*
> *Their minds, and muses on admired themes;*
> *If all the heavenly quintessence they still*
> *From their immortal powers of poesy,*

Wherein, as in a mirror, we perceive
The highest reaches of a human wit;
If these had made one poem's period,
And all combined in Beauty's worthiness,
Yet should there hover in their restless heads
One thought, one grace, one wonder, at the least,
Which into words no virtue can digest.

Soon after, other results of his ruthless brutality are seen. Preferring death to further dishonor, Bajazeth sends his queen out to fetch him a drink of water and dashes his brains out against his cage. When she returns and sees what has happened, Zabina goes mad and does the same. The sight is a shock to Zenocrate, as is the shedding of so much Egyptian blood, and not surprisingly she is somewhat torn between "shame and duty, love and fear," when she considers that her "father and [her] first betrothed love must fight against [her] life and present love." In the battle the Arabian king is mortally wounded and dies in Zenocrate's arms, and the Sultan is captured but spared, expressing himself as "pleas'd with this my overthrow, if as beseems a person of thy state, thou hast with honor used Zenocrate." Peace then is sealed by Zeno-crate's coronation as Queen of Persia, as well as of all the kingdoms and dominions Tamburlaine has conquered, and by her betrothal to the "Scourge of God."

THE BLOODY CONQUESTS
OF MIGHTY TAMBURLAINE

Part II

DRAMATIS PERSONAE

TAMBURLAINE, the Scythian conqueror and "the Scourge of God, . . . whose wrath is death, . . . that whips down cities and controlleth crowns, . . . the monster that hath drunk a sea of blood, and yet gapes still for more to quench his thirst." He is "a man greater than Mahomet, . . . that treadeth Fortune underneath his feet, . . . on whom Death and the Fatal Sisters wait, . . . [and] over whose zenith . . . Fame hovereth, sounding of her golden trump. . . . Nor [was he] made Arch-monarch of the world, crown'd and invested by the hand of Jove, for deeds of bounty or nobility."

ZENOCRATE, wife of Tamburlaine; "her sacred beauty hath enchanted Heaven, and, had she lived before the siege of Troy, Helen, whose beauty summoned Greece to arms, and drew a thousand ships to Tenedos, had not been nam'd in Homer's *Iliads.*"

AMYRAS, the heir,

CELEBINUS, a "tall stripling, . . . for person like to prove a second Mars. . . . How like his cursed father he begins to practice taunts and bitter tyrannies!"

CALYPHAS, their "lazy brother, . . . wherein was neither courage, strength, or wit, but folly, sloth, and damned idleness." He takes "no pleasure to be murderous, nor care[s] for blood when wine will quench [his] thirst. . . . [He'll] to cards,"

} Tamburlaine's sons, "more precious in [his] eyes than all the wealthy kingdoms [he] subdued. . . . They have their mother's looks, but when they list, their conquering father's heart."

THERIDAMAS, King of Argier [Algiers],
TECHELLES, King of Fez,
USUMCASANE, King of Morocco,

} Tamburlaine's generals, bugbears that "will make the hair stand upright on your heads."

CALLAPINE, son of Bajazeth, Emperor of Turkey, "born to be monarch of the Western World," but a prisoner of Tamburlaine. Later "by the aid of God and his friend Mahomet [he is crowned] Emperor of Natolia [i.e., Anatolia], Jerusalem, Trebizon, Soria [i.e., Syria], Amasia, Thracia, Illyria, Carmonia, and all the hundred and thirty kingdoms late contributory to his mighty father. Long live Callapinus, Emperor of Turkey!"

ALMEDA, Callapine's keeper, who escapes with his prisoner and is rewarded by being invested "King of Ariadan, bordering on Mare Roso near to Mecca."

ORCANES, King of Natolia, "he that with the cannon shook Vienna's walls."

THE KING OF AMASIA, ally of Callapine against Tamburlaine.

GAZELLUS, Viceroy of Byron.

URIBASSA, another viceroy of Asia.

SIGISMUND, King of Hungary,
FREDERICK,
BALDWIN,

} Lords of Buda and Bohemia,

} "Can there be such deceit in Christians, or treason in the fleshly heart of man whose shape is figure of the highest God?"

The KING OF TREBIZON,
The KING OF SORIA,

} Captive kings, harnessed to Tamburlaine's chariot. "Holla, ye pampered jades of Asia! What, can ye draw but twenty miles a day and have so proud a chariot at your heels and such a coachman as great Tamburlaine?"

The KING OF JERUSALEM, another captive of Tamburlaine.

The GOVERNOR OF BABYLON, a sturdy, brave defier of the conquerer, "for although [the] cannon shook the city walls, [his] heart did never quake, or courage faint."

A CAPTAIN OF BALSERA, mortally wounded fighting Tamburlaine.

OLYMPIA, his wife, "queen of chastity," whose "lord deceased was dearer unto [her] than any viceroy, king, or emperor." Loved by Theridamas, she resorts to a suicidal stratagem rather than "yield to his detested suit. . . . 'Twas bravely done, and like a soldier's wife."

Their Son, who prefers death to dishonor, and is slain by his mother.

MAXIMUS, citizen of Babylon.

PERDICAS, companion at cards to Calyphas.

Turkish Concubines, Physicians, Lords, Citizens, Messengers, Soldiers, and Attendants.

Setting: Western Asia and the Near East in the late fourteenth century.

"The general welcomes TAMBURLAINE *receiv'd,*
When he arrivéd last upon our stage,

Hath made our poet pen his Second Part
Where Death cuts off the progress of his pomp
And murderous Fates throws all his triumphs down."

Act I

The Turkish vassals of the conquered Bajazeth—Orcanes, King of Natolia; Gazellus, Viceroy of Byron; and Uribassa—gather to redeem the defeat of their emperor. Unable to fight on two fronts, however, and to attack Tamburlaine in the East, they join in a holy alliance against the common enemy with Sigismund, King of Hungary, their Christian foe in the West. Meanwhile, Callapine, the son and heir of Bajazeth, escapes from Tamburlaine's prison by bribing Almeda, his jailer, with promises; and Tamburlaine, now the father of three princely sons, receives the allegiance of his "contributory kings," Theridamas of Argier, Techelles of Fez, and Usumcasane of Morocco, all conquerors and plunderers in their own right.

Act II

On the theory that an oath is not binding when it is made to infidels, Sigismund of Hungary and his associates, Frederick and Baldwin, Lords of Buda and Bohemia, break their pledge and treacherously attack the Turks. Shocked at this perfidy, the Turks appeal, not to Mahomet, their own god, but to Christ, whose name the faithless Christians have dishonored by their broken oath, and in a fight with the Christians the Turks achieve a victory. Then they make haste to join the kings of Jerusalem, Soria, Trebizon, and Amasia in their league against Tamburlaine. But Fate begins to lay its icy hand upon the great Scythian conqueror. Zenocrate, his beloved wife, falls ill and dies; and, stricken to the heart with grief, "raving, impatient, desperate, and mad," the "Scourge of the immortal God," has her body "embalmed with cassia, ambergrice, and myrrh, not lapp'd in lead, but in a sheet of gold," and carries it about with him wherever he goes. With characteristic unrestraint he sets fire to the accursed town in which she died and lays the country waste.

Act III

With the aid of the kings of Natolia, Trebizon, Soria, and Jerusalem, the liberated Callapine is crowned emperor as successor to his father Bajazeth and gathers a huge united army to meet Tamburlaine. At the same time the ruthless and undaunted conqueror prepares his sons for the destiny which is theirs by training them in the rudiments of war, cutting his arm to show them his contempt for pain, and permitting them to wash their hands in his blood, "the God of War's rich livery." At Balsera, a stronghold which offers some resistance on the way, an incident occurs which in its conclusion demonstrates the greatness of human fortitude and devotion. A heroic captain is slain, and, preferring death to dishonorable survival, his wife Olympia kills their son, and is about to kill herself, when she is prevented by Theridamas, Tamburlaine's great general, who is so struck by her beauty that in spite of her pleas he carries her away with him. But his hope for her love is vain, as subsequent events prove. At Aleppo the two great armies meet, but for the moment content themselves with threatening taunts and warlike defiance.

Act IV

In the battle which follows, the hosts of Tamburlaine are victorious, and the kings of Natolia, Trebizon, Soria, and Jerusalem are captured. Unfortunately, too, during the battle one of Tamburlaine's sons, Calyphas—who, unlike his brothers, has no taste for fighting—remains in his tent to play at cards. In a rage his father seeks him out, denounces him as "the obloquy and scorn of [his] renown," and stabs him to death. So great is his contempt for his "effeminate brat," that he will not permit his soldiers to defile themselves by burying his body; instead he orders the captive Turkish concubines to perform the task and then has the concubines given to the common soldiers.

Meanwhile, Olympia is wooed by Theridamas, but rather than yield to the detested suit of the soldier-king, she pretends to have obtained from a cunning chemist an ointment which will protect from wounds the skin which is anointed with it. To prove that it will blunt the sharpest weapon, Olympia anoints her own throat; at her request Theridamas stabs her and she dies, achieving by stratagem what Theridamas had prevented before.

Further barbarity of Tamburlaine is seen on every possible occasion. Not satisfied merely to have them captive, the inhuman conqueror hitches to his chariot the "pamper'd jades of Asia," the kings of Trebizon and Soria, with the kings of Natolia and Jerusalem, scourging them with a whip and making them draw him on to Babylon.

Act V

The city of Babylon resists valiantly, and in revenge Tamburlaine orders the sturdy Governor to be hanged in chains from the walls, while the soldiers shoot at his body. Then he barbarously sentences all of the citizens of Babylon to be drowned. In open defiance of Mahomet, also, he gathers all the copies of the Koran he can lay hands on and has them burned in a great fire. It is not surprising, therefore, to hear that he feels suddenly ill. As he grows steadily weaker, he traces on a map the great extent of his conquests and to his boys he shows the vast lands lying westward which are still left for them to conquer. At the same time, the Emperor Callapine and the King of Amasia, who had escaped the conqueror at Aleppo, are seeking out the "tyrant of the world." But Tamburlaine is too weak to pursue them; he utters his defiance of them, orders his son Amyras crowned as his successor, and expires.

The Tragical History of

DOCTOR FAUSTUS

(1588–1592)

DRAMATIS PERSONAE

FAUSTUS, learned doctor of the University of Wittenberg, proficient in the liberal arts, in law, in physic, and "excelling all whose sweet delight disputes in heavenly matters of theology," but possessed of an inordinate desire for power as well as knowledge; "till swollen with cunning [i.e., learning], of a self-conceit, his waxen wings did mount above his reach, and, melting, Heavens conspired his overthrow. For, falling to a devilish exercise, and glutted now with learning's golden gifts, he surfeits upon cursèd necromancy. . . . Hell strives with grace for conquest in [his] breast, . . . [yet] the serpent that tempted Eve may be saved, but not Faustus."

LUCIFER, Prince of Hell, "chief lord and regent of perpetual night," to whom Faustus delivers himself by deed of gift, signed with his blood.

BEELZEBUB, his companion.

MEPHISTOPHILIS, onetime servant to great Lucifer, the agent of Faustus' damnation and his attendant, always obedient to his will.

VALDES, } magicians, infamous throughout the world as practitioners of the damned
CORNELIUS, } art, the friends and instructors of Dr. Faustus.

The EVIL ANGEL, } advisers of Dr. Faustus.
The GOOD ANGEL, }

An Old Man, who makes a final effort to reclaim Faustus from his loathsome life, but who, for his pains, is tormented by devils. His faith is great and triumphs over the vile fiends; "the heavens smiles at [their] repulse and laughs [their] state to scorn."

WAGNER, servant to Dr. Faustus, his famulus, or poor scholar.

A Clown, a boy hired by Wagner. "The villain is bare and out of service, and so hungry that I know he would give his soul to the Devil for a shoulder of mutton."

The Pope,
The Cardinal of Lorraine, } upon whom Dr. Faustus and Mephistophilis play pranks.
Friars attending them,

The Emperor of Germany [Charles V], } before whom Dr. Faustus demonstrates his
The Duke of Vanholt [Anhalt], } gifts of magic.
The Duchess of Vanholt,

Robin, the Ostler, a clownish conjurer.

Rafe, his man.

A Vintner, from whom Robin has stolen a goblet.

A Knight of the Emperor's court who scoffs at Faustus and is punished.

A Horsecourser, to whom Dr. Faustus sells his steed.

The Seven Deadly Sins: Pride, Covetousness, Wrath, Envy, Gluttony, Sloth, and Lechery, raised by Lucifer as a spectacle to amuse Dr. Faustus.

Spirits in the shapes of Alexander the Great and of his beauteous Paramour, raised by Dr. Faustus before the Emperor.

The Spirit of Helen of Troy, the "paragon of excellence," raised by Dr. Faustus for his scholar friends; later, Faustus' paramour. "Was this the face that launched a thousand ships, and burnt the topless towers of Ilium?"

Chorus, who serves as Prologue and Epilogue, and occasionally as commentator upon the action.

Balliol and Belcher, devils raised by Wagner.

Scholars, Devils, and other Attendants.

Setting: Germany and Rome in the early sixteenth century.

> *"Regard his hellish fall,*
> *Whose fiendful fortune may exhort the wise*
> *Only to wonder at unlawful things,*
> *Whose deepness doth entice such forward wits*
> *To practice more than Heavenly power permits."*

[*Scene i*] Faustus, learned doctor of the University of Wittenberg, sits brooding among his books, trying to decide upon a field of specialization. Although he has taken his degree in divinity, he has been attracted to other studies. He is a master of the liberal arts, particularly in the philosophy of Aristotle; he is a physician so learned in Galen that his prescriptions are "hung up as monuments, whereby whole cities have escaped the plague, and thousand desperate maladies been eased." He is learned in Justinian law and in Jerome's Vulgate. In short, Faustus has mastered all of the "four faculties" of the universities. But, as he examines each in turn, he finds all human learning hollow and unsatisfying when compared to the black art and the metaphysics of magicians—"O, what a world of profit and delight, of power, of honor, of omnipotence, is promised to the studious artisan" of these subjects. Accordingly, having made his choice, Faustus sends his servant Wagner with an invitation to Valdes and Cornelius, exponents of these sciences, who have been trying to convert Faustus to their study. In spite of the warning of his Good Angel to "lay that damned book aside" and read the Scriptures, Dr. Faustus follows the temptations of his Evil Angel and hopes to be the lord and commander of the elements, and "on earth as Jove is in the sky." His friends Valdes and Cornelius promise to begin his instruction immediately.

[*Scene ii*] Meanwhile, some of Faustus' friends have missed him, and, hearing from Wagner that his master is dining with the magicians Valdes and Cornelius, they fear that he has fallen into infamous ways from which nothing can reclaim him.

[*Scene iii*] At night, in the gloomy shadow of a grove, Faustus draws a magic circle and begins his incantations. He succeeds in raising a devil, Mephistophilis, servant of Lucifer, who is so ugly that Faustus bids him go and return in the garb of a Franciscan friar—"that holy shape becomes a devil best." From Mephistophilis Faustus learns that conjuring has been only the accidental cause of his appearance; actually devils come in hope of gaining a glorious soul whenever they hear a man abjure the Scriptures and the Trinity and pray to the Prince of Hell as Faustus has done. At the end of the interview, Faustus sends word to Lucifer that he is willing to surrender up his soul on condition that he be spared for four and twenty years, be permitted to live in all voluptuousness, and have Mephistophilis as a constant attendant upon him. The scholar and the devil agree to meet in Faustus' study at midnight.

[*Scene iv*] As a parody of the preceding scene, Wagner, Faustus' servant, who has learned to imitate his master, tries to bind the clown to him for seven years, raising two devils, Balliol and Belcher, to clinch the bargain.

[*Scene v*] At midnight, in Faustus' study, the Good and the Evil Angels again contend for Faustus' soul. When Mephistophilis arrives, however, Faustus draws up a deed of gift of his soul with his own blood. As he writes, his blood congeals rather than be used for this horrid purpose, and Mephistophilis must fetch a chafer of coals to dissolve it again. To seal the bargain, devils bring crowns and rich apparel to Dr. Faustus, and even a wife, whom he rejects as too foul.

[*Scene vi*] Filled with misgiving about his pact, a remorse which is increased by the promptings of the Good and the Evil Angels, Dr. Faustus engages in empty disputes with Mephistophilis. At last Lucifer and Beelzebub themselves come to rebuke his dissatisfaction and to offer him some pastime. They call up a pageant of the Seven Deadly Sins—Pride, Covetousness, Wrath, Envy, Gluttony, Sloth, and Lechery. As he leaves, Lucifer promises to satisfy Faustus' longing to see Hell and gives him a book from which he can learn to turn himself into any shape he likes. Thus the powers of evil overcome Faustus' regrets.

[*Scene vii*] Faustus now enters upon his promised years of power, travelling about the world on winged dragons and seeing all of the stateliest cities. In Rome, Faustus and Mephistophilis, invisible, play clownish tricks in the Pope's palace, snatching dishes and cups at a banquet, boxing the Pope's ears, and flinging fireworks among the friars who try to exorcise the evil spirits.

[*Scenes viii, ix*] Robin the ostler, having stolen one of Faustus' conjuring books, promises his man Rafe that he will do wonders, steals a silver goblet from a vintner, and tries to cover up his theft by incantations. But he is so frightened by the appearance of Mephistophilis, who sets squibs about, that he returns the stolen goblet. But, as punishment for the disturbance they have caused, Robin is transformed into an ape and Rafe into a dog.

[*Scene x*] Having returned home, Dr. Faustus finds his fame widespread. At the German court the magician is called upon by the Emperor Charles V to give a demonstration of his art, and summons up Alexander the Great and his paramour, punishing a knight who had scoffed at his power by fitting a pair of horns on his head.

[*Scene xi*] In Wittenberg again, Faustus sells his horse to a dealer for forty dollars, warning him not to ride the animal into the water.

[*Scene xii*] At night he is sought in his study by the horsecourser, who has ridden the horse into a pond, seen it transformed under him into a bottle of hay, and now demands his forty dollars back again. But in trying to awaken Dr. Faustus, the excited fellow pulls him by the leg, which comes off in his hands, and in his fright he runs away. Not, however, before he promises forty more dollars for being let off.

[*Scene xiii*] For the delectation of the Duke of Vanholt and his court Dr. Faustus in January brings a dish of fresh grapes from India by his magic.

[*Scene xiv*] Faustus' years of power have slipped by and his disintegration is complete. The learned man prepares for his end by giving all of his goods to his servant Wagner. But, in spite of approaching death, he continues to feast and to carouse with the students as of old. To satisfy their curiosity and to grace their feast, he even raises from the dead Helen of Troy, the most beautiful woman of antiquity. After his guests leave, however, one last time "Hell strives with grace for conquest in [his] breast," as a virtuous Old Man begs Faustus to repent his loathsome life and seek the mercy of his Savior. Faustus is about to recant, but Mephistophilis, determined not to be balked of his prey, acts quickly. The fiend drives Faustus to despair, offers him a dagger that he may take his life, and at last arrests his soul for disobedience to his sovereign lord. To atone for his defection, Faustus reaffirms in blood the pact which he had years before made to Lucifer, and, reinforced in evil, calls back fair Helen to be his paramour, so that "her sweet embraces may extinguish clean those thoughts that do dissuade [him] from his vow." Ordering the Old Man to be tormented by devils, thus at the last Dr. Faustus "excludes the grace of Heaven."

[*Scene xv*] As his hour approaches, Faustus rejects the kind offices of his friends who come to comfort him and to pray for him. It is too late. Alone, he hears the clock strike eleven; then the half-hour; and at the stroke of twelve, in thunder and lightning, devils carry Dr. Faustus off to Hell.

> *Cut is the branch that might have grown full straight,*
> *And burnéd is Apollo's laurel bough*
> *That sometime grew within this learnéd man.*
> *Faustus is gone.*

THE FAMOUS TRAGEDY OF THE RICH

JEW OF MALTA

(1589–1590)

DRAMATIS PERSONAE

The GHOST OF MACHIAVEL, unscrupulous, cunning Florentine politician, presenter and Prologue of the tragedy. He "weigh[s] not men, and therefore not men's words; . . . [he] count[s] religion but a childish toy, and hold[s] there is no sin but ignorance."

BARABAS, the Jew of Malta, "a merchant and a monied man, . . . wealthier far than any Christian. . . . More of the serpent than the dove," he is a dissembling caricature of pure atrocity. He "look[s] unto [him]self" and hates Christians, "for [he] can see no fruits in all their faith, but malice, falsehood, and excessive pride, which [he] thinks fits not their profession. . . . It's no sin to deceive a Christian, for they themselves hold it a principle faith is not to be held with heretics."

ABIGAIL, his "one sole daughter, whom [he] hold[s] as dear as Agamemnon did his Iphigen, . . . a fair young maid scarce fourteen years of age, the sweetest flower in Cytherea's field. . . . Tut, she were fitter for a tale of love than to be tired out with orisons." She is in love with Don Mathias. ("Are there not Jews enow in Malta, but thou must dote upon a Christian?")

ITHAMORE, a Turkish slave, Barabas' depraved, "trusty servant, nay [his] second self." They "are villains both."

FERNEZE, Governor of Malta.

DON LODOWICK, the Governor's son, in love with Abigail.

DON MATHIAS, a Maltese gentleman; "he loves [Barabas'] daughter and she holds him dear, but [the Jew has] sworn to frustrate both their hopes."

KATHERINA, widowed mother of Don Mathias.

SELIM CALYMATH, "proud-daring Calymath," son of the Grand Seignior of Turkey, demander of the tribute.

MARTIN DEL BOSCO, Spanish vice-admiral, who encourages the Maltese defiance of the Turks.

BELLAMIRA, a courtesan who curries favor with Ithamore for his gold.

PILIA-BORZA, the courtesan's man, a bully and "a shaggy-tatter'd staring slave, that when he speaks draws out his grisly beard and winds it twice or thrice about his ear; whose face has been a grindstone for men's swords; his hands are hackt, some fingers cut quite off; who when he speaks grunts like a hog, and looks like one that is employ'd in catzerie and cross-biting; such a rogue as is the husband to a hundred whores."

BERNARDINE, JACOMO, } friars of St. Jacques, "two religious caterpillars," avaricious and quarrelsome. "Will you turn Christian when holy friars turn devils and murder one another?"

An Abbess, Two Nuns, } through whom Abigail is admitted to the new-made nunnery.

Several Pashas of the Turk.

Two Merchants, business associates of Barabas.

Three Jews, acquaintances of Barabas.

A Reader of the Governor's Decree.

Officers, Janissaries, and Knights.

Setting: The Island of Malta in the sixteenth century.

> *"You shall find him still,*
> *In all his projects, a sound Machiavell;*
> *And that's his character."*

Act I

Barabas, Jew of Malta, sits in his countinghouse gloating over his wealth, when he has two groups of visitors—some merchants who report to him the safe arrival in Malta of several argosies "laden with riches, and exceeding store of Persian silks, of gold, and orient pearl"; and three Jews who summon him to an important meeting in the senate house. For years the Turks have imposed tribute upon the island, but cunningly have allowed the tax to accumulate for ten years until it is "such a sum as all the wealth of Malta cannot pay." Now, faced by the demand of the Grand Seignior for payment or surrender, the Christian governor of the island gains a month's grace in which to raise the money, and levies a special tax upon the Jews for the purpose. To be sure Jews are "strangers" in Malta, [i.e., not admitted to citizenship], but they have leave to get their wealth there, and the governor decrees that they shall contribute heavily—either pay over half of their estates to save the city from the Turks, or become Christians. Other Jews submit, but Barabas protests against this extortion, for half of his substance is a city's wealth. For at first refusing, and without being given an opportunity to recant, Barabas is deprived of his entire estate as a punishment for his unwillingness, and his house is to be converted into a nunnery. Of him alone is this cruel penalty exacted.

For tax purposes, however, Barabas makes a false declaration, and, under the floor of his house he has secreted "ten thousand Portuguese, besides great pearls, rich costly jewels, and stones infinite, fearing the worst of this before it fell." Accordingly, he persuades his daughter Abigail to pretend conversion, gain admission to the new-made nunnery, and recover for him the wealth which he has hidden there.

Act II

At night, from a window in the house Abigail tosses out the bags of gold to the exulting Barabas who waits below. Meanwhile, Martin del Bosco, vice-admiral to the King of Spain, puts into Malta's harbor with a shipload of Turkish slaves which he proposes to sell in the market there. At first the governor dares not give consent because of the tributary league with the Turks and the unpaid tax, but on promise of military aid from the Spanish, he is readily persuaded to risk withholding the tribute, defy the Ottomans, and permit the sale of slaves.

At the market Barabas buys a vicious slave named Ithamore, who was brought up in Arabia to all kinds of villainy and who is also a hater of Christians. Already Barabas has bought "a house as great and fair as is the governor's," and he now finds an assistant for his revenge upon the Christians. He instructs his slave, and to him he boasts about his past:

> *First, be thou void of these affections:*
> *Compassion, love, vain hope, and heartless fear,*
> *Be mov'd at nothing, see thou pity none,*
> *But to thyself smile when the Christians moan. . . .*
> *As for myself, I walk abroad a nights*
> *And kill sick people groaning under walls;*
> *Sometimes I go about and poison wells. . . .*
> *Being young, I studied physic, and began*
> *To practice first upon the Italian;*
> *There I enrich'd the priests with burials,*
> *And always kept the sexton's arms in ure*
> *With digging graves and ringing dead men's knells.*
> *And after that I was an engineer,*
> *And in the wars 'twixt France and Germany, . . .*

Slew friend and enemy with my stratagems.
Then after that was I an usurer,
And with extorting, cozening, forfeiting,
And tricks belonging unto brokery,
I fill'd the jails with bankrouts in a year,
And with young orphans planted hospitals,
And every moon made some or other mad. . . .
But mark how I am blest for plaguing them,
I have as much coin as will buy the town.

In the market place, also, Barabas meets Don Lodowick, the governor's son, and Don Mathias, another gentleman of good family, both of whom are in love with his daughter Abigail. Encouraging them both, Barabas permits them to follow him home, orders the girl—who is sincerely in love with Mathias—to show them both favor, and betroths her to both of them. At the same time, secretly, by means of a forged challenge and other lies, he provokes a deadly rivalry between the young suitors:

> *Why, was there ever seen such villainy,*
> *So neatly plotted, and so well perform'd?*
> *Both held in hand, and flatly both beguil'd?*

Act III

In a duel which the young Christians fight over Abigail, both Lodowick and Mathias are slain, and the girl, in despair at her lover's death, now turns sincerely to the church and becomes a genuine convert to Christianity, entering again the new-made nunnery of St. Jacques. To punish his recreant daughter Barabas sends a pot of poisoned rice porridge to the convent as a thank offering on the Eve of St. Jacques, when it is customary to send alms to the nunneries of Malta, and the whole abbey is poisoned. Before her death, however, Abigail confesses to Friar Jacomo and reveals to him her father's villainy and responsibility for the deaths of her two suitors.

Meanwhile, the Turks have returned for their tribute, which the governor now refuses to pay, and Malta prepares to withstand a siege.

Act IV

In violation of canon law, the friars make use of the information they have received in confession to exclaim against Barabas and his crimes. To save himself the Jew pretends that he too wishes to turn Christian and to give all of his wealth to the brother who converts him. Thus, he plays upon the avarice of the worthy friars and causes them to quarrel among themselves. Then he interviews each separately. With the aid of Ithamore, he strangles Bernardine, who converted Abigail, and props up the body so that Friar Jacomo, to whom she confessed, shall knock it down and be accused of murder.

The way is soon prepared, however, for Barabas' betrayal. His slave Ithamore has been a partner in his crimes and knows too much. Enticed by Bellamira the courtesan, Ithamore resorts to blackmail and demands more and more money from the Jew. In his cups the slave also talks, and Bellamira and her man Pilia-Borza resolve to go to the governor with their information. But Barabas discovers even these purposes and has his revenge. Disguised as a French lute player, he visits the courtesan's house, and poisons all three of his extortioners with a bouquet of flowers.

Act V

Before they die, however, Bellamira, Ithamore, and Pilia-Borza make their accusations to the governor. Busy as he is with preparations for war, the governor straightway arrests Barbaras and prepares to torture him. But again the crafty Jew escapes. By swallowing poppy and cold mandrake juice, he feigns death, and his body is thrown over the city walls to be the prey of vultures and wild beasts. There, free from his enemies, Barabas revives and engages in "a kingly kind of trade to purchase towns by treachery and sell 'em by deceit." He joins the Turks, and betrays Malta to them. In reward he is made governor. But, doubly perfidious, Barabas offers in turn to betray the Turks to the Christians for whatever sum the captive Christian governor can raise, perhaps a hundred thousand pounds. Mines are planted under a monastery outside the city where the bulk of the Turkish army is quartered, and a banquet is prepared for the Turkish commander and his staff at Governor Barabas' palace in a hall which has a collapsible floor under which the Jew has placed a boiling cauldron. At a given signal the Turkish army is blown up, but the Christian governor prefers to capture the Ottoman generals alive. In the nick of time, therefore, he betrays the villain, and Barabas himself plunges into the boiling cauldron, and so dies.

The Troublesome Reign and Lamentable Death of

EDWARD THE SECOND

King of England

With the Tragical Fall of Proud Mortimer

(1591–1593)

DRAMATIS PERSONAE

EDWARD II, King of England, the fundamentally unkingly son of Edward Long-shanks, weak and unfit to rule. "By nature he is mild and calm," possessed of many graces, but "never doted Jove on Ganymede so much as he on cursed Gaveston. . . . He claps his cheeks and hangs about his neck, smiles in his face, and whispers in his ears. . . . The idle triumphs, masques, lascivious shows, and prodigal gifts bestowed on Gaveston have drawn [his] treasury dry; . . . [his] court is naked, being bereft of those that makes a king seem glorious to the world; . . . libels are cast again [him] in the street, ballads and rhymes made of [his] overthrow." ("O miserable is that commonweal where lords keep courts and kings are locked in prison!")

ISABELLA, "sole sister of the Valois," King of France, and neglected queen of Edward II. "In vain [she] look[s] for love at Edward's hand, whose eyes are fixed on none but Gaveston." In despair her devotion to her husband gradually fades; she supports the rebellion against him; and, at last, Young "Mortimer and Isabel do kiss while they conspire."

PRINCE EDWARD, son of Edward II and Queen Isabella, afterwards King Edward III. He "is yet a child."

PIERS GAVESTON, the flattering favorite of the king, "a night-grown mushrump, . . . [the] proud disturber of [his] country's peace, corrupter of [his] king, [and] cause of these broils." ("His wanton humor grieves not me; but this I scorn, that one so basely born should by his sovereign's favor grow so pert, and riot it with the treasure of the realm. While soldiers mutiny for want of pay, he wears a lord's revenue on his back, . . . with base, outlandish cullions at his heels. . . . I have not seen a dapper Jack so brisk. He wears a short Italian-hooded cloak larded with pearl, and in his Tuscan cap a jewel of more value than the crown. Whiles other walk below, the king and he from out a window laugh at such as we, and flout our train, and jest at our attire. . . . 'Tis this that makes me impatient.")

LADY [MARGARET DE CLARE], niece of Edward II, "the only heir unto the Earl of Gloucester late deceased"; later married to Piers Gaveston.

"Inconstant Edmund," EARL OF KENT, brother to King Edward II.

The BISHOP OF COVENTRY, "only cause of [Gaveston's first] exile," and victim of his vengeance.

The ARCHBISHOP OF CANTERBURY, who protests to the Pope against this "violence . . . offered to the church" and crowns Prince Edward, Edward III.

OLD ROGER MORTIMER [of Chirk], a moderate noble, taken prisoner by the Scots while serving his king.

YOUNG ROGER MORTIMER [of Wigmore], his nephew, a haughty, ambitious, virile, but unprincipled young baron, more feared than loved, "who now makes Fortune's Wheel turn as he please. . . . More safety is there in a tiger's jaws than his embracements, . . . [but] the people love him well,"

GUY, EARL OF WARWICK, "that redoubted knight," rough and proud,

The EARL OF LANCASTER, "high-minded, . . . aspiring, . . . [and] inexorable, . . . that hath more earldoms than an ass can bear,"

The EARL OF PEMBROKE,

} "proud, overdaring peers," of the realm, opposed to Gaveston and King Edward II.

HUGH SPENCER THE YOUNGER, a "base upstart," formerly servant to the late Earl of Gloucester; later created Earl of Wiltshire and Earl of Gloucester by the king. "Like the lawless Catiline of Rome, [he] revelled in England's wealth and treasury"; he replaces Gaveston in the king's favor and becomes "a putrefying branch that deads the royal vine,"

HUGH SPENCER THE ELDER, his father,

BALDOCK, "that smooth-tongued scholar," formerly tutor to the late Earl of Gloucester's daughter; "curate-like in [his] attire, . . . [he is] inwardly licentious enough and apt for any kind of villainy." (His "gentry [he] fetched from Oxford, not from heraldry,")

} "the proud corrupters of the light-brained king."

The EARL OF ARUNDEL, supporter of the king.

BEAUMONT, clerk of the crown, the king's messenger to Gaveston in Ireland.

LEVUNE, a French diplomat, "faithful and full of trust," until bribed by King Edward and the Spencers. ("The lords of France love England's gold so well, as Isabel gets no aid from thence.")

SIR JOHN OF HAINAULT, "forward in arms," who befriends Queen Isabella.

RICE AP HOWELL,
The MAYOR OF BRISTOL, } captors of the king, the Spencers, and Baldock.
The EARL OF LEICESTER,

SIR THOMAS BERKELEY, of Berkeley Castle, messenger and gentle jailer of the king.

GURNEY, } creatures of Young Mortimer, and brutal jailers of the king.
MATREVIS,

LIGHTBORN, a murderer, hired by Mortimer to kill King Edward; " 'tis not the first time [he has] killed a man."

Berkeley, BISHOP OF WINCHESTER, witness for the church at King Edward's deposition.

SIR WILLIAM TRUSSEL, Proctor of Parliament; representative of the laity at King Edward's deposition.

JAMES, horseboy to the Earl of Pembroke.

The Abbot of Neath, at whose abbey King Edward II seeks refuge.

A Mower, who betrays the king to his enemies.

The King's Champion, who officiates at Prince Edward's coronation.

A Herald, messenger from the barons to King Edward.

Monks of Neath Abbey, Lords, Ladies, Poor Men, Posts, Messengers, Guards, Soldiers, and Attendants.

Setting: England and Paris in the early fourteenth century (London, Westminster, Tynemouth Castle, Boroughbridge Castle, Harwich, Bristol, Neath, Kenilworth Castle, Berkeley Castle, and the vicinity of these.)

"Misgoverned kings are cause of all this wrack."

Act I

During the reign of King Edward I, Piers Gaveston, favorite of the Prince of Wales, had been banished from the realm, but he hurries back to court from France on receiving the news that the old king is dead and an invitation to share the kingdom with his dearest friend, now King Edward II. Cynically, Gaveston plans to draw the pliant young monarch's mind which way it pleases him. Through wanton poets, pleasant wits, and tuneful musicians, he plans to enchant the king with Italian masques, sweet speeches, comedies, and pleasing shows. The weak king will be completely in his power. Gaveston's return disgusts both the nobles and the commons of the realm, who clash bitterly with their young sovereign on the subject, but King Edward receives his minion with open arms and creates him Lord Chamberlain, Chief Secretary of State, Earl of Cornwall, and Lord of the Isle of Man. Gaveston immediately exercises his influence over the king by avenging himself on the Bishop of Coventry, who had been the cause of his exile, having the churchman disrobed and flung into the Tower and his estates confiscated to himself. News of this highhanded treatment of the bishop, Gaveston's preferment, and the unhappiness of Queen Isabella, who has even more reason to object to the king's minion, arouses the Archbishop of Canterbury and confirms the barons—chiefly Warwick, Lancaster, and the Mortimers—in their opposition to the upstart. These nobles gather at the New Temple, order a renewal of Gaveston's banishment, and, sorely against his will, force the king to confirm the decree. But soon after, in spite of Gaveston's reflections upon the queen's character and the king's readiness to believe the worst about her, Isabella so pities her husband's sorrow at his separation from his favorite and is so hopeful of reclaiming the king, who has banished her from court, that she intercedes with the barons and procures Gaveston's recall. In anticipation of his return, King Edward announces that he has betrothed his favorite to his niece, the Earl of Gloucester's heir.

Act II

The death of the old Earl of Gloucester makes it necessary for his dependents, Young Spencer and Baldock, who are men of small ability and capable of any kind of hypocrisy, to seek a new patron. Hearing of Piers Gaveston's recall, and knowing that he is to marry the Earl's daughter, they resolve to cast their lot with him, and through him with the king. The return of Gaveston from exile in Ireland produces fresh dissension at court, even before he arrives. For the triumph which is to welcome him, two of the courtiers devise satirical impresa; Gaveston has hardly stepped from his ship at Tynemouth before the barons treat him with scorn and even try to kill him; and their embitterment flares into open rebellion when one of their number, the elder Mortimer, is captured by the Scots, and King Edward refuses to pay his ransom, although his captivity occurred in the royal service. The outraged nobles threaten the king with deposition; lay siege to Tynemouth Castle, Gaveston's stronghold; pursue the fleeing favorite; take him prisoner; and are about to execute him. But King Edward begs once more to see his minion, and, against Warwick's will, the barons agree to a meeting, placing their prisoner in the custody of the Earl of Pembroke. That noble, however, finding himself near his home, goes to visit his wife, leaving Gaveston for the night in the care of James, his horseboy. Meanwhile, Queen Isabella determines once more to try to reclaim the king, and, if she fails, to go to France with the Prince of Wales and there complain to the king, her brother.

Act III

On the road to Boroughbridge, the ruthless Warwick and some of his men seize their opportunity to ambush James and the other guardians of Gaveston, force surrender of the prisoner, and execute him. At the death of his minion, the foolish, weak king does not reform his manner, however; immediately he adopts a new favorite in Young Spencer, a haughty upstart who is as alarming to the barons as the old, and they continue their rebellion. But King Edward is reinforced by an army led by the elder Spencer, and, revealing a manly nature for the first time, he swears vengeance upon the rebels, joins battle with them, and is victorious. The prisoners include Kent, the king's brother, who had at first supported Gaveston but later joined the rebellion; Lancaster; Warwick; and Young Mortimer. Lancaster and Warwick are executed, Kent is banished, and Mortimer imprisoned in the Tower. After his triumph at Boroughbridge, the king is at the height of his power, and he purges his land of as many rebels as possible.

Meanwhile, however, other trouble is brewing. Because the weak king has failed to pay the customary homage for the duchy, the French have seized Normandy, and King Edward sends his wife and son as emissaries of peace to the French king. But Young Spencer by bribery takes care that the queen shall not make too many friends in France.

Act IV

The tide now turns against the unfortunate king. With the aid of Kent, Mortimer drugs his guards and escapes from the Tower to France, where he joins the neglected queen, who is befriended by Sir John of Hainault. By now Isabella's devotion to her husband has faded, and at last her wavering affections are transferred to Mortimer. With the aid of the queen, Mortimer lands near Harwich, raises the rebellion anew, and near Bristol defeats King Edward's army. The elder Spencer is taken prisoner, while King Edward, Young Spencer, and Baldock—having failed in their attempt to reach Ireland—disguise themselves and seek refuge in the Abbey of Neath. But a mower in the fields—"a gloomy fellow in a mead below"—leads the Earl of Leicester to their hideout, and they are surprised and captured.

Act V

At Kenilworth Castle, Leicester's seat, King Edward, now more sinned against than sinning, is forced to abdicate, and, in the custody of the gentle Sir Thomas Berkeley, is ordered to prison in Berkeley Castle. Before the transfer can be made, however, Mortimer places his plume-plucked sovereign in the hands of Gurney and Matrevis, cruel men, who keep their prisoner in a dungeon, starve him, and shave his beard in "puddle water." Here at Kenilworth, having changed sides again, Edmund, Earl of Kent, tries to release his brother, but is captured by the guards. Mortimer also realizes that the commons are already feeling pity for the deposed king and that Edward must die if he is to remain in power as proctector. Hence, Mortimer hires Lightborn to murder the king, sending his authorization in a riddling letter to Gurney and Matrevis—*Edwardum occidere nolite timere bonum est.* Without punctuation or with a comma before the last two words, the treacherous Latin says: "Fear not to kill the king, 'tis good to die." Move the comma back a single word and the message reads: "Kill not the king; 'tis good to fear the worst." Thus, if they follow Mortimer's intent, Gurney and Matrevis will bear the blame, especially since he sent them secret orders that when the deed was done, they murder Lightborn. Accordingly, in the dungeon of Berkeley Castle, where the unhappy king is now confined in mire and filth, Edward II is the victim of a peculiarly horrible murder. Lured by Lightborn to rest on a feather bed, the king is stifled and then pressed to death with a table.

Mortimer and the queen have gone too far. Young Edward III, who has just been crowned, is horror-struck at the crime, has Mortimer beheaded and quartered, and orders the queen, his mother, who is suspected of complicity, to be imprisoned in the Tower. Mortimer, who once made Fortune's Wheel turn as he pleased, goes off to execution with this melancholy reflection:

> *Base Fortune, now I see that in thy wheel*
> *There is a point to which when men aspire,*
> *They tumble headlong down. That point I touched,*
> *And, seeing there was no place to mount up higher,*
> *Why should I grieve at my declining fall?*

ROBERT GREENE
(1558–1592)

BIOGRAPHY. The most picturesque of the "University Wits," Robert Greene was born of middle-class stock in Norwich about 1558, entered St. John's College, Cambridge, as a sizar in 1575, and received the B.A. degree in 1578 and the M.A. in 1583. Greene was also Master of Arts of Oxford, 1588. His later career is known from his autobiographical pamphlets. Apparently he travelled in Spain and Italy where he learned to practice "such villainy as is abominable to declare." He married a good wife, but deserted her and their child for the sister of a notorious character of the London underworld. He became a "penner of love-pamphlets," in the Euphuistic-Arcadian manner, the best of which are *Pandosto* (1588) and *Menaphon* (1589); the writer of charming lyrics; the producer of repentance tracts and fiction which were intended to be thought thinly veiled autobiography; and the author of exposés of the London coney-catchers. Gradually Greene drifted into the theatre, always thinking himself above such occupation. It is not necessary to believe Greene quite as black as he painted himself; if he committed even a fraction of the evil he confessed to, he was the most unmitigated scoundrel that ever lived. He was simply a journalist who was born before the days of tabloids and cheap magazines and who capitalized upon his Bohemian existence and his bad reputation. He died after "a banquet of Rhenish wine and pickled herring," in a squalid lodging, penning on his deathbed a touching letter to his deserted wife and a pamphlet called *A Groatsworth of Wit Bought with a Million of Repentance* (1592).

CRITICAL COMMENT. At best Greene's career as a dramatist is brief; his earliest play cannot have been written before 1587, his latest was written about 1591. But in these few years he penned some of the most popular, as well as lastingly charming, plays of the age. *George a Greene* is his only by conjecture; it is a warmhearted, lusty drama for the English folk. *Friar Bacon* mixes magic, true love, patriotism, tragedy, and horseplay into an astonishing drama woven around the legends about Roger Bacon, a thirteenth-century scientist long reputed to have practiced an art as devilish and astounding as that of Dr. Faustus. In *James IV* there is the germ of tragi-comedy, a type of drama which was to have its full flowering later. All of these plays have real audience appeal, but Greene's greatest significance lies in his rare faculty for drawing sweet, lifelike, credible women. Margaret, the fair maid of Fressingfield, is the first thoroughly believable girl in English drama, and Queen Dorothea, if a Patient Griselda, and the Lady Ida are quite excellent portraits in their way. Greene may be forgiven if he liked his women a little sentimental and pathetic; he knew them that way.

SOURCES. All three of these plays by Greene have pseudohistorical backgrounds and introduce historical personages. But these elements which masquerade as fact will not bear critical examination for a moment. They are pure fiction, filled with anachronistic absurdities and a sublime indifference to historical truth. For example, the very title of *James IV* is absurd. The Scottish king was indeed slain at Flodden Field in 1513, but Greene's play begins in 1520, seven years after the historical James's death. The play does not deal with the battle at all, as the title seems to promise. It was the Scots who invaded England in 1513, not the English who invaded Scotland, as in the play. James IV was famous for his gallantries, and he did marry an English princess, but her name was Margaret, not Dorothea. But we're breaking a butterfly.

The source of *George a Greene* appears to have been an early version, now lost, of *The Famous History of George a Greene, Pinder of the Town of Wakefield*, . . . known only from a copy of much later date than the play. It also served as the source of a ballad which postdates the play.

Friar Bacon and Friar Bungay was also based upon a chapbook, *The Famous History of Friar Bacon*, written in the sixteenth century, but extant only in a quarto of 1627. Except for a hint the love story is original.

In *James IV* the romantic story of patient wifely love is derived from the *Hecatommithi* (III, i) of Giraldi Cinthio, who himself dramatized his story as *Arrenopia* (the name of his heroine). It purports to be a tale of a king of Ireland. The fantastic framework of the Scottish misanthrope and Oberon, King of Fairyland, is Greene's invention. Oberon comes originally from *Huon of Bordeaux*, a romance of the Charlemagne cycle.

BIBLIOGRAPHY

Collected Works:

The Plays and Poems of Robert Greene, edited by J. Churton Collins, 2 volumes, Oxford, 1905.

The Complete Plays of Robert Greene, edited by T. H. Dickinson, Mermaid
  Series, 1909.

Monograph: J. C. Jordan, *Robert Greene,* Columbia, 1915.

George a Greene:
  Early edition: 1599.
  Modern editions: Facs. J. S. Farmer (TFT, 1913); ed. F. W. Clarke (MSR,
  1911).

Friar Bacon and Friar Bungay:
  Early editions: 1594; 1630; 1655.
  Modern editions: Facs. J. S. Farmer (TFT, 1914); ed. W. W. Greg (MSR,
  1926).

James IV:

  Early edition: 1598.
  Modern edition: ed. A. E. H. Swaen and W. W. Greg (MSR, 1921).

A Pleasant Conceited Comedy of

GEORGE A GREENE
THE PINNER OF WAKEFIELD

(1587–1593)

DRAMATIS PERSONAE

GEORGE A GREENE, "right pinner [i.e., officer who impounds stray animals] of merry
  Wakefield town, . . . [and] true liegeman to [his] king. . . . For stature he
  is framed like to the picture of stout Hercules, and for his carriage passeth Robin
  Hood; . . . whoso resisteth bears away the blows, for he himself is good enough
  for three." ("I never saw the man, but mickle talk is of him in the country.")

BETTRIS, daughter to Grime and George a Greene's "lovely leman, as bright of blee
  as is the silver moon. . . . She may have many wealthy suitors, and yet she disdains them all to have poor George a Greene unto her husband." ("O, what is
  love? It is some mighty power, else could it never conquer George a Greene!")

MASTER GRIME, susceptible old father to Bettris, "a churl that keeps away [George
  a Greene's] love."

JACK JENKIN, a clown, underpinner, "a faint-hearted fellow . . .
  [that has] no stomach to fight. . . . There are few fellows
  in our parish so nettled with love as [he has] been of late. . . .
  There is some good will betwixt Madge the sousewife and [he], George a Greene's
  [but] marry, she hath another lover,"   servants.
WILY, a boy. ("I think this boy hath more knavery than all the
  world besides,")

WOODROFFE, the Justice of Wakefield.

Henry Momford, EARL OF KENDAL, "a mighty man, . . . yet for to be a traitor to his king is more than God or man will well allow," } rebels and "martial gentlemen."
LORD BONFIELD,
SIR NICHOLAS MANNERING, a "proud dapper Jack; . . . Nick, as you know, is haughty in his words,"
SIR GILBERT ARMSTRONG,

ROBIN HOOD,
SCARLET, } "three tall yeomen," who challenge George a Greene.
MUCH, the Miller's son,

MAID MARION, Robin Hood's "lovely leman."

EDWARD, King of England.

The EARL OF WARWICK, attending King Edward.

WILLIAM MUSGROVE, aged keeper of Sandown Castle, "fivescore and three at midsummer last past, . . . [who] whilom was thought the bravest horseman in all Westmoreland, . . . [but now] weak and forced to stay his arm upon a staff that erst could wield a lance." ("A stronger man I seldom felt before; but one of more resolute valiance treads not, I think, upon the English ground.")

CUDDY, his son.

A Shoemaker; "he knows where is the best ale."

JAMES, King of Scotland, "that oft hath sued and wooed [Mistress Barley] with many letters, . . . [though] little regard was given to [his] suit." ("But good King James is pleasant, as I guess.")

NED A BARLEY, a small boy, "son unto Sir John a Barley, eldest, and all that e'er [his] mother had."

JANE A BARLEY, his mother.

LORD HUMES, attending King James.

JOHNNY TAYLOR, post to King James.

Townsmen, Shoemakers, Soldiers, Messengers, and Attendants.

Setting: Wakefield, Bradford, and their vicinities at some indefinite time.

"Physic for a fool, [and] pills for a traitor that doth wrong his sovereign."

[*Scene i*] Under pretext of fighting to relieve the poor and to promote the general good of the country, a band of rebels headed by Henry Momford, Earl of Kendal; Lord Bonfield; Sir Nicholas Mannering; and Sir Gilbert Armstrong are in arms against King Edward of England. They seek the aid of James, King of Scotland, now ravaging the borderlands, and, having difficulty in getting provisions, they commission Mannering to go to Wakefield to see what effect threats of laying waste the country will have.

[*Scene ii*] Next day in Wakefield the citizens refuse the Earl of Kendal victuals because he is a traitor to his king and because by aiding him they would show themselves no less. Especially outspoken in support of this loyal decision is one George a Greene, the pinner of the town, who proclaims himself true liegeman to his king and a scorner of threats made by any traitorous squire. When Sir Nicholas Mannering waves his commission before him, George a Greene tears it up and makes him swallow the great wax seals as "physic for a fool, [and] pills for a traitor that doth wrong his sovereign."

[*Scene iii*] Equally loyal is Old William Musgrove, the aged keeper of Sandown Castle. Now that the wily Scots are again ravaging the border, this hoary fighter refuses to resign the hold to his son Cuddy and "give arms to youth," but resolves to remain on duty.

[*Scene iv*] While the Earl of Kendal and Sir Nicholas Mannering are concerned over supplies for their army, Lord Bonfield and Sir Gilbert Armstrong visit Master Grime in Bradford and are entertained royally by him. Master Grime is a collaborationist, but his daughter Bettris is not. By quirks and quiddities she evades all talk of love on the part of the traitors, and the poor father curses "the hour that e'er [he] got the girl, for . . . she may have many wealthy suitors and yet she disdains them all." Even when the Earl of Kendal arrives, she is no more gracious to him, and to all their wooing she has but one reply:

> *I care not for earl, nor yet for knight,*
> *Nor baron that is so bold;*
> *For George a Greene, the merry pinner,*
> *He hath my heart in hold.*

Promising to send the girl the pinner's head, the rebels resolve to go into Wakefield in some disguise and capture George a Greene.

[*Scenes v, vi*] Meanwhile, on his way to join the English rebels, King James of Scotland meets Jane a Barley's attractive young son Ned, and resolves to woo in person the mother who has given little regard to love letters sent her in the past. Sir John, her husband, is away from home, but the lady courageously defies the king's threats to raze her castle and kill her son unless she yields. Before James can make good his threats, however, an alarm sounds, and a messenger arrives with word that Old Musgrove is at hand.

The battle is soon over. King James is taken prisoner, and, at Jane's invitation, the Musgroves take him into Barley's castle to drink their fill, "for all this broil was 'cause he could not enter."

[*Scene vii*] Attended only by the clown Jenkin, whose mind runs on his love for Madge the sousewife and his rival Clim the sow-gelder, George a Greene meets the rebels in Wakefield. They have disguised themselves, turned their horses loose in George a Greene's wheat close, and gone into hiding. George orders the trespassing beasts impounded. The rebels then come forward and defy the honest pinner, insisting that they are gentlemen and that their horses shall eat their fill. Indeed, they say, they belong to Henry Momford, Earl of Kendal, and are men who before the month is out will be King Edward's betters in the land. At these words, the loyal George a Greene strikes the boaster a goodly blow. Told that it is an earl that he has struck, the pinner staunchly replies, "Why, what care I? A poor man that is true is better than an earl, if he be false." But George also finds that he is ambushed and surrounded by the Earl's men, who are about to arrest him. The pinner suggests a parley, is very logical in his own excuse, hears Kendal hypocritically explain that he is not rising against his king but is only trying to relieve the wrongs of the poor, and receives the offer of a captaincy in the Earl's band. George asks what the chances of victory are and hears of a miraculous prophecy that King James, Kendal, and King Edward shall meet in London and that the English king shall vail his bonnet to both the others. Professing to be half-convinced, George asks, however, that the three rebel leaders go in the morning to an old man who lives in a cave and tells fortunes. If his prediction is good and confirms the prophecy, George promises to join the rebels. They agree.

[*Scene viii*] To release Bettris from her father's vigilant eye, George a Greene's boy Wily disguises as a "sempster's maid" and goes to the house. The maid is met by Old Grime, who is suspicious of his visitor's covered face, but easily convinced that the girl is troubled with the toothache. Being susceptible to pretty wenches anyway, Grime admits the girl, and Bettris escapes in Wily's apparel to hasten straight to George a Greene.

[*Scene ix*] At the cave next morning the three rebels ask the blind old prophet who will win, King Edward or the Earl of Kendal. The hermit tells them the king, but warns them that they themselves shall be given the foil by a baser man than the prince, namely George a Greene. At the proper moment the old man seizes his walking staff and throws off his disguise. He is George a Greene, who has "only devised this guile to draw [them] on for to be combatants." After a sharp fight, George kills Sir Gilbert and takes the other two prisoners. Then Jenkin, too, pretends to do an act of magic and produces Bettris.

[*Scene x*] In London the Scottish king repents his breach of the league of truce with the English, the Earl of Kendal is brought in as prisoner, and mockingly King Edward fulfills the prophecy by vailing his bonnet to the rebels. But during the reports of both victories over his enemies, the king has heard so much about George a Greene, that he resolves to go to the North in disguise with a few followers to see this marvel. At George's request, conveyed by Cuddy Musgrove, the king pardons the Earl of Kendal.

[*Scenes xi, xiii*] Meanwhile, into Sherwood Forest news of the prowess of George a Greene and of the beauty of fair Bettris reach Robin Hood, Maid Marion, and the Merry Men, and several of the band set out for Wakefield to "try this pinner what he dares to do." In Wakefield they meet George a Greene, who vanquishes Robin Hood, Scarlet, and Much the Miller's son in combat, and receives an offer of two liveries and forty crowns a year to join the Merry Men in Sherwood Forest.

[*Scene xii*] In Bradford Jenkin the clown encounters a shoemaker, who asserts that it is a custom of the town that none shall pass through the streets with his staff on his shoulders unless he is willing to have a bout with him. Jenkin faintheartedly avoids trouble and takes his challenger to the alehouse instead.

[*Scene xiv*] To Bradford also, in search of George a Greene, come King Edward and King James in disguise, and they too are challenged by the shoemaker. Being men of peace, however, they are content to trail their staves. But while doing so they are met by Robin Hood and George a Greene, also disguised, and ordered to bear their staves on their shoulders. The result is a free-for-all fight with all of the shoe-makers in town, a contest in which George a Greene is decisively triumphant. Recognized by the shoemakers, George orders a stand of ale set up in the market place where all may drink. While they are celebrating, King Edward makes himself known. The Yorkshire men, "blunt of speech, and little skilled in court or such quaint fashions," beg their sovereign's pardon for any unintentional offense, and Edward graciously offers to "grace [them] with good deeds" before he goes. Hence, having drunk with the shoemakers, the king decrees that they no longer be called simply shoemakers, but the "trade of the gentle craft." Joined by Old Musgrove and his son Cuddy, he dubs the valiant old man knight and mends his poverty by granting him Middleham Castle. Then he sends for Old Grime and Bettris and obtains the father's consent for Bettris' marriage with George a Greene, on condition that Old Grime in turn be permitted to marry "this lovely lass," the semp-ster's maid, who turns out to be Wily in disguise. At last King Edward prepares to knight George a Greene. But that worthy asks that he first be granted a boon:

> *Let me live and die a yeoman still.*
> *So was my father, so must live his son.*
> *For 'tis more credit to men of base degree*
> *To do great deeds than men of dignity.*

Accordingly, King Edward spares the honest fellow the indignity of knighthood. King James is pardoned upon his promise to make full reparations to the citizenry for his plundering—a ransom set by George a Greene at the king's request. As the royal party sets out to sup at

George's house, His Majesty promises to see for himself if Jane a Barley is really as fair as good King James reports her to be. And he confirms the ancient Bradford custom of "vail staff," for "English Edward vailed his staff to you."

THE HONORABLE HISTORY OF

FRIAR BACON AND FRIAR BUNGAY

(1589–1592)

DRAMATIS PERSONAE

FRIAR BACON, master of Brazenose College, Oxford, versed in "pyromancy, to divine by flames; to tell by hydromantic, ebbs and tides; by aeromancy to discover doubts to plain out questions, as Apollo did. . . . A brave scholar, sirrah; they say . . . that he can make women of devils, and he can juggle cats into costermongers."

FRIAR BUNGAY, his rival and associate, a Suffolk conjurer.

DON JAQUES VANDERMAST, a learned magician from Hapsburg, "skillful in magic and those secret arts. . . . A German born, . . . [this doctor] passed into Padua, to Florence, and to fair Bologna, to Paris, Rheims, and stately Orleans, and, talking there with men of art, put down the chiefest of them all in aphorisms, in magic, and the mathematic rules."

BURDEN, ⎫ doctors of Oxford, "masters of our academic state, . . . whose heads
MASON, ⎬ contain maps of the liberal arts, spending [their] time in depth of learned
CLEMENT,⎭ skill."

MILES, Friar Bacon's unreliable subsizar, "the greatest blockhead in all Oxford, . . . as serviceable at a table as a sow is under an apple tree."

MARGARET, "the fair maid of Fressingfield," and the keeper's daughter, "fitter to be Lacy's wedded wife than concubine unto the Prince of Wales. . . . A bonnier wench all Suffolk cannot yield, . . . whose beauty tempered with her huswifery, makes England talk of merry Fressingfield."

ELINOR OF CASTILE, "one that overmatcheth Venus in her shape, . . . beauty's high-swelling pride, rich Nature's glory and her wealth at once," betrothed to Prince Edward.

EDWARD, Prince of Wales, "martial Plantagenet, . . . Henry's wanton son," in love with Margaret, and later betrothed to Elinor of Castile. ("His wooing is not for to wed the girl, but to entrap her and beguile the lass.")

EDWARD LACY, Earl of Lincoln, also in love with Margaret. "His ⎫
words are witty, quickened with a smile; his courtesy gentle, ⎬ friends of Prince
smelling of the court; facile and debonair in all his deeds," ⎭ Edward.
JOHN WARREN, Earl of Sussex,
WILLIAM ERMSBY, a gentleman,

KING HENRY III, "old Plantagenet that rules and sways the Albion diadem."

FREDERICK, "the Almain Emperor."

THE DUKE OF SAXONY, attending the Emperor.

THE KING OF CASTILE, father of Elinor.

RAFE SIMNELL, "King Henry's only lovéd fool."

A Constable, "ill-shaped and ill-faced, disdained and disgraced."

LAMBERT of Cratfield, } "brave neighboring squires, the stay of Suffolk's clime"; rival
SERLSBY of Laxfield,   } suitors to Margaret.

YOUNG LAMBERT, } "lusty younkers, . . . college mates, sworn brothers" of Broadgates
YOUNG SERLSBY, } Hall.

A Hostess at Henley, mistress of the Bell.

The Keeper of Fressingfield, father of Margaret, "frolic keeper of our liege's game, whose table spread hath ever venison and jacks of wine to welcome passengers."

His Friend.

THOMAS, } Suffolk rustics, acquaintances of Margaret's.
RICHARD, }

JOAN, a country wench, acquaintance of Margaret's.

A Devil, "Master Plutus; . . . I warrant you he's as yeomanly a man as you shall see. Mark you, masters, here's a plain, honest man without welt or guard."

The Brazen Head, which speaks.

The Fearful Dragon, "that watched the garden called Hesperides, subdued and won by conquering Hercules."

The Spirit of Hercules.

A Postboy, Lords, Country Clowns, Ladies, and Attendants.

Setting: Framlingham, Fressingfield, Harleston Fair, Oxford, and Hampton Court in the thirteenth century.

"See'st thou not great Bacon here,
Whose frown doth act more than thy magic can?"

Act I

While hunting near Framlingham, Edward, Prince of Wales, falls in love with the bonny Margaret, daughter of the keeper of Fressingfield. Realizing that the girl is so virtuous that it is "marriage or no market with the maid," Prince Edward resolves to go in haste to Oxford to enlist the necromantic skills of Friar Bacon and the charms of art to enchain her love. He leaves behind his friend Lacy to go in disguise to St. James's Fair at Harleston, court Margaret on behalf of "the courtier tired all in green," buy her fairings, and keep his royal friend informed of how she does.

Meanwhile, in Oxford, Bacon is at work upon a brazen head which will talk and deliver lectures on philosophy. With the aid of devils he means to compass England round about with a defensive wall of brass, so that no enemy may "touch a grass of English ground." To his university associates Bacon demonstrates his magic powers by bringing from

Henley on a whirlwind the hostess of the Bell, whom his sceptical friend Burden has been visiting with unbecoming frequency.

Act II

At Harleston Fair, instead of favoring the "green clad courtier" for whom Lacy woos, Margaret falls in love with Lacy himself. At Hampton Court, about the same time, King Henry entertains the beautiful Elinor of Castile, who has come to England to be betrothed to Prince Edward. The king hears that his son has gone to Oxford for a few days and proposes that the royal party go there too, especially since there is in the Emperor's train a German magician whom it would be interesting to see matched with the famous Friar Bacon of Brazenose. At Oxford Prince Edward prefers to be incognito. As a prank he changes clothes with his father's fool, Rafe Simnell, but the disguise does not for an instant baffle Friar Bacon, who not only recognizes the prince, but also tells him why he came to Oxford, and how his suit fares in Lacy's hands. By means of a "glass prospective" [i.e., a magic mirror, or a telescope], Friar Bacon even permits the prince to see but not hear a consultation between fair Margaret and the great Friar Bungay, Bacon's rival in magic. From Bungay Margaret learns that Lacy is not a simple wooer but the Earl of Lincoln, and to the friar she confesses that she is in love with Lacy. In a moment Lacy puts in his appearance properly disguised as a countryman. The earl is easily identified by Friar Bungay, he confesses to the old friar his mission and his own love for Margaret, and, in spite of his pledge to the prince, he is betrothed to the girl. In the magic glass Prince Edward sees this in pantomime, but does not hear what they say. He watches the lovers kiss, and is helpless to avenge himself upon them. But, just as Friar Bungay is about to marry the pair, Friar Bacon takes a hand. He strikes Friar Bungay dumb, and then on a devil's back conveys the rival magician to Oxford. Prince Edward vows to settle scores with his friend Lacy and hurries off to Fressingfield.

Act III

In Oxford elaborate plans are made for the entertainment of the king and his guests, the German Emperor, the King of Castile, and his lovely daughter, Elinor. "We must lay plots of stately tragedies, strange comic shows such as proud Roscius vaunted before the Roman emperors," say the university men, and in addition hold a test of skill between Friar Bacon and Jaques Vandermast, the Emperor's magician. Meanwhile, Rafe the fool, who is revelling it as prince, gets into trouble with the university proctors because of a tavern brawl.

In Fressingfield Prince Edward has sought out Lacy and with drawn sword is upbraiding him for his duplicity. Margaret, however, takes full responsibility for what has occurred; although Lacy had always wooed her for the courtier clad in green, she says, she fell in love with the wooer instead of the man for whom he spoke. But Edward vows that Lacy shall die as a traitor to his lord. Then Margaret again intervenes, asks what the prince hopes to gain by Lacy's death, vows to die with him, and begs Edward to keep "a friend worth many loves." Shamed by her words, the young prince conquers his unworthy desires and generously resigns the girl to Lacy for his wife. Then he hastens off to Oxford to meet the princess who has been selected for him by his father, taking his friend Lacy with him.

There at Oxford Friar Bungay and the German Vandermast engage in a discussion as to whether the spirits of pyromancy or those of geomancy are most predominant in magic, Vandermast maintaining the supremacy of the former, Bungay of the latter. As proof of his powers, Bungay conjures up the tree of the Hesperides, leaved with refined gold, together with the fire-dragon which sits thereon. In his turn Vandermast raises Hercules in his lion's skin and bids him break the branches of the tree. Friar Bungay cannot stop the destruction even by magic; Vandermast can by a mere command. But when Friar Bacon appears, Hercules admits that the mere frown of the Oxford friar is more potent than the German's magic art, and Bacon then bids Hercules take Vandermast back to Hapsburg. Thus is decided the question of supremacy among the friars.

At dinner, merely to show his guests "how little meat refines our English wits," Friar Bacon serves his guests a "friar's feeble fare," and finds the frugal meal taken as almost an insult by his royal guests. But the point made, Bacon has the table cleared, promising the diners Alexandria spices, rich wines, Afric dates, mirabiles of Spain, conserves and suckets from Tiberias, and choice cates from Judea.

Act IV

At Fressingfield, two neighbor squires, Lambert of Cratfield and Serlsby of Laxfield, who know nothing of the girl's betrothal, are rival suitors for fair Margaret's hand. They quarrel over her, and prepare to settle their claims by duel. Meanwhile, a letter comes to Margaret from Lacy, saying in the best euphuistic manner that their love affair has been a mistake, that by the king's command Lacy is marrying a Spanish lady-in-waiting to Elinor of Castile, and that he is atoning to Margaret by sending her a hundred pounds for her dowry.

More in pain than in anger Margaret gives the hundred pounds to the post who carried the letter and resolves to enter a nunnery.

In Oxford Friar Bacon has finished his seven years' work on the brazen head and is waiting for his creation to speak. By the enchanting forces of the Devil, the head should utter strange aphorisms and command a wall of brass to be built around all England. Bacon's honor and renown hang upon the performance of his brazen miracle. He and Bungay have waited and watched for threescore days, and both are now tired out. Hence, Friar Bacon has his servant Miles stay awake one night while Bacon sleeps, and instructs him to wake him immediately should the head utter a sound. The friar is hardly asleep before there is a great noise, and the head distinctly says "Time is!" To Miles, however, two words are a disappointing result of his master's great cunning and of seven years' labor. Hence, he decides to wait for better orations from it anon. A second time the head speaks—"Time was!"—and again Miles awaits important principles of philosophy and learned lectures. At last, to thunder and lightning, the head says "Time is past!" and is destroyed. Only then does Miles arouse his master, but it is too late. Friar Bacon's skill and labor are lying in the dust, and his reputation is gone. In his rage the disappointed friar casts off his stupid, but self-confident, servant to wander over the earth in cap and gown, but with hope that some fiend will haunt his steps and carry him off to Hell.

Act V

In his discouragement Friar Bacon is comforted by his friend Friar Bungay, but worse misfortune is still in store for the great magician. In Friar Bacon's prospective glass the scholar sons of Lambert and Serlsby seek news of their fathers, and, in horror, watch them fight their duel and kill each other. Then, enflamed to vengeance by what they have seen, the young friends stab each other dead. Perceiving that his magic has been the cause of these murders and that his mirror "worketh many woes," Friar Bacon smashes his prospective glass, repents the necromantic studies of his youth, and resolves to spend the rest of his life in pure devotion to God. In fulfillment of his last command, however, a devil seeks out Miles and efficiently carries him off to Hell.

But for the lovers present happiness and a bright future are in store. Prince Edward is betrothed to Elinor of Castile, and Lacy is so enthusiastic in praise of the fair maid of Fressingfield that King Henry sends him posthaste to Suffolk to bring the beauty to court. Lacy arrives in Fressingfield just as Margaret is about to enter the convent. Expressing astonishment that she should contemplate such an act, the lover explains his letter to the girl merely as a test "to try sweet Peggy's constancy." Fortunately, so much in love is Margaret that she readily accepts the explanation without question. At court with great ceremony and pomp a double wedding is solemnized, as the Prince of Wales marries Elinor of Castile and the Earl of Lincoln the fair Margaret of Fressingfield. In this royal union Friar Bacon sees a portent of much future peace and happiness for England, for there

> From forth the royal garden of a king
> Shall flourish out so rich and fair a bud
> Whose brightness shall deface proud Phoebus' flower,
> And overshadow Albion with her leaves. . . .
> Apollo's hellitropian then shall stoop,
> And Venus' hyacinth shall vail her top;
> Juno shall shut her gilliflowers up,
> And Pallas' bay shall bash her brightest green;
> Ceres' carnation, in consort with those,
> Shall stoop and wonder at Diana's rose. . . .
> This prophecy is mystical.

THE SCOTTISH HISTORY OF

JAMES THE FOURTH

SLAIN AT FLODDEN, INTERMIXED WITH A PLEASANT COMEDY, PRESENTED BY OBERON, KING OF FAIRIES

(1590–1591)

DRAMATIS PERSONAE

OBERON, King of Fairies, "not so big as the king of clubs, nor so sharp as the king of spades, nor so fine as the king of diamonds, . . . [but a] king of quiet, pleasure, profit, and content, of wealth, of honor, and of all the world, tied to no place,"

BOHAN, a Scottish misanthrope, though "a gentleman of the best blood in all Scotland. . . . Attired like a ridstall man," he dwells in a tomb and "reck[s] no friend, nor . . . reck[s] no foe, all's one to [him],"

SEMIRAMIS, "the proud Assyrian queen,"

STABROBATES, her conqueror,

CYRUS, King of Persia, "mighty in life, . . . whom Alexander once beheld entombed,"

SESOSTRIS, "conqueror of the world, slain at the last and stamped on by his slaves,"

Fairies, Antics, Kings, Lords, Ladies, Soldiers, and Dancers,

characters in the Induction or Frame-story, the Choruses, the Interscenes, and the Dumb Shows.

JAMES IV, the KING OF SCOTS, "overruled with parasites, misled by lust, and many circumstances too long to trattle on now; . . . [he] makes love by endless means and precious gifts, and men that see it dare not say't, my friend."

DOROTHEA, the "peerless Queen of Scots," and daughter to the King of England, "her father's honor and her country's hope, . . . poor unhappy queen."

ARIUS, KING OF ENGLAND, father to Dorothea.

IDA, a "lovely maid of modest mind," daughter of the Countess of Arran, and beloved by King James. "Europe can not match her for her gifts, of virtue, honor, beauty, and the rest." Her thoughts are "not in delights or pomp or majesty"; she "count[s] time misspent an endless vanity," and, could she choose, would "be honest poor; for she that sits at Fortune's feet a-low is sure she shall not taste a further woe; but those that prank on top of Fortune's ball still fear a change, and, fearing, catch a fall. . . . Her face is dangerous."

EUSTACE, an English gentleman, later married to Ida.

THE COUNTESS OF ARRAN, a Scottish noblewoman, widowed mother of Ida.

ATEUKIN, also called GNATO, a Machiavellian fox and parasite, "who lives by crafts, and sells king's favors for who will give most, . . . a fair-spoken gentleman that can get more land by a lie than an honest man by his ready money."

ANDREW SNOORD, servant to Ateukin, "by birth a gentleman, in profession a scholar,"

JAQUES, a Frenchman, "the wolf abroad, . . . a fit performer of our enterprise,"

} "greater vipers never may be found within a state than such aspiring heads."

SLIPPER, a clown and a loggerhead, also servant to Ateukin, a "shifting fellow . . . of many trades: the honest trade when [he] needs must, the filching trade when time serves, the cosening trade as [he] find[s] occasion, . . . [and he] can lift a pot as well as any man, and pick a purse as soon any thief in [his] country,"

NANO, a dwarf, his "little brother with the great wit," the faithful, goodhearted attendant of Queen Dorothea,

} Bohan's sons, sent out into the world by their father with "learning enough, both kinds, knavery and honesty."

The BISHOP OF ST. ANDREWS.

DOUGLAS, "wise and old in years, true to [his] king, and faithful in his wars,"

MORTON,

ROSS,

} Scottish nobles "that are, or should be, eyes of commonweal, . . . [and] that served in court in place of credit in [King James's] father's days."

SIR BARTRAM, a Scottish gentleman of "reverend years; . . . no labor, duty [has he] left undone to testify [his] zeal unto the crown, but now [his] limbs are weak, [his] eyes are dim, [his] age unwieldy and unmeet for toils."

SIR CUTHBERT ANDERSON, a courteous, gentle Scottish knight of "reverend years" who befriends Queen Dorothea; later, treasurer.

LADY ANDERSON, his wife.

LORD PERCY,
SAMLES,
} English peers.

The Scottish King's Purveyor.

An English Herald.

A Lawyer,   }
A Merchant, } who discuss the affairs of the commonwealth.
A Divine,   }

A Scout.

A Tailor,   }
A Shoemaker, } patronized by Slipper.
A Cutler,   }

Noblemen, Huntsmen, Soldiers, Ladies, Servants.

Setting: Scotland in the early sixteenth century.

> *"Thus wars have end; and, after dreadful hate,*
> *Men learn at last to know their good estate."*

INDUCTION OR FRAME-STORY

Oberon, diminutive King of Fairies, meets Bohan, an angry, misanthropic Scot, who, from sheer dissatisfaction with the world, lives in his tomb. Bohan, it appears, is a gentleman born, but is disillusioned; he has lived everywhere, but has found "the court ill, the country worse, and the city worst of all." He has two sons, Slipper and Nano, and these he sends forth into the world with more than ever Bohan's father gave him—"learning enough, both kinds, knavery and honesty." Upon Nano, the dwarf, as a blessing, King Oberon bestows quick wit, general attractiveness, and preferment to a prince's service; and upon Slipper, who will always be a clown, a wandering life, and a promise that he shall never be in want if he remembers whenever he is in distress to call upon Oberon. When his boys have gone, Bohan demonstrates to the little king why he hates the world. He begins: "In the year 1520 was in Scotland a king overruled with parasites"—a story he has set down and will show in action with the aid of some of his countrymen.

Act I

James IV, King of Scotland, is married with great ceremony to the matchless Dorothea, daughter to the King of England, and "England's choicest pride." But at the coronation—even in the chapel where his marriage is performed—King James permits himself to fall in love with a Scottish beauty named Ida, daughter of the Countess of Arran. He tries to persuade Ida to remain at court, but without success, for the lady is both virtuous and modest, with no delight in pomp or majesty, and a preference for simple, honest things. However, Ateukin, a parasitical timeserver who reads the king's mind, assures King James that the Lady Ida shall be his, and receives the royal promise of gold, honor, and worldly greatness if he attains his ends. Seeking for servants who can assist him and are commensurate with the new dignity that is his as servant of the king, Ateukin reads the bills which Slipper, Nano, and a needy gentleman named Andrew Snoord have set up in the market place, and hires all three. To curry favor with the new queen, Ateukin presents her with Nano the dwarf.

Meanwhile, Eustace, an English gentleman, visits a Scottish friend, Sir Bartram, bearing with him a letter of recommendation from the Countess Elinor of Carlisle, a portrait of the Lady Ida, and an inclination to fall in love with the blythe, "lewely," Scottish lass that all the world admires so much.

CHORUS TO ACT I

Oberon entertains Bohan with a fairy dance, and Bohan shows him three dumb shows: (1) the overthrow of Semiramis, "the proud Assyrian queen," by Stabrobates; (2) Cyrus the Great, before whom kings humbled themselves, lying at last in a marble tomb, the food for worms; (3) Sesostris, conqueror of the world, slain at last by his servants and stamped on by slaves—all revealing "in mirkest terms, . . . the loathe of sins, and where corruption dwells."

Act II

At home in Arran the fair Ida and her mother, content with simplicity and their needlework, receive Eustace, who finds "beyond report the wit, the fair, the shape" of the lady whose portrait he has seen and loved. Their interview is interrupted, however, by Ateukin and Slipper come to present gifts, and to impart in secret to the lady the love messages of King James. But Ida virtuously rejects these lawless overtures, and Ateukin's labor is lost.

About the same time at the Scottish court, the Bishop of St. Andrews, Douglas, Morton, and other of the Scottish peers who served at court in the days of King James's father, now see themselves accounted lightly while the king follows the "reckless course of youth, . . . his lawless and unbridled vein in love," and the advice of flatterers instead of that of his council and of his friends. Queen Dorothea, however, faithfully tries to smooth things over; the king is young, she points out, and even his infatuation for Ida may be only a trial of his wife's love. But the nobles remonstrate with King James, and, in anger, he bids them begone unless they can mend their talk.

With his faithful courtiers out of the way, James makes the most of his opportunities for evil. He calls Ateukin to him and receives from him the hopeful report that the Lady Ida is coy as yet, but that she would be receptive to the king's advances were she not afraid of Queen Dorothea. Accordingly, Ateukin suggests that an assassin put the queen out of the way, and mentions a Frenchman named Jaques, who is now at court, as the proper person to perform the deed. But the king must protect the murderer with a warrant to save his life.

Oberon comments upon the corruption of the king, the virtue of the country maid, and the opportunities the king has for evil now that the ancient lords have washed their hands of him. Then, to change his humor, Bohan has Slipper and a companion ("boy or wench") dance a hornpipe to amuse him.

Act III

In conversation with Slipper, Sir Bartram learns that the lease of a property at East Spring has been confirmed to a new tenant. Sir Bartram had wished to possess this land by patent, and, following custom, had bribed Ateukin to secure it for him. Now he perceives that the parasite, "injurious man, . . . lives by crafts and sells king's favors for who will give most." Angered at such double-dealing, and desirous of possessing the lease as evidence, Bartram promises Slipper a reward of a hundred pounds if he will bring him the letters from his master's pocket.

Ateukin rides high on the royal favor; his servants even defy the king's purveyor and refuse horses for his use. And the parasite has little difficulty in persuading the villain Jaques to undertake the queen's death. But in the course of his persuasions he reveals the fact that the king's warrant for the murder has somehow been lost from his pocket.

Meanwhile, at court, Sir Bartram has been trying to persuade Queen Dorothea that her life is not safe, and, to prove his fears, shows her the warrant for her death, which, along with other papers, the rascal Slipper has conveyed to him. Convinced at last of her husband's villainy, the queen agrees to seek safety by fleeing from court, disguised in man's clothes and accompanied only by her dwarf, Nano. At the same time the faithful Ross sends letters to her father in England, so that he may avenge the queen.

Bohan finds Oberon asleep and decides not to awaken him, because these treasons against the innocent would "make a marble melt and weep."

Act IV

Ateukin's villainy in the royal interest makes little progress and has many obstacles. At a hunt in the Countess of Arran's park, Eustace and the Lady Ida are betrothed. The escape of Dorothea and her page is discovered, and the murderer Jaques sets out in pursuit. Slipper, like the proverbial fool and his money, is seen making rich purchases of clothes with the reward he has received from Sir Bartram. But, eventually, he is robbed by his fellow knave, Andrew. At last, Dorothea and Nano are overtaken by the villain Jaques; the disguised lady defends herself as best she may, though she is inexperienced with weapons. But in the fray she is wounded by Jaques, who thinks her dead and flees. The faithful Nano, however, gets aid from Sir Cuthbert Anderson, who lives near-by to the site of the duel, and together they convey the wounded "squire" to safety. On receiving the news of Queen Dorothea's supposed death, King James has only a few pangs of conscience. But he orders Ateukin to promise Ida marriage, rewards Jaques, and has Andrew serve as scout at court to report any "least intent of muttering" in his train. But Andrew is sick of the wickedness he had been called upon to perform, and he sends secret letters to the English king to let him know of his daughter's misfortune and hopes perhaps to escape the scourge that will without doubt strike Scotland.

CHORUS TO ACT IV

Anticipating the end of all this villainy, Oberon reiterates to Bohan his willingness to stand the friend of Bohan's son Slipper, whatever happens.

Act V

Sheltered by the Andersons, Dorothea still maintains her disguise as a squire. But when she hears of the open rebellion in the country against the king, and of the English invasion, she sends her page Nano to court to tell Ross and Bartram that she is alive, in order that they may guard the king from harm. Ateukin and Jaques arrive in Arran just after Eustace and the Lady Ida have been married, and realize that their credit is completely lost. Jaques flees to France rather than be hanged in a strange country, and Ateukin is filled with regrets at having been responsible for the death of an innocent queen and for causing a war. But he is hardly repentant.

The progress of the English invasion is steady. They besiege Dunbar, which is surrendered by Douglas, whose defense of the place has been only halfhearted. They lay waste all the border, take Morton prisoner, and slay seven thousand Scottish lords. Indeed, they are so successful and their advance is so rapid, that when a lawyer, a merchant, and a divine gather to discuss the responsibility of each of their professions for conditions as they are in the commonwealth, they are routed by a scout with information that the English are already at hand and that the debaters had better flee for their lives.

In vain does the Scottish king try to appease his enemies. But his offer of a reward of a thousand marks for the return of his queen is taken by Dorothea as evidence that her husband still loves her. As a result the queen reveals herself to Lady Anderson, who has fallen in love with the convalescent squire, and sets out for court. There, King James receives the news of Ida's marriage, and, oppressed at last by his conscience, he rouses himself against the "flattering brood of sycophants" that fill his court. He orders the arrest and execution of Andrew and Slipper, and search for Ateukin. But true to his promise to Bohan, Oberon rescues the clown and carries him away. The English king arrives to avenge his daughter's death, for which he has the parasite's signed confession, and he challenges James to single combat. Just as the fight is about to begin, however, Dorothea and the Andersons make their appearance. There are explanations, reconciliations, and forgiveness for errors past, and the nobles are recalled to the court, for, as the long-suffering queen puts it:

> *Youth hath misled; tut, but a little fault!*
> *'Tis kingly to amend what is amiss.*

ARDEN OF FEVERSHAM

CRITICAL COMMENT. So far as is known, *Arden of Feversham* is the earliest domestic tragedy in English. Its subject is an episode from life in middle- and lower-class society, rather than from that of nobles and kings, and the treatment of that episode is realistic, not heroic. Hence, if *Arden* seems to lack dignity or real tragic feeling, or appears coarse or brutal or morally obtuse when compared with other Elizabethan tragedies, it is simply that a plain, unvarnished tale of lying, hypocrisy, crime, and horror can hardly be expected to rise to the level of high art. There is nothing noble about the drama; neither Arden the victim, nor Mistress Alice the murderess, are of true tragic calibre. The former is hard, unattractive, and stupid; the latter is hardly the "village Clytemnestra" Swinburne thought her. Her motives and her methods are cheap and low, but her diabolical persistence in crime, in spite of repeated failure and bad luck, is fascinating.

The author of *Arden* is unknown; in 1770 the play was attributed to Shakespeare by an uncritical and enthusiastic citizen of Feversham. But the attribution is not accepted today. Thomas Kyd has also been suggested, or some imitator of Kyd. The play was rewritten in the early eighteenth century by a Mrs. Haywood (1736) and by George Lillo, author of *The London Merchant*, whose version was acted at Drury Lane, July 12, 1759.

SOURCE. *Arden of Feversham* is founded on fact, a murder which took place on February 15, 1550/1, more than a generation before the drama was written. Holinshed's *Chronicles* (1577) devotes five whole pages to the story, and this account is the source which the author followed closely. There are other contemporary reports, like that in Stow's *Chronicles* (1580). A ballad, entitled "The Complaint and Lamentation of Mistress Arden of Feversham," was doubtless inspired by the play.

BIBLIOGRAPHY

Early editions: 1592; 1599; 1633.
Modern editions: Facs. J. S. Farmer (TFT, 1911); ed. A. H. Bullen (1887); Ronald Bayne (TD, 1897); C. F. Tucker Brooke (*Shakespeare Apocrypha,* 1908).

The Lamentable and True Tragedy of Master

ARDEN OF FEVERSHAM

in Kent, Who Was Most Wickedly Murdered by the Means of His Disloyal and Wanton Wife . . .

(1585–1592)

DRAMATIS PERSONAE

THOMAS ARDEN of Feversham in Kent, "by birth a gentleman of blood," and the long-suffering, if occasionally stern and gullible, husband of an erring wife. To some, too, Arden's successful land dealing seems sharp practice; "desire of wealth is endless in his mind, and he is greedy-gaping still for gain; nor cares he though young gentlemen do beg, so he may scrape and hoard up in his pouch."

MISTRESS ALICE, Arden's unfaithful wife, "rooted in her wickedness; perverse and stubborn, [she is] not to be reclaimed; good counsel is to her as rain to weeds, and reprehension makes her vice to grow." ("O, how cunningly she can dissemble!")

MOSBIE, Mistress Arden's lover, "a botcher and no better at the first; . . . by base brokage getting some small stock, [he] crept into service of a nobleman [Lord Clifford], and by his servile flattering and fawning is now become the steward of his house and bravely jets it in his silken gown."

RICHARD GREENE, a tenant of Arden's, one of Sir Anthony Ager's men, who fancies himself wronged by Arden in the transfer of the Abbey lands.

DICK REEDE, a sailor and "the railingest knave in Christendom," also a man who has a grievance against Arden.

SUSAN, Mistress Arden's "waiting maid," and sister of Mosbie, ⎤
CLARKE, a painter, "the only cunning man in Christendom, for he │ "a crew of har-
can temper poison with his oil," ⎬lots, all in love,
MICHAEL, Arden's servant, "a poorer coward . . . was never fos- │ forsooth."
tered in the coast of Kent," ⎦

BLACK WILL, a grim-faced, pitiless fellow, "he bears so bad a mind ⎤ murderers; "two
that for a crown he'll murder any man," ⎬ rougher ruffians
SHAKEBAG, "stern in bloody stratagem," ⎦ never lived in
                                                                    Kent."

BRADSHAW, once the fellow soldier of Black Will, now "a goldsmith [who has] a little plate in [his] shop," and is a receiver of stolen goods.

FRANKLIN, "Arden's dearest friend," and confidant.

LORD CHEINY, friend of Arden.

THE MAYOR OF FEVERSHAM.

ADAM FOWLE, landlord of the Flower-de-Luce in Feversham.

Attendants on Lord Cheiny, the Watch, a Sailor, a Prentice, and a Ferryman.

Setting: Feversham, London (St. Paul's and Aldersgate), near Rainham Down, the Kentish Coast, Southwark, and their vicinities in 1551.

"This naked tragedy,
Wherein no filed points are foisted in
To make it gracious to the ear or eye."

[*Scene i*] Thomas Arden, a gentleman of Feversham in Kent, has discovered that Alice, the wife he holds dear, is exchanging love letters and holding private meetings with one Mosbie, the upstart, good-for-nothing steward of Lord Clifford. On Mosbie's finger Arden has seen the wedding ring he gave his wife; he has heard her call on Mosbie in her sleep; and for these outrages Arden resolves to be revenged. His friend Franklin, however, urges him to do nothing desperate. With women like Alice, he believes, it is better to use gentle means and sweet words, and he suggests that Arden come with him to London for a while as if completely without suspicion, "for women, when they may will not, but, being kept back, straight grow outrageous." On hearing the news of Arden's journey, Alice is fulsome in her affection; but when her husband goes down to the quay to attend to some business preparatory to his departure, she sends a message to her lover by Adam Fowle, landlord of the Flower-de-Luce, and is impatient of his coming to her.

Already Alice and Mosbie have been planning Arden's death. Michael, Arden's servant, is the rival of Clarke the painter for the love of Susan, Mosbie's sister and a maid in the Arden household. By alternately supporting the hopes of these rivals, the pair have made both of Susan's lovers their accomplices. Michael has sworn secretly to put his master out of the way, and Clarke, who is such an amateur of poisons that, if report may be believed, he can temper venom with his oils, supplies them with a drug with which they can do the deed themselves.

As he comes from the quay Arden finds Alice and Mosbie together. He exchanges sharp words with Mosbie, takes away his sword, and orders him to keep away from his house. But so sincere does Mosbie seem in his insistence that all is over between Mistress Alice and himself, that he never again means to make love to her, and that he visits the place merely to see his sister Susan, that the credulous Arden is reconciled with him, and invites him in to breakfast to show the world how little he distrusts his wife.

At breakfast Mistress Alice makes her first attempt upon her husband's life. But Arden detects something wrong with the broth she serves him, throws it out, and borrows some mithridate from his friend Franklin as an antidote in case the dish has been poisoned. Mistress Alice hysterically assures her guests that she can do nothing to please her husband, offers to eat the broth herself, and melodramatically hopes that it is full of poison. This emotional outburst leads to the couple's making up again with ardent protestations of affection, and Arden and Franklin set out for London.

Having failed in her first attempt, Mistress Alice seeks means of having her husband disposed of as he walks the streets of London. She soon finds an ally in the person of Dick Greene. Greene holds a lease to some of the Feversham Abbey lands granted to Arden by a royal patent which voids all earlier claims. In his anger Greene calls to see Arden; speaks to Alice, who tells him confidentially how badly she is treated by her husband; and sympathetically agrees to hire cutthroats to commit the murder. In return, Alice gives Greene ten pounds and promises him twenty more as well as repossession of the leases he has lost. Then, to make assurance double sure, Mosbie and Alice visit Clarke again and ask him to prepare for them a poisoned crucifix, promising him the hand of Susan as reward.

[*Scene ii*] On the London road Greene seeks cutthroats fit for his purpose and finds them through Bradshaw, a goldsmith of sorts who is in trouble because of receiving stolen goods. They meet Black Will, with whom Bradshaw has once served in the army, and from this rascal the goldsmith learns the name of the thief who stole the plate he had bought. In Black Will and his mate Shakebag, Greene finds a pair of rogues who for gold are enthusiastically ready to undertake anything. As Bradshaw hurries home, however, Greene asks him to carry a letter to Mistress Arden—a favor which Bradshaw is later to regret.

[*Scene iii*] Then follow a series of missed opportunities and blunderings, as Greene, Black Will, and Shakebag stalk their prey. Greene serves as the brains of the team, but cautiously keeps out of the way as the thugs attempt to carry out his plans. For instance, the rogues lie in wait for Arden and his friend to come out of St. Paul's, but a prentice closing the window of his shop strikes Black Will on the head, and in the confusion the intended victim passes by unharmed. Greene and his ruffians then approach Michael, the servingman, offering to relieve him of the responsibility of killing Arden, which he has sworn, gain for him the friendship of Mosbie, and assure him of Susan. Michael readily promises to leave unlocked the doors of the house in which Arden is lodging.

[*Scenes iv, v*] When the time comes, however, Michael loses his nerve. The victim of conflicting thoughts—his master's kindness, his oath for Susan's sake, the threats of Black Will and Shakebag—Michael cries out in fear. Arden is awakened, accepts Michael's explanation that he has had a nightmare, scolds the boy for neglecting to lock up, and bars the doors himself. Hence, the ruffians fail a second time.

[*Scenes vi, vii*] Arden now has a dream which to him presages ill, and, discontented in London, he makes ready to return to Feversham, sending Michael down to Billingsgate to inquire about the tides. On the way Michael encounters Greene and his rogues, succeeds in explaining the failure of the night before, and suggests that the murderers meet their victim as he passes Rainham Down on his way home.

[*Scene viii*] Meanwhile, it is clear that the principals are beginning to fear their accomplices and one another. Mosbie is nervous and disturbed in mind about what Greene, and Michael, and the painter too, will know and blackmail him with. Even Alice herself is not to be trusted; she has planned to kill one husband and may try again. The lady herself is moody and on edge. The lovers quarrel, exchange recriminations, and then are reconciled. Arrival of Bradshaw with the letter from Greene, however, renews their hopes.

[*Scene ix*] Among the murderers too there is discord, and Black Will and Shakebag quarrel foolishly as they lie in wait for their victim near Rainham Down. As Arden and his companions approach the ambush, Michael gets out of the way by going back to Rochester to have his limping horse reshod. But just as the rogues are about to attack, Lord Cheiny appears with his men, engages in a friendly talk with Arden, and invites him on the morrow to dine at his house at Shorlow. He even recognizes Black Will and speaks to him, so that all possibility of carrying out the murder then is out of the question.

[*Scene x*] Arden's return home is uneventful, but early the next morning he and his friend Franklin set out for Lord Cheiny's. The departure is again an occasion for a quarrel between husband and wife, and Franklin's suggestion that they take Mistress Arden with them is merely fuel to feed the fire, for "begged favor merits little thanks." And once more the couple are emotionally reconciled. Knowing that Black Will and Shakebag wait in a broom-close near-by, Michael remains behind on the pretext of hunting for a lost purse, only to get his head broken in a fight with Clarke the painter over Susan.

[*Scenes xi, xii*] This time it is a thick fog that prevents the murder; Arden and his friend cross by ferry to the Isle of Sheppey before the ruffians realize that they have passed. Again Mistress Alice and her lover are disappointed, and Mosbie seriously doubts the ability of these knaves ever to do the crime. Alice then has a new suggestion. As Arden returns from Shorlow, she and Mosbie will meet him arm in arm, flaunting their love in his face, and in the quarrel which will doubtless follow, the cut-throats can do their work.

[*Scene xiii*] Near the Flower-de-Luce Dick Reede, a sailor who also has a grievance against Arden over the Abbey land, rails against the man and curses him, expressing the hope that that plot of ground be ruinous and fatal to him. Soon, as agreed, Alice and Mosbie appear in loving embrace. Also as predicted, swords are drawn, but Arden so ably defends himself that Shakebag and Mosbie are wounded, and the assault comes to naught. Again Mistress Alice convinces her husband that she has been misunderstood, and again the uxorious Arden forgives his wife and begs pardon, insisting also upon reconciliation with Mosbie, in spite of Franklin's good advice and Dame Alice's hypocritical protests.

[*Scene xiv*] To this end Arden sends invitations to his friends and neighbors to come to supper at his house. Undaunted by their many failures, the conspirators plan to make the party the occasion of their success. Greene is to delay Arden's home-coming for a while; Black Will and Shakebag are to conceal themselves in the countinghouse; when at last Arden arrives, Mosbie is to engage him in a game of backgammon, and at a given signal, with a towel Will from behind is to pull Arden to the ground, and the others are to stab him. Then they plan to carry the body out behind the Abbey, so that those who find it will suppose him slain by some footpad for his gold.

As planned, the fiendish plot at last succeeds. Shakebag, Mosbie, and Alice herself, all stab the trusting husband; the hired murderers flee; but before the body can be disposed of, the supper guests knock at the door. The corpse is hastily concealed in the countinghouse, rushes are strewn over the blood on the floor, and Dame Alice receives her neighbors. In spite of her agitation and the pangs of conscience, Alice carries off the situation fairly well, pretending to be very much worried about her husband's being out so late. The guests are seated, and Mosbie, in Arden's chair, drinks Arden's health. But at last to allay Mistress Arden's fears and his own suspicions, Franklin goes out to seek his friend, and Michael gets rid of the other guests.

Indecision about what to do with Arden's body is cut short by word that the Mayor and the watch are coming towards the house with glaives and bills (they are really seeking Black Will for an unrelated crime), and Alice and Susan carry the corpse to the fields. It is snowing, however, and the telltale tracks in the snow are important evidence of where the crime occurred. Franklin soon discovers Arden's body; the towel and the knife, neglected by Michael, are found in the house, as is the blood on the floor; and Mistress Alice is accused of the crime.

[*Scenes xv, xvii*] Justice for the murderers is reasonably swift and complete. Shakebag at first seeks refuge with the Widow Chambley in Southwark, but he quarrels with her, throws her downstairs, breaks her neck, and cuts her tapster's throat. After flinging their bodies into the Thames, he finds sanctuary for a time across the water. Hard pressed by pursuers, Black Will for a time finds refuge in Flushing. But justice is meted out to both later.

[*Scenes xvi, xviii*] Following popular belief that the victim's body bleeds in the presence of his murderers, Arden's corpse forces a confession from both Alice and Mosbie. At the trial, amid mutual recriminations and accusals, Alice is condemned to die at the stake in Canterbury, Mosbie and Susan at Smithfield, and Michael and Bradshaw (because of the letter he carried for Greene) at Feversham.

[*Scene xix*] It is Franklin as Epilogue who reveals what eventually happened to the rest. Shakebag was murdered in Southwark; Black Will was burned in Flushing; Greene was hanged in Osbridge; Clarke the painter fled and was never heard of again. But more notable than all the rest, the body of the murdered Arden was laid in that very plot of ground which he unjustly held from Reede, and in the grass the body's print was seen two years and more after the deed was done.

....•————◆————•....

HENRY PORTER
(Dates Unknown)

BIOGRAPHY. Almost nothing is known of Henry Porter, except that he was spoken of by Francis Meres in *Palladis Tamia* (1598) as among "the best for comedy amongst us." He may be the Henry Porter who matriculated at Brazenose College, Oxford, in 1589, or one of four other Henry Porters who were musicians. Porter's name first appears in the *Diary* of Philip Henslowe, manager of the Rose Theatre, as a writer for the Admiral's Men in 1596; payments are made to him until 1599. After that year he is no longer heard of. Of five plays mentioned in the *Diary* either as written by him alone or as written in collaboration, only *The Two Angry Women* has survived. It is usually assigned to 1598, but an allusion in Richard Harvey's *Plain Percivall* (c. 1589 or 1590) to a proverb-quoting "servingman of Abington" seems to point to an earlier date.

CRITICAL COMMENT.   Regardless of exactly when it was produced, *The Two Angry Women of Abington* is chiefly significant as a breezy picture of middle-class English life. The characters, to be sure, are only types; but the plot is simple and direct, and the whole is written in an easy, conversational style. No source is known.

BIBLIOGRAPHY

Early editions: 1599 (2).
Modern editions: Facs. J. S. Farmer (TFT, 1911); ed. W. W. Greg (MSR, 1912); Havelock Ellis (*Nero and Other Plays,* Mermaid Series, 1888).

The Pleasant History of

THE TWO ANGRY WOMEN OF ABINGTON

with the Humorous Mirth of Dick Coomes and Nicholas Proverbs, Two Servingmen

(1596–1598)

DRAMATIS PERSONAE

MISTRESS GOURSEY, "sore infected and heartsick with hate,"
MISTRESS BARNES, whose "jests grow too bitter; . . . malice lies embowelled in her tongue, and new-hatched hate makes every jest a wrong," } the angry women of Abington. "This is but short-lived envy. . . . 'Tis but a woman's jar. Their tongues are weapons, words their blows of war."

MASTER GOURSEY, "a wise and discreet gentleman,"
MASTER BARNES, "temperate, and ever free from such affections," } their husbands, "partners of two curst wives. O, where shall we find a man so blest that is not? . . . [They] esteem mere amity, familiar neighborhood, the cousin-german unto wedded love."

FRANCIS, or Frank, GOURSEY, "his father's son and heir. . . . I am much deceived in him, an if he be not sober, wise, and valiant. . . . Frank's young, and youth is apt to love. . . . Who would not love such a comely feature, nor high nor low, but of the middle stature?"

PHILIP BARNES, son of the Barneses, "a good wise young stripling for his years."

MARY, or Mall, BARNES, handsome daughter of the Barneses, "lusty guts, . . . seventeen and upward. . . . 'Twere pity to keep love and her asunder. . . . 'Tis a pretty wench, . . . and, like a well-lured hawk, she knows her call. . . . Her dowry, too, will be sufficient. . . . Why, she will flout the Devil; . . . nay, she will weigh your wit, as men weigh angels [i.e., gold coins], and, if it lack a grain, she will not change with ye."

SIR RALPH SMITH, "a virtuous knight, . . . a woodman," and a lover of sport.

LADY SMITH, his wife, who objects to hunting on humanitarian grounds. "Life is as dear in deer as 'tis in men. . . . Now, by my troth, I pity those poor elves."

DICK COOMES, a tipsy braggart. "O, this meat-failer Dick! . . . [with his] sword-and-buckler voice, and his 'swounds' and 'sblood' words! . . . Why, what a swearing keeps this drunken ass!—Canst thou not say but swear at every word?"

HODGE, the butler, also a "right maulster,"

} servants to Master Goursey.

NICHOLAS, alias PROVERBS, tripe-cheeked servant to Master Barnes. "He is not humored bluntly as Coomes is, yet his condition makes me often merry. . . . He's a fine neat fellow, a spruce slave; I'll warrant ye, he'll have his crewel garters cross about the knee, his woolen hose as white as th' driven snow, his shoes dry-leather neat, and tied with red ribbons. . . . Why, ye whoreson proverb-book bound up in folio, have ye no other sense to answer [one] but every word a proverb? No other English? . . . Alas, poor fool! He uses all his wit."

A BOY, "a pretty wag," witty servant to Frank Goursey; "'twas ne'er a good world since a boy could face a man so."

WILL, servant to Sir Ralph Smith.

Other Servants and Attendants.

Setting: Abington and the neighborhood at some unspecified time.

"Good Lord, what kind of creatures women are! Their love is lightly won and lightly lost; and then their hate is deadly and extreme. He that doth take a wife betakes himself to all the cares and troubles of the world."

Act I

After a dinner party given at the house of Master Barnes and his wife, and attended by Master Goursey, his wife, and son Francis, the wives for some unaccountable reason fall out. Jests are followed by innuendoes and sharp words, and the ruffled tempers of the ladies are not soothed by a game of backgammon at which the women insist upon playing for absurdly high stakes. The husbands have been close friends for years and good-naturedly do what they can to effect a reconciliation. But to no avail.

At the same time Philip Barnes, son of the host and hostess, entertains

Francis Goursey at bowls. Their game is friendly enough, though Philip loses heavily; but Francis does not take kindly the teasing of his boy or of Dick Coomes, his father's tipsy servant, about his amorous propensities. He loses his temper and offers to strike the one and fight the other, but Philip separates the combatants, and, having smoothed over his friend's anger, accompanies him somewhat on his way home. Where there is smoke there must be fire, and by his outburst of anger, Francis has revealed at least his inclination toward love and amorous adventure.

Act II

Later the same afternoon Master Barnes in his garden takes his wife to task for her behavior toward Mistress Goursey. Reasonably, and in perfect good humor, he reproves his lady mildly for her impatience with their guest, and the wrathful words she exchanged with her. But he only makes matters worse. One word leads to another; Mistress Barnes angrily calls Mistress Goursey strumpet, and accuses her husband of misconduct with her and of loving his neighbor's wife more than his own. "Knowing women's malice let alone will, canker-like, eat further in their hearts," Master Barnes ceases reproving her further and seeks a remedy. The Barneses have a daughter of marriageable age named Mall. The Gourseys have a son. Why not a match? By straining a little, Barnes can produce a dowry for his daughter equal to the Goursey land, and marriage between the children should be the means of making their mothers friends. He calls his daughter Mall to see how she is disposed to marriage. Mall is a frank, healthy wench with no false modesty about her, and she is not only disposed but eager. Forthwith, therefore, Master Barnes writes a letter to his friend Master Goursey, sends it by his old servant Nicholas, who speaks nothing but aphorisms and proverbs, and lets in on the secret his son Philip, who is so enthusiastic at the prospect that he follows on the messenger's heels to urge his friend to accept.

Meanwhile, the Gourseys' house is as much upset as the Barneses' by the day's events. Mistress Goursey pouts and will look merrily upon neither her husband nor her son. Nicholas soon arrives with Master Barnes's letter, followed by Philip, and father and friend have no difficulty in persuading Frank to agree to matrimony. The two young men hasten back to begin the wooing. But Mistress Goursey, in anger, snatches the letter from her husband, and he has difficulty in getting it back again. She does not read the contents, but—somehow—she knows about the proposed match, and is determined to cross it. Accordingly, she calls Dick Coomes, her servant, sees to it that he is armed, and sets out for the Barneses' house.

Act III

A little bashful about how to begin his wooing, Francis soon finds Mall Barnes "a wicked wench to make a jest, . . . [and] full of flouts and mocks." But, "like a well-lured hawk, she knows her call," and Mall is wooed and won in a very little time. The couple's love-making is interrupted, however, by Mistress Barnes, who perceives what is afoot, and opposes it vigorously. Soon her husband arrives and vainly tries to persuade her, and then Mistress Goursey appears with Coomes. In the resulting altercation, at Master Barnes's suggestion, Philip assists his friend and his sister to slip away separately, appointing as their meeting place the coney-green in a neighboring field, whence they can elope to Oxford and be married. By the time Master Goursey and his butler Hodge join the fray, the lovers have disappeared.

Act IV

Also by this time, the night is pitch dark. Mall finds her way to the warren without mishap, but before Francis can join her, Mistress Barnes, with a torch, apprehends her daughter and tries to force her to go home. But Mall eludes her by running away. Francis, in turn, narrowly escapes being caught by his mother and Coomes, but he too eludes the pursuers. Philip makes his way to the coney-burrow to assist the runaways, and, failing to find them, halloos to them. In the same field, however, are Sir Ralph Smith, the squire, and his man Will, who have been hunting late, and they answer Philip's calls. Frank's boy, Coomes, Hodge, and Nicholas, all join in the search; in the dark friend gets separated from friend, foe encounters foe, there is confusion and wrangling, until Master Barnes and Master Goursey, both vexed with their wives and the turmoil their rancor has caused, agree upon a plan for settling the quarrel.

Act V

Accordingly, when both the angry women and their servants are drawn together by the torch which Mistress Barnes still carries with her, the husbands put their plot into practice. As the wives rail at each other and repeat their charges of misconduct, Barnes and Goursey pretend to believe them and prepare to fight a duel. Their swords are out, Francis, Philip, Coomes, Will, and Hodge all rush in to part them, and the wives at last come to their senses. Had they not been foes, their husbands had remained friends; and all this killing strife, they see, is the result of women's malice. The sons at last effect a reconciliation, and the two angry women confess that their hate grew only from suspicion and no other cause. They join hands and cry, embrace and kiss, and end their quarrel.

Meanwhile, wandering in the dark, Mall has met Sir Ralph Smith, told him the whole story of her love for Francis Goursey and the opposition of their mothers, and the old knight, who approves of the match, promises to aid the young couple in every way he can. Accordingly, when Sir Ralph and Mall at last find the others, the old squire uses his best offices. He is too late to reconcile the two mothers, but he reproves them for trying to cross true love, gives the reunited young couple his blessing, and invites all to be his guests at dinner after their long night's labor.

THE PARNASSUS TRILOGY

CRITICAL COMMENT. The *Parnassus* trilogy of dramas offers an Elizabethan answer to the question, "After college, what?" Their author is unknown, but his plays were acted sometime between 1598 and 1603 at St. John's College, Cambridge, "that most famous and fortunate nurse of all learning," as Nashe called it. Whoever the playwright was, his works are by far the best of the university dramas that have come down to us, not only because of their local satire, but also because they touch upon a fundamental social problem which confronted many students in the Elizabethan universities.

In his essay "Of Seditions and Troubles" Sir Francis Bacon lists three things which do "speedily bring a state to necessity": (*a*) "the multiplying of nobility, and other degrees of quality, in an over-proportion to the common people"; (*b*) "an overgrown clergy, for they bring nothing to the stock"; and (*c*) "when more are bred scholars than preferments can take care off." All three of these causes of discontent and envy were minor anxieties in the sixteenth century, but the last named had already been significant in the development of the Elizabethan drama. The "University Wits"—Lyly, Marlowe, Greene, Peele, Nashe, Lodge, some of them graduates of St. John's—were all in one way or another scholars without perferment who turned to the theatre, not because they wanted to, but because there was nothing else to turn to.

In many ways the age of Elizabeth was an age of opportunity, and brilliant young men of all classes—like Marlowe, the shoemaker's son—found their way to Oxford or Cambridge on scholarship. Upon graduation the best men usually attracted the attention of the great, and statesmen like Burleigh, who was Chancellor of Cambridge University, or Walsingham, who was a patron of Oxford, were good judges of character on the lookout for bright young men. Even a tradesman's son had a good chance of advancement in church or state; some with more academic talents found patrons of other kinds.

But patrons always have more petitioners than they can satisfy; more graduates left the universities than could possibly attain their ambitions, and with
the best of intentions there simply was not enough preferment to go around.
Often educated beyond their stations in life, some of these young men had
accustomed themselves to a mode of living which rendered them incapable of
ordinary occupations or unwilling to try them. It is hardly to be expected
that Marlowe would become a shoemaker in Canterbury, or Greene a grocer
in Norwich. Some had learned to live wildly and thus become incapable of
any kind of steady employment.

What could become of these young hopefuls? That is the problem which
the *Parnassus* plays face. The author has no solution; he is inclined to complain and recomplain with his creations against the neglect of scholars, without suggesting any adjustment of attitude on the part of the young graduate
who thinks the world owes him a living. But he nevertheless presents a realistic, if satirical, illustration of what, it is to be feared, was often the actual
state of affairs. Some of these students, like Madido, fell by the wayside.
Some, like Ingenioso, gave promise, but were impatient of all restraints, left
college, and became pamphleteers, often venting their own personal venom
in the satires they penned. In an age when authorship had not yet become
a profession, some looked resentfully upon the rise of gentlemen authors as
unfair competition. Some became journalists in an age that had as yet no
real place for them. Some tried their luck at Rome or Rheims. Some, like
Luxurioso, lived a wild Bohemian life and depended upon their wits. Some,
like Philomusus and Studioso, tried everything and at last drifted into the
theatres either to act or to pen a part. Many came to London where competition was keen, and opportunities none too plentiful. Some just disappeared.
It is not a cheerful picture.

BIBLIOGRAPHY

Early editions: 1606 (2) [Part III only].
Modern editions: ed. W. D. Macray (Oxford, 1886) and J. B. Leishman
    (1949), all three parts from Bodl. Rawlinson MS. D 398; facs. J. S. Farmer
    (TFT, 1912). Part III only: facs. J. S. Farmer (TFT, 1912); ed. Edward
    Arber (English Scholars' Library, 1879); O. Smeaton (TD, 1905).

THE PILGRIMAGE TO PARNASSUS

(1598–1599)

DRAMATIS PERSONAE

PHILOMUSUS,⎫ two idealistic young pilgrims setting out to "trace this rough, this harsh,
STUDIOSO, ⎭ this craggy way that leadeth unto fair Parnassus hill."

CONSILIODORUS, their aged adviser who gives "gray-bearded counsel" to their "young
    untutored thought."

MADIDO, the votary of wine, whose "wit in drink is drowned,"
STUPIDO, the dullard, that slow-paced, "puling Puritan, . . .
  that earth-creeping dolt,"
AMORETTO, the voluptuary, "sworn Venus' servitor, . . .
  [who has] a wanton eye for a fair wench,"
INGENIOSO, the capable but fainthearted student, "showing
  philosophy a fair pair of heels,"

their schoolfellows whom they meet along the road.

DROMO, a stage attendant.

A Clown, dragged in with a cart-rope. ("Dost thou not know a play cannot be without a clown?")

Setting: The road to Parnassus, through the craggy mountains and thorny valleys of Logic, Rhetoric, Poetry, and Philosophy at some unspecified time.

*"Spectators, take you no severe account
Of our two pilgrims to Parnassus Mount."*

Act I

Two idealistic youths, Philomusus and Studioso, are about to set forth hopefully on a pilgrimage to the Muses' spring on Mount Parnassus to drink of learning. Before they begin their journey, however, they listen to the advice of a plain-dealing old hermit named Consiliodorus, after which they can have few illusions about what lies before them. Consiliodorus wisely warns them to expect to be poor, for "learning and poverty will ever kiss," and to be careful of the company they keep along the way—graceless topers who feed the tavern with their coin; lazy loiterers; "all foggy sleepers and all idle lumps"; smooth-faced voluptuaries; and others who "burn out their base inglorious days without or fruit or joy of their lost time."

The young men journey by way of the Trivium—Logic, Rhetoric or Poetry, and Philosophy—and the succeeding acts of this little play are devoted to each of these lands and the students' adventures there. Looking at "Jack Seton's map" (a recognized Cambridge textbook written by an orthodox Aristotelian fellow of St. John's College), the students see that the first country through which they must travel is Logic, "much like Wales, full of craggy mountains and thorny valleys," and frequented by two robbers "called *genus* and *species,* that take captive every true man's invention that come by them." Undismayed, they begin their journey.

Act II

The first person they meet is Madido, the taverner, who is turning Horace out of his "Roman coat into an English gaberdine," with the aid of sack, and seeking his inspiration in the alepot. To him travelling to

Parnassus is "not a pilgrimage for good wits," for "there is scarce a good tavern" on the way. "This Parnassus and Helicon are but fables of the poets: there is no true Parnassus but the third loft in a wine tavern, no true Helicon but in a cup of brown bastard." That alone will "make you speak leaping lines and dancing periods." Madido, too, has travelled— past the schoolmasters into the Land of Syntax, a country full of joiners; into Prosody, where there are men six feet long never mentioned by Sir John Mandeville; into Dialectics, where one can see nothing but ideas and phantasms. But here in Dialectics he was so confused by Ramus' map (a rival, anti-Aristotelian textbook on Logic), that he threw the book away in a chafe and gave up a tedious journey. "Stay with me," he urges, "and one pint of wine shall inspire you with more wit than all the Nine Muses." Philomusus is almost taken in, but saved by his more serious companion.

Act III

In the Land of Rhetoric the students find a more delicious earth, a smoother pathway, and a sweeter air. Here they listen to the sugared harmony and the tuneful melody of Tully's nightingale, and to Muretus, Bembus, Sadolet, Haddon, and Ascham chirp their pretty notes. And here they meet Stupido, a schoolfellow of theirs, who started out ten years ago, whom they have overtaken, and

> *Who, for he cannot reach unto the arts,*
> *Makes show as though he would neglect the arts,*
> *And cared not for the spring of Helicon.*

Logic makes Stupido's head ache; hence, this dull plodder has sought refuge in nonconformity and become a strait-laced Puritan. To ortho-doxy he prefers catechisms of Geneva's print and the writings of Giles Wiggington and John Penry ("Martin Marprelate"). He is content to follow the advice of his goodman uncle that there is no sound edifying knowledge in these vain arts of Rhetoric, Poetry, and Philosophy. They are rather the rags and parings of learning, and he hates all rhymers for their "diabolical ruffs and wicked great breeches full of sin." Stupido's seeming devotion, earnestness, and apparent honesty almost mislead Studioso, but he is saved in time by Philomusus.

Act IV

In the Land of Rhetoric and Poetry they also meet Amoretto, the Ovidian ladies' man, the horsy amorist, who almost misleads them both by his alluring descriptions of "Venus' sugaries," of wanton merriment, and of a land where there are plenty of Corinnas but a dearth of Ovids.

Act V

When the sweets of love have soured, and Philomusus and Studioso have escaped from "poetry's fair baits," they set foot in the Land of Philosophy. This is a rougher country than Poetry and Rhetoric, and at first it seems that their feet have grown too tender and unapt to travel over it. But they put their trust in Aristotle and continue. Here they meet another schoolfellow of theirs named Ingenioso, a brilliant but disillusioned student who is shaking the dust of Philosophy from his feet. He has burned his books, "splitted" his pen, torn up his papers, cursed learning, and declared Apollo a bankrupt. Philosophy is just a waste of good time; if a man is wise and means to live he will seek poverty no further; Parnassus is out of silver pitifully. It is too far to go there to fetch repentance. Ingenioso declares that he has studied so many years that his brain almost has consumption, and that he has looked so long for a Maecenas to reward his deserts and fed so long upon hope only that he has nearly starved. Hence, he bids these innocents turn home again, lest in their old age they curse their witless heads for picking no better trades in their youth. But Philomusus and Studioso are prepared for such discouragement, and they pass Ingenioso by the way.

Here there is a brief interlude. Merely because "clowns have been thrust into plays by head and shoulders ever since Kemp could make a scurvy face," Dromo, a theatre attendant, drags in a clown by a cart-rope for a few minutes of witticisms.

At last, after four years of travel, the two students arrive at the slopes of Parnassus and their journey's end, at the "laurel shady grove" they have sought so long:

> Now let us boldly rush among these trees,
> And hear the Muses' tuneful harmony.

THE RETURN FROM PARNASSUS
(1599–1600)
Part I

DRAMATIS PERSONAE

PHILOMUSUS,
STUDIOSO,
{ two scholars who "have sacrificed [their] youth" to learning, and spent some time on Parnassus, "the place of solace and true merriment. . . . Their tender years, much like a fruitful spring, promised a plenteous harvest should ensue."

INGENIOSO, who once "forswore the starved air" of learning, but who nevertheless carries "store of lands and livings in [his] head."

LUXURIOSO, or LUXURIO, "a vocal academic, . . . [who has] always more than naturally affected [the] poetical vocation, . . . [and has spent] much in rare alchemy in brewing of wine and burning sack to make [his] wit a philosopher's stone."

CONSILIODORUS, the wise adviser of Philomusus and Studioso; his "life's December, age's chilly frost."

LEONARDE, a carrier by whom Consiliodorus sends his pupils letters; "none of [his] kindred were fools."

A Patron of Ingenioso's, "Signior Barbarism," who enjoys a reputation as a Maecenas, but is "a mere man of straw, a great lump of drowsy earth, . . . [who has] besprinkled [some scholars] prettily with the drops of [his] bounty."

His Servingman, whose "obscure name . . . is known amongst none but hinds and milkmaids."

A Draper, }
A Tailor, } townsmen to whom Philomusus and Studioso owe money.

SIMSON, an innkeeper who has extended credit to Luxurioso.

GOODMAN WILLIAM PERCEVALL, a clown, later churchwarden in the village where Philomusus is sexton.

Studioso's Scholar, a "dandiprat; . . . the sire a clown, the son a fool will be."

Luxurioso's Boy, to sing ballads; his nose has lost its "sanguine complexion . . . for want of good company and good diet."

GULLIO, patron of Ingenioso, a fool of fashion, a braggart, and a pretender to learning and courtship—"this post put into a satin suit, this haberdasher of lies, this braggadocio, this ladymonger, this mere rapier and dagger, this cringer, this foretop." He speaks "pure Shakespeare and shreds of poetry that he hath gathered at the theatres."

Setting: The road back from Parnassus, and the country roundabout, at some unspecified time.

"But scholars still must live in discontent;
What reason then our scene should end content?"

Act I

Seven years have passed since Philomusus and Studioso, the two hopeful scholars, began their pilgrimage to Parnassus, and now, their studies completed, they must leave "these pleasant groves, . . . these Sisters Nine," to earn a living. With fewer illusions than at their original setting out, they resolve to wander through the world, "and reap [their] fortunes wheresoe'er they grow." Luck will be found if they but seek far and long enough.

The first person they meet is their old friend Ingenioso, who has become a pamphleteer in London with his name on every post in Paul's Churchyard. But he is not rich. He has wit, it is true, but that is merely "a quarreling shadow that will seldom dwell in the same room with a full purse." At the moment Ingenioso is in town trying to persuade a gouty old "lump of drowsy earth" to be his Maecenas. To get an interview with the old churl he has to promise the swine-faced servingman to write an elegant love letter for him to the chambermaid. When at last Ingenioso does see the man he is seeking, he must listen to his boasting of his liberality to scholars and to his wonder at what will become of them when their bounteous patron dies. Then Ingenioso receives two groats as reward for a fulsome dedication—a "fiddler's wages."

Next the scholars meet Luxurioso, who apparently has learned little in college except how to live beyond his means, and to love wine, women, song, and tobacco. He proposes to go to London, for "there is a great-nosed ballad maker deceased [William Elderton?], and [Luxurioso] is promised to be the rhymer of the City." The party sets out quietly and speedily, "lest *aes alienum* [i.e., their creditors] be knocking at [their] doors."

Act II

When the flight of Philomusus, Studioso, and Luxurioso is discovered, three townsmen gather to air their grievances against the delinquent gownsmen. To a draper Philomusus and Studioso are indebted twenty nobles for apparel; from a tailor they have borrowed forty shillings; and upon Simson the tapster's post Luxurioso's debts for drink stand chalked. An "Ita est" [i.e., a promissory note] is all the payment they shall get.

Meanwhile, Philomusus and Studioso obtain employment, but of an uncongenial sort. Philomusus is the sexton and the clerk in a village church, digging graves and using "a voice that was made to pronounce a poet or an orator . . . like a bellman in the inquiry of a strayed beast." Studioso earns five marks a year as a private tutor to the spoiled youngster of a family of *nouveaux riches,* at which post he is expected to wait at table and work all summer in the harvest field.

At the same time Luxurioso has become an itinerant ballad maker, writing verses full of poetical spirit for his boy to sing before an occasional auditory of gaping clowns. He is drinking harder than ever.

Act III

By now Ingenioso has attached himself to another patron named Gullio, a fool of fashion, an armchair traveller, a vainglorious pretender to learning and courtship, a "haberdasher of lies," a "ladymonger," and a Maecenas of the arts. In Paul's Churchyard, he boasts, he is pointed out as a poet, and in the tiltyard as a champion. In his days he has been likened to Sir Philip Sidney, he says, "only with this difference, that I had the better leg and more amiable face." As his own he quotes lines from Shakespeare's *Venus and Adonis* and *Romeo and Juliet,* as well as "shreds of poetry that he hath gathered in the theatres." And, because he is busy in weightier affairs, he commissions Ingenioso to write some New Year's verses for his mistress, which he will afterwards peruse, polish, and correct.

Acts IV and V

In the end evil befalls all of them. Studioso loses his place because he refuses to allow one of the bluecoat servants to perch above him at the dinner table and because his pupil complains to mother when the tutor insists that he do some work. Philomusus is sent packing because he is too proud to whip dogs out of church and is negligent about his janitor work. Ingenioso is cashiered and bequeathed "to the travelling trade," because, after submitting to the overbearing criticism of his verses and serving as messenger with them to Gullio's mistress, he truthfully reports to his patron how his messages have been received by the lady, and adds some choice billingsgate of his own. Luxurioso and his page are even worse off than before, travelling about like beggars and keeping just one jump ahead of the village constable.

At last all four decide to go abroad in hope of finding a kinder world, Luxurioso and his page to seek beggary elsewhere, Ingenioso to write satire and do hackwork to maintain him, and Philomusus and Studioso to hie to Rheims or Rome to mend their state—i.e., turn traitor to their church and country—as did many a poor scholar of the day.

THE RETURN FROM PARNASSUS

OR

THE SCOURGE OF SIMONY

(1601–1603)

Part II

DRAMATIS PERSONAE

A Boy to speak the Prologue,
The Stagekeeper, or Prompter,
MOMUS, a mocking critic of the piece,
DEFENSOR, a defender of the play.
} characters in the Induction, or Prologue.

PHILOMUSUS (for a time disguised as Theodore, a French quack doctor),
STUDIOSO (for a time disguised as Jaques, the doctor's man and tutor in French),

the two scholars, returned from their wanderings abroad, thoroughly disillusioned and out to gull the world. "Cockle their harvest is and weeds their grain, contempt their portion, their possession pain." ("See how a little vermin poverty altereth a whole milky disposition!")

INGENIOSO, "a pretty inventer of slight prose, . . . possessed with the spirit of malediction, . . . [and] like a great schoolboy giving the world a bloody nose,"
FUROR POETICUS, "the Devil in the likeness of a poet, . . . [and] a nimble swaggerer with a goose quill, . . . [who has] a very terrible roaring muse, nothing but squibs and fireworks,"
PHANTASMA, his "holy swain, that night and day sit[s] . . . rubbing [his] wrinkled brow, studying a month for one fit epithet,"

"This is their share in happiness, to torment the happy."

ACADEMICO, a real scholar seeking a living in the church, and "one that made an oration for [Amoretto] once on the Queen's Day, and a show that [he] got some credit by."

A Burgess, a butcher and a public magistrate, who has "disturbed [himself] studying the penal statutes," and is therefore a patient of Theodore, the French physician.

The Burgess' Man.

Another Patient of Doctor Theodore's.

DICK BURBAGE, the great tragedian,
WILL KEMP, the great comedian. ("Is it not better to make a fool of the world as [he has] done, than to be fooled of the world as [these] scholars are?")

members of the Lord Chamberlain's Company of actors. "He is not counted a gentleman that knows not Dick Burbage and Will Kemp; there's not a country wench that can dance Sellenger's Round but can talk of Dick Burbage and Will Kemp."

RICHARDETTO, a pupil of Jaques's, learning French.

Fiddlers, with whom Philomusus and Studioso become associated.

IUDICO, a critic and corrector for the press; friend of Ingenioso's.

JOHN DANTER, a London printer and stationer for whom Ingenioso writes.

AMORETTO, the Ovidian, now a Templar, "a broker for a living and a bawd for a benefice," and still "a spruce gartered youth, . . . the chief carpenter of sonnets, a privileged vicar for the lawless marriage of ink and paper, . . . [and one that] talks of nothing all day long but his hawk, his hound, and his mistress." ("There is no fool to the satin fool, the velvet fool, the perfum'd fool.")

SIR RODERICK, a squire and a justice of the peace, father of Amoretto, and "one that loves alife a short sermon and a long play." He hates scholars and yet is fain to give them good words, for he hopes "at length England will be wise enough—[he] hope[s] so i'faith—then an old knight may have his wench in a corner without any satires or epigrams."

SIGNIOR IMMERITO, an ass-headed fellow, "that hath taken all his learning on his own head, without sending to the university," and who aspires to be a parson. "The time hath been when such a fellow meddled with nothing but his plowshare, his spade, and his hobnails, and so to a piece of bread and cheese, and went his way."

STERCUTIO, his simple father. ("You must pardon [him]; he wants bringing up.")

MASTER RECORDER, whose "two neat's feet . . . wear no socks, . . . [who] lives like a summoner upon the sins of people, . . . [and who] hate[s] a scholar because he descries [his] ass's ears."

JACK, Amoretto's page; "there's no felicity to the serving of a fool."

RICHARD, page to Sir Roderick.

MASTER PRODIGO, whose land is forfeit to Sir Roderick.

Echo, replying to Academico's complaints.

Setting: London and the country in the late sixteenth century.

> *"Wonder at thine own bliss, pity our case*
> *That still do tread ill fortune's endless maze."*

Act I

The final play in the trilogy traces remorselessly "the scholars' progress in their misery" as they fall still lower in fortune. With the aid of Juvenal, Ingenioso is writing satire, but is afraid to let himself go. His friend Iudico, a corrector for the press, advises him to give it up, and the two amuse themselves by flipping over the pages of John Bodenham's *Belvedere, or The Garden of the Muses* (1600), the latest poetical miscellany, containing contributions by the leading poets of the day. Iudico has a pretty talent for epigrammatic criticism: Spenser is "a sweeter swan than ever sung in Po"; "sweet honey-dropping Daniel" is advised more sparingly to "make use of others' wit, and use his own the more"; Drayton's "sweet muse is like a sanguine dye able to ravish the rash gazer's eye"; Marston "is a ruffian in his style," and brings "the great battering ram of terms to . . . the walls of the old flinty world"; Marlowe was "happy in his buskined muse, . . . [and] a tragic penman for a dreary plot"; Jonson is "a mere empiric, one that gets what he hath by observation"; Shakespeare is praised for *Venus* and *Lucrece,* "his sweeter verse contains heart-throbbing line, could but a graver subject him content without love's foolish languishment"; and, as to Nashe —"for a mother wit, few men have ever seen the like of it." Some of these fellows, of course, write because of an inward urge; others, as Ingenioso does, "exchange words for money."

Indeed Ingenioso has a manuscript now which he offers to his publisher, John Danter. But the stationer protests that he lost by Ingenioso's last book, and that there are many who pay him handsomely for printing their inventions. Yet, for all that, Ingenioso shall have forty shillings and a bottle of wine. But when Danter hears that the book is *A Chronicle of Cambridge Cuckolds,* with much salt and pepper in the nose and "will sell sheerly underhand," he is willing to talk further.

About the same time Philomusus and Studioso have found that "discontented clerks" do not get a cardinal's hat as easily as they had expected, or indeed any mercenary preferment at Rheims or Rome, and conclude that

> It's as good to starve mongst English swine,
> As in a foreign land to beg and pine.

They have resolved now to try dishonest means at making a livelihood, to "run through all the lewd forms of lime-twig purloining villainies" and turn "coney-catchers, bawds, or anything," to gull the world. At the moment Philomusus poses as Theodore, a French doctor, and Studioso is his man Jaques, who gives French lessons on the side.

Act II

But doctoring is not the way to riches either. From a burgess, who has "disturbed [him]self by studying the penal statutes," they receive only a groat as a fee and eightpence bounty. Hence, it is not surprising to hear these scholars in a melancholy lament that they have "run through every trade, yet thrive by none," and that they cannot succeed "by virtue nor by sin."

A new recruit to the disillusioned graduates and a real scholar is Academico, who fares no better than Philomusus and Studioso. He seeks a church living which is in the gift of Squire Roderick, the father of Amoretto, the Ovidian, now a Templar, with a smattering of law as well as of wanton versifying. Academico has once at college ghostwritten an oration for Amoretto one Queen's Day, but the man of the world professes to have forgotten and turns the scholar's request for assistance to ridicule. The competitor for the place is Signior Immerito, a man without parts or education, who has never been at the university, but who with his father is prepared to bid a hundred pounds for the benefice.

Act III

To make sure that he is conferring his kindness upon a sufficient and a worthy incumbent, Sir Roderick and the Recorder give Immerito a farcical examination, which tests both his learning and his virtues, and which proves him well versed in logic, grammar, astronomy, philosophy, poetry, arithmetic, as well as a man of good utterance. Then the squire gives the new parson a few exhortations—to abstain from controversy; not to gird at men of worship, such as himself; and to use his wit discreetly. So, having committed simony of the worst sort, the squire and his legal adviser congratulate themselves upon their appointment of a safe clergyman.

Meanwhile, in the tavern, Ingenioso, who has a reputation as a "pretty inventer of light prose," meets his friends Furor Poeticus and Phantasma, who devote their wits to Latin epigrams. The three direct their attention to Sir Roderick and his family and what they call "a gentlemanlike kind of begging"—flattery and blackmail. It shall be Furor's task first to give the worldly, wenching old Sir Roderick "some sugar candy terms," and then if he does not untie his purse strings, cudgel him with "thick terms" and sting him with others "laid in *aqua fortis* and gunpowder." At the same time Phantasmo is to direct his "sugar ends of verses" to Amoretto, Sir Roderick's son, who "will draw out his pocket glass thrice in a walk, . . . [and] loves no scholar but him whose tired ears can endure . . . his flyblown sonnets to his mistress." It is Phantasmo's task "to cut this gull's throat with fair terms," or, if these fail, to "fall at defiance with him, and the poking stick he wears."

About the same time, pursuivants are out looking for the French doctor and his man, having bespoken lodgings for them in Newgate.

Act IV

Not content with taking money for a vacant benefice, Sir Roderick and his legal adviser, Master Recorder, confiscate some property belonging to Master Prodigo, solely because it is lawful for them to do so, and Sir Roderick means to be a good subject and obey the law. But while Sir Roderick is justifying his forfeiture and Amoretto is learnedly arguing a point of law with the Recorder, Ingenioso, Furor, and Phantasmo interrupt them, at first with veiled insults, and then with the most astonishing outbursts of rant, billingsgate, obscenity, and vituperation in Latin and English. The satirists put their victims to flight, but they also know better than to stay around too long to laugh at the jest, lest Sir Roderick's bailiffs be sent to apprehend them.

About the same time, having run afoul of the authorities by their quack doctoring, Philomusus and Studioso—like the dramatists known as the "University Wits"—now turn for relief to the theatre, which they call "the basest trade." "Must we be practic'd to these leaden spouts, that naught do vent but what they do receive?" Accordingly, Richard Burbage and Will Kemp, leading members of the Lord Chamberlain's company of actors, put them through tryouts for the stage, and hope that they "can entertain these scholars at a low rate; . . . they have oftentimes a good conceit in a part. . . . Few of the university men pen plays well, [however]; they smell too much of that writer Ovid, and that writer *Metamorphoses,* and talk too much of Proserpina and Jupiter. Why, here's our fellow Shakespeare puts them all down." Acting, the players assure the young graduates, is "the most excellent vocation in the world for money," and Burbage thinks that Studioso, the serious one, might do well after a while as Hieronimo in *The Spanish Tragedy,* and that Philomusus—judging by the proportion of his body—might do for Richard III. Kemp, however, judges from his face that Philomusus might be good as a foolish mayor or justice of the peace.

Act V

But, even if acting is nothing but "mouthing words that better wits have penned," Philomusus and Studioso soon give it up and join a troupe of wandering fiddlers. On New Year's Day they call on Sir Roderick, watch the pages mimic their masters, but come away with "not so much as the usual Christmas entertainment of musicians, a black-jack of beer and a Christmas pie." Hence, because they bring nothing but bad luck to the band they have joined, the two scholars go their own way.

Soon they meet with their old friends Ingenioso, Furor Poeticus, Phantasmo, and Academico—all having the worst luck possible. Writs are out for Ingenioso because of some satirical plays he has written, and he is bound for refuge in the Isle of Dogs, accompanied by his two cronies—"Fury and Fancy on good wits attend." Academico is returning to a post at his old college—to his "Cambridge cell again." Philomusus and Studioso, having run through many trades, "poor in content, and only rich in moan," head for the downs of Kent to seek "a shepherd's poor secure contented life,"

> Sure footing we shall find in humble dale;
> Our fleecy flocks we'll learn to watch and ward,
> In July's heat and cold of January,
> We'll chant our woes upon an oaten reed,
> Whiles bleating flock upon their supper feed. . . .
>
> So shall we shun the company of men,
> That grows more hateful as the world grows old,
> We'll teach the murmuring brooks in tears to flow,
> And steepy rock to wail our passed woe.

MICHAEL DRAYTON

(c. 1563–1631)

BIOGRAPHY. Michael Drayton, better known as a narrative, historical, topographical, and lyric poet, than as a playwright, was born at Hartshill in Warwickshire about 1563 and brought up as a page in the household of Sir Henry Goodyere of Polesworth, to whose daughter, Anne, Drayton later addressed his pastorals and his sonnet sequence *Idea*. He wrote busily for the Admiral's Men, invariably as the collaborator of Dekker and others from 1597 to 1599, and less regularly from 1599 to 1602. By 1598 he was classed by Francis Meres in *Palladis Tamia* as among the "best for tragedy." Most of the plays in which he had a hand are lost, and *The Merry Devil of Edmonton* is assigned to him for no very good reason. The play has also been attributed to Shakespeare. Drayton cannot be traced as a playwright after 1608. He died in 1631.

CRITICAL COMMENT.   Whoever its author, *The Merry Devil of Edmonton* is one of the most amusing and lively of Elizabethan comedies, and its jolly host, its love story, its elopement, its nocturnal scenes on Enfield Chase all suggest comparison with *The Merry Wives of Windsor*. That the play was popular in the theatre is clear from Jonson's allusion to it as "your dear delight, the Devil of Edmonton," in the Prologue to *The Devil Is an Ass* (1616).

SOURCE.   The main plot of *The Merry Devil* bears some relation to *The Famous History of Friar Bacon,* which served as the source of Greene's famous comedy, but the love story is probably the author's own invention. The comic underplot bears a close resemblance to T[homas] B[rewer's] *The Life and Death of the Merry Devil of Edmonton, with the Pleasant Pranks of Smug the Smith.* But the earliest edition of this prose chapbook is dated 1631, though it was entered for publication as early as 1608. Even so, the play is known to have been in existence earlier than that, and unless one assumes an early edition of the novel, it cannot be the source. Yet the chapbook explains much that is left confused in the play, especially the gentlemen's mix-up of inns. The text of the play as we have it is obviously corrupt and abbreviated.

BIBLIOGRAPHY

Early editions: 1608; 1612; 1617; 1626; 1631; 1655.

Modern editions: Facs. J. S. Farmer (TFT, 1911); ed. Hugh Walker (TD, 1897); C. F. Tucker Brooke (*Shakespeare Apocrypha,* 1908); W. Amos Abrams, 1942.

THE MERRY DEVIL OF EDMONTON
(1599–1604)

DRAMATIS PERSONAE

PETER FABEL, a renowned scholar of Cambridge University, "that for his fame in sleights and magic, . . . was called the merry fiend of Edmonton; . . . whilst he lived he could deceive the Devil." At this time, however, he uses "no conjurations, nor such weighty spells as tie the soul to their performancy."

MILLICENT CLARE, "this sweet beauty," daughter of Sir Arthur and Lady Dorcas Clare, and beloved of Raymond Mounchensey. ("Well, go thy ways; if ever thou prove a nun, I'll build an abbey.")

RAYMOND MOUNCHENSEY, pupil of Peter Fabel, and betrothed of Millicent Clare, "as fine a mettled gentleman, of as free spirit, and of as fine a temper as is in England."

SIR ARTHUR CLARE, father of Millicent, "the false fox, . . . [and a] villainous old gouty churl." ("Damnation dog thee and thy wretched pelf!")

DORCAS, Lady Clare, and Millicent's mother.

Young HARRY CLARE, Millicent's brother and friend of Raymond Mounchensey.

SIR RICHARD MOUNCHENSEY, father to Raymond; "the riotous old knight hath o'errun his annual revenue in keeping jolly Christmas all the year."

SIR RAFE JERNINGHAM, "dwelling in the forest," more provident friend of Sir Arthur's.

FRANK JERNINGHAM, "a gallant boy, . . . the lusty heir of Sir Rafe, . . . [and] zealous friend" of Raymond Mounchensey.

BLAGUE, the merry host of the George Inn, Waltham, a "good sinful innkeeper, . . . [who] can scarce bear the sin of [his] flesh in the day, 'tis so heavy." ("Away with punctilioes and orthography! [He] serve[s] the good Duke of Norfolk,")

BANKS, the miller of Waltham,

SMUG, the "honest smith of Edmonton, . . . a boor, a boor of the country, an illiterate boor, and yet the citizen of good fellows." ("An thou touchest liquor, thou art foundered straight,")

SIR JOHN, the merry vicar of Enfield. ("A hem, grass and hay! We are all mortal; let's live till we die and be merry, and there's an end,")

} tippling boon companions, and poachers of the king's venison.

The PRIORESS of Cheston Nunnery.

FRIAR HILDERSHAM of Waltham Abbey, Frank Jerningham's old friend and "ghostly father, . . . a reverend man."

BENEDICK, young novice of Waltham Abbey.

COREB, a spirit, to whom Fabel sold his soul and who "many years attended his command."

BRIAN, Raymond Mounchensey's "honest friend, . . . [and] the mad keeper" at Enfield Chase.

RAFE, Brian's man.

BILBO, "my soldier of St. Quentin's," now footman to the Mounchenseys. He has "a villainous sharp stomach to slice a breakfast."

The Chamberlain of an inn across the way from the George at Waltham.

The Sexton of Enfield church.

Ostlers, Nuns, and Attendants.

Setting: Waltham, Cheston, Enfield, and vicinity, about 1500.

"Let us alone, to bustle for the set;
For age and craft with wit and art have met."

PROLOGUE AND INDUCTION

Peter Fabel, renowned magician and "merry devil of Edmonton," has made a compact with the Devil signed in blood. The period of the agreement has now expired, and Coreb, the angry and impatient spirit through whom the pact was signed, now comes to claim his own. Lamenting that his soul should have been sacrificed for the attainment of a power which when achieved was found to be relatively contemptible, Fabel begs for more time, and finally tricks the fiend into sitting in a necromantic chair, where he is held fast and obliged to grant a respite of seven years. (This Induction has little relevance to the play itself, however, in which the element of magic trickery is slight.)

Act I

Some two years ago Sir Arthur Clare betrothed his lovely daughter Millicent to Raymond Mounchensey by handfasting, and this morning is the time appointed when the affiance made between the young people shall be confirmed and sealed. For this purpose the Clare family has repaired to the George Inn at Waltham to await the arrival of the Mounchenseys and their friends. Sir Arthur, however, has repented somewhat of the match, because Sir Richard Mounchensey has run through his annual revenues by riotous living and generosity, and by paying the debts of his brother, who is a Turkey merchant. Without telling their daughter—who overhears their plans, however, and disapproves—Sir Arthur and Lady Clare determine to break off the match under pretext of entering the girl as a probationer in Cheston Nunnery. Then, after some three months time, Sir Arthur will compass a fairer, wealthier match between his daughter and young Frank Jerningham, the heir of Sir Rafe, and the friend of the Mounchenseys. In due time the Mounchenseys arrive, accompanied by the Jerninghams and Peter Fabel, once Raymond Mounchensey's tutor at Cambridge. The old magician has discovered Sir Arthur's foxy scheme against his former pupil, and at the proper moment reveals it to Raymond, Frank, and young Harry Clare, who are all fast friends willing to pledge their aid to the old scholar's plan to thwart the graybeards. Anyway, Frank is already in love with an Essex girl. Thus, "age and craft with wit and art have met."

Act II

Meanwhile, another intrigue is afoot. Banks, the miller of Waltham; Smug, the tippling smith of Edmonton; Sir John, the vicar of Enfield; and Blague, the "good sinful innkeeper" of the George in Waltham—an incomparable quartette of rogues—meet to plan a raid by night upon the king's deer at Enfield Chase. The host's byword is "I serve the Duke of Norfolk," by which he means such mild peccadilloes as poaching an occasional deer from the park. The party are to assemble at nine, secure their venison, and, if surprised by the keepers in the forest, all meet at the earliest opportunity in the church porch at Enfield.

At about the same time, Sir Arthur has told Sir Richard that the marriage is off, and the generous old spendthrift has not taken the news too kindly. Raymond has been forbidden to see his Millicent, the girl is being hurried off to the nunnery, but Fabel reassures his pupil and promises the young men some merry pranks among the nuns of Cheston (which, happily, are not further alluded to in the play). As Millicent is taken away, a most unwilling nun, Fabel sets out with Raymond for Waltham Abbey, where he promises his sometime pupil he shall become a beardless novice.

Act III

Fabel is as good as his word. In the guise of Friar Hildersham of Waltham Abbey, he instructs Raymond in the duties of visitant to the nunnery, helps him to pose as Benedick the novice, and to deceive Sir Arthur, whom he meets at the entrance to the convent. Thus, Fabel secures for the lover an interview with his beloved, who proves a most unpromising nun. The lovers agree to elope by night to the upper lodge in Enfield Chase, owned by Brian the keeper and the friend of Raymond. Fabel, Harry, and Frank are to assist at the elopement.

Act IV

It is in Enfield Chase, too, that the poachers seek some of the king's venison. Young Harry Clare and Frank Jerningham have succeeded in effecting the escape of Millicent from the nunnery, and are making their way in the dark to Brian's lodge where they are to meet Raymond. They hear the poachers tramping in the woods, think they have been discovered by their father's men, and hide, getting separated among the trees. Blague, Smug, Banks, and Sir John hear the runaways, think the gamekeepers are up, and flee toward Enfield Church. Brian the keeper is aroused by both groups of trespassers, hears Millicent calling softly for her brother and young Jerningham, and succeeds in reuniting them. When indeed Sir Arthur and Sir Rafe do arrive in pursuit, the friendly Brian directs the young people to Enfield, whither he promises to send young Mounchensey should he come. Then, by acting the indignant keeper who has found trespassers on his ground, Brian keeps the fathers at bay and covers the retreat of the elopers.

At Enfield church porch the poachers meet, but not before all of them have seen harrowing shapes moving about the churchyard—white bulls, devils, and spirits dressed in sheets—so that Mine Host of the George at last resolves to "serve God in the night hereafter afore the Duke of Norfolk."

Act V

The next morning stranger things still are revealed. Sir Arthur and Sir Rafe, smarting at their failure to apprehend the runaways, interview both Friar Hildersham of Waltham Abbey and his novice Benedick, but both of them are mystified by the parts they are supposed to have played in the affair. More singular still, the knights then discover that they have spent the night in the wrong inn. Instead of at the George, they have slept in the inn across the way, the signs having been confused. But at the George the runaway lovers have been married during the night by Sir John, the merry Enfield priest, and there is nothing for the disappointed fathers to do but accept the fact. Explanations reveal that everything was done at the direction of Peter Fabel, who has "used some pretty sleights," even removing the sign of the George Inn to confuse the oldsters. Chased by the keepers, the tipsy Smug had escaped by climbing upon the sign of the White Horse across the road, thus converting it falsely into the George and so mystifying Sir Arthur and Sir Rafe.

* * *

THOMAS DEKKER
(c. 1572–1632)

BIOGRAPHY. Although Ben Jonson called him a "rogue," Thomas Dekker is one of the most attractive of the dramatists of the period; he is known almost entirely as he reveals himself in his writings. Probably a Londoner of Dutch extraction, almost nothing is known of his personal life, except that he was always impecunious, and nothing of his education. He first emerges in 1598 as a playwright for the Admiral's Men, and until 1602 he wrote busily and usually in collaboration for this company or for Worcester's Men. He had a hand in more than seventy-five plays, most of which are lost. In addition to drama, Dekker also wrote pamphlets and other ephemera in the manner of Nashe, and these are among the best records of London life of his day. By 1613 he fell upon evil days, was arrested for debt, and languished in prison until 1619. He returned to the theatre to collaborate with Ford, Massinger, Rowley, and others. But he is not traceable after 1632, when a Thomas Dekker householder, was buried at St. James's, Clerkenwell.

CRITICAL COMMENT. In drama Dekker is notable for his vivid realism, his Dickensian humor, and his tender sympathy and pathos. No one knew London better or loved it more than he did. Among his dramas *Old Fortunatus* has a quaint, old-fashioned flavor and is related to the old morality plays. His masterpiece is *The Shoemakers' Holiday,* a boisterous, rowdy comedy of London life as seen through the eyes of a romanticist, and emphatically a play of the heart, not the head. *The Honest Whore* is a tender-hearted play in which fun and irony, homely virtue and heartache, pity and whimsy, satire and humor are blended.

SOURCES. *Old Fortunatus* is a dramatization of a German folk tale, printed in 1509, which had already been put on the stage by Hans Sachs in 1553; ultimately it stems from the East. There is no English translation of the original.

The Shoemakers' Holiday is based upon Thomas Deloney's *The Gentle Craft* (1598), a romanticized story of a fifteenth-century Lord Mayor. Here Dekker found most of the details of his play, from the hiring of the foreign workman to the feasting of the apprentices, even the tale of Crispine and Crispianus, whose story suggested the Rose and Lacy plot—indeed everything except the breezy character of Simon Eyre himself and his relations with his apprentices. These are Dekker's own.

For *The Honest Whore* no source is known; it is compounded of Dekker's own observation of London life, a conventional intrigue story of the type employed by Middleton, who collaborated with Dekker on the first part, and a subplot of humor characters.

BIBLIOGRAPHY

Collected Works:

The Dramatic Works of Thomas Dekker, Pearson Reprints, edited by R. H. Shepherd, 4 volumes, 1873.

The Best Plays of Thomas Dekker, edited by Ernest Rhys, Mermaid Series, 1887.

Monographs:

Mary L. Hunt, *Thomas Dekker,* Columbia, 1911.

K. L. Gregg, *Thomas Dekker, a Study in Economic and Social Backgrounds,* University of Washington, 1924.

Old Fortunatus:

Early edition: 1600.
Modern edition: ed. Oliphant Smeaton (TD, 1906).

The Shoemakers' Holiday:

Early editions: 1600; 1610; 1618; 1624; 1631; 1657.
Modern edition: ed. J. R. Sutherland (1928).

The Honest Whore:

Early editions: Part I: 1604; n.d. [known only from imperfect copies]; 1605; 1615-16; 1635. Part II: 1630.

THE COMEDY OF

OLD FORTUNATUS

(1599)

DRAMATIS PERSONAE

FORTUNE, a goddess, "most powerful Queen of Chance, dread sovereigness; . . . true center of this wide circumference, sacred commandress of the destinies. . . . This world is Fortune's ball wherewith she sports. . . . This hand hath written in thick leaves of steel an everlasting book of changeless fate, showing who's happy, who unfortunate."

VIRTUE, "immortal Aretë," whose "looks want cunning to entice. ⎫
. . . The world laughs her to scorn,"   ⎬ goddesses who
VICE, "foul, hell-bred fiend, . . . [Virtue's] sergeant, her jailer, and ⎬ contend with
her executioner,"   ⎭ one another.

FORTUNATUS, an old man, "very poor and very patient. . . . Sorrow's heir and eldest son to Shame," who becomes "one of Fortune's minions."

AMPEDO, "my brother Virtue here," ⎫ the star-crossed sons of Fortunatus,
                                   ⎬ originally "two knights of the post. . . .
ANDELOCIA, his younger "brother Vice," ⎬ But fools have always this loose garment
                                   ⎬ wore, being poor themselves, they wish all
                                   ⎭ others poor."

SHADOW, their servant, "my little lean Iniquity. . . . When thou provest a substance, then the tree of virtue and honesty, and such fruit of Heaven, shall flourish upon earth."

The SOLDAN OF BABYLON, owner of a magic wishing hat, who is visited by Old Fortunatus.

His Noblemen.

ATHELSTANE, King of England.

AGRIPYNE, a princess, daughter of King Athelstane; "the ruby-colored portals of her speech were closed by Mercy; but upon her eye, attired in frowns sat murdering Cruelty. . . . She's full of beauty, full of bitterness, . . . [but] seems to shun love's gentle lure. . . . Tush, man, be bold, were she a saint, she may be won with gold." ("Is't not a shame that a king's daughter, a fair lady, a lady not for lords, but for monarchs, should for gold sell her love, and when she has her own asking, and that there stands nothing between, then to cheat [her] sweetheart? O fie, fie, a she coney-catcher!")

ORLEANS, a French nobleman, "born to be her beauty's slave, and her ⎫
love's scorn . . . [He has] in Sorrow's jail been long tormented." ⎬
("You look lean, and likest a lover,")   ⎬ Agripyne's
INSULTADO, her "Castilian prisoner, . . . [who] has sworn to [her] by ⎬ lovers.
the cross of his pure Toledo, to be [her] servant,"   ⎬
The PRINCE OF CYPRUS,   ⎭

GALLOWAY,
MONTROSE, } Scottish nobles,

CORNWALL,
CHESTER, } English nobles,
LINCOLN,

LONGAVILLE, a French noble, } at King Athelstane's court.

HENRY THE FIFTH [Fourth?], "a German emperor, . . . who being first deposed, was after thrust into a dungeon and thus in silver chains shall rot to death,"

FREDERICK BARBAROSSA, "Emperor of Almaine once, but by Pope Alexander now spurned and trod on when he takes his horse, and in these fetters shall he die his slave,"

LEWIS THE MEEK; "this wretch once wore the diadem of France, . . . but through his children's pride, thus [is he] famished,"

Poor BAJAZET, "old Turkish Emperor, and once the greatest monarch in the East, . . . yet must [he] in a cage of iron be drawn in triumph at [the] heels [of Tamburlaine] and there in grief dash out [his] brains,"

} four kings ruined by Fortune. "These [she] created emperors and kings, and these are now [her] basest underlings, . . . chained like Tartarian slaves."

A Shepherd—"Viriat, a monarch now, but born a shepherd; . . . these hands have conquered Spain, these brows fill up the golden circle of rich Portugal,"

A Carter—"Primislaus, a Bohemian king, last day a carter,"

A Monk, "Gregory, now lifted to the Papal dignity,"

A Tailor, "this Dutch botcher wearing Munster's crown, John Leyden, born in Holland poor and base, now rich in empery and Fortune's grace,"

} exalted by Fortune.

Two Old Men for the Prologue and Epilogue at Court.

Chorus for Acts II and IV.

Echo, a voice that answers Fortunatus.

A Boy with a lute, attending Orleans.

The Three Destinies,
A Priest,
A Company of Satyrs, } attending Fortune.
Nymphs,

Soldiers and other Attendants.

Setting: Cyprus, Babylon, and England in some mythical time during the reign of Athelstane in England.

"Good gifts abused to man's confusion turn."

Act I

An old beggar named Fortunatus, who is "very poor and very patient," encounters the goddess Fortune, the "most powerful Queen of Chance," who is just receiving the curses of several kings—Henry the Fifth [Fourth ?], a German emperor; Frederick Barbarossa; Lewis the Meek of France; and Bajazet, the Turkish emperor—all of whom

have now fallen from their high estates. At the same time Fortune
receives the grateful homage of others to whom she has been kind—
Viriat, once a shepherd, but now monarch of Spain and Portugal;
Primislaus, a carter become King of Bohemia; Gregory, a monk who
has attained the papacy; and John Leyden, a Dutch tailor who now
wears Munster's crown. The goddess smiles upon the beggar and offers to make old Fortunatus one of Fortune's minions and to give him
his choice of wisdom, strength, health, beauty, long life, or riches. In
spite of the warnings of the kings and the encouragement of the others,
the old man accepts Fortune's favor and foolishly chooses wealth. He
receives from her a purse from which at any time he can draw forth
ten pieces of gold, current in any realm in which he may find himself.
With elated heart, Fortunatus sets out on his travels, first to visit his
sons in Cyprus, and without regard to the ringing words Fortune sends
after him:

> *Farewell, vain covetous fool, thou wilt repent*
> *That for the love of dross thou hast despised*
> *Wisdom's divine embrace; she would have borne thee*
> *On the rich wings of immortality.*
> *But now go dwell with cares and quickly die.*

At the same time, Fortune and her attendants (Virtue and Vice, who
are mortal enemies of each other) also come to Cyprus to consecrate a
grove to their deities and to plant the trees of good and evil. Vice's
tree is a fair and flourishing one of gold with apples on it, but Virtue's
tree is withered and almost without fruit. Because of her ill success,
Virtue must bear the taunts of Vice, but she resolves hopefully once
more to try to find a wholesome climate for her tree, and to attract the
love of men. Fortune, however, is indifferent; she cares not which tree
flourishes, because she advances both virtuous souls and vicious. But
she agrees, nevertheless, to judge which of her attendants wins this
sovereignty.

Act II

In the course of his travels Fortunatus visits the court of the Soldan
of Babylon, who is covetous of Fortunatus' famous purse. The old man
promises him one just like it, and in return is shown the Soldan's marvellous treasure, a hat which transports the wearer wherever he wishes
to go. Innocently, the Soldan permits his guest to try the hat on; the
old rascal wishes himself in Cyprus with his sons and disappears. In
Cyprus Fortunatus lives a life of luxury and revelry. But when the old
fellow is at the height of his success, Fortune and the Destinies cut his

time short. Before he dies, however, he tries to return his magic purse to Fortune that she may give wisdom to his sons, Ampedo and Andelocia. But it is too late, and he can only bequeath to them his purse and his hat. These treasures the boys agree to possess by turns; one shall have the purse for a year and the other the hat and so much gold as he can ask. Then they will change about.

Act III

Possessed of the inexhaustible purse, but heedless of his father's fate, the younger son, Andelocia, makes his way to the court of Athelstane, King of England, whose heartless daughter Agripyne has many suitors, but "she seems to shun love's gentle lure." To Andelocia, who seems the "golden lord," the princess shows favor, but it is only to betray him. She drugs the foolish spendthrift with a soporiferous juice, and while he lies sleeping in her lap steals his magic purse and substitutes another like it in its place. When he awakens the disillusioned Andelocia resolves to return to Cyprus, rob his more virtuous brother of his wishing hat, seek out Misery, "and where she dwells . . . languish and die."

Act IV

Andelocia does indeed succeed in robbing his brother Ampedo of the Soldan's wishing hat, but he does not seek out Misery, as he vowed. Instead, with the magic cap he hopes to win his purse again. Disguised, he returns to England, bargains for jewels with the beauteous Agripyne, who wears the purse at her side, kidnaps her, and transports her to a desert place. There, regardless of the purse, he attempts to seduce the princess. She evades him, however, and professes to be dying of hunger and thirst. There is neither food nor drink in the desert, but Andelocia spies some apple trees. The fruit of one is withered; that of the other looks like gold, is delicious to the taste, but bitter as gall when one has downed it. The trees are those planted by Virtue and Vice. In order better to reach one of the fair apples which grows on a high branch, and also to shield Agripyne who complains of the hot sun, Andelocia bids her take his hat, and the girl promptly puts it on and wishes herself back in England.

Cheated of both purse and hat, Andelocia is transformed into an absurd horned beast by the apples of Vice which he has eaten. He wishes for death and falls asleep beneath the trees. Fortune, attended by Virtue and Vice, appears; Vice mocks his misery, but Virtue offers to cure him of his deformity. The fruit of her tree is bitter to the taste, but once downed it is delicious. He accepts Virtue's fruit, undergoes a reformation, and wishes for his hat and purse again that he might put them to better use. Fortune grants him the opportunity, bidding him gather fruit from both the trees, by help of which he may regain his property, and promising to transport him to England where his virtuous brother and their servant Shadow now reside. But Fortune warns Andelocia that if he loses her favor once again, he shall rue it. Virtue claims a victory, but Vice cynically bids her wait to see who triumphs at last.

Once in London, Andelocia and his servant Shadow pretend to be Irish costermongers and dispose of their fruit at court as fine Damascus pippins. Here, too, Andelocia meets his brother Ampedo, who resolves to burn both purse and hat, should they be found again, and so end his grief, his brother's riot, and both their shames.

Act V

As a result of eating the apples of Vice, the Princess Agripyne, together with Montrose and Longaville, two courtiers, are all transformed into horned monsters. A marriage with the Prince of Cyprus is broken off; only the true lover Orleans will accept the princess as she is. Physicians try their art in vain, until there is brought in a French doctor who has been drawn to court by the report of the princess' grief. He is Andelocia in disguise. He produces a cure—the apples of Virtue —which he is permitted to try first on Longaville and then on the princess. But Andelocia is more interested in finding his purse and his hat than in making the cure. The princess still wears the former on her person, and when he finds the latter lying on the floor unguarded, he seizes the lady by the hand, abducts her once more, and joins his brother. But he releases Agripyne once she yields up the inexhaustible purse to him. To Ampedo he now resigns the wishing hat, and the virtuous elder brother at least in part makes good his vow to burn the talismans:

> Count what good and bad
> They both have wrought, the good is to the ill
> As a small pebble to a mighty hill. . . .
> Good gifts abused to man's confusion turn.

Covetous pursuers from the court, however, overtake the pair; the hat which might have helped them to escape has been destroyed; Ampedo and Andelocia are put into the stocks, and there perish miserably.

Their captors, Montrose and Longaville, then fight over the purse, until Fortune appears and claims the prize. The conflict between Virtue and Vice is not so easily settled; the two goddesses still contend before Fortune, each claiming the victory. At last Virtue appeals for judgment to Queen Elizabeth, who is present at the performance. In consternation, Vice runs away from Her Majesty's virtuous presence, and Fortune resigns to her all power bestowed by Heaven, acknowledging Elizabeth as the true Queen of Chance and commander of the Fates. Even Virtue herself professes to be a counterfeit and falls at the feet of the true personification of goodness. With hymns in praise of Virtue's deity, the drama closes.

THE SHOEMAKERS' HOLIDAY

OR

The Gentle Craft

with the Humorous Life of Simon Eyre Shoemaker and Lord Mayor of London

(1599)

DRAMATIS PERSONAE

SIMON EYRE, "the mad shoemaker of Tower Street," in succession alderman, sheriff, and Lord Mayor of London, and "one of the merriest madcaps in [the] land; . . . prince [is he] none, yet near a princely mind." ("O brave shoemaker, O brave lord of incomprehensible good-fellowship! . . . I had rather a thousand pound I had an heart but half so light as yours. . . . Let's be merry whiles we are young; old age, sack, and sugar will steal upon us, ere we be ware.")

DAME MARGERY, his vain, talkative, but good-natured wife, "Lady Clapperdudgeon, . . . this wench with the mealy mouth that will never tire; . . . you bombast cottoncandle quean, . . . you Islington white-pot, . . . you hopper-arse, . . . Mother Miniver-cap." ("How like a new cartwheel my dame speaks, and she looks like an old musty ale bottle going to scalding.")

ROGER, commonly called HODGE, Eyre's "brisk foreman," later master of the shop,

FIRK, his "fine firking journeyman,"

RAFE DAMPORT, "a young man, and but newly entered" into his trade, impressed for the wars—"a good workman and a tall soldier,"

"all gentlemen of the gentle craft, . . . true Trojans, courageous cordwainers; they all kneel to the shrine of holy Saint Hugh. . . . Be as mad knaves as your master Sim Eyre hath been, and you shall live to be sheriffs of London."

JANE, the "sweet, . . . loving, lovely" wife of Rafe.

ROWLAND LACY, nephew of Sir Hugh Lacy, and "chief colonel of all those companies mustered in London and the shires about to serve His Highness in those wars in France"; later, Hans Meulter, "a Fleming butterbox, a shoemaker." ("'Twas not a base want of true valor's fire that held him out of France, but love's desire.")

ROSE, "Mistress Damask Rose," the fair-cheeked daughter of Sir Roger Oteley, and beloved of Rowland Lacy, "young, wellborn, fair, virtuous, a worthy bride for any gentleman."

SYBIL, her simpering maid.

MASTER HAMMON, "a proper gentleman, a citizen by birth, fairly allied, . . .[and] of fair revenues," suitor first of Rose and then of Jane.

MASTER WARREN, Hammon's brother-in-law.

SIR HUGH LACY, Earl of Lincoln and uncle of Rowland Lacy.

ASKEW, his nephew.

DODGER, a servant to the Earl of Lincoln, a "parasite [and] the arrant'st varlet that e'er breathed on earth; he sets more discord in a noble house by one day's broaching of his pickthank tales than can be salved again in twenty years."

SIR ROGER OTELEY, Lord Mayor of London and father of Rose.

MASTER SCOTT, citizen of London and kinsman of Sir Roger's.

The KING of England.

The EARL OF CORNWALL, attending the King.

LOVELL, a courtier, messenger from the King.

A Dutch Skipper.

A Boy, Courtiers, Officers, Soldiers, Huntsmen, Shoemakers, Apprentices, Servants, and Attendants.

Setting: The City of London and the adjacent village of Old Ford in the mid-fifteenth century.

> *"By the Lord of Ludgate, it's a mad life to be a Lord Mayor;*
> *it's a stirring life, a fine life, a velvet life, a careful life."*

[*Scene i*] Rowland Lacy, nephew of Sir Hugh Lacy, Earl of Lincoln, is in love with Rose, the daughter of Sir Roger Oteley, Lord Mayor of London. Both Sir Roger and Sir Hugh disapprove of the match, for Rowland has shown himself an unthrift who does not know the value of money. Once, while travelling on the Continent, he squandered the allowance his uncle had made him and became a shoemaker in Wittenberg to earn money with which to get home. Moreover, Sir Hugh has ambitions for the boy at court, and, to discourage the love affair, he has had His Majesty appoint Rowland colonel-in-chief of the companies of troops mustered in London and the vicinity for service in the wars with France. The army is equipped and ready, and so glad are the two guardians to get rid of the young man that the Lord Mayor and the Council give him twenty pounds as a parting gift, and Sir Hugh gives him thirty Portuguese. Rowland, however, has some serious private business to attend to before he can sail; he gives his cousin Askew the twenty pounds and ten of his uncle's Portuguese, promising to catch up with the expedition in a few days, either at Dover or in Normandy.

At the same time in other circles other true lovers are being separated by the war. Rafe Damport, journeyman in the shop of Simon Eyre, mad shoemaker of Tower Hill, and the new-married husband of Jane, has been impressed as a soldier. Rafe's bluff but kindly old master and all of Rafe's fellow journeymen try to get him released from service; Eyre even offers to provide Colonel Lacy with boots for seven years if he will leave Rafe behind. But when they fail in their appeal, the honest shoemakers encourage their soldier and give him gifts. Rich men in parting present their wives with jewels and rings; Rafe gives his Jane a pair of shoes, made up and pinked with letters of her name, bidding her wear them for his sake:

> *And every morning when thou pull'st them on,*
> *Remember me, and pray for my return.*
> *Make much of them, for I have made them so*
> *That I can know them from a thousand mo.*

With these words, which are to have great future significance, Rafe leaves for the wars.

[*Scene ii*] In the garden at Old Ford, whither she has been sent by her obdurate father, Rose weaves a garland of flowers for her Lacy's head and laments their separation. Then she sends her maid Sybil off to London to learn for sure whether Lacy has gone to France or not.

[*Scene iii*] Rowland Lacy, however, has no intention of leaving Rose, even if he incurs the King's displeasure and his uncle's wrath. The gods have taken many shapes to gain their loves; Lacy will once more adopt the trade of a Dutch shoemaker to work with Eyre in Tower Street, in hope occasionally of seeing Rose.

[*Scene iv*] Hence, early in the morning as Simon Eyre arouses his apprentices and maids to their daily tasks, there passes by a workman, singing of the gentle craft. He is so carefree and quaint of tongue that Hodge and Firk urge their master to hire him. Both Simon and Dame Margery think they have enough journeymen in these hard times, but when both the foreman and the best workman threaten to leave the shop, Simon Eyre engages the stranger. His name is Hans Meulter (alias Rowland Lacy), and he knows what is expected of him. Although it is before breakfast, he sends a boy out for half a dozen cans of beer.

[*Scene v*] Sir Roger loses no time in finding another suitor for his daughter Rose. One day while out hunting near Old Ford, Master Hammon, a well-to-do citizen of London, loses a deer in the Lord Mayor's orchard, where Rose and Sybil are walking. While his companion Warner flirts with Sybil, Hammon bandies words with Rose, and by the time her father appears, he has fallen in love. Sir Roger bids the young men welcome, resolved to do all he can to match his daughter to this gentleman.

[*Scene vi*] In Tower Street, not only does Hans prove a competent workman; he encourages his master in other business ventures as well. On one occasion he lends Simon Eyre enough for a down payment on the cargo of a Dutch ship from Candia, full of sugar, civet, almonds, cambric, and a thousand thousand things, puzzling his fellow journeymen as to where he got the twenty Portuguese to make the bargain. And, as time goes on, the garrulous Eyre prospers and becomes alderman, with a garded gown and a damask cassock. "Lord, Lord, to see what good raiment doth!"

[*Scene vii*] About the same time, however, Dodger, Sir Hugh's tattling servant, brings news from France of a battle between the English and the French, and, of course, word that Rowland Lacy never had been there, his cousin Askew serving as deputy commander in his stead. Certain that love for Rose is the distracting force which explains Rowland's neglect of his military duty, Sir Hugh sends Dodger to his nephew's old haunts and to the Lord Mayor's house in hope of getting news of the young scapegrace.

[*Scene viii*] In spite of the Lord Mayor's support, Master Hammon's suit to Rose does not prosper. The young people quarrel. Rose vows she will live a maid; and, rather than permit Sir Roger to force his daughter into marriage, Hammon steps aside. It is not wealth he seeks; there is a wench who keeps a shop in the Old Change; perhaps she will marry for love. At least Hammon can ask. Rose is packed off to Old Ford again, but soon after Dodger arrives seeking Lacy. If Lacy is lurking in London, no doubt Rose knows about it, and to her father that explains her refusal of Master Hammon. Meanwhile, Simon Eyre has continued to prosper surprisingly; the Lord Mayor and his friend Master Scott are now Eyre's partners, and the shoemaker's gains in one venture alone will rise at least to full three thousand pounds. There is every likelihood that he will soon be chosen sheriff of London.

[*Scene ix*] Dame Margery Eyre begins to put on airs, ordering a pair of shoes with cork soles and inquiring about periwigs, French hoods, and farthingales—"I must enlarge my bum, ha ha! . . . How costly this world's calling is!" Then Rafe returns from the wars—badly crippled, alas—seeking his wife Jane. "She was here awhile," Dame Margery explains, "and, because she was married, grew more stately than became her; I checked her, and so forth; away she flung, never returned, nor said bye nor bah." But, more sympathetic than his arrogant dame, Hodge offers Rafe work and assistance in finding the girl. And on the same day, Simon Eyre is elected sheriff. Decked in the scarlet robes and the gold chain of his office, Eyre resigns his shop to Hodge, makes Firk foreman, promises Hans a hundred for his twenty Portuguese, and sets out for Old Ford to dine with the Lord Mayor.

[*Scene x*] There Eyre makes merry with his lordship, and the "merry Mesopotamians" from his shop honor the occasion in a morris dance.

There, too, Hans sees Rose, who recognizes him and drinks his health; and Sybil wagers that in spite of all her father's scheming, Rose will yet marry her Lacy.

[*Scene xi*] Meanwhile, Master Hammon has sought out the sempster in the Old Change. She is Jane Damport, and Hammon makes as little progress with her as with Mistress Rose. His suit is honorable, but when he learns that Jane is married to a soldier, he shows her a letter from a friend of his which contains a casualty list, and on it she finds Rafe's name. Grief-stricken, Jane finds in Hammon a persistent suitor, but at last she promises that if ever she marry again, it shall be with him.

[*Scenes xii, xiii*] On the day following the holiday occasioned by the Lord Mayor's dinner, the shoemakers work with extra vigor. Into the shop comes Sybil, Rose's maid, with an order that Hans the Fleming go to Cornhill to fit some shoes for her mistress. Soon after, a serving-man enters the shop with a rush order for a pair of wedding shoes to be delivered to Master Hammon at the Golden Ball in Watling Street, bringing with him an old shoe as a pattern. Rafe recognizes the shoe he gave to Jane when he was pressed for France, and he resolves to be on hand with a lusty crew of honest shoemakers to watch the bride go to St. Faith's Church.

[*Scene xiv*] At the Lord Mayor's house in Cornhill Hans and Rose have a happy reunion and are planning an elopement when Sybil warns them that Sir Roger is at hand. Hans must play the shoemaker to avoid detection. Then a prentice announces the Earl of Lincoln, and while Sir Roger is out of the way for a moment, Rose and Lacy steal off forthwith. Sir Hugh is seeking his nephew, and even as they talk, Sybil hurries in with word that her mistress has just run away with a shoemaker. At first Sir Hugh is amused and Sir Roger angry at this lowly alliance for his daughter, but Sir Hugh then remembers that his nephew once before played Dutch shoemaker—he speaks the language and he knows the trade. After some quibbling with Firk, who has come to deliver shoes and is a past master at wasting time, they learn that Hans and Rose will be married the next morning at St. Faith's Church under Paul's Cross. Actually they are to be married at the Savoy, and Firk knows it.

[*Scene xv*] At last Simon Eyre is Lord Mayor—"By the Lord of Ludgate, it's a mad life to be a Lord Mayor; it's a stirring life, a fine life, a velvet life, a careful life. . . . [And] Lady Madgy, thou hadst never covered thy Saracen's head with this French flap, nor loaden thy bum with this farthingale; . . . Simon Eyre had never walked in a red petticoat, nor wore a chain of gold, but for [his] fine journeyman's Portuguese." Hence, his lordship is only too ready to assist his bully Hans, now Rowland Lacy again, in his wedding. And, because years before, when he was but an apprentice himself, he vowed that if ever

he came to be Mayor of London he would feast them all, "by this beard,
Sim Eyre will be no flincher." Moreover, he has decreed that upon
every Shrove Tuesday at the sound of the pancake bell shoemakers
shall shut up their shops for a holiday:

> *Boys, that day are you free, let masters care,*
> *And prentices shall pray for Simon Eyre.*

[*Scene xvi*] At St. Faith's Church, Rafe is supported by his fellow
shoemakers, and in spite of Hammon's offer of twenty pounds for Jane,
Rafe is reunited with his wife. At the same time, Sir Hugh and Sir
Roger wait in vain for Rowland and Rose, only to learn from Dodger
of their marriage at the Savoy with the support of the Lord Mayor.
They resolve to appeal to the King. And, as the pancake bell rings,
the apprentices celebrate the first "St. Hugh's Holiday."

[*Scenes xvii, xviii, xix*] Having heard so much about the madcap
Mayor of London, the King at last sets out to meet him. In a great new
hall erected for the purpose, the shoemakers are feasting when word
reaches Simon Eyre of His Majesty's proposed visit. Promising Rowland
and Rose that he will gain for them a free pardon, he goes to meet the
King. His Majesty is so delighted with the jolly shoemaker that without question he pardons Lacy's neglect in the wars; in spite of the
accusations of Sir Hugh and Sir Roger, he knights the young man and
approves the marriage. Then he decrees that the new hall erected at
Simon Eyre's cost in Cornhill shall be called *Leadenhall*, because in
digging the foundations for it he found the lead to make the roof,
grants the shoemakers two lawful market days a week to buy and sell
leather in Leadenhall, and goes with Simon to taste the banquet that
stands waiting, where, on this day, the apprentices emptied a hundred
tables five times covered.

THE HONEST WHORE

Part I

WITH THE HUMORS OF THE PATIENT MAN AND THE
LONGING WIFE

(1604)

DRAMATIS PERSONAE

COUNT HIPPOLITO, "a most successful gentleman, [and] as gallant a spirit as any in
Milan, . . . [but] he betrays his youth too grossly to that tyrant melancholy" be-

cause of his devotion to Infelice, daughter of the Duke. "Their love is just, 'tis good," but ancient hatred between the two houses prevents their marriage. Yet Hippolito is a man, "did not [his] enemies' blood boil in his veins, whom [the Duke] would court to be [his] son-in-law."

INFELICE, "a delicate piece," daughter of the Duke of Milan.

GASPARO TREBAZZI, Duke of Milan, opposed to the marriage of Hippolito and Infelice.

BELLAFRONT, a whore, a "little marmoset, . . . [a] good, pretty rogue," who turns honest for love of Hippolito. ("I have heard many honest wenches turn strumpets, . . . but for a harlot to turn honest is one of Hercules' labors!")

CANDIDO, a rich linen draper, "a grave citizen, [and a] patient man, nay, [a] monstrous patient man . . . linked with a waspish shrew. . . . He's so mild, so affable, so suffering, . . . a man in print for all things else save only in this: no tempest can move him. . . . He has no more gall in him than a dove, no more sting than an ant." (" 'Twere sin all women should such husbands have, for every man must then be his wife's slave.")

VIOLA, his wife, who "often beat[s] at the most constant rock of his unshaken patience and . . . long[s] to vex him. . . . Many times [she is] ready to bite off [her] tongue, because it wants that virtue which all women's tongues have, to anger their husbands." ("A woman to long to turn a tame man into a madman, why, the Devil himself was never used so by his dam!")

MATHEO, Hippolito's bosom friend, and "the first [who] gave money for [Bellafront's] soul, . . . [she] was led by [his] temptation to be miserable."

CASTRUCHIO,
SINEZI,
PIORATTO, } gallants, or court "butterflies."
FLUELLO,

BENEDICT, a doctor, friend of Hippolito.

ANSELMO, "a most reverend friar" of Bethlem Monastery.

FUSTIGO, the seafaring brother of Viola, returned to Milan, having "sowed his wild oats."

GEORGE, servant and apprentice to Candido, "the headman; you shall taste him by his tongue; a pretty, tall, prating fellow, with a Tuscalonian beard."

First Apprentice, } "flatcaps" in Candido's shop. ("I tell you here are boys more
Second Apprentice, } tough than bears.")

CORPORAL CRAMBO, } "arrant knaves" employed by Fustigo. ("I would not be
LIEUTENANT POLI, or POH, } the devil to meet Poh.")

ROGER, "a withered, artichoke-faced, . . . panderly sixpenny rascal," servant to Bellafront.

MADONNA FINGERLOCK, a bawd, "Lust's factor, and Damnation's orator! Gossip of Hell!"

A Servant to Hippolito.

The Doctor's Man.

A Porter, a Sweeper, Madmen, Servants, and Attendants.

Setting: Milan and the vicinity in the late sixteenth century.

*"Thou wert yesterday a simple whore, and now th'art a
cunning, coney-catching baggage today."*

In Milan there are in progress three intrigues which eventually in-
tertwine and resolve one another: (*a*) that of Count Hippolito to
marry Infelice, the duke's daughter, in spite of parental opposition;
(*b*) that of the courtesan Bellafront to entangle many lovers; and (*c*)
that of Mistress Viola Candido to vex her patient husband.

[*Scenes i, iii*] As the play opens the love story of Hippolito and
Infelice has apparently already come to an unhappy conclusion, for the
funeral procession of the girl is passing through the streets, and the
frantic young nobleman, restrained by his friend Matheo, is repeatedly
interrupting it in his grief and in his efforts to have one last look at
his beloved. Calmed at last, Hippolito vows to the sceptical Matheo
that every Monday—Infelice's death day—he will avert his eyes so that
they shall not gaze on any female cheek, lock himself in his chamber,
and meditate on nothing but Infelice's end or on a dead man's skull.

Soon after, in her father's palace, Infelice returns to life, for she has
only been under the influence of a sleeping potion administered by her
father's physician to oppose her love for Hippolito, whose family the
duke hates. On recovering from her stupor, Infelice is told that Hippolito
has died, and her father now sends her to the country to Bergamo
to recover from her illness and from the shock of her lover's death. At
the same time he suborns the physician, Doctor Benedict, to remove
Hippolito completely by death.

[*Scenes ii, iv, v, vii*] Meanwhile, Mistress Viola's longing to vex her
patient husband becomes critical. Candido the linen draper is in every
way a model husband; he "has wealth enough and wit enough, [but]
no loss of goods can increase in him a wrinkle; no crabbed language
make his countenance sour; the stubbornness of no servant shake him,
[and he] is so free from anger that many times [his wife is] ready to
bite off [her] tongue, because it wants that virtue which all women's
tongues have, to anger their husbands." The arrival of Viola's brother
Fustigo, however, suggests an opportunity for arousing this "mirror
of patience" that is not to be overlooked. Fustigo is a seafaring man
whom his brother-in-law has never met. Viola puts him up at the
Tortoise and supplies him with money, in return for which he is to
come to the shop and in Candido's presence to "swagger worse than a
lieutenant among fresh-water soldiers, . . . take up wares, but pay
nothing, . . . snatch rings, jewels, or anything," and kiss his sister.

About the same time, some young gallants of the court have also
heard of Candido's imperturbability, and, seeking amusement to pass
the time, lay wagers that they can upset the merchant. Accordingly,

they visit the shop—arriving before Fustigo—make Candido take down his goods, disparage their quality, haggle about the price, and then purchase a pennyworth of lawn, insisting that it be cut, not from the end, but from the middle of the bolt. To the amazement of his customers Candido is unmoved, merely taking refuge in a proverb that

> *he that means to thrive, with patient eye*
> *Must please the Devil if he come to buy!*

He even offers to drink the health of the gentleman who made the purchase. The courtiers drink several rounds, but Candido is a one-drink man who refuses to pledge when another toast is proposed, and one of the gallants in reprisal carries away the silver-gilt beaker from which he had been drinking. Still Candido remains unmoved, but he sends a constable after the jokesters to recover his property. It is his wife who is in a rage at the prank.

When Fustigo arrives at the shop, his conduct is an exaggeration even of that of the courtiers. He swaggers; he treats Mistress Viola with familiarity, calling her "coz," pulling off her wedding ring, and kissing her repeatedly. He disparages and insults the shopkeeper, and he enrages the apprentices by calling them "flatcaps" and making them unnecessary work. Still Candido is unmoved, but the apprentices, after duly warning Fustigo, cudgel him with their clubs and give him a bloody coxcomb. Then Fustigo confesses everything, much to Viola's vexation, and is welcomed cordially by his brother-in-law.

In a little while an officer summons Candido to a meeting at the senate house. In a pique his wife refuses to give him the key to the chest in which his official gown is kept, feeling that "this trick will vex him sure, and fret his heart." But with the help of his senior apprentice George, Candido improvises a substitute from a table cover, puts on a nightcap as if he had just come from a sickbed, and hopes to evade the fine for attending meeting without his gown—still without anger. Hence, Mistress Viola enlists the aid of George the apprentice to help her vex her husband.

[*Scenes vi, viii, ix, x*] Still in search of pastime, the young courtiers visit Bellafront, a handsome, witty, and popular courtesan, sending out for wine to make merry. To the same establishment Matheo brings Hippolito, who has abandoned the court and is still grief-stricken and exceedingly melancholy because of the death of his beloved Infelice. He cannot stand the affected gaiety of the place, and leaves, promising to return in half an hour for Matheo. Bellafront acts capricious and clears the house, so that she is alone when Hippolito returns. But it is no use; Hippolito insists upon constancy in love, and even gives the courtesan a long lecture on the inconstancy, the deceit, the misery of harlots. But so eloquent is he and so charming that Bellafront falls in love with him. He is no sooner gone than she resolves to become pure-honest for his true love, and even prepares to stab herself with the sword he has forgotten and left there. But he returns for his weapon and prevents her desperate suicide. She declares her love for him, yet he is crueler than his sword; he treats her with utter disdain.

Bellafront's conversion to chastity is no passing whim; it lasts. She turns away even the "sweetest, prop'rest, gallantest gentleman, . . . [who] smells all of musk and ambergris, his pocket full of crowns, flame-colored doublet, red satin hose, carnation silk stockings." She astonishes her former clients by lecturing them on chastity and the evils of incontinence; she sends away Matheo, who had been her first lover; she even tries to compose love lyrics to Hippolito. At last she resorts to stratagems.

One day as Hippolito sits in his chamber before a skull, a taper, a book of devotions, and a portrait of Infelice, a messenger disturbs his meditations by bringing a letter and insisting upon delivering it personally. It is Bellafront, disguised as a page. Pointing to Infelice's picture, Hippolito again explains that he cannot love another, and when Bellafront tells him that the guilt will fall on his head should she sin again, the count bids her read his book, ask counsel of his death's-head, and so take physic for temptation. He leaves to meet Doctor Benedict, who has asked to see him.

[*Scenes xi, xii*] His head still smarting from the cudgeling Candido's apprentices gave him, Fustigo hires two ruffians, Crambo and Poli, to avenge him, "blood for blood, bump for bump, nose for nose, head for head, plaster for plaster." Especially does he wish to settle scores with George, the headman, that "voluble-tongued villain."

Meanwhile, in the shop, George and his mistress are awaiting Candido's return from the senate. George has on his master's best apparel—gown, chain, cap, ruff, everything. The junior apprentices have been instructed to keep countenance and to treat their senior fellow as if he were master. Candido takes one look at his shop as he hurries through, but Mistress Viola sees for the first time the fantastic costume her husband has on, and thinks him girt like a madman. Surely he is vexed now; this trick has angered Candido, because he said nothing. But in a moment Candido returns dressed like an apprentice, just as Crambo and Poli arrive. The knaves pretend to shop, drawing the senior apprentice (i.e., Candido) aside and trying to pick a quarrel with him. Failing, they attack him anyway, but the apprentices disarm the rogues and cudgel them soundly. Still Candido remains unperturbed, letting the rascals off without a word. But his wife has gone out for officers to carry her husband to a madhouse:

If this move not his patience, nothing can;
I'll swear then I have a saint, and not a man.

[*Scene xiii*] Having a secret plan of his own, Doctor Benedict meets the duke and assures him that Hippolito has been poisoned, and is repudiated by his employer and banished forever for his pains. But the honest doctor finds the young count, tells him that his Infelice lives, and will meet him in Bethlem Monastery, where they can be married on the morrow.

[*Scene xiv*] Almost immediately repentant at having incarcerated her long-suffering husband, Viola appeals to the duke for his release. But she and George arrive just as His Excellency receives the news that his daughter has escaped from Bergamo and expects to be married to Hippolito that very day. At least the duke is not impossible to vex! He orders his courtiers to go in immediate pursuit.

[*Scene xv*] At Bethlem Monastery the various threads of this story are tied together. The lovers arrive safely, but find that they cannot be married by Friar Anselmo until afternoon; a friend of Hippolito's warns them, however, that their secret is out, and they prepare to escape dressed as friars. The duke and his courtiers come dressed as country gentlemen who wish to see the sights of the madhouse, and are disarmed by Friar Anselmo—for safety's sake. Here her former clients encounter Bellafront, the honest whore, now mad for love. It is she who plucks off the friar's disguise and reveals Hippolito, Infelice, and Matheo to the duke and his friends. But the couple have already been married, and Anselmo begs pardon for being the means of turning "the ancient hates of your two houses to fresh green friendship." Bellafront has only put on her mad disguise to win Hippolito. But, having failed, she instead accepts Matheo, her first lover, whom the duke forces into matrimony. And here, among the lunatics, is Candido the patient man, who knows that he is not mad, that the duke is not mad; indeed, that "none is mad here but one—how do you, wife?"

The Second Part of

THE HONEST WHORE

With the Humors of the Patient Man, the Impatient Wife; the Honest Whore, Persuaded by Strong Arguments to Turn Courtesan Again; Her Brave Refuting Those Arguments, and Lastly, the Comical Passages of an Italian Bridewell

(1604–1605)

DRAMATIS PERSONAE

BELLAFRONT, now completely reformed; "she has been more common than tobacco; this is she that had the name of the Honest Whore; . . . this is she, that, if any of her religion can be saved, was saved by my lord Hippolito."

MATHEO, reckless, unscrupulous, incorrigible husband of Bellafront who flies high. "He riots all abroad, wants all at home; he dices, whores, swaggers, swears, cheats, borrows, pawns," and withal is a malicious "black-mouthed devil." ("This varlet's able to make Lucrece common.")

ORLANDO FRISCOBALDO, father of Bellafront, disguised as PACHECO, a bluecoat serving-man. "When children from duty start, parents from love may swerve."

COUNT HIPPOLITO, husband of Infelice, who converted Bellafront to chastity, and is now "turned ranger. . . . Is't possible the Lord Hippolito, whose face is as civil as the outside of a dedicatory book, should be a muttonmonger?"

INFELICE, daughter of the Duke and wife of Hippolito.

GASPARO TREBAZZI, Duke of Milan.

LODOVICO SFORZA, "a notable-tongued fellow, . . . [who] discourses well, . . . [and] is well valued by my lord."
BERALDO,
CAROLO,
FONTINELL,
ASTOLFO,
}courtiers.

BRYAN, "little St. Patrick," a redheaded Irish footman in the service of Hippolito, who "talk[s] so like a pagan."

ANTONIO GEORGIO, a poor scholar who dedicates a book to Hippolito.

SIGNIOR CANDIDO, "the linen draper, he that's more patient than a brown baker upon the day when he heats his oven and has forty scolds about him."

CANDIDO'S BRIDE, a fine young wife, who soon learns submission and detests to wear the breeches.

LUKE, Candido's apprentice.

LIEUTENANT BOTS, "an arrant knave, . . . one of Fortune's bastards, a soldier and a gentleman," turned pander. ("Oh, an apple-squire!")

MADAM HORSELEECH, a bawd, "burnt [i.e., branded] at fourteen, seven times whipped, six times carted, nine times ducked, searched by some hundred and fifty constables."

DOROTHEA TARGET, ⎫
PENELOPE WHOREHOUND, ⎬ harlots in Bridewell, "past shame, past penitence."
CATHARINA BOUNTINALL, ⎭

Governors and Masters of Bridewell, Constables, Billmen, Beadles, Vintners, Guests, Prentices, and Servants.

Setting: Milan in the late sixteenth century.

> *"To turn a harlot*
> *Honest, it must be by strong antidotes;*
> *'Tis rare as to see panthers change their spots."*

[*Scene i*] Bellafront, the courtesan converted from her mode of life by Hippolito and married to her seducer Matheo, has become the devoted wife of her worthless husband. As the play opens, Bellafront is the bearer of a petition to her husband's friend Hippolito, now happily married to Infelice, the duke's daughter. The petition is on behalf of her husband, who is now in prison for killing a man. Hippolito promises to be the advocate for his friend to the duke, and assures him of pardon. Then, for the first time, he recognizes the petitioner, is struck by her beauty, asks a few perfunctory questions about her father, and suggests that she return to see him again on the morrow.

[*Scene ii*] Next day old Orlando Friscobaldo, father of Bellafront, calls upon Hippolito. He is stoically unconcerned about his daughter, supposing her to be still what she once was. But from the count, who first pretends that the girl is dead, Orlando learns of her poverty and the imprisonment of her husband. Orlando has not seen Bellafront for seventeen years, but deep in his heart there is still a great affection for his erring child. Before the count he is hard; but left alone, he resolves to help the girl, disguises himself in the blue coat of one of his servants, has his beard shaved off, and sets out to seek his daughter.

[*Scene iii*] On the same day, Candido, the patient linen draper, who has lost his first wife, is marrying again. Some of his friends from the court, Lodovico, Carolo, and Astolfo, particularly, wonder whether he is letting himself in for worse trouble than before when he married a shrew, and they visit the merchant's shop during the wedding breakfast to have a glimpse of the bride. Her conduct is not very promising; as Luke the apprentice offers her wine, she strikes him, breaks the glass, and leaves the table in a pique. Candido passes the incident off as a mere mistake and a sign of nervousness, but Lodovico calls him aside to warn him that this wench, his new wife, "will take you down to your wedding shoes, unless you hang her up in her wedding garters."

He offers to assist at the wife-taming, if Candido can fit him with an apprentice's suit.

[*Scene iv*] Meanwhile, Matheo has been set free and has returned home. He is a reckless blackguard, given to dicing and swaggering, and not a whit the better for his experience in jail—except that he is full of good resolutions. Nor would he be averse to seeing Bellafront return to her old way of life, if he could get money for himself by her doing so. The reunion of the couple is interrupted by the knocking of Orlando, disguised as a servant, and presenting himself as Pacheco, who last served Bellafront's father. He asks no wages, but offers his services and gives Matheo twenty pounds—his savings—to keep for him. Soon the Count Hippolito also calls, following a diamond and a letter he had sent before him. But he leaves when he finds Matheo at home, giving Pacheco a handsome tip and a purse for his mistress. Obviously, Hippolito's interest in Bellafront is no longer innocent. The faithful servant gives the purse to the lady at the earliest opportunity, and is forthwith sent to return it, the ring, and the letters Hippolito has written. Obviously, too, Bellafront is over her infatuation for the handsome young nobleman. But ironically, the man who rescued Bellafront from her life of sin now becomes her greatest tempter.

[*Scene v*] Lodovico is as good as his word to Candido. He serves in the linen shop as an apprentice, encourages Candido to cross his wife's whims, and supports him when their differences come to a crisis. But instead of fighting back as expected, the good wife kneels submissively, denies any ambition to wear the breeches, and by so doing wins the day.

[*Scene vi*] To thwart the evil intentions of Hippolito, the old servant Pacheco goes to Infelice and reveals to her her husband's derelictions. Confessing a pretended infidelity herself, Infelice waits until Hippolito denounces her self-righteously before handing him the tokens he had given to Bellafront and returning to him his own words of denunciation. But even though he has been caught, Hippolito resolves to go on with the affair.

[*Scene vii*] In Matheo's household things go from bad to worse. Money is scarce; dicing has taken all the ready cash the ne'er-do-well can raise; his cloak and rapier have already been pawned, and but for Pacheco his doublet had gone too. The honest servant's savings, it is to be feared, have long ago been spent up. To get gold Matheo even pawns his wife's satin gown from off her back. He is not above asking Bellafront to borrow from some of his friends, and he accepts a satin suit from Lodovico. Pacheco tries to protect Bellafront, but she is too dutiful a wife to approve of his efforts. Never was a wife more sorely tempted.

[*Scene viii*] At the linen draper's, too, efforts are being made to seduce a faithful wife. For sport, Carolo, a courtier, offers Mistress Horseleech, a bawd, and Bots, a pander, twenty crowns for an assignation with the bride. But the good wife scorns the pander who proposes it. At the same time the young gallants of the town, having nothing better to do, try Candido's patience yet again. With Bryan, Hippolito's Irish footman, they price cambric, but Candido cannot understand Bryan's brogue, and in anger the Irishman tears the cambric in two. But the patient Candido simply remarks that there is always a call for remnants at his shop, and thanks his customers for their patronage.

[*Scene ix*] Meanwhile, Matheo struts about in the new suit for which Lodovico has provided the satin. The tailor is still unpaid for making it, and there is little to live upon. It is then that Orlando, no longer in disguise, visits his daughter, who is meekly submissive to the stern old man and does what she can to curb her husband's disrespectful tongue. Orlando has come to rebuke his son-in-law for his prodigality, to accuse him of harboring an old servant of his (Pacheco), and to charge them both with having robbed two poor country peddlers (really Orlando's servants in disguise). But Matheo defiantly brazens it out, even during the heated denunciation urging his wife to kneel to her old father and beg money from him. When Bellafront does do so, it is all that the broken-hearted old man can do to remain implacable and seem indifferent to her poverty. After Orlando has gone, and Bellafront brings her husband food which has been given to her by the neighbors, Matheo calls her whore, accuses her of begging, and threatens to beat her with a stool. She is protected only by the return of old Orlando, who has resumed his disguise of Pacheco. Surely no woman had greater provocation to return to a life of sin.

Shortly after Matheo and Pacheco leave the house for the avowed purpose of robbing old Orlando, Hippolito returns and tries to seduce Bellafront again. As convincingly as he had once argued against harlotry and incontinence, he now argues for them, but Bellafront stoutly resists his blandishments and flees from her tempter.

[*Scene x*] Instead of meeting Matheo as agreed, the disguised Pacheco goes instead to the duke to secure assistance in reclaiming his daughter's feckless husband. The duke penetrates Orlando's disguise, and sends Lodovico along with him to serve a warrant against Matheo and at the same time to apprehend all suspected persons in his house. In addition, in the hope of shaming his own son-in-law and of reclaiming him, the duke orders the purging of the city of all women known to be light. If the law will not frighten Hippolito, perhaps his love for the girl will prevent his subjecting her to such jeopardy.

[*Scene xi*] When the officers arrive at Matheo's to arrest him and his man for robbery, they find the house full. Several courtiers have dropped in, so have Bots the pander and Mistress Horseleech the bawd, and there is even Candido the linen draper. This respectable citizen has come to see some pieces of lawn, which now are shown to be stolen goods. A temperate man, he has been obliged while there to drink the health of bawds; now he must go along to Bridewell.

[*Scene xii*] Seeing Hippolito in the street, Lodovico tells the count that Bellafront has been arrested and sits in Bridewell, wearing the blue gown of penance. The young count is outraged at this injustice and resolves to go to her immediately.

[*Scene xiii*] At Bridewell all of the loose threads of this story are brought together. Several of the governors serve as guides to the duke, Infelice, and a party of courtiers who pay the institution a visit. Bellafront appears to plead for her husband. The shameless Matheo accuses her of infidelity with his friend Hippolito. The count defends his own innocence and hers, and Pacheco throws off his disguise to corroborate their honesty. In spite of Matheo's lies and mistreatment, like a dutiful wife Bellafront forgives her husband; Orlando gives the couple his blessing; and Matheo is warned to mend his ways. Even Candido is little the worse for the practical joke which has been played upon him. Still unruffled, he reasons:

> *I was in Bedlam once, but was I mad?*
> *. . . am I bad because I'm with bad people?*

Only Bots is punished; too many of Bridewell's incorrigible inmates identify him, and he is sentenced first to whipping and then to banishment.

BEN JONSON
(1572–1637)

BIOGRAPHY. The posthumous son of a minister of Scottish origin, Ben Jonson was born in Westminster and attended Westminster School under William Camden, the famous antiquary. Unfortunately, he never enrolled at either university, but "he was Master of Arts in both, . . . by their favor not his study." For a time he may have followed his stepfather's occupation of bricklaying—something his enemies never permitted him to forget—but if so he soon escaped to the wars in the Low Countries, distinguishing himself by killing an enemy in single combat between the lines. By 1597 his connection with the stage had begun, and he was writing and acting for Henslowe at the Rose. In the same year he was imprisoned for his share in an outrageous satire, *The Isle of Dogs;* and in 1598 he killed Gabriel Spencer, a fellow actor, in a duel, for which he was again imprisoned—escaping the death penalty only by the plea of benefit of clergy. After 1600 he wrote for various companies, including the Chapel Children, participated in the notorious Stage Quarrel (1600–2), and after 1605 became famous at court for his masques. In 1612–13 he visited France as the tutor to the son of Sir Walter Raleigh, then a prisoner in the Tower; the youth was knavishly inclined, made his tutor drunk, and carted him about Paris to the accompaniment of lewd remarks. At least such is the story Jonson told on himself when he took a walking tour to the North in 1619 and visited Drummond of Hawthornden. In 1625 at the death of James I, Jonson resumed playwriting, which he had dropped in 1616; in 1631 he quarreled with Inigo Jones, the architect who designed the sets for his masques at court. In 1637 he died.

CRITICAL COMMENT. Ben Jonson is without rival as a dramatic satirist, an observer of human weaknesses, and a manipulator of ingenious, complicated plots. There is hardly a folly, an affectation, or a fraud of his day upon which he does not wield his lash of steel. His comedies are so many social documents, and his skill in play architecture is amazing. As a result, Jonson was the inspiration of English comic writers for more than two centuries. But his appeal is to the head rather than the heart; we admire Jonson, but we love Shakespeare.

Every Man in His Humor was an innovation in its day, no romantic fancy, but a racy comedy of contemporary life. It is the first comedy in the language written in accord with a critical theory, and it is the first comedy of *humors.* As he explains in his Prologue to the play, Jonson believed comedy should be a realistic

> *image of the times*
> *And sport with human follies not with crimes.*

In his Induction to *Every Man Out of His Humor* he explained his conception of comic caricature:

> *As when some one peculiar quality*
> *Doth so possess a man, that it doth draw*
> *All his affects, his spirits, and his powers,*
> *In their confluctions all to run one way,*
> *This may be said to be a humor.*

Jonson's comic theory, therefore, is allied to both the morality tradition and classical example. His characters are types actuated by some dominating trait and tagged by suitable names; the situations are drawn from the conventions of Roman comedy—intrigues of mistaken identity and disguise involving the deceived father and the sporting son, the clever guileful servant, the jealous husband, the braggart captain, the gull, the would-be wit, and a clandestine marriage. *Every Man in His Humor* had a long and honorable career on the stage. Kitely was one of David Garrick's famous roles, and Charles Dickens played Captain Bobadill in amateur performances.

Sejanus, just as surely, represents Jonson's conception of tragedy, which, as he explained in an address "To the Readers" of the printed play, he conceived of as consisting of "truth of argument, dignity of persons, gravity and height of elocution, fullness and frequency of sentence." But the play failed on the stage; the characters were not diversified and were too many in number, and action was lacking.

In *Volpone* Jonson abandoned his earlier theories. Vice rather than mere folly is his subject now, and he does not sport with it; he castigates it savagely. The baseness of human nature, not mere eccentricity is what he lays bare—avarice, love of power, lust, pride, cunning, deceit, credulity. To this end he creates a whole animal world, the characters of which are labelled with names from the old beast epic. Only Sir Politic Would-be and his Lady are survivors from the old comedy of humors. *Volpone,* therefore, is the least realistic of Jonson's plays, but its plot is one of his best, and in Mosca and Volpone himself the author has created two virtuosos in rascality unsurpassed on the stage. The play was originally performed by the King's Men at the Globe and at both Universities. It was performed frequently throughout the seventeenth, eighteenth, and even nineteenth centuries, and an adaptation had considerable success in Germany, France, and the United States in the twentieth. It was produced by the Theatre Guild in New York with Alfred Lunt and Lynn Fontaine in 1928, and by the Actors' Laboratory in Hollywood in 1945.

Epicoene, Jonson's gayest comedy, is a kind of Elizabethan *Charley's Aunt,* a riotous combination of farce, comedy of humors, and comedy of manners, singled out for especial analysis and praise by Dryden in his *Essay of Dramatic Poesy* (1668). This play, too, has held the stage in modern times.

From Jonson's point of view, *The Alchemist* is the most nearly perfect example of his kind of comedy. Its plot has been described by Coleridge as one of the three finest ever devised by the mind of man (*Oedipus the King* and *Tom Jones* being the other two); certainly it is a marvel of ingenuity. The characterization is brilliant and diversified. The dialogue is lively, and everything moves at a breathless pace, as the weakness of each of the dupes is played upon. The play is still satirical, but unlike *Volpone* its concern is not seriously with fundamental defects in human nature. Rather it is with the gullibility of the lazy few who lack common sense and who seek a short cut to their heart's desires by charlatanism and quackery. As a result *The Alchemist* is one of the most brilliant comedies of manners in English. One of Garrick's famous vehicles was an adaptation which made the role of Abel Drugger the star part. He also played Face.

Bartholomew Fair, the last of Jonson's great comedies, is one of the rowdiest, noisiest, most Rabelaisian dramas in the language, with a whole gallery of Hogarthian rogues, hypocrites, and fools. It is a vivid and striking presentation of the life of the Fair; the author literally takes his reader to a circus—side shows and all.

The Staple of News, written after Jonson's nine years' absence from the theatre, is nevertheless an effective satire with two main themes: (*a*) money worship, the use and abuse of riches, and the extravagance, folly, and intriguing which wealth and the desire for it often entail; and (b) the public appetite for gossip of all sorts, and the credulity which made possible the new journalism embodied in the first English newspapers: *Weekly News* (1622), *Mercurius Britannicus* (1625), and similar pamphlets, published by Nathaniel Butter and others. The "news staple" of this play is an early seventeenth-century news exchange—a kind of Reuters or Associated Press—for the collection and dissemination of news and gossip—"authentical and apocryphal." Needless to say, the enterprising proprietors of even the first newssheets were not altogether such unreliable, unprincipled exploiters of public gullibility as tinkling Cymbal and Nathaniel the butterman in Jonson's play. (But see also Fletcher's *Fair Maid of the Inn,* 1626, which likewise satirizes the new journalism.)

SOURCES. For *Every Man in His Humor* no specific source has been found, but its adaptations of the conventions of Roman comedy to contemporary English life are apparent. *Sejanus,* on the other hand, is heavily documented from Tacitus, Dion Cassius, and other Roman authors. *Volpone* is as original as Jonson could be, but it is based upon the game of legacy-hunting which is satirized in many books from Lucian's *Dialogues* to Erasmus' *Praise of Folly.* *Epicoene* is a composite of the *Casina* of Plautus, which introduces a boy-bride, and the Sixth Declamation of Libanius, a Greek author of the fourth century of the Christian era, where Morosus suffers from a talkative wife. The dialogue of the play echoes many classical authors. *The Alchemist* likewise is a composite of disparate sources—the *Mostellaria* of Plautus, which may have suggested the deserted house used by rogues for their practices, the quarrel scene which opens the play, and the unexpected return of the master of the house; Erasmus' *De Alcumista,* Ariosto, and perhaps even Giordano Bruno's *Il Candelaio* (1582), which has a similar theme. The play may also contain thinly veiled allusions to well-known London quacks of the time; Subtle may be a satirical portrait of Dr. Simon Forman, disreputable physician, astrologer, and necromancer of the time. *Bartholomew Fair* has no source but the Fair itself and the human types who frequented it. *The Staple of News* is a patchwork. The central theme of money-worship is based upon Aristophanes' *Plutus,* but there are echoes from other classical authors, as well as from Jonson's own earlier work, notably *Cynthia's Revels* (1601), where Lady Argurion also personifies money, and several of his masques, one of which, *News from the New World* (1621), contains a news staple. More important is *The London Prodigal,* a play of unknown authorship once attributed to Shakespeare, which contains characters like the three Pennyboys, and a father who pretends to be dead in order that he may reclaim a spendthrift son. Jonson may have had a hand in writing this play; certainly it was piratically printed for Nathaniel Butter in 1605. Hence, in his very choice of source, Jonson was dredging up an old shady business scandal in which the butt of his satire had been involved twenty years before.

BIBLIOGRAPHY

Collected Works:

The Works of Ben Jonson, edited by C. H. Herford and Percy Simpson, 10 volumes, 1925-51 (to be completed in 11).

The Best Plays of Ben Jonson, edited by B. Nicholson and C. H. Herford, 3 volumes, Mermaid Series, 1893–94.

Monographs:

C. H. Herford and Percy Simpson, *Ben Jonson: The Man and His Work,* 2 volumes, 1925.

M. Castelain, *Ben Jonson, l'homme et l'œuvre,* Paris, 1907.

C. R. Baskervill, *English Elements in Jonson's Early Comedy,* University of Texas Bulletin, 1911.

R. G. Noyes, *Ben Jonson on the English Stage, 1660–1776,* 1935.

Esther C. Dunn, *Ben Jonson's Art: Elizabethan Life and Literature Reflected Therein,* Smith College Publications, 1925.

Every Man in His Humor:

Early editions: 1601 [with a Florentine setting and an Italian dramatis personae]; 1616 [First Folio, revised and Anglicized]; 1640 and 1692 [in collected works].

Modern editions: 1601 quarto, W. Bang and W. W. Greg (Materialen zur Kunde des älteren englischen Dramas, 1905); W. M. Dixon (TD, 1901, Folio text); H. H. Clark (Yale Studies, 1921, both texts).

Sejanus:

Early editions: 1605; 1616, 1640, 1692 [in collected works].

Modern edition: ed. W. D. Briggs (Belles Lettres Series, 1911).

Volpone:

Early editions: 1607 (2); 1616, 1640, 1692 [in collected works].

Modern editions: ed. Henry de Vocht (quarto text, Bang's Materialen, n.s., 1935); J. D. Rea (folio text, Yale Studies, 1919).

Epicoene:

Early editions: 1616 [First Folio; there may have been printings in 1609 and 1612]; 1620 (2); 1640 and 1692 [in collected works].

Modern edition: ed. A. Henry (Yale Studies, 1906).

The Alchemist:

Early editions: 1612; 1616, 1640, 1692 [in collected works].

Modern editions: Facs. Noel Douglas Replicas (1927); ed. C. M. Hathaway (Yale Studies, 1903); F. E. Schelling (Belles Lettres Series, 1903).

Bartholomew Fair:

Early editions: 1631 [really a part of the Second Folio of 1640]; 1692 [Third Folio].

Modern edition: ed. C. S. Alden (Yale Studies, 1904).

The Staple of News:

Early editions: 1631 [really a part of the Second Folio of 1640]; 1692 [Third Folio].

Modern edition: ed. De Winter (Yale Studies, 1905).

$\mathcal{E}VE\mathcal{R}Y$ $\mathcal{M}A\mathcal{N}$ $I\mathcal{N}$ HIS $HU\mathcal{M}OR$

A Comedy

(1598)

DRAMATIS PERSONAE

EDWARD KNOWELL SENIOR, a "hoary-headed" old gentleman, "of a thousand a year, Middlesex land."

BRAINWORM, "a successful merry knave," and contriver of intrigues, old Knowell's man, but more loyal to the son.

EDWARD KNOWELL JUNIOR, "a handsome young gentleman . . . of an exceeding fair disposition, and of very excellent good parts."

GEORGE DOWNRIGHT, a plain squire; "he is of a rustical cut, I know not how, he doth not carry himself like a gentleman of fashion," and thinks his brother Wellbred's Bohemian companions "a sort of lewd rakehells that care neither for God nor the Devil."

WELLBRED, his half brother, "a young gentleman, . . . Master Kitely married his sister." Harmless himself, he makes Kitely's house "common as a mart, a theatre, a public receptacle for giddy humor and diseaséd riot. . . . Counsel to him is as good as a shoulder of mutton to a sick horse."

CAPTAIN BOBADILL, "a Paul's man" [i.e., a lounger around St. Paul's] who lodges with Cob, "that rogue, that foist, that fencing Burgullion, . . . [that] bragging coistrel! . . . O, he swears admirably! 'By Pharoah's foot!' 'Body of Caesar!' I shall never do it, sure. . . . No, I ha' not the right grace. . . . O manners! That this age should bring forth such creatures! That Nature should be at leisure to make hem!"

MASTER MATTHEW, the town gull, who "think[s] himself poet-major o' the town," in love with Mistress Bridget, "and there he will sit you a whole afternoon sometimes, reading of these . . . abominable, vile, . . . rascally verses, 'poyetry,' 'poyetry,' . . . And the wenches they do so jeer and tee-hee at him." But his is "the pocket muse; . . . body o' me, he carries a whole realm, a commonwealth of paper, in's hose, . . . [and his verses are nothing but] stolen remnants, . . . [or parodies], with a kind of miraculous gift to make it absurder than it was!"

Wellbred's "two hangbys, . . . [his] wind instruments."

MASTER STEPHEN, a country gull, nephew to old Knowell, "a prodigal, absurd coxcomb . . . [who seeks] to make a blaze of gentry to the world; . . . he is stupidity itself. . . . 'Slight, he shakes his head like a bottle to feel an there be any brain in it!' "

KITELY, "the rich merchant i' the Old Jewry," lately married. His "house is so stored with jealousy there is no room for love to stand upright in." But "horns i' the mind are worse than o' the head."

DAME KITELY, his equally suspicious wife, sister to Downright and Wellbred.

MISTRESS BRIDGET, "a maid of good government and much modesty," sister to Kitely and dwelling in his house.

THOMAS CASH, Kitely's trusted cashier, "a toward imp; . . . he's no Precisian, that I am certain of; . . . he'll play at fayles and ticktack; I have heard him swear."

OLIVER COB, "a water-bearer that dwells by the Wall, . . . [of] an ancient lineage and a princely, . . . herring, the king of fish, . . . one o' the monarchs o' the world."

TIB, his wife.

JUSTICE CLEMENT, "a City magistrate, a justice here, an excellent good lawyer, and a great scholar, but the only mad, merry old fellow in Europe; . . . they say he will commit a man for taking the wall of his horse, . . . [but] the honestest old brave Trojan in London; I do honor the very flea of his dog." He resolves the intrigues.

ROGER FORMAL, his clerk.

Servants.

Setting: Knowell's House, Cob's House by the Wall, Kitely's Shop in the Old Jewry, Moorfields, the Windmill Tavern, Clement's House in Coleman Street, and the Streets of London in the sixteenth century.

"Deeds and language such as men do use,
And persons such as Comedy would choose,
When she would show an image of the times,
And sport with human follies, not with crimes."

Act I

Old Edward Knowell, gentleman of London, has a son, Edward, who is quiet, civil in demeanor, and studious; indeed, "a scholar, if a man may trust the liberal voice of fame in her report, of good accompt in both our Universities, either of which hath favored him with graces [i.e., degrees]." His absurd nephew, Stephen, on the other hand, cares for nothing but hawking and hunting, and, like a prodigal, spends his coin on every bauble and melts away himself in flashing bravery just "to make a blaze of gentry to the world." Young Edward, however, has one shortcoming—if indeed it may seriously be thought a flaw—he dreams "on naught but idle poetry, that fruitless and unprofitable art, good unto none, but least to the professors." Old Knowell himself had had this very failing when a youth, but since then time and truth have waked his judgment, and reason taught him better to distinguish vain from useful learning.

One day, by mistake, the old man intercepts a letter written to his son by one Master Wellbred, whom young Edward had idolized "for the happiest wit, the choicest brain the times hath sent us forth." Overcome by curiosity, Old Knowell breaks the seal—"be it but for the style's sake and the phrase." He finds wit enough, but also some disparaging allusions to himself, and an invitation to the Windmill

Tavern in the Old Jewry, the whole couched in such terms that the old father is instantly suspicious that young Edward is consorting with gamesters, dissolute fellows, and worse. Old Knowell resolves to take no extreme measures; he will not prevent his son's going to the Windmill, but gradually win him back to virtue.

The ever-vigilant Brainworm, however, reveals to his young master the fact that his letter has been opened, and when young Edward reads it with great amusement, he has a pretty shrewd guess as to what his parent thought of it. He takes his cousin Stephen with him to the Windmill; a man of parts, carriage, and estimation—a miracle of nature—like him, may "do well for a suburb humor" and add to the sport.

Meanwhile, Master Matthew, melancholy poetaster and fishmonger's son who creeps and wriggles "into acquaintance of all the brave gallants about the town," seeks out at his lodging with Cob the water-bearer one Captain Bobadill, gentleman, literary critic and fencer extraordinary, swearer of dainty oaths, and drinker of "this same filthy, roguish tobacco." Already Matthew has had a brush with Squire Downright, Wellbred's half brother from the country, apparently a man who does not suffer fools gladly. Downright has threatened to cudgel Matthew, —to give him the *bastinado,* as Matthew prefers to term it for more grace—and now Captain Bobadill does not find Matthew at all a promising practitioner of fencing, as they make ready to call upon their friend, young Wellbred.

Act II

Young Wellbred, it appears, is no more in the graces of his brother-in-law Kitely, with whom he lives, than of his elder brother Downright. Kitely complains that he has greatly changed from what he was when first he came to town. He now follows loose, irregular courses, is disrespectful and inconsiderate of others, and, what is worse, turns the house into a tavern or a stews with his wild associates, repeating lascivious jests, swearing, drinking, and reveling by night. The two men agree that there is no use in talking to him, and their sober conference is interrupted by the appearance of Master Matthew and Captain Bobadill, two of Wellbred's comrades come to seek him. Downright is all for letting his younger brother hear about his riotous courses, but he is persuaded by Kitely to go about it in a milder, gentler, more subtle way. Kitely's fears, it becomes clear, are for his wife and sister. Where there is such a resort of wanton gallants and revelers, how can any woman remain honest long? To put it more specifically, Kitely, who is no longer young and but lately married to a young wife, is afraid he will be made cuckold. Indeed, the suspicion is already planted in his mind.

Meanwhile, Brainworm appears on Moorfields disguised as a disabled veteran of the wars. To curry favor with Young Knowell he hopes somehow to intercept his old master in his journey to the Windmill. The rascal first meets young Edward and Master Stephen, very skillfully gets their sympathy with his long story of his hardships, and, in spite of Edward's caution, sells Stephen a sword which he represents as "a most pure Toledo." Later, Brainworm meets the elder Knowell, whose mind is filled with how youth has declined in manners and breeding since he was a young man. Brainworm gives his name as Fitzsword, receives a lecture against begging, but in the end succeeds even better with the elder Knowell than with his son— he is engaged as a servant by the old man, with opportunities for knavish mischief that are unlimited.

Act III

At the Windmill Wellbred, Matthew, and Bobadill are joined by Young Knowell and Stephen, and the two gentlemen thoroughly enjoy the affectations and the melancholy of the would-be wit, the braggart, and the ape of fashionable folly. Among other things, Captain Bobadill proves the blade which Stephen has just bought from the soldier no Toledo, but "a poor provant [i.e., strictly G. I.] rapier, no better," and Stephen is so out of patience that he "could eat the very hilts for anger." When, by miracle, the old soldier puts in his appearance, is faced with his knavery, and confesses his deception blandly, poor Stephen is at a complete nonplus. Secretly, however, Brainworm reveals himself to Young Knowell, explains his disguise, and warns him that the father is following the son and has only stopped for a moment at Justice Clement's house in Coleman Street. Taking Brainworm with them, the young men resolve not to be outstripped by one old plodding brain.

Meanwhile, Kitely's suspicions grow; he resolves to trust Cash, his man, with his secret, then thinks better of it; decides to postpone an errand, and then thinks better of that, too; and at last leaves word that he is to be sent for to the Exchange or to Justice Clement's in Coleman Street, in case Wellbred should bring any gentlemen home with him before Kitely gets back. As he goes out he passes Cob the water-bearer, grumbling about Ember days, Fridays, fasting days, and their ruination of fish. Soon Wellbred and his party from the Windmill make their appearance, and Cash seeks someone to send for Kitely. In the general hubbub of loud talk and the filling of tobacco pipes, Cash at last commissions Cob for the errand. But Cob, who dislikes tobacco, gets into an altercation with Bobadill over smoking and is cudgelled, while Stephen, in admiration, learns the art of swearing from the braggart captain. Cob finds Kitely at Justice Clement's, and the jealous merchant hurries home, but Cob seizes the opportunity while he is at the law-yer's of taking out a warrant binding Captain Bobadill to keep the peace. Learning that the trouble arose over Cob's speaking against tobacco, the merry old Justice pretends to be a lover of the weed, and orders the plaintiff forthwith to jail. But after he has frightened Cob, the old fellow lets him go and grants his petition. In the same way he is inclined to think his friend Knowell, still waiting for the return of his soldier-servant, over serious about his young son and worried with-out reason.

Act IV

At Kitely's, Squire Downright has been speaking his mind to his sister Dame Kitely about her young brother's friends, and when Master Matthew, who is in love with Mistress Bridget, begins to read verses to his sweetheart, the good squire leaves the room in disgust. But Mat-thew's poetry is a particular delight to Wellbred and Young Knowell, who recognize it as plagiarized—"he utters nothing but stolen rem-nants. . . . And from the dead! It's worse than sacrilege." Wellbred teases his sister Bridget about her poetical lover, and even wonders pleasantly why his sister Kitely doesn't get herself a servant that can rhyme and do tricks, too. This is too much for Downright, who has no sense of humor whatever; he denounces the crowd; swords are drawn, and a fight is averted only by the intercession of Cash and the servants, and by old Kitely himself. The young men withdraw, but the two women protest to the stern Downright and Kitely against such treatment of Wellbred's friends, praising especially the appearance and the deportment of Young Knowell. Kitely's suspicions are confirmed; this handsome young gentleman is his wife's lover.

Meanwhile, the counterintrigue begins to operate. Back at the Windmill Young Knowell confesses to Wellbred the love he has con-ceived for Bridget, and has his friend's promise of his best offices. "Fitzsword" at last returns to Justice Clement's for Old Knowell, with a breathless story of a feast at which there were many rich merchants' and brave citizens' wives, with one of whom Young Knowell made an appointment to meet at Cob's house by the Wall. The father hastens away to prevent the rendezvous, and "Fitzsword" turns his attention to Formal, the lawyer's clerk, on whose invitation he goes back to the Windmill for "a cup of neat grist, as we call it." Cob also has had his warrant served upon Captain Bobadill, but being bound to keep the peace does not protect the braggart from a beating when he and Matthew meet Downright in the street. But in his anger, Downright drops his handsome cloak, and, in spite of warning from Young Knowell that it will be challenged, Stephen picks it up and wears it. Kitely the merchant becomes more and more suspicious, until he is sure he is in danger of poisoning by his wife. Successful at the Windmill, Brainworm, dressed in Formal's clothes, comes to call Kitely away so that Wellbred can send word to Young Knowell to meet him and Bridget at the Tower, where they can be married without delay. As he hurries away he calls for Cob to stand sentinel, and the wag Wellbred assures his sister that Cob's wife is a bawd, and that Kitely frequently goes to her house. Dame Kitely hurries away to apprehend her husband. When Kitely returns from a false errand and learns that his wife has gone to Cob's, he is beside himself.

At Cob's, Knowell, Dame Kitely, and Kitely meet. But none finds what he seeks. There are recriminations every way, and all go to Justice Clement's to settle the matter. Disgraced by their beating, Matthew and Bobadill also decide to resort to the law. They pawn a jewel and a pair of silk stockings to the lawyer's man (Brainworm in disguise) for a writ against Downright, whom they identify by his silk russet cloak, laid with russet lace. Then, having pawned Formal's clothes to procure a sergeant's gown, Brainworm goes with Matthew and Bobadill to serve their warrant. They encounter Stephen in Downright's cloak, but soon correct their error, meet Downright himself, and leave poor Stephen arrested at the squire's suit. He can hardly hang because he appropriated the cloak; it is but a whipping matter, sure!

Act V

At Justice Clement's house all of the entanglements are loosed. The good-natured old judge listens patiently to the complaints of Old Knowell, Kitely, Dame Kitely, Cob, Tib, Bobadill, Matthew, Downright, and Stephen. It soon appears that all have been fooled most grossly, that the warrants served the squire and the gull haven't even been signed. Clement threatens the sergeant with jail, and Brainworm reveals himself, confesses all his peccadilloes, and tells of the elopement of Young Knowell and Mistress Bridget. Even Formal turns up, apologetic and clad only in the rusty armor left him by the ill company into which he had fallen by chance. The bogus poet and the braggart soldier are exposed. The young lovers are forgiven. Then the merry old Justice sentences Brainworm—in a cup of sack. "Pledge me. Thou hast done, or assisted to, nothing, in my judgment, but deserves to be pardoned for the wit, o' the offense. If thy master, or any man here, be angry with thee,

I shall suspect his ingine [i.e., wit], while I know him, for't." All retire
to supper, to dedicate the night to friendship, love, and laughter.

SEJANUS, HIS FALL

A TRAGEDY

(1603)

DRAMATIS PERSONAE

THE ROMAN EMPEROR, "scarce-seen TIBERIUS, . . . dull heavy Caesar, . . . [a man
of] cunning and fine words, . . . an emperor only in his lusts," but still the Emperor, "howe'er he hath forgone the dignity and power. . . . If this man had
but a mind allied unto his words, how blessed a fate were it to us, and Rome!
. . . His grace is merely but lip-good; . . . he permits himself be carried like a
pitcher by the ears to every act of vice."

AELIUS SEJANUS, a Roman of "obscure and almost unknown gentry, . . . [now be-
come] court god, . . . well applied with sacrifice of knees, of crooks, and cringe;
. . . Rome, senate, people, all the world have seen Jove but [his] equal, Caesar
but [his] second." ("This Sejanus, trust my divining soul, hath plots on all; no tree
that stops his prospect but must fall.")

SERTORIUS MACRO, the Emperor's organ in the overthrow of Sejanus, "though none
less apt for trust; need doth allow what choice would not. He hath a spirit too
working to be used but to th' encounter of his like."

DRUSUS SENIOR, "th'Emperor's son, . . . a riotous youth, . . . [but an] excellent
brave prince, . . . [who] bears himself each day more nobly than other, and wins
no less on men's affections than doth the father lose, . . . chiefly for opposing to
Sejanus."

AGRIPPINA, noble, high-minded widow of Germanicus, and a "male-spirited dame."

NERO,
DRUSUS JUNIOR, "the noble issue of Germanicus" and grandnephews of Tiberius. "Ger-
CALIGULA, manicus lives in their looks, their gait, their form, t'upbraid us with
his close death, if not revenge the same. . . . The youths are of themselves hot, violent, full of great thought."

LUCIUS ARRUNTIUS, an old man of "frank tongue; . . .
he only talks,"

CAIUS SILIUS, "the most of mark, . . . in power and
reputation equal strong,"

TITIUS SABINUS, "so white, so full of years," a one-   principal opponents of
time "follower of Germanicus, and still . . . an   Sejanus, "that discontented
observer of his wife and children, though they   list . . . [who] want the fine
be declined in grace,"   arts . . . should make [them]

MARCUS LEPIDUS, "grave and honest, [and of] mod-   graced or favored of the
eration still in all his censures,"   times."

CREMUTIUS CORDUS, "a most tart and bitter spirit, . . .
that has writ annals of late, . . . and very well,"

ASINIUS GALLUS, not trusted by Tiberius, "howe'er he
flatters,"

REGULUS, a consul and "no friend unto Sejanus."

SOSIA, wife of Caius Silius, "bold and free of speech," loyal to Agrippina; "she hath a fury in her breast more than Hell ever knew."

GRACINUS LACO, provost of the watch; "he hath the voice to be an honest Roman," though no factionary.

LATIARIS, a senator, "the spy, the reverend spy," of Sejanus.

VARRO, a splenetic consul of Sejanus' faction; formal accuser of Caius Silius before the senate.

DOMITIUS AFER, "the orator! One that hath phrases, figures, and fine flowers to strew his rhetoric with, and doth make haste to get him note or name by any offer where blood or gain be objects."

SATRIUS SECUNDUS, } "two of Sejanus' bloodhounds," and accusers of Cordus. "There
PINNARIUS NATTA,   } be two know more than honest counsels. . . . These can lie, flat-
                   } ter and swear, foreswear, deprave, inform, smile, and betray; . . .
                   } cut men's throats with whisp'rings."

RUFUS,   } hopeful agents of Latiaris in spying on Sabinus.
OPSIUS, }

LIVIA, light wife of Drusus Senior, seduced by Sejanus.

EUDEMUS, physician to Livia.

MARCUS TERENTIUS, }
COTTA,   }
HATERIUS,   }
SANQUINIUS,   } flatterers, "sponges," or "officious friends" of Sejanus.
POMPONIUS,   }
JULIUS POSTHUMUS, }
MINUTIUS,   }
FULCINUS TRIO, a consul, }

A Messenger who brings news of the horrible sequel to Sejanus' death.

Tribuni, Praecones [public criers], a Flamen [priest], Tubicines [trumpeters], Lictores, Ministri [servitors], Tibicines [flute-players], and Attendants.

Setting: Rome, 23–31 A.D.

*"O violent change,
And whirl of men's affections!"*

Act I

Aelius Sejanus, a Roman of obscure parentage who was once a serving boy and worse, is much in favor with Tiberius Caesar, the Emperor. So completely has this ambitious upstart won the Emperor by his flattery, that he has risen "to the highest and most conspicuous point of greatness; . . . [he is] the partner of the empire—hath his image reared equal with Tiberius, borne in ensigns; commands, disposes every dignity. Centurions, tribunes, heads of provinces, praetors, and consuls, all that heretofore Rome's general suffrage gave, is now his [for] sale." So unscrupulous is he that through her physician Eudemus, Sejanus plans to seduce the beautiful but light Livia, wife of Drusus Senior, son of the Emperor. Hence, because of Sejanus' insatiable ambition, "men murmur at his greatness, and the nobles stick not, in public, to upbraid [his] climbing." Chief among these are the senators Lucius Arruntius, Caius Silius, and Titius Sabinus, but especially Drusus Senior. One day after the Emperor has approved a proposal to erect Sejanus' statue in Pompey's theatre, and Sejanus flaunts his power in the streets, Drusus can bear him no longer and strikes Sejanus in the face.

Act II

Partly to avenge this disgrace, and partly to remove opposition to his love for Livia, Sejanus plots with the lady, her physician Eudemus, and one Lygdus, a eunuch who serves as cupbearer, to poison Drusus. Further to clear the way, Sejanus divorces his wife Apicata, but these are only the beginnings of "a race of wicked acts" which flow out of his anger and ambition, and which he hopes will lead to empire. By flattery and insinuation he plants suspicions in the mind of Tiberius against other obstacles in his way to the throne—the widow Agrippina; "her proud race," the sons of Germanicus; and their supporting friends, Silius, Sabinus, Arruntius, Gallus, Regulus, and others, who frequently attend banquets at Agrippina's house and talk of the virtues of her dead husband. To further these ends, Sejanus enlists the aid of Augusta, the Emperor's mother, to repeat malicious gossip in her son's ear. He even plants his spies, Satrius and Natta, in Agrippina's very house, to inquire out secrets and report to him. Meanwhile, Sejanus' faction multiplies, and the first of the obstacles to the crown is removed. Drusus Senior dies, and it begins to be clear that Sejanus has other plots—"no tree that stops his prospect but must fall."

Act III

Still unsuspecting, at Drusus' death the Emperor Tiberius asks the senate to undertake the guardianship of the young princes, Nero and Drusus Junior, and as a body to take the place of their uncle whose wards they were. At the same meeting of the senate Sejanus strikes his next blows, by having the most powerful of his opponents, Caius Silius and Cremutius Cordus, arrested on trumped up charges. Silius, publicly accused by the consul Varro and the orator Afer, Sejanus' creatures, is declared guilty of fomenting war in Gaul and dragging it out for his own personal profit, as well as making censorious and boastful remarks at Agrippina's table. The charges are all a lie, but, realizing that he will

not get a fair trial, Silius stabs himself. Cordus is accused by Satrius
Secundus and Pinnarius Natta, "two of Sejanus' bloodhounds" who
have also been spying on Agrippina's guests. He is declared to be "a
man factious and dangerous, a sower of sedition in the state, a turbulent
and discontented spirit," charges which can be proved from his writings
about Julius Caesar's time and his praise of Brutus and Cassius. Cordus
is carried off to prison, and his books are ordered burned.

Only when Sejanus suggests to Tiberius that he be permitted to marry
the widowed Livia does the Emperor begin to suspect his favorite's
motives and designs. Out of his proneness to voluptuous living, Tiberius
falls in with Sejanus' recommendations that he leave Rome and retire
to the country. But at the same time he leaves behind him Macro to be
his eye and ear and to keep strict watch on Agrippina and the princes,
but also on Sejanus as well. Macro is sharp, subtle, "wise, well-read in
man and his large nature," and the assignment as spy and informer is
perfectly suited to him. Macro, perhaps, is not too trustworthy, and
he has ambitions himself, but necessity does not permit the Emperor
to be choicy. Hence it is not startling to hear Macro resolve:

> *If then it be the lust of Caesar's power*
> *T' have raised Sejanus up, and in an hour*
> *O'erturn him, tumbling, down from height of all,*
> *We are his ready engine, and his fall*
> *May be our rise.*

Act IV

An accident at Spelunca, when a natural grot caved in and Sejanus
saved the Emperor's life, seems to have fixed the favorite in Tiberius'
graces more than ever before. When he returns to Rome, leaving the
Emperor to his own devices, Sejanus' tyrannies continue with renewed
fury. Sabinus, an old campaigner with Germanicus, is seized by Sejanus'
spies, fettered, and executed. Agrippina and two of her sons, Nero and
Drusus Junior, are cited to the senate for treason. Gallus is imprisoned.
Caligula, the youngest of Germanicus' sons, however, is spirited off to
Capreae by Macro. In his country retreat Tiberius seems to take no note
of these "forkéd tricks"; but reports from him, "feigning now ill, now
well, raising Sejanus and then depressing him," convince those who
know the Emperor that he has found his favorite grown too great, that
he is counterintriguing, and that he is delaying and playing double, in
order to make Sejanus odious to the common people, whose aid he
hopes to use when they turn against the favorite.

Act V

At last, when Sejanus feels most secure, Tiberius prepares to strike. Urgent letters are sent to all senators bidding them assemble at a given time, and rumors circulate through Rome that Sejanus is to receive the tribunitial dignity in open senate. But at the same time Macro, Regulus, and Laco, the provost of the watch, secretly get control of the guard. Numerous bad omens, however, presage a frowning Fortune for Sejanus —his statue in Pompey's theatre belches forth black smoke, and, on being opened, is found to contain a monstrous serpent. At his last augury instead of the bird of good luck, croaking ravens flew up and down and rested all night on the prison. At a special sacrifice, the statue of Fortune herself averts its face, and Sejanus, who professes no faith in these things, overturns both statue and altar. There are other portents. But Sejanus ignores them, rehearsing with great satisfaction his victories over one after the other of his enemies. At the Temple of Apollo, where the senate meets, Sejanus is surrounded by flatterers and troupes of officious friends. Under pretext of conferring upon Sejanus the tribunitial dignity and power, a long and deferential letter from the Emperor to the senate veers from praise of the favorite to dispraise. It wishes that he had run a calmer course against Agrippina and the princes, charges that his public severity, under pretext of service to the Emperor, was but personal ambition, desires that Sejanus' offices be seized by the senate, and orders that he be placed under arrest. "O violent change, and whirl of men's affections! . . . Who would trust slippery Chance?" As Sejanus is being led away to prison, "the eager multitude, who never yet knew why to love or hate, but only pleased t'express their rage of power," in wild fury, "crying that they are glad; say[ing] they could ne'er abide him, . . . protest[ing] they ever did presage h'would come to this, . . . and not a beast of all the herd demand[ing] what was his crime, or who were his accusers," wrest him from his captors and rend him limb from limb. Worse, under direction of the cruel Macro, who bids fair to be a greater prodigy in Rome than was Sejanus, the mob wreaks its rage upon the young son and daughter of Sejanus, while Apicata, their half-crazed mother, vows to prove to Caesar and the senate the guilt of Livia, Lygdus, and Eudemus in the death of Drusus.

> *How Fortune plies her sports, when she begins*
> *To practise them! . . .*
> *Let this example move th'insolent man*
> *Not to grow proud and careless of the gods, . . .*
> *For whom the morning saw so great and high,*
> *Thus low and little, fore the even doth lie.*

VOLPONE, OR THE FOX

A COMEDY

(1605–1606)

DRAMATIS PERSONAE

VOLPONE [*the Fox*], an "old magnifico [and] a brave clarissimo" of Venice who glories "more in the cunning purchase [i.e., underhand gain] of [his] wealth than in the glad possessions; . . . [he] use[s] no trade, . . . wound[s] no earth with plowshares, . . . fat[s] no beasts to feed the shambles, . . . [has] no mills for iron, oil, or corn, . . . blow[s] no subtle glass, expose[s] no ships to threatenings of the furrow-facéd sea, . . . turn[s] no moneys in the public bank, nor usure private. . . . [He] know[s] the use of riches."

MOSCA [*the Gadfly*], his parasite, "a fellow of no birth or blood, . . . the chiefest minister, if not plotter, in all these lewd impostures." ("Almost all the wise world is little else, in nature, but parasites and sub-parasites.")

VOLTORE [*the Vulture*], an advocate, "that can speak to every cause, and things mere contraries, till [he is] hoarse again, yet all be law; that with most quick agility [can] turn, and re-turn, make knots and undo them, give forkéd counsel, take provoking gold on either hand, and put it up; . . . this fellow for six sols more would plead against his Maker,"

CORBACCIO [*the Carrion Crow*], a very old gentleman, "avarice's fool," the deaf old "Croaker, . . . old round-back, . . . old glazen-eyes, . . . with the three legs." ("What horrid, strange offence did he commit against Nature in his youth worthy this age?")

CORVINO [*the Raven*], "our spruce merchant, . . . a chimera of wittol, fool, and knave; . . . he would have sold his part in Paradise for ready money, had he met a copeman [i.e., buyer],"

"greedy and full of expectation."

CELIA, the merchant Corvino's "own most fair and proper wife, . . . a wench o' the first year, a beauty ripe as harvest. . . . All her looks are sweet as the first grapes or cherries, and are watched as near as they are."

BONARIO, a young gentleman, old Corbaccio's son; an honest good man.

SIR POLITIC WOULD-BE, an English knight, whose mind and notebook are filled with projects and with "grave affairs of state; . . . though [he] live[s] free from the active torrent, yet [he'd] mark the currents and the passages of things for [his] own private use, and know the ebbs and flows of state." ("This knight had not his name for nothing.")

Fine LADY WOULD-BE, the knight's beauteous wife, "my madam with the everlasting voice. The bells, in time of pestilence, ne'er made like noise, or were in that perpetual motion. . . . The sun, the sea will sooner both stand still than her eternal tongue. . . . Howe'er [she] affect strange airs, she hath not yet the face to be dishonest."

PEREGRINE, a gentleman traveller from England.

Nano, a dwarf,
Androgyno, a hermaphrodite and a professional fool, } servants to Volpone.
Castrone, an eunuch,

Grege [or Mob].

Four Avocatori, or magistrates.

Commandadori, officers of justice.

Notario, the registrar of the court.

Three Mercatori, known to Peregrine.

Servitore, a manservant.

Several Women-servants.

Setting: Venice at some unspecified time.

> *"It cannot be, sir, that you should be cozened.*
> *'Tis not within the wit of man to do it."*

Act I

Old Volpone, a magnifico of Venice, has no wife, no children, no parents, and no relative to whom to leave his fortune; whoever he names will be his heir. This fact draws new clients to his house daily, men and women, who bring presents or send plate, coin, and jewels, in the expectation that when Volpone dies the gifts shall return tenfold upon them. Several rivals even try to outgive one another, and, with the co-operation of his clever parasite, Mosca, the old fox encourages the attentions of these harpies, gloating over his prospective deception of them all. He even feigns illness, with a cough, phthisic, gout, apoplexy, palsy, and catarrhs, and for three years now he has "milked their hopes." Chief among Volpone's expectant heirs are Voltore, a lawyer; Corbaccio, an old miser with one foot in the grave; Corvino, a rich merchant; and Lady Would-be, the affected wife of an English knight, Sir Politic Would-be, who lives in Venice that his wife may study the fashions and that he may advance his projects and observe politics—"the spider and the bee ofttimes suck from one flower." Each of these prospects visits Volpone, usually bringing some rich gift; each hopefully inquires about the progress of Volpone's maladies; each is played off against the others by Mosca; and each receives from Mosca assurances that he is the heir. With Corbaccio Mosca even goes so far as to suggest that as a gesture the old crow draw up a will disinheriting his own meritorious son and naming Volpone his heir. At the bold English who "dare let loose their wives to all encounters" unchaperoned, Volpone never ceases to wonder. But Mosca knows that however affected she may be, Lady Would-be is safe enough. If she were Signior Corvino's wife, however, he says to his master, the case might be different, and he paints an enthusiastic picture of the perfections of this lady "whose skin is whiter than a swan all over, [whose] soft lip would tempt you to an eternity of kissing, . . . [but who] never comes abroad, never takes air but at a window, . . . [because] there is a guard of ten spies thick upon her." Volpone resolves to see this paragon.

Act II

Disguised as the mountebank Scoto of Mantua, Volpone sets up a platform in St. Mark's Place, gathers a crowd to hear about medicines and cures, and succeeds in attracting the attention of Celia, Corvino's wife, as she looks out of her window. But the jealous husband drives the quacksalver away, upbraids his wife for looking out at "a juggling, toothdrawing, prating mountebank, . . . [while] a crew of old, unmarried, noted lechers stood leering up like satyrs," and threatens her with closer incarceration than before. "But angry Cupid, bolting from her eyes, hath shot himself into [Volpone] like a flame"; he must have the lady, and he appeals to Mosca to release him from his torment. Accordingly, Mosca calls on Corvino to report that while he was busy in the outer room, Voltore and Corbaccio brought some of Scoto's oil and administered it to Volpone, who is now showing signs of recovery. They have even called in for consultation, and at great expense, the College of Physicians, and they have agreed that there is no means of keeping the old man alive "but some young women must be straight sought out, lusty, and full of juice, to sleep by him." On this search Mosca says he is engaged; he has stopped to acquaint Corvino with the fact that all the others are now trying to see which one shall first present Volpone with a cure. Corvino, of course, suggests that they hire a common courtesan, but Mosca rejects this plan because age is so doting and courtesans so full of art, that a quean might cheat them all. Moreover, Signior Lupo, the physician, who knows Volpone's physical condition, has offered his own daughter. Convinced that it is safe, Corvino offers his wife, and sends Mosca home to tell Volpone how willingly he agreed to it, while he himself bids Celia don her best attire and her choicest jewels and accompany him "to a solemn feast at old Volpone's."

Act III

Meeting Bonario in the street, Mosca reveals to him his father's wicked purpose of disinheriting his son, and promises to bring Bonario, who does not trust the parasite, where he shall hear the deed, if not actually see it. Meanwhile, Lady Would-be, "my madam with the everlasting voice," visits the invalid Volpone and nearly talks the impatient

Mountebanks in the Piazza San Marco, Venice
From an engraving by Giacomo Franco, 1609.

The Duel in *The Maid's Tragedy*
From the title page of the edition of 1619.

Scene from *Philaster*
From the title page of the edition of 1620.

old man to death. Mosca is able to get rid of her only by telling her that Sir Politic is rowing in a gondola with the most cunning courtesan in Venice. Corvino arrives with his wife, to whom he now reveals his purpose. But he finds that commands, threats, and coaxing are no persuasives to the virtuous lady. Nevertheless, at length he leaves her alone with Volpone. But the old fox is no more successful in his persuasions, and just as he is about to force the lady, Bonario leaps from the hiding place where he had expected to spy upon his father, rescues Celia, and denounces the imposter. "Unmasked, unspirited, undone, betrayed to beggary, to infamy," the old rascal fears he will be turned over to the police. But Mosca is equal to the occasion, even when Corbaccio and Voltore put in their appearance. To Corbaccio Mosca explains that Bonario accidentally discovered the old man's purpose of changing his will and sought by violence to prevent it, and he succeeds in making the old man disinherit his son indeed. When Voltore, coming from behind, overhears the whole story and suspects that Mosca is playing double, the parasite also succeeds in placating the lawyer by explaining that Celia had come to visit the invalid and was awaiting her husband, that Bonario, growing impatient at so long a wait to see Volpone, seized the lady and made her swear, on threat of death, that the old fox had done her rape. To avoid further infamy, Voltore suggests that they all go to the Scrutineo for a legal investigation and an injunction against Bonario.

Act IV

Meanwhile, Sir Politic Would-be has been regaling Peregrine, a fellow countryman and a traveller like himself, with his acquaintance of the world, his knowledge of secret intelligence, and his projects—for supplying Venice with red herring direct from Rotterdam; preventing arson by permitting only known patriots to own tinderboxes; saving delay for quarantine by fumigating ships with onion-water. Were he a traitor, Sir Politic adds confidentially, he knows how to sell Venice to the Turks in spite of the Venetian navy. He even shows Peregrine his diary wherein he notes the activities of the day—his putting on new spurs, his purchase of toothpicks, his bargaining for sprats—truly politic notes. His conversation is interrupted by Lady Would-be seeking her husband and his courtesan. When, innocently the knight introduces her to Peregrine, the lady is certain that he is a wench dressed in man's apparel. Although she apologizes when she learns the truth, the invitation with which Lady Would-be accompanies her apology, and her husband's earlier and apparently significant withdrawal, leads Peregrine to think but one thing—that Sir Politic is a bawd to his own wife, and he resolves upon revenge for the knight's attempt upon his inexperience.

At the senate the accusations and counteraccusations confuse the magistrates and the registrar. But Voltore conducts the case in so masterly a fashion that he gulls the whole court and convinces everyone that Bonario is an ungrateful son, saved only by accident from being a patricide; that Celia is a creature of "most professed and prostituted lewdness"; that Bonario is her lover; and that they have invented their story to cover up their guilt. He even calls witnesses to prove it—Mosca to testify that he saw the woman in a gondola with a foreigner, Lady Would-be to confirm the fact, and Volpone himself on a stretcher to show how impotent he really is. The guiltless Celia and Bonario have no witnesses but Heaven—which is not acceptable in a court of law, "where multitude and clamor overcomes."

Act V

Flushed by their success in diverting the torrent upon the innocent and away from themselves, and in cozening these rascals who were so stuffed with their own avarice and so divided among themselves that they were beyond suspicion, both the old fox and his parasite go too far. Volpone sends his servants out into the streets to spread the news that he is dead, writes a will in which he makes Mosca his heir, and dresses the parasite in his own gown that he may sit before an account book and take inventory of his properties, while Volpone hides behind a curtain and watches the faces of those whose hopes have come to naught. They come —Voltore, Corbaccio, Corvino, Lady Would-be—but Mosca knows so much to the discredit of each that not one can open his mouth in protest. So delighted is Volpone at what he has seen, that he urges Mosca to go out into the streets, flaunt his good fortune, and torment them more. He wishes he could see the sport, and Mosca offers to get a police officer drunk and bring Volpone his uniform as a disguise. "Sir, you must look for curses," warns Mosca, but the fox is delighted.

Meanwhile, Peregrine succeeds as well in his revenge upon Sir Politic. Disguised as a merchant friend of the knight's, he pretends to warn Sir Politic that Peregrine is a secret agent and has reported to the Venetian authorities Sir Politic's plot to sell the state to the Turks. He advises Sir Politic to flee or to hide, and helps him to get inside a contrivance which the knight has constructed out of tortoise shell and which he hopes will make him look like a strange fish. Impersonating search officers, some merchants enter Sir Politic's house and discover the remarkable beast; and when Peregrine has tired of his sport, he reveals himself to Sir Politic, and with laughter leaves the place. The knight will become "the fable of all feasts, the freight of the *gazetti* [i.e., the theme of the newspapers], . . . and, which is worst, even talk for ordinaries." The only incriminating papers Sir Politic possesses are notes drawn out of playbooks!

But to return to Volpone. By declaring himself dead, signing a new will, giving the parasite his keys, and adopting the disguise of a police officer, the fox has ventured out of his hole—and Mosca knows it. While Volpone enjoys himself in the streets, gloating over his prospective heirs, Mosca is preparing the "fox trap." At the same time, Voltore, Corbaccio, and Corvino are not content to be thus outstripped by a parasite. Making common cause, they resolve to tell as much of the truth as they dare, return to the senate and confess for conscience sake to assistance at a sad miscarriage of justice, and accuse Mosca of being the instrument of all these deceptions. More confused than ever, the magistrates send for Mosca. When he arrives he tries to spring his fox trap; to escape Volpone throws off his disguise; and the court sentences both. As a fellow of no birth and blood, Mosca shall first be whipped and then live a perpetual prisoner in the galleys. As a gentleman, Volpone shall have his goods confiscated, and, because most were got by feigning horrible diseases, given to the hospital of the Incurabili. He himself is to lie in prison until he is sick and lame indeed. In addition, Voltore is disbarred and banished the state. Corbaccio is immediately to turn over his estate to his son Bonario and retire to the monastery of San Spirito, where he may learn to die well. Corvino is to be rowed through the Grand Canal wearing a cap with long ass's ears instead of horns, and so to stand in the pillory. And to expiate the wrongs done his wife, Corvino is to send her back to her father, with her dowry trebled.

EPICOENE; OR, THE SILENT WOMAN
(1609)

DRAMATIS PERSONAE

MOROSE, "that stiff piece of formality," a gentleman who "can endure no noise. . . . They say he has been upon divers treaties with the fishwives and orangewomen; . . . a brazier is not suffer'd to dwell in the parish, nor an armorer. . . . The waits of the City have a pension of him not to come near that ward. . . . He hath chosen a street to lie in so narrow at both ends that it will receive no coaches, nor carts; . . . [he has devised] a room with double walls and treble ceilings. . . . He turned away a man last week for having a pair of new shoes that creak'd." When he marries Epicoene, Morose sells his "liberty to a distaff," and discovers that "strife and tumult are the dowry that comes with a wife."

SIR DAUPHINE EUGENIE, his "next of blood and his sister's son, . . . sick o' the uncle," because he is threatened with disinheritance. "A very worthy gentleman in his exteriors, . . . he shows he is judicial in his clothes. . . . Sir Dauphine's carelessness becomes him."

NED CLERIMONT, a gentleman, a frank open friend of Sir Dauphine's; "here's a man that can melt away his time, and never feels it!"

TRUEWIT, another friend of Sir Dauphine's, "a very honest fellow . . . [who has] many plots."

EPICOENE, the supposed "silent gentlewoman, . . . but she is a woman of excellent assurance and an extraordinary happy wit and tongue."

SIR JOHN, or JACK, DAW, "the only talking sir in the town, . . . a fellow that pretends only to learning, buys titles, and nothing else of books in him! . . . No mushroom was ever so fresh,"

SIR AMOROUS LA FOOLE, of "as ancient a family as any is in Europe, . . . but let that go; antiquity is not respected now. . . . O, that's a precious mannikin! . . . He is one of the braveries, though he be none of the wits. . . . Did you ever hear such a wind-sucker as this?"

> Some men kiss and tell, but "these adulterate knights" tell and never kiss.

CAPTAIN TOM OTTER, "a kind of gamester, but he has had command both by sea and by land, . . . [an] *animal amphibium*. . . . He is his wife's subject; he calls her 'princess,' and . . . follows her up and down the house like a page, with his hat off. . . . [Yet], he will rail on his wife, with certain commonplaces, behind her back, and to her face— . . . Alas, what a tyranny is this poor fellow married to!"

CUTBEARD, a barber, Morose's agent in his search for a dumb wife. "The fellow trims him silently."

LADY HAUGHTY, a "grave and youthful matron, . . . [with an] autumnal face [and] pieced beauty, . . . lady of the College,"

LADY CENTAURE, who "has immortalized herself with "her taming her wild male." shadows"

MISTRESS DOLL MAVIS,

> Ladies Collegiates, "an order between courtiers and country-madams that live from their husbands and give entertainment to all the wits and braveries of the time. . . . All their actions are governed by crude opinion, without reason or cause; they know not why they do anything; but, as they are inform'd, believe, judge, praise, condemn, love, hate, and in emulation one of another do all things alike. Only they have a natural inclination sways them generally to the worst, when they are left to themselves."

MISTRESS OTTER, the Captain's termagant wife and kinswoman of La Foole. She was "the rich chinawoman that the courtiers visited so often, that gave the rare entertainment. She commands all at home,"

MISTRESS TRUSTY, Lady Haughty's woman; "she is a Fidelia,"

> pretenders.

A Parson, "a fine quick fellow, and an excellent barber of prayers; . . . [he] has catch'd a cold . . . with sitting up late and singing catches with cloth workers."

MUTE, one of Morose's servants, trained to communicate by signs without speaking.

Page to Clerimont.

Pages and Servants.

Setting: London in the early seventeenth century.

"Why, did you think you had married a statue, or a motion only? One of the French puppets, with the eyes turn'd with a wire?"

Act I

Because he suspects the young man and his friends of ridiculing him, Morose, a cantankerous old bachelor with an insane aversion to noise, has vowed to disinherit his nephew, Sir Dauphine Eugenie. To this end Morose determines to marry and beget an heir, and for half a year now he has employed one Cutbeard, his barber, to seek out a suitably dumb woman to be his wife. One has at last been found, lodged in the next street from the old man, a girl, "exceedingly soft-spoken, thrifty of her speech, that spends but six words a day." But Cutbeard is also the friend of Sir Dauphine and has kept him fully informed. Sir Dauphine, however, seems to accept the situation philosophically, and to some of his friends, especially Truewit, with whom he is discussing it, his apparent complacency is exasperating. Truewit demands to know where this phenomenal lady may be seen, and resolves to make her talk, but Dauphine is evasive. When he hears that the girl lives in the same house with Sir Jack Daw, a talkative pretender to learning and composer of verses, Truewit is sure she'll soon learn to speak, and, on the pretext of pressing business, leaves his friends. When he is gone, Sir Dauphine talks more freely to Ned Clerimont; Truewit is an honest fellow, but not a keeper of secrets. The nephew, it seems, has not been so complacent as he appears; he has met the silent woman, been present when Sir Jack Daw courted her and read verses to her, and has been invited to a dinner, which is to be given by Sir Amorous La Foole, another windbag and ladies' man, at the house of Captain Tom Otter, a kind of amphibian who has been both a sea and a land captain, and whose wife is a kinswoman of La Foole's.

Act II

Officious in his friend's behalf, Truewit has sought out not the silent woman, but Morose, and done all in his power to break up the match. Posing as a courier from court, Truewit interrupts a household conference between Morose and his servant Mute, who is being trained to communicate by signs without uttering an offending sound. Truewit blows on a post horn, expresses volubly the solicitude of Morose's friends at court over his rumored marriage, and almost talks the poor man out of his wits, by thundering at him "the incommodities of a wife and the miseries of marriage." He even offers Morose a halter, which he says these friends have sent him, desiring him to commit his neck to this knot rather than to the noose of wedlock.

Meanwhile, Dauphine and Clerimont have gone to Sir John Daw's house to visit Epicoene, the silent woman. There Sir John reads the "Madrigal of Modesty" he has composed to the lady; glibly dismisses Plutarch and Seneca as "mere essayists," Aristotle as a "commonplace fellow," Plato as "a discourser," Thucydides and Livy as "tedious and dry," and Homer as "an old, tedious, prolix ass"; and entertains the company by his criticism of literary taste. Here Truewit joins his friends, well-satisfied that he has forbidden the banns and broken off the marriage. But Dauphine receives his news with a singular lack of enthusiasm. Why? For four months now this gentlewoman Epicoene has been lodged here on purpose to deceive the uncle, and has pretended this obstinate silence solely for Dauphine's sake and profit. If his most malicious enemy had studied to inflict an injury upon Sir Dauphine, he could have thought of nothing worse than this rash action of a friend.

Providentially, however, Truewit's prank does not have the expected result. Cutbeard brings word that old Morose thinks the joke one of Dauphine's procuring, and is resolved to meet the lady and marry her instantly, if she is as silent as she has been represented. When the barber introduces Epicoene to Morose, the girl exceeds his expectations. She barely whispers, and utters her few words with such divine softness and modesty, that the old fool sends forthwith for a silent minister to marry them.

Act III

At the Otters', preparations go forward for Sir Amorous La Foole's feast and the reception of ladies, wits, and braveries. Mistress Otter is a social climber and a pretender to gentility who likes to fill her house with fools of fashion. But her husband, Captain Tom, has been a great man at the Bear Garden in his time. He even designates his chief carousing cups the "Bull," the "Bear," the "Horse," and so on down according to size. He thinks no entertainment perfect until these be brought out and set on the cupboard—much to the vexation of Mistress Otter. He calls his wife "princess" and always speaks under correction in her presence. But occasionally, as at present, he gets out of hand in the matter of what liquid refreshment is suitable. Dauphine, Truewit, and Clerimont arrive early, flatter their hostess a little, and learn from Cutbeard that the wedding is taking place. Then for further sport, Clerimont tells Sir John Daw that his mistress Epicoene has deserted him for a fortune, but that Sir Dauphine has made her so repentant of the injury she has done her lover that she has asked to be forgiven, bid him come to the wedding feast, and sent him a message that she will be able to do him "more favors, and with more security, now, than before." To stir up strife between Daw and La Foole, Clerimont suggests that La Foole has planned his feast to disgrace Sir John and urges the knight to divert all of the company to the bride's house. Then he tells Sir Amorous what Sir John is planning to do in honor of his mistress and as a disgrace to him, advising him to dress as a waiter and himself transfer his feast to the house of the newly married couple.

Poor Morose, however, hardly knows what is in store for him. No sooner is she married than Epicoene finds her tongue and uses it vigorously and sharply on her husband. A sea of friends pours in to offer good wishes and to celebrate the happy occasion. Sir John Daw introduces Epicoene to the Collegiate Ladies, a group of gossips and scandalmongers. Clerimont brings in a band of musicians. La Foole conducts in his servants bearing the wedding dinner. And Captain Otter brings with him his Bull, his Bear, and his Horse in anticipation of a big evening of carousing.

Act IV

So great is the tumult that poor Morose puts on a whole nest of nightcaps and locks himself up at the top of his house to escape the noise. His bride, or rather the fury he has married, takes every occasion to speak or rather to shout, and at last withdraws in private with the Collegiates for some special instruction in their arts. Captain Otter has filled the Bull for himself, the Bear for Sir John Daw, and the Horse for Sir Amorous, and foot to foot, the three drink toasts as the kettledrums and trumpets sound out in token of their pledge. In his cups Otter makes disparaging remarks about his wife which she overhears and punishes with beating. In vain does Morose appear with his long sword and try to clear his house. In vain does Sir Dauphine try to comfort him. Epicoene inquires solicitously about his health, but is snarled at, cries out that her husband is distracted, and precipitates a tumultuous chatter about remedies for madness. Meanwhile, Truewit, who is a man of many plots, contrives to frighten the half-tipsy and cowardly Sir Jack Daw and Sir Amorous La Foole of one another, and to reconcile them with honor. With Epicoene's aid he even promises to cause all of the Collegiates to fall in love with Sir Dauphine. At last Morose is ready to trust himself in the hands of his nephew and Truewit, who promise to procure "a very sufficient lawyer and a learned divine" to advise the old man about a divorce.

Act V

The doctor and the parson are none other than Cutbeard and Captain Otter in disguise, both of whom smatter Latin, and with a little coaching by Truewit wrangle over minute points most realistically. Morose is ready to seize upon anything if it will prove grounds for divorce. Epicoene beseeches all the women present to assist her against such a wrong conspired against a poor bride on her wedding day. At last the old churl confesses that he is impotent; surely this will be cause enough for immediate divorce. But Epicoene declares herself willing to take Morose with all his faults. Then both Sir Jack Daw and Sir Amorous La Foole are prevailed upon to confess to carnal knowledge of the bride. The lady weeps, but the lawyer and the divine reject the fact as a cause for divorce because it occurred before the marriage. Finally, Morose accepts his nephew's offer to rid him of his wife for five hundred pounds a year during life and reversion of his property at his death. Sir Dauphine simply pulls off Epicoene's peruke and reveals her as a boy he has trained for the purpose—a cause for divorce, *error personae, in primo gradu*. Even the Collegiate Ladies are mute at the revelation, for they have talked much to Epicoene; and as for Sir John and Sir Amorous, "no drunkards, either with wine or vanity, ever confess'd such stories of themselves."

THE ALCHEMIST

A COMEDY

(1610)

DRAMATIS PERSONAE

SUBTLE, the ALCHEMIST, "the chymical cozener, . . . an excellent Paracelsian."

JEREMY, the butler, the housekeeper, a "groom arrogant; . . . [alias] CAPTAIN FACE, that parcel broker and whole bawd, all rascal; . . . [alias] LUNGS, [the alchemist's] fire-drake, . . . he that puffs his coals."

DOLL COMMON, their colleague, "a Bradamante, a brave piece, . . . royal Doll, . . . my dainty Dolkin, . . . my little God's gift."

DAPPER, "a fine young quodling, . . . [a] lawyer's clerk [whom Face] lighted on last night in Holborn at the Dagger, . . . nor any melancholic underscribe shall tell the vicar, but a special gentle that is heir to forty marks a year, consorts with the small poets of the time, is the sole hope of his old grandmother, that knows the law and writes you six fair hands, . . . has his ciph'ring perfect, . . . and can court his mistress out of Ovid."

ABEL DRUGGER, "a seller of tobacco, . . . free of the Grocer's [Guild]." (A "miserable rogue, and lives with cheese, and has the worms.")

SIR EPICURE MAMMON, a covetous and credulous gentleman of
   voluptuous mind, "slow of his feet, but earnest of his tongue," } "the fat knight and
PERTINAX SURLY, an incredulous gamester, "Monsieur Caution, } the lean gentleman."
   that will not be gulled, . . . [and] a bachelor, worth
   naught. . . . This gentleman hath a parlous head,"

TRIBULATION WHOLESOME, a "very zealous pastor" of Amsterdam,
ANANIAS, "a very faithful Brother, . . . the sanctified elder . . . } a "brace of little
   of the exiled Brethern that deal with widows' and with orphans' } John Leydens."
   goods and make a just account unto the Saints—a deacon."
   ("A botcher, and a man by revelation that hath a competent
   knowledge of the truth,")

KASTRIL, "the angry boy, the heir that [would] carry quarrels as gallants do and
   manage 'em by line, . . . a gentleman newly warm in his land, . . . a man . . .
   of some three thousand a year, . . . [who has] heard some speech of the angry
   boys and seen 'em take tobacco, . . . and would fain be one of 'em, and go down
   and practice i' the country."

DAME PLIANT, his sister, and a neighbor of Drugger's, "a rich young widow, . . .
   nineteen at the most, . . . soft and buxom, . . . [and] a delicate dabchick, . . .
   [but] a good dull innocent" when compared to Doll.

LOVEWIT, the indulgent master of the house, a widower who loves mirth and "a
   teeming wit as [he] love[s his] nourishment."

A Parson, Neighbors, Officers.

Setting: A house in the Blackfriars district of London, one day in the autumn of 1610.

"Alchemy is a pretty kind of game,
Somewhat like tricks o' the cards, to cheat a man
With charming."

Act I

During the hot summer months while the plague rages in London, a
householder in the Blackfriars district of London quits his house in town
and goes to his hopfields in the country, leaving behind one servant,
Jeremy the butler, to look after his possessions. With little to do, and
secure in the knowledge that, as long as even one a week dies of the sickness, his master will not return home, Jeremy becomes acquainted with a
cheater named Subtle and his punk Doll Common, then suffering from
lean days. He lends them the house to practice in, furnishes them with
equipment for an alchemical laboratory, and enters into an agreement with
them to share the take. Many persons patronize the place—ladies and
gentlewomen, citizens' wives, knights in coaches, other gallants, oyster
women, sailors' wives, tobacco men, even Puritan Brethren from
Amsterdam—for casting horoscopes, telling fortunes, raising familiar
spirits, making philosopher's stones, and practicing flat bawdry.

As the play opens Jeremy and Subtle are quarreling with violence over their relative importance to the enterprise and the size of their cuts, each beroguing the other. Only Doll realizes the seriousness of what they are doing if their "sober, scurvy, precise neighbors, that scarce have smiled twice sin' the king came in," should hear them, and she restores harmony just as a client rings the doorbell. He is Dapper, a lawyer's clerk, that Jeremy (disguised as Captain Face, an apocryphal suburb-captain) has picked up in Holborn at the Dagger. He wants a familiar spirit to help him win at raffles, horse races, and gaming. Pretending to be very reluctant and to accommodate the strange youth only at Face's earnest persuasion, does Doctor Subtle agree. After several gold angels change hands, Subtle reveals to Dapper that a rare star reigned at the young man's birth, for he is allied to none other than the Queen of Fairy.

The second client is another acquaintance of Face, Abel Drugger, a tobaccoman who has just opened a shop at the corner and who would like to know by necromancy where to place his door, where his shelves, which to use for boxes, which for pots. Before Drugger leaves, he also hears of a good fortune, how despite his youth he will soon wear the livery of his company and become an alderman by spring—all in exchange for a gold Portuguese he has carried this half year. The rogues spy Sir Epicure Mammon making his way along the far end of the lane, and Face hastens to change into the clothes he wears as Lungs, the alchemist's helper, for this is the day on which Subtle has promised Sir Epicure "the *magisterium*, [or] *great work*, the [philosopher's] stone" itself.

Act II

Sir Epicure is a most enthusiastic believer in the alchemical mystery, and he has brought with him a friend, Pertinax Surly, a sceptic on guard against being gulled, whom he hopes to convert. Accordingly, Sir Epicure paints an optimistic picture of what he hopes to do with the stone when he gets it—tonight transform all the base metal in his house into gold; in the morning send to the plumbers and pewterers and coppersmiths and buy up all the lead, tin, and copper; purchase Devon and Cornwall and make them perfect Indies; restore old men to perfect youth; cure all diseases regardless of cause; and rid the kingdom of the plague in three months. When Surly still remains incredulous—untransmuted by the stone—Sir Epicure offers to convince him by documents—a book written by Moses and his sister and King Solomon on the art of alchemy, a treatise in High Dutch penned by Adam on cedar wood treating the philosopher's stone, a book which proves that such stories as those about Jason, Pandora, the Hesperian Garden, and Cadmus are but abstract riddles and allegories about the stone.

While he talks with Lungs about the progress which that devout holy man Subtle is making with the stone he is creating for Sir Epicure, that knight continues to retail the luxuries he expects to have—a list of wives and concubines equal with Solomon's; the best bawds and paramours that money can buy; shirts of taffeta-sarsnet; gloves of fish- and bird-skin, perfumed; and so on. But Subtle's piety and the scientific jargon of the laboratory all fail to impress Master Surly, to whom alchemy is still a charming cheat, and nothing more. Sir Epicure, however, pays willingly for extras and even promises to send for transmutation his household brass and pewter, his andirons, and the very jacks that turn spit in his kitchen—especially after he has had a glimpse of Doll. Doll, Lungs explains confidentially, is a lord's sister and a most rare scholar now being treated by the doctor for madness induced by studying Broughton's rabbinical books. To get rid of Surly, who is now convinced that the place is nothing but a bawdyhouse, Lungs gives him a message that one Captain Face wishes to meet him at Temple Church, and then whispers to Sir Epicure a promise of conversation with the learned lady if he will but return in the afternoon.

The rascals then prepare to meet still another client, the Puritan Ananias, one of the holy Brethren of Amsterdam, who deal with widows' and orphans' goods, and are negotiating for the philosopher's stone in hope of increasing their influence by its use, and to propagate "the glorious cause" by bribing any lords spiritual or temporal that shall oppose them. But when Ananias reports that the Brethren refuse to invest any more money until they see results, having heard that an alchemist of Heidelberg made the stone out of an egg and a paper of pin filings, Subtle drives him away in indignation.

Finally, Abel Drugger calls again, with a gift of tobacco. There is something more, he remembers. Near him there lives a rich young widow, but nineteen at the most, who has come down to London to learn the fashions and who longs to have her fortune told. With her is her brother, newly come into his inheritance of three thousand a year, who wants to learn to quarrel like the London gallants and to live by his wits as they do, so that he may return to the country to practice these arts. Drugger is urged to bring them both to see the doctor; the learned man may even make a match between the widow and the tobacconist, in spite of her brother's vow that she shall marry none under a knight. At Face's urging, Drugger promises Doctor Subtle a damask suit. But secretly the rogues see in the rich widow a wife for one of themselves; they'll draw lots, taking care that Doll hears nothing of it.

Act III

As Subtle has predicted, his treatment of Ananias produces that worthy's speedy return with his elder, Tribulation Wholesome, and more money to implore the alchemist to go on. Professing concern now for the care of the widows and orphans, Subtle suggests that if the saints need a present sum they might consider buying a tincture which will transform pewter into Dutch dollars. There is some difference of opinion between the two Brethren on the ethical point as to whether such coining—or casting—even of foreign money, is lawful; and Tribulation and Ananias depart to lay the question before the Brethren. Meanwhile, Captain Face has been to Temple Church, but unable to find the costive Surly. While there, however, he has met a noble count, a don of Spain, who is coming to the house straight, under pretext of taking the doctor's curative baths, to visit Doll.

Soon clients come in droves, as Dapper, Drugger, and "the angry boy" all arrive at once. The latter goes back with Drugger to fetch his sister when he learns how successful the doctor has been in making matches all over England, and for the moment the way is cleared for Dapper. This young man has put on a clean shirt, fasted, and "vinegared his senses" (i.e., put vinegar up his nose) as Subtle instructed him to do, and now is ready to meet face to face his aunt the Queen of Fairy, alias Doll Common. First they blindfold him, then bind him, and to make sure that he is absolutely stripped of coin have the fairies pinch him thoroughly. But while they are at these ceremonies and before they can introduce Dapper to the Queen, Sir Epicure knocks at the door, and they must get rid of Dapper. Hence, they caution him not to speak for two hours, gag him with a piece of gingerbread to make sure, and lock him in the privy while they receive a more important customer.

Act IV

Cautioning the knight that the doctor is very scrupulous and violent against the least act of sin, and that the scholarly lady can talk intelligently on any subject—physic, mathematics, poetry, politics, or bawdry—provided there is no word of ecclesiastical controversy introduced to bring on her madness, Lungs introduces Sir Epicure to Doll and leaves them together. Then quickly changing back into his uniform, Face joins Subtle in receiving Dame Pliant, the "soft and buxom widow," and Kastril, the "child of wrath and anger." Even before they begin their instruction, the two scoundrels begin to quarrel over this "delicate dabchick." But again they are interrupted by the arrival of a client, this time the solemn Spaniard—Surly in disguise. Obviously the Spaniard can speak no English; hence, in their politest manner both Face and Subtle load him with insult and assure him that he shall be cozened, emptied, pumped, drawn dry, and milked before he leaves. But Doll is already busy; the don becomes impatient, and there is nothing to do but introduce him to the young widow—after all, whichever one of the rogues should finally win her, it is but one man more. Congratulating Dame Pliant upon her good fortune, and overcoming her scruples about Spaniards, they leave the pair in the garden, while Subtle gives a quarreling lesson to the "angry boy," who sees in the match a great advance for the house of the Kastrils.

Meanwhile, the rendezvous between Sir Epicure and the learned lady has gone wrong. By chance the knight has barely alluded to the philosopher's stone, and the scholar has begun discoursing volubly out of Broughton's works, and nothing will stop her mouth. Dressed again as the alchemist's drudge, Lungs tries to quiet the couple; Subtle discovers their "deeds of darkness" (in spite of Sir Epicure's protest that there was no unchaste purpose in their conversation); work on the philosopher's stone will be retarded for a month; the retort bursts, and all is ruined— just because of Sir Epicure's voluptuous mind.

At the same time, too, Master Surly has revealed all the knavery of the scientists to the Widow Pliant and seriously proposed marriage to her. He throws off his disguise, denounces Subtle and Face (who has changed back into his uniform again), and further exposes their carryings-on. Face presents the angry boy Kastril with a first-class opportunity to fight; expecting a real Spanish count, the doctor and the widow have been deceived by an imposter employed by a conjuring competitor.

But the quarreler will neither fight, nor be convinced by Surly that these men are rascals. Drugger arrives with the damask cloth; so does Ananias with word that the Brethren have concluded casting dollars is lawful. The zealous Puritan spies the ruff of pride about the don's neck and the lewd, superstitious, and idolatrous Spanish breeches he wears. Hence, with this reinforcement Face is able to rout Surly, and get him out of the house. But his triumph is but momentary. Doll brings news that the master of the house has returned home.

Act V

Talking to the neighbors, Lovewit receives a circumstantial account of the men and women of all sorts, tagrag, which have flocked to his premises during the past weeks—surely his servant must be exhibiting bawdy pictures or a flea-circus to have attracted such hordes. At last, as Lovewit is about to break in the door, Jeremy the butler appears. He tries to outface the neighbors, pretending that the place has been locked up for three weeks, and almost succeeds. But Surly and Sir Epicure have made common cause and return, calling for the rogues and cheaters; Kastril the angry boy demands his sister; Ananias and Tribulation beat on the door; and all go out for officers. It is vain for Jeremy to pretend that these people have all broken loose "out of St. Kather'ne's, where they use to keep the better sort of madfolks," or that they are all optical illusions. The neighbors recognize some of them as the people who have called at the house in recent days, and, inside, Dapper calls for his aunt the Queen of Fairy, the gingerbread gag having melted in his mouth. Master Lovewit promises to be indulgent if Jeremy will make a clean breast of everything, dismisses the rabble that has collected, and accepts Jeremy's promise to help him to a rich widow that will make him seven years younger, if he will let him work things out in his own way.

Accordingly, Dapper meets the Queen of Fairy face to face, and in a cage about his neck receives the familiar spirit he hoped for. Still hopeful of marrying the widow, Drugger brings a Spanish costume, and is sent out to fetch a parson. Subtle and Doll pack up all the booty preparatory to flight, but Jeremy holds the keys and claims the loot in the name of his master. As officers pound on the door, the rascally pair are glad to escape empty-handed. Meanwhile, Lovewit has donned Drugger's Spanish costume and married the Widow Pliant, thereby gulling both the tobacconist and the cautious Surly. The master gives the officers of the irate Sir Epicure, Ananias, and Tribulation free leave to search the premises. But the rogues have fled, and Lovewit demands a certificate of how they were cozened—or cozened themselves—before he will return any goods they claim. Only the angry boy remains. Lovewit does what he can to provoke him to a quarrel, but all fight is gone out of him in honor of the fine match his widowed sister has made. The indulgent, rascally master pays his compliments to the masterly rascal, and Jeremy, who has got off clean "from Subtle, Surly, Mammon, Doll, hot Ananias, Dapper, Drugger, all with whom [he] traded," throws himself upon the mercy of the audience, for a plaudite.

BARTHOLOMEW FAIR

A COMEDY

(1614)

DRAMATIS PERSONAE

The STAGEKEEPER,
The BOOKHOLDER, or prompter, } characters in the Induction.
A SCRIVENER,

URSULA, "mad, merry Urs, . . . the fatness of the Fair," a Falstaffian vendor of liquor and roast pig, "a plain, plump, soft wench of the suburbs, . . . having the marks upon her of the three enemies of man: the World, as being in the Fair; the Devil, as being in the fire; and the Flesh, as being herself. . . . Here you may ha' your punk and your pig in state, sir, both piping hot. . . . Out upon her, how she drips! . . . [She does] water the ground in knots, as [she goes], like a great garden pot; you may follow by the S's [she] make[s]. . . . Two stone o' suet a day is [her] proportion. . . . Fie upon't; who would wear out their youth and prime thus in roasting of pigs that had any cooler vocation? Hell's a cold cellar to't, a very fine vault, o' my conscience! . . . Her language grows greasier than her pigs."

MOONCALF, "you thin, lean, . . . grasshopper's thighs, . . . child o' the bottles"; tapster to Ursula.

LANTHORN LEATHERHEAD, "parcel poet and . . . inginer," a hobbyhorse seller [i.e., a toyman] and "profane professor of puppetry, little better than poetry. . . . What do you lack? What is't you buy? . . . Rattles, drums, halberts, horses, babies o' the best? . . . What do you lack? A fine horse? A lion? A bull? A bear? . . . A fine hobbyhorse, to make your son a tilter? A drum, to make him a soldier? A fiddle, to make him a reveller? . . . What is't you lack, gentlemen? Fine purses, pouches, pincases, pipes? . . . [And] O, the motions that [he has] given light to, in [his] time! . . . *Jerusalem* was a stately thing, and so was *Nineveh*, . . . and *Sodom and Gomorrah,* with the rising of the prentices, and pulling down the bawdyhouses there upon Shrove Tuesday. But the *Gunpowder Plot!* There was a get-penny."

FILCHER, } doorkeepers to Leatherhead's puppet show.
SHARKWELL,

MASTER DANIEL KNOCKEM JORDAN, the ranger of Turnbull, . . . captain of the roarers [i.e., bullies], . . . a strutting horsecourser, . . . strong debaucher and seducer of youth,"

VAL CUTTING, "that helps Captain Jordan to roar, a circling boy,"

CAPTAIN WHIT, a bawd, "esquire of dames, madams, and twelvepenny ladies,"

NIGHTINGALE, "a sweet singer of new ballads allurant. . . . Hear for your love, and buy for your money, 'A Delicate Ballad o' the Ferret and the Coney'; 'A Preservative again' the Punk's Evil'; another of 'Goose-green Starch and the Devil'; 'A Dozen of Divine Points'; and 'The Godly Garters'; 'The Fairing of Good Counsel,' of an ell and three quarters. What is't you buy?"

EZECHIEL EDGWORTH, "a civil cutpurse searchant, . . . that keeps company with the roarers and disburses all still. He has ever money in his purse; he pays for them, and they roar for him; one does good offices for another. They call him the 'secretary.' . . . A great friend of the ballad-man's; they are never asunder. . . . A very quick hand, sir,"

ALICE, mistress o' the game, "your punk of Turnbull, ramping Alice. . . . The poor common whores can ha' no traffic for the privy rich ones; your caps and hoods of velvet call away [the] customers,"

JOAN TRASH, a gingerbread-woman, "lady of the basket; . . . though [she] be a little crooked o' [her] body, [she'll] be found as upright in [her] dealing as any woman in Smithfield,"

"right Bartholomew birds."

A TINDERBOXMAN, vendor of mousetraps. "Buy a mousetrap, a mousetrap, or a tormentor for a flea?"

A COSTERMONGER. "Buy any pears, very fine pears, pears fine!"

A CORNCUTTER. "Have you any corns i' your feet and toes?"

JOHN LITTLEWIT, "Proctor John Littlewit, one of the pretty wits o' Paul's, the Littlewit of London. . . . A pox o' these pretenders to wit! Your Three Cranes, Mitre, and Mermaid men! Not a corn of true salt, nor a grain of right mustard amongst them all. . . . When a quirk or a quiblin does scape thee, and thou dost not watch and apprehend it, and bring it afore the constable of conceit . . . let 'em carry thee out o' th' archdeacon's court into his kitchen, and make a Jack of thee, instead of a John,"

WIN-THE-FIGHT LITTLEWIT, his wife, "a pretty little soul, . . . with a strawberry breath, cherry-lips, apricot cheeks, and a soft velvet head, like a melicotton. . . . She has as little wit as her husband, it seems,"

DAME PURECRAFT, "the sober matron," mother of Mistress Littlewit. "She is not a wise wilful widow for nothing, nor a sanctified sister for a song,"

ZEAL-OF-THE-LAND BUSY, suitor to Dame Purecraft, "a stone puritan with a sorrel head and beard, . . . [and] an old elder come from Banbury, . . . that puts in here at meal-tide, . . . says a grace as long as his breath lasts him; . . . he breaks his buttons and cracks seams at every saying he sobs out. . . . He is more than an elder; he is a prophet, sir. . . . He was a baker, sir, but he does dream now and see visions. . . . By his profession he . . . derides all antiquity, defies any other learning than inspiration, and what discretion soever years should afford him, it is all prevented in his original ignorance. . . . He eats with his eyes as well as his teeth,"

"These are Banbury bloods, o' the sincere stud, come a-pig-hunting. . . . They are all sippers, sippers o' the City; they look as they would not drink off two penn'orth of bottle-ale amongst 'em."

SOLOMON, Littlewit's man.

NED WINWIFE, Rabbi Busy's rival, a gentleman.

TOM QUARLOUS, a gamester, companion to Winwife; "he is the more madcap of the two."

MASTER BARTHOLOMEW COKES, of Harrow o' the Hill, i' th' county of Middlesex, Esquire, "resolute Bat, i' faith." Brother of Mistress Overdo, betrothed to Grace Wellborn, and but nineteen years old, "he is now upon his making and marring. . . . His foolish schoolmasters have . . . almost spoiled him; he has learned nothing but to sing catches and repeat 'Rattle, bladder, rattle!' and 'O Madge.' I dare not let him walk alone for fear of learning of vile tunes, which he will sing at supper and in sermon-times! . . . He has a head full of bees. . . . If he go to the Fair, he will buy of everything to a baby there, and household stuff for that, too. If a leg or an arm on him did not grow on, he would lose it in the press. . . . And then he is such a ravener after fruit!" ("A delicate great boy! Methinks he outscrambles 'em all. I cannot persuade myself but he goes to grammar school yet, and plays the truant today. . . . Was there ever green plover so pulled!")

HUMPHREY WASPE, "Master Numps," his "dry nurse; . . . he is his master's both hands, I assure you." ("Sir, if you have a mind to mock him, mock him softly, and look t'other way. . . . A terrible testy old fellow, and his name is Waspe, too. . . . How now, Numps! Almost tired i' your protectorship? Overparted? Overparted? . . . Hold thy hand, child of wrath, and heir to anger, make it not Childermas Day in thy fury, or the feast of the French Bartholomew, parent of the massacre!")

ADAM OVERDO, "a wise Justice of Peace meditant," and guardian of Grace Wellborn. Disguised as "a certain middling thing between a fool and a madman," he plays Junius Brutus or Haroun al Rachid at the Fair to see for himself what "enormities" are being practiced there. Being a fool himself, he misinterprets much of what he sees and hears. ("Of all beasts I love the serious ass; he that takes pains to be one.")

DAME ALICE OVERDO, the Justice's wife and the sister of Bartholomew Cokes, "goody she-justice, Mistress French-hood! . . . She does so love them all over in terms of justice and the style of authority, with her hood upright, that I beseech you come away, gentlemen, and see't."

GRACE WELLBORN, ward to Justice Overdo and betrothed to Bartholomew Cokes. "What a pity 'tis yonder wench should marry such a Cokes! . . . She seems to be discreet, and as sober as she is handsome. . . . Ay, and, if you mark her, what a restrained scorn she casts upon all his behavior and speeches!"

TROUBLEALL, "a fellow that is distracted, they say. . . . He was an officer in the court of pie-pouldres [i.e., a court of justice to settle disputes between persons resorting to the Fair] here last year, and put out of his place by Justice Overdo, . . . upon which he took an idle conceit, and is run mad upon't, so that ever since he will do nothing but by Justice Overdo's warrant. He will not eat a crust, nor drink a little, nor make him in his apparel ready. His wife . . . cannot get him . . . shift his shirt, without his warrant." ("A madman that haunts the Fair. . . . It's a marvel he has not more followers after his ragged heels.")

NORDEN, a clothier and a northern man, "my galloway nag, . . . [who] does change cloth for ale in the Fair here."

PUPPY, a westerner, "a strong man, a mighty man, my Lord Mayor's man, and a wrestler. He has wrestled so long with the bottle here that the man with the beard hash almosht streek up hish heelsh."

DAVY BRISTLE, also called Oliver, "a Welsh . . . runt; . . . you stink of leeks, metheglin, and cheese, you rogue," }
TOBY HAGGISE, } "His Majesty's watch."
POCHER, a beadle, }

PUPPETS: Cast of *Hero and Leander:*

Leander of Puddlewharf,
Hero of the Bankside,
Cole, a sculler,
Cupid, "distinguished like Jonas the drawer, . . . [who] strikes Hero in love . . . with a pint of sherry,"
       } two friends, "lodged in that alehouse in
Damon, | which fair Hero does do. . . . They are
Pythias, [whoremasters both, sir, that's a plain
       } case,"
The Ghost of their friend Dionysius, "not like a monarch, but the master of a school, in a scrivener's furred gown,"

"They are civil company; . . . they offer not to fleer, nor jeer, nor break jests, as the great players do. And then, there goes not so much to the feasting of 'em, or making of 'em drunk, as to the other."

Officers, Porters, Boys, and Visitors to the Fair.

Setting: Smithfield, London, at some unspecified time.

"Would I might lose my doublet, and hose too, as I am an honest man, and never stir, if I think there be anything but thieving and coz'ning in this whole Fair."

Act I

It is August 24—St. Bartholomew's Day—and John Littlewit, a featherbrained proctor of London, is looking for an excuse to attend Bartholomew Fair, eat pig, and see performed a puppet play which he has secretly written for production there. Littlewit needs an excuse because his mother-in-law, Dame Purecraft, is a lady of Puritan propensities, and any suggestion that a member of her family visit so profane a place is sure to meet with disapproval. Littlewit's pride is his ability to play upon words, and to some extent his desire to attend the Fair has arisen while writing out a license to marry for Master Bartholomew Cokes, Esquire, of Harrow o' the Hill, and Mistress Grace Wellborn, ward to Adam Overdo, Justice of the Peace: "Bartholomew upon Bartholomew!" His wish to see the Fair is only increased by those who are on their way there: Master Winwife, a suitor to Dame Purecraft, temporarily out of favor because of the influence of the reverend elder, Zeal-of-the-Land Busy; Master Quarlous, his friend; Waspe, the choleric, quarrelsome servant of Cokes, who has come for his young irresponsible master's marriage license; Cokes himself; Grace, his fiancée; and Mistress Overdo, his sister. All stop by on their way to Smithfield.

Hence, with all this stimulation, Master Littlewit resorts to strategy. His wife, who glories in the Puritan appellation of Win-the-Fight Littlewit, is with child, and ready enough, at her husband's suggestion, to profess a great longing to eat roast pig—Bartholomew pig—at Bartholomew Fair. She screams and seems to swoon; Dame Purecraft, her doting mother, runs to her assistance, urges her to resist these carnal provocations, and at last calls in Rabbi Busy, for his faithful fortification against the adversary. That worthy is also fond of eating—indeed, he is found "fast by the teeth i' the cold turkey pie i' the cupboard with a great white loaf on his left hand and a glass of malmsey on his right." In spite of his Puritan disapproval of the Fair, Busy readily reasons that there can be no harm in going there to eat pig, especially when Dame Purecraft urges him to "think to make it as lawful as he can." "It is subject to construction," he decides; pig "may be eaten in the Fair, . . . in a booth, the tents of the wicked. The place is not much, not very much; we may be religious in the midst of the profane; so it be eaten with a reformed mouth, with sobriety and humbleness, not gorged in with gluttony or greediness, there's the fear. For, should she go there, as taking pride in the place, . . . to feed the vanity of the eye or the lust of the palate, . . . it were not well, . . . it were abominable."

Accordingly, the whole Littlewit family make haste to go to the Fair, taking with them Brother Busy, who resolves by public eating of swine's flesh to profess his loathing of Judaism. But the Littlewits, on pleasure bent, plan to lose him somewhere in a booth.

Act II

Bartholomew Fair is filled with booths and stalls, barrows and baskets, belonging to vendors of divers wares, and with a motley array of stall-keepers, balladmongers, bullies, bawds, and cutpurses. Lanthorn Leatherhead has an assortment of trinkets and toys as well as a puppet show; Joan Trash, "the lady of the basket," sells her gingerbread progeny; Ursula, herself "a walking sow of tallow," sells bottle-ale and roast pig, with the assistance of her lean tapster, Mooncalf, and lets out an inner room of her booth for purposes of iniquity. Nightingale, the ballad singer, works with Ezechiel Edgworth, the cutpurse, there; there are roarers, like Knockem Jordan, "the ranger of Turnbull," and his companion, Val Cutting; bawds and punks, like Captain Whit and ramping Alice; and costermongers, corncutters, tinderboxmen, and other petty chapmen—all plying their trades, crying their wares, renewing old acquaintance, and quarreling among themselves. Watching over all this hubbub is Justice Overdo, in disguise, playing Junius Brutus or Haroun al Rachid in the Fair, in order that he may see for himself what "enormities" are being practiced there. He is only an overzealous fool, who, fortunately, absurdly misinterprets what he hears and sees, and, like other well-intentioned meddlers, only gets into trouble for his pains.

While the good justice looks on, Tom Quarlous, Ned Winwife, and Knockem Jordan get into an altercation as they drink and smoke together; Ursula, who has become a little tipsy, falls down with a pan of hot grease, and "resolute Bat" Cokes comes to see everything in the Fair. To Adam Overdo all these confusions are "the fruits of bottle-ale and tobacco, the foam of the one, and the fumes of the other." To restrain young Cokes, he begins a lecture on the creeping venom of these subtle serpents, fascinates the young simpleton, gathers a crowd, and enables Edgworth to relieve Cokes of his purse, which the pickpocket covertly conveys to his confederate Nightingale. When the loss is discovered, everyone talks at once, and in the end, led by Waspe, all shower blows upon the innocent but misguided justice. "To see what bad events may peep out o' the tail of good purposes!"

Act III

A little later in the day the Littlewits, Dame Purecraft, and Brother Busy at last find their way to Ursula's booth. "The place is Smithfield, . . . the grove of hobbyhorses and trinkets, the wares are the wares of devils, and the whole Fair is the shop of Satan; they are hooks and baits, very baits, that are hung out on every side, to catch you, and to hold you, as it were, by the gills." But here is pig, savory pig, and Busy puts aside his caution, following the scent and leading the party into the tents of the unclean for once, where Littlewit may satisfy his wife's frailty and longing for roast flesh. To Ursula these guests are just sippers who "look as they would not drink off two penn'orth of bottle-ale amongst 'em." But to Knockem and Whit, who are hanging about the pig-woman's booth, they are "Banbury bloods o' the sincere stud, . . . fine ambling hypocrites, . . . good gluttons," and they turn tapster and waiter to serve them.

Meanwhile, young Bartholomew Cokes is buying up everything in the Fair and loading poor Numps down with the trinkets he has bought. To furnish out a masque at his prospective wedding, Cokes buys out Leatherhead's stock of toys and Joan Trash's gingerbread men, trustingly leaving these purchases to be picked up later. But Edgworth and Nightingale spy him as he boastfully shows another purse and defies all pickpockets. The ballad singer gathers a crowd with a song of warning against cutpurses; Cokes again is fascinated, and a second time his pocket is picked. Around the ballad singer Justice Overdo is still hovering because from the beginning he has taken a fancy to this civil young man. When Cokes's second loss is discovered, the good man is again beaten and carried off to the stocks. So disgusted is Waspe with his foolish charge that he takes from him for safe keeping the box containing his marriage license.

But Winwife and Quarlous, from a distance, have seen everything. In admiration of his skill rather than in censure, they call Edgworth to them and promise not to betray him to the law; the condition is that he get the little black box away from Waspe and bring it to them. The rogue undertakes the mission gladly; he values a gentleman's good opinion.

By now the Littlewits have finished feasting on pig, and are ready to see the sights of the Fair. But they shall never do so unless Win longs again, this time to see hobbyhorses, fine devices, the bull with five legs, and the great hog. "Now you ha' begun with pig," argues the husband, "you may long for anything, Win, and so for my motion [i.e., puppet show], Win." Brother Busy, too, is ready for other occupations. Having filled his belly with pig, he is moved by the Spirit to reprove sin and to denounce this wicked and foul Fair and all "Bartholomew abominations." He rails at Leatherhead's toys as rank idols, and destroys Joan Trash's gingerbread men as a nest of popish images. Hence, he, too, is carried off to the stocks, followed by Dame Purecraft. At last the Littlewits are left to their own devices. But overeating and drinking bring their natural consequences, and the pair seek accommodation in Ursula's booth. Meanwhile, Joan Trash and Leatherhead get out of the way lest their customer Cokes return for his purchases.

Act IV

For most of the habitués of the Fair, complications are only beginning. In the stocks the disguised Justice Overdo resolves to bear his adversity patiently as an example to his enemies. But his conscience is soon disturbed by Troubleall, a demented creature who has conceived an absurd veneration for the justice—not because Overdo has ever used him compassionately, but rather because once, in his severity, the justice displaced the poor fellow from a minor office he held. Now Troubleall insists upon Justice Overdo's omnipotent warrant for everything, to the annoyance of everyone he meets.

Once more the irresponsible Cokes is victimized by Nightingale and Edgworth. They trip up a costermonger, who is their confederate; Cokes falls a-scrambling for the pears he upsets from his basket; Nightingale offers to hold his hat, cloak, and sword, and then runs off with them. Grace Wellborn's disgust with her fiancé Cokes has grown as his childish irresponsibility has got him into scrape after scrape, and she has shown it. Now she finds herself wooed by both Winwife and Quarlous, who are prepared to fight one another over her. To prevent anything untoward, Grace agrees to accept one or the other of her new suitors by lottery. Each is to write a name he has a fancy to in a notebook, and the choice shall be left to the next person who comes that way. He is Troubleall, the madman, who demands Justice Overdo's warrant for what they would have him do, but at last is persuaded to make a choice. But Grace insists that for the time being it remain secret.

Meanwhile, Edgworth has been seeking an opportunity to filch the marriage license away from Waspe. He finds him in a drunken altercation with Puppy, a wrestler, and Nordern, a clothier; the altercation becomes a fight, and in the melee Edgworth gets the box and passes it on to Quarlous. For rioting, Waspe is also carried off to the stocks where he joins Justice Overdo and Brother Busy, who is rejoicing in his affliction and prophesying the destruction of all fairs and May games, wakes and Whitsun ales. But as the officers open the stocks to receive him, Waspe cleverly puts his shoe on his hand and slips it in for his leg; hence, when the backs of the watch are turned he easily makes his escape. In the confusion which follows, the stocks are left unlocked, and Overdo and Busy likewise run off.

As time goes on, Mistress Overdo also has need of a jordan, and calls at Ursula's booth, only to get into a quarrel with "ramping Alice, . . . the tripe of Turnbull," who misunderstands her needs and objects strenuously to amateur competition. And Tom Quarlous, possessed of the marriage license from which Cokes's name can easily be erased, is not sure that it is his name that Troubleall picked. Hence, he sets out in search of the madman who has served as fortuneteller.

Act V

Late afternoon at the Fair brings with it numerous transformations. Lanthorn Leatherhead has given up his toy-booth and turned puppeteer. Justice Overdo changes his disguise to that of porter in order that, in another form, he may "break out in rain and hail, lightning and thunder, upon the head of enormity." Quarlous persuades Troubleall to lend him his rags, and in the disguise he discovers that Winwife and not he has been the lucky man with Grace. But at the same time Quarlous finds himself followed by Dame Purecraft, who remembers a prophecy about her marrying a madman and now earnestly proposes to the madman in hand. Why shouldn't Quarlous marry six thousand pounds, and a good trade, too, now that Winwife has the other wench?

At last all of the principals meet at the puppet show, which is a gross mixture of the stories of *Hero and Leander* and *Damon and Pythias*. Master Littlewit the author has taken "a little pains to reduce it to a more familiar strain for our people," and has "made it a little easy and modern for the times." Cokes is present; so are Winwife and Grace; Mistress Littlewit and Mistress Overdo in the bad company of Knockem, Edgworth, and Whit; Waspe and Justice Overdo, still seeking for enormities. The absurd play is interrupted by the inrush of Brother Busy, who has scented that bête noire of the Jacobean Puritan, theatricals, and has gaped, "as the oyster for the tide, after their destruction." His denunciation is both unreasonable and violent and includes most of the stale arguments which the Puritans employed against plays and players. But Lanthorn Leatherhead, who is a ventriloquist as well as a puppeteer, cleverly gets Busy into an argument with one of the puppets, who was cast as Dionysius. The little creature refutes all of Busy's arguments, even his objection that on a stage men dress as women and women as men. It will not hold against puppets, and by the plain demonstration of lifting its garment the puppet proves that there is neither male nor female amongst them. Brother Busy is converted, but before the play can be resumed, Justice Overdo reveals himself and in his denunciations not only characterizes some of the rascals accurately, but also exposes his own folly. Quarlous, who turns up with his bride, Dame Purecraft, sets him right about Nightingale, the "innocent" young man the justice has been so solicitous of all day. The rogues, the hypocrites, and the fools all come off scot free, and Adam Overdo invites everyone home with him to supper, for, after all, his intentions—like the author's—are *ad correctionem, non ad destructionem; ad aedificandum, non ad diruendum.*

THE STAPLE OF NEWS

A COMEDY

(1626)

DRAMATIS PERSONAE

THE PROLOGUE, "gentleman-usher to the play,"

MISTRESS MIRTH, "daughter of Christmas and spirit of Shrovetide,"

MISTRESS TATTLE,

MISTRESS EXPECTATION; "we would entreat your ladyship expect no more than you can understand."

CURIOSITY, my Lady Censure,

"persons of quality, . . . and women of fashion, and come to see and to be seen; . . . such as had a longing to see plays and sit upon them, . . . and arraign both them and their poets. . . . They say 'it's merry when gossips meet.' "

characters in the Induction and the Intermeans, or Choruses.

The BOOKHOLDER, or prompter,

Tiremen, to mend the lights, and "to give light to the business,"

LADY AURELIA CLARA PECUNIA DO-ALL, "a gentlewoman sojourning with [Pennyboy Junior's] uncle, Richer Pennyboy, . . . a Cornish gentlewoman; . . . a great lady, indeed she is, and not of mortal race. Infanta of the Mines. Her grace's grandfather was duke and cousin to the King of Ophir the Subterranean. Let that pass. . . . A great princess, of mighty power, though she live in private with a contracted family. . . . She is the talk o' the time! The adventure of the age! . . . All the world are suitors to her. . . . All sorts of men and all professions. . . . You shall have stall-fed doctors, cramm'd divines, make love to her, and with those studied and perfumed flatteries, as no room can stink more elegant than where they are. . . . And by your leave, good master's worship, some of your velvet coat make corpulent curtsies to her till they crack for't." ("All this nether world is yours, you command it, and do sway it; the honor of it, and the honesty, the reputation, ay, and the religion, . . . is Queen Pecunia's.")

PENNYBOY JUNIOR, "a prodigal, a tub without a bottom, . . . top of our house, the flourishing and flaunting Pennyboy. . . . This Pennyboy is now the heir, . . . the lord and the prince of plenty." He is chief suitor to Lady Pecunia.

FRANCIS, or FRANK, PENNYBOY, father to Pennyboy Junior, who pretends to have died, but disguises as a canter [i.e., a beggar or vagabond], and attaches himself to his spendthrift son. "A loving and obedient father, . . . a right kindhearted man, to die so opportunely, . . . and to settle all things so well! . . . This canter would make a good brave burgess in some barn."

RICHER PENNYBOY [called PENNYBOY SENIOR], "Old Harry Pennyboy, and, to make rhyme, close wary Pennyboy, . . . who is a crafty knave enough, believe it." He is the miserly uncle of Pennyboy Junior, and the guardian of Lady Pecunia. "A notable tough rascal, this old Pennyboy! Right City-bred! . . . In Silver Street, the region of money, a good seat for an usurer. . . . He has the monopoly of sole-speaking. . . . Old money-bawd!"

CYMBAL, "the Governor of the Staple; . . . he is the chief, and after him the emissaries, . . . their tinkling captain. . . . A wit, sir; . . . but he has brave wits under him. [He is] a courtier, sir, or somewhat more, [to] have this tempting language." He is also "grand-captain of the jeerers," a group of idle, sharp-tongued, social parasites.

REGISTER OF THE STAPLE. " 'Tis the House of Fame, sir, where both the curious and the negligent, the scrupulous and careless, wild and staid, the idle and laborious, all do meet, to taste the cornucopia of her rumors, which she, the mother of sport, pleaseth to scatter among the vulgar,"

NATHANIEL, first clerk of the office of the Staple; "a decay'd stationer he was, but knows news well, can sort and rank them, . . . and for a need can make them. . . . True Paul's, bred in the churchyard. . . . Would Butter would come in and spread itself a little to us!"

"They manage all at home, and sort, and file, and seal the news, and issue them."

TOM, Pennyboy Junior's barber, made second clerk of the office, "a pretty scholar, and a Master of Arts was made—or went out Master of Arts in a throng—at the university. . . . He's a nimble fellow, and alike skill'd in every liberal science, as having certain snaps of all; a neat quick vain in forging news, too. I do love him,"

MASTER FITTON [i.e., Liar], "emissary Court; . . . this is a moth, a rascal, a court-rat. . . . He's a jeerer, too. What's that? . . . A wit, . . . or half a wit, some of them are half-wits; two to a wit, there are a set of them,"

MASTER AMBLER, "emissary Paul's, a fine paced gentleman as you shall see walk the middle aisle,"

FROY HANS BUZ, a Dutchman; "he is emissary Exchange,"

[They do not appear in person.]

"Emissaries? Stay, there's a fine new word! . . . Pray God it signify anything!"

DOMINE PICKLOCK, "a pettyfogger," Pennyboy Junior's scheming "man of law and learn'd attorney," appointed emissary Westminster. "A fine pragmatic. . . . Thou seem'st by thy language no less a courtier than a man of law. . . . Tut, [he is] Vertumnus [a classical divinity who could change shape as he pleased]; on every change, or chance, upon occasion, a true chameleon, [he] can color for it. [He] move[s] upon [his] axle like a turnpike, fit[s] [his] face to the parties, and become[s] straight one of them. . . . A fine round head, when those two lugs are off, to trundle through a pillory! . . . My gowned vulture!"

DR. ALMANAC, a quacksalver, "this dog-leech," who pretends to be "a fine physician, one of the jeerers,"

SHUNFIELD, a cowardly "man of war. He was our muster-master, . . . but a sea captain now," and jeerer,

MADRIGAL, an insipid but popular poetaster and jeerer, "the crowned poet of these our times. . . . He has an odd singing name, . . . is . . . an heir to a fair fortune, . . . a dainty scholar, and a pretty poet, . . . [but he is] freshman in the world. . . . My egg-chinn'd laureate, . . . he's of years, though he have little beard,"

YOUNG MASTER PIEDMANTLE, a mercenary pursuivant at arms, "an apprentice in armory. . . . No herald yet, a heraldet,"

suitors to the Lady Pecunia. They "are all cogging Jacks, a covey of wits, . . . or rather an aery, for [they] are birds of prey. . . . [They] jeer all kind of persons [they] meet withal, of any rank or quality, and if [they] cannot jeer them, [they] jeer [them]selves. . . . A pretty sweet society, and a grateful. . . . This is a very wholesome exercise, and comely, like lepers showing one another their scabs, or flies feeding on ulcers."

BROKER, secretary and gentleman usher to the Lady Pecunia; "thou hast a sweeping face; thy beard is like a broom."

MOTHER MORTGAGE, old nurse to Lady Pecunia. "If you have a tenement, or such a morsel, though she have no teeth, she loves a sweetmeat, anything that melts in her warm gums."

MISTRESS ROSE WAX, chambermaid to Lady Pecunia; "she's a good pliant wench, and easy to be wrought, sir."

MISTRESS STATUTE, "a judge's daughter, but somewhat stately,"
MISTRESS BAND [i.e., Bond]; "her father's but a scrivener, but she can almost as much with my lady as the other," } gentlewomen to Lady Pecunia.

PAWN and his Fellow, two grooms to the Lady Pecunia. [They do not speak and appear only as part of her train.]

FASHIONER, the tailor of the times, "a silkworm [who] deal[s] in satins and velvets and rich plushes. . . . [He is] an ass, old Aesop's ass" [i.e., he was never meant to be a lap dog, like Tom the Barber]. ("Pray, thee, peace; I cannot abide a talking tailor,")
LEATHERLEG, a shoemaker,
A Haberdasher, or Hatter,
A Linener [i.e., a shirtmaker],
A Spurrier, } "A brave troop, all billmen" to Pennyboy Junior.

LICKFINGER OF THE DEVIL TAVERN, "mine old host of Ram-alley," master-cook and parcel-poet. "A saucy Jack you are, that's once. . . . The glory of the kitchen! . . . He holds no man can be a poet that is not a good cook, to know the palates and several tastes of the time. He draws all arts out of the kitchen, but the art of poetry, which he concludes the same with cookery. . . . A master-cook! Why he's the man of men! . . . He has Nature in a pot, 'bove all chemists; . . . he is an architect, an engineer, a soldier, a physician, a philosopher, a general mathematician."

A Porter to Richer Pennyboy.

BLOCK,
LOLLARD, } dogs belonging to Richer Pennyboy.

A Country Butterwoman, and other Customers of the Staple, male and female.
Fiddlers.
NICHOLAS, a singing boy.
Setting: London in 1625.

> "*Baits, sir, for the people! And they will bite like flies!*"

INDUCTION AND INTERMEANS

Like the citizens in *The Knight of the Burning Pestle,* four impromptu
critics, "lady-like attired," and named Mirth, Tattle, Expectation, and
Censure, interrupt the Prologue, take seats on the stage, and at the end
of each act comment upon what occurs. The play is a scurvy thing; there
is neither a fool nor a devil in it; the news given out is monstrous and
stale, "ill-cook'd and ill-dished"; and the poet is "a decay'd wit, . . .
broken, . . . nonsolvent, . . . and forever forfeit, . . . to scorn of
mirth, . . . censure, . . . expectation, . . . tattle!"
Moreover, their blundering gabble about the play, and their lively
gossip about current affairs contrast strikingly with the semiallegory of
the drama and impart a flavor of reality to the whole.

Act I

Surrounded by his shoemaker, tailor, linener, haberdasher, barber, and
spurrier—"all billmen"—Pennyboy Junior, a carefree young prodigal,
prepares to face the world. He is just twenty-one, and the hour has come
which he has long anticipated. Gone are his pupilage and vassalage together, liberty at last is his; his father is dead and he has come into his
property, "an heir t'above two thousand a year." From Tom the barber,
who has a pretty talent himself in spreading gossip and is a Master of
Arts of sorts, Pennyboy Junior hears of the establishment—in the very
house in which he has chambers—of a Staple of News, "where all the
news of all sorts shall be brought and there be examined, and then
registered, and so issued under the seal of the office as Staple News—
no other news be current. . . . A place of huge commerce it will be!"
Promising to gratify Tom's wish for a clerkship in this news office, even
if it cost fifty or a hundred pounds, Pennyboy Junior resolves to visit the
Staple. Without so much as examining their bills, he pays all of his
parasites and sets out, taking with him an old canter or vagabond in a
patched and ragged cloak whom he fancifully calls his "founder," because the fellow first brought him news from the country of his father's
death. "The difference 'twixt the covetous and the prodigal!" sighs the
old beggar. "The covetous man never has money, and the prodigal
will have none shortly!" The canter is really Pennyboy Junior's father
in disguise.

At the Staple, Register and clerks are examining and filing all sorts of news, "authentical and apocryphal, . . . barbers' news and tailors' news, porters' and watermen's news, . . . vacation news, term news, and Christmas news, . . . Protestant news and pontifical news." Even *Mercurius Britannicus* gains by the monopoly, for "where he was wont to get in hungry captains, obscure statesmen, . . . fellows to drink with him in a dark room in a tavern, . . . now all that charge is saved."

Pennyboy Junior is much impressed by news which may be stored for use as needed, which doesn't have to be printed to be true, and which can in a few years, "as the age doats," be used over again. "Why," he says to Cymbal, "if the common honest people *will* be abused, why should they not have their pleasure in the believing lies are made for them? . . . Sir, I admire the method of your place. All things within't are so digested, fitted, and composed, as it shows Wit had married Order."

He has no difficulty in purchasing Tom the barber a clerkship for fifty pounds.

At the same time Pennyboy Junior learns secretly from Picklock his attorney who has purchased a post as "emissary"—the grand name by which reporters are designated—that Master Cymbal, the proprietor of the establishment, has designs upon a gentlewoman once intended for Pennyboy Junior. She is the Lady Pecunia, who is the ward of his uncle Richer Pennyboy. The great lady has many suitors—Dr. Almanac, Captain Shunfield, Master Piedmantle, and Master Madrigal—and Pennyboy Junior resolves to cut out all rivals.

Act II

Richer Pennyboy is a cantankerous, covetous old usurer who has been a strict and careful guardian of the Lady Pecunia. But he is her grace's martyr, as he himself admits, and now that he is aging, he prepares this "noble, young, free, gracious lady" for the reception of suitors. "They are a few that know your merit, lady," he tells her, "and can value it. Yourself scarce understands your proper powers." Richer Pennyboy's wealth attracts gifts; he has venison sent him, fowl, and fish, in such abundance that he is sick to see it. It thrusts a sin upon him he was ne'er guilty of. "Nothing but gluttony, gross gluttony," he complains, "will undo this land," and the reduction of interest rates, which eats up the poor and devours their inheritance. "When moneys went at ten in the hundred," he argues, "I, and such as I, the servants of Pecunia, could spare the poor two out of ten, and did." Now he can spare them nothing.

Soon the suitors appear—Piedmantle the heraldet, Almanac the doctor, Fitton the courtier, Shunfield the man of war turned sea captain, Madrigal the poetaster—all to see Lady Pecunia. But Richer Pennyboy contemptuously puts them off: "Provide you better names, [then] Pecunia is for you." Though they taunt him with being the jailer, the slave, the idolator of Pecunia, he is obdurate. "I remember, too, when you had lands and credit, worship, friends, ay, and could give security. Now you have none, or will have none right shortly. . . . I have all these, . . . and am right heartily glad of all our memories, and both the changes."

But he welcomes Pennyboy Junior, the flourishing and flaunting heir of his house, and introduces him to Pecunia, who instantly shows the young man ardent favor. She accompanies him to dine in the Apollo Room of the Devil Tavern and to visit the Staple of News.

Act III

Far from loyally supporting the interests of Pennyboy Junior alone, the two-faced attorney Picklock hastens to the Staple to prepare Cymbal and his associates for the Lady Pecunia's visit, and to urge that all there "make court unto her, that she may first but know, then love the place. . . . She will be weary of the prodigal quickly." Hence, when Pennyboy Junior and the lady arrive, they see the Staple at its busiest. They ask for news—"any, any kind, so it be news"—and hear the newest there: the King of Spain has been made both Pope and Emperor; a burning glass has been found in Galileo's study which will set fire to any fleet at sea, and by moonlight, too; the Dutch have invented a kind of submarine, an invisible eel to swim the haven at Dunkirk and sink the shipping there; perpetual motion has been discovered by an alewife at St. Katherine's; the Turk has turned Christian; a colony of cooks has been sent to America to convert the cannibals; a recipe has been discovered for growing hair on bald pates from seed.

Meanwhile, the Master of the Staple surreptitiously tries to win Pecunia away from Pennyboy Junior, and his associates use their blandishments upon Statute, Band, Mortgage, and Wax, her gentlewomen attendants. But in vain; they are "the family of scorn." The party leaves for the Apollo, followed soon by the discarded, parasitic suitors—Fitton, Almanac, Shunfield, and Madrigal. At Lickfinger's establishment they are sure of a good dinner and a jeer, perhaps.

But Cymbal, the master, hastens to call upon Richer Pennyboy, presents himself as a suitor to Lady Pecunia with six thousand pounds a year, and offers the old money-bawd half of the profits of his moiety in the Staple if he will only let his ward sojourn at the office. But, though Richer Pennyboy during the interview recovers miraculously from deafness and other ailments, the old fellow launches into a vehement tirade against the decay of honest trade and the folly and the extravagance of the age. His visitor timidly protests at his monopoly of the conversation, the old fox loses his temper, and the interview ends with each calling the other names.

Act IV

In the Apollo Room of the Devil Tavern, in spite of the mockery of the old canter, the jeerers join the party of Pennyboy Junior and Lady Pecunia. All court her and heap praise upon her. Aware at last of her great power, the lady confers kisses all around—at the bidding of the foolish Pennyboy. Madrigal makes verses in her honor, fiddlers and a singer are fetched in, and the whole party is intoxicated with the liberty they enjoy. Only the canter sees how the prodigal is prostituting his mistress, and only he is sick of indignation at these rascals.

At last, alarmed by the long absence of his ward and fearful that his trust has been wronged, Old Richer Pennyboy comes to the Apollo to seek Lady Pecunia and take her home. But she refuses to leave Pennyboy Junior and her other lewd companions and to return to her prison. She exposes the old man's churlish treatment of her, and in the end he is kicked and thrown out of doors, to return to his kennel and consult his dogs, "the Lares of [his] family." The fiddlers drown out the noise, the riot continues, Piedmantle brings in the flattering pedigree he has drawn up for Lady Pecunia, and is soundly kissed for his pains.

At last in disgust because he can bear these goings on no longer, the old canter denounces all present, their jeering, their project of forming a college, their presumptuous folly. Pennyboy Junior has demonstrated his inability to take care of Lady Pecunia when he had her and to treat her worthily. Accordingly, the old man throws off his disguise and takes the lady in charge. Turning to his son he vents his contempt for him thus: "Thou prodigal, was I so careful for thee to procure . . . this noble match for thee, and dost thou . . . scatter thy mistress' favors . . . on such rascals who are the scum . . . of men?"

> If thou hadst sought out good and virtuous persons
> Of these professions, I had loved thee and them.
> For these shall never have that plea against me,
> Of color of advantage, that I hate
> Their callings, but their manners and their vices.

Money cannot make noble; it may "give place, and rank, but it can give no virtue." The indignant father bequeaths his ragged cloak to his prodigal son.

Act V

Penitent at last in his rags, Pennyboy Junior hears the news that the Staple has gone bankrupt, "wretchedly broke, . . . all to pieces, quite dissolved, . . . soon as they heard the Infanta was got from them." It is little consolation, but the news that his father and Lawyer Picklock have fallen out stirs him from his lethargy. The fraudulent attorney denies the feoffment and the trust Old Frank Pennyboy made out to him of his whole estate which he was to administer for the boy's benefit. While professing friendship for Pennyboy Junior and consoling him in his misfortune, the shyster secretly plans to ruin both father and son. But to the boy Picklock unguardedly does admit having such a deed, and by a stratagem Pennyboy Junior gets possession of it.

Meanwhile, because of his loss of Lady Pecunia and his other misfortunes, Richer Pennyboy has gone mad and is arraigning his poor dogs, Block and Lollard, for what has happened to him. In his affliction he is set on by the jeerers, led now by Cymbal. But he holds his own against them until he is rescued by his brother and his nephew, Pennyboy Junior. The jeerers are put to flight, father and repentant son are reconciled, the dishonest Picklock is set in the pillory, Pennyboy Junior is made the heir of Richer Pennyboy, and he and the Lady Pecunia are united in marriage.

••••——◆——••••

THOMAS HEYWOOD
(1573?-1641)

BIOGRAPHY. Pamphleteer, poet, translator, compiler, as well as pageant-writer and playmaker, Thomas Heywood was the most prolific of Elizabethan dramatists; he confessed to having had "either an entire hand or at least a main finger" in some two hundred and twenty plays. Only a small fraction of this number has survived or is known to be his work; and in spite of his industry, Heywood never amounted to more than a literary journeyman.

Born about 1573, the son of a country parson, Thomas Heywood came of a Lincolnshire family, probably the same one to which the earlier dramatist John Heywood belonged. He was educated at Cambridge and was said to have once been fellow of Peterhouse. The first certain record of him in London dates from 1596, when he was writing for the Admiral's Men, usually in collaboration. In 1598 he was mentioned by Meres in Palladis Tamia as among the "best for comedy." Later references to him show him to have been both a playwright and an actor and to have transferred his services from company to company. For years he wrote Lord Mayors' pageants and turned his hand to almost every kind of literary hackwork. He projected but did not finish a *Lives of All the Poets,* died in 1641, and was buried in St. James's, Clerkenwell.

CRITICAL COMMENT. Called by Charles Lamb "a sort of prose Shakespeare," Thomas Heywood was intentionally much more popular in his appeal than was his great contemporary. Romance and chivalric adventure, historical and pseudohistorical action, as well as contemporary life, were his subjects, all of them treated with a great deal of vitality. Heywood both loved and understood people; he also knew what they liked when they went to the theatre.

A Woman Killed with Kindness is that rare thing in Elizabethan drama, a domestic play which depicts English country home life and treats the human relationships of ordinary people, rather than of the great. What is more rare still, the play is a tragedy of pathos without bloodshed. It even breaks with ethical convention which demands death for the guilty wife; for justifiable revenge on the part of the husband, Frankford substitutes Christian forgiveness. But the effect upon poor Mistress Anne is the same; to her sensitive heart her husband's restraint from violence is as fatal as a sword. Sympathy and understanding come too late. Strangely modern in its psychology, *A Woman Killed with Kindness* is one of the few Elizabethan plays revived in recent years on the stage—in 1887 in London; in 1914 in both New York and Paris; and in 1922 by the Birmingham Repertory Company.

The two-part *Fair Maid of the West,* on the other hand, is one of the few Elizabethan plays which breathe the very salt air of the time when all the youth of England were on fire. It is filled with astonishing people and fantastically heroic deeds in far places. Unlike the author's *Four Prentices of London, The Far Maid of the West* cannot be justified as having been written "in my infancy of judgment." Yet it belongs to the same sort of popular dramatic fare as that satirized by Beaumont in *The Knight of the Burning Pestle.*

SOURCES. *A Woman Killed with Kindness* is based upon several stories in Painter's *Palace of Pleasure,* but treated with considerable freedom. For *The Fair Maid of the West* no more satisfactory source has been found than Heywood's own inventive imagination.

BIBLIOGRAPHY

Collected Works:

The Dramatic Works of Thomas Heywood, Pearson Reprints, 6 volumes, 1874.

The Best Plays of Thomas Heywood, edited by A. W. Verity, Mermaid Series, 1888.

Monographs:

O. Cromwell, *Thomas Heywood: A Study in the Elizabethan Drama of Everyday Life,* New Haven, 1928.

A. M. Clark, *Thomas Heywood: Playwright and Miscellanist,* Oxford, 1931.

Henry Hitch Adams, *English Domestic or Homiletic Tragedy, 1575-1642,*

Being an Account of the Development of the Tragedy of the Common Man, Columbia, 1943.

F. S. Boas, *Thomas Heywood,* London, 1950.

A Woman Killed with Kindness:

Early editions: 1607; 1617 [called the "third edition" on the title page].

Modern editions: ed. A. W. Ward (TD, 1897), Katherine Lee Bates (Belles Lettres Series, 1917).

The Fair Maid of the West:

Early edition: 1631 (both parts).

Modern editions: ed. J. P. Collier and B. Field (Shakespeare Society, 1842–51), Katherine Lee Bates (Belles Lettres Series, 1917—Part I only).

A WOMAN KILLED WITH KINDNESS
(1603)

DRAMATIS PERSONAE

MASTER JOHN FRANKFORD, "the most perfect'st man that ever England bred a gentleman, . . . possessed of many fair revenues, . . . studied in all arts," and apparently happily married—"there's music in this sympathy [in years, descent, and education]; it carries consort and expectation of much joy."

MISTRESS ANNE FRANKFORD, "a wife so qualified, and with such ornaments both of the mind and body, . . . [that she seems] Beauty and Perfection's eldest daughter." But after her fall she is "the wofull'st wretch on earth, a woman made of tears." ("Is all this seeming gold plain copper?")

MASTER WENDOLL, friend to Frankford, "full of quality and fair desert; . . . he's affable, and seen in many things; discourses well, a good companion, and, though of small means, yet a gentleman." But he proves "a villain and a traitor to his friend. . . . [He has] divorced the truest turtles that ever lived together!" ("Man, woman, what thing mortal can we trust, when friends and bosom wives prove so unjust!")

SIR CHARLES MOUNTFORD, friend of Frankford; "it was not [he], but rage, did this vile murder" for which he must atone with many misfortunes.

SUSAN, pretty sister to Sir Charles Mountford, "an angel in a mortal's shape, . . . [whose] heart's so hardened with the frost of grief Death cannot pierce it through."

SIR FRANCIS ACTON, brother to Mistress Frankford; "all his wild blood [his] father spent on [him], . . . all his mad tricks were to his land entailed, and [Frank is] heir to all."

MASTER SHAFTON, "this flinty man," false friend to Sir Charles.

OLD MOUNTFORD, uncle to Sir Charles,
MASTER SANDY, former friend to Sir Charles, "men all of flint, pictures of marble
MASTER RODER, former tenant to Sir Charles, and as void of pity as chaséd bears."
MASTER TIDY, cousin to Sir Charles,

MASTER CRANWELL, friend to Frankford and Sir Charles.

MASTER MALBY, friend to Sir Francis.

Frankford's Two Little Children.

NICHOLAS, or NICK, the groom, "though blunt, yet he is honest,"

JENKIN, later assigned to Master Wendoll,

SPIGOT, the butler,

} household servants to Frankford.

SISLY MILKPAIL, cook and chambermaid to Mrs. Frankford.

ROGER BRICKBAT,
JACK SLIME,
} country fellows,

JOAN MINIVER,
JANE TRUBKIN,
ISBEL MOTLEY,
} country wenches,

} who dance at the Frankford wedding.

The Sheriff.

The Keeper of the Prison in York Castle.

Sheriff's Officers, Sergeant, Huntsmen, Falconers, Coachmen, Carters, Servants, and Musicians.

Setting: Yorkshire at some unspecified time.

"*Look for no glorious state; our Muse is bent
Upon a barren subject, a bare scene.*"

[*Scenes i, ii*] At his marriage to Mistress Anne, sister to Sir Francis Acton, Master John Frankford receives the hearty congratulations of his friends. By birth, upbringing, age, and taste the couple seem perfectly suited to each other, and Mistress Anne already the perfect wife. As Sir Charles Mountford remarks to his friend, "this lady is no clog, as many are, . . . to tie your neck, and curb ye to the yoke; but she's a chain of gold to adorn your neck. You both adorn each other. . . . There's equality in this fair combination." After the bride and bridegroom have withdrawn, some of the guests, particularly Sir Charles and Sir Francis, arrange to meet the next day for sport, laying wagers on their hawks and hounds.

Meanwhile, as in the parlor so in the yard, the dancing goes forward. Master Frankford's servants make merry with the mad lads and country lasses, every mother's child with nosegays and bridelaces in their hats, footing it to "Sellenger's Round" and all their country measures, rounds, and jigs.

[*Scene iii*] Next day, at the hawking, Sir Francis' falcons fly badly and miss their prey, luck seems generally against him, and he proves a bad loser. Hot words are exchanged between Sir Francis and Sir Charles, and then blows. There is a fight in which, unfortunately, Sir Charles kills two of Sir Francis' men, his falconer and his huntsman, and the rest flee. Deserted by his friends and aghast at what he has done in heat of blood, Sir Charles is deeply penitent and fully cognizant of his responsibilities. In his trouble the unhappy man is joined by his beautiful sister Susan, who first urges Charles to flee; and when he honorably refuses, the faithful girl lovingly resolves to stand at his side in every adversity. In a moment the sheriff, sent by Sir Francis, comes to convey him to prison.

[*Scene iv*] Master Frankford, on the other hand, has continued reason to congratulate himself upon his sweet felicity, his fortunate life, and, best of all, his chaste and loving wife. His meditations are interrupted, however, by Master Wendoll, who brings news of the hunting fray and the imprisonment of Sir Charles. Master Wendoll has for some time made a most favorable impression upon Frankford—he is affable, accomplished, pleasant in discourse, generally companionable—and, knowing that the man has small means and is somewhat pressed by want, Frankford takes the opportunity this visit affords of welcoming Wendoll to his house, his table, and his purse as if they were his own, offering him horse and servant, and bidding his dutiful wife, Anne, to "use him with all [her] loving'st courtesy." For all of these favors, Wendoll is properly grateful, but Nick the groom, without knowing why, just somehow does not like the man.

[*Scene v*] At his trial Sir Charles is cleared, in spite of his enemies, but to gain his freedom he has been obliged to spend all his patrimony, and he is left the poorest knight in England. His house and a bare five hundred pounds are all that are left to maintain him and his sister. Hence, he is glad enough to accept the friendship of Master Shafton, and the loan of three hundred pounds additional. But he little knows that Shafton plans his utter ruin.

[*Scene vi*] In quite another way does Wendoll prove a traitorous friend, and Frankford too trusting. Although Frankford has heaped untold kindnesses upon Wendoll, that disloyal villain cannot put from him thoughts of Mistress Anne's divine perfections. One day when Frankford is from home, Wendoll makes love to his wife, sweeping her completely off her feet and utterly overwhelming her innate honesty and devotion to her husband. They are seen, however, by Nick the groom, who never has trusted Wendoll, and who now resolves to keep an eye upon them for his master's sake.

[*Scene vii*] Meanwhile, by hard work and strict economy, Sir Charles and Susan have been able to make ends meet and to live well. As they are looking over their farm one day, however, Shafton appears with a sergeant and offers to buy it. Sir Charles refuses, explaining that the place has been in the family for three hundred years, that his great-great-grandfather who founded the present line had dwelt there, and that there his father had made the wealth he left his son. In brief, Sir Charles replies that he would not sell the farm for more gold than would pave the ground. Thereupon Master Shafton demands his three hundred pounds, with interest, calls the sergeant, and arrests him. As Sir Charles is carried off to prison again, his old enemy, Sir Francis Acton, and Master Malby are passing and rejoice at this new misfortune. In spite of Malby's warning that he has already had more revenge than he is entitled to, Sir Francis resolves to seduce Sir Charles's pretty sister, flout her poverty, and deride her fortunes. But as he turns to the girl Sir Francis is enchanted by Susan's beauty, and when she flees from him as from one who seeks her blood, he resolves by honest means to gain her love or die trying.

[*Scene viii*] At last Nick has seen so much that he can no longer refrain from telling Frankford that his friend is false and his wife dishonest. At first Frankford refuses to believe the accusation and strikes his servant for suggesting it, but later, during a card game, the suspicion is confirmed. Accordingly, Frankford orders a new set of keys made for his house, so that he may sometime surprise the lovers.

[*Scene ix*] Meanwhile, the devoted Susan goes to her kinsmen and her friends seeking aid for her brother. Her Uncle Mountford; Master Sandy, the friend of their prosperity; Master Roder, the tenant who has once lived rent-free on one of their farms; Master Tidy, their cousin— all turn away and refuse to help. By Malby Sir Francis sends her gold, but mistaking Sir Francis' honesty, she spurns it in her need; never shall her honor be sold. But the more Susan spurns his love the more Sir Francis admires her, and at last, since other means fail, he sends for the keeper of the prison to pay Sir Charles's debts.

[*Scene x*] Thinking that he has wronged his kinsmen and his friends by calling them ingrate and unthankful, Charles accepts his freedom with moving gratitude. But Susan soon disillusions him about their relatives. Puzzled at release, they ask the keeper and learn the truth. Charles is even more puzzled to find a motive for this favor from his enemy, but Susan knows, and tells her brother of Sir Francis' love, the gifts, the letters, and the tokens he has sent and she refused. Sir Charles resolves in some way to pay the debt.

[*Scenes xi, xii*] Meanwhile, with the aid of Nick, Frankford makes ready to get conclusive evidence of the infidelity of his wife and his friend. Just as the household is settling down to supper one dark and stormy evening, Nick brings his master a letter, and Frankford immediately prepares to make a journey to York. His wife, Wendoll, and Cranwell, who is a guest that night, try to persuade him to wait until morning, but to no avail. Cranwell does not feel well and begs to be excused; Wendoll rejoices in the opportunity which is theirs, but Mistress Anne has misgivings. When her lover accuses her of talking like a Puritan she replies: "You have tempted me to mischief, Master Wendoll; I have done I know not what. Well, you plead custom; that which for want of wit I granted erst, I now must yield through fear." That night the pair have their supper served in Anne's bedroom, careless of the gossip of the servants.

[*Scene xiii*] About midnight, when the house has gone to rest, Frankford and Nick return, admit themselves with the duplicate keys, and find the lovers sleeping in each other's arms. Pursued by Frankford with drawn sword, Wendoll flees in his shirt, saved only by a maid who stays her master's hand and prevents his killing the villain. Mistress Anne, shamed beyond endurance, swoons but recovers, and, abjectly contrite, begs for death. Instead of killing her, Frankford prays God for patience and reasons with her, asking why she was unfaithful, what in his treatment of her merited so foul a return, what he had failed to provide her that justified this deed. Then, as the unhappy wife dies ten thousand deaths, he confronts her with their infant children—"these young, harmless souls, on whose white brows [her] shame is charactered, and grows in greatness as they wax in years."

Then, lest he do anything rash, Frankford retires to his study. When he returns, a terrible calm has settled on him, and he announces Anne's sentence. He will not martyr her, nor mark her as a strumpet, "but with usage of more humility torment [her] soul, and kill [her] even with kindness." Accordingly, he orders her to gather all of her belongings, leaving nothing in the house that would ever remind him of such a woman; select a bed and furnishings for her chamber; choose servants to attend on her; within two hours get out of his sight; and never see him or communicate with him or their children again.

[*Scene xiv*] To requite the enemy who released him from jail, Sir Charles Mountford decks out his sister Susan like a bride and begs her with her honor at least to offer to repay the debt. "With full five hundred pounds [Sir Francis] bought your love, and, shall he not enjoy it?" So great is her devotion to her brother that Susan at last agrees, but she carries with her a dagger "to save [her] honor [and] slice out [her] life." Deeply touched by a man whose integrity is such that he will pawn his only treasure to pay a debt, and by a girl whose sense of duty to her brother leads her to risk the forfeit, Sir Francis accepts the gift as a jewel to wear next his heart, and takes the dowerless sister as his bride.

[*Scene xv*] While love is being born at the Acton house, in that of the Frankfords it is wholly dead. Searching the place so that nothing whatever which once belonged to Mistress Anne may remain to remind him of his erring wife, Frankford finds the lute upon which she often sweetly played. He puts sentiment aside and sends it after her.

[*Scene xvi*] Anne is uncomplaining at her punishment, but she is weighed down by guilty sorrow. As she rides toward the manor Frankford has assigned to her, she receives the lute. Once more she plays, while from the wood where he is hiding Wendoll creeps out to hear and to reveal his penitent soul. When she has finished her song, Anne orders the lute broken against a wagon wheel, and vows never again to eat or drink or taste of any food that may preserve her life. As she commends her spirit to her Savior when it shall be washed white by her tears, Wendoll comes forward and calls to her. But she flees from him as from the temptation of the Devil and goes on her way.

[*Scene xvii*] One day Sir Francis and his Susan, Sir Charles, and several of their friends go to the manor house to visit the unhappy Anne, wishing that there was some way in which she could overcome her woes as they have theirs, and commending the mild spirit and strange virtue with which Frankford has met his griefs. But Anne is dying. Touched by her great repentance, Frankford at last forgives his wife, restores to her the names of wife and mother which she forfeited by her crime, and with a kiss weds her again, declaring her honest in heart. Upon her marble tomb in golden letters he orders that these words be writtten:

Here lies she whom her husband's kindness killed.

THE FAIR MAID OF THE WEST

OR A GIRL WORTH GOLD

(1607–1630)

Part I

DRAMATIS PERSONAE

BESS BRIDGES, the Fair Maid of the West, a tanner's daughter from Somersetshire, "not fully yet seventeen," barmaid at the Castle in Plymouth; later, hostess at the Windmill in Fowey, and "a pattern to all maids hereafter of constancy in love. . . . A sweet lass, if I have any judgment, . . . honest, . . . [and] wondrous modest, . . . but withal exceeding affable. . . . She'll laugh, confer, keep company, discourse, and something more, kiss; but beyond that compass she no way can be drawn. . . . 'Tis a virtue but seldom found in taverns. . . . That English earth may well be termed a Heaven, that breeds such divine beauties. . . . Were her low birth but equal with her beauty, here would I fix my thoughts. . . . This wench would of a coward make a Hercules."

SPENCER, a gentleman-adventurer, Bess's "worthy and approved . . . friend." ("These Englishmen, nothing can daunt them.")

CAPTAIN THOMAS GOODLACK, friend of Spencer and of Bess; captain of Bess's ship the *Negro*.

ROUGHMAN, a swaggerer who thinks himself "the only approved gallant of these parts, a man of whom the roarers stand in awe." He beats Bess's "servants, cuffs them, and, as they pass him by, kicks [her] maids, nay, domineers over [her], making himself lord o'er [her] house and household." But in reality he is a "base, white-livered, . . . hare-hearted fellow." ("I never yet heard man so praise himself, but proved in the end a coward.") Nevertheless, he becomes lieutenant of Bess's ship the *Negro*.

FAWCETT, friend of Spencer and of Bess.

CLEM, a vintner's apprentice at the Windmill in Fowey, "newly come into [his] teens," who has "scraped trenchers this two years, and the next vintage . . . hope[s] to be bar-boy. . . . [His] father was a baker; and, by the report of his neighbors, as honest a man as ever lived by bread. . . . When did you see a black beard with a white liver, or a little fellow without a tall stomach?"

CARROL, a quarrelsome gentleman, slain by Spencer in a duel.

Two Captains, friends of Carrol.

The MAYOR OF FOWEY, who wishes to marry his son to Bess.

An Alderman of Fowey.

A Surgeon who attends Spencer in Fayal.

A Kitchenmaid at the Windmill.

"Mighty MULLISHEG, . . . amorous KING OF FEZ . . . and great Morocco, . . . pride of our age and glory of the Moors, . . . that ne'er before had English lady seen."

PASHA ALCADE, "great Monarch of the Mauritanians."

PASHA JOFFER, "great Signior of the Saracens."

A London Merchant bound for Barbary, who befriends Spencer, and later is captured by the Spanish, rescued by Bess, and then "by a cunning quiddit of the law, [finds] both ship and goods made forfeit to the King [of Fez],"
A French Merchant, "run into relapse and forfeit of the law [of Fez] . . . for dealing in commodities forbid,"
A Florentine Merchant, some of whose men, "for a little outrage done, are sentenced to the galleys" by the King of Fez,
} for whom Bess intercedes with Mullisheg.

A Spanish Captain who captures Spencer.

A Christian Preacher, a "grave old man . . . that would convert [the] Moors, and turn them to a new belief."

The GENERAL [i.e., the Earl of Essex],
The MAYOR OF PLYMOUTH,
Captains,
Petitioners,
} characters in the dumb show, Act I, scene v.

Chorus, Drawers, English Sailors, Spaniards, Moors, Servants, and Attendants.

Setting: Plymouth and Fowey in England; Fayal in the Azores; Morocco; and the High Seas at the time of the Island Voyage against the Azores and the Spanish Indies (1597).

"Peruse it through, and thou mayst find in it
Some mirth, some matter, and, perhaps, some wit."

Act I

In Plymouth, where the people "are all of fire to purchase [i.e., take booty] from the Spaniard," preparations are on foot for the Island Voyage. The General is there in readiness to set forth; the town "swells with gallants. . . . You cannot meet a man but tricked in scarf and feather, that it seems as if the pride of England's gallantry were harbored here." The "flower of Plymouth," however, is Bess Bridges, barmaid of the Castle, whose "beauty hath upheld that house and gained her master much; . . . [it] draws to them more gallant customers than all the signs i' the town else." Bess is as affable as she is popular, but her virtuous heart belongs to gallant Master Spencer, a gentleman-adventurer about to put to sea, and she loves none but him. In a tavern brawl, however, Spencer has the misfortune to kill Master Carrol, a bully, while protecting Bess from incivility, and for the crime he must fly the country. But before he goes, the lovers meet a last time on the Hoe; and Spencer, declining Bess's offer to return the hundred pounds he once gave her, makes ample provision for the girl during his absence. He bestows upon her all of his wealth, including the Windmill Tavern at Fowey in Cornwall, and enjoins her to keep his picture ever with her. Bess gives him her ring, and sets out for Fowey to await her Spencer's safe return from the Azores. In dumb show the General setting out takes leave of the Mayor of Plymouth, receiving petitioners as he goes aboard, and, like the great gentleman he is, paying the tavern reckoning of Master Carrol, which death had left on score.

Act II

In Fowey Bess conducts her own inn as she had conducted the Castle. With only Clem, an apprentice "newly come into [his] teens" to help her, she has in a week "almost undone all the other taverns; the gallants make no rendezvous now but at the Windmill." She has some tough customers, however, among them Roughman, who thinks he is "a man of whom the roarers stand in awe, and must not be put off." He beats her servants, kicks her maids as they pass him, and even domineers over the hostess, "making himself lord o'er [her] house and household." To cure him, however, Bess dons male attire, lies in wait for the ruffian in the fields, and exposes his cowardice, by taking away his sword, making him tie her shoe, and ordering him to lie down while she strides over him.

Meanwhile, in Fayal, Spencer becomes involved in another quarrel and is wounded to the point of death while trying to stop a duel between two captains. The fleet is bound for England, Spencer has time only to send his friend Goodlack aboard with his ring as a token, a message of farewell to Bess, and his will which provides her with five hundred pounds a year, if on his arrival Goodlack finds Bess well reported and free from scandal. As his ship sails, Goodlack hears a great bell toll and learns that it is for one Spencer who has died of a mortal wound. But he does not know that the man who died was another Spencer and that his friend was to survive and take passage on an English merchant ship, homeward bound by way of Mamorah, a town in Barbary. Ten months hence, Spencer hopes to visit England.

Act III

In Fowey, Bess bears herself so well that she is "without stain or blemish, well reputed," so virtuous is she that the Mayor of the town hopes to marry his only son to her. When Goodlack arrives, therefore, he can find nothing at all to Bess's discredit—though he tries, in hope of having Spencer's legacy for himself. The devotion which Bess shows Spencer's picture convinces Goodlack of the girl's fidelity, and he at last reveals himself and delivers his message. Grief-stricken at his news, Bess buys a good tight ship for eight hundred pounds, fits it out as a privateer, puts Captain Goodlack in charge of it, but will not reveal even to him the purpose of the voyage she plans. It is enough that "though some may blame, all lovers will commend" her act.

Act IV

In token of her sorrow, Bess paints her ship black, fits it with black sails, and christens it the *Negro*. She answers the marriage proposal of the Mayor of Fowey by committing to his trust her last will and testament, in which she leaves generous legacies to young beginners in their trades, those who have loss by sea, dowerless maidens, maimed soldiers, and the poor, demonstrating to the good man that she is now too poor herself to bring a dowry with her fit for his son. Then, having feasted the whole town of Fowey, Bess sets sail with Captain Goodlack, the boy Clem, and Fawcett, another friend of Spencer's, having appointed as lieutenant of the expedition the reformed Roughman, in whom this matchless girl has kindled the dead fire of courage.

Soon, Bess's purpose in making the voyage is revealed; the devoted maid is bound for Fayal to bring home to English soil the body of her dead lover. But her hope is vain. When she arrives off shore at the Azores, from Spanish prisoners she learns that Fayal has been retaken by the Spaniards, that Spencer's body was removed from holy ground because he was a heretic, first buried in the fields, and then exhumed and burned. Hence, Bess's mourning now it turned into revenge, and her first act is to command her gunners to shell the church. Then she sets out to look for Spanish ships.

Meanwhile, on the high seas, the vessel in which Spencer is sailing is captured by a Spanish ship, which by a strange coincidence is itself taken by the *Negro* in an encounter off Fayal. Captain Goodlack is wounded and below decks when the prisoners are brought aboard; Spencer recognizes something familiar in the young officer—for Bess is dressed as a sea captain—but cannot remember where he saw him. Bess, in turn, recognizes Spencer, but thinks he is a ghost urging her on to avenge his death and disgrace at the enemy's hands.

While all this is happening, another event is shown in anticipation of what is yet to occur. In Morocco King Mullisheg establishes laws to enrich his treasury, decreeing, among other things, that any Christian merchant in the country who conceals the least part of his custom shall forfeit ship and goods. Also, His Majesty seeks new concubines, and orders his attendants to procure the fairest Christian damsels they can hire or buy for gold; Moors and Negroes he can procure on command.

Finally, because the stage "so lamely can express a sea," a Chorus describes what should have been seen in action. Bess has recovered from her sight of the ghost; Goodlack has been cured of his wound; their ship has taken many prizes from the rich Spaniard and the barbarous Turk; they have become wealthy. But for lack of water the *Negro* is forced to put into Mamorah. News of Bess's arrival has been brought to Mullisheg, "that ne'er before had English lady seen," and he sends for her to come ashore.

Act V

At the court of Mullisheg Bess conducts herself with perfect decorum. She visits the palace only on condition of safe conduct; the amorous King of Fez is smitten with her beauty, begs a kiss, and has her sit with him in state to beautify his throne and to judge causes. Here, His Majesty grants Bess her slightest wish on behalf of the poor unfortunates brought before them, and, with the aid of Clem, who quickly learns the ways of courtship, she assists a French and a Florentine merchant who have got into difficulties in Fez, as well as the English merchant who rescued Spencer and failed to pay the duty on his cargo. Here, too, Bess and Spencer are reunited by Captain Goodlack and married by a Christian preacher come to convert the Moors. King Mullisheg provides the wedding banquet and bestows upon the couple rich and sumptuous gifts.

THE FAIR MAID OF THE WEST
Part II

The second part of *The Fair Maid of the West* suffers the fate of most sequels; it outdoes itself and is a poor thing when compared with the spirited Part I. Hardly have Bess and Spencer been married, than the King of Fez repents his magnanimous behavior toward them, and the lovers are involved in the worst kind of bedroom farce. The king is infatuated with Bess, his queen Tota with Spencer. Their intrigues fail; in the dark they are deceived and find themselves in each other's arms. The bride and groom contrive to escape to their ship, are recaptured, and sentenced to death. But by a series of quixotic circumstances they are at last pardoned and leave Fez. Presently they are separated by piracy and shipwreck, and poor Bess is "as soon a widow as [she] was a bride." She loses all her wealth; she is captured by bandits; she is rescued by the Duke of Florence, who gives her ten thousand crowns and makes love to her. Finally, the supposedly lost Spencer also makes his way to Florence, and there, after many surprises and coincidences, the lovers are reunited.

----◆----

JOHN MARSTON
(c. 1576–1634)

BIOGRAPHY. John Marston was the son of a well-to-do lawyer of Shropshire origin who had settled in Coventry; his mother was Italian, the daughter of a physician. Marston was educated at Brazenose College, Oxford, and took his degree in 1594. He joined the Middle Temple, but soon abandoned the study of law, and in 1599 his father left law books to him "whom I hoped would have profited by them in the study of law, but man proposeth and God disposeth." But John Marston had already begun his literary career. By 1598 he had won a reputation for his satiric verses; by 1599 his career as a playwright had begun. He wrote originally for the Admiral's Men, but his chief work was for Paul's boys and after 1604 for the Children of the Queen's Revels. In 1616 he took orders and became vicar of Christchurch, Hampshire, a living he resigned in 1631. He died in Aldermanbury parish in 1634.

CRITICAL COMMENT. Marston is known for his bitter, cynical dramas. His *Dutch Courtesan,* for example, is a satirical representation of the courtesan which should be placed beside Dekker's romantic depiction in *The Honest Whore.* The play was adapted to the Restoration stage by Thomas Betterton [or Aphra Behn?] as *The Revenge, or a Match in Newgate* (1680). *The Mal-*

content, Marston's masterpiece, is a bitter melodrama which stands halfway between the satiric comedy of Jonson and the disillusioned tragedy of Webster and Tourneur. The characters, especially Malevole, are humor characters.

SOURCES. *The Dutch Courtesan* is derived from Bandello's famous story of the Countess of Celant, translated by Painter and by Fenton. Parts of the comic subplot, featuring the pranks of Cocledemoy, are drawn from a story of Masuccio, also translated by Painter. For *The Malcontent* no source is known.

BIBLIOGRAPHY

Collected Works:

   The Works of John Marston, edited by A. H. Bullen, 3 volumes, 1887.
   The Plays of John Marston, edited by H. H. Wood, 3 volumes, 1934-39.

The Dutch Courtesan:
   Early editions: 1605; 1633 (2) [in the collected editions of Marston].

The Malcontent:
   Early editions: 1604 (3), but the position of the date on none of the title pages necessarily refers to the year of printing.
   Modern edition: ed. G. B. Harrison (TD, 1933).

THE DUTCH COURTESAN
(1603-1605)

DRAMATIS PERSONAE

FRANCESCHINA, "a pretty nimble-ey'd Dutch tanakin, . . . a plump-rump'd wench, . . . [but] a fair devil in shape of woman, . . . as false as prostituted, and adulterate as some translated manuscript. . . . O, thou unreprievable, beyond all measure of grace damn'd irremediably! . . . To what devilish end [will] this woman of foul soul . . . drive her plots? . . . For know [the] deepest Hell as a revenging woman's naught so fell. . . . Woman corrupted is the worst of devils."

BEATRICE, betrothed of Young Freevill, a maid of "sweetness, quiet modesty, yet deep affection, . . . the admired glory of [her] sex. . . . Heaven! To have such a wife is happiness to breed pale envy in the saints! Thou worthy dove-like virgin without gall, cannot that woman's evil, jealousy, despite disgrace—nay, which is worse, contempt—once stir thy faith?"

CRISPINELLA, her lighthearted, mocking, diminutive sister. "What a tart monkey is this! By Heaven, if thou hadst not so much wit, I could find in my heart to marry thee! Faith, bear with me for all this! . . . You are grown a proud, scurvy, apish, idle, disdainful, scoffing—God's foot! Because you have read *Euphues and his England, Palmerin de Oliva,* and *The Legend of Lies!* . . . Fie, Crispinella, you speak too broad!"

Sir Hubert Subboys' daughters.

YOUNG FREEVILL, Sir Lionel's son, "a well-shaped, clean-lipp'd gentleman, of a handsome, but not affected, fineness, a good faithful eye, and a well-humored cheek. Would he did not stoop in the shoulders. . . . A fool, an unthrift, . . . a constant drab-keeper," he discards his mistress Franceschina when he is betrothed to Beatrice.

MALHEUREUX, "ill-fortuned Malheureux," Young Freevill's unhappy friend, "a man of snow, . . . [and one] that 'gainst Nature would seem wise. . . . When woman's in the heart, in the soul hell."

TYSEFEW, a blunt gallant, suitor to Crispinella.

COCLEDEMOY, "the foulest mouth'd, profane, railing brother, . . . that man of much money, some wit, but less honesty, cogging Cocledemoy, . . . a thick, elderly, stub-bearded fellow," a knavishly witty City companion [i.e., coney-catching rascal], a debauched scholar who has "read Tully's *Offices*, . . . [and] a flatt'ring knave; . . . 'tis a good thriving trade; it comes forward better than the seven liberal sciences or the nine cardinal virtues. . . . Hang toasts!" ("Whatsoever he has done has been only *euphoniae gratia*—for wit's sake. . . . Lord, that he has but one neck!")

"Cheaters and bawds go together like washing and wringing."

MISTRESS MARY, or MALL, FAUGH, an old woman, Cocledemoy's "moveable chattel, his instrument of fornication, . . . [his] blue-tooth'd patroness of natural wickedness." ("One of the Family of Love [i.e., a Puritan sect], and, as they say, a bawd that covers the multitude of sins, yet . . . none of the wicked that eat fish o' Fridays,")

MASTER MULLIGRUB, "hardly-honest Mulligrub, . . . a sharking vintner" of Cheap, a "gouty-barm'd spiggot-frigging jumbler of elements," victim of Cocledemoy's pranks.

MISTRESS MULLIGRUB, his "good yoke-fellow," who vows not to "leave . . . [her] poor Mulligrub . . . until [she has] seen [him] hang." She notes all new and wellspoken phrases; "thus 'tis to have good education, and to be brought up in a tavern. [She keeps] as gallant and as good company, though [she] say[s] it, as any she in London."

SIR LIONEL FREEVILL, a widower, father of young Freevill, ⎫
SIR HUBERT SUBBOYS, father of Beatrice and Crispinella, ⎬ two old knights.

PUTIFER, nurse of Beatrice and Crispinella.

CAQUETEUR, "that prattling gallant of a good draught, common customs, fortunate impudence. . . . For grief's sake keep him out; his discourse is like the long word *Honorificabilitudinatatibus*, a great deal of sound and no sense; his company is like a parenthesis to a discourse."

MASTER BURNISH, a goldsmith-jeweller, from whom Mulligrub buys a cup.

LIONEL, his man.

HOLIFERNES REINSCURE, a barber's boy, "apprentice to surgery."

Three Watchmen; "God's-so, what good members of the commonwealth do [they] prove."

Pages, Gentlemen with Music, Masquers, Officers, Halberds, and Servants.

Setting: London, at some unspecified time.

> *"The difference betwixt the love of a courtesan and a wife is the full scope of the play, which, intermixed with the deceits of a witty City jester, fills up the comedy."*

Act I

Now betrothed to Beatrice, the matchless daughter of Sir Hubert Subboys, Young Freevill determines to break off his connection with Franceschina, a Dutch courtesan living in London. To Freevill, a carefree youth, an unthrift, and a "constant drab-keeper," the relationship has been casual; "they sell but only flesh, no jot affection." But he has some reasons for believing that Franceschina will not break off so easily. To his strict friend Malheureux, on the other hand, the affair ought never to have begun; he is "a man of snow," to whom "the most odious spectacle the earth can present is an immodest vulgar woman." Nevertheless, "to make her loathe the shame she's in," Malheureux permits Young Freevill to introduce him to his mistress, and the unlucky friend is instantly infatuated by the wit, the charm, the wantonness of Franceschina. Freevill is amused that his "cast garment must be let out in the seams" for Malheureux, when all is done. "The sight of vice augments the hate of sin," indeed!

At the same time, on a lower social level, a duel of wits between a dishonest vintner Mulligrub and the clever knavish Cocledemoy has its beginning. Having engaged a room at Mulligrub's tavern and ordered supper, Cocledemoy has made off with a nest of goblets, and Mulligrub has vowed vengeance for the theft.

Act II

So much in love is Freevill with his Beatrice, who has given her beloved a ring to wear for her, that he is unable to understand Malheureux's infatuation with Franceschina, and tries to dissuade him from her. But in vain; his friend's passion for her grows. At a second visit which the two young men make to the courtesan's, Franceschina notices the ring on Freevill's finger. She begs it; he refuses to give it to her, and, instantly jealous, she finds all the news she has heard of Sir Hubert Subboys' daughter confirmed. The Dutch courtesan flies into a rage, sends Freevill away, and with a facile change of mood exercises her blandishments upon Malheureux. Would the pretty fair-eyed youth enjoy her? He may, she no longer loves Freevill. What a pity she has made a vow—so long as Freevill lives, she must not love. Thus by promising to gratify her new lover she incites him to kill the old, and bring his ring to her as token of his death.

In his quarrel with Master Mulligrub, Cocledemoy continues the aggressor. Borrowing a basin, razor, and apron from Holifernes Rein-scure, a barber's apprentice, the rogue gains entrance to Mulligrub's house as a talkative barber named Andrew Shark, lathers the vintner's face, and while he is helpless, puts a cockscomb on Mulligrub's head, and makes off with a bag of cash containing fifteen pounds.

Act III

Even though Franceschina's demand that he kill Freevill has shocked Malheureux into a realization of his folly, the infatuated man still persists in his course; he must have the courtesan. But he does disclose her plot to Freevill, who promises to help him attain his ends. At a masque which is to be given in honor of the wedding, the two friends are to pretend to fall out, give seeming challenge, and retire as if to fight a duel. With the ring, Malheureux is to go to Franceschina's, and the friends are to meet later to laugh at folly.

In the comic subplot, Master Mulligrub has new cause to rail at the rascal Cocledemoy and to threaten him with punishment. But there is greater reason still in store. Disguised as a French peddler, Cocledemoy watches the vintner buy a standing cup from Master Burnish the gold-smith and order it sent home to Mistress Mulligrub. Then the rascal follows the delivery boy, pretends to be another servant of Master Burnish's, delivers a jole of fresh salmon, announces that Mulligrub has invited the Burnishes to dinner, and asks that the cup be sent back to have Mulligrub's arms engraved on the side. The vintner's wife unquestioningly complies. But even when she learns that she has been cozened, Mistress Mulligrub is unprepared for the knave's return. This time he gets back his salmon, too.

Act IV

At the masque Malheureux and Freevill seem to quarrel as they had arranged and retire, apparently to fight. In case Malheureux should be arrested for murder, however, they agree that Freevill is to lie hidden at Master Shatewe's the jeweller's, whence he can be produced at need. And Malheureux hastens to Franceschina with the ring. Free-vill, however, is disturbed by his friend's strange infatuation and de-termines if possible to cure him of it. He will go to no jeweller's, but withdraw and watch what happens.

When Malheureux arrives at Franceschina's with the ring, he is put off for two hours while the harlot makes herself ready. Freevill she thinks is dead; Malheureux shall hang; and her rival, Beatrice, will go mad. Hence, with treacherous heart she hastens to reveal the news to Sir Lionel Freevill and Beatrice, Young Freevill serving as her escort disguised as a pander, Don Dubon. Thereupon Sir Lionel and Sir Hubert, accompanied by officers, go to Franceschina's lodging, conceal themselves behind a curtain, and await the coming of Malheureux at the appointed hour.

At night, in the street, Master Mulligrub catches up at last with Cocledemoy, who flees from his enemy in pretended terror and leaves his cloak behind him. But before Mulligrub can pursue the rascal, Cocledemoy returns with the watch, accuses the vintner of robbery, and sees him put into the stocks for safekeeping until his hearing in the morning. Then, disguised as a bellman, Cocledemoy accepts a bribe from Mulligrub to identify him to the constables. Cocledemoy does so, and, convinced that they have apprehended both a cutpurse and the keeper of a bawdyhouse, the constables drag their man off to prison; they'll trust no stocks with him.

Act V

From his own lips the officers in hiding hear Malheureux's confession to Franceschina that he murdered Freevill, and take him away to prison. Only now that the courtesan has betrayed him are the young man's eyes opened to her perfidy and devilishness. Franceschina scorns the ring Freevill has worn, and sends it to Beatrice by the pander Dubon, in the hope that it will make the girl run mad. In prison, Malheureux protests his innocence, but his confession stands against him. Freevill is not to be found at Master Shatewe's, and the day of execution is set.

At the same time poor Mulligrub is convicted of stealing the cloak. He too has confessed, after a fashion;

> the rest of his defense
> The choler of a justice wrong'd in wine,
> Join'd with malignance of some hasty jurors.

In short, "the knave was cast."

At the last moment, before the gallows, however, Freevill reveals himself and explains his scheme of "suffering this fair devil in shape of woman to make good her plot," and of giving her line, until, "with her own vain strivings," she has entangled herself and Malheureux has been cured of his passion. In the same way, Cocledemoy reveals himself, has Master Mulligrub released, and is reconciled with him, on the ground that whatever he has done had "been only *euphoniae gratia*— for wit's sake." Franceschina is condemned "to the extremest whip and jail"; Beatrice and Freevill are to be married, as are her merry sister Crispinella and her suitor Tysefew. Faith, in this play, "marriage and hanging are spun both in one hour."

THE MALCONTENT
(1604)

DRAMATIS PERSONAE

A Fool of Fashion (played by WILLIAM SLY),
His Cousin, "Master Doomsday's son, the usurer" (played by JOHN SINKLO),
A Tireman,
DICK BURBAGE,
HARRY CONDELL,   } members of the King's Company of players,
JOHN LOWIN,

frequenters of plays,

characters in the Induction.

GIOVANNI ALTOFRONTO, "Genoa's last year's duke," living at court as the low-born, plain-tongued MALEVOLE, a disguise that affords him "that which kings do seldom hear, or great men use, free speech. . . . More discontent than Lucifer when he was thrust out of the presence, . . . his highest delight is to procure others' vexation, . . . for 'tis his position, whosoever in this earth can be contented is a slave and damned. . . . Th' elements struggle within him; his own soul is at variance within herself; his speech is halter-worthy at all hours. I like him; faith, he . . . makes me understand those weaknesses which others' flattery palliates." ("That a duke should be forced to fool it! . . . Better play the fool lord than be the fool lord.")

MARIA, the "true-faithed, . . . grave duchess of banished Altofronto. . . . She was a cold creature ever; she hated monkeys, fools, jesters, and gentlemen-ushers extremely; . . . not only . . . truly modestly honorable in her own conscience, . . . she would avoid the least wanton carriage that might incur suspect. . . . God bless me, she had almost brought bed-pressing out of fashion." ("I tell thee, I have found an honest woman!")

PIETRO JACOMO, "the too-soft, . . . honest fool, . . . weak-brained Duke [of Genoa], who only stands on Florence' stilts, . . . a most plain-breasted man."

AURELIA, the "subtle lascivious duchess" to Duke Pietro Jacomo, daughter of the Medicis, who "can desire nothing but death, nor deserve anything but Hell."

MENDOZA, a minion of the Duchess Aurelia, later Duke of Genoa; the "sharp-nosed lord that made the curséd match linked Genoa with Florence. . . . [He is a] treacherous, damnable, monster, . . . [an] egregious devil, . . . [a] murdering politician, . . . [a] whoreson, hot-reined, he-marmoset, . . . scant of honor, full of devilish wit, . . . [his] brain is in labor till it produces mischief, . . . [an] ignoble villain, whom neither Heaven nor Hell, goodness of God or man, could once make good. . . . Like a pair of snuffers, [he] snibs filth in other men, and retains it in himself."

FERNEZE, a young courtier enamored of the Duchess Aurelia, a "silly novice, . . . [who] treads . . . the dangerous path of lust. . . . The fool grasps clouds."

COUNT CELSO, a friend to Altofronto, a "constant lord, [whose] star's oppressed, . . . one of full ten millions of men that loves virtue only for itself."

BILIOSO, an old choleric marshal, "Master Make-pleas," "Marshal Make-room," a "burr that only stick[s] to nappy fortunes; . . . [one whose inviolable maxim is] flatter the greatest and oppress the least, a whoreson flesh-fly, that still gnaws upon the lean, galled backs." ("Did you ever see a fellow whose strength consisted in his breath, respect in his office, religion in his lord, and love in himself? Why, then, behold!")

PASSARELLO, court fool to Bilioso, "as common in the court as an hostess' lips in the country; knights, and clowns, and knaves, and all share [him]; the court cannot possibly be without [him]."

EMILIA, "How many servants think'st thou I have?"⎫
BIANCHA, Bilioso's young wife. ("I do wonder how thou, having⎬ladies attending the
for the most part of thy lifetime been a country lady, shouldst⎟Duchess Aurelia.
have been so good a wit,")⎭

MAQUERELLE, an "old crone in the court, . . . a cunning bawd, . . . [and] sentinel" to the Duchess Aurelia; the "picture of a woman, and substance of a beast!"

FERRARDO, a minion to Duke Pietro Jacomo, a "little ferret, he goes sucking up and down the palace into every hen's nest, like a weasel."

COUNT EQUATO, "a scholar by art, [and a] ridiculous fool by nature,"⎫two courtiers.
GUERRINO, "a most loathed flatterer,"⎭

PREPASSO, "Sir Tristram Trimtram," a gentleman-usher.

MERCURY, "the god of ghosts, . . . [who] presents the masque" at court.

The Captain of the Citadel, dwelling of the Duchess Maria.

A Perfumer, Pages, Suitors, and Halberts.

Setting: Genoa in the late sixteenth century.

> *"In night all creatures sleep;*
> *Only the malcontent, that 'gainst his fate*
> *Repines and quarrels, alas, he's goodman tell-clock!"*

INDUCTION

Two members of the audience seek accommodations on the stage of the theatre and engage in banter with prominent members of the King's Company, alluding to the satirical dramatic fare which is the attraction at Blackfriars, rival house of the boy actors, and to some retaliatory theft of dramatic property involving this play, but now obscure: "Why not Malevole in folio with us, as Jeronimo in decimo-sexto with them?" [i.e., why not this play, *The Malcontent,* which was once the property of the Blackfriars' children's company, but lost, played by our adult actors at the Globe, as *The Spanish Tragedy,* King's Company property, played by these half-pints, these 16mo actors, these children?]

One of the spectators insists that *The Malcontent* is a bitter play; Condell, a player, insists that it is neither satire nor morality, but just a story, yet there are people who will twist around innocent happenings or speeches on the stage and find hidden meanings in them. Another of the spectators doubts that Burbage can play the role of the Malcontent as well as it has been played elsewhere. At last, because sitting on the stage is not permitted at the Globe, the spectators are taken to a "private room" or box, and the play begins.

Act I

In the decadent and debauched court of Genoa, now presided over by the craven Duke Pietro Jacomo and his frivolous Florentine Duchess Aurelia, lives the deposed Duke Giovanni Altofronto, disguised as a baseborn, gross-tongued malcontent named Malevole. A kind of cynical court jester, Malevole is tolerated but not taken seriously. Under cover of his disguise, he is as fetterless as an emperor, railing misanthropically at the flattering knaves, the lecherous courtiers, the egregious wittols, and the adulterous women-in-waiting who frequent the court. And he is biding his time to get his throne back again. Only the honest Celso knows who Malevole is, and only Celso has remained faithful to the old duke throughout the political intrigue which Altofronto was too virtuous to suspect until he found himself deposed and his faithful Duchess Maria close imprisoned in the citadel. It was a strong alliance by marriage with Florence that placed Pietro on the throne, and the treacherous Mendoza, who engineered the match and is still the power behind the throne, now cuckolds the duke. Out of the discord which is sure to result, Malevole plans to work. Moreover, Mendoza has a rival in Ferneze, who plies the old crone Maquerelle well with jewels, and completely replaces Mendoza in Aurelia's favor. Hence, when Pietro with drawn sword upbraids Mendoza for dishonoring his bed, Mendoza can shift the blame to Ferneze, easily convince the stupid Pietro, and together plan at night to surprise the adulterers. They can then kill Ferneze without too much dishonoring the duke and the duchess or supplying the lady with a cause for revenge. But Mendoza expects to forward his own ends and avenge himself on his rival.

Act II

At night Ferneze is conveyed to Aurelia's chamber by the bawd Maquerelle, and is seen by the spying Mendoza. Upon the stroke of twelve Mendoza is joined by Pietro and several of his courtiers, who go over again the details of the plan in which they have been instructed. In gratitude to Mendoza Duke Pietro, who is childless, names him his heir. The women-in-waiting retire, leaving Maquerelle as sentinel in an anteroom; then at the proper moment as agreed, the lovers are surprised, Ferneze flees in his shirt, and is received upon Mendoza's rapier. Also, as agreed, Mendoza protects the body and prevents any further outrage, especially to the duchess. Willing to forgive and to forget, Pietro makes no scene, but bids his duchess good night and retires with his courtiers. But Mendoza remains behind, hypocritically to reproach Aurelia with the wrong she has done to one who loves her much, gets her to admit her error in believing the slandering tongue of Ferneze and in granting Ferneze her favors, and promises to assist her in murdering her husband, lest he try to avenge himself and further publicize her honor's much-known blot. Florence will help them, and in the end Mendoza shall be duke. The plan suits this schemer perfectly and he retires for the night. Ferneze, however, is not dead; left alone he calls for a surgeon, and Malevole, being by, conveys him to safety.

Act III

Less satisfied than he had hoped to be by the knowledge of his own dishonor, Duke Pietro commissions Bilioso, the absurd old wittol who is his marshal, to go to Florence and report Aurelia's disgraceful conduct to the duke, her father. To Malevole and Celso this move seems a turning point in fortune; Florentine power alone is responsible for Altofronto's banishment and Pietro's accession, and it is likely that the Florentine will now forsake his puppets and withdraw his support. Moreover, "that beast with many heads, the staggering multitude," has grown dissatisfied with the change in government it helped to produce. Malevole resolves to lie in wait and watch Mendoza. Fooled completely by the disguise of the caustic malcontent, that villain suggests that Malevole murder the weak-brained duke, and reveals to him his whole plan—to seize the throne, banish the duchess (because Florence will no doubt forsake her), then marry Maria, the wife of banished Altofronto, and so strengthen his claims by joining her faction to his. Malevole agrees to undertake the whole intrigue, and Mendoza promises in reward to make him a great man. Accordingly, while Pietro is out hunting, Malevole gets him alone; but, instead of using his advantage for murder, he reveals Mendoza's devilish scheme to the foggy, duped princeling, and suggests that Pietro go into disguise for a while as the Hermit of the Rock.

Act IV

Defying infamy; the Duchess Aurelia revels and dances at court, attended by Mendoza, and their merrymaking is interrupted by Malevole and the hermit bringing news that the Duke Pietro is dead, the hermit having heard him exclaim against female faith and seen him fling himself into the sea. It is Celso who wishes "a better fortune to our Duke Mendoza"; the court acclaims the adopted heir, and the new duke takes office. But Mendoza cannot so lightly pass over Pietro's death as to leave his woes without revenge; hence, his first act is to banish the shameless Aurelia to the cave whence the good hermit comes. Then he sends Malevole with his ring to the citadel to woo for him the grave Maria. In the absence of the malcontent, Mendoza becomes confidential with the hermit, telling him how dangerous the broadspoken Malevole is, and asking him to poison Malevole at supper. The blame can be laid upon Maria, who then must either yield love or die. When Malevole returns for better warrant to enter the citadel, Mendoza takes him aside, tells him how perilous a fellow the hermit is, who makes religion his stalking-horse, and commissions the misanthrope to poison him. Maria will bear the suspicion, on which she must either yield her love or die. Pietro and Malevole, of course, promptly reveal this villainy to each other. Meanwhile, both Aurelia and Pietro have a change of heart. In mourning attire and with a contrite spirit, the former duchess makes ready to go to her cell of shame, and Pietro, touched by her penitent and loving words about the husband she has wronged, weeps bitter tears and bears patiently the barbed remarks of the malcontent who has vowed to be his affliction. Hence, when Bilioso returns with word that the great Duke of Florence has decreed that his lascivious daughter shall die, Duke Pietro be banished, and the deposed Duke Altofronto be restored, the thoroughly repentant Pietro renounces forever the rule of Genoa. In true contrition he dedicates himself to holiness and prayer for the restoration of Altofronto. Thereupon Malevole for the moment throws off his disguise, and, joined by Celso and Ferneze, the four plot their new fortunes.

Act V

As agreed with Mendoza, Malevole releases Maria from the citadel, brings Mendoza word that the hermit is dead, and seems to fall dead himself when Mendoza deliberately opens under his nose an empty poison pouncet-box which Malevole has just given him. Ordering Celso to bury "the good Malevole" who is dead on sudden, Mendoza also commands a masque as the entertainment for the evening. The faithful

Maria, of course, resists all of Mendoza's threats and blandishments, remains true to her banished husband, and is accused of poisoning the hermit. As Mendoza threatens Maria's life, Aurelia adds to the confusion by appearing in her mourning habit, and, at the same moment Mercury with loud music introduces the masque Mendoza has commanded. It consists of four high-famed dukes of Genoa come from Elysium to congratulate Mendoza on his happy fortune. But the masquers are Malevole, Pietro, Ferneze, and Celso, dressed in white and concealing pistolets and short swords under their robes. Malevole takes his wife Maria as a dancing partner, Pietro takes Aurelia, Ferneze takes Maquerelle, and Celso, Biancha. As they dance, Duke Altofronto reveals himself to his duchess, and then at the proper moment the masquers surround Mendoza, cover him with their weapons, and unmask. Mendoza begs for his life, which Altofronto scornfully grants him, and the rightful duke assumes his throne again.

GEORGE CHAPMAN
(c. 1560–1634)

BIOGRAPHY. George Chapman was born near Hitchin in Hertfordshire; nothing is known of his education, though he is said to have studied at Oxford, Cambridge, or both the universities. Like Jonson he was a soldier in the Low Countries and began his career as a playwright about 1596, when he was writing for Henslowe at the Rose. Chapman's *Humorous Day's Mirth* (1597) to some extent anticipated Jonson's method of using a single plot and humor characters. His plays were popular, and by 1598, when Meres wrote *Palladis Tamia,* his reputation for both comedy and tragedy was established. In the same year he completed Marlowe's *Hero and Leander.* From about 1600 or soon after until 1608 he wrote for the Chapel Children, later known as the Queen's Revels. In 1624 he completed his translation of Homer, which, excellent as it is, would certainly be less well-known were it not for Keats's sonnet. Chapman also wrote court entertainments, and Jonson told Drummond that "next himself, only Fletcher and Chapman could make a masque." He died in 1634 and was buried in St. Giles-in-the-Fields.

CRITICAL COMMENT. Akin to Jonson in both comedy and tragedy, Chapman is more good-natured than Jonson and more ready to laugh at the follies of mankind than to lash them. In tragedy he wears his learning somewhat more lightly, though his serious dramas are a combination of history, philosophy, and classical learning with a Senecan technique.

All Fools is Chapman's comic masterpiece and is more carefully constructed than most of his plays. It is an excellent comedy of intrigue in the classical manner.

Bussy D'Ambois is Chapman's most famous play, and its flamboyant hero is an example of the aspiring, energetic titans produced by the Renaissance. Bussy is more than a loudmouthed braggart, however; as Chapman takes pains to present him he is the self-sufficient, self-reliant, virtuous individualist defying the world. But the play in which this character figures is full of fustian— what Dryden called "glaring colors, . . . gigantic words, repetition in abundance, looseness of expression, and gross hyperboles" (Preface to *The Spanish Friar*). The play is a Senecan melodrama of blood and a good deal of thunder. Yet *Bussy* was popular on the stage until the end of the seventeenth century, and was adapted to new tastes by Tom D'Urfey as *Bussy D'Ambois, or The Husband's Revenge* (1691).

The Revenge of Bussy D'Ambois, on the other hand, is an entirely different kind of play because its hero is a different kind of man. If Bussy suggests Tamburlaine, his brother and avenger Clermont suggests Hamlet. He is the "Senecal man" of good breeding, a stoic in philosophy who accepts the duty of revenge, but performs it in his own way without haste or passion. Like its predecessor, this play is filled with splendid declamation, but it is richer in thought, and as a whole is a better exemplification of Chapman's theory of tragedy, as he explains it in his dedication. The subject is "not truth, but things like truth, . . . material instruction, elegant and sententious excitation to virtue, and deflection from her contrary, being the soul, limbs, and limits of an authentical tragedy."

SOURCES. *All Fools* is a clever combination of two plays of Terence, *Heautontimoroumenos* (The Self-Tormentor) and *Adelphi* (The Brothers), with an English subplot dealing with the humors of a jealous husband. The classical material has been altered considerably; the courtesan of Terence is transformed into a secret wife, and the intriguing slave into a scholar and younger brother who has attained cynical detachment and who likes to manage other people's affairs. The contrast between the two fathers—worldly wise and opinionated, and kindly and easygoing—is also more fully carried out than in the Latin comedies.

Bussy D'Ambois is based upon contemporary French history as told in Jacques Auguste de Thou's *Historiae sui Temporis,* Rosset's *Histoires tragiques,* and the memoirs of Brantôme and Marguerite de Valois. The precise source which Chapman used is unknown. Bussy's story has also been made the subject of a novel by Dumas père, *La Dame de Monsoreau* (1846).

The Revenge of Bussy D'Ambois is based upon Grimeston's *General Inventory of the History of France* (1607).

BIBLIOGRAPHY

Collected Works:

The Tragedies of George Chapman (1910), and *The Comedies of George Chapman* (1913), both edited by T. M. Parrott.

The Best Plays of George Chapman, edited by William Lyon Phelps, Mermaid Series, 1895.

Monograph: P. V. Kreider, *Elizabethan Comic Character Conventions as Revealed in the Comedies of George Chapman,* University of Michigan Publications, 1935.

All Fools:

Early edition: 1605.
Modern edition: ed. T. M. Parrott (Belles Lettres Series, 1907).

Bussy D'Ambois:

Early editions: 1607-8; 1641 (2) ["corrected and emended by the author"]; 1646; 1657.
Modern edition: ed. F. S. Boas (Belles Lettres Series, 1905).

The Revenge of Bussy D'Ambois:

Early edition: 1613.
Modern edition: ed. F. S. Boas (Belles Lettres Series, 1905).

ALL FOOLS

A COMEDY

(1599–1604)

DRAMATIS PERSONAE

GOSTANZO, an "old politic dissembling knight, . . . a Machiavel," and a hard dictatorial father who is gulled by his children, Valerio and Bellanora, and made instrumental in promoting their love affairs. ("Y'are too severe, i' faith,")

MARC ANTONIO, "an honest knight, . . . [and] no good politician—plain believing, simple honesty, is [his] policy still." In the opinion of his neighbor Gostanzo, he is "not acquainted with the fine sleights and policies of the world, . . . [and] much too indulgent to his presuming children," Fortunio and Rinaldo,

} neighbors and friends.

RINALDO, "the scholar," younger son of Marc Antonio, who likes to manage other people's affairs and manipulates the plot of the play. Once in love himself, he is now disillusioned with women. "The poor fox that lost his tail persuaded others also to lose theirs; [he] for one perhaps that for desert or some defect in [his] attempts refused [him], revile[s] the whole sex, beauty, love, and all. . . . [He whose] fortune is to win renown by gulling" others, is at last gulled by his own greed.

FORTUNIO, elder son to Marc Antonio, in love with Bellanora, daughter to Gostanzo. "Like the turtle all in mournful strains wailing his fortunes, . . . [Fortunio] love[s] and never can enjoy the sight of her [he] love[s], . . . all passages to [her are] so strongly kept by strait guard of her father."

VALERIO, son of Gostanzo, secretly married to Gratiana. "Like the lark mounting the sky in shrill and cheerful notes, chanting his joys aspired, . . . Valerio loves, and joys the dame he loves." Transformed by his father's covetous humor and education into a bailiff and overseer of his pastures, Valerio's "skill extends to something more than sweaty husbandry, . . . cards, tennis, wenching, dancing, and what not. . . . Yet all this while, [his] father apprehends [him] for the most tame and thrifty groom in Europe, . . . so seasoned with obedience even from his youth, that all his actions relish nothing but duty." ("O father, pardon; [he] was born to gull thee.")

GRATIANA, "beauty's little world," stolen wife to Valerio, "a gentlewoman, but her unnourishing dowry must be told [i.e., counted] out of her beauty. . . . One that is rich enough: her hair pure amber; her forehead mother-of-pearl; her fair eyes two wealthy diamonds; her lips mines of rubies; her teeth are orient pearl; her neck pure ivory. . . . Would not a son hazard his father's wrath, his reputation in the world, his birthright, to have but such a mess of broth as this?"

BELLANORA, daughter to Gostanzo and beloved of Fortunio, her "dear choice,"

Unlike Gazetta, they "have loves and wish continual company with them in honor'd marriage rites, which [she] enjoy[s]. But seld' or never can [they] get a look on those [they] love."

CORNELIO, a start-up gentleman, who is more a "jealous jailer" than a husband, and who has "a vigilant eye to the main chance still. . . . [He] lives . . . abroad at great expense, turns merely [i.e., completely] gallant from his farmer's state, uses all games and recreations; runs races with the gallants of the court, feasts them at home, and entertains them costly, and then upbraids [his wife] with their company. . . . Jesus! What moods are these? Did ever husband follow his wife with jealousy so unjust? . . . Will you blow the horn yourself, when you may keep it to yourself? Go to, you are a fool; understand me."

GAZETTA, "the new-turn'd gentleman's fair wife, . . . with whom the amorous courtier Dariotto is far in love, and of whom her sour husband is passing jealous. . . . There's no man's eye fix'd on [her], but doth pierce [her] husband's soul. . . . Indeed, such love is like a smoky fire in a cold morning." She envies Gratiana and Bellanora because they are "still being woo'd and courted, still so feeding on the delights of love, . . . where [she is] cloy'd."

DARIOTTO, "the amorous courtier, . . . a neat spruce slave, . . . esteemed a witty gentleman, . . . [who plays] the stallion ever where [he] come[s], . . . no woman's honor unattempted by [him]." But he protests that "alas, alas, faith, [he has] but the name; [he] love[s] to court and win, and the consent without the act obtain'd, is all [he] seek[s]. [He] love[s] the victory that draws no blood. . . . Who would steal out of a common orchard?"

CLAUDIO, "the twin-courtier, his companion," another "secret lecher, . . . true in nothing else,"

gentlemen of the court.

CURIO, a page, "a young Mercurio, [and] an excellent-spoken boy," who parodies the Euphuism of John Lyly and chivalrously undertakes the defense of Gazetta, "and in her of all that name (for 'lady' is grown a common name to their noble sex), which sex [he has] ever loved from [his] youth, and shall never cease to love, till [he] want[s] wit to admire."

FRANCIS POCK, "a practitioner in surgery."

KYTE, a scrivener or notary. "He's a shrewd fellow indeed. I had as lief have his head in a matter of felony, or treason, as any notary in Florence."

A Drawer at the Half Moon Tavern.

Setting: Florence, at some unspecified time.

"Heaven, Heaven, I see these politicians
(Out of blind Fortune's hands) are our most fools."

Act I

Fortunio, elder son of Marc Antonio, an honest simple knight, and an indulgent father to his children, is in love with Bellanora, the only daughter of Gostanzo, his covetous neighbor, a "wretched Machiavellian," and a harsh disciplinarian. In turn the "lusty Valerio," only son of Gostanzo, has secretly married Gratiana, a girl who is pretty enough but who has no dowry. Through his covetous humor Gostanzo has denied Valerio the customary recreations of a gentleman's son and transformed him into a bailiff and overseer of his farms; consequently the old man thinks the lad "the most tame and thrifty groom in Europe," who hardly dares to look a woman in the face. But, unknown to his father, Valerio has skill in something more than sweating husbandry—"dice, cards, tennis, wenching, dancing, and what not"; he is "known in ordinaries and tobacco-shops, trusted in taverns and vaulting houses," and now has acquired a wife he is afraid to take home to his father.

It is Rinaldo, the younger son of Marc Antonio, who, though a woman-hater himself, at one stroke assists both of the couples. Meeting Gostanzo just before the latter has seen all of the young people together, Rinaldo cannot evade the old man's questioning about Gratiana, and pretends that she is the bride of his brother Fortunio, who is afraid to take his wife home to his father, and who now threatens to join the army rather than face parental displeasure. As Rinaldo expects, Gostanzo cannot keep a secret. The old trickster tells Marc Antonio, whom he takes to task for his easygoing, indulgent ways; and he offers at his house to discipline Fortunio by precept and the example of Valerio, and in the end to send Fortunio home "both dutiful and thrifty." Thus both young couples will be housed under the same roof.

At the same time, in contrast to these young people who are in love but who must love in secret, there are Gazetta and her upstart husband Cornelio for whom love has turned to ashes. More of a jailer than a husband, Cornelio lavishly entertains gallants at home and then suspiciously upbraids his wife for being hospitable to his guests.

Act II

As agreed, the young people all repair to Gostanzo's house—until Marc Antonio's "black anger's storm be overblown," so Gostanzo says,

and some amusement is created when the old man insists that his
sheepshead son Valerio welcome the lady Gratiana in courtly fashion
with a kiss. Did it ever happen before that a disapproving father—and
a Machiavel at that—commanded his son to kiss his stolen bride and
chided him for not kissing? Or to welcome to his house his daughter's
lover, "where it had been her undoing t'have him seen?" If only the
truth can be kept from old Gostanzo.

Meanwhile, the relations between Gazetta and her jealous husband—
unlike those of the other couples of young lovers—become worse instead of better. Cornelio accuses her of misconduct with Dariotto, a
courtier who frequents Cornelio's house. Valerio belongs to the same
company of irresponsible roisterers; among them he makes up for his
enforced good behavior while under his father's eye. When, under pretext of modesty, he swaggers and boasts about his prowess in dancing
and singing, Cornelio determines to betray him to his father. First, however, Cornelio shows Valerio up by insisting that he sing to the theorbo,
or double-necked lute. Never did "dog howl with worse grace." "By
Heaven, Valerio," exclaims one of his listeners, "an I were thy father,
and loved good qualities as I do my life, I'd disinherit thee!" Rinaldo,
however, sees the prank for what it is, and warns his friend. Valerio
then determines to play a counter-joke upon the suspicious husband
that will make him mad "and turn his wife divorced loose amongst us,"
i.e., among the young gallants of the town.

Act III

At Gostanzo's, however, the bride and groom have not been discreet in
their behavior, and the strict old man begins to have misgivings about
the arrangement he has made. As he snooped about the house, he has
seen an ardent encounter between Gratiana and Valerio. His son, who
was "last day so bashful that he durst not look on a wench, now courts
her, and by'r lady, will make his friend Fortunio wear his head of the
right modern fashion [i.e., horned]" unless something is done. Hence,
for everyone's good, Gostanzo determines to send Gratiana away for a
time, but to keep Fortunio with him until he has time to save face with
the young man who believes his lenient old father disapproves of the
marriage. About the plan Gostanzo consults Rinaldo, who must think
fast. The deception, it is clear, is not yet discovered; without suspicion
Fortunio can still be with Bellanora, but bride and groom will be
separated. Hence, Rinaldo suggests that if he must send Gratiana away,
Gostanzo send her to Marc Antonio's as the wife of Valerio, married
without his father's knowledge. Thus, when the truth is known, simple
wit will triumph over Machiavellian scheming. For the time being,

however, Gostanzo will think his friend gulled and still account Marc Antonio simple. At the same time, in the interests of sport, the rascally Gostanzo is not above permitting his son to steal out to visit the girl occasionally at his neighbor's house; "spirit will break out, though never so suppress'd and pinioned." But the old fellow does warn Marc Antonio that caution is necessary.

Meanwhile, Rinaldo is involved in another intrigue, the "black ball of debate Valerio's wit hath cast betwixt Cornelio and the enamor'd courtier," Dariotto. Cornelio's jealousy has always sought occasion for divorce; now Valerio's casual mockery of the old fool seems sure to present it. Ignoring all pleas that he behave reasonably, Cornelio will not be pacified; he insists upon a divorce from Gazetta, and attacks Dariotto in the streets. But he is inexperienced in the gentlemanly art of dueling, and in the encounter he is slightly wounded.

Act IV

Gostanzo is no more able to keep his second secret from Marc Antonio than his first, and the indulgent old man, bearing Valerio's penitent submission to his father and joining his own persuasions to appease parental fury, learns from Gostanzo himself of the "deception" which is being practiced by and for the young lovers. Pretending at first to be angry at Valerio's wedding, the deceived Gostanzo is easily persuaded to forgive his son and accept his daughter-in-law. "Gulled I my father," asks Valerio in private of Rinaldo, "or gulled he himself? Thou told'st him Gratiana was my wife, I have confessed it, he has pardoned it." Whatever the answer to the question, the way is now cleared for these lovers to meet daily.

But the debate which Valerio has set between Cornelio and his wife is not so easily solved. The jealous fool has hired a notary to draw up articles of divorce which he insists upon having read publicly. As he prepares to sign the document, however, his nose bleeds, and Cornelio defers signature till the next court day. It is then that Claudio tells him that the whole affair has been engineered by Valerio, assisted by Rinaldo, not because there was any just cause for the divorce, but only because Valerio had been shown up as a vain boaster in the matter of singing to the theorbo. Cornelio, only partially convinced, resolves to conclude the matter with "a counterbluff given to these noble rascals."

Act V

Rinaldo has now successfully gulled Gostanzo, Dariotto, and Cornelio, all of whom had the full possession of their wits, and he waits to see what Cornelio will at last do about his divorce. But as Rinaldo enjoys the consequence in anticipation, Cornelio seeks him out, however, to warn him that Valerio has been arrested for debt, that they are both in danger as Valerio's security, and that it is best that Rinaldo explain everything to the young man's father and fetch him to release the boy from prison. He will find both the officers and the prisoner at the Half Moon Tavern. Thus, the gulled husband will be revenged upon his gullers; here at this tavern will Gostanzo find a merry riotous company, "and amongst them the ringleader, his son, . . . his Saint Valerio, that knows not of what fashion dice are made nor ever yet look'd toward a red lattice [i.e., a tavern], . . . at drinking and at dice with all their wenches, and at full discover his own gross folly and his son's distempers." As Cornelio hopes, so events fall out. When the drunken party is at its height, Gostanzo arrives and for some minutes watches his "innocent" son in action. There he is joined by Marc Antonio. The latter has already discovered who is the true husband of Gratiana, and in the explanations which follow, it is learned that Fortunio and Bellanora are also secretly married. As for Cornelio, the grounds for his suspicions of Gazetta may not be removed, but they can be extenuated, and what man will proclaim his shame abroad when he can keep it to himself? The jealous husband is reconciled with his lady and the company, as the tipsy Valerio mounts a chair to make a speech in praise of this harmony and in honor of "the most fashionable and authentical" symbol, the horn.

BUSSY D'AMBOIS

A TRAGEDY

(1600–1604)

DRAMATIS PERSONAE

HENRI III, King of France, so much "in fear to make mild virtue proud, [that he] use[s] not to seek her out in any man."

MONSIEUR, [the Duc d'Alençon], "the politic Monsieur," brother of the king, who "did never good, but to do ill, . . . [and whose] tongue [is] so scandalous, 'twill cut the purest crystal. . . . A bachelor and a courtier, ay, and a prince," but he is an importunate, troublesome lover, "of all dames hated. . . . There's but a thread betwixt [him] and a crown."

BUSSY D'AMBOIS, "Fortune's proud mushroom shot up in a night," a young, haughty, truculent, blunt adventurer, who "dares as much as a wild horse or tiger" to win recognition, "and to feed the ravenous wolf of [his] most cannibal valor. . . . [He's] for honest actions, not for great. . . . Like a laurel put in fire, [he] sparkled and spit."

The COUNT OF MONTSURRY, a courtier.

TAMYRA, his "matchless wife, . . . her virtues are so renowned." ("O, the infinite regions betwixt a woman's tongue and her heart! Is this our goddess of chastity?")

PERO, her maid; "a man may go a whole voyage with her, and get nothing but tempests from her windpipe."

The DUKE OF GUISE, a violent man, "only great in faction."

ELENOR, Duchess of Guise.

ANNABELLE, maid to Elenor. "Here's a peacock seems to have devoured the Alps, she has so swelling a spirit, and is so cold of her kindness."

BEAUPRÉ, niece to Elenor.

CHARLOTTE, maid to Beaupré. "Here's one, I think, has swallowed a porcupine, she casts pricks from her tongue so."

BARRISOR, once the courtly lover of Tamyra,⎫ courtiers, three "famous soldiers," who
L'ANOU,   ⎬ are the enemies of D'Ambois.
PYRRHOT,   ⎭

BRISAC,   ⎫ courtiers who are the "brave friends" of D'Ambois.
MELYNELL,⎭

MAFFÉ, officious steward to Monsieur. "What qualities have you, sir, beside your chain and velvet jacket? . . . A barbarous groom grudge at his master's bounty!" ("Never was any curious in his place to do things justly, but he was an ass; we cannot find one trusty that is witty.")

BEAUMOND, a lord attending King Henri.

PYRA, a court lady.

FRIAR COMOLET, "a most learned and religious man," but the go-between for D'Ambois and the Countess Tamyra.

UMBRA, or GHOST, of Friar Comolet.

BEHEMOTH, "Prince of Darkness,"   ⎫ spirits.
CARTOPHYLAX, who has in his power all papers,⎭

Nuntius, a messenger who reports the combat of D'Ambois and his enemies.

Murderers, Lords, Ladies, Pages, and Servants.

Setting: Paris in the late sixteenth century, before 1579.

> "Farewell, brave relics of a complete man!
> Look up and see thy spirit made a star."

Act I

Poor and neglected by Fortune, Bussy D'Ambois, an adventurer "of spirit beyond the reach of fear," is introduced at the court of Henri III of France by Monsieur, Duc d'Alençon, brother to the king and secret aspirant to the throne, who thinks it good to get "resolved spirits" about him. But Bussy is also haughty and "apt to take fire at advancement," and his sudden rise to dignity, his blunt behavior, and his lack of courtship, as well as his insolence, soon earn for him the jealousy and hatred of many at court. He even antagonizes the Guise, and finds aggressive enemies in Barrisor, L'Anou, and Pyrrhot, three famous soldiers and gentlemen of the court. But he also finds favor with the courtiers Brisac and Melynell, and with some of the court ladies, especially the Countess of Guise to whom he is attentive.

Act II

Envy of Bussy D'Ambois' sudden rise and great spirit quickly breaks forth in a desperate quarrel in which Bussy and his two friends, Brisac and Melynell, engage in a fierce combat with Barrisor, L'Anou, and Pyrrhot. From the fight only Bussy D'Ambois survives, and from it he emerges as "the bravest man the French earth bears." For participating in such an encounter Bussy's life is forfeit, but through the intercession of Monsieur, the king pardons his offense, much to the disgust of the Guise. Monsieur and Bussy—patron and protégé—are then free to continue their courtly love intrigues; Bussy with Elenor, Duchess of Guise; Monsieur with Tamyra, Countess of Montsurry. For some time, Monsieur, who is gross-mannered and far from handsome, has been the troublesome, importunate suitor of the countess, who seems wholly devoted to her husband and is renowned for her virtue. But it is this lady to whom Bussy's love has secretly long been vowed in heart, and Bussy now becomes the rival of his patron.

The slain Barrisor had also been the countess' courtly lover, and from him she keeps a love letter written in his blood. On the ground that a report is spreading through the court that this affair was the cause of their quarrel, Bussy D'Ambois seeks an interview with the lady, and trusts to fortune and his own cunning to see him through. Moreover, Tamyra has made an old friar her confidant; he is versed in dissembling feminine nature, and he alone knows a secret subterranean passage to Tamyra's chamber. This friar serves as Bussy's guide.

Act III

Fearful for her honor and her life, Tamyra parts from Bussy at dawn before her husband arrives home, and, as a token of her love, presents Bussy with a chain of pearl—which had earlier been the gift of Monsieur. As time passes, Bussy grows in the king's favor, but Monsieur becomes as bitterly envious of his protégé as does the Guise. He regrets that he has raised Bussy to power, and all his outward favor to him is turned to inward hate. The hatred of the Guise not only smolders but occasionally flares out, and King Henri tries to reconcile the two. Upstarts, however, "should never perch too near a crown," and the

Guise and Monsieur join forces to plot the downfall of Bussy D'Ambois.
They resolve to set snares for "his ranging greatness . . . amongst
[the] greatest women, . . . for there is no such trap to catch an upstart
as a loose downfall." Bussy is no longer as attentive as he had been to
the Duchess of Guise, and his courtly neglect of her has been noted. It
is even suspected that he loves another lady. But whom? Publicly,
Tamyra takes no notice of him. It is Pero, Tamyra's maid, who at last
reveals to Monsieur the astounding news that Bussy is in fact his rival
for the favor of the Countess of Montsurry, and that he has had a midnight rendezvous with the lady.

Monsieur now has the information he needs, but before he can reveal
it to the Guise or the countess' husband, the truculent Bussy appears to
talk rather frankly of Monsieur's royal ambitions. The prince, of course,
disclaims them, but he asks Bussy without flattery to tell him fairly "the
full and plain state of me in thy thoughts." Bussy agrees on condition
that Monsieur first tell what he thinks of him. When both have finished
their characterizations, neither can have any illusions about the other.
With a spontaneous show of friendship, they go to a banquet given by
the king to celebrate the reconciliation of the Guise and Bussy D'Ambois.

Act IV

At the banquet Tamyra still acts as if she and Bussy were unacquainted,
but it is clear that Monsieur knows more than he will openly tell. When
all but the Guise and Montsurry have retired, Monsieur makes horns at
the count and has the bad taste to taunt him with having a wife who
seems "a mere [i.e., an absolute] Cynthia." But he dares not charge the
lady more specifically. He does offer Montsurry a letter, however, which
purports to tell more, but he insists that the count pawn his honor to
return it after he has read it. The conversation is interrupted by the
return of Tamyra, and Monsieur and the Guise leave the couple alone.
Finding that swooning and dissembling take all of the righteous indignation out of her weak husband, Tamyra urges him to see Monsieur's
paper and to question her maid Pero; indeed, she will herself write to
Monsieur for the letter.

Bussy D'Ambois has also become suspicious that Monsieur knows
of his love for the countess. He visits Tamyra with the friar. The latter
offers to put their fears at ease by calling up spirits who can tell the
lovers what the secret paper contains. But Behemoth and Cartophylax,
who respond to his incantations, are prevented by counter-exorcism from
giving them the information. The lovers, however, are permitted by
magic through space to see but not hear Monsieur, the Guise, and
Montsurry consult the letter, see the Guise advise Montsurry if he seeks

revenge to force his wife to write Bussy an invitation to come to see her, and see the count in a jealous fit stab Pero who brings Monsieur Tamyra's note.

To the friar's natural question, "what shall become of us?" Behemoth can only reply darkly:

> If D'Ambois' mistress dye not her white hand
> In her forced blood, he shall remain untouched;
> So, father, shall yourself, but by yourself.
> To make this augury plainer, when the voice
> Of D'Ambois shall invoke me, I will rise,
> Shining in greater light, and show him all
> That will betide ye all. Meantime be wise,
> And curb his valor with your policies.

Act V

This ambiguous advice holds sealed the doom of Bussy D'Ambois. There are bound to be repercussions from what Monsieur has revealed to Montsurry, and Bussy is far from being a wise or a patient man. The friar remains behind to temper as best he can the insane fury which the jealous husband showers upon his wife, while Bussy goes to strew his hate of Monsieur with smiles and to play the politician with those who seek his ruin. But all in vain. As the Guise has advised, Montsurry tries to wring from Tamyra the name of the go-between for the lovers, and to insist that she write an invitation to her lover. She stolidly refuses, and, in spite of his solemn oath to the friar that he would not harm his guilty wife, the count in his frenzy stabs Tamyra repeatedly. At this "rape of honor and religion" represented by the broken promise, the friar drops dead. Tamyra admits that the cleric was the go-between, and begins the letter, but with her blood instead of ink so that Bussy will know the lines come from her wounds and not from herself. When she has finished, Montsurry disguises himself in the friar's robe and serves as the messenger, with the aid of Monsieur and the Guise hiring murderers to kill Bussy when he arrives. But the Umbra, or Ghost, of the friar tries to warn Bussy. As agreed, Bussy again raises Behemoth, who also warns him. Yet when the false friar brings him the letter, Bussy suspects the spirits of deceiving him, accepts the blood-written note as a sacred witness of his mistress' love, and follows his guide.

Twice more the Umbra of the friar tries to save his friend. He warns Tamyra, but Bussy in bravado refuses to retreat from her chamber while there is still time. The Umbra frightens off the murderers when they first attack Bussy. Even when Montsurry rallies his hirelings, Bussy momentarily has the advantage; he fights and gets Montsurry down, granting him his life only when Tamyra begs it. But the pistol shots of reserve assassins off stage give Bussy D'Ambois his mortal wound. At the bidding of the Umbra of the friar, Bussy forgives his murderers, urges the reconcilement of Montsurry and the countess, and expires. But the penitant Tamyra realizes that she cannot be reconciled to Montsurry and remain true to her lover; hence, she merely begs her husband's forgiveness, promising never more to grieve him with her sight until Death has cured her wounds.

THE REVENGE OF BUSSY D'AMBOIS
(1607–1612)

DRAMATIS PERSONAE

CLERMONT D'AMBOIS, "dear minion to the Guise," brother to Bussy D'Ambois, and called upon to avenge his murder. "Men affirm though this same Clermont hath a D'Ambois spirit, and breathes his brother's valor, yet his temper is so much past his that you cannot move him. . . . France never bred a nobler gentleman for all parts. . . . Besides his valor, he hath the crown of man, and all his parts which learning is, . . . which Bussy, for his valor's season, lack'd. . . . He will be fiery, . . . yet when he lists he can contain that fire, as hid in embers. . . . In all, Rome's Brutus is revived in him. . . . In his most gentle and unwearied mind, . . . in his contempt of riches and of greatness, . . . in . . . his scorn of all things servile and ignoble, . . . this Senecal man is found in him. He may with Heaven's immortal powers compare." ("How strangely thou art loved of both the sexes; yet thou lovest neither but the good of both.")

The COUNT OF MONTSURRY, murderer of Bussy D'Ambois, "passing covetous with that blind greediness that follows gain. . . . His lady by his suit (wooing as freshly as when first love shot his faultless arrows from her rosy eyes) now lives with him again. . . . He will lie like a lapwing."

TAMYRA, wife to Montsurry and former mistress of Bussy D'Ambois.

BALIGNY, Lord Lieutenant, treacherous brother-in-law of Bussy and Clermont D'Ambois, and searcher for malcontents and their designs against the king. "Oh, Baligny, who would believe there were a man that . . . could bear a mind so more than devilish?"

CHARLOTTE, wife to Baligny and "the brave virago, . . . manly sister" of Bussy and Clermont D'Ambois. Her "heart stands with haste of the revenge, being . . . full of her brother's fire."

The COUNTESS OF CAMBRAY, mistress to Clermont D'Ambois. "I never witness'd a more noble love, nor a more ruthful sorrow. . . . She wept her fair eyes from her ivory brows, and would have wept her soul out."

HENRI III, King of France. "Never trust a man for any justice that is rapt with pleasure. . . . 'Tis more than Nature's mighty hand can do to make one humane and a lecher too. . . . Kings may do what they list; . . . there's no disputing with the acts of kings."

MONSIEUR, the "vicious Monsieur," his brother. "You did no princely deeds ere you were born, I take it, . . . nor did any since that I have heard; nor will do ever any, as all think."

The DUKE OF GUISE, "that bore a chief stroke in [Bussy's] death," but is nevertheless the admiring patron of Clermont D'Ambois. He is not trusted by King Henri.

RENEL, "the malcontent, decay'd Marquis Renel," friend to Clermont.

MAILLARD,
CHALON,   } captains sent by King Henri to apprehend Clermont D'Ambois.
AUMALE,

ESPERNON,
SOISSON,   } courtiers attending the king.
PERRICOT,

The UMBRA, or GHOST, of Bussy D'Ambois, victim of "the cruel'st murder that e'er fled the sun," now come up "from the chaos of eternal night, to which the whole digestion of the world is now returning."

GHOSTS of { Monsieur.
            Guise.
            Cardinal Guise.
            Chatillon.

RIOVA, a maidservant to the Countess of Cambray.

A Gentleman-Usher to the Countess of Cambray.

Messengers, several Captains, Soldiers, the Guard, Servants, and other Attendants.

Setting: France in the sixteenth century.

*"Woe be to that state
Where treachery guards, and ruin makes men great."*

Act I

Clermont D'Ambois, brother of Bussy, but very different from him in temperament, has been urged by the ghost of the murdered man to avenge his death. Although Bussy was killed in adultery, other members of the family have also vowed to avenge the murder, but Clermont now insists upon carrying it out himself, and only by the honorable method of a duel, "in the noblest and most manly course." But the cowardly Count of Montsurry, who slew Bussy, evades Clermont's challenge, surrounding himself with an armed guard and barricading his house. There he lives, outwardly reconciled with his wife Tamyra, who, however, does not love her husband and longs for revenge of her lover's death. At least, if Clermont himself is above trickery, his brother-in-law Baligny is not. Baligny has been accepted as a husband by Charlotte D'Ambois only on condition that he avenge Bussy's death, and with the aid of Renel, a treacherous friend whom Montsurry trusts, Baligny succeeds in delivering Clermont's challenge.

At the same time, Clermont's close friendship with the Duke of Guise has aroused jealousy and antagonism at court, especially in the mind of the king. And it is this same Baligny who fosters the suspicion.

Act II

"Treachery for kings is truest loyalty"—this, at least, is the principle which animates the double-dealing Baligny. The faction of the Guise is growing in strength, and King Henri's fears of it animate intrigues for its suppression. Clermont D'Ambois belongs to the Guise party, and the unscrupulous Baligny proposes to the king that on a journey into Cambray which Clermont is to make with Baligny to review a muster of the king's troops, the former might be arrested and Baligny's hand never be discerned therein. At the same time Baligny flatters the Guise and praises Clermont to his patron. To Clermont, in turn, Baligny subtly suggests the Guise's responsibility for the St. Bartholomew Massacre. Upon being rebuffed, however, for his innuendoes, Baligny brings the conversation around to the challenge which has been delivered to Montsurry, but which is still being evaded. Perhaps while they are in the country, the traitor suggests, the Countess Tamyra and Lord Renel will find some means of making sure that Clermont meets the murderer. Meanwhile, in Cambray they are sure of welcome and high honor.

Act III

In Cambray, however, plans are afoot for the ambush and capture of Clermont D'Ambois. Although the arrest is to be made at the king's command, the soldiers who are to undertake the task have misgivings, and they know their assignment will not be an easy one. Clermont is strong and quick, and if he rides his Scotch horse, "all France put at the heels of him will fail to take him." Hence, the captains determine to disguise a couple of their best men as lackeys so that at the proper moment they may lay a sure hand on their prospective prisoner and pluck him from his horse.

Clermont is welcomed by his sister Charlotte, and while at her house receives an anonymous letter which warns him of the treachery about to be practiced against him, and which specifically accuses his brother-in-law Baligny and his lieutenant of complicity. But Clermont refuses to heed; though he accuses Maillard of the scheme, he nevertheless accepts the captain's word that no harm is meant to him. But he is not deceived by the officer's protestations, and he receives the two lackeys who come with a message for him.

Act IV

Attempts to capture Clermont at first fail, for "who can hold light-ning?" The disguised lackeys are thrown aside as if they were autumn leaves; even two companies of men, enclosing Clermont, as "in two half moons," are unable to hold him. But at last the man is captured, and led in in the custody of the perjured Maillard, his bonds, however, "honor'd more than all the freedom he enjoy'd before." Stoically he ac-cepts arrest, and asks only that he be permitted to send a messenger to his mistress, the Countess of Cambray, explaining his inability to be present at her house at night. When Aumale, Clermont's messenger, re-ports to the countess what has occurred, she sends her noble lover a chest of jewels, and weeps bitterly for his misfortune. "Tears are all the vent [her] life [has] to 'scape death."

But when word of Clermont's arrest reaches the court, the Guise loses no time by forceful pleading in obtaining the release of his protégé from the weak and vacillating king. Meanwhile, part of the dying prophecy of Bussy D'Ambois has been fulfilled. Monsieur, who betrayed him, is dead. But Bussy had prophesied more—he had also predicted the end of the Guise.

Act V

While he talks to the Guise concerning the scheme for propagating Catholicism in which his whole faction is involved, Clermont receives a second visit from his brother's Ghost, come to whet his almost blunted purpose of revenge. "Use the means thou hast to right the wrong I suf-fered," urges the Ghost; "what corrupted law leaves unperform'd in kings, do thou supply. . . . Danger, the spur of all great minds, is ever the curb to your tame spirits." Although he can hear and see nothing, the Guise is terrified by Bussy's spirit, for he too had participated in Bussy's downfall. His reasoning is logical: "Would he rise, and not be thundering threats against the Guise?" But Clermont assures the duke that his friendship for himself makes amends for the enmity he once showed to Bussy. Spurred by the Ghost's taunts, as well as by news that the Countess of Cambray has literally wept her eyes out for him and has gone blind, Clermont determines to carry out the revenge he has sworn, as his sister Charlotte, disgusted at Clermont's long delays and disguised as a man, offers her services to Tamyra as an avenger. Aided by the Ghost, Clermont gets into Montsurry's house, forces the murderer to fight, and at last kills him, while Renel, Tamyra, and Charlotte look on. But not before he exchanges forgiveness with his victim. The score at last is settled.

Meanwhile, however, King Henri has repented his release of Cler-mont and his weakness before the Guise. He finds a willing accomplice

in Baligny, and, as he is called to the king's council, the Guise is put
to death by murderers concealed behind an arras. Bussy's prophecy is
now fulfilled completely, and his ghost, leading in the ghosts of
Guise, Monsieur, Cardinal Guise, and Chatillon (who are also dead),
dances about the body of Montsurry. This spectral celebration is Clermont's first intimation that his patron has met with foul play. When his
fears are confirmed, Clermont refuses to live alone in a world where
such a deed is possible, amid "all the horrors of the vicious time." Revenge
upon the king is unthinkable; but "friendship is the cement of two
minds," and Clermont kills himself. Tamyra and Charlotte resolve to
retire to a cloister and spend their remaining days in penance; "too
easy 'tis to die."

GEORGE CHAPMAN, BEN JONSON, AND
(c. 1560–1634)   (1572–1637)
JOHN MARSTON
(c. 1576–1634)

For biographies see above: Chapman, p. 239; Jonson, p. 168; and Marston,
p. 228.

CRITICAL COMMENT. In its contrast between two apprentices and their
associates, *Eastward Ho!* to some extent anticipates Hogarth's famous series of
prints called "Industry and Idleness" (1747), and may indeed have given the
artist the hint for them. The play also presents a more attractive side of the
sterling London citizen and shopkeeper than is usual, on the whole, in early
seventeenth-century drama, with his tiresome bourgeois code and his con-
sciousness of rectitude. The social climbers, the carpet knights, the usurers, the
lawyers, even the adventurers for Virginia—all are the subject of telling satire.
Indeed, the authors went too far in their fun, and for some remarks upon
the Scots parvenus—which sound innocent enough today—they were imprisoned for a time.

Eastward Ho! was adapted to Restoration taste by Nahum Tate as *Cuckolds'*
Haven, or an Alderman No Conjurer (1685), with some scenes from Jonson's
The Devil Is an Ass. Charlotte Lennox transformed it into *Old City Manners*
(1775), which was produced by Garrick, who had revived the original in
1751. The play also supplied Sir Walter Scott with details for the realistic
background for *The Fortunes of Nigel* (1822).

SOURCE. No source is known for the main plot of *Eastward Ho!*, but the
play belongs to the tradition of the repentant prodigal-son stories. The intrigue involving Sir Petronel and Winifred draws upon two novels of Masuccio.

BIBLIOGRAPHY

Early editions: 1605, 1605 (twice, with passages offensive to the Scots omitted).

Modern editions: Facs. J. S. Farmer (TFT, 1914); ed. F. E. Schelling (Belles Lettres Series, 1904); Miss J. H. Harris (Yale Studies, 1926).

EASTWARD HO!

(1605)

DRAMATIS PERSONAE

MASTER WILLIAM TOUCHSTONE, goldsmith of London, a sterling citizen and a trades-man. "Did [he] gain [his] wealth by ordinaries? No! By exchanging of gold? No! By keeping of gallants' company? No! [He] hired . . . a little shop, fought low, took small gain, kept no debt-book, garnished [his] shop, for want of plate, with good wholesome thrifty sentences, as 'Touchstone, keep thy shop, and thy shop will keep thee'; 'Light gains makes heavy purses'; ' 'Tis good to be merry and wise.' . . . [He] grew up, and [he] praise[s] Providence, [he] bear [s his] brows now as high as the best of [his] neighbors. . . . Work upon that now!"

MISTRESS TOUCHSTONE, his wife, who "has been [his] cross these thirty years, and [he'll] now keep her to fright away sprites, i' faith." ("Come, why dost thou weep now? Thou art not the first good cow hast had an ill calf, I trust!")

GERTRUDE, his elder daughter and his "wife's dilling, . . . proud, lascivious, and a fool, . . . [who] must be ladified, forsooth. . . . So a woman marry to ride in a coach, she cares not if she ride to her ruin." Gertrude is betrothed and later married to Sir Petronel Flash. "Would the Knight o' the Sun, or Palmerin of England, have used their ladies so? . . . Or Sir Launcelot, or Sir Tristram?" ("Surely, in my mind, your ladyship hath fished fair and caught a frog, as the saying is,") } Touchstone's two daughters, "the eldest of a proud ambition and nice wantonness, the other of a modest humility and comely soberness."

MILDRED, his younger daughter. "She is not fair, well-favored or so . . . [but she] had rather make up the garment of [her] affections in some of the same piece, than, like a fool, wear gowns of two colors, or mix sackcloth with satin." She is be-trothed, and later married, to Golding, Touchstone's younger apprentice,

FRANCIS QUICKSILVER, "a prodigal coxcomb, . . . a drunken whore-hunting rakehell, . . . thou common shot-clog, gull of all companies, . . . thou most madly vain, whom nothing can recover but that which reclaims atheists, and makes great persons sometimes religious—calamity," } Touchstone's two apprentices, "the one of a boundless prodigality, the other of a most hopeful industry."

GOLDING, his younger, more prudent fellow; "as good a gentle-man born, . . . nay, and better meaned. But does he pump it, or racket it? . . . Note but the reward of a thrifty course. . . . From trades, from arts, from valor, honor springs; these three are founts of gentry, yea, of kings." Later he is married to Mildred, Touchstone's youngest daughter,

SIR PETRONEL FLASH, a new-made knight, "our Virginian colonel," betrothed and later husband to Gertrude. "I ken the man weel; he's one of my thirty-pound knights. . . . No, no, this is he that stole his knighthood o' the grand day for four pound. . . . He says he has a castle in the country. . . . Alas, all the castles [he has] are built with air."

MISTRESS SINDEFY, Quicksilver's mistress and later waiting-gentlewoman to my Lady Flash; "stolen from [her] friends which were worshipful and of good accompt, by a prentice in the habit and disguise of a gentleman, . . . brought up to London and promised marriage, and now likely to be forsaken, for he is in possibility to be hanged!"

BETTRICE, a waiting woman, attending Gertrude Touchstone.

POLDAVY, "most edifying [ladies'] tailor! I protest you tailors are most sanctified members, and make many crooked thing go upright."

POTKIN, a tankard bearer, attending my Lady Flash.

A Coachman to my Lady Flash.

HAMLET, Lady Flash's footman. ("But must this young man, an't please you, madam, run by your coach all the way a-foot?")

MISTRESS FOND, } who see my Lady Flash take her coach. "O God, an we citizens
MISTRESS GAZER, } should lose such a sight!"

SECURITY, a covetous old usurer and bawd, newly married to a young wife. His "house is, as 'twere, the cave where the young outlaw hoards the stolen vails of his occupation; and here, when he will revel it in his prodigal similitude, he retires to his trunks, and (I may say softly) his punks. He dares trust [the usurer] with the keeping of both, for [the old rascal is] Security itself. . . . How the old villain joys in villainy! . . . 'I do hunger and thirst to do you good, sir!' "

WINIFRED, wife of Security, "prisoned with his stern usurous jealousy."

MASTER BRAMBLE, a lawyer. "Worshipful Master Bramble, how far do you draw us into the sweetbrier of your kindness! . . . God send you fortunate pleas, sir, and contentious clients."

A Scrivener.

SEA-GULL, a sea captain,
SCAPETHRIFT, } adventurers for Virginia.
SPENDALL,

Page to Sir Petronel Flash.

SLITGUT, apprentice to "a poor butcher of Eastcheap."

Drawer of the Blue Anchor Tavern, near Billingsgate, who rescues Winifred from the Thames.

WOLF, } officers of the Counter Prison.
HOLDFAST,

Two Gentlemen, a Messenger, a Constable, two Prisoners in the Counter and their Friend, Officers, and Attendants.

Setting: Goldsmith's Row; The Blue Anchor Tavern, near Billingsgate; Cuckolds' Haven; the Counter Prison; and elsewhere in London and on the Thames-side, at some unspecified time.

"*Look not westward to the fall of Dan Phoebus, but to the east—Eastward Ho!*

> *Where radiant beams of lusty Sol appear,*
> *And bright Eoüs makes the welkin clear.*"

Act I

William Touchstone, honest, substantial goldsmith of London, has two apprentices, Quicksilver and Golding, both gentlemen born, the former a young man "of a boundless prodigality, the other of a most hopeful industry." He also has two daughters, the elder, Gertrude, "of a proud ambition and nice wantonness," the younger, Mildred, "of a modest humility and comely soberness." Quicksilver is a swaggering unthrift, who keeps fast company, apes the fashions of London gallants, is already sevenscore pounds behind in his accounts, gets drunk, and, in his master's opinion, "is running directly to the Prodigal's hog's-trough." Gertrude, an ill-natured, immodest, vain minx, is about to be ladified, i.e., to marry a knight, Sir Petronel Flash, who, she thinks, will give her a coach to ride in, and share with her a title that will enable her to "take place" of her mother and her sister. The match is entirely of Mistress Touchstone's making; Gertrude has a piece of land, valued at a hundred pounds, which her grandmother left her; this she and Sir Petronel may flash out, if they will. But nothing will the blunt and outspoken Touchstone give to augment this dowry; his hand and his eyes open together. He does not give blindly.

Touchstone's disgust at Quicksilver, at his elder daughter's choice, and at her contempt for everything pertaining to the City, is mitigated somewhat by the trust and the hope he has in his virtuous apprentice Golding, and his plain, unassuming daughter Mildred. "Thou art towardly, she is modest," he says to the young man; "thou art provident, she is careful." Accordingly, the honest goldsmith makes a match between the two with intent

> *to prove*
> *Which thrives the best, the mean or lofty love.*
> *Whether fit wedlock vowed 'twixt like and like,*
> *Or prouder hopes, which daringly o'erstrike*
> *Their place and means.*

Act II

The next morning, on Sir Petronel and Gertrude's wedding day, Quicksilver has early drunk deep of the bridebowl and behaves so impudently and noisily, quoting scraps from popular plays, that his master casts him off; Touchstone can no longer dishonest his house, nor endanger his stock by this wastrel's license. At the same time the goldsmith gives his industrious apprentice his freedom, and a portion that makes it possible for Golding and Mildred to marry forthwith. Touchstone also offers the couple a marriage feast equal to that which Gertrude and her knight enjoyed, but they frugally profess themselves content with what is left over from the earlier nuptials.

Quicksilver finds refuge in the house of the unscrupulous usurer Security, who is a bawd and a receiver of stolen goods, with whom Quicksilver has had dealings before. Here the young scapegrace decks himself out in a gallant's clothes, meets his mistress, Sindefy, and with her and Security plots to bring Knight Petronel into the usurer's parchment rolls. The bride's estate is a fine seat, with fertile, well-wooded land. The knight needs money—let him have it. As soon as his lady's signature is affixed to the deed of sale of her inheritance, and he has been furnished with cash, Sir Petronel plans instantly to desert his bride, hoist sail, and away for Virginia. Quicksilver undertakes to engineer the scheme for Security, and Sindefy is preferred to the post of her ladyship's gentlewoman and is presented to Gertrude as the daughter of a friend, newly come to town from the country to study fashions.

Act III

As planned, Sir Petronel and Security come to terms. Master Bramble, the pettifogger, draws up writings for Gertrude to sign before she takes coach into the country to her bridegroom's imaginary castle. At the same time the knight makes arrangements at night to meet Captain Sea-gull, Scapethrift, and Spendall, his fellow adventurers, at the Anchor in Billingsgate, fill their skins with vintage, and with all expedition, take boat to their ship.

As Golding and Mildred return from their simple wedding, the snobbish Gertrude, with much fanfare, takes coach, but not before she has signed away her dowry. Her husband's pretext is that he needs her consent to dispose of one of his poor tenements that he may supply some necessary furnishings for his castle. "It goes down without chewing, i' faith," and the foolish girl doesn't look at what she is signing. Sir Petronel also uses the occasion for further knavery. Like himself, the accommodating usurer Security is just married to a young wife, Winifred, whom the knight has found fair. Under pretext of being enamored of Master Bramble's wife, who also is "prisoned with . . . stern usurous jealousy," Sir Petronel contrives it that Security shall assist at his own deception. So delighted is the old fool at Sir Petronel's project of stealing the lawyer's wife, that Security offers his own wife's best clothes as a disguise. Thus attired Winifred is brought by Quicksilver to the Anchor.

There, the Virginia adventurers, with the usurer and the lawyer, carouse and make merry. Outside, a storm rises. As the party takes boat to go aboard ship, Security and Bramble return home, where the former discovers his wife's absence, and in the tempest sets out for Billingsgate again in pursuit.

Act IV

In his nightcap and soaked to the skin, Security at last makes shore, not at Billingsgate his destination, however, but ominously at Cuckolds' Haven. In the meantime the boat bearing the adventurers has come to grief in the storm. A penitent and very wet Winifred is fished out of the Thames by the drawer of the Anchor Tavern, who recognizes her, supplies her with dry clothes of her own that have been left at the tavern, and finds lodging for her at the house of a friend in St. Catherine's. When at last Security finds his wife, the witty wench turns the tables against him. She pretends to have spent the night searching for him, upbraids him for rioting in taverns, and accuses him of robbing her of her clothes. Meekly the fool begs pardon.

One by one the other adventurers are washed ashore, thinking they have landed in France. They are utterly destitute, but when they learn where they are, Quicksilver—who has not lived among goldsmiths and goldmakers for nothing—undertakes within four and twenty hours to make passable gold coins from copper.

Meanwhile, Master Touchstone has discovered Sir Petronel's principal knaveries, and chastened, though not yet penitent, Lady Flash has returned to London via "Weeping Cross," from her husband's "castle in the country." Touchstone's other son-in-law Golding—on the first day of his freedom, too—has been taken into the livery of his company, and scarcely a week later made deputy to the alderman of the ward wherein he dwells. Golding, too, has heard of the mishap at Billingsgate and sent officers to the Anchor to apprehend the adventurers. To Touchstone's great satisfaction, as rogues and masterless men the offenders are brought before the young magistrate and committed to the Counter.

Act V

Hence, events have more than borne out both Touchstone's premonitions and his hopes. Within a week his ladified daughter Gertrude has lost her dowry, been deserted by her husband, and left destitute, with

nothing but her ladyship to pawn. And there is question that ?
will lend anything on that. His daughter's maid, Sindefy, w
first brought to London by an apprentice in the habit of a g'
and promised marriage, is now forsaken and her abducto
sibility of being hanged. The scapegrace knight who is his son
been committed to prison, with his thriftless apprentice.
dustrious and trustworthy son-in-law in the plain course
his snobbish, immodest daughter must now humbly seek
the roof of her virtuous, modest sister.

Touchstone refuses to help anyone, and is deaf to
the penitent prisoners. In their extremity both Sir Pe
silver have grown devout, especially the latter. "He
all the stories of the *Book of Martyrs* and speak you
Salve, without book." Quicksilver has converted o
and has brought him so far on the road to sal
nails and say his prayers, and 'tis hoped he wi
and become an intelligence [i.e., an informe
written a woeful ballad of farewell, rehears
repenting them.

In contrast to his obdurate father-in-law
by the prisoners' distress and willing to do
is no means, however, of making Touc
ceed as bringing him to the prisoners w
Hence, Golding has himself arrested a
his bail. In the prison the goldsmith
well, Security—who is also in jail—s
on his knees humbly beg forgivene
trude, Sindefy, and Winifred. Th
ciliations. Even Gertrude admits
begs her parents' blessing. Goldi
to Sindefy and that Security
Winifred are reunited, for, as
it's an argument you have a
if you be a cuckold, and kn
it and endure it, a true m

And in this
Behold the
The solem
The usur
The pro

GEORGE WIL (fl. c. 1604-1608)

Nothing is known about George Wi
about 1604 to 1608, and towards the end
for both the King's and the Queen's M
...on of the story in 1608. A George Wilkins o
who described himself as a victualler, aged thirty
with Shakespeare in the suit of Belott *vs.* Mountjoy
dramatist.

Both *The Miseries of Enforced Marriage,* by George
Tragedy, by an unknown author, were based upon
alter Calverly, as executed for his crime at York in August,
...verly's life up to 1604 and has a happy ending;
...es the story, and its puzzling opening scene is
wife, and the characters which the two plays have
husband is an unreasonable fool inclined to
...ces and upon the world. Neither of the adults
...The minor characters are no less types.
...r of *The Miseries,* have some attractions.
...rawn, are not wholly understandable, and the
...certain effectiveness, and *A Yorkshire*
...tributed to Shakespeare. It is only a

...*Timothy Tawdry* (1677), a com-
...e *Miseries of Enforced Marriage.*
...ed in Hazlitt's re-edition)
...t is included in no mor

MISTR cook,
MISTRESS Jo to learn fast
SAM FREEDOM, Mist ... he's a fool, but
MONEYLOVE, "a scholar:
ONESIPHORUS HOARD, brot
LIMBER,} country frie
KIX,
LAMPREY,} Lon
SPICHCOCK,}
HARRY D lawy

except that he
at period was
has been
he pro-
parish
was

THE *MISERIES* OF *ENFORCED* *MARRIAGE*
(1605–1607)

DRAMATIS PERSONAE

WILLIAM SCARBOROW [Walter Calverly], the victim of enforced marriage, "young and unsettled, though of virtuous thoughts by genuine disposition. . . . He is one, whom older look upon as on a book wherein are printed noble sentences for them to rule their lives by. . . . All emulate his virtues, hate him none."

THOMAS SCARBOROW, "a merry gentleman," and a student at the Inns of Court,
JOHN SCARBOROW, an Oxford student,
} brothers of William Scarborow, all "issue of one father, . . . an honest gentleman . . . whose hopes were better than the son he left should set so soon unto his house's shame."

A Sister of William Scarborow, whose marriage portion is in her brother's keeping.

LORD FALCONBRIDGE, William Scarborow's stern guardian.

SIR WILLIAM SCARBOROW, uncle to young William.

SIR JOHN HARCOP, a well-to-do gentleman of Yorkshire, "keeps a wine-cellar, has travelled, been at court, known fashions."

CLARE HARCOP, "a very perfect, proper gentlewoman, . . . young, fair, rich, honest, virtuous," only daughter of Sir John Harcop, the "kernel, hope, and comfort of [his] house," and trothplight wife to William Scarborow.

KATHERINE, "a maid, . . . both fair and chaste," niece to Lord Falconbridge, later married to William Scarborow.

DOCTOR BAXTER, Chancellor of Oxford and friend of Lord Falconbridge, the divine who marries Katherine and young Scarborow.

SIR FRANCIS ILFORD, "a scurvy-proud-prating prodigal, licentious, unnecessary . . . ass, . . . a slave that feeds upon [young Scarborow] like a fly, poisoning where [he] do[th] suck. . . . 'Sfoot, the knight would have made an excellent zany in an Italian comedy." ("Gulled, by this hand! An old coney-catcher and beguiled!")
WENTLOE,
BARTLEY,
} his companions, a "couple of smell-smocks,"
} "These men, like fish, do swim within one stream, yet they'd eat one another, making no conscience to drink with them they'd poison; no offense betwixt their thoughts and actions has control, but headlong run, like an unbiased bowl."

MASTER GRIPE, a usurer, who lives "by the fall of young heirs, as swine by the dropping of acorns."

A Couple of Sergeants, who pretend to arrest Sir Francis Ilford at Gripe's suit.

Butler, faithful, "old, tough, and unwieldy" servant to the Scarborow family.

ROBIN, a clown, Sir John Harcop's man; "this is a philosophical fool."

OLIVER, drawer at the Mitre in Bread Street, a "scrape-trencher, stair-wearer, wine-spiller, metal-clanker, rogue by generation."

Secretary to Lord Falconbridge.

Steward to Lord Falconbridge.

Page to Sir Francis Ilford.

Scarborow's two Children.

Servants and Attendants.

Setting: Yorkshire, near Wakefield, and London, sometime before 1605.

> *"For I have heard those matches have cost blood,*
> *Where love is once begun, and then withstood."*

Act I

Although William Scarborow of Yorkshire is but an orphan eighteen years of age, he is possessed of fifteen hundred pounds a year, and hence considered "a young gentleman of good parts and a great living," eligible for marriage. And, as his worldly-wise acquaintances, Sir Francis Ilford, Wentloe, and Bartley, warn him, a young man like that is particularly liable to be inveigled into marriage by some ambitious father who has a daughter to dispose of. Indeed, young Scarborow has been invited down into his native county by a "hoary knight," Sir John Harcop, to meet his daughter Clare and to arrange a wedding. And, just as the London gallants had predicted, so matters fall out. Sir John introduces the young people to each other, and contrives to leave them together; young Scarborow, who has never before been left alone with a gentlewoman, is instantly smitten by her beauty and modest behavior, and to make conversation—hardly for any other reason—he forthwith proposes marriage. With more maturity and common sense than her lover, Clare accepts the offer, exchanges vows with Scarborow, and becomes his trothplight wife in the sight of Heaven. For three more years, however, the young heir will be a ward, and those years must elapse before he and Clare are married.

Hardly has this betrothal been completed, however, before Scarborow is recalled to London by his guardian, Lord Falconbridge, and his uncle, Sir William Scarborow. Young William, they admit, bears himself with gravity, and is a model youth, but he is young and unsettled. There are daily precedents of hopeful gentlemen, trusted in the world with their own wills, who divert to ill the good which is expected of them, and keep company with revellers, panders, parasites, and knaves. "Marriage restrains the scope of single life," they reason, and to prevent young William from following courses of excess, the old men resolve to match him with a wife. Indeed, Lord Falconbridge has already found just the girl—his niece Katherine, a maid both fair and chaste—and appointed Doctor Baxter, Chancellor of Oxford, to draw up the marriage contract. Young Scarborow protests that he is already affianced to Sir John Harcop's Clare. But neither uncle nor guardian will recognize a troth made by the lad himself, and with threats and other coercion, they force young Scarborow to marry Katherine.

Act II

Young Scarborow is married to Katherine, has all his land in his own hand, is entrusted with his brothers' and his sister's portions, and has received four thousand pounds in ready money with his wife. But he is far from happy; he stalks about "like a cashiered captain discontent," and is the ready prey of sharpers of all sorts. A letter from Sir John Harcop reminds him of his enforced perfidy to Clare, and by return of messenger he sends the girl a simple note—"Forgive me, Clare, for I am married"—deserts his wife in London, and returns to Yorkshire. Sincerely in love with the youth, Clare also knows that as a jilted Elizabethan girl, whatever the cause of the desertion may be, she is

> *A wretched maid, not fit for any man;*
> *For being united his with plighted faiths,*
> *Whoever sues to me commits a sin,*
> *Besiegeth me; and who shall marry me,*
> *Is like myself, lives in adultery. . . .*
> *Let me live ne'er so honest, rich or poor,*
> *If I once wed, yet I must live a whore.*

Accordingly, Clare takes her own life, leaving only the note, "Forgive me, I am dead." In his grief, and forgetful of his own responsibility for the match, her old father curses young Scarborow for what has occurred, calling the boy a murderer, poor Katherine his wife a strumpet and an accessory to the crime, and their children bastards. With all of these accusations the desperate and penitent young man is readily in accord. Scarborow sends his brothers and his despised, but innocent, wife back to his estate near Wakefield, and sets out for London, vowing such a course of riot that warned by the example of "his life so foul, men ne'er should join the hands without the soul."

Act III

In London, through drink young Scarborow goes from bad to worse, wastes his substance like the Prodigal Son, and easily falls the victim of his erstwhile acquaintances, the coney-catching Sir Francis Ilford, Wentloe, and Bartley, who trick him into standing security for them with

Master Gripe the usurer. His brothers, Thomas and John, and their sister become alarmed about the patrimony which their father left them and come to London to claim their own. But in his resentment, William fights with his brothers and wounds them with his sword. He cracks the crown of the faithful old butler who brings him news out of Yorkshire of the birth of two sons, and, "more like a brute beast than a gentleman," even draws his sword on his guardian and his uncle.

It is to the old butler, not to Lord Falconbridge or Sir William Scarborow, who are responsible for young William's riots, that the young prodigal's brothers and sister turn for help. For the sake of their father, his old benefactor, the butler promises somehow to assist them and save them from want or an evil life:

> To keep you honest, and to keep you brave,
> For once an honest man will turn a knave.

Act IV

Accordingly, the butler assists Thomas and John to rob the now heirless Sir John Harcop of three hundred pounds, justifying the crime with disarming whimsicality:

> To steal is bad, but taken where is store,
> The fault's the less, being done to help the poor.

Then, without too close scrutiny of the niceties involved, but with the aid of her brothers, he marries off the penniless sister to Sir Francis Ilford, who has come into Yorkshire to take possession of Scarborow's land, and is tricked into believing the girl a rich heiress. Thus, those who were directly or indirectly responsible for beggaring young Scarborow are made the means of relieving his brothers and his sister.

Act V

Half an hour after marriage, however, Sir Francis discovers that he may have wed a modest, dutiful wife, but that she hasn't money enough to hire him a horse to run away from her. In his anger he calls her every foul name he can think of, kicks her, takes away the jewels and bracelets her brothers have bought her with their stolen wealth, and drives her out of the house, vowing to seek out and kill her brother William, whom he holds responsible for the match. Also blaming his elder brother for what has occurred, Thomas sets out to avenge his wrong upon William, and John follows to prevent one brother from killing the other. Again, it is the faithful butler, with his poor servingman's allowance of twelvepence a day, who undertakes to preserve his young mistress from want and shame.

The resentment of the brothers has an unexpected conclusion, however. Thomas is the first to meet William Scarborow, drunk as usual, but before they can fight their duel, Ilford, Wentloe, and Bartley put in their appearance, and the two brothers join to drive away the foe. William, then, thanks Thomas for saving his life, offers to repent, and asks that they live at peace together. Thomas refuses, however, but the duel is again interrupted by the appearance of John, who strives to reconcile the combatants and prevents the fight. So great is Thomas' fury against William, however, that Thomas vows to reveal the robbery he and John have committed, only to avenge himself on John for hindering his revenge on William. William's repentance in turn is interrupted by the butler with word that the house is surrounded by creditors, and that Katherine and the children have come to join the husband. But his wife's patience and forgiveness only infuriate the unhappy William the more. He denounces the poor lady, refuses to acknowledge his children, and curses and casts off the faithful old butler who intercedes and prevents further violence still.

It is Doctor Baxter, the learned divine from Oxford who married William Scarborow, who now brings him to his senses and "disrobe [s his] thoughts of this wild frenzy that becomes [him] not." To his righteous chiding, Scarborow responds by heartfelt repentance. But it is the old butler who intercepts Thomas and prevents his confession of the robbery, who reconciles the brothers, who rejoins Sir Francis Ilford and his wife, and who brings together William, Katherine, and the children. In his turn, William promises to see all portions paid, and the miseries of enforced marriage, temporarily at least, are at an end.

A YORKSHIRE TRAGEDY

For critical comment see above, p. 262.

BIBLIOGRAPHY

Early editions: 1608; 1619; also included in the Third (1664) and Fourth (1685) Folio editions of Shakespeare.

Modern editions: Facs. J. S. Farmer (TFT, 1910); ed. C. F. Tucker Brooke (*Shakespeare Apocrypha,* 1908).

A YORKSHIRE TRAGEDY

NOT SO NEW AS LAMENTABLE AND TRUE

(1605–1608)

DRAMATIS PERSONAE

HUSBAND [Walter Calverly], of "an honored stock and fair descent, till this black minute without stain or blemish, . . . [but] an unclean rioter, [whose] lands and credit lie now both sick of a consumption. . . . He has consumed all, . . . and made his university brother stand in wax for him; . . . puh, he owes more than his skin's worth. . . . 'Tis lost at dice what ancient honor won." ("Here's weight enough to make a heart-string crack.")

WIFE [Mistress Calverly], his virtuous, docile, and devoted spouse, who "never yet spoke less than words of duty and love. . . . Was it in man to wound so kind a creature?"

FIRST SON, Calverly's "white boy."

SECOND SON, a child in arms.

THE MASTER OF A COLLEGE, a "plain and effectual" man, friend of Calverly's younger brother who is a student at the university.

A Knight, Justice of the Peace, who "deserve[s] the worship of [his] place, . . . [for in him] the law is grace."

A Gentleman who reproves Calverly.

OLIVER,
RALPH, } servingmen in the Calverly household.
SAM,

A Lusty Servant who interferes with Calverly's fury, "thinking to prevent his quick mischiefs."

A Maidservant, attending Calverly's second son.

Other Servants, Officers, and Gentlemen.

Setting: Calverly Hall, Yorkshire, and vicinity, 1605.

> *"And 'tis set down by Heaven's just decree*
> *That Riot's child must needs be Beggary."*

In Yorkshire a virtuous and devoted young woman is betrothed to a young man about whom even the servants are gossiping. Unknown to her, the man is a gambler and a spendthrift, having mortgaged his property, and even bound his brother, a student at the university, security for his debts. What is worse, the scoundrel is already married to another woman, "beats his wife. and has two or three children by her."

In time the young wife has reason to bewail the recklessness and extravagance of her husband. Dicing, voluptuous living, and midnight revelry have consumed his fortunes; his credit is gone; and his riotous meetings are invariably followed on the morning after by sullen fits of godless sorrow and despair as the young husband recounts his losses. Then, the depraved fellow takes out his troubles on his poor loving wife, calling her harlot and their children bastards, and demanding money, money, money from her. At last he persuades her to sell her dowry, "to give new life unto those pleasures which [he] most affect[s]." Friends remonstrate with him to give up his wild courses; one even fights a duel with him for disparaging the virtue of his wife and insinuating that the friend is more than just the champion of the lady. But even a wound does not bring him to his senses.

Meanwhile, the wife has travelled to London to see her uncle-guardian, smoothed over her husband's brutality, said nothing of his riotous living, and obtained for him from the indulgent uncle something better than the sale of the dowry—a place at court "of worth and credit." But the unreasonable wastrel spurns his lady for it, calls the post "base servitude," and even threatens his wife with his dagger.

Soon the Master of the College which the younger brother is attending calls upon the spendthrift with word that the boy has been seized by the creditors and thrown into prison. At last the gamester seems to realize that by his recklessness, "five are made miserable beside myself: my riot is now my brother's jailer, my wife's sighing, my three boys' penury, and mine own confusion." But the discovery only maddens him.

Bidding the Master walk in the garden while he furnishes "a sufficient answer" for him to take back with him, the shame-crazed man kills two of his young sons, wounds his wife and a servant who tries to interfere, and then takes horse for the house at which the youngest child is out at nurse. On the way, however, providentially he is thrown by his horse, captured by the Master and officers who have pursued him, and brought before a justice. Sobered by what he has done, the young man has only this defense, that, having consumed everything he "thought it the charitablest deed [he] could do to cozen beggary, and knock [him] o' the head." After a remorseful interview with his devoted wife, who has only been wounded, and a sight of the bodies of his murdered babes, he is led off to prison to await trial.

THOMAS MIDDLETON
(1580-1627)

BIOGRAPHY.   Thomas Middleton was the son of a London bricklayer who
had a coat of arms and wrote himself "gentleman." Nothing is known of the
dramatist's education, but it has been conjectured that he studied at Oxford
and afterward entered Gray's Inn. His dramatic career began about 1599 and
for many years he wrote for various companies, usually in collaboration with
Drayton, Munday, Webster, Dekker, and later, William Rowley. In 1620 he
was appointed chronologer to the City of London. In 1627 he died at Newing-
ton Butts and was buried in the parish church there.

CRITICAL COMMENT.   Thomas Middleton was the Hogarth of the early
seventeenth century; he knew his London well, and he excelled in realistic,
satirical dramas which have a background of low life in the great metropolis.
His plays all illustrate the trend away from both the romantic comedy of
Shakespeare and the moral satire of Jonson, and the trend toward the irresponsible comedy of Etherege and Congreve.

A Trick to Catch the Old One is a comedy of manners second to none in
the language. It stems from Jonson, but it is more lighthearted and less surely
on the side of the angels.

Michaelmas Term is "a trick to catch the young one." The play is a picture
of London in the season, but it is not at all concerned with polite society; it
deals with the practices of usurers and lawyers on the shady side of the law,
and with fools, pretenders, and other dupes of the sharper.

SOURCES.   Both plots are presumably Middleton's own invention from his
knowledge of London life. Tricks like those employed by Quomodo had been
described before in books satirizing usurers.

BIBLIOGRAPHY

Collected Works:

  The Works of Thomas Middleton, edited by A. H. Bullen, 8 volumes,
    1885-86.
  The Best Plays of Thomas Middleton, edited by A. C. Swinburne, 2 volumes,
    Mermaid Series, 1887.
Monograph: W. D. Dunkel, *The Dramatic Technique of Thomas Middleton
  in the Comedies of London Life*, University of Chicago Press, 1925.

A Trick to Catch the Old One:

  Early editions: 1608 (2); 1616.

Michaelmas Term:

  Early editions: 1607; 1630.

A TRICK TO CATCH THE OLD ONE
(1604–1607)

DRAMATIS PERSONAE

THEODORUS WITGOOD, "a rioter, a wastethrift, a brothelmaster, . . . a midnight surfeiter," but, withal, a gentleman, and a clever contriver.

A COURTESAN, a "round-webbed tarantula, that [dries] the roses in the cheek of youth, . . . [and] the secret consumption of [his] purse"; later, JANE MEDLER, late widow of Anthony Medler, . . . four hundred a year valiant in woods, in bullocks, in barns, and in rye stacks, . . . a Dutch widow."

PECUNIUS LUCRE, Witgood's fox-brained, ox-browed uncle, "a severe extortioner; a tyrant at a forfeiture; greedy of others' miseries; one that would undo his brother, nay, swallow up his father, if he can, within the fadoms of his conscience,"

WALKADINE HOARD, another old skinflint, "rich in money, moveables, and lands, . . . able to buy three of Lucre, . . . [and] ˄n old, doting fool,"

"these three years mortal adversaries. Two old, tough spirits they seldom meet but fight, or quarrel when 'tis calmest. I think their anger be the **very** fire that keeps their age alive."

˅INNY LUCRE, Old Lucre's "second wife, old, past bearing; . . . a fine ⌐her] first husband married [her] out of an alderman's kitchen."

˅oard's niece. "She now remains at London with . . . her uncle, ˄ractice music. . . . A thousand good pound is her portion."

˅cre's "t'other husband's son; ˄h," ˅'s wise, but he's poor,"

rivals for the love of Mistress Joyce, Hoard's niece. ("Pray now, is not a rich fool better than a poor philosopher?")

˅r of Walkadine, ˅s of Old Hoard's, "the right worshipful seniors of our country."

˄n friends of Old Hoard's. (Their fathers and his "were all free ˄n' Fishmongers'.")

˅PIT, "a famous, infamous trampler of time [i.e., ˅: his own phrase; . . . [his] clients, . . . the ˄miny and coxcombry of the country," ˄g GULF, "his fellow caterpillar, . . . the little dive-dapper of damnation, . . . for his time worse than t'other,"

usurers, and "the most prodigious rascals that ever slipped into the shape of men."

AUDREY, Dampit's servant, "thou kitchen-stuff drab of beggary, roguery, coxcombry."

Three Creditors of Witgood's, "short pig-haired, ram-headed rascals."

A Mad Host, in league with Witgood, and later "the widow's man."

GEORGE, Lucre's servant.

ARTHUR, Hoard's servant.

SIR LANCELOT, a client of Dampit's.

LADY FOXTONE, a wedding guest.

A Tailor,
A Barber,
A Perfumer, }engaged by Old Hoard.
A Falconer,
A Huntsman,

A Vintner.

A Drawer at a Tavern, "a pretty, familiar, priggin rascal."

WILLIAM, at the bar.

A Scrivener, a Boy, Gentleman, Sergeant of the Law, and Servants.

Setting: Leicestershire and London, in the early seventeenth century.

"Who seem most crafty prove ofttimes most fools."

Act I

Theodorus Witgood has at last come to his senses. His wasteful spending, his riotous living, his surfeiting, and his wenching have reduced him to beggary. He dares not show his face in London for fear of his creditors, and his recklessness has lost him "a virgin's love, her portion, and her virtues." Those estates he once had are mortgaged, and to his fox-brained, wealthy old uncle, Pecunius Lucre, who is somewhat the wealthier for his nephew's follies, and who is the cunningest usuring rascal in London. In short, Theodorus Witgood is broke, he has earned for himself the name of "bully Hadland," and his repentance comes somewhat late.

As he meditates upon his folly, he is greeted by the Courtesan upon whom he has lavished his substance, and at first he upbraids her as the secret consumption of his purse, and the cause of his ruin. But he suddenly thinks of a plan in which she can help him—a trick to catch the old one—and his tone changes. Why not take the girl to London as a rich country widow with four hundred a year to whom he is about to become engaged? The covetous old fox might make some amends; he will certainly supply his nephew's immediate needs in London; and the wile might even conjure up a kind of usurer's love in him. Witgood knows the state of the old man's affections well: "if his nephew be poor indeed, why, he lets God alone with him; but, if he be once rich, then he'll be the first man that helps him."

With the aid of a merry host of his acquaintance, who not only supplies horses but also comes along as the widow's servingman and general manager of the business, the couple set out for London. There they lodge the "Widow Medler" in a respectable house, and Witgood and the host call on Dampit and Gulf, two notorious usurers with whom Witgood has done business in the past. From then on word of the young spendthrift's presence in town spreads rapidly.

Old Pecunius Lucre, it should be said, has a mortal enemy in old Walkadine Hoard, who is much like him, and these tough old spirits seldom meet without clashing violently. The trouble between them started three years ago about "a purchase fetching over a young heir." Hoard made the bargain, but Lucre knew the client, and at the last minute stepped in and cozened him himself.

Also, one might add, in Hoard's house lives his niece, Mistress Joyce, who learns the London fashions, practices music, and has a thousand good pound as her portion. For her hand Moneylove, a poor scholar, and Sam Freedom, the foolish son of Lucre's wife, are rivals.

Act II

With Old Lucre the plan succeeds in every point as Witgood had predicted. Disguised as a confidential servant seeking legal advice for his mistress who is a stranger in London, the host calls upon Witgood's uncle. There he plays the role of good blunt honesty so convincingly and permits the old fox to pump out of him so much information about the country gentlewoman and her suitor, that the old man is instantly enthusiastic. Hopeful that some of the widow's lands may one day fall his way, if things are carried wisely, Lucre sends for his nephew, all but overwhelms him with cordiality, insists upon defraying the cost of his wooing in London, has him bring the widow to his house, speaks of Witgood as his heir, and does everything in his power to make up the match. Indeed, so much is Lucre taken with the Widow Medler, that Mistress Lucre calls aside her son Sam, bids him give up his wooing of Mistress Joyce, and sends him dogging the widow home to her lodging with a gold chain and a diamond, together with assurance to the lady that he has two hundred a year of his own, besides a proper person and a lovely.

And, as the happy rumor spreads, Madame Medler acquires still other suitors. Master Moneylove also gives up his suit for Mistress Joyce, offering Old Hoard, the girl's guardian, two hundred angels if he will speak a good word for him that will help him cut out Witgood. But the young fool has left his treasure with a thief—"trust a widower with a suit in love!"—for Old Hoard sees his opportunity not only "extremely to cross [his] adversary and confound the last hopes of his nephew, but thereby to enrich [his own] state, augment [his] revenues and build [his] own fortunes greater." He, too, will become a suitor to the widow!

Meanwhile, as the rumor spreads further, Witgood's creditors, like harpies, begin to bestir themselves.

Act III

But Witgood is as successful with his creditors as he had been with his uncle. They want their money, but they also understand the young man's logic when he assures them that if they press him now he will be discredited with the widow and all hope of his ever paying up will be lost. Hence, the creditors are not only willing to be patient, but also each secretly presses a new loan upon the young rascal lest be borrow from strangers.

The widow is so haunted with suitors that she does not know which to dispatch first. "Here comes one old gentleman, and he'll make her a jointure of three hundred a year, forsooth; another wealthy suitor will estate his son in his lifetime, and make him weigh down the widow; here a merchant's son will possess her with no less than three goodly lordships at once which were all pawns to his father." But when Witgood hears that Old Hoard, his uncle's adversary, is among them, he advises the girl to make up her own fortunes now and do herself a good turn. "He's rich in money, moveables, and lands, . . . [and] he's an old, doting fool. . . . Marry him." It can do the Courtesan no harm, and good fortune may come to Witgood by it. Hence, when the widower arrives with friends to support his words, the widow receives him graciously. The old rascal's idea of wooing is to upbraid the prodigal Witgood and his tyrannical uncle, but Mistress Medler permits herself to be impressed, accepts a rich jointure, and agrees to elope with him to Cole Harbor. But all the while she protests that herself has nothing.

For Hoard the belief—actively encouraged by Witgood—that he is outwitting his old adversary Lucre sweetens his success. But his neglect of his niece permits Mistress Joyce to indulge her predilections for Theodorus Witgood, and for that young man to reassure her that reports about him will alter shortly.

Act IV

Hardly are the widow and Hoard secretly married than an irate Lucre seeks out the lady to obtain justice for his nephew. Knowing that they are safe from any act of his, Hoard permits his wife to receive him, and stands by, enjoying his laugh. The widow defends her preference of the older suitor on the grounds that, though she loved young Witgood and believed his promises, investigation proved that his wealth was but words. His estates lay mortgaged in his uncle's hands. Thereupon Lucre promises to restore his nephew's wealth immediately and adopt him as his heir, taking along the host as pledge from the widow that she will remain as she is until his promises are performed. And Lucre is as good as his word. Before witnesses he delivers the mortgages to his nephew, and, confident that he will enjoy the last laugh, orders the wedding breakfast for Thursday morning.

Meanwhile, however, rumors of Witgood's loss of the widow have already begun to circulate; the young rogue's good fortune is short-lived, and he falls into the hands of his creditors. But as Old Hoard is engaging tailors, barbers, perfumers, falconers, and huntsmen to serve him, and contemplating with satisfaction the vexation he will cause Old Lucre as he drives past with his equipage on the way to the country, the host brings Mistress Hoard a letter. It is a threat on Witgood's behalf of legal action based upon precontract, which at the time constituted an impediment to marriage unless it was set aside by the mutual consent of both parties. Reluctantly, Mistress Hoard admits its validity, but suggests that perhaps the action can be quashed. Witgood is now caught by his creditors. Rather than rot in prison the wastrel will probably agree to a release if his debts are paid. Hence, in haste, lest Old Lucre hear of it first, Hoard sends for Witgood and his creditors, and pays the young man's debts in return for his signing a legal quitclaim to all or any of the Widow Medler's "manors, manor houses, parks, groves, meadow grounds, arable lands, barns, stacks, stables, dove-holes, and cunny-borrows, together with all her cattle, money, plate, jewels, borders, chains, bracelets, furnitures, hangings, movables or immovables." Hoard is a happy man to be so easily free of a difficulty—so happy that before witnesses he pledges himself Witgood's perpetual friend and even invites Old Lucre to the wedding dinner.

And Witgood's cup is also running over. The last of his financial worries is at an end, and, as he leaves the house, Mistress Joyce drops him a note directing him to meet her presently.

Act V

At the wedding feast Old Lucre has the last laugh, for it is only by telling him that his old enemy was married to a "Dutch widow"—a penniless common whore—that Witgood could prevail upon his uncle to accept Hoard's invitation. But Mistress Hoard is equal to her unmasking. On the ground that she never boasted of lands or wealth, but took a plainer course and told the truth, she blames whatever error has been committed upon her crafty husband. She justifies her sin by saying that worse has been forgiven, insists that she is not too bad a wife for an old man, and, kneeling, promises to reform. Hoard accepts his shame with surprising good grace. Finally, Witgood announces his marriage to Joyce, kneels to confess his follies, and also vows to reform, as the company retires to dinner which celebrates a double wedding.

MICHAELMAS TERM
(1604–1606)

DRAMATIS PERSONAE

MICHAELMAS TERM, the first, or autumn, session of the London courts, "new come up from the country. . . . From wronger and from wronged [he has] fee; and what by sweat from the rough earth they draw is to enrich this silver harvest, law; and so through wealthy variance and fat brawl, the barn is made but steward to the hall,"

His Boy,

The Other Three Terms,

A Poor Fellow, "wrapped in silk and silver" by the Three Terms; "so well appointed too with page and pander,"

A Page,

A Pander,

> characters in the Induction.

RICHARD EASY, who "has good land in Essex; a fair freebreasted gentleman, somewhat too open—bad in man, worse in woman, the gentry-fault at first—he is yet fresh, and wants the City powdering." He is the victim of Quomodo's cozening. "Beshrew my blood, a proper springal, and a sweet gentleman,"

REARAGE, friend of Easy; in love with Susan Quomodo. His suit has the support of Mistress Thomasine, the girl's mother,

SALEWOOD, }
COCKSTONE, } gentlemen, and friends of Easy,

> "Are you not knights yet, gentlemen? . . . No? That must be looked into; 'tis your own fault."

EPHESTIAN QUOMODO, rich citizen and woolen draper of London, "a most merciless devourer, the very gull o' the City, . . . merely enriched by shifts and cozenages, believe it. . . . He's such a nature, look; let him owe any man a spite, what's his course? He will lend him money today, o' purpose to 'rest him tomorrow. . . . [But] deceit is her own foe; craftily gets, and childishly lets go. . . . The Devil grind thy bones, thou cozening rascal!"

MISTRESS THOMASINE, "sweet honey-thigh," the wife of Quomodo; when her husband pretends to be dead, she becomes "the happiest widow that ever counterfeited weeping." Afterwards she is married to Richard Easy.

SIM QUOMODO, ungrateful son of the woolen draper, "that lately commenced at Cambridge, . . . but now he's a Templar. Has he not good grace to make a lawyer? . . . Thus [those] that seldom get lands honestly, must leave [their] heirs to inherit [their] knavery."

SUSAN, daughter of Quomodo and Thomasine, "with seven hundred pounds in her purse."

SHORTYARD, alias BLASTFIELD, etc.,
FALSELIGHT, alias IDEM, alias YEOMAN
SPIDERMAN, etc., } Quomodo's attendants and his "two spirits, . . . that have so enriched [him]." They adopt various disguises to assist their master's villainies.

ANDREW GRUEL, alias LETHE, an adventurer, son of Mother Gruel; he "has forgot his father's name, . . . [being] crept to a little warmth, and [is] now so proud that he forgets all storms; one that ne'er wore apparel, but, like ditches, 'twas cast before he had it; [he] now shines bright in rich embroideries. . . . His father was an honest, upright toothdrawer. . . . 'Tis well known his father was too poor a man to bring him up to any virtues; he can scarce write and read." Lethe poses as "a gentleman of most received parts, forgetfulness, lust, impudence, and falsehood, and one especial courtly quality, to wit, no wit at all." He is the rival of Rearage for the hand of Susan Quomodo, whom he woos "for her happy portion." His suit has the support of the girl's father.

DICK HELLGILL, a "saucy, pestiferous pander," in the service of Andrew Lethe.

A Country Wench, a Northampton lass seduced by Lethe, "young, beautiful, and plump; a delicate piece of sin. . . . How easily soft women are undone! . . . What base birth does not raiment make glorious? And what glorious births do not rags make infamous?"

The Country Wench's Father, "though [he] be poor, 'tis [his] glory to live honest."

DUSTBOX, a scrivener called in by Quomodo to draw up a bond for Blastfield and Easy to sign.

A Judge, who decides the complaints of Quomodo, Easy, and Thomasine.

MOTHER GRUEL, who assists in unmasking her graceless son.

Thomasine's Mother, who has "buried four husbands."

A Tailor,
MISTRESS COMINGS, a tirewoman, } who outfit Lethe's Country Wench.

WINEFRED, maid to Mistress Thomasine.

GEORGE, Mistress Thomasine's manservant.

A Drawer at the Horn Tavern.

A Boy, servant to Blastfield.

A Beadle, Liverymen, Mourners, Officers, and Attendants.

Setting: London—St. Paul's, the Horn Tavern, Fleet Street, the City, etc.—at some unspecified time.

"He that expects any great quarrels in law to be handled here will be fondly deceived; this only presents those familiar accidents which happened in town in the circumference of those six weeks wherof Michaelmas Term is lord. Sat sapienti: I hope there's no fools i' th' house."

Act I

Covetous of the estates of Richard Easy, a simple country gentleman from Essex, Ephestian Quomodo, an unscrupulous usurer of London,

plots his ruin. With his confederates, Shortyard and Falselight, Quomodo hopes to make him the victim of dissipation, and arranges that
Shortyard shall disguise as Blastfield, become the intimate of Easy,
train him in every wasteful sin, and in short undo him.

At the same time Quomodo encourages the suit for his daughter's
hand of one Andrew Lethe, a graceless adventurer, who has changed
his name upon coming to London and poses as a gentleman. The girl
is also taken in by Lethe, but Mistress Thomasine, Quomodo's wife,
opposes the match and supports the suit of Master Rearage. Accordingly,
the impudent pretender writes a letter to Thomasine, suggesting that
her unwillingness to consent to his marriage with her daughter is mere
jealousy and the result of the mother's doting upon the daughter's suitor,
and assuring her that such a union will afford him better means and
opportunity of making love to her without the least suspicion. This outrageous letter Andrew sends to Mistress Quomodo by Mother Gruel, his
simple old parent who has come to London to seek him. She fails to
recognize her son because of his fine clothes, and Andrew, who does
recognize her, merely pretends not to be a stranger to her. At the same
time the pander Hellgill in Lethe's employ has lured a Country Wench
from Northampton to London with promises of silken dresses and advancement to gentility.

Act II

As planned, Blastfield (Shortyard in disguise) succeeds in making
the acquaintance of Easy in a gambling den, where the Essex gentleman
loses his whole quarter's rent. Blastfield befriends the loser, and as part
of the scheme, also finds himself out of cash. Pretending a very great
credit in the City, the rascal sends to Quomodo for a loan of several
hundred pounds, receives from him a gracious promise of accommodation, and brings Easy with him to the usurer's shop. There a loan is
negotiated for Blastfield, not in ready cash, but, as the rascally custom
of the time was, in commodities, which it proves impossible to sell for
more than a small fraction of their full value. Blastfield receives only
threescore pounds, furnishing bonds for several hundred, and Easy
signs as security—"for form's sake" only. Already Quomodo is jubilant
at the prospect of becoming a landed proprietor. But Mistress Thomasine,
unobserved, watches the transaction, and finds herself attracted to Easy.

Meanwhile, like Mother Gruel, the father of the Country Wench
Lethe is trying to seduce comes to the City in disguise to seek his
child and to become her servant if necessary, in order that he may be
near her and protect her.

Act III

In a short time, Blastfield becomes deeper and deeper indebted to Quomodo, until the usurer holds bonds of his worth seven hundred pounds, for all of which Easy has stood security. Then, one day the landed gentleman from Essex finds himself arrested by Shortyard and Falselight disguised as sergeant and yeoman, at the suit of Master Quomodo. Blastfield is nowhere to be found. When Easy is brought before the usurer, Quomodo is most sympathetic, granting him time to seek his friend, and dismissing the bailiffs. Then Shortyard and Falselight return, dressed as rich citizens willing, by persuasion, to become security for Easy on his bond of body, goods, and lands. Again Thomasine, in hiding, overhears everything.

Meanwhile, the Country Wench, outfitted like a gentlewoman, and attended by her disguised father, is introduced by Andrew Lethe to his riotous companions. But through Mother Gruel, who openly reports her ill success in delivering Andrew's impudent letter to Thomasine, the girl discovers that Master Lethe is hopeful of marriage to another, and is planning to desert her. She vows to be avenged.

Act IV

By his shifty dealings the usurer now has possession of Easy's estates, has the satisfaction of calling himself "landed Master Quomodo," and anticipates with his mind's eye the ostentatious holiday journeys he and his friends will make into Essex. But such contemplation is not enough for the fellow; he wishes to see how his wife, Thomasine, his family, and his friends and associates, will conduct themselves in the face of the new dignity. Hence, he feigns death. But he is dismayed at the result. Master Rearage and the Country Wench's father expose Andrew Lethe and upset Quomodo's hope that his daughter Susan will marry the pretender who would make him rich in custom. Disguised as a beadle at his own funeral, Quomodo meets his own son Sim, who shows little respect for his late father and contradicts any praise of the departed as belying the dead. Worse still, Mistress Thomasine may weep copiously and even fall down in a swoon as the coffin is carried out, but she quickly recovers and deserts her husband's funeral procession to elope with Easy. To Easy Thomasine had promptly sent a love token immediately upon her husband's demise. But Quomodo has seen only her apparent grief; his complete disillusionment comes later.

Act V

As might be expected, a rascal who is as clever as Shortyard will not long remain inactive in his own behalf. He soon cheats Sim Quomodo out of his inheritance. But, confronted by the accusations of Easy and the knowing Thomasine, Shortyard is willing enough to return to their rightful owner all the bonds and deeds he has cozened Sim of. His hope of complete escape fails, however; he is arrested along with Falselight. Still in ignorance of his wife's precipitant remarriage, Quomodo disguised still as a beadle, calls at his own house to collect his funeral fee. Asked to sign a quit-bill for the sum, Quomodo uses his own name as a surprise to his wife, only to find that he has signed a memorandum stating that he has received of Richard Easy everything due him in the house, and releasing the young man from all future obligations.

The tricker himself has been tricked; indeed he has set the trap for himself. In a rage Quomodo hastens to seek judgment before a magistrate. But Easy and Thomasine visit the judge first, and the shifty usurer finds that coming back to life presents unpleasant consequences. He must either be thought a counterfeit, or confess to cheating an innocent gentleman of his lands. "Deceit is her own foe; craftily gets, and childishly lets go."

Before the same judge the other offenders are brought in and condemned. Shortyard and Falselight are banished; Andrew Lethe is made to fulfill his promise of marriage to the Country Wench, and to receive his mother's curse. Meanwhile, Rearage and Susan have been married. "After some penance and the dues of law," his lordship grudgingly admits, Quomodo may legally reclaim Thomasine as his wife. But there is no suggestion that the lady will acknowledge his claim.

THOMAS MIDDLETON
(1580–1627)
AND
THOMAS DEKKER
(c. 1572–1632)

For a biography of Middleton see above, p. 270; for one of Dekker, p. 146.

CRITICAL COMMENT. *The Roaring Girl* is a romantic portrait of a notorious character of the day, idealized for dramatic purposes against the background of contemporary life. Mary Frith, upon whose story the comedy is founded, was the daughter of a shoemaker born about 1584. Even as a child, her biographer tells us, she "delighted and sported only in boys' play and pastime; . . . she could not endure the sedentary life of sewing or stitching; . . . her needle, bodkin, and thimble she could not think on quietly, wishing them changed into sword and dagger for a bout at cudgels." Naturally, she failed when sent into domestic service, and, seeking her fortune in the world, she became a pickpocket, a fortuneteller, and a forger. She dressed as a man, wore a sword, and used it. She is said to have been the first woman to smoke. In 1612, the year after this play was produced, Moll was forced to do penance at Paul's Cross for some unknown offense. She seemed red-eyed and contrite enough, until it was discovered that she had "tippled off three quarts of sack before she came to do her penance." Mary Frith lived to an old age, dying about 1660.

There is therefore nothing realistic about the portrait of "Mad Moll" which one finds in this play—more sinned against than sinning, and ever willing to help poor lovers in distress. As the Preface to the first printed edition remarks disarmingly, the play is "a light-color summer stuff, mingled with divers colors. . . . Worse things, I must needs confess, the world has taxed her for than has been written of her. But 'tis the excellency of a writer to leave things better than he finds 'em. . . . We rather wish in such discoveries where reputation lies bleeding a slackness of truth than fullness of slander."

It is characteristic of Dekker that it should have been so.

BIBLIOGRAPHY

Early edition: 1611.
Modern editions: Facs. J. S. Farmer (TFT, 1914); most editions of Middleton.

THE ROARING GIRL

OR MOLL CUTPURSE

(1611)

DRAMATIS PERSONAE

MARY FRITH, alias MOLL CUTPURSE, "mad, merry Moll," the Roaring Girl, a knowledgeable lass who uses her knowledge not to practice, but to defeat vice. She is "a good, personable creature, . . . [but] so strange in quality, a whole city takes note of her name and person. . . . Here's her worst: sh'as a bold spirit that mingles with mankind, but nothing else comes near it; and oftentimes through her apparel somewhat shames her birth. But she is loose in nothing but in mirth. Would all Molls were no worse!" ("Thou'rt a mad girl, and yet I cannot now condemn thee. . . . In troth, . . . I'm sorry now the opinion was so hard I conceived of thee.")

SEBASTIAN WENGRAVE, son of Sir Alexander and suitor to Mary Fitzallard; for strategic reasons he pretends to be bewitched by the Roaring Girl.

MARY FITZALLARD, "a virtuous gentlewoman," daughter to Sir Guy, and betrothed to Sebastian Wengrave.

SIR ALEXANDER WENGRAVE, the covetous father of Sebastian; "the god of gold has been to [him] no niggard."

SIR GUY FITZALLARD, father of Mary.

SIR DAVY DAPPER, "as damned a usurer as ever was," and friend to Sir Alexander.

JACK DAPPER, unthrift son of Sir Davy, "a noise of fiddlers, tobacco, wine, and a whore, . . . dice, and a water spaniel with a duck— . . . when his purse jingles, roaring boys follow at's tail, fencers, and ningles." ("He looks for all the world, with those spangled feathers, like a nobleman's bed-post.")

SIR THOMAS LONG,
SIR BEAUTEOUS GANYMEDE, } friends of Jack Dapper.
LORD NOLAND,

SIR ADAM APPLETON, "old muzzle-chops," friend to Sir Alexander.

MASTER GREENWIT, friend to Sir Alexander; he's "not yet so mellow in years as" Sebastian.

RALPH TRAPDOOR, "honest Ralph, . . . a poor ebbing gentleman, . . . with a full-charged mouth, like a culverin's voice," preferred into Sir Alexander's service to confound Moll Cutpurse. "Faith, a good well-set fellow, if his spirit be answerable to his umbles." ("Hold thy hand up. What's this? Is't burnt [i.e., branded]? . . . No, sir, no; a little singed with making fireworks.")

TEARCAT, his companion, "a mere whipjack, and that is, in the commonwealth of rogues, a slave that can talk of sea fight, name all your chief pirates, discover more countries to you than either the Dutch, Spanish, French, or English ever found out; yet indeed all his service is by land, and that is to rob a fair, or some such venturous exploit." Tearcat is "but a maunderer upon the pad [i.e., a highway beggar] . . . and a ruffler [i.e., a first-class rogue] is [his] style, [his] title, [his] profession."

NEATFOOT, "this formal ape," Sir Alexander Wengrave's man. ("You're kissing [the] maids, drinking, or fast asleep!")

GULL, "a sweet-faced boy," page to Jack Dapper. ("Troth, [Jack Dapper] whistled the poor little buzzard off o' [his] fist, because, when he waited upon [him] at the ordinaries, the gallants hit [him] i' the teeth still, and said [he] looked like a painted alderman's tomb, and the boy at [his] elbow like a death's-head.")

MASTER HIPPOCRATES GALLIPOT, an apothecary.

MASTER TILTYARD, a feather-seller.

MASTER OPENWORK, a sempster.

MISTRESS PRUDENCE GALLIPOT, wife of the apothecary; "she's a gentlewoman born, I can tell you, though it be her hard fortune now to shred Italian pot herbs. . . . 'Tis such a wasp!"

MISTRESS TILTYARD, wife of the featherer,

MISTRESS ROSAMOND OPENWORK, wife of the sempster. "Sh'as a tongue will be heard further in a still morning than Saint Antling's bell. She rails upon [her husband] for foreign wenching, that [he] being a freeman must needs keep a whore i' the suburbs, and seek to impoverish the liberties,"

" 'Tis impossible to know what woman is thoroughly honest, because she's ne'er thoroughly tried; I am of that certain belief, that there are more queans in this town of their own making than of any man's provoking."

GOSHAWK, a young man about town who "goes in a shag-ruff band, with a face sticking up in't which shows like an agate set in a cramp ring. . . . A goshawk? A puttock; all for prey. He angles for fish, but he loves flesh better." Goshawk pays court to Mistress Openwork,

LAXTON, another wolf. ("Thou'rt one of those that thinks each woman thy fond flexible whore. If she but cast a liberal eye upon thee, turn back her head, she's thine; or amongst company by chance drink to thee, then she's quite gone, there is no means to help her.") Laxton pays court to Mistress Gallipot.

"Happy is the woman can be rid of 'em all! 'Las, what are your whisking gallants to our husbands, weigh 'em rightly, man for man?"

CURTLEAX, a sergeant, HANGER, his yeoman, "They look for all the world like two infected malt-men coming muffled up in their cloaks in a frosty morning to London."

A Fellow with a long rapier by his side, "goodman swine's face," challenged by Moll Cutpurse.

A Tailor to Moll Cutpurse.

A Porter, "goodman hog-rubber."

A Coachman.

A Cutpurse, very gallant. "'Tis one that cumbers the land indeed; if he swim near to the shore of any of your pockets, look to your purses."

Four or five other Cutpurses, his companions.

Setting: London in 1611.

"If all that have ill names in London were to be whipped, and to pay but twelvepence apiece to the beadle, I would rather have his office than a constable's."

Act I

Sebastian, son and heir of Sir Alexander Wengrave, has been betrothed to Mary Fitzallard, daughter of Sir Guy. The covetous Sir Alexander, however, has "reckoned up what gold this marriage would draw from him," scorned the girl's dowry of five thousand marks, and done all he can to dissuade his son from the match. The young people love each other, however, and, partly to vex the old man, and partly to bring him to terms, they determine to sail "with a side wind." Sebastian pretends to have fallen desperately in love with Moll Cutpurse, a notorious London character who often dresses as a man and is known as "the Roaring Girl." Upon her Sebastian publicly lavishes all the affection that he owes to Mary Fitzallard, and Moll good-naturedly lends herself to the deception. The boy's hope, however, is that when Sir Alexander is faced with a choice of daughters-in-law, he will gladly consent to the original marriage arrangement.

Meanwhile, by hiring Trapdoor to spy upon Moll, Sir Alexander has taken steps to end his son's infatuation with the girl. "Play thou the subtle spider," says the old rascal to his tool; "weave fine nets to ensnare her very life. . . . Twist thou but cords to catch her; I'll find law to hang her up."

Act II

At the same time in London there are several apparently less innocent intrigues than that of Sebastian and "Roaring Moll." Laxton has for some time been trying to seduce Mistress Gallipot, the apothecary's wife, and has succeeded at least in getting her to supply him with money. The shallow lecher Jack Dapper lays siege to Mistress Tiltyard, the featherer's wife, who yet "seems like Kent unconquered," but has many wiles in her. Goshawk's technique is to plant in the mind of Mistress Openwork, the scolding wife of the sempster, suspicion of her husband's infidelity, in order that he may become the instrument of her revenge.

With all of these bragging wolves Moll Cutpurse holds her own. She knows them thoroughly without illusion, and is on familiar terms with all of them. But she inspires respect by the way in which she picks quarrels with overbold gallants in the streets, and she makes assignations with the more ardent only to bring them to scorn. Even Trapdoor is tripped up by the heels in his first encounter with her, but after enjoying his discomfiture, Moll makes amends by promising to hire him as her own servant.

Meanwhile, in the street Sir Alexander observes an encounter between Sebastian and Moll, reproves his son for his folly, is unimpressed by his defense, and remains unrelenting. As a result, since plain dealing is ineffective, Sebastian determines to ask Moll for more active assistance in his love affair; " 'twixt lovers' hearts she's a fit instrument, and has the art to help them to their own."

Act III

In Gray's Inn Fields where Moll has appointed him a meeting, the amorous Laxton is discomfited in a duel by the Roaring Girl, who is dressed in man's clothing and is capable of defending her honor with her sword. Trapdoor, also, is deceived by Moll's disguise into believing her a quarrelsome young Templar, before she good-humoredly relents and hires the double-dealer as her servant.

In the City, on the other hand, Mistress Gallipot succeeds in deceiving her uxorious husband into believing that Laxton is a young man she was betrothed to in her youth and who for thirty pounds black-mail will give up his claim to her. The poor fool of a husband pays it without question. The second City intrigue also reaches a crisis. At the end of his tether with his unthrifty, rakish son, Jack, Sir Davy Dapper determines to catch this woodcock in a springe, and to send the lad "to Wood Street College [i.e., to the Wood Street Counter, or sheriff's prison]." Accordingly, the father hires two officers, Curtleax and Hanger, to attach his person as he comes out of a tavern, but Moll and Trapdoor effect a rescue before young Dapper is even arrested. The third intrigue—that between Mistress Openwork and Goshawk—by contrast is ominously dormant.

Act IV

But to return to the Roaring Girl. As servant to both Moll and Sir Alexander, Trapdoor is in an advantageous position to share all Moll's secrets and to report them to the old knight, his other master. To-gether Sir Alexander and his man try to trap the girl by putting out a watch, a chain, a ruff-band, and other trinkets in the hope of tempt-ing Moll to steal. But she is not to be caught. By now, too, the Roaring Girl is the complete confidante and assistant of the lovers. "Without touch of either sin or shame," she has done them a kind office; Mary Fitzallard is disguised as a page in Moll's service, and Sebastian has every opportunity of meeting his betrothed. At home, the young man continues to torture his father by passing off Moll as a music master for whom he borrows money. But the old man knows her only too well and gives his son four uncurrent gold angels with holes in them, the better to bring the girl to ruin.

Meanwhile, the City intrigues which survive are found to be the results of practical jokes. Through a trick played by Master Openwork, Goshawk is exposed as both a liar and a prospective lecher, and Mistress Openwork repents of suspecting her husband. With the aid of Greenwit, who disguises as a summoner, Laxton has continued to blackmail the Gallipots. But when they refuse to pay further and he is exposed, every-one accepts his explanation that his pursuit of Prudence was innocent and only a trial of her virtue because she seemed so confident and so devoted to her husband. Laxton repays the gold he has extorted from the couple, and all the gallants dine with the citizens and their wives.

Act V

Moll, too, continues her exposure of fraud and deceit, revealing among other accomplishments her knowledge of thieves' cant, and unmasking Trapdoor and his companion Tearcat, who have disguised as broken-down soldiers returned from the wars. And at last she is able actively to assist Sebastian in marrying Mary Fitzallard.

Rumor reaches Sir Alexander that his son is about to marry the Roaring Girl. Nearly distracted at the news, the old man must bear the taunts and reproaches of his friends and the pangs of his own conscience for breaking up the original match. He does not know where to turn to prevent this new misfortune, and he gladly offers anything— even half of what he owns—when Sir Guy Fitzallard undertakes to stop the elopement and stakes his whole estate on the result. Word comes that the bridal party is on the way home, and hope that rumor is false arises when Moll puts in a momentary appearance in man's clothes. Apparently the couple are not yet married, and no priest would marry a bride in that garb. Perhaps after all, the young scapegrace has married someone else.

But when Sebastian leads in his masked and veiled lady, in spite of all, she is found to be Moll, now changed to female attire. Sir Alexander has a roaring girl as a daughter-in-law. But even so, the covetous old rascal will not release his friend Sir Guy from his rash bargain to reclaim the prodigal—he works "upon advantage, as all mischiefs do upon [him]." All contention ends, however, when Sir Guy reveals that the real bride is Mary, and that Sir Alexander has been gulled—as he deserved to be— with the aid of the Roaring Girl. He gladly gives his blessing to the happy pair and repents his low opinion of mad Moll. But the girl herself has a last laugh:

> *He was in fear his son would marry me,*
> *But never dreamt that I would ne'er agree.*

When will Moll marry?

> *When you shall hear*
> *Gallants void from sergeants fear,*
> *Honesty and truth unslandered,*
> *Woman manned, but never pandered.*

The Roaring Girl remains the champion of virtue and of her sex. "This sounds like Doomsday," observes Lord Noland.

THOMAS MIDDLETON
(1580–1627)
AND
WILLIAM ROWLEY
(?–1626)

BIOGRAPHIES. For a biography of Middleton see above, p. 270.

Concerning William Rowley's birth and education nothing is known. He first appears as a dramatist in 1607, and he continued to write until his death, usually as the collaborator of Middleton, Ford, or Heywood. The date of his death is conjectural; he simply disappears.

CRITICAL COMMENT. *The Changeling* is one of the most powerful plays of its time, an astonishing psychological study of a beautiful, but fickle and unscrupulous girl and an ugly man who is in the grip of an almost uncontrollable passion for her. At first Beatrice Joanna is filled with loathing for Deflores, who worships her from afar; but in her own interest she incites him to crime, and finds herself in the power of one who is as evil as he is odious. The result is a sensational tragedy of blood and intrigue, a series of variations on a theme and a living pun upon the differing meanings of the word "changeling":

a) the ill-favored Deflores suggests the unnatural repulsive creature which might result by the growing up of an ugly, ill-tempered babe which had been substituted by fairies in its cradle for a beautiful one stolen away;

b) Beatrice Joanna, spoiled, fickle, and inconstant in love, is another variety of "changeling," a waverer and a renegade.

c) Antonio and Frederick and the disguise they adopt for amorous purposes of imbeciles and inmates in a hospital for half-wits represent pseudo and real varieties of still a third kind of "changeling."

Yet most critics to this day persist in believing the drama named from a character in the underplot. In the original *dramatis personae* Antonio alone is described as a "changeling," and the word occurs nowhere else in the text of the play. But the word had several meanings for the seventeenth century, and not to apply them singly or collectively to the major characters of this drama, as well as to the minor, is only imperfectly to understand the play and the technique of the playwrights.

SOURCE. The Beatrice Joanna–Deflores plot is derived from Book I of John Reynolds' *The Triumphs of God's Revenge against the Crying and Execrable Sin of Murther* (1621). For the subplot, laid in a sanatorium for mental cases, no source has been discovered.

BIBLIOGRAPHY

Early editions: 1653; 1668.

THE CHANGELING
(1622)

DRAMATIS PERSONAE

VERMANDERO, governor of the castle of Alicante, and father of Beatrice Joanna.

BEATRICE JOANNA, beautiful daughter of Vermandero, who finds "a giddy turning in [her]. . . . O cunning devils! How should blind men know you from fair-faced saints?"

DIAPHANTA, her waiting woman, "as good a soul as ever lady countenanced." ("These women are the ladies' cabinets, things of most precious trust are locked into 'em.")

TOMASO DE PIRACQUO, a noble lord.

ALONZO DE PIRACQUO, his brother, suitor to Beatrice. "The gentleman's complete, a courtier and a gallant, enriched with many fair and noble ornaments."

ALSEMERO, a Valencian traveller and "a complete gentleman, . . . one both ennobled in blood and mind, so clear in understanding"; later, married to Beatrice Joanna. He loves "her beauties to the holy purpose."

JASPERINO, friend of Alsemero, in love with Diaphanta. ("How wise is Alsemero in his friend! It is a sign he makes his choice with judgment.")

DEFLORES, a gentleman-servant to Vermandero, "the fellow that some call honest Deflores—but methinks honesty was hard bestead to come here for a lodging; as if a queen should make her palace of a pesthouse. . . . [His hairy, pimply, dog face] loathes one; . . . he's so foul one would scarce touch him with a sword he loved; . . . so most deadly venomous, he would go near to poison any weapon that should draw blood on him. . . . The very sight of him is poison to [Beatrice]; . . . some twenty times a day . . . do[es he] force errands, frame ways and excuses to come into her sight, and [he has] small reason for 't and less encouragement, for she . . . does profess herself the cruelest enemy to [his] face in town." Later, he becomes her lover.

ALIBIUS, a jealous old doctor married to a young wife. He specializes in madmen and idiots. ("You are a jealous coxcomb, keep schools of folly, and teach your scholars how to break your own head.")

ISABELLA, his beautiful wife.

ANTONIO, called the changeling, who has assumed the disguise of an idiot and become an inmate of the doctor's sanatorium because he is "the truest servant to [Isabella's] powerful beauties." (" 'Tis a gentle nidget,")

FRANCISCUS, disguised as "the handsomest, discreetest madman. . . . [He] was changed from a little wit to be stark almost for the same purpose,"

\right\} two of the chiefest men Vermandero kept about him.

LOLLIO, an "usher of idiots," the doctor's man.

PEDRO, the friend of Antonio.

Madmen, Idiots, and Servants.

Setting: Alicante at some unspecified time.

"I see in all bouts, both of sport and wit,
Always a woman strives for the last hit."

Act 1

Beatrice Joanna, beautiful daughter of Vermandero, governor of the castle of Alicante, has discovered that her eyes and her heart could be mistaken. Only five days ago she was betrothed to Alonzo de Piracquo, a young courtier enriched with many fair and noble ornaments. But as she leaves church today and again finds waiting for her Alsemero, a nobleman of Valencia whom she met only yesterday, she realizes that her mind has changed, and that this is the man who was meant for her. Hitherto, Alsemero has been unsusceptible to beauty, but now he is so much in love that he is delaying a voyage for one more glimpse of Beatrice Joanna. She introduces Alsemero to her father, who discovers him to be the son of an old friend. But from Vermandero the young lover learns for the first time that Beatrice is engaged, and that the wedding is to be held within a week.

Also, without meaning to, Beatrice Joanna has inspired love in still another man. In her father's service there is a gentleman named Deflores, ugly of face and deformed of mind, who is attentive to Beatrice's every whim and who "some twenty times a day . . . force[s] errands [and] frame[s] ways and excuses to come into her sight. But [he] has small reason for't and less encouragement." For Beatrice Joanna loathes Deflores and would rather see him "dead than living"; she has never spoken a civil word to him, "and yet she knows no cause for't but a peevish will."

About the same time in Alicante, Alibius, a jealous old doctor who specializes in mental diseases, takes precautions that the affections of his beautiful young wife Isabella shall have no opportunity to waver. Alibius does not fear the brainsick unfortunates in his house—they are but idiots and madmen—but rather the daily visitants to these inmates, especially comely, well-dressed young gallants with quick, enticing eyes. These are most shrewd temptations to clandestine love affairs, and he cautions his trusty man Lollio to watch his lady and to take care that those who come to see idiots and madmen see no more than what they came for.

But the suspicious doctor does not reckon upon a lover's stratagem. Disguised as a half-wit, Antonio is brought to the sanatorium by his servant Pedro. The patient is a gentleman and an heir, Pedro explains, with whose family money is no object, if only his wits can be improved. The assistant assures Pedro that he will make the idiot fit to bear public office in five weeks' time and give him the brain of a constable or even a justice before he is through. He may even make him as wise as himself.

Act II

Through his friend Jasperino, who is in love with Diaphanta, Beatrice's waiting woman, Alsemero and his lady communicate by letter. But during separation Beatrice perceives more clearly still the merits of her second lover— "a true deserver like a diamond sparkles; in darkness you may see him; that's in absence." Hence, she asks that her marriage to Alonzo be postponed three days—a request her fiancé readily agrees to. But his brother Tomaso sees in the girl's general behavior a coolness of affection which makes him suspect that she loves another. When at last the lovers do meet, in secret, it is to lament that there is such a man as Piracquo and such a tie as the commands of parents. Arguing that one blow can remove both fears, Alsemero suggests that he send Alonzo a challenge. But Beatrice cannot bear the risk; Alsemero might be killed. Anyway, bloodguiltiness becomes a fouler visage than his. At the words her thoughts turn to Deflores—"the ugliest creature Creation framed for some use!" But she does not reveal anything to Alsemero. Instead, she has Diaphanta conduct him out the private way he came.

But Deflores has been watching the meeting of the lovers. He knows that both of the men in Beatrice Joanna's life "cannot be served unless she transgress." Once she has fallen, Deflores argues, a woman's sin is progressive, first with one and then with more. Who knows, perhaps even he may become one of Beatrice's lovers? The thought is as wine to his blood. Hence, when for the first time Beatrice Joanna calls him fairly by his name—"Deflores"—and neither rogue nor rascal, he is overjoyed. When she sighs and addresses him as "my Deflores," wishing Creation had but formed for her one man to free her from marrying the man she hates, then Deflores readily undertakes to murder Alonzo de Piracquo. Finally, when Beatrice accepts his service and gives him gold to encourage him, promising that his reward shall be precious, Deflores' reply is ominous: "That I have thought on; I have assured myself of that beforehand; . . . the thought ravishes!"

Hence, Deflores makes an immediate opportunity to commit the crime.

Act III

While Vermandero's household thinks him on a gondola excursion about the town, Alonzo de Piracquo decides instead to go on a tour of inspection of the fortifications, with Deflores as his guide. Taking care to disarm the man, Deflores lures him to a distant vault, stabs him to death, and then cuts off his ring finger to bear witness to the deed. But however much she wished Alonzo's death, Beatrice Joanna is shocked at Deflores' token of his crime—the ring was the first gift the girl had sent her lover. And she is even more horror-stricken at Deflores' price for murder—he scorns the diamond ring, refuses three thousand golden florins, and then double the sum. At last his meaning is clear—it is not fit that "two, engaged so jointly, should part and live asunder." Beatrice and he are equally dipped in blood; the price of Piracquo's murder is the changeling lady herself:

> *Do you urge me,*
> *Though thou writ'st "maid," thou whore in thy affection?*
> *'Twas changed from thy first love, and that's a kind*
> *Of whoredom in thy heart; and he's changed now*
> *To bring thy second on, thy Alsemero,*
> *Whom, by all sweets that ever darkness tasted,*
> *If I enjoy thee not, thou ne'er enjoy'st!*
> *I'll blast the hopes and joys of marriage;*
> *I'll confess all. My life I rate at nothing.*

About the same time, in Doctor Alibius' sanatorium another lady has every reason to rebel against the fetters laid upon her freedom. Isabella is kept in a pinfold, watched at every turn, and dependent for her social life upon idiots and madmen. But as the saucy Lollio shows her Franciscus, their latest arrival—"the handsomest, discreetest madman," who is a poet, mad for love—the supposed lunatic sings the lady a love song. When for variety of entertainment Lollio brings out Antonio and is called away, the disguised idiot reveals himself to Isabella as a gentleman whose love for her has wrought his transformation, and he kisses her. But however great her provocation may be for revenge upon her suspicious old husband, Isabella does not succumb to the stratagem. She merely assures Antonio that she will not expose him, but that that is all the favor he may expect.

Their encounter, however, has been witnessed by Lollio, who was concealed while it occurred. When he returns from putting Antonio away, he too makes love to his mistress. Hence, there develops in this subplot an innocent parallel to the situation in the main plot, as the servant tries to blackmail his lady for a share in her supposed frailty. Although Isabella threatens Lollio with death unless he holds his tongue, their further bargaining is interrupted by the return of the doctor. He has been asked to supply a troupe of dancing madmen as entertainment at Beatrice Joanna's wedding.

Act IV

A dumb show fills the interval of happenings between Act III and Act IV. Vermandero and his friends express wonder at what seems to be the flight of Alonzo de Piracquo. But the friends applaud the father's choice of Alsemero as a substitute bridegroom for Beatrice Joanna, and the couple are married. Deflores, following after the procession, smiles at the event, but he is sobered by the appearance of Alonzo's ghost, showing the hand from which the finger had been cut.

———————

Never was there a bride so filled with fears as is Beatrice Joanna on her wedding night. The man she has married is of noble mind and clear understanding. To deceive such an one is both shameful and dangerous. As she muses upon her plight, she spies the key to the door to Alsemero's closet, goes in, and discovers the laboratory of an amateur scientist. On the table lies a manuscript entitled *The Book of Experiment, Called the Secrets in Nature,* which contains chapters on "How to Know Whether a Woman Be with Child or No," and "How to Know Whether a Woman Be a Maid or Not." Beatrice Joanna is now more afraid than ever. But a trick comes to her mind. Pretending bride-night fear, Beatrice bribes Diaphanta, her waiting woman, with a thousand ducats to take her place, and steal forth quickly about midnight. But she makes sure that Diaphanta is a maid by drinking with her a spoonful of the liquid from Glass M on Alsemero's medicine shelf, and carefully noting the symptoms.

It is well she does so. The more easily to succeed in her own stratagem, Diaphanta reveals her mistress' timorosity to Alsemero; Jasperino overhears an interview between Beatrice and Deflores which he reports to the husband; and the result is that Alsemero becomes suspicious of his bride. He gives her the test, and when Beatrice exhibits all the proper symptoms, the husband's fears seem unfounded.

Meanwhile, Tomaso de Piracquo seeks satisfaction for his brother Alonzo's disappearance and Alsemero's marriage in his place, and suspicion begins to rest upon Antonio and Franciscus, two gentlemen in Vermandero's service who left the castle some ten days since, pretending voyages to distant ports.

At Doctor Alibius' house the two counterfeit madmen are completely oblivious of their danger. By Lollio they send love missives to Isabella. Lollio in turn takes enthusiastically to the role of bawd, and encourages rivalry by building up the hopes of each. And he has Isabella's promise that if she should prove frail, he will be given first place in her affections. Taking a cue from Lollio that the best way to deal with half-wits is to deceive them, Isabella dresses as a madwoman and rehearses with the madmen the dance which they are to perform at the castle. But if ever she had any intention of beguiling "the nimble eye of watchful jealousy," it is completely dispelled by Antonio's stupid inability to penetrate her simple disguise.

Act V

As planned, Diaphanta takes Beatrice's place beside Alsemero, but she stays too long. Torn both by jealousy and by fear of discovery, Beatrice appeals to Deflores, who advises extreme measures. To get Diaphanta back to the lodging where she belongs, he sets fire to her chamber, and under pretext of scouring the chimney with a fowling piece, kills the frightened girl as she returns to her room and makes it appear that she has burned to death. But if Beatrice and Deflores escape suspicion at this time, they soon fall into it unexpectedly in another quarter. Both Alsemero and his friend Jasperino observe an incriminating encounter between the two in the garden. Successively the husband faces both his wife and her lover. With only the excuse that all was done for Alsemero's sake, and still professing her loathing for Deflores, Beatrice confesses to adultery, deception, and murder; and Deflores confirms her admissions.

Hence, when Vermandero brings in the suspected Antonio and Franciscus, whose subterfuge the virtuous Isabella has at last revealed to the doctor, Alsemero is able to deliver over to justice the real murderers of Alonzo. But to prevent torture, Deflores stabs Beatrice and himself to death. The grief-stricken Alsemero summarizes the effects which the changeling moon has had upon them:

> Here's beauty changed
> To ugly whoredom; here servant-obedience
> To a master-sin, imperious murder;
> I, a supposed husband, changed embraces
> With wantonness. . . .
> [Tomaso's] change is come to, from an ignorant wrath
> To knowing friendship.—Are there any more on's?

Yes; Antonio and Franciscus repent the folly which nearly brought them to the gallows; and Doctor Alibius, prompted by the faithful Isabella, promises to change now into a better husband and never again keep scholars that are wiser than himself.

CYRIL TOURNEUR

(1575?–1626)

BIOGRAPHY. Of Cyril Tourneur little is known; he first appears as the author of a satire called *The Transformed Metamorphosis* (1600). His career as a dramatist was over by 1613. Later he was employed in foreign service, mainly in the Low Countries and at Cadiz, where he was Sir Edward Cecil's secretary on the unsuccessful expedition of 1625. He was disembarked among the sick in Ireland and died there in 1626.

CRITICAL COMMENT. Of the two plays here attributed to Tourneur, only *The Atheist's Tragedy* is certainly his, but the dramas have a great deal in common. Together they are among the most horrible, grotesque, bloody, and ingenious melodramas of all time. Both are revenge plays, employing all of the dramatic conventions of the type, sometimes wrenched to new uses and significance. One cannot imagine more morbid dramas on the stage or off.

SOURCES. For neither *The Atheist's Tragedy* nor *The Revenger's Tragedy* are sources known; one episode in the former seems based upon a story in Boccaccio's *Decameron* (VII, 6).

BIBLIOGRAPHY

Collected Works:

   The Plays and Poems of Cyril Tourneur, edited by J. Churton Collins, 2
      volumes, 1878.
   The Complete Works of Cyril Tourneur, edited by Allardyce Nicoll, 1930.
   The Best Plays of Webster and Tourneur, edited by J. A. Symonds, Mermaid Series, 1888.

The Revenger's Tragedy:
   Early editions: 1607; 1608.
   Modern edition: ed. G. B. Harrison (TD, 1933).

The Atheist's Tragedy:
   Early editions: 1611; 1612.

THE REVENGER'S TRAGEDY

OR THE LOYAL BROTHER

(1606–1607)

DRAMATIS PERSONAE

The DUKE, "grey-haired adultery; . . . it well becomes that judge to nod at crimes, that does commit greater himself, and lives." ("O, that marrowless age should stuff the hollow bones with damned desires, and, 'stead of heat, kindle infernal fires within the spendthrift veins of a dry duke, a parched and juiceless luxur! O God! one that has scarce blood enough to live upon!")

LUSSURIOSO, the Duke's legitimate son and heir, "as impious stupid as he. . . . His heat is such were there as many concubines as ladies he would not be contained; he must fly out. . . . O thou almighty Patience! 'Tis my wonder that such a fellow, impudent and wicked, should not be cloven as he stood; or with a secret wind burst open!"

SPURIO, the Duke's illegitimate son, a "hate-all, . . . true begot in evil; . . . indeed, a bastard by nature should make cuckolds, because he is the son of a cuckold-maker."

VINDICI; " 'tis a good name that. . . . It does betoken courage; thou shouldst be valiant, and kill thine enemies." He is the idealistic, cynical, cruel avenger, who mourns the beautiful and virtuous Gloriana, his betrothed, poisoned by the Duke because her "purer part would not consent unto his palsied lust." The better to attain his ends he disguises as PIATO, a "strange-digested fellow, . . . of ill-contented nature, . . . a man that were for evil only good, . . . whose brain time hath seasoned," and who serves as the blunt "slave-pander" to Lussurioso, the Duke's son.

HIPPOLITO, also called CARLO, brother of Vindici and Castiza, and son of Gratiana.

CASTIZA, daughter of Gratiana and sister of Vindici and Hippolito. ("O angels, clap your wings upon the skies, and give this virgin crystal plaudities!")

GRATIANA, mother of Castiza, Vindici, and Hippolito. "Yon dam has devils enough to take her part; . . . golden spurs will put her to a false gallop in a trice." She tempts her virtuous daughter to be "the Duke's son's great concubine! A drab of state, a cloth-o'-silver slut, to have her train borne up, and her soul trail i' th' dirt. . . . Who shall be saved, when mothers have no grace? . . . Why does not the earth start up, and strike the sins that tread upon't? O, were't not for gold and women, there would be no damnation. Hell would look like a lord's great kitchen without fire in't."

The DUCHESS, "that foul incontinent duchess, . . . that will do with the Devil"; in love with Spurio, the Duke's bastard son.

AMBITIOSO, the Duchess' eldest son,
SUPERVACUO, the Duchess' second son, ⎱ "Here's envy with a poor thin cover on't; like
The Duchess' Youngest Son, "that ⎰ scarlet hid in lawn, easily spied through."
moth to honor,"

ANTONIO, whose wife was raped by the Duchess' youngest son, ⎱ nobles of the court.
PIERO, his friend, ⎰

DONDOLO, servant to Gratiana.

NENCIO, ⎱ servants to Lussurioso.
SORDIDO, ⎰

The Keeper of a Prison, Judges, Officers, Nobles, Gentlemen, and Servants.

Setting: a city in Italy in the Renaissance period.

> *"Thus much by wit a deep revenger can,*
> *When murder's known, to be the clearest man."*

Act I

Holding in his hands the skull of his dead mistress, Gloriana, a lady to whom he has been betrothed but whom the lecherous old Duke has poisoned because she would not be his concubine, Vindici watches the

Duke and his train pass by, and bitterly vows vengeance for the crime. An opportunity is presented, he hopes, when his brother Hippolito, asked by Lussurioso, the Duke's son, to recommend a pander to him, thinks that Vindici might disguise as "some strange-digested fellow" and perform the office. Soon it is clear that the whole ducal family is corrupt. The Duke himself is as great a lecher as his son Lussurioso; the Duchess, his second wife, is incestuously in love with the Duke's illegitimate son Spurio; and the Duchess' youngest son—who is unnamed—has raped the wife of Antonio, a nobleman of the court, and rather than bear the shame the virtuous lady has taken her life by poison. At the prince's trial for rape, the Duke pretends a virtuous severity, and, in spite of the Duchess' pleading, leaves the judgment to his magistrates. But when he perceives that sentence is about to be passed, he defers the judgment until the next sitting of the court and orders the offender to be kept close prisoner.

Meanwhile, disguised as Piato, a malcontent, Vindici meets Lussurioso and is employed by him to seduce his own sister Castiza and bring her to the prince's bed.

Act II

Pretending to fall in with this villainous purpose, Vindici—still in disguise—offers his mother Gratiana money to assist in winning over Castiza, but the girl virtuously refuses to be seduced. The pander reports his success to Lussurioso, describing the greed of the mother and holding up his hopes for the daughter, and Lussurioso impatiently resolves to visit her forthwith that night. Meanwhile, however, gossip about the Duchess' affair with Spurio is circulating; Spurio hears of Lussurioso's villainous plans and resolves to disinherit his brother by murdering him at his lust. To prevent Lussurioso from visiting Castiza, however, Piato reveals to the prince his stepmother's infamy. In a fury Lussurioso bursts into the Duchess' bedroom shouting "Villain" and "Strumpet." But only the Duke is there, and the father mistakes his son's indignation for an intention to murder him and succeed to the throne. Before he can explain or make any accusations, however, Lussurioso is hurried off to prison. Supervacuo and Ambitioso, his envious brothers, pretend to take his part with the Duke, urging his pardon and then reversing themselves. Thus they merely reveal their own dangerous aspirations. The Duke gives these villains his signet ring and an order for Lussurioso's execution, but no sooner are they gone than he orders his son released. "It well becomes that judge to nod at crimes, that does commit greater himself, and lives."

Act III

In haste, Supervacuo and Ambitioso make the most of their opportunities and present the Duke's signet as warrant for the execution of their brother. But Lussurioso has already been released, and the officers, mistaking the intention, execute instead the younger brother of the ambitious plotters. Thus a villain is by accident brought to a well-deserved doom, and by his own kin.

Soon after, Vindici has a perfect opportunity to avenge the death of Gloriana. As Piato the pander, Vindici has been hired by the Duke to conduct him to a lady in a dark, secluded place. Dressing up the skull of his betrothed in rich attires and poisoning its mouth, Vindici and his brother Hippolito bring the Duke to the grove in which Spurio and the Duchess have an assignation, present him to this puppet as to a bashful country lady, and bid him kiss her. Then, as the poisoned man sinks to his knees, Hippolito stamps on him, Vindici throws off his disguise and denounces him, and the brothers take care that he shall see his bastard son Spurio embracing the Duchess. Only then do they permit their victim to die.

Meanwhile, Ambitioso and Supervacuo meet Lussurioso abroad, and to their great chagrin and fury learn that they have been responsible for their own brother's execution.

Act IV

Disturbed by the crime he almost committed on his father, and resentful against Piato for his responsibility in the mistake, Lussurioso now seeks means to be rid of the fellow. Accordingly, he again approaches Hippolito, who introduces Vindici in his own guise to the young prince, as a brother who has become a malcontent by the study of law. To Hippolito and Vindici the prince now accuses Piato of seeking to corrupt their sister, and is satisfied to hear them vow his death. Left alone they resolve to dress up the body of the Duke in Piato's disguise to make it seem that Piato killed the Duke and then fled. Then the brothers—each with a dagger in his hand—set about conjuring the base devil out of their mother.

Act V

As planned, when the body of the Duke is at last discovered, the absent Piato is accused of murder, and Lussurioso succeeds to the throne. Vindici and Hippolito, however, approach Piero and other noblemen to plot with them against Lussurioso and his supporters. Meanwhile, a blazing comet in the sky forbodes evil to the kingdom. At his installation the new duke banishes the Duchess and condemns his illegitimate brother as well as his stepbrothers to death. But during the revels, two groups of malcontents plan to kill the new duke. That of the revengers, including Vindici, Hippolito, and two lords, arrives first and successfully carries out the murder; that of Ambitioso, Supervacuo, and Spurio finds their work already done. In the quarrel that follows Spurio kills Ambitioso, and a nobleman kills Spurio before Antonio and a guard can rush in to restore order. Hippolito and Vindici at first pretend innocence, but they soon betray themselves by boasting. As Vindici and Hippolito are led away to execution, the virtuous Antonio succeeds to the crown.

THE ATHEIST'S TRAGEDY

OR THE HONEST MAN'S REVENGE

(1607-1611)

DRAMATIS PERSONAE

LORD D'AMVILLE, brother of Lord Montferrers, and "confirmed an atheist. . . . With all [his] wisdom [he's] a fool, not like those fools that we term innocents, but a most wretched miserable fool which instantly, to the confusion of [his] projects, with despair [he does] behold. . . . [He has] no feeling of another's pain."

ROUSARD, elder son of D'Amville and later husband to Castabella; "disease and weakness have disabled him for issue."

SEBASTIAN, younger son of D'Amville; "a lusty blood! Has both the presence and spirit of a man. . . . Verily his tongue is an unsanctified member. . . . His loose humor will endure no bond of marriage."

BORACHIO, D'Amville's echo and instrument of evil, "a most delicate, sweet, eloquent villain, . . . a lonely night raven, . . . read in Nature and her large philosophy."

LORD MONTFERRERS, a baron of France. "He was a man of such a native goodness, as if regeneration had been given him in his mother's womb. So harmless that rather than ha' trod upon a worm he would ha' shunned the way. So dearly pitiful that ere the poor could ask his charity with dry eyes he gave 'em relief with tears. . . . His life's example was so true a practique of religion's theory that her divinity seemed rather the description than the instruction of his life. And of his goodness was his worthy son a worthy imitator."

CHARLEMONT, son of Montferrers and "the man whom Castabella loves. . . . The father held open war with sin, the son with blood; this in a war more gallant, that more good." Torn between love and honor, he goes to the wars.

LORD BELFOREST, a baron of France.

LEVIDULCIA, lascivious wife of Belforest; "she has a perpetual appetite. . . . She's very affectedly inclined to young Sebastian's company o' late."

CASTABELLA, chaste daughter of Belforest and Levidulcia, betrothed of Charlemont, but later enforced wife of Rousard. "That gentlewoman is most sweetly modest, fair, honest, handsome, wise, wellborn, and rich. . . . She's like your diamond, a temptation in every man's eye, yet not yielding to any light impression herself."

LANGUEBEAU SNUFFE, a tallow chandler turned Puritan. "My Lord Belforest, taking a delight in the cleanness of [his] conversation, withdrew [him] from that unclean life and put [him] in a garment fit for his society and [his] present profession" of chaplain to his lordship. "His own profession would report him pure. . . . Yet, but compare's profession with his life; they so directly contradict themselves, as if the end of his instruction were but to direct the world from sin, that he more easily might ingross it to himself." ("Verily your gravity becomes your perished soul as hoary mouldiness does rotten fruit.")

CATAPLASMA, a maker of periwigs and attires, "but under color to profess the sale of tires and toys for gentlewomen's pride, [she] draw[s] a frequentation of men's wives to [her] licentious house." ("Her rent is great. The good gentlewoman has no other thing to live by but her lodgings. So she's forced to let her forerooms out to others.")

SOQUETTE, a seeming gentlewoman, working in Cataplasma's shop.

FRESCO, manservant to Cataplasma.

The GHOST OF MONTFERRERS.

A Sergeant and a Musketeer attending Charlemont.

Judges, Officers, Watchmen, Soldiers, and Servants.

Setting: France at some unspecified time.

"Now I see
That patience is the honest man's revenge."

Act I

Because "wealth is lord of all felicity," D'Amville, younger brother of Lord Montferrers and a professed atheist, is bent upon increasing his family fortunes. To this end he enlists the aid of his villainous servant Borachio, who is "read in Nature and her large philosophy," and this rascal becomes his "oracle" and agent of evil. As a first step, D'Amville encourages his nephew Charlemont to follow the wars and to ignore his father's fears for his safety. He even lends the young man a thousand crowns to make possible his departure. Then as soon as Charlemont is out of the way, D'Amville connives with Belforest and Levidulcia, the parents of Castabella, Charlemont's betrothed, to force the girl into marriage with his own sickly elder son Rousard, thus joining the houses of Belforest and D'Amville in a wealthy alliance. Only Sebastian, D'Amville's younger son, supports Castabella in opposing the match.

Act II

At the wedding feast, as arranged, Borachio appears disguised as a wounded soldier with a false report that Charlemont is dead. He gives a circumstantial account of Charlemont's drowning on a foreign field, and exhibits a scarf which leaves no doubt of the young man's death. Deeply moved by his son's tragedy, Montferrers retires from the banquet with Languebeau Snuffe, the chaplain, to remake his will and to name his brother D'Amville his heir. Meanwhile, D'Amville and Borachio have encouraged Montferrers' servants to get drunk. On the way home, the attendants quarrel among themselves and extinguish their torches in the drunken scuffling. D'Amville and Borachio thrust Montferrers into a gravel pit and knock out his brains with stones, and the crime appears to be a mere accident. Suspicion falls on no one, yet the whole was the hellish design of the atheist villain, "and those that saw the passage of it made the instruments, yet knew not what they did."

The wedding feast is also the occasion of further evil. Levidulcia, mother of the bride, makes an assignation with young Sebastian, who is in disfavor with his father for his spirited opposition to the marriage. She also makes advances to Fresco, the servant she has borrowed to escort her home, is obliged to hide him behind the arras upon Sebastian's arrival, and contrives to get both lovers safely out of the house when her husband returns home unexpectedly. But the lascivious lady has merely postponed the evil she has planned.

In camp, the Ghost of his father appears to Charlemont, informs him of his disinheritance by murder, bids him return to France, and exhorts him to

> *Attend with patience the success of things,*
> *But leave revenge unto the King of Kings.*

Act III

With hypocritical mourning, D'Amville conducts funerals for both his brother and his nephew Charlemont, and erects a flattering epitaph to each. Charlemont returns to find his beloved Castabella dissolved in tears at his cenotaph, receives from her the confirmation of the Ghost's report of his father's death and his own disinheritance, and learns of her enforced marriage to his cousin. He seeks out his uncle D'Amville, and arrives just as the atheist is refusing his son Sebastian his customary annuity because of his insubordination in opposing the wedding of Rousard and Castabella. D'Amville pretends to take his nephew for a ghost, but Sebastian fights. In haste the Ghost of Montferrers appears to restrain young Charlemont. Once again the father exhorts the son to leave revenge to Heaven, but not before Sebastian is wounded. For his daring, as well as for the sum of money he has lent the boy, D'Amville has Charlemont thrown into prison, and relents toward Sebastian sufficiently to compensate him for his wound by giving him a thousand crowns. This sum the impetuous but honest youth uses to release his cousin Charlemont from prison. When the two young men confront D'Amville, the villain temporizes. The open liberality of his son Sebastian, D'Amville maintains, has but made known his friendly disposition toward his nephew. He professes to be Charlemont's guardian, not his dispossessor, offers to take his father's place to guide the green improvidence of his youth, and to make him ripe for his inheritance. In his turn Charlemont confesses that he has been rash, and uncle and nephew embrace in token of their reconciliation.

But from Castabella and the invalid Rousard themselves, Charlemont and D'Amville learn that their marriage has been one in name only.

Act IV

The evil intrigues which had their beginning earlier now reach their climax. Escorted by her husband's hypocritical chaplain, Languebeau Snuffe, who serves as a screen for her unholy purposes, Levidulcia meets Sebastian in the home of Cataplasma, a tiremaker. Snuffe himself makes advances to Soquette, a needleworker in Cataplasma's shop. D'Amville engages Borachio to murder Charlemont and gives him a pistol for the purpose. Acting upon Castabella's own revelation, the atheist resolves to insure the continuation of his line by seducing his daughter-in-law and begetting a child of his own.

In a churchyard at midnight, Borachio attacks Charlemont, who has come to meditate among the tombs. The villain's pistol misses fire, however, and in self-defense, Charlemont kills his assailant. Determined to give himself up to the authorities, but nevertheless fleeing from the scene of the killing, Charlemont surprises Snuffe and Soquette, who have sought the seclusion of the churchyard for their amours. They flee, leaving behind the false wig and false beard with which the Puritan has disguised himself. These Charlemont appropriates for possible use later, and hides himself in a charnel house. To the same churchyard D'Amville conducts Castabella. At the proper moment Charlemont answers his beloved's prayer for help by rising in disguise from a grave and frightening away his uncle, who thinks he sees a ghost. After explanations, the lovers lie down to rest—each with a death's-head for a pillow—and are found in these compromising circumstances by the returning D'Amville and Snuffe. The latter has also discovered the body of Borachio. Charlemont accepts responsibility for the villain's death, Castabella falsely confesses to misconduct in order that she may share her lover's punishment, and amid D'Amville's hypocritical protests, they are taken away to prison.

At the same time Belforest learns from Fresco of his wife's misconduct with Sebastian, and with the watch surprises the lovers at Mistress Cataplasma's. Belforest and Sebastian fight, and both are slain. To complete the holocaust, Levidulcia then stabs herself:

> *O with what virtue lust should be withstood!*
> *Since 'tis a fire quenched seldom without blood.*

Act V

Vengeance at last is overtaking the atheist D'Amville. As he fingers the golden revenues that have come to him since his brother's death, the Ghost of Montferrers appears to him with a message of despair. Then a servant brings in the body of Sebastian, and another in terror calls him to the bedside of Rousard. Physicians are as powerless to cure the elder as to revive the younger son. D'Amville has "not a brat left to succeed" him.

Distraught by grief, he interrupts the trial of Charlemont and Castabella by bringing in the hearses of his two sons, and mounts the bench to sit in judgment on his long-suffering nephew. He is even granted the privilege himself of carrying out the execution of Charlemont, who has made little effort to defend himself and patiently awaits his fate. But as D'Amville raises the axe, Heaven achieves its revenge. By accident he strikes out his own brains and staggers from the scaffold. With his last breath he confesses to his manifold crimes and acknowledges the justice of the judgment which has overtaken him. Charlemont is united to Castabella; the wealth and honors of Montferrers are increased by those of Belforest and D'Amville; and the young couple are duly grateful. As Charlemont observes:

> *Only to Heaven I attribute the work,*
> *Whose gracious motives made me still forbear*
> *To be mine own revenger. Now I see*
> *That patience is the honest man's revenge.*

••••——◆——••••

JOHN WEBSTER
(c. 1575?–1634 or 1638)

BIOGRAPHY. Nothing is known of John Webster, except through his own casual allusions to himself and a few scattered records. The title page of his pageant, *Monuments of Honor* (1624), describes him as "merchant-tailor," and in the epistle he states that he was born free of the company. His dramatic career began in 1602 when he was writing for Henslowe, usually in collaboration with Dekker. His dates are known only by conjecture.

CRITICAL COMMENT. John Webster has been called both "a master poet in the realm of the horrible" and "a Tussaud-laureate." His reputation rests almost wholly upon the two plays represented here; both are melodramas filled with mental as well as physical horror, and with amorous and political intrigue; both are concerned with actual events which occurred in Italy, to Renaissance Englishmen a land where anything could happen. But withal, Webster was one of the best psychologists of the time. *The White Devil* is an amazing study of infatuation, illicit love, Machiavellian intrigue, revenge, and murder. *The Duchess of Malfi* is an even more intense treatment of unconventional virtue, suffering, and diabolical revenge of kin upon kin.

Both of these plays were adapted to early eighteenth-century taste; the first as *Injured Love, or The Cruel Husband* by Nahum Tate (1707), the latter as *The Unfortunate Duchess of Malfi, or The Unnatural Brothers* by an unknown author (1707). Lewis Theobald also published an adaptation of the latter called *The Fatal Secret* (1735).

SOURCES. Both of Webster's plays here outlined were based upon fact. *The White Devil* is the tragic life story of Vittoria Accoromboni, who was murdered on December 22, 1585. Several accounts of her were published, but whether Webster knew any of them is not known. More probably he based directly upon an oral account of the lives of the persons of his play. *The Duchess of Malfi* is also historical and covers the years from 1504 to 1513. Bandello, who tells the story (I, 26), says he knew the principals and he may himself have been the prototype of Delio in Webster's play. The tale was retold elsewhere; Webster's immediate source was Painter's *Palace of Pleasure*, handled freely in accordance with the conventions of the Elizabethan tragedy of blood. The story had even been dramatized before Webster's time by Lope de Vega, *El Mayordomo de la Duquesa de Amalfi*, but the English author was unacquainted with this Spanish version.

Webster's *Duchess of Malfi* was revived in London in 1945 with John Gielgud, Peggy Ashcroft, and Leon Quartermaine in the principal roles.

BIBLIOGRAPHY

Collected Works:

> *The Works of John Webster,* edited by F. L. Lucas, 4 volumes, 1927.
> *The Best Plays of Webster and Tourneur,* edited by J. A. Symonds, Mermaid Series, 1888.

Monograph: Rupert Brooke, *John Webster and the Elizabethan Drama,* 1916.

The White Devil:

> Early editions: 1612; 1631; 1665; 1672.
> Modern editions: ed. M. W. Sampson (Belles Lettres Series, 1904); G. B. Harrison (TD, 1933).

The Duchess of Malfi:
  Early editions: 1623; 1640; 1678; n.d.
  Modern editions: ed. C. E. Vaughan (TD, 1896); M. W. Sampson (Belles
    Lettres Series, 1904); George Rylands and Charles Williams (1945).

THE WHITE DEVIL

Or The Tragedy of Paulo Giordano Ursini, Duke of Brachiano, with the Life and Death of Vittoria Corombona, the Famous Venetian Courtesan

(1609–1613)

DRAMATIS PERSONAE

VITTORIA COROMBONA, "the devil in crystal, . . . born in Venice, honestly descended
from the Vitelli, . . . [she] came from thence a most notorious strumpet, and
so [has] continued. . . . You see . . . what goodly fruit she seems; yet, like
those apples travellers report to grow where Sodom and Gomorrah stood, I will
but touch her, and you straight shall see she'll fall to soot and ashes. . . . I am
resolved, were there a second Paradise to lose, this devil would betray it." A
woman of brave spirit, if of wicked life, Vittoria is at least faithful to the profligate
Brachiano, but at the same time she remains true to her own nature. "Oh, [her]
greatest sin lay in [her] blood; now [her] blood pays for't."

PAULO GIORDANO URSINI, DUKE OF BRACHIANO, who was "held the famous politician,
whose art was poison . . . and whose conscience, murder! . . . By close pan-
derism [he] seeks to prostitute the honor of Vittoria Corombona. . . . O thou fool,
whose greatness hath by much o'ergrown thy wit!"

CAMILLO, husband of Vittoria Corombona, "a fine capricious, mathematically jealous
coxcomb. . . . A gilder that hath his brains perished with quicksilver is not more
cold in the liver; the great barriers moulted not more feathers than he hath shed
hairs; . . . an Irish gamester that will play himself naked, and then wage all
downward at hazard is not more venturous; so unable to please a woman, that,
like a Dutch doublet, all his back is shrunk into his breeches." ("If I had such a
dove-house as Camillo's, I would set fire on 't, were 't but to destroy the polecats
that haunt to it.")

ISABELLA, sister of Francisco de Medicis and wife of Duke Paulo of Brachiano, "our
phlegmatic duchess. . . . Those are the killing griefs which dare not speak."

GIOVANNI, son and heir of Brachiano, "forward lapwing! He flies with the shell on's
head. . . . Did you e'er see a sweeter prince?"

FLAMINEO, unscrupulous, politic villain, brother of Vittoria and secretary to Brachiano.
He is "Brachiano's pander, . . . made his engine and his stalking-horse to undo
[his] sister. [He] made a kind of path to her and [his] own preferment. . . .
As rivers, to find out the ocean, flow with crook bendings beneath forcéd banks, or as
we see, to aspire some mountain's top, the way ascends not straight, but imitates
the subtle foldings of a winter's snake; so who knows policy and her true aspect

shall find her ways winding and indirect." Later, Flamineo becomes "a politic madman."

FRANCISCO DE MEDICIS, Duke of Florence, hypocritical and cunning; "that old dog-fox, that politician Florence"; later, disguised as MULINASSAR, a Moor. ("Oh, the rare tricks of a Machiavellian!")

COUNT LODOVICO [Ursini], "the engine for [Francisco's] business. . . . 'Tis gold must such an instrument procure; with empty fist no man doth falcons lure. . . . I know that thou art fashioned for all ill; like dogs that once get blood, they'll ever kill. . . . He did most passionately dote upon [the] Duchess [Isabella], . . . though she ne'er knew on't."

MARCELLO, virtuous brother of Vittoria and attendant upon Francisco de Medicis. "Thou art a soldier, follow'st the great duke, feed'st his victories, as witches do their serviceable spirits, even with thy prodigal blood. What hast got, but, like the wealth of captains, a poor handful, which in thy palm thou bear'st as men hold water? Seeking to gripe it fast, the frail reward steals through thy fingers."

LORENZO DE MONTICELSO, a cardinal, later Pope [Sixtus V]. "O poor charity! Thou art seldom found in scarlet."

DOCTOR JULIO, "a poor quacksalving knave, . . . one that should have been lashed for's lechery, but that he confessed a judgment, had an examination laid upon him, and so put the whip to a *non plus.*"

CORNELIA, virtuous, noble mother of Vittoria, Flamineo, and Marcello.

ZANCHE, a Moor waiting woman to Vittoria. Flamineo loves the "witch, very constrainedly," and should have married her. He "made her some such dark promise. . . . [But] lovers' oaths are like mariners' prayers, uttered in extremity."

A Lawyer at the arraignment of Vittoria; "your learned verbosity!"

Matron of the House of Convertites—"a house of penitent whores"—to which Vittoria is sent.

"All the Grave Lieger Ambassadors" in Rome, including those of France, Spain, Savoy, and England.

The CARDINAL OF ARRAGON, who announces the election of a new Pope.

HORTENSIO, an officer of Brachiano.

ANTONELLI,
GASPARO,
CARLO,   } friends of Count Ludovico.
PEDRO,

A Conjurer who shows Brachiano the success of his plots to murder Isabella and Camillo.

JAQUES, a Moorish boy, servant to Giovanni.

CHRISTOPHERO, the doctor's assistant in the dumb show (II, iii). He does not speak.

GUIDANTONIO, attendant upon the Duchess Isabella in the dumb show (II, iii).

FARNESE, attending Francisco and Lodovico at Brachiano's palace in Padua. He does not speak.

The GHOST OF ISABELLA.

The GHOST OF BRACHIANO.

Lords, Physicians, Officers, Guards, Servants, and Attendants.

Setting: Rome and Padua towards the close of the sixteenth century.

"If the Devil
Did ever take good shape, behold this picture."

Act I

While visiting at the home of Camillo and Vittoria Corombona, Paulo Giordano Ursini, Duke of Brachiano, becomes deeply enamored of his beautiful and accomplished hostess. No love exists between Vittoria and Camillo, her jealous, impotent, ridiculous old husband, and Brachiano has grown weary of Isabella, his devoted but phlegmatic duchess, who is the sister of Francisco de Medicis, Duke of Florence. Hence, aided by Flamineo, Vittoria's unscrupulous and ambitious brother, Brachiano engages in an intrigue with Vittoria. At their first interview the shameless lady relates to her lover a dream which she has had, the purpose being to incite him to murder both her husband and his own duchess. Cornelia, the mother of Vittoria, has overheard the story, however; but in vain does she reprove her daughter and shame the seducer. Though unsuccessful in curbing it, Cornelia has at least opposed with vigor a course of mischief which can only lead to crime.

Act II

In an effort at reconciliation with her neglectful husband, the Duchess Isabella comes to Rome with her young son, Giovanni, and is welcomed to the town house of her brother, the Duke of Florence. Here the duchess' brothers, Francisco and the Cardinal Monticelso, interview Brachiano, reprove him for his adulterous life, and for the sake of his young son Giovanni try to shame Brachiano into becoming a model of virtue. In vain; a subsequent interview between the duke and his long-suffering, forgiving duchess leads only to a solemn vow on Brachiano's part that henceforth he will never lie with his wife, and that this divorce shall be as truly kept as if a judge had decreed it. To prevent further enmity between her husband and his brothers, however, Isabella makes herself the author of Brachiano's vow, refusing to be reconciled to the duke, pretending utterly to reject patience, and earning her brothers' belief that she is a foolish, mad, and jealous woman. Hence, they turn to other business and appoint Camillo, the husband of Vittoria, and Marcello, Francisco's secretary and a virtuous brother of the lady's, joint commissioners to rid the coast of pirates led by the banished Count Lodovico, a distant relative of Brachiano's. Meanwhile, Brachiano engages the quack doctor Julio and Flamineo to commit the murders he is bound to perform.

With the aid of a conjurer who puts a magic nightcap on his head, Brachiano in dumb show sees his confederates succeed at their work. Doctor Julio and an assistant poison a portrait of Brachiano, and his faithful duchess dies as she kisses it, following her devoted custom nightly before she goes to bed. As if by accident, Flamineo contrives to break Camillo's neck as he exercises in a gymnasium on a vaulting horse. But Vittoria is promptly arrested by the duke and the cardinal, as an accessory to her husband's death, and preparations are made for her trial. From the dumb shows, too, Brachiano learns that Count Lodovico the pirate "did passionately dote upon [his] duchess, . . . though she ne'er knew on't."

Act III

Before all the lieger ambassadors in Rome and a host of other spectators, and with the Cardinal Monticelso as accuser, Vittoria is tried as a "debauched and diversivolent woman," an adultress, and a murderess. In spite of her brave spirit, and a scorn and a boldness that seem like innocence, she is condemned; for Brachiano, who is present, confesses to having lodged beneath her roof the night her husband met his death. Other evidence of her guilt is also produced. "Sum up my faults," she prays at last, "and you shall find that beauty and gay clothes, a merry heart, and a good stomach to [a] feast, are all, all the poor crimes that you can charge me with." But her sentimental bid for sympathy is vain, and she is sentenced to confinement in a house of convertites.

To divert suspicion from himself, Flamineo, Vittoria's guilty brother now feigns madness and gets into a quarrel with Lodovico the pirate and the secret lover of Brachiano's duchess. On the discovery of their sister Isabella's death, Francisco and the cardinal do not see eye to eye upon a policy to pursue toward Brachiano. Francisco is not willing openly to seek revenge upon his guilty brother-in-law and so provoke a war between their two states, nor does he wish to follow the cardinal's advice that they treacherously bide their time. Instead, Francisco writes a pretended love letter to Vittoria in verse, makes sure that it will be delivered only when some of Brachiano's followers are by, and plans, by gold, to make Count Lodovico the instrument of his revenge. Lodovico's motives are adequate for the role.

Act IV

Francisco's stratagem succeeds wonderfully. The letter falls into Brachiano's hands; he jealously upbraids Vittoria with having a secret love for the Duke of Florence; there is weeping and wild protestation. The consequence is that in defiance of everything, Brachiano carries Vittoria out of her prison disguised as a page and marries her. Francisco has caused his hated brother-in-law to marry a whore!

Meanwhile, the Cardinal Monticelso has been elected Pope, and his first act, upon hearing of the elopement, is to excommunicate Brachiano and Vittoria. At the same time, his suspicions are aroused by his brother's zeal in obtaining a pardon for Lodovico's piracy. Meeting the count in the palace, Monticelso wrings from him the secret that he has been engaged to avenge the duchess whom he loved and to murder Brachiano. The new Pope, of course, condemns the plot as damnable and dissuades Lodovico from it. But to confirm his agent's resolution, Francisco sends Count Lodovico a thousand ducats as if they came from the Pope, and by accident these reach the prospective avenger immediately after his interview with the pontiff. Lodovico is convinced that Monticelso's piety is cunning pretense, and the murderer is now doubly armed for his deed of blood.

Act V

Disguised as Mulinassar, a Moorish knight, and accompanied by Lodovico and his friend Gasparo disguised as Knights of Malta, Duke Francisco is received in Brachiano's palace in Padua. Impatiently, he awaits the opportunity for an ingenious revenge upon his hated brother-in-law. Meanwhile, Vittoria's brothers, Flamineo and Marcello, quarrel because of the Machiavell's general wickedness, and particularly over his reflection upon their mother's honor. Treacherously and without warning, Flamineo stabs his virtuous brother in the back and runs him through. The crime is committed in Cornelia's presence, and the frenzied mother runs at her unnatural child with a knife. But in remorse she lets her weapon fall, goes mad with grief at what has occurred, and in her distraction sings the beautiful dirge over Marcello's corpse:

> Call for the robin redbreast and the wren
> Since o'er shady groves they hover,
> And with leaves and flowers do cover
> The friendless bodies of unburied men.
> Call to his funeral dole
> The ant, the field mouse, and the mole,
> To rear him hillocks that shall keep him warm,
> And (when gay tombs are robbed) sustain no harm;
> But keep the wolf far thence, that's foe to men,
> For with his nails he'll dig them up again.

When, at last, the revenge is practiced upon Brachiano, it is as ingenious as Francisco could wish. Lodovico sprinkles poison in his victim's helmet as he is about to enter the lists to fight at barriers; the drugs combine with perspiration to produce a lingering agony and a madness from which physicians are powerless to save the duke. Lodovico and Gasparo, now disguised in the holy garb of Capuchins, attend the dying man and perform the last rites. But, having cleared the room, they reveal themselves to their victim, and strangle him before the eyes of Vittoria, who has rushed back to his bedroom in answer to his cries. Flamineo, his secretary, happily, also comes to a bad end. Little moved by his mother's madness and still hopeful of a rich reward for his villainy, he is visited by Brachiano's ghost, who warns him of a horrible death. To his sister Vittoria he makes his claim for reward, but she gives him the portion Cain groaned under and no other. Disappointed, Flamineo fetches two pairs of pistols and threatens Vittoria and her Moorish maid Zanche with death and proposes to commit suicide after their murder. But he permits the women to persuade him to die first; they fire at him and he falls, only to rise in a few minutes unwounded and newly armed. His threats have only been a ruse. The screams of the women, however, attract Lodovico, Gasparo, and their followers, still disguised as Capuchins. They throw off their holy garments, and under the supervision of Lodovico they stab all three. "Oh, my greatest sin lay in my blood"; exclaims the dying Vittoria, "now my blood pays for't. . . . My soul, like to a ship in a black storm, is driven, I know not whither." The murderers do not escape, however; led by the young prince Giovanni, a posse wounds and apprehends Lodovico, who "limned this night piece." He confesses his fault, implicating Francisco, and Giovanni promises to bring to justice all who have had a hand in this melancholy affair.

THE TRAGEDY OF

THE DUCHESS OF MALFI

(1612–1614)

DRAMATIS PERSONAE

The DUCHESS OF MALFI, a virtuous widow who has "youth and a little beauty," and whose worth "stains the time past, lights the time to come,"

FERDINAND, Duke of Calabria, her twin brother, but the Devil's own wolvish child, and "a most perverse and turbulent nature. What appears in him mirth is merely outside; if he laugh heartily, it is to laugh all honesty out of fashion." ("You have bloodily approved the ancient truth that kindred commonly do worse agree than remote strangers,")

The CARDINAL, another brother, "a melancholy churchman, . . . [and] an old fox [of hypocrisy and evil]. . . . Some fellows, they say, are possessed with the Devil, but this great fellow were able to possess the greatest devil and make him worse. . . . [He] will play his five thousand crowns at tennis, dance, court ladies, . . . [and] he strews in his way flatterers, panders, intelligencers, atheists, and a thousand such political monsters." ("When thou killed'st thy sister, thou took'st from Justice her most equal balance, and left her naught but her sword,")

of "the royal blood of Aragon and Castile; . . . you never fixed your eye on three fair medals cast in one figure, of so different temper."

ANTONIO BOLOGNA, steward of the Duchess' household, her "upright treasurer"; later her husband, who has "long served virtue and ne'er ta'en wages of her; . . . both his virtue and form deserved a far better fortune. . . . Say that he was born mean, Man is most happy when's own actions be arguments and examples of his virtue." ("We are merely the stars' tennis balls, strook and banded which way please them. . . . In all our quest of greatness, like wanton boys whose pastime is their care, we follow after bubbles blown in th' air. Pleasure of life, what is't? Only the good hours of an ague; merely a preparative to rest, to endure vexation.")

DANIEL DE BOSOLA, provisor of the Duchess' horse, a melancholy, cynical malcontent, "a very quaint invisible devil in flesh—an intelligencer" for Duke Ferdinand. "His railing is not for simple love of piety. Indeed he rails at those things which he wants, would be as lecherous, covetous, or proud, bloody, or envious as any man, if he had means to be so. . . . A politician is the Devil's quilted anvil; he fashions all sins on him, and the blows are never heard. . . . There are a many ways that conduct to seeming honor, and some of them very dirty ones." At best, Bosola "rather sought to appear a true servant than an honest man."

DELIO, Antonio's "loyal, . . . lovéd and best friend," and "one of [Julia's] old suitors."

CARIOLA, the Duchess' faithful maid.

CASTRUCHIO, an old lord who "would fain be taken for an eminent courtier [i.e., jurist]."

JULIA, "a witty false one," frail wife of Castruchio and mistress of the Cardinal, who has grown weary of her.

A Doctor attending on Duke Ferdinand; "physicians are like kings—they brook no contradiction."

FOROBOSCO, servant to the Duchess; he "keeps the key o' th' park gate."

The COUNT MALATESTE, "a mere stick of sugar candy, . . . horribly afraid gunpowder will spoil the perfume on . . . [his] mistress' scarf,"

The MARQUIS OF PESCARA, "under whom [Antonio] hold[s] certain land in cheat; . . . here's a man now would fright impudence from sauciest beggars,"

attendants upon Ferdinand and the Cardinal.

SILVIO,
RODERIGO, } lords attending the duke.
GRISOLAN,

An Old Lady of the Duchess' court.

Three Young Children of Antonio and the Duchess.

Two Pilgrims to the Shrine of Our Lady of Loretto.

Several Madmen.

Court Officers, Executioners, Ladies, Soldiers, Servants, and Attendants.

Setting: Amalfi, Rome, Loretto, and Milan, in the early sixteenth century.

> *"We are merely the stars' tennis balls, strook and banded Which way please them."*

Act I

From motives of mere avarice and family pride, the Cardinal and the Duke of Calabria do not wish their widowed sister, the Duchess of Malfi, to marry again. Accordingly, these unscrupulous, worldly men persuade her to appoint as her purveyor of cavalry one Daniel de Bosola, a returned soldier, but a fellow who has served "seven years in the galleys for a notorious murder," and a man who has no scruples against acting as their spy. On occasion before, the Cardinal has employed Bosola for evil work, and, hence, avoids him. But even so, for their purpose they prefer Bosola to Antonio Bologna, master of the Duchess' household, who, the Cardinal thinks, is "too honest for such business." Duke Ferdinand, therefore, employs Bosola, whose duties are "to live i' th' court here and observe the Duchess; to note all the particulars of her havior, what suitors do solicit her for marriage, and whom she best affects." And, departing for home, the brothers let the lady know their disapproval of a second marriage for her.

The Cardinal, however, is not the only one who has observed the honorable conduct of Antonio. The Duchess herself has noted Antonio's many virtues, and, despite his humble birth, has fallen in love with him. But because of the difference in their rank and her brothers' disapproval of any match for her, the Duchess does her own wooing. One day, taking care that her maid Cariola is concealed behind the arras and can overhear everything they say, she calls Antonio to her, and proposes marriage, at first in riddles, and then openly, placing upon his finger the wedding ring which she "did vow never to part with . . . but to [her] second husband." Then she calls to Cariola and has her witness a contract *per verba de presenti* between them as they kneel, declaring that they "now are man and wife, and 'tis the church that must but echo this."

Act II

Some time later the spy Bosola notices unmistakable signs of pregnancy in the Duchess, and resolving to test his findings, obtains some apricots, which pregnant women are supposed to crave, and presents them to the lady as a delicacy. The Duchess eats them with relish—a sure proof to Bosola of her being with child—and at the same time the fruit induces labor before the Duchess can be removed to a place of seclusion. To prevent anyone's hearing any noise, Antonio pretends that there has been a theft in the palace, and orders the gates shut and everyone at court to remain in his rooms. But when a son is born, Antonio goes out to have its horoscope cast immediately. As he returns he is met by Bosola, and in the ensuing altercation accidentally drops the paper on which the horoscope is written. His suspicions confirmed, Bosola sends a letter to the brothers in Rome, informing them of what has occurred, but being unable to name the father of the child. The brothers control their anger, resolving to find out who made their sister a strumpet and to be revenged upon him.

Act III

In the course of time the Duchess bears two more children, and still no suspicion of the marriage falls upon Antonio, who continues to manage the Duchess' household. Suggestion by Ferdinand that the Duchess marry the Count Malateste, who is a perfect milksop—"a mere stick of sugar candy"—is met by the Duchess' dry remark that when she chooses a husband she will marry for her brothers' honor. Bosola, however, has obtained a duplicate key to the Duchess' bedchamber, and one night while she is preparing to retire (Antonio fortunately having stepped out of the room), the Duchess is surprised by her brother Ferdinand. Ferdinand's rage is deep and quiet; he shows no interest in explanations, warns his sister to keep her lover out of his sight, and leaves with her a poniard, bidding her die—quickly. Then he takes horse and rides back to Rome, "in a whirlwind." Husband and wife have little time to consider what is best for their safety; Bosola knocks at the door. Pretending that Antonio has mismanaged her affairs and is behind in his accounts, the Duchess sends Bosola for officers. Then she refuses to prosecute the swindler and only wishes to be rid of him, having arranged that Antonio flee to Ancona, buy a house there, and await her coming. But she makes the mistake of believing Bosola's high praise of the dismissed steward sincere, and to this villain she reveals her marriage and the secret she has kept for years, even appointing Bosola to follow Antonio to Ancona with coin and jewels. Thus, unwittingly and ironically, the Duchess of Malfi places herself in Bosola's power.

Meanwhile, wars make it necessary that the Cardinal turn soldier, and at the Shrine of Our Lady of Loretto, at which the lovers meet, this diabolical churchman participates in two ceremonies—his own install-ment as a warrior, and the formal banishment from Ancona of Antonio, the Duchess, and their children. Suspicious of ambush, in spite of an equivocal letter from Ferdinand, the family separates. Antonio flies with his eldest son to Milan, and none too soon, for the Duchess is overtaken on the road by Bosola and a guard, and returned as prisoner to her own palace.

Act IV

Here the noble lady endures the hellish ingenuity of her brother Ferdinand's revenge, all under pretext of reconciliation and atonement.

Because he has vowed never to see her again, Ferdinand comes to her in the dark, presenting her with a dead hand with a ring upon it, and pretending that it is Antonio's. Next, he reveals to her a chamber of horrors of wax figures of Antonio and the children as if they were dead. Immediately after, he has all the mad folk released from the common hospital so that they can interrupt her sleep by singing and dancing to the full o' th' moon. Finally, conducted by Bosola in the garb of a tomb maker, executioners bring in a coffin, toll a bell, and strangle the Duchess, Cariola, and the two children. These devilish murders are no sooner over, however, than both Bosola and Ferdinand begin to have pangs of conscience. "Mine eyes dazzle; she died young," cries the latter, "O, I'll tell thee, the wolf shall find her grave, and scrape it up, not to devour the corpse, but to discover the horrid murder."

Act V

Soon after, Duke Ferdinand is ill with "a very pestilent disease . . . [called] lycanthropia," which causes those who are afflicted with it to think themselves wolves, steal forth to churchyards in the dead of night, and dig dead bodies up. Even in the presence of his brother's delirium, the Cardinal maintains his calm, never revealing even to Bosola any knowledge of its cause or his own guilt. He orders Bosola to seek out Antonio and kill him, but he gives no sign of knowledge of his sister's death. It is Julia, wife of Castruchio and mistress of the Cardinal, who wheedles the secret out of him. The Cardinal is growing tired of Julia; Julia falls in love with Bosola; and to prove her love for him she agrees to find out the cause of the Cardinal's recent melancholy. To her the churchman confesses his secret guilt that by his appointment the Duchess and two of her young children were murdered. But he makes Julia swear secrecy by kissing a book which is poisoned, and thus her curiosity kills her. But Bosola has overheard everything, and the fellow-murderers recognize each other.

Meanwhile, Antonio knows nothing of his wife's death and is still hopeful of a reconciliation with the brothers. He plans to surprise the Cardinal in his room at night—as Ferdinand once did the Duchess— and so force a friendly reconcilement. But an echo from what is his wife's grave warns him of danger. Nevertheless, he makes the attempt. In the Cardinal's palace at night the whole untidy affair reaches its conclusion. Fearful of what Ferdinand may reveal in his madness, the Cardinal persuades his attendants not to go to the duke's assistance—or his own—should they hear a call. Bosola overhears the Cardinal meditate his murder, and, hearing some one prowling in the dark, by mistake stabs Antonio, whose life, as atonement, he had resolved to save. Bosola then seeks out the Cardinal, who cries for help but is ignored as he had ordered. Duke Ferdinand joins in the scuffle, and all three receive their death wounds. But once the bloodshed is over, a happier day is ahead. The noble Delio, loyal friend of Antonio's, introduces to the amazed court the little son of Antonio and the Duchess of Malfi, and all resolve "to establish this young hopeful gentleman in's mother's right."

FRANCIS BEAUMONT
(1584–1616)

For a biography of Beaumont see below, p. 321.

CRITICAL COMMENT. *The Knight of the Burning Pestle,* written apparently for the Children of the Queen's Revels, is the earliest first-rate mock-heroic play on the English stage, and it is unequalled except for Buckingham's *The Rehearsal* and Sheridan's *The Critic.* But, whereas the plays just named satirize authors and types of popular drama, *The Knight of the Burning Pestle* ridicules as well the taste of one variety of Elizabethan playgoer, the London citizen who knows what he likes when he goes to the theatre. The play is a gay, uproarious, rowdy piece, consisting of three main elements: (*a*) a frame-plot around George the London grocer and his family, who are real if ridiculous people, with pronounced likes and dislikes, and pronounced reactions to what they see on the stage; (*b*) a parody of romantic love, called *The London Merchant,* with a clever scapegrace apprentice who loves his master's daughter; and (*c*) the burlesque romance of chivalry, not unlike Heywood's *Four Prentices of London,* with another English apprentice, a squire of low degree, performing brave deeds. We may forgive the author his superior airs for the riotous fun he has created.

The Knight of the Burning Pestle failed when it was originally produced, but by 1635, when it was revived before an aristocratic audience, there were sufficient differences in taste between the audiences of the public and private houses for the play to succeed. It continued to be produced during the Restoration, but has seldom been seen on the professional stage since. It is sometimes revived by college and university dramatic clubs.

SOURCE. The problem of the source of *The Knight of the Burning Pestle* is bound up with problems of date. The general resemblance of the plot to *Don Quixote,* as well as the specific episodes of the inn taken for a castle and of the barber's basin are easily recognized. But Shelton's translation of the great Spanish burlesque was not published until 1612. There is no evidence that Beaumont had ever read Cervantes' story in the original; he may have heard about it, however.

BIBLIOGRAPHY

Early editions: 1613; 1635 (2) [one edition so dated is probably several years later]; 1679 [Second Beaumont and Fletcher Folio].
Modern editions: ed. F. W. Moorman (TD, 1898); H. S. Murch (Yale Studies, 1908); R. M. Alden (Belles Lettres Series, 1910); W. T. Williams (1924); M. Joan Sargeaunt (1928); J. K. Peel (1929).

THE FAMOUS HISTORY OF

THE KNIGHT OF THE BURNING PESTLE
(1607–1610)

DRAMATIS PERSONAE

Characters in the Induction and Interscenes

The PROLOGUE.

George, A CITIZEN of London, "an honest man and a true Christian grocer," as well as a freeman of his guild,

Nell, HIS WIFE, who is "a stranger here; [she] was ne'er at one of these plays, as they say, before,"

RAFE, their apprentice, "a fatherless child, . . . [who] will act you amongst the sometimes at our house that all the neighbors cry out on him; spectators. he will fetch you up a couraging part so in the garret, . . . that . . . we'll fear our children with him; if they be never so unruly, do but cry, 'Rafe comes, Rafe comes,' to them, and they'll be as quiet as lambs,"

A Boy who sings and dances between acts.

Other Boys, attendants at the theatre.

Cast of THE LONDON MERCHANT

VENTUREWELL, a rich merchant of London.

LUCE, his daughter, "so young, so fair, so kind, so trim."

MASTER HUMPHREY, a friend of the merchant's and suitor to Luce, whom "love hath tossed . . . in furious blanket like a tennis ball, . . . [but] a fellow of so lame a presence, one that hath little left of nature in him." (Luce loves "him dearly, even as [she] love[s] an ague or foul weather.")

JASPER MERRYTHOUGHT, Venturewell's apprentice, who has "the wits of twenty men about [him]. . . . Dost not see . . . how a swaggers and flies at the very heads o' folks; . . . his very ghost would have folks beaten. . . . If the wag in's lifetime played the knave, can you forgive him, too?" ("But, . . . as I remember, you had never charge to love your master's daughter.")

OLD CHARLES MERRYTHOUGHT, his father, "a merry old man, . . . [who] can not work, and . . . has not forty shillings left, and . . . eat[s] good meat, and drink[s] good drink, and laugh[s]." ("If you would consider your state, you would have little list to sing, iwis.")

MISTRESS MERRYTHOUGHT, Old Merrythought's wife, who "walk[s] upon adventures, and forsake[s her] husband, because he sings with never a penny in his purse."

MICHAEL, younger son of the Merrythoughts, and his mother's "white boy."

A Coffin Bearer.

Servants.

Cast of THE KNIGHT OF THE BURNING PESTLE

"The Right Courteous and Valiant KNIGHT OF THE BURNING PESTLE, . . . Mirror of Knighthood," alias RAFE, the Grocer's apprentice, "an Englishman, as true as steel, . . . confounding ladies' enemies."

His "Trusty SQUIRE," otherwise TIM, his elder apprentice. ("Whoreson blockhead, cannot remember!")

His "DWARF," otherwise "little GEORGE," his younger apprentice. ("It's a fine child.")

"The Old KNIGHT OF THE MOST HOLY ORDER OF THE BELL, who gives to all knights-errant entertain," otherwise Mine Host of the Bell Inn, Waltham.

The "Merry SQUIRE TAPSTERO," otherwise Tapster at the Bell.

"Huge BARBAROSO, that insulting giant," alias NICK the barber.

Three Knights,
A Lady from Turnbull Street, } captives of Barbaroso.

POMPIONA, daughter of the King of Moldavia, who falls in love with the Knight of the Burning Pestle.

A Lieutenant,
An Ancient,
A Sergeant,
WILLIAM HAMMERTON, pewterer,
GEORGE GREENGOOSE, poulterer, } Rafe's soldiers, "brought . . . from the shops of security and the counters of content to measure out . . . honor by the ell and prowess by the pound."

Setting: London, Waltham, Moldavia, and their vicinities, once upon a time.

"Our intent was at this time to move inward delight, not outward lightness, . . . soft smiling, not loud laughing."

INDUCTION

An audience is assembled in a London theatre to see a play called *The London Merchant.* The Prologue has come forward to describe the piece when he is interrupted by a Grocer, a member of the noble City and a freeman of his guild, who has attended plays there these seven years and has grown tired of the constant girds at citizens. "Why could not you be contented," he demands, "as well as others, with *The Legend of Whittington;* or *The Life and Death of Sir Thomas Gresham, with the Building of the Royal Exchange;* or *The Story of Queen Eleanor, with the Rearing of London Bridge upon Woolsacks?"* He'll have them present "something notably in honor of the commons of the City"; he'll have a citizen, and of his own trade, too, do admirable things. And so, in spite of the embarrassment of the Prologue, he brings his Wife and their apprentice Rafe up beside him on the stage to help devise a plot for a play, with Rafe in the hero role. To try out before the gentlemen who sit on the stage, and to prove his quality, Rafe thunders out a huffing speech—an inaccurate version of Hotspur's remarks on honor from Shakespeare's *1 Henry IV*—the good Grocer digs into his pockets for two shillings to provide shawms for the stately part Rafe is to enact, and soon the romantic scenes of *The Knight of the Burning Pestle* are intermixed with those of *The London Merchant,* while the Grocer and his Wife sit among the spectators on the stage, comment on the action, and interrupt it on occasion.

Act I

Venturewell, a merchant of London, has a beautiful daughter, Luce, for whom he has provided a suitor named Humphrey, who is of gentle blood, but, withal, "a fellow of so lame a presence, . . . [that he] hath little left of nature in him." At the same time Venturewell has an apprentice, Jasper, who has earned his master's displeasure by falling in love with his daughter, and she with him. For his audacity Jasper is dismissed from the merchant's house and service, and the lovers plan to elope. At her father's insistence, however, the romantic Luce receives the addresses of Master Humphrey, accepts from him a pair of embroidered gloves which cost "three and twopence or no money," and assures him that she will never marry any man unless he steals her hence. Humphrey is resolved "to venter life and limb for one so young, so fair, so kind, so trim," as Luce, and he agrees to elope with her through Waltham Forest.

At last Rafe appears. He is in his shop with two apprentices, Tim and little George, reading the romance of *Palmerin of England*. So impressed is he with the "courteous and fair well-spoken knights" of old, neglecting their possessions, wandering through deserts to relieve distressed damsels, that he too resolves to leave his grocer's shop, both for the credit of himself and of the company, and pursue feats of arms. His elder apprentice Tim will be his trusty Squire, little George will be his Dwarf, yet, in remembrance of his former trade he will have emblazoned on his shield a burning pestle, and be known as "the right courteous and valiant Knight of the Burning Pestle." After coaching his young attendants, he sets out.

Meanwhile, the discharged Jasper returns home. The Merrythoughts have agreed that the old wastrel Charles shall provide for his elder son, and the mother will lay up for Michael the younge.. Hence, Mis tress Merrythought refuses to give her blessing to Jasper—who apparently takes after his father—and reserves it for Michael. Old Merrythought, however, in spite of misfortune, gives Jasper ten shillings as his portion, adds to it some good advice, and sends him on his way.

Throughout, the Grocer and his Wife comment upon what occurs, especially upon Jasper's justification of himself to his mother, which seems to them saucy choplogic; upon Old Merrythought, whose songs make him an instant favorite, but whose economic philosophy is too unsure for these provident folk; and upon the boy who dances at the end of the act, whose performance wins the good Wife's heart.

Act II

Disgusted at her husband's lack of responsibility and his cheerfulness in spite of it, Mistress Merrythought gathers up the money and jewels she has been scraping together for Michael, and leaves the old reprobate. In Waltham Forest mother and son are frightened by the Knight of the Burning Pestle and his fierce attendants, mistake them for giants, and misunderstand their chivalric efforts to relieve poor errant gentlewomen. They flee, leaving a casket of valuables behind them, and, before the Knight can reassure the lady and her son and properly offer to assist them, Jasper comes that way and takes the casket with him as spoil.

Meanwhile, to make sure that the elopement will not be embarrassingly interrupted, the unromantic Humphrey has told old Venturewell all about the plan, and carried away the girl. But in Waltham Forest the elopers too get lost and are met by Jasper—as Luce had planned. Humphrey gets a beating, and the apprentice runs away with the beauty.

Then it is that the good Grocer and his Wife can restrain themselves no longer. They denounce the insufferable swaggerer who always succeeds in his escapades; honest Nell comforts poor Master Humphrey, and the Grocer demands that Jasper meet Rafe in a fight. When the Prologue protests that that is not according to the plot of their play, the Grocer's remark is significant: "Plot me no plots! I'll ha' Rafe come out; I'll make your house too hot for you else." Accordingly, Rafe challenges "the caitiff wretch hath done this deed." But Jasper, who has also been reading romances, has in the course of things acquired more than a book knowledge of fighting. Hence, in spite of encouragement from the side lines of "Break 's pate, Rafe; break 's pate," the poor Knight of the Burning Pestle has his weapon snatched away and is knocked down. Greatly disappointed at the result of the encounter, the good Wife threatens "if there be any law in England, [to] make some of them smart for 't," and the more experienced Grocer is quick to sense exactly what is wrong—Jasper is enchanted. He'll have a ring to discover all enchantments, and Rafe shall beat him yet.

Smarting from his defeat, but undiscouraged, Rafe conducts Mistress Merrythought and Michael to "an ancient castle, held by the Old Knight of the Most Holy Order of the Bell," otherwise known as the landlord of the Bell Inn at Waltham, and there the adventurers and their charges spend the night.

Meanwhile, Humphrey has reported the abduction to old Venturewell, and the merchant goes to talk with Jasper's father. But Old Merrythought's carefree singing and unwillingness to listen to anything that spoils his mirth, enrages Venturewell and he vows revenge.

During the entre-act music the Grocer and his Wife disagree as to whether "Baloo" or "Lachrymae" is the better tune, and discuss the story depicted in the painted cloth which forms part of the stage hangings.

Act III

After having lost their way and wandered about all night in Waltham Forest, Jasper and Luce sit down to rest. The girl is persuaded to sleep, but the romantic Jasper decides that the time is right to test her love and constancy. Accordingly, he draws his sword and pretends to be about to kill Luce—much to the alarm of the Grocer's Wife, who calls upon her husband to raise the watch at Ludgate and upon the gentlemen about her to see the king's peace kept and prevent manslaughter upon his harmless gentlewoman. Luce is submissive, but Jasper's test is interrupted by the arrival of Venturewell, Humphrey, and their men, who take Luce away and leave Jasper, who has not had an opportunity to explain to the girl that he was only fooling. After this encounter, the poor Grocer's Wife trembles like an aspen leaf and has to be comforted in the arms of her husband.

At the Bell Inn the day also begins inauspiciously. The Knight of the Burning Pestle prepares to take his leave and in good storybook fashion thanks his host the good Knight of the Holy Bell for his hospitality. But there are twelve shillings to pay, and as he is a true knight, the host refuses to bate a penny. It is the honest Grocer who comes to the rescue and pays the tavern shot, so that his boy Rafe may be beholden to no one. Mistress Merrythought and Michael take their leave to return home, but, at the suggestion of the Knight of the Bell, the Knight of the Burning Pestle undertakes his second adventure. Within this wilderness in a cave there dwells an ugly giant called Barbaroso, alias Nick the barber, who also serves as toothdrawer and surgeon, and Rafe resolves to undertake the quest. At this point Mistress Merrythought appears to continue her part in the play, but she is persuaded by the Grocer's Wife to postpone her entrance until Rafe has got the giant out of the way. In the encounter Rafe is victorious, rescuing at the same time several wretched prisoners which the giant had lured to his loathsome den under pretext of curing them of the itch and other diseases. The giant Barbaroso recants and promises to reform, and Mistress Nell calls Mistress Merrythought to come on now and continue her role. But, alas, old Charles, making merry with his "lads of mettle" refuses to have her back, and thus precipitates an altercation between the Grocer and his Wife, whose sympathies are all with Mistress Merrythought, the staff of her husband's age, his yokefellow, his own rib, with whose help he draws through the mire of this transitory world. By this time Mistress Nell needs a drink; her husband sends out for beer, and she drinks the health of the gentlemen around, while a boy dances a jig between acts. Unfortunately he cannot tumble or eat fire, but the good woman tips him nevertheless.

Act IV

By now the Grocer and his Wife are becoming bored and at loose ends as to what Rafe shall do next. The Grocer suggests that they "let the Sophy of Persia come and christen him a child," but is told that this episode is stale and has been seen before at the Red Bull Theatre. Then the Citizen's Wife has an idea of which Hollywood might be proud: "Let Rafe travel over great hills, and let him be very weary and come to the King of Cracovia's house covered with velvet: and there let the king's daughter stand in her window, all in beaten gold, combing her golden locks with a comb of ivory; and let her spy Rafe, and fall in love with him, and come down to him, and carry him into her father's house; and then let Rafe talk with her." Rafe's conversation on this occasion may not be edifying, but his conduct in the situation which develops satisfies his master and mistress. He refuses to wear the favor of a lady "that trusts in Antichrist and false traditions," and prefers Susan, the black-thumbed cobbler's maid of Milk Street, to a Moldavian princess. And the honest Grocer again sees to it that his boy shall do the right thing about tipping the servants in the household of the King of Cracovia, when the Knight of the Burning Pestle takes his departure. Rafe even gives the princess threepence for herself to buy pins at Bumbo Fair.

Meanwhile, Jasper has resorted to trickery to regain his beloved Luce. He sends a letter to old Venturewell, confessing the wrong he has done his master, but asking as a dying request that his body be brought to his daughter that she may know at last the true love he bore her. Plans are going forward for the marriage of Luce and Humphrey, but old Venturewell is so glad his prentice is at last quiet that he grants the request. He permits Jasper's coffin to be brought to the girl; Jasper hears her pathetic expression of love for him and then arises from the dead, places Luce in the coffin, and has her carried out to his old father's.

Having by now lost all interest in knight-errantry, the Grocer and his Wife again think up a very notable matter for Rafe to do to the eternal honor and glory of all grocers. Something must be laid on the altars of patriotism and civic pride. Rafe shall "come out on May Day morning upon a conduit, with all his scarfs about him, and his feathers, and his rings, and his knacks." Accordingly, for want of other adventures, Rafe becomes Lord of the May.

Act V

Disguised as his own ghost Jasper causes old Venturewell to repent his hardheartedness to the young lovers, and to "beat fond Humphrey out of doors." Rafe calls "all the youths together in pompous fashion" and conducts a review of the trained bands. Meanwhile, Old Merrythought accepts the coffin and even Jasper's ghost in his old carefree manner, opens the door of his house to his wife and son Michael only if they sing, admits the repentant Venturewell on the same condition, and is present, still singing, at the reunion of Luce and Jasper with old Venturewell's blessing.

Finally, Rafe's part, too, must come to an end, and the Grocer and his Wife must enjoy some pathos. Rafe must die. Accordingly, he comes on stage with a forked arrow through his head, gives a long summary of his virtues and of his adventures, commends his soul to Grocer's Hall, and piteously expires.

Old Merrythought sings another song as epilogue, and Mistress Nell asks the applause of the audience for her boy Rafe.

FRANCIS BEAUMONT AND JOHN FLETCHER
(1584–1616)   (1579–1625)

BIOGRAPHIES. Francis Beaumont was the third son of a distinguished lawyer and Justice of Common Pleas from Leicestershire. He was educated at Broadgates Hall (Pembroke College), Oxford, but left without a degree, and was admitted to the Inner Temple in 1600. But he was unsuited to the law, and drifted into literature. His dramatic career began about 1606, possibly through Michael Drayton, who was a family friend. His first connection with Fletcher was when they both contributed commendatory verses to Jonson's *Volpone* in 1607. The two began to collaborate in 1608 or 1609 and wrote at most only half a dozen plays together. But their collaboration left their names so closely associated that more than fifty plays are linked with them, in most of which Fletcher may have had a hand, but in which Beaumont could not have had. In 1613 Beaumont married an heiress and retired from the theatre, although in the same year he did compose the magnificent masque which the Inner Temple in conjunction with Gray's Inn presented in honor of the marriage of the Princess Elizabeth and the Elector Palatine. In 1616 he died, a month before Shakespeare, and was buried in Westminster Abbey.

John Fletcher came from an even more distinguished family. Born in Rye, Sussex, he was the son of Richard Fletcher who was chaplain to Queen Elizabeth, Dean of Peterborough, chaplain at the execution of Mary Queen of Scots, Bishop of Bristol, of Worcester, and later of London (1594). Giles and Phineas Fletcher, the poets, were cousins. Nothing is known of Fletcher's education, but it has been surmised that he went to Cambridge. After 1596 when his father died, heavily in debt and leaving eight children, nothing is known of Fletcher until he emerged as a playwright, more than a decade later. As a dramatist he was the successor of Shakespeare with the King's Men, and he wrote industriously, usually in collaboration. He died of the plague in 1625, and was buried in St. Savior's.

CRITICAL COMMENT. Beaumont and Fletcher are significant in English drama because they popularized the "romance" or "tragi-comedy," the two greatest examples of which are *The Maid's Tragedy* and *Philaster*. The chief characteristics of the type are: a highly romantic and ingenious plot, which falls apart under critical examination; characters which grow out of the plot and are brilliant but often shallow; a rapid chain of events; spectacular scenes; a mixture of humor and seriousness; the contrast of love and lust, with some intermediary varieties of affection; sentimentality rather than sentiment; and, usually though not always, a happy conclusion. As the name implies, *The Maid's Tragedy* has a tragic ending; *Philaster* ends happily. In their sophistication and their high-flown sentiment, Beaumont and Fletcher's plays are forerunners of the heroic drama of the Restoration.

Both *The Maid's Tragedy* and *Philaster* are of their age rather than for all time, but both were very popular before and after the Restoration. Edmund Waller revised the last act of *The Maid's Tragedy,* eliminating the killing of the king (1664), and Elkanah Settle transformed *Philaster* into an opera in 1695, "the last two acts new written." Another adaptation of *Philaster* called *The Restauration, or Right Will Take Place* has been ascribed to the Duke of Buckingham and was printed in 1714. But both plays continued to be acted as originally written.

SOURCES. For neither *The Maid's Tragedy* nor *Philaster* is any precise source known, but episodes in both have been referred to Sidney's *Arcadia* or its continuation by Alonzo Perez. The girl disguised as a boy, a device which appears in both plays, is a romantic commonplace in both fiction and drama.

BIBLIOGRAPHY

Collected Works:

The Works of Beaumont and Fletcher, a variorum edition under the general direction of A. H. Bullen, 1904-12, but incomplete.

The Works of Beaumont and Fletcher, edited by A. Glover and A. R. Waller, 10 volumes, 1905-12.

The Best Plays of Beaumont and Fletcher, edited by J. S. L. Strachey, 2 volumes, Mermaid Series, 1904.

Monographs:

C. M. Gayley, *Beaumont the Dramatist,* 1914.

O. L. Hatcher, *John Fletcher: a Study in Dramatic Method,* 1905.

E. H. C. Oliphant, *The Plays of Beaumont and Fletcher: An Attempt to Determine Their Respective Shares and the Shares of Others,* 1927.

A. C. Sprague, *Beaumont and Fletcher on the Restoration Stage,* 1926.

J. H. Wilson, *The Influence of Beaumont and Fletcher on Restoration Drama,* 1928.

The Maid's Tragedy:

Early editions: 1619; 1622 [enlarged]; 1630; 1638; 1641; 1650 [60?]; 1661; 1679 [Second Folio]; 1686.

Modern edition: ed. A. H. Thorndike (Belles Lettres Series, 1906).

Philaster:

Early editions: 1620; 1622 [corrected and emended]; 1628; 1634; 1639; 1652 (2); n. d. [1663?]; 1687.

Modern editions: ed. A. H. Thorndike (Belles Lettres Series, 1906); F. S. Boas (TD, 1898).

THE MAID'S TRAGEDY

(1608–1611)

DRAMATIS PERSONAE

ASPATIA, trothplight wife to Amintor, and "prouder that [she] was once [his] love though now refused, than to have had another true to [her]. . . . Nothing but sad thoughts in her breast do dwell. . . . She carries with her an infectious grief that strikes all her beholders; she will sing the mournful'st things that ever ear hath heard, and sigh, and sing again."

EVADNE, "young and handsome, a lady of a sweet complexion," married to Amintor; she "love[s] with [her] ambition, not with [her] eyes. . . . [Her] whole life is so leprous, it infects all [her] repentance." ("Thou hast death about thee—h' has undone thine honor, poisoned thy virtue, and, of a lovely rose, left thee a canker.")

AMINTOR, a noble gentleman of the court, once betrothed to Aspatia and now married to Evadne. "Alas, [he is] nothing but a multitude of walking griefs!"

MELANTIUS, the "stout and able" friend of Amintor, "who is as slow to fight with words as he is quick of hand. . . . [To him] the name of friend is more than family or all the world besides,"

DIPHILUS,

} brothers of Evadne.

The KING OF RHODES, "a shameless villain, a thing out of the overcharge of Nature, sent like a thick cloud to disperse a plague upon weak, catching women—such a tyrant that for his lust would sell away his subjects, ay, all his heaven hereafter."

LYSIPPUS, brother of the King and his successor.

CALIANAX, "an old man and a councilor," father of Aspatia and keeper of the fort; "he's so humorous [i.e., temperamental, unpredictable] since his daughter was forsaken. . . . When [he] was a youth [he] kept [his] credit with a testy trick [he] had amongst cowards, but durst never fight."

CLEON,
STRATO,

} gentlemen of the court.

ANTIPHILA,
OLYMPIAS,

} waiting gentlewomen to Aspatia.

DULA, a mirthful lady, attendant on Evadne.

DIAGORAS, a servant.

Two Gentlemen of the King's Bedchamber.

"Swarthy Face[d] . . . Night, . . . great queen of shadows,"
Cynthia, goddess of the moon,
Neptune, "great master of the flood and all below,"
"Blue Proteus," Tritons, and other Sea Deities,
Aeolus, god of the winds,
Favonius and the Milder Winds,

} characters in a wedding masque given before Amintor and Evadne.

Lords, Ladies, Gentlemen, Messengers, Spectators at the Masque, Musicians, and Servants.

Setting: Rhodes at some indefinite time.

"Look, look, wenches,
A miserable life of this poor picture!"

Act I

Although once betrothed to Aspatia, daughter of old Calianax, the noble young Amintor is now about to marry the fair Evadne, sister of Melantius, his closest friend. So sudden has been the change of brides that Melantius, newly returned from the wars to be present at Amintor's wedding, mistakenly greets the beautiful Aspatia as the bride. Without meaning to he has hurt her to the quick, and from his friends at court and from Amintor himself he learns that it was not fickleness on the young noble's part, or falseness of heart, which caused the shift in plans, but the royal command. To honor Melantius—so it is given out—

the King dissolved the original betrothal and expressly commanded the substitution of the warrior's sister as the bride. Surprised, but more than pleased to have his friend as his brother-in-law, Melantius accepts the situation; but the deserted Aspatia is cast into melancholy, "walks discontented, with her wat'ry eyes bent on the earth" in the unfrequented woods, and has lost all her mirth.

At the masque with which the King has the wedding celebrated, an old enmity breaks forth again between Melantius and old Calianax, the father of Aspatia, who always was a coward and has grown somewhat testy and moody since his daughter was forsaken. The King, however, commands their reconciliation; a masque involving Night, Cynthia, Neptune, and the Winds is produced before the court, with an epithalamium; and the bride and the bridegroom are conducted to their bedchamber with the hearty felicitations of the whole court.

Act II

When at last the couple are alone, Evadne reveals to her astonished husband the real reason for the royal interest in their marriage. What has seemed maidenly coyness in the bride is not that at all; instead, Evadne's reserve is the result not only of a total absence of love on her part for her newly married husband, but also of a vow which she has made never to share his bed. For a long time now Evadne has been the secret mistress of the King, and this marriage with Amintor has been jointly planned by the lovers so that for protection the girl might have some worthy man to bear the name of husband to her, to father children, and to make her sin more honorable. And, because the King is her fellow in this villainous deception, Amintor is deprived of revenge for his dishonor, for what frail man dares lift his hand against the King? "Let the gods speak to him when they please; till when, let us [i.e., ordinary men] suffer and wait." Hence, there is nothing for Amintor to do but to dissemble and to bear his wrong with patience.

Meanwhile, at her father's house forlorn Aspatia spends the hours at needlework with her maids, embroidering the stories of unhappy women who were cast off by their lovers—Oenone, Dido, Ariadne, and, finally, the lost Aspatia of Rhodes, "Sorrow's monument."

Act III

Next morning the young couple endure the witticisms of their friends, and so well do they dissemble that the King calls them aside to seek reassurance from Evadne that she has remained faithful to him. Amintor, meanwhile, must endure the pair brazenly flaunting their love before him.

But Melantius is not deceived; under the carefree manner of Amintor he suspects that his friend bears some secret grief, and he determines to know the cause. At length he wrings from the young man his awful secret. To Melantius, however, "the name of friend is more than family or all the world besides," and, once convinced of what has occurred, the soldier is resolved to avenge his wronged friend, his sister's honor, and the reputation of his house. The doctrine of the divine right of kings does not restrain the warrior as it did the wronged courtier. Through his loyal brother Diphilus, Melantius gathers what friends will join his faction without knowing the cause they are to fight for, collects arms, and prepares by force to right the wrong. He even tries to effect the surrender of the fort, which is in the hands of his old enemy, Calianax. Earlier in the day the old dotard challenged Melantius to a duel, and now, frankly affirming his purpose of killing the King who has wronged the old man and his daughter Aspatia, Melantius demands the fort. But from Calianax' hesitancy and his request of an hour to think the matter over, Melantius knows the old man will go directly to the King.

Act IV

Melantius' plot of revenge rapidly gains head. In an interview with his sister, Melantius turns her eyes into her very soul, hears her penitent confession of her guilt, and exacts from her a promise at the first opportunity to kill the devil-king who tempted her frailty. So contrite is Evadne that she even begs pardon of her wronged husband, who finds her change of heart hard to believe. But there are dangers of discovery, too. As Melantius has supposed, Calianax reports to the King the demand for the surrender of the fort. But the King doubts whether, without first putting the matter to test, he should believe so serious a charge from an old dotard like this councilor, especially when he is a known enemy to the warrior. Hence, at a banquet the King faces Melantius with the accusation. So skillful is the soldier at dissimulation and intrigue, however, that he readily convinces everyone that the story is the result of Calianax' distraction, and, amid laughter, hears the King threaten to remove the old man from his offices. Accordingly, when they are left alone, old Calianax in disgust surrenders the fort to Melantius; a king who is so incredulous and a traitor who is so clever deserve such treatment. Besides Calianax wants to be on the winning side.

The whole conspiracy is almost overthrown from another direction, however. The King has sent for Evadne, and, knowing nothing of what is afoot, Amintor is almost beside himself lest his wife's penitence come to naught. He demands that his friend Melantius forthwith draw sword, and hand in hand with him, "rush to the chamber of this hated King and sink him with the weight of all his sins to Hell forever." But the wily Melantius bids him with reason plot revenge, and not with passion, and, knowing the loyalty which prevented his undertaking revenge in the first place, Melantius sobers Amintor by a reminder that it is against the King that he proposes to fight.

Act V

The revenge plot succeeds remarkably. As planned, Evadne stabs the King in the very bed which he had dishonored; Melantius seizes the fort, and from the wall with loud voice disclaims personal ambition and announces the innocence of his act. So strong, indeed, is his position, morally and militarily, that Lysippus, brother of the dead King and his successor on the throne, throws Melantius and his supporters a blank pardon, certified by his seal.

But some events which follow hard upon this success could not have been foreseen. Disguised in man's apparel and disfigured with counterfeit scars, Aspatia poses as her soldier brother, returned from the wars and seeking to avenge the slight done his sister. Actually, Aspatia hopes for her own death at the hands of Amintor. But only by striking and kicking the young lord does the pretended soldier provoke him to draw his sword, and then she handles her weapon so clumsily that Amintor cannot keep from wounding her. As the disguised Aspatia falls, Evadne exultantly appears with bloody hands and news that the King is dead. But the loyal Amintor accuses her of having taken a life "the very name of which had power to chain up all [his] rage, and calm [his] wildest wrongs," and refuses to grant his wife forgiveness. Hence, Evadne stabs herself. Almost overcome by grief, and preparing for his own death, Amintor vows not to leave his wrong to Aspatia unsatisfied. The wounded girl thereupon reveals herself to her lover, but she is too weak to survive, and dies in his arms. As Melantius and the new king arrive with news of what has occurred at the fort, Amintor stabs himself, dying in the arms of his friend. Melantius tries to commit suicide, but is prevented by his brother; and the new king Lysippus sees in all these events a lesson he can profit by:

> May this a fair example be to me
> To rule with temper; for, on lustful kings,
> Unlooked-for, sudden deaths from God are sent,
> But cursed is he that is their instrument.

PHILASTER

OR LOVE LIES A-BLEEDING

(1609–1610)

DRAMATIS PERSONAE

PHILASTER, heir to the crown of Sicily, a "Mars of Men," and "the king of courtesy." His father "was by our late King of Calabria unrighteously deposed from his fruitful Sicily, . . . [and] this would have been a pattern of succession, had he ne'er met this mischief."

PHARAMOND, Prince of Spain and suitor to the Princess Arethusa, "Sir Prince of Popinjays" who is "naught but a valiant voice. . . . He looks like an old surfeited stallion after his leaping, dull as a dormouse. . . . O, he's a precious limehound! Turn him loose upon the pursue of a lady, and, if he lose her, hang him up i' th' slip." ("O thou pernicious petticoat prince, are these your virtues?")

ARETHUSA, fair and virtuous daughter of the King of Calabria, and betrothed to Prince Pharamond; "many that will seem to know much say she looks not on him like a maid in love."

EUPHRASIA, daughter of Dion, and supposed to be spending "the springtime of her life in holy pilgrimage" undertaken "for the penance but of an idle dream." Actually she is disguised as the "pretty, sad-talking" page BELLARIO, who is "the trustiest, loving'st, and the gentlest boy that ever master kept."

The KING OF SICILY AND CALABRIA, a "tyrant king, that languishing hears his sad bell and sees his mourners, . . . [and knows] the injuries [he has] done must be revenged."

DION, a lord of the court and the father of Euphrasia (Bellario).

CLEREMONT,
THRASILENE,} noble gentlemen, his associates.

GALATEA, "the court star, . . . a wise and modest gentlewoman that attends the princess."

Another Lady attending the princess.

MEGRA, "Lady Towsabel," a lascivious lady of the court, "made by a painter and a pothecary. . . . She has a garrison of devils in her tongue." ("That's a firker, i' faith, boy.")

An Old Wanton Lady or Crone; "her name is common through the kingdom."

An Old Captain, "an old gray ruffian," who leads the insurrection in favor of Philaster.

Five Citizens, "my ding-dongs, my pairs of dear indentures, kings of clubs, . . . dainty duckers, . . . rose-nobles, . . . myrmidons, . . . roarers."

Two Woodmen of the forest in which the King hunts.

A Country Fellow who wounds Philaster.

The King's Guard and Train.

Setting: Sicily at some indefinite time.

"Let princes learn
By this to rule the passions of their blood;
For what Heaven wills can never be withstood."

Act I

At the court of the combined kingdoms of Sicily and Calabria, there lives the manly, high-minded young prince Philaster, true heir to the throne of Sicily and son of the ruler whom the late King of Calabria unrighteously deposed. Dependent upon the present King, but a potential opponent to existing authority, Philaster is saved from imprisonment or worse by his great popularity with the uncertain but right-hearted "rods of vengeance, the abuséd people." Now, partly "to bring in the power of a foreign nation to awe his own with," and partly to affect the political union of the two kingdoms, the King has betrothed his beautiful and virtuous daughter to Pharamond, Prince of Spain, and proposes to bestow upon the couple both Sicily and Calabria as a dowry. Against this proposal and in defense of his rightful inheritance, Philaster speaks boldly, much to the secret admiration of the court, making the foreign prince, who is a vainglorious talker, a "Prince of Popinjays," and a lecher of the worst order, look "like a toothdrawer" beside him.

The virtues of the unfortunate Philaster are happily not overlooked by the Princess Arethusa herself. She sends for him, secretly declares for him a love which he returns, and accepts from him the promise of a trustworthy page in his employ who will wait upon her and carry messages between them. At the same time, the contrast between the noble Philaster and his ignoble rival is clearly seen in the encounter which the two have as Philaster is leaving the princess, and in the dishonorable proposal which the lascivious Spaniard makes to Arethusa before marriage.

Act II

To his surprise, Philaster finds his page Bellario most reluctant to accept preferment to the service of Arethusa, the faithful boy persisting in his belief that he is being turned off because of some fault he has committed, and begging for another chance. Even Philaster's assurance that Bellario's service of the princess will really be service of his master does not convince the lad. Nevertheless, Bellario obeys and takes service with Arethusa, who fits him out in a handsome livery and finds him a quiet, tender, confidential servant.

Meanwhile, the lecherous Pharamond seeks a courtesan among the maids of honor. This "pernicious petticoat prince" first assays the

virtuous and witty Galatea, who, for his presumption, cheats him of the
gold he offers her. Then he tries Megra, who has a weakness for foreigners, and who promises to find the means of slipping into his lodging at
night. But Galatea has overheard the arrangements and reports to her
mistress Arethusa, who is glad of an opportunity to break off the un-
welcome match with Pharamond. Accordingly, late at night she sends
the King and his guard to the Spaniard's lodging, and, though the
prince tries to prevent discovery, there they find Megra. But the shameless creature seeks to escape calumny by accusing the Princess Arethusa
to the King of keeping a handsome, eighteen-year-old boy, the page
Bellario, and threatens to let all the world know of it.

Act III

Word of the princess' shameful conduct soon spreads through the
court and is readily believed by those who see in it a "punishment to
scourge the King with his own issue." Indeed, some of the courtiers
believe that this disgrace, added to the unpopular betrothal of Arethusa
and an unprincely foreigner, has created the proper opportunity for
Philaster to cast off his backwardness and claim his rightful heritage.
Those who know the young prince best believe that the only cause
of his hesitation has been his secret love for Arethusa, and this admiration they can now confute. But his friends find Philaster hard to convince, even when Dion, a lord of loyalty and trust, assures the young
prince that he took Arethusa and her page together. Filled with misgivings, Philaster questions Bellario and then threatens him with
death, but so sincerely does the boy protest his innocence, that Philaster
believes him. Nevertheless he dismisses the page, bidding him never
come into his sight again.

At the same time the King tells his daughter of the foul whispers
stirring about her and warns her to dismiss the boy, advice in which
Philaster also concurs when he next sees Arethusa and finds her in
tears. But so passionately does the princess defend her page, his loyalty,
and his devotion, that Philaster is again suspicious, denounces the lady
for her infidelity, and leaves her forever, in disillusionment. Hence,
when the unhappy Bellario comes to take leave of his mistress, Arethusa
accuses him of collusion with his master in her ruin, and the faithful
boy, too, goes forth to seek out some forgotten place in which to die.

Act IV

At hunting, the princess separates herself from the rest of the party
in the forest, and there, far from the haunts of men, by accident the

principals in this triangle meet—Arethusa, Philaster, and Bellario. There in despair Philaster offers the lady and the page his sword, bidding each kill him, or worse will follow. When they both refuse, and Bellario has been sent out of the way, Philaster "perform[s] a piece of justice," wounding Arethusa. Before he can kill her, however, he is prevented by a country fellow, who bursts upon the scene only to be met by Arethusa's astonishing and haughty inquiry:

> *What ill-bred man art thou, to intrude thyself*
> *Upon our private sports, our recreations?*

Undaunted by such a quixotic notion, the rescuer wounds Philaster in a fight, but permits him to escape. There the princess is found by a searching party from the court, which continues to seek her assailant. The princess professes to believe that he is a distracted fellow that she does not know.

In another part of the forest the discarded Bellario falls asleep, and is found by Philaster. But the pursuers are hot on the prince's trail. If Arethusa is true, he knows that they have no means of identifying her assailant except by the wounds he bears. To escape, therefore, with his sword he gives similar wounds to the sleeping boy; and, when the pursuers arrive, Bellario takes upon himself his master's guilt in having hurt the princess. But so circumstantial is his confession, which he says was motivated by revenge, that Philaster creeps from hiding to protect innocence, begs Bellario's forgiveness, and assumes the blame himself—"you know she stood betwixt me and my right." This is the opportunity for which the King has been waiting. "Thou ambitious fool," he cries, "thou that hast laid a train for thy own life! Now [that] I do mean to do, I'll leave to talk. Bear him to prison." But, on the ground that it is against her life they have plotted, the Princess Arethusa begs her father for the custody of the prisoners, their tortures, and their deaths. He grants her request, assuring Pharamond that now they may with more security go on with the intended marriage, but leaving Philaster's friends to fear that by his violent act the young prince may have lost the hearts of the people.

Act V

Philaster's death is ordered, and prisoner and headsman are sent for by the King. From the prison, however, the Princess Arethusa brings Philaster as her husband, Bellario in robe and garland serving as the conductor of a marriage masque. The King threatens to throw both bride and bridegroom into the citadel, but his rage is cut short by word of a rising in the city and of the capture of Prince Pharamond by the citizens in reprisal for the imprisonment of Lord Philaster. Finding that there is no other way to calm the mutiny, the King bids Philaster show himself to the people, "and be what you were born to. Take your love, and with her my repentance, all my wishes, and all my prayers." Accordingly, Philaster receives the enthusiastic greetings of the insurgents, rescues Prince Pharamond, and, with a handsome tip, disperses the mob.

But the old spectre continues to haunt the couple. As Pharamond prepares to return home, Megra again accuses the princess and the page. The King insists that Arethusa clear herself. After some melodramatic gestures in which Bellario is threatened with torture, and Philaster offers twice to stab himself, the page is discovered to be Euphrasia, daughter of the courtier Dion. For love of Philaster, whose worth her father often praised, and whose virtues she idealized, the romantic girl pretended to go on a holy pilgrimage, but instead dressed as a boy to serve the prince. Vowing never to marry, Euphrasia accepts Arethusa's friendship free of jealousy. Megra escapes unpunished for her scandal; Prince Pharamond takes passage home, knowing that his faults cost him both wife and kingdom; and Arethusa and Philaster receive the blessings of the King.

JOHN FLETCHER
(1579–1625)

For a biography, see p. 322.

CRITICAL COMMENT. Serious drama was not Fletcher's strong suit; he was best in tragi-comedies that offered opportunity for rich contrasts or in lively comedies of manners, and the four plays here summarized are representative of his work at its best.

The Faithful Shepherdess is a tragi-comedy which attempted to popularize pastoral conventions on the public stage, and failed. There is in it variety enough in both character and sentiment, the latter ranging all the way from ideal devotion to brutish lust. But, as Fletcher complained in his preface to the printed play, the audience noting that the characters were shepherds, "concluded [it] to be a play of country hired shepherds in gray cloaks, with curtailed dogs in strings, . . . and, missing Whitsun ales, cream, wassail, and morris dances, began to be angry." In short, a popular audience expected shepherds to behave like shepherds in real life. Later, the play enjoyed considerable vogue, particularly at court, where realism was less expected.

The Wild-Goose Chase is a sprightly comedy of manners, with wit, sophistication, and a brilliant dialogue that anticipates the careless grace of "easy Etherege" and the comic writers of the Restoration. The play is a merry duel of sex in which the hero, a rake who is merely trying to live his own scarlet life, is at last tricked into matrimony with a charming, but determined, woman. The theme became common after 1660. *The Wild-Goose Chase* was adapted to early eighteenth-century tastes by George Farquhar as *The Inconstant* (1702).

The Island Princess is a tragi-comedy which likewise has an excellent plot, a romantic Pacific setting, and a heroine who changes her mind. It is often charming, and always ingenious. The play was revised as *The Island Princess, or The Generous Portugal* (1669), and first printed in this form. It was again rewritten by Nahum Tate in 1687, and an operatic version by Pierre Motteux with music by Purcell and others was issued in 1699.

Rule a Wife and Have a Wife, another comedy of manners, is a delightful variation of the old shrew-taming theme and Fletcher's best comedy, well-constructed and full of lively scenes.

SOURCES. *The Faithful Shepherdess* is in the tradition of Guarini's *Il Pastor Fido,* itself modelled on Tasso's *Aminta,* but there is no precise source. For *The Wild-Goose Chase* no original is known, but the play is made up of sure-fire situations, cleverly put together. *The Island Princess* may be based upon Bartolome Leonardo de Argensola's *La Conquista de las Islas Malucas* (1609), the fourth book of which outlines the story as Fletcher followed it for three acts, except that the hero of the original is a native islander and a Mohammodan. Hence, the change of race and religion accounts for Acts IV and V of the play. But Fletcher may not have read Spanish. *Rule a Wife* in its main plot is Fletcher's own. But the story of the copper captain and his gulling is derived from a story in Cervantes' *Exemplary Novels* (1613), considerably modified and disinfected.

BIBLIOGRAPHY

The Faithful Shepherdess:
   Early editions: n.d. [1608–10]; 1629; 1634; 1656; 1665; 1679 [Second Folio].
   Modern edition: ed. F. W. Moorman (TD, 1897).

The Wild-Goose Chase:
   Early editions: 1652; 1679 [Second Folio].

The Island Princess:
   Early editions: 1647 [First Folio]; 1679 [Second Folio].

Rule a Wife and Have a Wife:
   Early editions: 1640; 1679 [Second Folio]; 1696 [separately]; 1697.

THE PASTORAL OF

THE FAITHFUL SHEPHERDESS

(1608–1609)

DRAMATIS PERSONAE

CLORIN, the faithful shepherdess, and "the Virgin of the Grove, . . . [who] hath long since buried her chaste love, and now lives by his grave, for whose dear soul she hath vowed herself into the holy roll of strict virginity."

THENOT, who has "forgot what love and loving meant; rhymes, songs, and merry rounds that oft are sent to the soft ear of maid are strange to [him]. . . . Did ever man but he love any woman for her constancy to her dead lover?"

AMORET, beloved of Perigot and the "fairest bud of maiden virtues, . . . fairer far than the chaste blushing morn, or that fair star that guides the wand'ring seaman through the deep,"

PERIGOT, "the true admirer of [her] chastity, . . . the prime of our young grooms, even the top of all our lusty shepherds, . . . [and] as free from ill as he whose conversation never knew the court or city. . . . [His] affections are as pure as those chaste flames that burn before the shrine of the great Dian,"

"The great powers will not let their virtuous love be crossed."

AMARILLIS, another, more wanton, shepherdess that is in love with Perigot, "and would be gladder to be loved again than the cold earth is in his frozen arms to clip the wanton spring." ("Do not love him then that cannot love again; on other men bestow those heats . . . that may return you fire for fire. . . . These neighboring plains have many a comely swain.")

THE SULLEN SHEPHERD, who "dwells down by the moor, [and] whose life hath ever shown more sullen discontent than Saturn's brow, . . . one that doth wear himself away in loneness and never joys, unless it be in breaking the holy plighted troths of mutual souls; one that lusts after every several beauty, but never yet was known to love or like. . . . All to [him] in sight are equal, be they fair or black or brown, virgin or careless wanton." ("Ye are better read than I, I must confess, in blood and lechery.")

CLOE, a bright-eyed, amorous shepherdess who seeks a lover. Her "face has foil enough; nor can they lay justly too strict a coyness to [her] charge. . . . Their coldness, not [her] virgin-modesty, makes [her] complain. . . . Give [her] him dare love at first encounter, and as soon dare prove!" ("It is impossible to ravish [her], [she is] so willing.")

DAPHNIS, a bashful, shamefast, modest shepherd wooed by Cloe, "that only dare salute, but ne'er could be brought to kiss any, . . . and could be well content to covet graces were they not got by boldness. . . . Let other men set up their bloods to sale; [his] shall be ever fair as the soul it carries, and unchaste never." ("Thou art too cold, unhappy boy. . . . 'Tis not fear to offend in boldness wins. . . . Let men that hope to be beloved be bold.")

ALEXIS, a more willing shepherd, also wooed by Cloe; "in all my life I have not seen a man in whom greater contents hath been than thou thyself art."

A Satyr, servant of Pan, who assists Clorin. "They wrong thee that do term thee rude; though thou be'st outward-rough and tawny-hued, thy manners are as gentle and as fair as he who brags himself born only heir to all humanity."

The GOD OF THE RIVER, "immortal power that rul'st this holy flood," which heals Amoret of her first wound.

A Priest of Pan.

An Old Shepherd.

Shepherds and Shepherdesses.

Setting: Thessaly in some mythical time.

> *"Mortal, you must leave your wooing;*
> *Though there be a joy in doing,*
> *Yet it brings much grief behind it."*

Act I

Forsaking all pastoral sports, delights, and games, as well as "all ensuing heats and fires of love," the faithful shepherdess Clorin dwells in a shady glade in a wood beside the grave of her lover, "the truest man that ever fed his flocks by the fat plains of fruitful Thessaly." There she forgets all the joys of former times, studying "the dark, hidden, virtuous use of herbs," and with her knowledge striving to alleviate the ills of men and beasts. And there her purity and devotion inspire the homage of a rough satyr, the servant of the great god Pan, who offers her fruit.

While Clorin keeps her lonely vigil, other shepherds and shepherdesses, however, have been attending a great festival in honor of Pan, and after the rites are over are purified by the priest with holy water, "from all hot flames of lust" and "the wanton quick desires" which may have been kindled by the ceremonial feasting and drinking. As the shepherds and shepherdesses go their ways, there emerge several individuals or pairs of lovers who illustrate all of the gradations of love from the most chaste to the most sensual. Perigot and Amoret represent pure, ideal love; and they agree to meet at night to plight their troths beside the holy well "in that fair grove where all true shepherds have rewarded been for their long service." Amarillis, in turn, represents greater ardor than Amoret. As chaste as Amoret where others are concerned, Amarillis is also in love with Perigot and determined to have him. But he suggests that she choose another—"these neighboring plains have many a comely swain"—and the spurned shepherdess remembers the Sullen Shepherd, who dwells alone near the moor, who lusts but never loves, and whose only joy is in breaking off the trothplights of true lovers. Amarillis, therefore, finds him ready to agree to destroy the strong faith of Perigot and Amoret, and promises herself to him when he shall succeed. Then there is Cloe, the frank sensualist, who is in no way coy, and who finds cold chastity a "dull humor, most unfit to be the friend of man." She is seeking a lover of quick soul, "whose words may tend to some free action." First she encounters the constant Thenot, the idealist, who is in love with the faithful Clorin, and for the very fact of her fidelity to her dead lover. Then she meets the bashful, modest Daphnis, who is just as unpromising. He agrees to seek her in the grove at night, but misunderstands her purpose so far as to assure her that she need have no fear to be alone with him in the dark. Finally, Cloe meets Alexis, a handsome, lusty swain more to her liking, and with him she also makes an assignation in the holy wood at night.

Act II

In the forest toward nightfall these lovers meet as they have agreed. Thenot visits Clorin as she sorts out her herbs and contemplates their healing properties. To her he declares his love, but shows some relief at being rejected. "If ye yield," he explains, "I die to all affection; 'tis that loyalty ye tie unto this grave I so admire." He asks merely that the faithful shepherdess grant him permission to dwell near her bower in "yon same dell o'ertopped with mourning cypress and sad yew," a request to which Clorin accedes, expressing the hope that the gods will give Thenot a quick release and happy cure for his disease. The Sullen Shepherd meets Amarillis and tells her the plans he has already made to destroy the love of Perigot and Amoret. But Amarillis has her own method. From her grandam she has learned a secret to be used if she be crossed in love. The holy well here in the forest has power to change the form of any creature which is thrice dipped overhead into its waters, provided that he take some herbs to produce a proper sleep, and have pronounced over him the proper charm. Amarillis proposes that the Sullen Shepherd assist her in assuming the shape of Amoret, leave her to her own affairs during the night, and then assist her to return to her own shape in the morning and take his reward. Cloe, too, comes early to her assignation, and hears both Daphnis and Alexis call her. But, meeting the former and finding him too fearful of being bad-mannered, she bids him wait for her at an old oak, "whose hollowness may bind us both within his body." Then she follows her preference for Alexis.

Act III

As planned the Sullen Shepherd lowers the sleeping Amarillis into the holy well and transforms her into the likeness of Amoret. But the transformation has consequences that were originally undreamed of. As planned, when Perigot appears and calls his love by name, Amarillis responds and follows the shepherd into the forest. And, when the real Amoret arrives the Sullen Shepherd sends her off in a direction opposite to that which Perigot and Amarillis have taken. But at the same time the Sullen Shepherd falls in love with Amoret and starts in pursuit. So doing, he happens upon Alexis and Cloe seeking a proper place for their love-making. To the Sullen Shepherd all women are alike; accordingly, he attempts to seize the one at hand, and wounds Alexis when he tries to defend Cloe. Before he can carry the girl off, however, the satyr appears, frightens the Sullen Shepherd away in one direction and Cloe in another, and carries the bleeding Alexis off to his "goddess in the wood," Clorin, to be healed.

When poor Cloe recovers from her fright sufficiently to return, she finds neither Alexis nor her would-be ravisher. The only hope left her is Daphnis in the hollow tree, a lover she had scorned before, but whom she now goes to seek. More tardily the Sullen Shepherd returns for Cloe, but finds instead Perigot with Amarillis in the shape of Amoret. Perigot, however, has found the shepherdess too ardent for his taste, and in his disillusionment he first offers to kill himself and then with drawn sword runs after the girl to pierce her lustful heart. Seeing the turn events have taken, the Sullen Shepherd strews herbs in the air to uncharm Amarillis, and the shepherdess reassumes her own shape. But Amoret appears at the moment, and Perigot turns his wrath upon her, wounding her with his sword. Lest some honest night-traveller cure her wound and save her life, the brutal Sullen Shepherd throws poor Amoret into the holy well to drown. But the God of the River rises with the body in his arms, heals the wound immediately because the victim is a virgin pure, and even makes love to the girl, offering her many inducements if she will live with him and be his love. In spite of all that has occurred, however, Amoret remains true to her betrothed Perigot.

Act IV

Certain that his Amoret has been "untrue, unconstant, and unkind," Perigot prepares to fall upon his boar-spear, but is prevented by the contrite Amarillis, who assures him that his Amoret's love in untainted. She explains how all of the confusion occurred, and even promises to show the sceptical shepherd herself turned again into Amoret, if he will but wait for her an hour. Hence, when Amarillis meets the real Amoret, healed of her wound and wandering about the wood in search of her Perigot, she directs her to her lover, but Perigot is loath to trust his eyes. The forlorn shepherdess freely forgives the shepherd before he asks it and tries to win back his love, but he is unconvinced. At last Perigot wounds Amoret a second time, and the satyr and Clorin have another patient.

Meanwhile, the physicians have dressed Alexis' wound and found that he will be difficult to cure until he lays aside all heats, desires, and lustful thoughts, and repents his unrestraint. But with another patient the faithful shepherdess affects a final cure. The hapless Thenot is resigned to death for love of Clorin's very constancy, and when she perceives that fact Clorin pretends to break her holy vow for his sake and to return his love. The effect is instant. Thenot denounces Clorin and all womankind as light and fickle, leaving the lady to rejoice that her stratagem has succeeded, for it is better that a man be a cynic than that he die.

While these events have been occurring, the Sullen Shepherd, having performed his promise, seeks Amarillis to claim his reward. But, as he attempts to seize her, she slips away and bids him catch her first.

Act V

At last it is dawn, and the priest of Pan and his companion, an old shepherd, come to arouse the shepherds from sleep only to find that none has been to bed. Hence, the two set out to search for them in their usual daytime haunts.

In her cabin the faithful Clorin has almost purified the thoughts of Alexis, and his wound begins to heal. But as with spotless hand she applies her drugs to Amoret's breast, the herbs fall off, indicating that the shepherdess is impure and full of lust—a deduction which is unthinkable—or that some uncleanness is lurking near. It proves to be the amorous Cloe and Daphnis. Tested in a magic flame which burns anyone who lusts, Daphnis is unspotted, and he is exonerated. But when Cloe is tested, the taper eagerly darts at her fingers' ends. So sensual is she in mind, that when she and Alexis recognize one another, and Cloe goes to embrace him, his wound reopens, and she must be taken away.

Meanwhile, the priest and the old shepherd meet Thenot and Daphnis, who are able to tell them something of the events of the night, and rescue Amarillis from the Sullen Shepherd, who must suffer penance for the wrong he has done.

At Clorin's bower all of the remaining difficulties are resolved. Unable to wash away the blood of Amoret from off his hand, Perigot seeks the aid of the faithful herbalist, finds Amoret, and discovers, when he has asked pardon and been reconciled to the girl, that the stain easily disappears. At Clorin's bidding the priest of Pan cleanses the environs of all unchastity, punishes the Sullen Shepherd, and brings in Amarillis. But so completely has that shepherdess reformed that the magic flame, which detects the slightest trace of unchastity, hurts her not at all, when she holds her hand in it. All join in praise of Clorin and in a song to Pan.

THE WILD-GOOSE CHASE

A COMEDY

(1619–1622)

DRAMATIS PERSONAE

MIRABEL, the Wild-Goose, heir to La Castre, "a travell'd monsieur, and great defier of all ladies in the way of marriage, otherwise their much loose servant; at last caught by the despis'd Oriana. . . . He marry! He'll be hanged first!. . . [He has] tales of all sorts for all sorts of women, and protestations likewise of all sizes. . . . He makes a common scorn of handsome women; modesty and good manners are his May games; he takes up maidenheads with a new commission—the church warrant's out of date." ("You have the gift of impudence; be thankful. Every man has not the like talent.")

PINAC, "his fellow traveller, of a lively spirit, and servant to the no less sprightly Lillia Bianca. . . . A little modesty he has brought home with him, and might be taught, in time, some handsome duty. . . . They say he is a wencher, too."

BELLEUR, "companion to both, of a stout blunt humor, in love with Rosalura. . . . But [he is] so bashful, so naturally an ass! . . . Travel three years, and bring home such a baby to betray ye as bashfulness!" ("Of a great thing, I have not seen a duller.")

ORIANA, "the fair betroth'd of Mirabel, and witty follower of the chase. . . . 'Tis a lusty wench, . . . as modest as she is fair; . . . of those happy parts and carriage, a good man's tongue may be right proud to speak her,"

ROSALURA, "a merry, . . . plain-spoken gentlewoman; . . . will make, no doubt, a good wife. . . . She speaks to th' matter, and comes home to th' point,"

LILLIA BIANCA, "Lady Learning, . . . of a more demure way, . . . no often-speaker, but, when she does, she speaks well; nor no reveller, yet she can dance, and has studied the court elements, and sings, as some say, handsomely. . . . She is a little haughty; of a small body, she has a mind well mounted, . . . [and] will . . . speak things that no man understands, nor herself neither,"

"the airy daughters of Nantolet. . . . Beshrew my blood, they are fair ones! . . . But of so strange behaviors,"

"They are coz'ning mad, they are brawling mad; they are proud-mad; they are all, all mad, . . . mad as March hares. . . . There's no trusting of 'em!"

DE GARD, "a noble, staid gentleman, that, being newly lighted from his travels, assists his sister Oriana in her chase of Mirabel the wild-goose."

LA CASTRE, "the indulgent father to Mirabel, . . . rich both in land and money."

NANTOLET, father to Rosalura and Lillia Bianca.

LUGIER, "the rough and confident tutor to the ladies, and chief engine to entrap the wild-goose; . . . a man well bred and learn'd, but blunt and bitter, yet it offends no wise man. . . . Many fair gifts he has."

MARIANA, "an English whore, a kind of fling-dust, one of your London light o' loves, a right one; come over in thin pumps and half a petticoat, one faith and one smock, with a broken haberdasher. . . . Her name is Jumping Joan, an ancient sin-weaver; she was first a lady's chambermaid." But she is passed off by Pinac as a goodly lady "of a loving mind, a quiet, and one that weighs the worth of him that loves her."

PETELLA, waiting woman to Nantolet's daughters.

Four Women, assisting Rosalura in gulling Belleur. "What are these? Whirlwinds? Is Hell broke loose, and all the Furies flutter'd?"

A Servant to Lillia Bianca, saucy and unreliable.

A Young Man disguised as FOSSE, a factor to an Italian Merchant named Leverdure, who is a friend of Mirabel's.

Two Gentlemen, a Page or Footboy attending De Gard, a Singing Boy in Nantolet's household, Two Men disguised as Merchants, a Priest, Servants, and Attendants.

Setting: Paris at some unspecified time.

"What a world's this! Nothing but craft and cozenage!"

Act I

Called home from his travels in Italy, Mirabel, the wild-goose and a Don Juan utterly averse to marriage, determines to evade the wishes of his father, La Castre, that he settle down and marry. "There's no reason," Mirabel argues, "a gentleman, and a traveller, should be clapp'd up (for 'tis a kind of bilboes to be married), before he manifests to the world his good parts; tug ever, like a rascal [i.e., a galley slave], at one oar? Give me the Italian liberty!" Oriana, to whom he is betrothed but whom he has shamefully deserted, confides to her brother De Gard, however, that she is still in love with the wild young scapegrace and determined to reclaim him to good and honorable ways and to marry him. Sceptical of the result, De Gard nevertheless promises not to oppose her efforts.

Returned with Mirabel are his two friends, Pinac and Belleur, both roisterers and wenchers like Mirabel, and, like him also, rakes who know "no more what the conditions and the ties of love are, the honest purposes and grounds of marriage, . . . than I do how to build a church." All three are introduced to Rosalura and Lillia Bianca, the young but beautiful daughters of Nantolet, the hope of La Castre being that if his son is dissatisfied with Oriana, he will make his choice between these girls. They are "no gypsies," their proud father maintains, "they have been trained well" by their tutor Lugier, and they are ready to make their debuts in the world. At first Mirabel haughtily treats them in a highly patronizing manner, as if they were both children. But the elder, Rosalura, is a merry, plain-spoken wench who recognizes a braggart when she sees one and gives Mirabel back witticisms as audacious as she gets. Her frank ardor repels even as great a rake as the wild-goose. Her sister Lillia Bianca, on the other hand, has a reputation for starched austerity and learning, and in her turn she chills the vain talker with a philosophical and moral lecture instead of repartee. Hence, the worldly Mirabel dislikes both of the young women, and he asks his father for more time in which to make up his mind. His two friends, however, are attracted to the girls, Belleur to Rosalura, and Pinac to Lillia Bianca. Oriana and her brother watch Mirabel's encounters with her rivals and have left little hope for her success.

Act II

When the young men call upon the girls a second time, however, they find them much changed and trying different techniques. Pinac, who is attracted by the grave Lillia Bianca, encounters her in a lighter mood, dancing energetically to merry songs and drinking wine; while Belleur, nervously prepared to woo Rosalura by impudent and saucy means, finds her frigidly veiled and reading a prayer book. Indeed, Nantolet's fair daughters "are compounded of free parts, . . . sometimes [they] are grave and silent and put on sadder dispositions, . . . sometimes too [their] lighter, airy, and [their] fiery mettles break out, and show themselves." Hence, neither wooer knows what to think or to make of the young women who know both codes of the chase, pursued and pursuing. To obey their father they have made a tender of their beauties to the travelled monsieur, "yet, two words to a bargain. He slights [them] as skittish things, and [they] shun him as curious." But to some extent the change in them is traceable to their sympathy with the lovesick Oriana; they care nothing for her Mirabel, but women can be as capricious as men.

Act III

Reasonable persuasions having failed to retrieve "the insolent licentious carriage of this outfacing fellow Mirabel," Oriana's brother De Gard enters into a scheme with Lugier to bring the wastrel to terms by making him jealous. Accordingly, De Gard disguises as a lord of Savoy, nephew of the duke, and pretends to be a suitor for the hand of Oriana. Mirabel is almost taken in. But a disgruntled servant, angered at being beaten by Lugier, gives the whole trick away, and De Gard and his sister must bear the jeers of the shameless Mirabel.

Nantolet's young daughters have also found their tutor's precepts about courtship wanting and reprove him for it. For his teachings, they expected husbands, they say, excellent husbands; they expected men of all ages and states to run mad over them and to inundate them with offers—a torrent of trim suitors. But the results have not been what they were led to look for.

> We follow'd your directions, we did rarely,
> We were stately, coy, demure, careless, light, giddy,
> And play'd at all points; this, you swore would carry. . . .
> We made love, and contemn'd love; now seemed holy,
> With such a reverend put-on reservation
> Which could not miss, according to your principles;
> Now gave more hope again; now close, now public,

—but to no avail. They are resolved, therefore, to follow their own devices henceforth. But before they can put their plans to practice the men use a few tricks of their own. Pretending not to care, but really indignant at having had his legs danced off and his self-esteem ruffled by Lillia Bianca's treatment at his last visit, Pinac introduces her to Mariana—really an English courtesan bribed for the purpose—whom he passes off as the lady he expects to marry. And in his turn Belleur pretends to be smarting still from the scorn Rosalura heaped upon him, threatens everyone who smiles in his presence with retaliation, and tries to frighten the girl out of her wits by threatening her:

> Till I receive a satisfaction
> Equal to the disgrace and scorn ye gave me
> You are a wretched woman; till thou woo'st me,
> And I scorn thee as much, . . . I will proclaim thee, . . .
> Because ye are a woman, ye are lawless,
> And out of compass of an honest anger.

It is all very discouraging to girls so young, but it rouses them to vengeance.

Act IV

Accordingly, Lillia Bianca and Rosalura enter into other stratagems devised by Lugier for their benefit. Bearing a willow garland and pretending to repent her levity, Lillia Bianca lures Pinac into a declaration of love and a resolution to forsake his pretended fiancée, Mariana; then she wittily unmasks him, by exposing the true character of Mariana and the deception to which she is a part. Similarly, Rosalura, with Lugier's aid, lures Belleur into upbraiding her into repentance. Then she laughs him to scorn again, and with her sister and four other women armed with knives, succeeds in turning the tables on the braggart and making a ridiculous ass and a coward out of him. Thus the girls are avenged upon their lovers and have the last laugh. At the same time they have betrayed the young men into declaring themselves in love.

Lugier's second trap for the wild-goose, however, succeeds no better than the first. Oriana pretends madness and appears to be at death's door. At first Mirabel is deeply touched; is it possible that his nature should be so damnable as to let her suffer? He begs the girl's pardon. But at the wrong moment Belleur puts in his appearance denouncing all women as cozening mad; and the tricky Mirabel, still feigning solicitude, asks to be left alone for a moment with Oriana. She recovers too quickly and confesses her stratagem too soon. Hence, the elusive wild-goose shames her publicly as "only mad for marriage" and disclaims her utterly unless she has a better trick than this.

Act V

Disillusioned with decent women, the three young men prepare to to travel once more and to follow their old rakish pursuits. But Lugier and De Gard have yet another trick to try, and this they play with the aid of La Castre, Mirabel's father. To Mirabel there comes a young man who presents himself as Fosse, factor to one Leverdure, an Italian merchant who is the friend of Mirabel. Fosse bears a commission, he says, from Alberto of Genoa, another merchant whose life Mirabel once saved near Bologna. Alberto is now dead, but on his deathbed in gratitude he has left Mirabel some jewels, commanding his sister, as she loved him and his peace to see the legacy delivered. This lady, young and handsome and well-attended, is now in Paris and desires to meet her brother's benefactor. The young rake scents another adventure.

But the Italian lady is Oriana, and her attendants, Nantolet's impatient daughters. Before he knows it, Mirabel is tricked into a declaration of love and a proposal of marriage, and the wild-goose at last is caught. So are Pinac and Belleur, who are somewhat less reluctant bridegrooms.

THE ISLAND PRINCESS

A Tragi-Comedy

(1619–1622)

DRAMATIS PERSONAE

QUISARA, the Island Princess, sister to the King of Tidore, an islet in the East Indies. "She is a princess, and she must be fair; that's the prerogative of being royal. . . . As I live, a rare wench; . . . she has a noble spirit. . . . This woman's cunning, but she's bloody, too; although she pulls her talons in, she's mischievous; form'd like the face of Heaven, clear and transparent."

The KING OF TIDORE, brother of the Island Princess, and prisoner of the Governor of Ternata. "I ne'er saw before a man of such a sufferance; . . . load him with irons, oppress him with contempts, which are the governor's commands, give him nothing, or so little to sustain life 'tis next nothing, they stir not him; he smiles upon his miseries, and bears 'em with such strength, as if his nature had been nursed up and fostered with calamities. . . . He gives no ill words, curses, nor repines not, blames nothing, hopes in nothing."

The GOVERNOR OF TERNATA, captor of the King of Tidore. "That Governor's a fierce knave, unfaithful as he is fierce, too; there's no trusting. . . . Has dangerous eyes, . . . a perilous thief and subtle, . . . and to that subtlety a heart of iron. . . . [He] had paid [them] all, but Fortune played the slut."

ARMUSIA, a noble, daring Portuguese, in love with the Island Princess. "Now as I live, a gentleman at all inches, so brave a mingled temper saw I never; . . . and no doubt, truly valiant, for he that dares come hither dares fight anywhere." He rescues the King, and eventually marries the Princess.

The KING OF BAKAM, "that lofty sir that speaks far more, and louder in his own commendations, than a cannon," } suitors to the Princess Quisara.

The KING OF SYANA, "that hopeful man, . . . a brave temper'd fellow, and more valiant,"

RUY DIAS, a valiant but dilatory captain of Portugal; "he stands in . . . good favor in the list too of privy wooers. . . . The captain's jealous—jealous of that he never durst deserve yet." ("I am glad to see this man's conversion; I was afraid fair Honor had been bedrid or beaten out o' th' island.")

PYNIERO, merry nephew to Ruy Dias and "our mad lieutenant. . . . He's a soldier sure, his rudeness sits so handsomely upon him, . . . a good blunt gentleman."

QUISANA, aunt to the princess, "the old hen, the brood-bird! . . . How like an inventory of lechery she looks!" } "my great lady's followers, her riddle-founders, and her fortune-tellers, her readers of her love lectures, her inflamers."

PANURA, waiting woman to the princess. ("Marriage and mouldy cheese will make [her] tamer,")

CHRISTOPHERO, PEDRO, } soldiers and friends of Pyniero.

SOZA, EMANUEL, } companions to Armusia, and his valiant followers.

A Captain of Ternata.
A Keeper of a Prison in Ternata.
Several Moors attending the Keeper.
A Guard at the Prison in Ternata.
A Guard at the Prison in Tidore.
Soldiers of Ternata, Bakam, Syana, and Portugal.
Citizens of both Ternata and Tidore, and their Wives.
Townsmen of Tidore.
The Princess' Train.
Singing Boys and other Attendants.
Setting: India [i.e., the East Indies] at some unspecified time.

"We are arriv'd among the blessed islands, where every wind that rises blows perfumes, and every breath of air is like an incense. The treasure of the sun dwells here; each tree, as if it envied the old Paradise, strives to bring forth immortal fruit."

Act I

While rowing for his recreation, the King of Tidore, a native princeling favorable to foreign traders, has been taken prisoner by his neighbor, the Governor of Ternata, who is fierce and untrustworthy. Quisara, the noble-minded sister of the captive King, now rules in his stead and has made every effort to secure her brother's freedom. But in vain. Her beauty has attracted many suitors—the haughty King of Bakam, the sprightly King of Syana, and even the Governor of Ternata, her mortal enemy and the captor of her brother. In addition to these native princes, there is a brave Portuguese commander, Ruy Dias, who because of his valor is in special favor with the Island Princess. At an audience which she grants her suitors, the princess cuts short their competitive wooing with a simple announcement: he who would marry her must win her with his worth. Her royal brother is a prisoner in Ternata; "therefore, that man that would be known [her] lover must be known his redeemer, and must bring him either alive or dead to [her] embraces." The wicked Governor promptly accepts her offer; the king is his prisoner and nothing would please him better than to exchange his captive for such a bride. But, to the great satisfaction of the assembled suitors, Quisara spurns the Governor's proposal and vows ere she would so basely win her brother's liberty, she would forget he was her brother. "By force he was taken; he that shall enjoy me, shall fetch him back by force, or never know me."

Particularly impressed by Quisara's rare and noble manner is one

Armusia, a new arrival among the Portuguese adventurers, and a daring man. Instantly in love, he determines to win the princess.

Act II

Disguised as merchants, Armusia and two valiant followers have no difficulty in landing on Ternata, setting fire to the prison, and, in the ensuing turmoil, rescuing the captive King, whose treatment at the hands of the Governor has been increasingly cruel and inhumane. But so confident has Quisara been that her favorite Ruy Dias would undertake the expedition and win her hand by his success, that she is unprepared for the success of another. While she is mildly taking the captain to task for his dilatoriness, news is received that the King has returned and the princess finds herself betrayed by fortune. Armusia claims his reward, and the grateful King is ready to bestow it upon him. But the princess hesitates to keep her word, and Ruy Dias bids her "despair not; something shall be done yet, and suddenly and wisely." But he "looks as though he were sick o' the worms."

Act III

Hence, inconsiderate of the fact that Armusia has done a glorious deed which deserves reward, and mindful only of his own disappointment, Ruy Dias approaches his nephew Pyniero and suggests that he put Armusia out of the way. Pyniero's advancement may be dependent upon Ruy Dias, but the young lieutenant is an honest man and no mere uncle's agent. To gain time, he insists upon hearing from Quisara's own mouth her wish that violence be done. Ruy Dias gives him a letter to the princess, and, by flattering Quisana, the aunt, and Panura, her waiting woman, Pyniero gains access to Quisara. He finds her ready to commission such an act as Ruy Dias has suggested, and even more cunning and bloodthirsty than he feared. Quisara has no scruples about how she can be released from her promise, and Pyniero, therefore, perceives that he must pretend to undertake the task, bearing up the hopes of both the princess and his uncle, lest some bloody slave perform indeed the crime they wish for.

Meanwhile, Armusia is no longer content to be put off and denied the prize he merited. Encouraged by his followers, he appeals to the King and receives assurance—a king's word—that he shall have the princess as she promised. But he is still almost in despair, when the appearance of Panura the princess' waiting woman suggests a stratagem to him. By flattery and a bribe, he gets Panura to admit him to the princess' bedchamber, and there confronts her, not with violence, but only to plead his case against her perfidy and fierce cruelty. The princess, however, is expecting Ruy Dias, and the rivals soon are facing each other. Dias' jealousy and blustering possessiveness are in such marked contrast to the modest, respectful behavior of Armusia, that the princess denounces Dias as a coward and a fool, "being nothing but a sound, a shape, the mere sign of a soldier—of a lover. . . . I scorn thee, and condemn thee."

Act IV

Hence, Ruy Dias must now re-establish himself in his lady's favor, and to do so he resolves to challenge Armusia to a duel—much to the relief of his nephew Pyniero. A duel is more becoming to a gentleman; "to kill men scurvily, 'tis such a dogtrick, such a ratcatcher's occupation." At the same time Quisara has had a change of heart; she too calls Pyniero aside and begs him not to carry out her earlier orders to attempt the life of Armusia. When the duel is fought, however—on ground selected by Ruy Dias behind the palace where the princess will surely see it—Armusia participates reluctantly. But once in, he bears himself manfully, and Ruy Dias is defeated and falls. At this accident Quisara, who has indeed been watching, stops the fight. And by now she is convinced of Armusia's noble nature, and arranges to meet him in the garden an hour hence.

In the meanwhile, the wicked Governor of Ternata has been laying the foundations for ambitious mischief and revenge. Disguised as a holy Moorish priest, he has visited the King of Tidore and sown in his mind evil suspicions that these smooth-faced Portuguese have only come to Tidore to exploit the island and to ruin it. Specifically, he warns the King against Armusia, who aspires to marry the princess, and he asks what reverence their gods shall have when a foreigner is on the throne, and what justice the miserable people can expect? Then, having succeeded with the King, the seeming holy man talks with Quisara.

Hence, when the princess meets her lover as appointed, King and priest are in hiding where they can overhear the interview. Quisara offers to fulfill her promise if Armusia will but change his religion, and be of one belief with her. But, as the priest knew beforehand, this Armusia steadfastly refuses to do; he'll be hanged first. Casting aside all restraint, Armusia denounces both the princess and all she worships, and thus convinces the King of the truth of his suspicions. But the scene only makes certain for Quisara that Armusia is for her the proper husband: "Oh how I love this man, how truly honor him!"

Act V

As a consequence of his zealous outburst, Armusia is thrown into prison. The noble-minded King reproaches himself with ingratitude toward his manly rescuer, but the priest at his side prevents any generous impulse to release him. Quisara, on the other hand, now completely in love, has grown so frantic in the stranger's behalf that she must be bound for her own preservation. When, at last, tortures are prepared for Armusia, the princess offers to share them with him, "a virgin won by [his] fair constancy, and glorying that she is won so." But before the fire can be prepared, Captain Ruy Dias thoroughly redeems his honor by leading a rescue party, having vowed that he would "not leave a stone here—no, not the memory here stood a city—unless Armusia be deliver'd fairly." The impious Governor of Ternata is exposed, sent to prison, and deprived of his throne (which he had usurped anyway); the King of Tidore is reconciled with Armusia; and in token of renewed friendship, he bestows upon him the hand of the Island Princess.

RULE A WIFE AND HAVE A WIFE

A COMEDY

(1624)

DRAMATIS PERSONAE

DONNA MARGARITA, "the orient heiress, *the* Margarita, sir. . . . How happy were that man could catch this wench up and live at ease! She's fair and young, and wealthy, infinite wealthy, and as gracious too in all her entertainments, as men report. . . . But she is proud, . . . that I know for certain, and that comes seldom without wantonness. He that shall marry her must have a rare hand. . . . 'Tis a good lady, and a wise young lady, . . . and virtuous enough, too, I warrant ye. . . . [But] she fears her youth will not hold out. . . . They say, too, she has a greedy eye that must be fed with more than one man's meat. . . . [Hence she seeks] a husband of an easy faith, a fool, made by her wealth and moulded to her pleasure, . . . a shadow, an umbrella, to keep the scorching world's opinion from [her] fair credit."

DON LEON, who seems to "make the goodliest shadow for iniquity! . . . He's a man at all points, a likely man! . . . He is made as strong as brass, is of brave years, too, and doughty of complexion, . . . yes, and a soldier; as gentle as you would wish him; a good fellow, wears good clothes. . . . He will not quarrel with a dog that bites him; let him be drunk or sober, he's one silence." ("He cannot be *all* fool. . . . Sure they dare fight in fire that conquer women.")

ALTEA, attendant upon Donna Margarita and Don Leon's "best sister, for she proved so, . . . when she deceived [her mistress] with a loving husband."

Three Old Ladies who advise Margarita. "She does well and wisely to ask the counsel of the ancient'st; . . . [their] years have run through many things she knows not."

The DUKE OF MEDINA; "great men are fools sometimes as well as wretches, . . . and find what 'tis to play the fool in vice."

Attendants upon the Duke.

LORENZO, a servant in Margarita's household.

ESTIFANIA, attendant upon Donna Margarita, and "the prettiest rogue that e'er you looked upon, the loving'st thief! . . . You cannot find in all this kingdom, if you had need of cozening, . . . a woman that can cozen you so neatly. . . . The rogue is witty." This merry wench has "firked a living from men these five years."

MICHAEL PEREZ, the conceited copper captain, "a man of copper, a kind of candle-stick, . . . [who loves] a sweet young wench. . . . Go, silly fool! Thou may'st be a good soldier in open field, but for our private service thou art an ass. . . . [Yet] the most kind man and the ablest also to give a wife content. He's sound as old wine." (Has he "so long studied the art of this sex and read the warnings to young gentlemen?")

CACAFOGO, "an usuring jeweller's son," and a fat man. "Another pumpion; let him loose for luck sake. . . . This rascal will make rare sport! How the ladies will laugh him! . . . If ye have no money, ye're an ass."

DONNA CLARA, "a pretty gentlewoman," companion to Estifania.

JUAN DE CASTRO, a colonel,
SANCHIO,   officers in the army.
ALONZO,

A Servant to Michael Perez.

A Coachman, an Old Woman, a Maid, a Boy, Servants, and Attendants.

Setting: Valladolid and a country house near it, at some unspecified time.

> *"I'd rather guide a ship imperial*
> *Alone, and in a storm, than rule one woman."*

Act I

It is rumored about Valladolid that the Donna Margarita, who is young, fair, and infinitely wealthy, desires to marry. Gossip adds that she is proud, probably wanton, and hard to control. But in spite of possible risks, there are many suitors who adore her—great men, princes, and princes' fellows—and who would gladly be her spouse. Indeed, the word is that she has bought a brave house in town and asked counsel of several old and experienced ladies in the selection of a husband.

At the same time Margarita's servant, Estifania, is also seeking a husband and capably selecting him without advice from anyone. Accompanied only by Donna Clara, who has an errand to Colonel Juan de Castro, an officer about to depart for the wars, Estifania attracts the attention of a conceited copper captain, Michael Perez. She modestly evades his advances by posing as "some young unmanaged thing," but at the

same time leads him on by suggesting that she is not averse to his addresses if he will let his servant follow her to learn where she lives. In
spite of the fact that Michael Perez poses as an unsusceptible lady-tamer
who boastfully lectures his friends on how to handle women, and in
spite of warnings that he may be caught, the captain calls on Estifania.
He is so impressed by the goodly house in which she dwells, the rich-
ness of its furnishings, and the lady's inclination to marriage and to him,
that he marries her forthwith, pretending to be possessed of "jewels,
chains, such as the war has given [him]," and a thousand ducats in
ready gold.

Act II

Meanwhile, Donna Margarita, in conference with her experienced
advisers, makes clear the conditions prompting her decision to marry.
She wishes liberty for her amorous proclivities; hence, she must marry
a husband who is a man of easy faith and a fool. At first there is some
doubt that such a man can be found, but Altea, Margarita's companion,
has discovered one, "a right one and a perfect." He is as lusty, as handsome, as docile, as stupid, as simple, and as innocent as anyone could
wish. "He will not quarrel with a dog that bites him; let him be drunk
or sober, he's one silence." Accordingly, the maid of honor presents her
lady with Don Leon, her brother, who has been coached in his role by
his sister and has already won such a reputation for simplicity that he
has been rejected by Colonel de Castro for even an ensign's commission,
he is so unsuitable for military service. Don Leon certainly seems a
perfect milksop. He professes complete subservience to the lady, answers
satisfactorily all of her questions, meets all of her conditions, and is at
last accepted by Margarita, who resolves to move to the city forthwith and
occupy her new house.

Then it is that Estifania must use her wits or lose her husband. To
catch Michael Perez she has posed as the owner of Margarita's house.
Now, on Margarita's arrival, Estifania pretends that her mistress is a
poor kinswoman who wants to borrow the fine house in order to play
upon her suitor the same trick that she has played upon Perez. Unsuspecting, but by no means willing, Michael Perez agrees to move to a poor-
house for a few days until the stratagem shall succeed.

Act III

By marriage to Don Leon, Margarita has got what she desired, "a
shadow, an umbrella, to keep the scorching world's opinion from [her]
fair credit," and she soon prepares to receive her admirers at her town

house, and to give feasts and banquets, revels and masques. But in the presence of her guests, including the Duke of Medina, Don Leon surprisingly asserts his authority over his wife. Vexed to the soul, Margarita and the Duke know that they must resort to stratagems if they are to deceive Don Leon and carry on the intrigue they have begun.

Meanwhile, Michael Perez is most uncomfortable in the hovel to which he has moved. His wife disappears, taking all of his possessions with her; and the poor man, who has long studied the arts of women and warned young gentlemen of them, learns from the neighbors and from Margarita herself that Estifania has always been a wild young girl, poor, and of scant fame.

Act IV

The Duke's first stratagem to get Margarita's bridegroom out of the way is to give Don Leon a commission to command a troop of horse. But instead of going alone to the wars, Don Leon begins to pack up plate, jewels, hangings, furniture—everything that is portable—and proposes to take his bride with him to camp. Margarita's hypocritical weeping at their possible parting now changes to protests, excuses, and wiles in which the Duke seconds her. Margarita even supports Michael Perez's claims to her house, but the pretense fails to dissuade her husband from his desire to travel. At last there is no other way but to inform Don Leon that he has no command, and that the whole was a trick to try his jealousy.

Meanwhile, Estifania, too, has resorted to stratagems, but to retain her foolish husband, not to get rid of him. She confesses to Michael Perez that she has deceived him about the house; the chains with which he wooed her have also turned out to be mere pinchbeck—that is why Perez is called the "copper captain." Each has cozened the other, and the couple quarrel violently and separate. But, meeting on the street with Cacafogo, the fat usuring jeweller's son, Estifania pretends to be acting for the Lady Margarita and borrows from him a thousand ducats on some of the worthless glass and copper stuff.

Act V

If, after the events of Act IV, the Donna Margarita seems conformable to her husband's will, her former associates do not recognize her reformation. But the lady joins her husband in a practical joke that convinces them. Cacafogo, the cheated usurer, comes to protest about the jewels Estifania has passed off on him. The Duke of Medina pretends to be wounded in a duel before Margarita's door that he may be given first aid in her house and have access to the lady. Husband and wife entertain both suitors with hopes. Cacafogo is taken to the cellar and made drunk. Then the Duke is entertained by the lady, frightened by the carousing in the cellar, which he is made to believe is the noise of devils, accepts Margarita's rebukes for his attempts upon her honesty, and her assurances of devotion to her husband, and is reconciled to Don Leon, granting him a true commission as captain.

Estifania, too, at last wins her husband's love as completely. Irreconcilable over the cheat she has practiced on him, Michael Perez threatens his wife's life. But she pulls a pistol on the coward, and when he has become more reasonable, she pacifies him with the thousand ducats she has cheated Cacafogo out of. The drunken usurer is let out to rail or hang himself as he chooses.

----◆----

JOHN FLETCHER
(1579–1625)
AND
WILLIAM SHAKESPEARE
(1564–1616)

BIOGRAPHY. For a biography of Fletcher, see above, p. 322.

"Gentle Shakespeare," the greatest of the Elizabethan dramatists, was born of good middle-class stock in Stratford-upon-Avon in April, 1564. His dramatic career began about 1590; by 1592 he had made his mark sufficiently in his profession of actor and playmaker to arouse the resentment of one of the "University Wits." In 1594 he became a sharer in the Lord Chamberlain's Men, one of the best and most stable of acting troupes. In 1598 he was mentioned by Francis Meres in *Palladis Tamia* as among the best in both comedy and tragedy for the stage, commended for his "fine-filed phrase," and praised for his lyric poetry, especially for "his sugared sonnets among his private friends."

To the Chamberlain's company, which became the King's men at the coming of the Stuart dynasty, Shakespeare devoted his talents until 1611 or 1612 when he retired. For them he wrote the whole or the major part of thirty-seven plays for production in the famous Globe Theatre (built in 1599), or at Blackfriars (acquired by the company as a winter house in 1608). He died in 1616 and was buried in the chancel of the Church of the Holy Trinity in Stratford.

CRITICAL COMMENT. *The Two Noble Kinsmen,* if indeed Shakespeare had a hand in it, belongs to the end of his career, and like *Henry VIII* represents the collaboration of an older playwright with one whose career had only begun. The play is a "romance" in the manner of Fletcher, the characterization is rather poorer than what one would expect of Shakespeare, but there are many passages which stylistically suggest the master. While not a great play, *The Two Noble Kinsmen* has some attractions and several spectacular scenes, like that of the interrupted wedding (I, i), that of the duel (III, vi), and that at the altars (V, i).

The Two Noble Kinsmen was adapted to the Restoration stage by Sir William Davenant as *The Rivals* (1664).

SOURCE. The main plot of the play is a dramatization of Chaucer's *Knight's Tale,* condensed and altered, notably by the addition of the parallel underplot of the jailer's daughter and her love for Palamon. Of this there is no trace in Chaucer. *The Knight's Tale* had already served twice as a source for drama —as early as 1566 when a play on the story by Richard Edwards was produced before the Queen at Christchurch, Oxford, and in 1594 when another play on the theme is mentioned in Henslowe's *Diary*. Both are lost, but it is unlikely that either was known to Fletcher or Shakespeare.

BIBLIOGRAPHY

Early editions: 1634; 1679 [Second Beaumont and Fletcher Folio].
Modern editions: Facs. J. S. Farmer (TFT, 1910); ed. Harold Littledale (New Shakespeare Society, 1876); C. H. Herford (TD, 1897); C. F. Tucker Brooke (*Shakespeare Apocrypha,* 1908); G. L. Kittredge (*The Complete Works of Shakespeare,* 1936).

THE TWO NOBLE KINSMEN
(1613–1616)

DRAMATIS PERSONAE

PALAMON, "what a bold gravity, and yet inviting, has this brown, manly face! . . . His brow is grav'd and seems to bury what it frowns on; . . . melancholy becomes him nobly. . . . He has a tongue will tame tempests and make the wild rocks wanton," the two noble kinsmen, nephews of King Creon of Thebes, and close friends; "it is a holiday to look on them. Lord, the diff'rence of men!

ARCITE, "I have not seen since Hercules, a man of tougher sinews. . . . If wise Nature, with all her best endowments, . . . were here a mortal woman and had in her the coy denials of young maids, yet doubtless she would run mad for this man. What an eye, of what a fiery sparkle and quick sweetness, has this young prince! . . . What a brow, of what a spacious majesty, he carries! . . . Arcite is gently visag'd; yet his eye is like an engine bent, or a sharp weapon in a soft sheath; mercy and manly courage are bedfellows in his visage," . . . Can these two live, and have the agony of love about 'em and not kill one another?"

THESEUS, Duke of Athens, whose "fame knolls in the ear o' th' world, . . . [whose] first thought is more than others' labored meditance, [and whose] premeditating more than their actions," PIRITHOUS, an Athenian general, kinsmen and friend of Duke Theseus, and "half his own heart. . . . How his longing follows his friend!"

"They two have cabin'd in many as dangerous as poor a corner, peril and want contending; they have skiff'd torrents whose roaring tyranny and power i' th' least of these was dreadful; and they have fought out together where Death's self was lodg'd; yet Fate hath brought them off. Their knot of love tied, weav'd, entangled, with so true, so long, and with a finger of so deep a cunning, may be outworn, never undone."

HIPPOLYTA, bride to Theseus, "most dreaded Amazonian . . . [and] soldieress that equally can . . . poise sternness with pity."

EMILIA, sister of Hippolyta, beloved of both Palamon and Arcite. "Behold and wonder! By Heaven she is a goddess, . . . fresher than May, sweeter than her gold buttons on the boughs or all th' enamel'd knacks o' th' mead or garden. . . . She is all the beauty extant, . . . the victor's meed, the price and garland to crown the questant's title."

The JAILER'S DAUGHTER, who loves Palamon "beyond love and beyond reason, or wit, or safety," and goes mad for love. "To marry him is hopeless, to be his whore is witless. . . . That intemp'rate surfeit of her eye hath distemper'd the other senses. . . . It is a falsehood she is in, which is with falsehoods to be combated."

Three Queens in Black, "whose sovereigns fell before the wrath of cruel Creon; [and] who endure the beaks of ravens, talons of the kites, and pecks of crows in the foul fields of Thebes. . . . For [their] crowned heads [they] have no roof save this, which is the lion's and the bear's, and vault to every thing! . . . [They] come unseasonably; but when could grief cull forth, as unpang'd judgment can, fitt'st time for best solicitation?" ("This world's a city full of straying streets, and Death's the market place, where each one meets.")

ARTESIUS, an Athenian captain, attendant upon Duke Theseus.

VALERIUS, a Theban nobleman at the court of King Creon.

Six Knights, "all the sons of honor," to accompany Palamon and Arcite and fight in their cause.

A Waiting Woman, attending Emilia.

JAILER to Palamon and Arcite, also called KEEPER. "Alas! the prison [he] keep[s], though it be for great ones, yet they seldom come; before one salmon, you shall take a number of minnows. [He is] given out to be better lin'd than it can appear to [him] report is a true speaker."

A Brother of the Jailer's.

Two Friends of the Jailer's.

A Wooer of the Jailer's Daughter.

A Doctor who administers to the Jailer's Daughter.

HYMEN, god of marriage,
Nymphs, with wheaten garlands and wheaten chaplets on their heads,
A Boy to sing and strew flowers,

} characters in a marriage masque, honoring Theseus and Hippolyta.

MASTER GERROLD, "the dainty domine, the schoolmaster, . . . our thing of learning, . . . the rectifier of all, by the title pedagogus, that let[s] fall the birch upon the breeches of the small ones and humble[s] with a ferula the tall ones." He presents the entertainment before the court. "He's excellent i' th' woods; bring him to th' plains, his learning makes no cry."

Four Countrymen as morris dancers,
A Countryman as the bavian [i.e., baboon]. "My
    friend, carry your tail without offense or scandal
    to the ladies; and be sure you tumble with audac-
    ity and manhood; and when you bark, do it with
    judgment,")
Five Wenches (Friz, Maudline, little Luce, bounc-
    ing Barbary, and freckled Nell),
Timothy, a taborer,

"a few of those collected here that ruder tongues distinguish 'villager' "; they provide May-day entertainment in the forest for Duke Theseus and his court.

A Herald, a Gentleman, an Executioner, a Guard, Messengers, Servants, Train, and Attendants.

Setting: Athens, Thebes, and their neighborhoods, in the mythical past.

"Never Fortune
Did play a subtler game. The conquer'd triumphs,
The victor has the loss, yet in the passage
The gods have been most equal."

Act I

Three queens "in black, with veils stained, [and] with imperial crowns," interrupt the marriage ceremonies of Duke Theseus of Athens and his Amazonian bride, Hippolyta. One falls at the feet of Theseus, another before Hippolyta, and the third before Emilia, sister of the bride, to plead for aid against "the wrath of cruel Creon," King of Thebes, against whom their husbands had died fighting. Now the tyrant will not permit the burning of their bodies, but leaves them unburied to "endure the beaks of ravens, talons of kites, and pecks of crows in the foul fields of Thebes." Moved at last by the pleas of the mourners, as well as by the added entreaties of his wife and sister-in-law, Duke Theseus undertakes the widows' cause and hastens to Thebes with his army. In the battle Creon is defeated, and the queens honor their dead lords with full funeral ceremony. At the same time the Athenians take prisoner Palamon and Arcite, King Creon's nephews, who have no illusions about their uncle, but who have been wounded fighting for their native land. Duke Theseus has seen them in the battle "like to a pair of lions smear'd with prey, make lanes in troops aghast," and in admiration for their valor he orders for them the best medical care. Then he hastens back to Athens and his bride.

Act II

In prison the young men astonish their Jailer and his Daughter by "making misery their mirth and affliction a toy to jest at. . . . They eat well, look merrily, discourse of many things, but nothing of their own restraint and disasters." The reason is that the two are self-sufficient; their friendship has made them "an endless mine to one another; [they] are one another's wife, even begetting new births of love; [they] are father, friends, acquaintance. . . . Is there record of any two that lov'd better than [they] do? . . . [And they] do not think it possible [their] friendship should ever leave [them]."

But one day as they look out of their prison window, they see the Princess Emilia gathering flowers in the garden. Both young men fall in love with her, and "friendship, blood, and all the ties between [them]" are turned to bitter hate in their rivalry. As they quarrel over which saw Emilia first and upbraid each other with treachery and filching affection from his rival, Arcite is released from prison, but is banished from the kingdom. But instead of returning to Thebes, the young warrior disguises himself, learns from a group of countrymen that games are being held before the duke, and joins the company as a wrestler in hope of catching a glimpse of Emilia. By his athletic prowess, Arcite wins a garland, attracts the attention of the royal party, and not only sees Emilia face to face, but also kisses her hand and is appointed her attendant "to do observance to flow'ry May, in Dian's wood."

Meanwhile, and entirely unknown to the young man, the Jailer's romantic Daughter has fallen in love with Palamon. "To marry him is hopeless; to be his whore is witless"; the girl therefore resolves to risk everything pertaining to herself and to her father and to permit him to escape from prison.

Act III

From the May games Arcite separates himself to meditate upon his good fortune in enjoying Emilia's favor and upon the wretchedness of his friend and fellow captive, when Palamon, still in shackles, emerges from the wood. He has been released by the Jailer's Daughter. But Palamon's bitterness has by no means abated. From his cousin he now demands food to restore his strength, files to free him from his gyves, and a sword with which to fight and to make good his claim to Emilia. All these things Arcite chivalrously supplies, and as the friends eat and drink together, they recall the wenches they have known in former days, and in wine pledge them one after another. But it is only "strained mirth"; their thoughts and their sighs are all for Emilia, and the two prepare to fight to the death to sustain their claims to the Amazonian princess.

Meanwhile, the Jailer's Daughter has been forgotten. She seeks Palamon at the place appointed for their meeting and does not find him. Wolves howl, crickets chirp, and the screech owl calls in the dawn; the girl is nearly dead with fear and cold, and is certain that her Palamon has been killed by wild beasts. The poor wench goes mad, falls in with a May-day company of morris dancers, and participates in a May-day entertainment they offer before the duke, his duchess, and their trains.

In the interim, Palamon and Arcite have harnessed one another in armor stolen from the duke's armory. But as they begin their duel, hunting horns are heard, and the duke's party approaches. It is too late, dishonorable, and also useless to hide—their lives are forfeit anyway—and the two knights continue their combat until they are discovered. Out of hand, Theseus condemns them both for fighting without permission, but their boldness in identifying themselves and in explaining their quarrel wins them many admirers in the duke's train. His bride, Hippolyta, Emilia herself, and his friend Pirithous all plead for the lives of the young princes. But Emilia's substitute suggestion that they be punished by banishment is no solution; "can these two live and have the agony of love about 'em and not kill one another?" The young men scorn to take an oath never to fight over the girl again, even if their suits are vain. They cannot both have her. Emilia cannot choose between them. But she does agree, if one is dead to accept the other as a husband. Accordingly, Duke Theseus appoints a day when the two, each accompanied by three fair knights, shall appear again in the lists in which he'll build a pyramid,

> *and whether,*
> *Before us that are here, can force his cousin*
> *By fair and knightly strength to touch the pillar,*
> *He shall enjoy her; the other lose his head,*
> *And all his friends!*

Act IV

To his surprise, the Jailer goes unpunished for the escape of Palamon; indeed, in gratitude the former prisoner has given a large sum of money toward the Daughter's marriage portion. But, alas, the girl is mad; "she is continually in a harmless distemper, sleeps little, . . . dreaming of another world," and singing snatches of songs. "What broken piece of matter soe'er she's about, the name Palamon lards it, that she farces ev'ry business withal, fits it to every question." Hence, the doctor who attends her suggests to the young man who has been her wooer that perhaps a cure can be effected if he will but take the name of Palamon, make love to her, sing her such songs as Palamon sang in prison, eat and drink with her, and encourage her friends to talk to her of Palamon. "It is a falsehood she is in, which is with falsehoods to be combated."

Emilia, meanwhile, awaits the day of combat with great perturbation. She gazes first upon the portrait of one of the young lovers and then upon the other. She cannot decide between them; "what a mere child is fancy, that, having two fair gauds of equal sweetness, cannot distinguish, but must cry for both!" While she is thus deep in her dilemma, word comes that the knights have arrived.

Act V

Before the tournament the two friends Palamon and Arcite embrace and take a last farewell of one another, and each of the principals in the triangle says his prayers to an appropriate deity. Arcite and his followers worship at the altar of Mars and receive a token of his approval. Palamon and his knights kneel at the altar of Venus, and are blessed with a sign of her pleasure. Emilia, all in white, humbles herself at the altar of Diana, praying that the prince who loves her best and has the truest title to her may be successful. She too receives a gracious sign from the goddess.

But from the contest itself Emilia stays away; she cannot bear to watch. In the fight Palamon at first is successful, only to fail in the end. Arcite is proclaimed victor and brought to the lady for his reward, while Palamon the loser prepares for his execution. As he mounts the scaffold he hears the welcome news that the Jailer's Daughter who gave him freedom has fully recovered and is to be married shortly. He and all of his knights add their purses to her marriage portion. But before the headsman can lift his axe, Pirithous rushes in with word that Arcite has been thrown from his horse—the black steed that Emilia first gave him—and killed when the spirited animal fell on him. With his last breath, Arcite confers the matchless Emilia upon his friend, who from the prison window really had seen the girl first and even then proclaimed his love for her. Thus, the favors of all three of the deities to whom the trio paid their homage are sustained.

JOHN FLETCHER

(1579–1625)

AND

PHILIP MASSINGER

(1583–1640)

BIOGRAPHY. For a biography of John Fletcher, see above, p. 322.

Philip Massinger was born in Salisbury, the son of a confidential servant of the second Earl of Pembroke. He was educated at St. Alban Hall, Oxford, but left the university without a degree in 1606. While at Oxford, according to Anthony à Wood, he "applied his mind more to poetry and romances than to logic and philosophy." His dramatic career began about 1613 when he was in the employ of Henslowe, and from that time until the close of his life he wrote about three dozen plays, mostly in collaboration—with Field, Daborne, Tourneur, Dekker, and Fletcher. His best work belongs to the last years of the reign of James and to that of Charles. He died in 1640 and was buried in St. Savior's.

CRITICAL COMMENT. "I could read the *Beggars' Bush* from morning to night," said Coleridge in *Table Talk* (February 17, 1833). "How sylvan and sunshiny it is!" The play has frequently been compared with *As You Like It,* and the similarity of its serious-minded merchant hero to Antonio in *The Merchant of Venice* is inescapable. The play as a whole is an engaging romance of tyrants, honest outlaws living a vagabond life, a glorified merchant prince, separated lovers, intrigues amorous and political, regained thrones, and united dukedoms.

Apparently the play was popular on the stage. Under the title of *The Lame Commonwealth* the farcical first scene of Act II was played during the Puritan Commonwealth, and the complete comedy was soon revived on the Restoration stage. An adaptation called *The Royal Merchant, or Beggars' Bush* by H. N., probably Henry Norris the comedian, was produced in 1705; an opera called *The Royal Merchant* by Thomas Hull was produced in 1768; and *The Merchant of Bruges, or Beggars' Bush* by Douglas Kinnaird was put on in 1815 with Edmund Kean as Florez.

SOURCE. No source is known for *Beggars' Bush,* though such books as Dekker's *Lanthorne and Candlelight* (1608) may have contributed some of the thieves' cant.

BIBLIOGRAPHY

Early editions: 1647 [First Beaumont and Fletcher Folio]; 1661 [quarto]; 1679 [Second Beaumont and Fletcher Folio].

BEGGARS' BUSH

A COMEDY

(1615–1622)

DRAMATIS PERSONAE

BERTHA, called GERTRUDE, daughter to the Duke of Brabant and heiress to the title, who passes as the daughter of Burgomaster Van Dunck and is "the dainty black-ey'd belle" beloved of Goswin [Florez]. "She is such a wonder, such a mirror for beauty and fair virtue Europe has not. . . . Her mind is ten times sweeter, ten times nobler, and but to hear her speak, a Paradise."

VAN DUNCK, "noble Burgomaster" and merchant of Bruges, reputed father of Gertrude [Bertha, heiress of Brabant] and "a true statesman. . . . Give me my bottle, and set down the drum. . . . Are we not in Bruges? Under the rose here?"

MARGARET, wife to Van Dunck.

FLOREZ, rightful Earl of Flanders, but known only as GOSWIN, "the young spruce merchant in Bruges," in love with Gertrude, the burgomaster's daughter. "He bears himself with such a confidence as if he were the master of the sea. . . . He's young, and rich, at least thus far reputed so, that since he liv'd in Bruges, there was never brought to harbor so rich a bottom, but his bill would pass unquestion'd for her lading. . . . To doubt him would be held an injury or rather malice with the best that traffic. . . . For his outward habit, 'tis suitable to his present course of life; his table furnish'd well, but not with dainties that please the appetite only for their rareness or their dear price; nor given to wine or women, . . . and so loves his state he will not hazard it at play. . . . [But] when desert or reason leads him to be liberal, his noble mind and ready hand contend which shall add most to his free courtesies. . . . At some times we fear he will be bankrupt; he does stretch tenter his credit so, embraces all, and to't, the winds have been contrary long."

WOLFORT, "usurping Earl of Flanders, . . . a rank traitor, as ever breath'd, . . . a prince in nothing but [his] princely lusts and boundless rapines." ("And still, would Wolfort were an honest man; under the rose, I speak it.")

GERRARD, stepfather to Florez, Earl of Flanders, disguised as CLAUSE and chosen king of the beggars and "Monarch o' th' Maunders. . . . The man with the grave beard."

JACQUELINE, daughter to Gerrard and beloved of Hubert, living among the beggars under the name of MINCHE.

HEMPSKIRKE, a "roaring rascal [and a] huffing sir"; favorite of Wolfort and one of his captains, pretended uncle to Gertrude [Bertha].

HUBERT, "honest, noble Hubert," a lord of Flanders, "no man more lov'd, nor more deserv'd it, being the only man that durst be honest in this court." He is the friend of Gerrard and the lover of Jacqueline, Gerrard's daughter, and he joins Clause's band disguised as a huntsman.

VAN LOCK,
Four Other Merchants,} of Bruges to whom Goswin is in debt.

MISTRESS FRANCES, a frow, daughter to Vanlock the merchant. "She dreams apace; . . . that's but a drowsy fortune."

HERMAN, a courtier,⎫
A Merchant,   ⎬ inhabitants of Flanders.

HIGGEN, "an excellent orator; . . . give him leave
   to spit, the fine, well-spoken Higgen,"
PRIGG, an upright man; "will ye see any feats of
   activity, some sleight of hand, legerdemain?" ⎫ beggars, and "princes of the ragged
FERRET,   ⎬ regiment."
SNAP; he stammers. (" 'Slid, they did all speak
   plain ev'n now, methought!")

LORD ARNOLD of Benthuisin, alias GINKES, a deaf and dumb man, ⎫ lords of Flanders
LORD COSTIN, alias COZEN,   ⎬ disguised as beggars
                                                               ⎭ in Clause's band.

A Beggar Boy who sings a song.

Boors, or country yokels, "you most abominable stinking rascals, you turnip-eating
   rogues."

Young Merchants and others, guests at Goswin's wedding.

A Sailor.

A Guard.

Servants and Attendants.

Setting: Flanders—Bruges and the country near it—at some unspecified time.

*"A civil habit oft covers a good man, and you may meet in
person of a merchant with a soul as resolute and free and all
ways worthy as else in any file of mankind."*

Act I

Many years ago, when Florez, the rightful heir to the earldom of
Flanders, was but a child, negotiations were begun about a match between the infant daughter of the Duke of Brabant, heiress to the crown,
and the young Earl of Flanders. During the negotiations, however, the
little princess was kidnapped from court—by the treachery of the men
of Flanders, it was charged—and instead of amity between the two prin-
cipalities, war broke out. As a result of seven years of fighting, Brabant
was defeated and ruined, but an even greater calamity befell Flanders.
Wolfort, the original ambassador to arrange the marriage between the
heirs of the two countries and later an able Flemish general in the war,
took advantage of his popularity with the army to seize complete
power. In an effort to purge away all persons loyal to the crown, the
usurper put many men to death, and, hence, to save the young prince his
stepfather Gerrard fled with the boy. Nothing has been heard of them in

Flanders since. Loyal feeling, however, is not dead, and as the play opens, Hubert, "the only man that durst be honest in this court," has just been apprehended by Wolfort's agents as he was attempting to escape to Bruges, a city which still holds out against the usurper. Besides loyalty to the rightful heir, Hubert has a personal reason for his attempted flight. He had been engaged to Jacqueline, the daughter of Gerrard who accompanied her father into exile, and Hubert is still hopeful of finding her. Indeed, so eloquent and outspoken is he to Wolfort, that he seems to melt the heart of the tyrant, who promises to resign what he has usurped and to send with Hubert his captain Hempskirke to assist him in finding out his loyal friends.

At the same time there lives in Bruges a prosperous young merchant named Goswin, who is honored and respected for his mercantile ventures and his generosity to his fellow citizens. He is really Florez, the missing heir to the Flanders earldom, but he is ignorant of the fact. Indeed, in spite of his wide business acquaintanceship, Goswin is a man apart with few intimates. An old beggar named Clause, however, who is really Gerrard in disguise, has been recipient of Goswin's bounty for many years and now asks a favor of his master. On the morrow the beggars of Bruges are electing a new king. If Goswin will but walk out to Beggars' Bush and, if asked by the fellows assembled there which of them he likes best, point out Clause, the old fellow believes it will give him pre-eminence of candidacy over the rest. The young man agrees to do so.

Act II

On the morrow Goswin's recommendation secures for Clause the kingship of the beggars, as he had hoped, and during the celebration Hubert and Hempskirke pass along the road. Among the beggars Hubert thinks he recognizes Jacqueline, but she eludes him, and his inquiry about her yields information from the beggars which is as contradictory and confusing as it is intended to be. Also, at the house of Burgomaster Van Dunck, Hubert and Hempskirke fare no better. Van Dunck is unquestionably loyal to the old cause and a hater of Wolfort —under the rose of course. He drinks healths, but he is also more than a little contemptuous of Hempskirke, who in seven years has not found leisure to visit his niece, a beautiful girl named Gertrude whom Van Dunck is bringing up as if she were his own daughter. She is really Bertha, the kidnapped heiress of Brabant, but only Hempskirke knows it. Relations between uncle and guardian are not improved by Hempskirke's objections to a merchant as a suitor for the girl, especially when he has not troubled to meet the young man. The suitor is Goswin, who soon appears and bears up nobly under the insults of Hempskirke and is encouraged by the girl herself and by the tipsy Van Dunck. When Hempskirke in helpless anger strikes Goswin with his sword, the young merchant takes his weapon away from the seasoned captain and accepts a challenge to meet him in a duel next day. To all this Hubert is a silent witness.

Act III

Next day at the appointed place Hempskirke seeks out Goswin, taking care, however, to bring with him a gang of boors to assist him. But Clause and his beggars rescue the young merchant and take Hempskirke prisoner. He admits that he is Wolfort's follower, and in the lining of his doublet the beggars find evidence that he is a spy-knave, seeking to discover certain loyal gentlemen who are in hiding, and that when his companion Hubert has done his best and worthiest service, his throat is to be cut. Soon the beggars are joined by Hubert disguised as a huntsman, and so readily does he appeal to the beggars that they not only make him a member of their band, but also appoint him the custodian of their prisoner.

But in spite of his good fortune in escaping ambush, Goswin is not happy. His mind is troubled with such sadness as will sink him, and to Clause and later to Gertrude he explains that unless his ships make port, or he can raise a hundred thousand crowns, by the next day, he must go bankrupt and face prison.

Act IV

Goswin's creditors are obdurate and will not grant him an extension of time, but before his loans are due, Clause and his band bring their patron a hundred thousand crowns in gold—their savings, they say, from the alms they have collected by the roadside. The old fellow refuses to take a note for his loan, asking only for Goswin's ring and his promise, when the time shall come, that he will grant the beggar freely but one petition. The young merchant has scarcely repaid his loans, however, when word arrives of the safety of several of his ships, one of them saved from the Turks by a valiant captain Goswin had once redeemed from prison. Thus his kind acts pay dividends. And old Van Dunck insists upon an immediate wedding for his ward. But somewhat unaccountably, when he hears of the plan, Clause appears with Goswin's ring and insists upon taking the young man away from his own wedding ceremony. Like Hempskirke, Clause too objects to such an alliance.

Meanwhile, in his huntsman's disguise, Hubert has for certain identified Jacqueline, and because of her, knows that all the nobles he seeks are here in Bruges. As for Hempskirke, he unwittingly assists in another project which the honest huntsman undertakes. In exchange for freedom Hempskirke promises to make the huntsman chief ranger over all the earl's parks, but his promises are nothing to the service which it is within the power of the huntsman to perform. Here, near Bruges, the rascal reveals, are the old lords who rebelled against Earl Wolfort; they are very crafty, and only the authority and the person of the earl himself is sufficient to make them yield. At midnight on the morrow, the huntsman promises to betray them to the earl. But he privately reveals himself to Clause, whom he has identified as Gerrard, and the beggars are ready when the time comes.

Act V

Convinced that Goswin's guide is a disguised agent of some other love who has command of the young merchant's affections, Gertrude follows her lover to Beggars' Bush. But on the way she falls into the hands of Wolfort and Hempskirke, led by Hubert and several of the beggars disguised as boors. Wolfort congratulates himself upon his good fortune, for it had been his intention from the beginning to marry the heiress of Brabant and so to unite the two nations. Soon they capture Florez and Gerrard, who has explained everything to his stepson, and later other members of the loyal band. But when it is most apparent that Hubert is a traitor, the exulting party is surprised by Van Dunck and an armed force of merchants and beggars from Bruges. Hubert is exonerated and married to Jacqueline, Wolfort and Hempskirke are banished, and the ruling houses of Flanders and Brabant are united at the marriage of Florez and Bertha.

----◆----

PHILIP MASSINGER AND NATHAN FIELD
(1583–1640)   (1587–?)

BIOGRAPHIES. For a biography of Massinger, see above, p. 359.

Nathan Field was the son of a Puritan preacher and castigator of the stage. He was born in 1587, educated at St. Paul's School, and about 1600 impressed as one of the Children of the Chapel Royal, ostensibly to sing, but actually to perform in plays. Later he acted in adult companies, first the Lady Elizabeth's and then the King's Men, joining the latter in 1615. As a boy actor Field played in Ben Jonson's comedies and acted the title role in Chapman's *Bussy D'Ambois*. Later, as an adult he played in Shakespeare's, Jonson's, and Beaumont and Fletcher's plays and is alluded to in *Bartholomew Fair* as "your best actor." Jonson told Drummond that "Nid Field was his scholar, and he had read to him the Satires of Horace and some Epigrams of Martial." Field was the author of several plays besides this collaboration with Massinger on *The Fatal Dowry,* and perhaps he had a hand in some of the Beaumont and Fletcher plays. His later life is obscure, and the date of his death is unknown; he is sometimes confused with his brother Nathaniel, who died in 1633 and was a bookseller and stationer.

CRITICAL COMMENT. Although Massinger called *The Roman Actor* "the most perfect birth of my Minerva," the best tragedy in which he had a hand is *The Fatal Dowry,* written in collaboration with Nathan Field. The play is a domestic tragedy, highly effective in its irony and brilliant in its contrasts of character. It held the stage exceptionally well, and was last revived at Sadler's Wells in 1845 when Samuel Phelps played Romont and John Marston Charalois.

Even more significant is the fact that *The Fatal Dowry* was transformed into a she-tragedy by Nicholas Rowe and renamed *The Fair Penitent* (1703). In accordance with the sentimental taste of the early eighteenth century, greater emphasis was given to the heroine; the tragedy became Calista's [Beaumelle's], not her husband's; and Novall Junior became the "haughty, gallant, gay Lothario," the model for Richardson's Lovelace in *Clarissa Harlowe. The Fair Penitent* was extremely popular; it was played by David Garrick, and later Mrs. Siddons was a famous Calista.

SOURCE. No source is known for *The Fatal Dowry,* but the story of the voluntary imprisonment of a son to secure decent burial for his father is told by Valerius Maximus of Miltiades and his son Cimon. The condemnation of a guilty wife by her strictly just father and her execution by her husband may be Spanish.

BIBLIOGRAPHY

Monograph: C. Beck, *Philip Massinger, The Fatal Dowry: Einleitung zu einer neuen Ausgabe,* Erlangen Diss., 1906.
Early edition: 1632.
Modern edition: C. L. Lockert, Jr. (1918).

THE FATAL DOWRY

A TRAGEDY

(1618–1619)

DRAMATIS PERSONAE

ROCHFORT, ex-Premier-President of the Parliament of Dijon, a "reverent old man," and father of Beaumelle. "His life transcends all fair examples of such as were before him in Dijon."

BEAUMELLE, "star of Dijon, the lustre of all France," only child of Rochfort who "would meet love and marriage both at once." But she "must do as [she] may, not as [she] would; [her] father's will is the goal [she] must fly to. . . . [With] music, language, courtship, . . . her education follows not any [i.e., is inferior to none]; for her mind, I know it to be fairer than her shape. . . . If she were well declined, to keep her so deserved not thanks; and yet, to stay a woman spurred headlong by hot lust to her own ruin, is harder than to prop a falling tower with a deceiving reed. . . . Bold enough to be a strumpet, [she] dare[s] not yet live one. . . . Ten dissemblers are in this subtle devil!"

CHARALOIS, a noble gentleman, son of the deceased Marshal, "from whom he inherits his fame and virtues only. . . . A braver hope of so assured a father did never comfort France— . . . young, yet old in judgment; theoric and practic in all humanity [i.e., the humanities, polite learning]; and, to increase the wonder, religious yet a soldier. . . . Nought but a fair tree could such fair fruit bear. . . . I am strangely taken with this Charalois. Methinks, from his example the whole age should learn to be good, and continue so."

NOVALL SENIOR, successor to Rochfort as Premier-President of the Parliament of Dijon, and a "corrupt elder," onetime enemy of Charalois' father. " 'Tis true, this boil of state wears purple tissue, is high-fed, proud; so is his lordship's horse, and bears as rich caparisons. I know this elephant carries on his back not only towers, castles, but the ponderous republic, and never stoops for't; with his strong-breathed trunk snuffs others' titles, lordships, offices, wealth, bribes and lives, under his ravenous jaws. . . . Helps he the poor, in a just business? Nay, does he not cross every deserved soldier and scholar, as if, when Nature made him, she made the general antipathy of all virtue?"

NOVALL JUNIOR, son of the Premier-President, and the lover of Beaumelle. He is his tailor's "creature, and did he not each morning new create [him], [he'd] stink, and be forgotten. . . . [As to fighting], he fears his clothes more than his flesh. . . . Wedlock? No, padlock, horselock! [He] wear[s] spurs to keep it off [his] heels. . . . Like a free, wanton jennet in the meadows, [he] look[s] about, and neigh[s], take[s] hedge and ditch, feed[s] in [his] neighbors' pastures, pick[s] [his] choice of all their fair-maned mares. . . . What a perfume the muskcat leaves behind him!"

COLONEL ROMONT, a brave officer, "an honest man and worthy," and the "faithful and tried friend" of Charalois, the son of his old commander. But his "skill . . . consists in camps, not courts," and his blunt, outspoken honesty makes him sometimes appear a contemptuous, uncivil busybody and a "seditious sower of debate."

PONTALIER, "the hopeful Pontalier," who, as captain in the field, has done "such service as then made [him] their envy that commanded; here at home, however, [he plays] the parasite to a gilded knave," } friends of Novall Junior.

MALOTIN, his companion,

LILIDAM, a "court spider, . . . [and] a long thing with an unpromising face, . . . [Novall Junior's] dressing block, upon whom my lord lays all his clothes and fashions ere he vouchsafes them his own person." He was once apprentice to Le Robe, tailor at Orleans, but is now received here "for a complete monsieur,"

AYMER, "a good, foolish, knavish, sociable gallimaufry of a man, and has much caught my lord with singing; he is master of a music house. . . . Some tricks and crotchets he has in his head, as all musicians have, and more of him I dare not author," } parasites, dependent on Novall Junior. "If my lord deny, they deny; if he affirm, they affirm. They skip into my lord's cast skins some twice a year, and thus they lie to eat, eat to live, and live to praise my lord."

FLORIMEL, "Goody Wisdom, whom nobody regards, . . . [and who] thinks to be mother of the maids here, and mortify them with proverbs,"

BELLAPERT, secret agent of Novall Junior, and "the cabinet to all Beaumelle's counsels, . . . [who] know[s] the cause that makes [her] lady wither thus in youth." ("By this light, madam, this wagtail will spoil you, if you take delight in her licence!")

ladies-in-waiting to Beaumelle. "What an electuary [i.e., a sweet, blended medicine] found [this] father out for his daughter when he compounded [these] two [her] women! For . . . Florimel [is] even a grain too heavy, simply, for a waiting gentlewoman, . . . and . . . Bellapert, a grain too light."

DU CROY, President of the Parliament of Dijon, and a judge *pro tem* at Charalois' trial.

CHARMI, an advocate who pleads for the Marshal's funeral and is checked for it by Novall Senior; later he is also a judge *pro tem* at the trial of Charalois.

BEAUMONT, secretary to Rochfort. "You are a scholar, . . . and can search deeper into the intents of men, than those that are less knowing."

Three Creditors of the old Marshal's, "usurers, bred by a riotous peace, . . . the worst of spirits that strive to rob the tombs of what is their inheritance, the dead."

A Priest who conducts the old Marshal's funeral.

A Captain, a Lieutenant, and an Ensign, to whom Charalois gives the spurs, the scarf, and the cuirass of the deceased Marshal.

A Tailor, a Barber, a Perfumer, and a Page, attendants upon Novall Junior.

Presidents of the Parliament, Court Officers, Captains, Soldiers, Mourners, Jailers, Bailiffs, Servants, and Attendants.

Setting: Dijon, in Burgundy, at some unspecified time.

> *"The wrong that's done to the chaste married bed,*
> *Repentant tears can never expiate."*

Act I

In spite of valiant and faithful service to the state, the Marshal of Burgundy has been permitted to die in debtors' prison, and his ungrateful country has not supplied him even with the means of satisfying his creditors for the sums which he borrowed for the public good—all of two hundred thousand crowns. These usurious rascals now impound his body, refuse to permit its burial, and come into court to defend their claims. Charalois, the son of the old general, represents his father's cause, but he and his advocate Charmi are honest men who will not stoop to court the favors of the judge's parasitic followers, and hence, are easily rebuffed by the court and denied their petition. Only Romont, a blunt, outspoken soldier who is Charalois' loyal friend, is so outraged at the injustice and dishonor done his old commander that he speaks his mind and is arrested for contempt of court. Since the law has failed him, it is then that Charalois nobly proposes that in prison he replace his father's body, if the creditors will release the corpse on such conditions. Against the advice of his father's friends, who are loath to see a young man throw away his liberty and the joys of life together, Charalois insists, the offer is eagerly accepted by court and creditors, and the young man enters what appears "a lively grave" to make himself prisoner to "bail his father's death."

Although strictly in accordance with the law, the court's unfavorable decision in the case is palatable to few who hear it, and even the advocates for the creditors return their fees to their clients rather than have any part in what has occurred. Also, the verdict is to some extent traceable to the fact that Rochfort, a grave and just old patriarch and a friend of the Marshal's, has resigned his post of Premier-President of the Parliament and that his successor, Novall Senior, is "a corrupt elder" devoid of mercy, and an enemy of the dead more interested in settling an old grudge than in justly doing "the office that [he] sit[s] for." But Rochfort has been present during the trial and is so touched by the filial piety of young Charalois and the honest indignation of his faithful friend Romont that he determines to procure their release.

Act II

Soon after the funeral of the Marshal, therefore, Rochfort discharges his old friend's debts, pays Romont's fine, and not only offers Charalois untold wealth, but also the hand of his only child, Beaumelle, in marriage. Beaumelle is a beautiful girl, "the fairest virgin in Dijon," well brought up and obedient to her father's wishes. But she is frivolous and spoiled, and she has already been carrying on a flirtation with an empty-headed fop, the son of the new Premier-President, Novall Junior. Charalois instantly falls in love with the charming Beaumelle, who without hesitation accepts her father's choice of a husband for her, and he receives with joy both the dowry and the girl. But even as the couple are being married, it is apparent that Novall Junior has no intention whatever of forsaking the pursuit of this lady's honor, even though he sees "her made another man's, and such a man's, so good, so popular." And Beaumelle, alas, is all too foolishly prone to accept the philosophy of her waiting woman Bellapert that love and marriage are not necessarily the same thing and that women wed to lie with other men.

Act III

Hence, aided by Bellapert, who is his secret agent, Novall Junior gains a private meeting with the lady, exchanges kisses with her, and receives promises of further favors at a future meeting. But, guided by Florimel, another and more honorable of Beaumelle's maids, Romont witnesses the whole interview. Ever blunt and direct, as well as devoted to his friend, Romont speaks to Beaumelle forthwith. It is not that as yet he suspects her of gross misconduct, but rather that what he had seen is quite enough, and that he wishes her to prove such a wife to Charalois, "and such a one he merits, as Caesar, did he live, could not except at—not only innocent from crime, but free from all taint and suspicion." Beaumelle, however, haughtily scorns his good advice, and brazenly informs him that she "will revel, feast, kiss, embrace, perhaps grant larger favors," taunting him with living upon her means and then murmuring at her conduct. Then, when Romont, again in his direct and honest way, speaks to old Rochfort, the daughter contrives by dissembling and subtlety to turn his suspicious accusations to ridicule, and to earn for her husband's friend the displeasure of her father. Willing even to risk a breach of friendship for Charalois' honor, Romont goes to the young husband. But Charalois is incredulous of these suspicions, at first laughingly, and then angrily.

Act IV

As Romont seeks for something on which to assuage his wrath, he meets Novall Junior, gets rid of the train of fops which always attends him, and at the point of a pistol makes him write a promise, under oath, never again to see Beaumelle except by chance, much less allure her, and never to send token, message, or letter "to incline this too much prone already yielding lady." Trembling with fear, Novall agrees. But Romont has hardly gone before Bellapert arrives in haste to summon him to Beaumelle's, and the dishonorable rascal cheerfully breaks his vow:

> No pain is due to lovers' perjury;
> If Jove himself laugh at it, so will I.

This time, however, Charalois himself finds the lovers together, completely compromised. With deliberate calm he forces Novall Junior to draw sword and defend himself, killing him in fair fight instead of in passion. Then with even more astonishing restraint he sends back to Rochfort in a casket the fatal dowry of his daughter, as freely as, unasked, it had been given to him, bidding his father-in-law come to him instantly. Only then does he turn to Beaumelle, whose eyes at last are opened to how worthy her husband was both of love and duty, now that she has lost him. There are no emotional recriminations; still calm Charalois raises from her knees the penitent lady, hears her confess that she "was bold enough to be a strumpet, [and] dare[s] not yet live one," and sees her prepare to die. When Rochfort appears, Charalois clothes him in his judicial robes, informs him that "there is a cause to be determined of that does require such an integrity as [he] has ever used," and binds his eyes so that he may be impartial. To her father the erring wife confesses her guilt; the old judge, no longer blindfolded, condemns his child, even barring possible forgiveness for such a sin; and the righteous, if melodramatic, husband serves as executioner of his sentence. Only after the girl has been stabbed to death before him does the upright judge display any emotion. Turning to his son-in-law, Rochfort cries out against his heartlessness:

> *I, in your cause, put on a scarlet robe*
> *Of red-dyed cruelty; but in return,*
> *You have advanced for me no flag of mercy.*
> *I looked on you as a wronged husband; but*
> *You closed your eyes against me as a father.*
> *O Beaumelle! My daughter!*

For a second time in Charalois' life strict justice has triumphed over compassion, and on this occasion the young man himself has been its executor.

Officers, led by Novall Senior, soon put in their appearance to arrest Charalois and to bring him to justice for double murder.

Act V

At the trial, Charalois is reconciled with his faithful friend Romont; dispassionately and ably he presents his case, serving as his own accuser when old Rochfort's devotion to justice renders the role impossible for him, and he is quickly acquitted of Beaumelle's death. But tried for Novall's murder, he honorably refuses "for the dignity of the court and [his] own honor" to testify in detail concerning how he came by knowledge which made certain the lovers' guilt. Only when Romont places in evidence the written oath he extracted from Novall Junior and calls in the bawd Bellapert, does the court decide in Charalois' favor.

But almost immediately after, Charalois is stabbed to death by Pontalier, the only one of Novall's followers who shows in any way his sorrow for the passing of the libertine. Then in quick succession, Pontalier is himself stabbed by Romont, who is promptly banished by the court for his act of revenge. Right at last has triumphed. "What's fallen upon me," says Charalois as he dies,

> *Is by Heaven's will, because I made myself*
> *A judge in my own cause, without their warrant.*

And Romont's case is another

> *sad precedent, how just soever*
> *Our reasons are to remedy our wrongs,*
> *We are yet to leave them to their will and power*
> *That, to that purpose, have authority.*

PHILIP MASSINGER

(1583–1640)

For a biography of Massinger, see above, p. 359.

CRITICAL COMMENT. Massinger is one of the cleanest and most high-minded of the early dramatists, and these qualities are nowhere better illustrated than in *The Maid of Honor*. Camiola the maid is a masterly characterization, virtuous, loving, brave, and gifted with a self-respect that makes her stand out among associates of lesser calibre. The fickle Bertoldo is entirely unworthy of her devotion, and the resolution with which she acts when her hopes are wrecked by his duplicity is touching.

A New Way to Pay Old Debts has the honor of contributing a great and a popular character to the English stage. Sir Giles may be overdrawn; but he is a compound of lion and fox, and it is his monomania which lends force to the play. As a result, *A New Way* is the only non-Shakespearean drama prior to *The Beggar's Opera* which has held the boards consistently to the present day. Revived by David Garrick in 1748, it has been the vehicle for almost every great actor, English and American, since that time. John Philip Kemble, both of the Keans, Edwin Forrest, both of the Booths, Samuel Phelps, Henry Irving, all have played Sir Giles. In recent years it has been produced at the Old Vic in London and by Walter Hampden in America (see R. H. Ball, *The Amazing Career of Sir Giles Overreach*, 1939).

SOURCES. *The Maid of Honor* is based upon a story in Painter's *Palace of Pleasure*, but the original has been surely and freely transformed. The rich widow of the source is replaced by the maid of the play; the duchess whose infatuation for the soldier-hero explains without justifying his desertion of the heroine, is an addition to the story; so is the surprise ending in which the jilted girl takes the veil. But above all the high moral tone of the drama and the conclusion as the inevitable result of a selfish worldly dispensation of holy vows—which Camiola herself had foreseen but neglected to remember—this is Massinger's improvement of the story. The hero is not a Knight of Malta in the original; this added circumstance makes a great deal of difference to the story.

A New Way to Pay Old Debts is merely a rewriting of Middleton's *A Trick to Catch the Old One,* but inevitably the treatment is different in Massinger's hands. Middleton's play is pure comedy, hard and realistic, with few moral questions asked, little feeling, and reconciliations and a dinner at the end. Massinger's play, on the other hand, is hardly a comedy at all. Its tone is serious; it is morally earnest in its overthrow of a villain who richly deserves what he gets. But Sir Giles is committed to a madhouse in the end, without any prospect of recovery. Indeed, Massinger all but identifies his leading character with a rapacious contemporary, Sir Giles Mompesson (1584–1651?), whose abuse of privilege as the controller of licenses to innkeepers and supervisor of the manufacture of gold and silver thread was exposed and punished in 1621. His legal associate, Sir Francis Michel, is thought to be the Greedy of this play. Hence, *A New Way to Pay Old Debts* had considerable contemporary significance, and may to some extent have been drawn from life.

BIBLIOGRAPHY

Collected Works:

> *The Plays of Philip Massinger,* edited by W. Gifford and F. Cunningham, 1868.
>
> *The Best Plays of Philip Massinger,* edited by Arthur Symons, Mermaid Series, 2 volumes, 1887–89.

Monographs:

> A. H. Cruickshank, *Philip Massinger,* Oxford, 1920.
>
> M. Chelli, *Le Drame de Massinger,* Lyon, 1924.

The Maid of Honor:

> Early edition: 1632.
>
> Modern edition: ed. Eva A. W. Bryne (Bryn Mawr Diss., 1927).

A New Way to Pay Old Debts:

> Early edition: 1633.
>
> Modern edition: ed. A. H. Cruickshank (1926).

THE MAID OF HONOR

A TRAGI-COMEDY

(1621–1632)

DRAMATIS PERSONAE

CAMIOLA, the Maid of Honor, "an heir sprung from a noble family, fair, rich, young. . . . You may search through the world and meet not with such another phoenix."

CLARINDA, Camiola's waiting woman.

ROBERTO, King of Sicily, a "good and gracious . . . king of peace."

BERTOLDO, natural brother of King Roberto, "a Knight of Malta by [his] Order bound to a single life, . . . a goodly gentleman . . . so trained up and fashioned for noble uses. . . . Behold this man, and . . . know that 'tis safer far to play with lightning than trifle in things sacred. . . . The heavy curse that waits on perjury and foul ingratitude pursue thee ever!"

ASTUTIO, a Sicilian councilor of state.

ANTHONIO, sometime ward of Astutio,⎱ two rich heirs; city bred; "loose carpet knights,
GASPARO, nephew of Astutio, ⎰ . . . gaudy butterflies," followers of Bertoldo.

SIGNIOR SYLLI, a foolish self-lover, a suitor to Camiola and "the pitifullest animal of the lineage of the Syllis! . . . His father was the banker of Palermo, and this the heir of his great wealth; his wisdom was not hereditary. . . . Was there ever such a piece of motley heard of?"

FULGENTIO, the minion of King Roberto, "a suit-broker in court, . . . [and] the Devil, I fear, in his holiday clothes, . . . [who] neither speak[s] nor hold[s his] peace for nothing. . . . A gentleman, yet no lord, he hath some drops of the king's blood running in his veins, derived some ten degrees off; . . . 'tis not impossible but a king may have a fool to his kinsman. . . . His revenue lies in a narrow compass, the king's ear, and yields him every hour a fruitful harvest. . . . [He's] rich, . . . devilish rich, as 'tis reported, and sure [has] the aids of Satan's little fiends to get it. . . . He has the worst report among good men I ever heard of for bribery and extortion. In their prayers widows and orphans curse him for a canker and a caterpillar in the state." With King Roberto's support, Fulgentio is a suitor to Camiola.

ADORNI, a "gentleman . . . of a noble temper," once a follower of Camiola's father, and "a man that at a reverend distance loves" Camiola. "There are a thousand ladies, and of good fame, . . . would be proud of such a servant. . . . Was there ever poor lover so employed against himself to make way for his rival?"

AURELIA, Duchess of Siena, "dispossessed by violence of what was her true inheritance."

GONZAGA, a Knight of Malta and "the honor of his Order," general to the Duchess of Siena.

PIERIO, a colonel to Gonzaga.

RODERIGO,⎱ captains to Gonzaga.
JACOMO, ⎰

FERDINAND, Duke of Urbino; "he too late is conscious that his ambition to encroach upon his neighbor's territories with the danger of his liberty, nay, his life, hath brought in question his own inheritance; but youth and heat of blood . . . may both plead and mediate for him. . . . [His] offense grew from excess of love."

DRUSO,⎱ captains to Duke Ferdinand.
LIVIO, ⎰

An Ambassador from the Duke of Urbino to Roberto of Sicily.

A Page, "Hercules . . . bound up in *decimo sexto!* . . . Tamburlaine in little!"

FATHER PAULO, a priest, Camiola's confessor.

A Bishop, a Jailer, a Scout, a Dwarf, Officers, Soldiers, Servants, and Attendants.

Setting: Palermo, Siena, and their vicinities in the fourteenth century.

> *"May she stand*
> *To all posterity a fair example*
> *For noble maids to imitate, since to live*
> *In wealth and pleasure is common, but to part with*
> *Such poison'd baits is rare."*

Act I

To his friend Roberto of Sicily, Ferdinand, Duke of Urbino, sends an ambassador asking assistance in his desperate fortunes. Disappointed in love by Aurelia, Duchess of Siena, Ferdinand foolishly has sought to force affection from the lady by attacking and capturing her principal city of Siena. Now, too late, the young hothead is aware of his mistake. The great Gonzaga, Knight of Malta and general of the duchess' armies, has rallied her scattered troops and laid siege to the captured town, admitting no parleys and ignoring all flags of truce. Gonzaga insists upon unconditional surrender of Siena and all in it. Reduced by his indiscretion to a starving prisoner within the city, Duke Ferdinand now begs aid from Sicily. Roberto, however, is a king of peace. On the ground that Ferdinand's cause is unjust and foolish, and that he took up arms without first taking counsel, Roberto refuses to aid him. He will not gild an unjust invasion with the trim of glorious conquest.

The king's decision, however, is not universally favored by his courtiers. Bertoldo, his natural brother, also a Knight of Malta and the leader of a party of empty-headed younglings and malcontents who take fire from him, ignores the present issue and argues that since Sicily is an overpopulated island ringed by the sea, Nature designed her people to be warriors. Sicily cannot be self-supporting. Even though it were more fruitful now than when it was called "the granary of great Rome," the island must provide itself with colonies or it must starve. Sicilian sinews must not shrink up through sloth, nor want of employment transform younger brothers into thieves. Their swords must sow and reap their harvest somewhere. And Bertoldo cites the example of England, "the empress of the European isles," whose navies have made her the mistress of the ocean.

Responding to this pressure, the gentle Roberto does not retract, but he follows instead a course of equivocation. He will not himself engage in Ferdinand's quarrel nor press his subjects to maintain it. But if there are gallants in Sicily who are weary of the happiness of peace and desire the bitter sweets of war, the king consents to let them go as adventurers and volunteers, wholly on their own responsibilities. From him they must expect no aid, and if any should miscarry in this rash undertaking, Roberto says he will hear of it merely as disaster fallen on a stranger.

Moreover, he will esteem that man no subject who in purse or person aids those who come to grief.

Near Palermo lives a "maid of honor," named Camiola, "sprung from a noble family, fair, rich, young." She is beset by many suitors, mostly fools, like Signior Sylli, who has sworn "never to take a wife but such a one . . . as can hold out a month against [him]." He is now trying his charms on Camiola, who has no difficulty in withstanding them. With the noble excellencies of Bertoldo, however, Camiola is in love, and he with her. But even if they would, the lovers cannot marry; their social stations are not equal, and by his Order Bertoldo is bound to a single life. The prince does, indeed, suggest a dispensation, but the honorable lady will not hear of it, and Bertoldo is too noble to propose a dishonorable alliance. As the girl herself observes:

> *When what is vowed to Heaven is dispensed with*
> *To serve our ends on earth, a curse must follow*
> *And not a blessing.*

Of Camiola Bertoldo now takes his leave, bidding all thoughts of women perish in him, and letting "the glorious light of noble war extinguish Love's dim taper." He leaves the life of Camiola empty by his going.

Act II

So precipitate, indeed, is the departure of Bertoldo's expedition that the knight does not even take leave of his king. But when Roberto learns that the force is larger than at first he thought it might be, and that it is composed of "all ill-affected spirits in Palermo, . . . turbulent swordsmen, [and] such whose poverty forced 'em to wish a change," the king writes a letter to the Duchess of Siena in excuse of the army of Sicilians operating against her. Also taking advantage of Bertoldo's absence, Fulgentio, the king's minion, enlists the royal assistance in his suit for the hand of Camiola. But even though he wears the king's ring, the overbearing, vainglorious favorite has no success, and only earns the enmity of Adorni, a noble gentleman who sincerely loves the lady from a distance.

The army of Sicilians no sooner arrives in Siena than, far from relieving the siege of the city, it is ignominiously defeated in a brilliant assault led by Gonzaga. Bertoldo and several other prominent Sicilians are taken prisoner. Of such captives as Anthonio and Gasparo, "at the best loose carpet knights [and] gaudy butterflies," the great Sienese leader is justly contemptuous. But he is thunderstruck at the apostasy of so great a soldier as Bertoldo—a crusader, vowed to guard weak ladies from oppression and never to draw sword against them, for gain or glory espousing an ill quarrel and doing his utmost to uphold the falling enemy of such a princess as Aurelia. And the general weeps as at the funeral of virtue, faith, and religion when he strips from Bertoldo's breast the cross of the Knights of Malta.

Act III

In the Sienese camp with letters from King Roberto, Astutio, the king's councilor, assures Gonzaga of His Majesty's friendship to the general and of his service to the duchess. But he also takes the opportunity of ransoming, at two thousand crowns apiece, his sometime ward and his nephew, Anthonio and Gasparo. Bertoldo, however, is Gonzaga's personal prisoner, and the ransom fixed for his release is nothing less than fifty thousand crowns. Certain that Roberto would rather thank Gonzaga to detain the prisoner than to give one crown to free him, Astutio lets Bertoldo know that he has no authority to release his bonds and that the king has seized all of his brother's patrimony so that it will be impossible for him to ransom himself. Then, though he is rich himself and might pay the sum down, Astutio declines to do so. Hence, though such creatures as Anthonio and Gasparo go free, the renowned Bertoldo must remain in fetters.

In Palermo the faithful Adorni rids Camiola of a pestilent suitor by challenging the coward Fulgentio to a duel and as a birthday gift presents the lady with a retraction signed in the braggart's blood of all the malicious lies he has been spreading about her. Adorni is wounded in the encounter, and the maid of honor thus learns of his devotion. Hence, when Anthonio and Gasparo return from the wars without Bertoldo but with news of his cruel imprisonment, it is to Adorni that Camiola turns. With him as messenger she will risk the king's displeasure; ransom Bertoldo herself, if it takes two parts of her estate; and ask in exchange nothing but a solemn contract that he will make her his lawful wife. In her eagerness to free Bertoldo, Camiola has forgotten his vows and the curse which she foresaw attending dispensations. In addition, lest the prisoner want accommodations, she sends money with which Adorni is to furnish him according to his birth, and a kiss, printed on Adorni's lips, which he is to deliver on Bertoldo's hand. "Was there ever poor lover so employed against himself to make way for his rival?"

Act IV

Unable in his prison cell to accept the consolations of such philosophers as Seneca, Bertoldo has given way to absolute despair when Adorni ransoms him. The prince's gratitude to Camiola knows no bounds, and her request of a contract of marriage is to him only an increase of obligation—" 'twas my *nil ultra* ever—the end of my ambition." But he is soon to forget.

Meanwhile, the Duchess Aurelia has returned to Siena, received King Roberto's letters endeavoring to mitigate the affront offered by the Sicilian expedition to Siena, and reserved judgment on the question, though she finds it hard to think of "but as a wrong, with purpose to detain us from our own." But when she receives the rehabilitated Bertoldo in audience, her tone changes; she is instantly smitten by his fine clothes and goodly bearing, and falls in love with him. The duchess' attentions to the Sicilian prince are noticeable to everyone at court and disapproved of. To Bertoldo himself, "grown up in a moment a favorite," it is clear that except for Camiola "there is no step between [him] and a crown." Then in spite of Adorni's reminder, Bertoldo puts all thought of the girl aside, and makes ready to journey home accompanied by the duchess to be reconciled with his brother and to obtain a dispensation for his marriage with Aurelia. Adorni hastens ahead to Palermo, for, once Camiola knows of Bertoldo's duplicity her love must change to just disdain, and perhaps she will show some compassion for her faithful servant.

In Palermo King Roberto himself comes to Camiola's house to charge her with stubborn disobedience to his will, and scorn and disrespect for Fulgentio, the suitor favored by him. But so impressed is the king by the dignity and the virtue of the maid of honor, and by the justice of her charges against the malicious favorite, that in anger Roberto casts aside Fulgentio and shows Camiola every honor and consideration.

Act V

When Adorni brings the news from Siena, Camiola receives it with similar dignity. Bertoldo is not worth her sorrow, it is true; "ingratitude and perjury at the height cannot express him." But Camiola accepts her disappointment calmly. She merely asks Adorni for the contract in which Bertoldo swore to marry her, sends Signior Sylli for her confessor Father Paulo with written directions, attires herself like a virgin bride, and announces that she will this day do something that shall deserve men's praise—and wonder, too.

At court Roberto and his brother are quickly reconciled, and preparations for the wedding of Bertoldo and the duchess are nearly complete. But, attended by Fulgentio, Sylli, and Adorni, her rejected suitors, Camiola interrupts the ceremonies, demanding justice to an injured maid. To King Roberto she presents the marriage contract which

Bertoldo has signed, claims the prince as her husband, and tells the whole story. All acknowledge Camiola's worth and honor. The Duchess Aurelia disclaims all interest in Bertoldo, the knight in contrition begs pardon and offers to make recompense, and Camiola calls in the holy friar. But instead of marrying her to Bertoldo or to any of the other suitors, Father Paulo claims her for the church. The maid of honor has taken the veil and renounced the world—this is the marriage, this the port to which her vows have steered her.

Her estate she divides into three parts—one to be given to the nunnery to which she will retire, a second to pious uses, and the third to Adorni for his true and faithful service. She reconciles Roberto and Fulgentio, bids Bertoldo reassume his Order and redeem his mortgaged honor fighting against the enemies of faith, and, finally, asks him to be an arbiter between Duke Ferdinand and the Duchess Aurelia. Then, in token of their reunion once more as brothers in arms, Gonzaga restores to Bertoldo's breast the white cross of the Knights of Malta.

A NEW WAY TO PAY OLD DEBTS

A COMEDY

(1621–1625)

DRAMATIS PERSONAE

SIR GILES OVERREACH, a cruel extortioner who is "both a lion and a fox in his proceedings. . . . Of all the griping and extorting tyrants I ever heard or read of, I ne'er met a match to Sir Giles Overreach. . . . [He] feeds high, keeps many servants, who must at his command do any outrage. Rich in his habit, vast in his expenses, . . . he frights men out of their estates, and breaks through all law nets, made to curb ill men, as they were cobwebs. No man dares reprove him."

FRANK WELLBORN, a prodigal nephew of Sir Giles Overreach, and the true friend of Tom Allworth's dead father. Once "a lord of acres, the prime gallant, . . . [Wellborn] had a merry time of 't—hawks and hounds, with choice of running horses, mistresses of all sorts and all sizes." But now he is "in his manners so debauched and hath to vicious courses sold himself. . . . [Yet], howe'er his outside's coarse, his inward linings are as fine and fair as any man's."

LADY ALLWORTH, a rich widow, "being descended nobly and allied so," and stepmother to young Allworth. "There are few such stepdames. . . . 'Tis a noble widow, and keeps her reputation pure and clear from the least taint of infamy; her life, with the splendor of her actions, leaves no tongue to envy or detraction."

LORD LOVELL, "a true-born Englishman, . . . an honorable man, . . . [who] commands a regiment of soldiers, . . . [and] the gallant-minded . . . minion of the people's love."

TOM ALLWORTH, "a handsome and a hopeful youth, . . . his father's picture in little,

. . . that lives at the devotion of a stepmother, . . . [and is] by want compelled to serve" Lord Lovell as a page.

MARGARET, or MEG, "the only child and heir of Cormorant Overreach, . . . a maid well qualified and the richest match our north part can make boast of. . . . If ever the queen of flowers, . . . the rose, sprang from an envious brier, I may infer there's such disparity in their conditions between . . . the daughter, and the base churl of her father."

TIMOTHY TAPWELL, an alehouse keeper, once Wellborn's underbutler,
FROTH, his wife,
⎱ "Of all the scum that grew rich by [Wellborn's] riots, this, for a most unthankful knave, and this, for a base bawd and whore, have worst deserved."

"A decayed Vintner,"
"A Tailor once, but now [a] mere botcher,"
A Surgeon,
⎱ creditors of Wellborn.

JUSTICE GREEDY—Greedy Woodcock—"the lean skeleton, . . . the thin-gutted squire, . . . justice of peace and quorum, . . . [who loves] choice dishes and plenty of 'em. . . . Meat's cast away upon him. It never thrives. . . . His stomach's as insatiate as the grave. . . . Some fury's in that gut! Hungry again!"

JACK MARALL, a "term driver [i.e., a solicitor who travels from court to court during sessions], . . . this snip of an attorney, . . . [Overreach's] pupil . . . in the art of undoing men"; later, Wellborn's assistant. ("Is not this a true rogue that, out of mere hope of a future coz'nage, can turn thus suddenly?")

PARSON WILLDO, incumbent at Overreach's manor of Gotham.

ORDER, a steward, in "chain and double ruff,"
AMBLE, an usher, "my lady's go-before,"
FURNACE, a conscientious, choleric cook,
WATCHALL, a porter,
⎱ servants to the Lady Allworth.

A Waiting Woman,
A Chambermaid,
⎱ attending Lady Allworth, and devoted to young Tom.

Servants and Attendants.

Setting: The country near Nottingham in the early seventeenth century.

"Such a spirit to dare and power to do were never Lodged so unluckily."

Act I

Partly through his own folly and prodigality, and partly through the trickery and extortion of his uncle, Sir Giles Overreach, Frank Wellborn has been reduced to poverty. Once he had twelve hundred a year, was the lord of acres, and had a merry time of it—"hawks and hounds, . . . running horses, mistresses of all sorts and all sizes." But soon his manors began to melt, his land was gone, his credit was not worth a token, and he became a common borrower—"no man scaped [his] paper pellets [i.e., I.O.U.'s] from the gentleman to the beggars on highways." For a time his uncle Overreach took up the mortgages and supplied his nephew with funds, but his motive was not relief of misfortune in his kin so much as profit to himself. Now, at Sir Giles's bidding, the very tapsters Wellborn once made rich refuse to serve him; his clothes are in tatters, and he has very few friends.

One of these is Tom Allworth, whose father, Wellborn's close friend, was also ruined by Sir Giles. In spite of this fact, however, young Tom is secretly in love with Margaret, the only child of the old cormorant. But he knows that his suit is hopeless, for "to make her great in swelling titles," Sir Giles Overreach, "without touch of conscience, will cut his neighbor's throat." Tom Allworth would relieve Wellborn's need if he were able, but compelled by his own poverty, he is dependent upon his stepmother and the uncertain favor of a lord, whom he serves as page. Lord Lovell is a soldier, commander of a regiment about to depart for the Low Countries, and he is more of a father to the boy than a master. Lady Allworth is also solicitous of her stepson's welfare, still mourns his father's death, and is highly regarded by everyone. Hence, because she is well-to-do in her own right, she has as many suitors as Ulysses' Penelope, and with no more encouragement, they eat her out of house and home.

For the sake of the friendship Wellborn bore her husband, this lady now receives the prodigal. He refuses her gracious offer of a hundred pounds, will not beg nor borrow sixpence from her, and has but one request to make, which she denies not to strangers. He whispers it, and she agrees.

Act II

Hence, a few days later, by paying a social call Frank Wellborn interrupts his uncle's schemes for ruining his neighbors. The old man orders his nephew out of his sight, but Wellborn astonishes the rascal's assistant, Jack Marall, by pushing aside all the temptations to suicide and despair which Sir Giles had suggested that Marall plant in the young man's mind, and by inviting the solicitor to dine with him— gratis—at the house of a gallant lady, the Widow Allworth. So courteous is Wellborn's reception there, so solicitous are the servants for his comfort, so gracious is the lady, and so excellent is the fare, that Marall is ready to believe the young man the successful suitor for the lady's hand and to respect him again as "worshipful." He even offers Wellborn a gelding and twenty pounds to buy a riding outfit, but such favors the young man artfully declines. Marall breathlessly reports everything to Sir Giles—that, far from hanging or drowning himself, his prodigal nephew lives, "lives once more to be made a prey to you, a greater prey than ever."

Meanwhile, Sir Giles has also been full of schemes for bettering his own social position by marriage. His daughter, Mistress Margaret, "must part with that humble title, and write 'honorable,' 'right honorable,' . . . if all [he has], or e'er shall get, will do it." For the gallant-minded, popular Lord Lovell is coming to dine on the morrow.

Act III

But Lord Lovell already knows that his page is in love with Margaret and reassures the lad, who is beset by jealous doubts and fears. On his part, Sir Giles has turned the supervision of his kitchen over to his collaborator Justice Greedy, who, in his own conceit, is "archpresident of the boiled, the roast, the baked." Sir Giles has the room perfumed; he orders out the choicest linen and gold plate. Then he sees to it that Margaret is trimmed up with orient pearls and diamonds, and instructs her how to conduct the wooing, lest all be spoiled by coyness and modesty —which the girl inherits from her mother, for Sir Giles was ever forward. And, left alone with his lordship Margaret is charmingly frank and bold. Her father's haste, she tells Lord Lovell, holds no power over her will. She urges the disparity in their years and in their social ranks; she could say more, but she dares not trust the walls. Eavesdropping a moment later, Sir Giles rejoices to see the couple whispering. But their confidence concerns young Allworth and the "amorous carriage" toward Lord Lovell which Margaret must put on to delude her subtle father.

The Overreach dinner is a great success for still another reason. A coach is heard, and Lady Allworth—"the garments of her widowhood laid by"—arrives unexpectedly with Wellborn. He still looks like a tatterdemalion, but the lady introduces him as one who "may ere long with boldness rank himself with some that have contemned him." What if Justice Greedy and Marall must eat with the servants because there is no room for them at the main table? If Lady Allworth marries Wellborn, all that is hers will be Sir Giles's, as he will manage his nephew. Lord Lovell, too, seems obviously smitten by Margaret. He gives her a parting kiss and proposes to send her daily letters by his faithful page. But Lovell leaves with Lady Allworth, and old Sir Giles has Wellborn remain behind to compliment him on his success with the rich widow. Sir Giles, however, is not content that the lady shall say she married Wellborn like a beggar or in debt. Sir Giles redeems from pawn a trunk of his nephew's rich clothes and gives him a thousand pounds to pay his petty debts—"this done, sir, out of love, and no ends else." The old fellow even sends Wellborn home in his own coach.

Act IV

To make the match sure between Lord Lovell and his daughter, early next day Sir Giles seeks out his lordship at Lady Allworth's house, promises with Margaret all his lands and leases, ready coin, and goods as dowry, and assures the nobleman that as long as he lives, each year he will add something to the heap. He even offers Lovell the house in which they stand—so confident is he that the Allworth estates will soon be mortgaged to him.

But when the shrewd old rascal is gone, Lord Lovell and Lady Allworth have some questions to ask each other. The widow is assured that "were Overreach's states thrice centupled, his daughter millions of degrees much fairer than she is," Lord Lovell has no intention of marrying her; and his lordship is relieved to hear that in spite of appearances, Lady Allworth's intentions concerning Wellborn are honorable and good.

Meanwhile, having found out a new way to pay old debts, Wellborn is once more richly dressed and discharging his obligations. And, acting to the life what Lord Lovell has planned for them, Tom Allworth and Margaret meet frequently. One day, pretending anger at a letter suggesting elopement, Margaret insists to the messenger that she will never marry without her father's full consent. Overhearing, as he was intended to do, Sir Giles forthwith orders Margaret to accompany the page, sends his ring to identify her to the chaplain at Gotham, and writes a note which reads simply: "Marry her to this gentleman." As Margaret kneels for her father's blessing, the old man congratulates the page—"Good Master Allworth, this shall be the best night's work you ever made."

Act V

The problem now for all concerned is how to let Sir Giles know he has been deceived, for he is "both a lion and a fox in his proceedings." Through Lady Allworth's favor, "the plots and projects of the downtrod Wellborn" have succeeded; his debts are paid, and he is once more furnished for fair employment. Through Lord Lovell, Tom Allworth and Margaret have been married; and, matched in years, birth, estates, and alliance, his lordship and the widow join in solemn contract. But thus far Sir Giles Overreach knows nothing of all this.

What Sir Giles hears first is only "a certain buzz of a stol'n marriage . . . in which, 'tis said, there's somebody hath been cozen'd." But it is enough to stir him into action. Armed by his document box he tries to take his anger out on Wellborn, whom he believes married, demanding immediate security for the thousand pounds he lent him recently "in pure love, and no ends else." Wellborn in turn demands his lands, and the old man exultantly relies upon his deeds. But when the document box is opened, it contains only a clean sheet of parchment—all of the writing has been obliterated and the seals turned to dust. Then by flattery the old extortioner tries to persuade Marall to testify that he was present when the deeds were drawn and delivered. But the knavish notary, who has been responsible for the deterioration of the document by his cunning incorporation of chemicals with the ink and the wax, rebels against his master. Sir Giles's hopes are momentarily raised when Parson Willdo reports Margaret's marriage, but his exaltation is short-lived, and his rage increases when he learns that she is not "right honorable," but the happy wife of young Allworth. Having overreached himself in every way, and been deceived by those he hoped to cozen, Sir Giles goes mad. He tries to kill his daughter, but luckily she is protected. At last he is carried off to Bedlam, frothing at the mouth and helplessly flourishing a sheathed sword. As umpire between him and the undoubted heir of Sir Giles, Lovell promises to recover Wellborn's land, and Wellborn, in turn, asks a commission in Lord Lovell's regiment so that by service to king and country he may make all right again.

JOHN FORD, WILLIAM ROWLEY, AND
(1586–c. 1639)   (?–1626)
THOMAS DEKKER
(c. 1572–1632)

For a biography of Ford, see p. 389; for one of Rowley, p. 287; for one of Dekker, p. 146.

CRITICAL COMMENT. Not only did the Elizabethan theatre furnish its audiences with entertainment, but it frequently provided also a rostrum for the discussion of current topics, and occasionally, in an age without newspapers, brought before the public the latest sensational happenings. *The Witch of Edmonton*, written jointly by John Ford, William Rowley, and Thomas Dekker in 1621, is one of the most interesting examples of this journalistic function of the early theatre. On April 19, 1621, Elizabeth Sawyer of Edmonton was executed for witchcraft; by the end of the year the play was on the boards and had been produced at court.

The Witch of Edmonton is an astonishingly sympathetic treatment of such a suspected creature in an age which knew many witch-scares. Mother Sawyer is presented on the stage as a wretched old woman who is harassed by slander and hounded by persecution until she makes a pact with the Devil in self-defense. Obviously the authors believed in witchcraft; they were not so far ahead of their time as to disbelieve. But the sympathy shown the old woman and the pitiful creature's justification of herself is unusual in its day.

Beside the story of Mother Sawyer, and bound up with it, there is a domestic tragedy on the well-worn theme of the miseries of enforced marriage.

SOURCE. For the portions of this play which deal with the witch the authors drew upon a contemporary pamphlet: Henry Goodcole's *Wonderful Discovery of E. Sawyer, a Witch* (1621). For the domestic tragedy no source is known.

BIBLIOGRAPHY

Early edition: 1658.

THE WITCH OF EDMONTON

A KNOWN TRUE STORY, COMPOSED INTO A TRAGI-COMEDY BY DIVERS WELL-ESTEEMED POETS

(1621)

DRAMATIS PERSONAE

SIR ARTHUR CLARINGTON, a "right worshipful knight," seducer of his maidservant, Winnifride. "He that will feast at others' cost must be a bold-faced guest."

WINNIFRIDE, Sir Arthur's maid and a "much-wronged woman, . . . [who] change[s her] life from a loose whore to a repentant wife."

FRANK THORNEY, also in the service of Sir Arthur Clarington, and an "untimely-lost young man, . . . [whose] plots aim but to keep [his] father's love. . . . O, that [his] example might teach the world hereafter what a curse hangs on their heads who rather choose to marry a goodly portion than a dower of virtues!"

OLD THORNEY, a gentleman, Frank's father.

OLD JOHN CARTER, a wealthy, "honest Hertfordshire yeoman."

SUSAN; "virtue and beauty hold fair mixture in her; she's rich, no doubt, in both. . . . 'Tis a mannerly girl, . . . though but an homely man's daughter," / Old Carter's daughters, "a pair of arrows drawn out of one quiver."

KATHERINE, "a sweet, lovely maid, . . . rich in goodness," /

WARBECK, "a very unthrift, . . . one of the country roaring lads," / SOMERTON, "the honester man of the two by five pounds in every stone weight; a civil fellow. He has a fine convenient estate of land in West Ham, by Essex," / suitors to Old Carter's daughters.

JANE, Carter's maid.

The Ghost of Susan.

MOTHER ELIZABETH SAWYER, an old crone, "poor, deformed, and ignorant," called the witch of Edmonton, and "hated like a sickness, made a scorn to all degrees and sexes. . . . Reverence once had wont to wait on age; now an old woman, ill-favored grown with years, if she be poor must be called bawd or witch. . . . If every poor old woman be trod on thus by slaves, reviled, kicked, beaten, as [she is] daily, she to be revenged had need turn witch."

TOM, a familiar spirit in the shape of a Dog, which has "seen and pitied [Mother Sawyer's] open wrongs, and come, out of [his] love to give [her] just revenge against [her] foes." ("It seems you devils have poor, thin souls, that you can bestow yourselves in such small bodies.")

ANN RATCLIFFE, "who for a little soap licked by [Mother Sawyer's] sow, struck and almost had lamed it"; she runs mad and beats out her own brains.

OLD RATCLIFFE, her husband.

OLD BANKS, a countryman, "a kind of God-bless-us, as they say, . . . one of [Mother Sawyer's] chief adversaries, . . . [and] ground of all [her] scandal. . . . Fie, to abuse an aged woman!"

YOUNG CUDDY BANKS, a clown, his son, in love with Kate Carter, "up to the very hilts."

A Spirit in the shape of Kate Carter.

Several Countrymen as morris dancers, "the nimble-footed youth of Edmonton."

FATHER SAWGUT, an old fiddler for the morris dancers.

POLDAVIS, the barber's boy, to play the witch in the morris dance, "because he can show his art better than another." [He is merely referred to in the text.]

A Justice, a Constable, Officers, and Servingmen.

Setting: Edmonton and vicinity, and Tyburn, London, in the early seventeenth century.

> *"The whole argument is this distich:*
> *Forced marriage, murder; murder, blood requires.*
> *Reproach, revenge; revenge, Hell's help desires."*

Act I

To discharge "the true part of an honest man" and to give a name to the child she carries, Frank Thorney has married Winnifride, a servant with him in the household of Sir Arthur Clarington of Edmonton. But, because merely on the rumor of such an alliance Old Thorney has threatened to disinherit his son, Frank cannot acknowledge his bride openly, and hopes to win his father over by degrees. Hence, temporarily, he has arranged for Winnifride to live with her uncle Selman near Waltham Abbey. He promises, however, to visit her frequently, and vows that nothing shall cause him to be false to the bridal oath that binds him to the girl.

No sooner have the couple parted than Sir Arthur Clarington, who knows nothing of the wedding, reproaches Frank for shamefully undoing a modest maid, urges him to marry Winnifride, and offers to make the girl a marriage portion of two hundred pounds. Young Thorney accepts, tells his master of the marriage, and asks him to write Old Thorney a letter denying the rumors which have reached him. Sir Arthur agrees to the deception, telling Frank to write his own letter, and he will sign it. But when the young man has gone and Winnifride returns, it is apparent that the motives of Sir Arthur's solicitude for the young people are neither high nor unselfish. It was Sir Arthur and not Frank Thorney who first seduced the girl, and the knight now sees in the marriage of two of his dependents free scope for his intrigue with his maidservant, without control or fear. But, in spite of her master's blandishments, Winnifride resolves to remain honest, now that she is married, and to change her "life from a loose whore to a repentant wife."

Meanwhile, to disencumber his estate and to prevent the sale of his lands, Old Thorney has been making overtures of marriage between their heirs to Old Carter, a rich Hertfordshire yeoman who will give handsome dowries with his daughters. The girls, Susan and Katherine by name, already have suitors in young Warbeck and Somerton, and their father has promised that when husbands are selected his daughters may choose for themselves. Susan and Frank Thorney are already acquainted, and the girl is already in love with him. Hence, when the young man arrives at his father's bidding and satisfies Old Thorney that he is unmarried, a betrothal is quickly arranged between Frank and Susan, the marriage money to be paid "before your wedding shoes can be pulled on." Thus, Young Thorney wades "deeper into mischief than virtue can avoid."

Act II

Near Edmonton, also, in an old cottage ready to fall from age, lives Mother Sawyer, a poor, deformed, bad-tongued old crone, upon whom the envious world has thrown all its scandalous malice. "Hated like a sickness, made a scorn to all degrees and sexes," the old woman is by some believed to be a witch. Chief among them is Old Banks, who misses no opportunity to abuse and beat her, especially when Mother Sawyer trespasses on his ground—as she does occasionally—to gather a few rotten sticks to keep herself warm. So often has Banks called her hag that Mother Sawyer half believes she is one and can bewitch cattle, crops, and babes at nurse. She has heard old beldames talk of familiar spirits in the shape of mice, rats, ferrets, weasels, and the like, and the old woman longs for one, at any price, so that she may be revenged upon "this miser, this black cur that barks and bites and sucks the very blood of [her] and of [her] credit. 'Tis all one to be a witch as to be counted one."

To Gammer Sawyer's surprise her wish is granted by the appearance of a black dog, named Tom. He has the power of speech, and he tells the old woman that he is a devil who has pitied her wrongs, and, out of love for her, come to give her just revenge upon her foes. The only condition is that Mother Sawyer make a deed of gift to the Devil of her body and soul, and sign it in her blood. Instantly, the old woman orders the spirit to kill Old Banks. But his power is disappointingly circumscribed; he cannot take life unless he finds his intended victim cursing and swearing. He can kill cattle and mildew corn, however, and with this form of retaliation the old woman must rest content.

Mother Sawyer's first real opportunity of getting even with Old Banks, however, comes when she meets his son Cuddy, who is even a bigger clown than his father. Cuddy confesses that he is bewitched already by the beauty of Kate Carter, the wealthy yeoman's daughter, and he asks Mother Sawyer to make the girl love him, too. Calling her familiar spirit, the old woman tells Cuddy to be at the stile at the west end of his father's peasfield tomorrow at sunset and to follow the first living thing he sees. It will bring him to his love. Then, Mother Sawyer plans to wreak the father's wrong upon the son.

Meanwhile, Old Carter brushes aside the prior claims of Young Warbeck to his elder daughter, and Frank Thorney and Susan are married. But soon the devoted bride notices sudden distractions and strange behavior in her husband. She asks the cause, and, half evasively, Frank tells her that he had once been told by a skillful palmist that he should have two wives. By a slip of the tongue he calls Susan "Winnifride," and in riddles he tells her the whole truth. But Susan's love for Frank is such that she pushes his words aside, thinks Frank is trying to dissemble his uneasiness about a duel with Young Warbeck, and resolves that they shall be friends. His second wife is much more fond of him than Frank Thorney had at first imagined.

Act III

The next day at sunset, when Cuddy Banks slips away from his fellow morris dancers and approaches the rendezvous appointed, he sees a black dog and follows it. Before him there appears suddenly a spirit in the shape of Katherine Carter, who trips enticingly away. But when the clown tries to embrace her, he falls into the water and gets wet. Afterwards the dog is very friendly to Cuddy and becomes his ingle, but the beast has other work to do that night.

Frank Thorney is unable to endure the duplicity to which his second, adulterous marriage has led, and he determines to end it. Taking the dowry for which he sold himself, and disguising Winnifride as a horseboy, he determines to seek happiness with her abroad. But Frank must take leave of Susan as if he were only going on a long journey. This loving girl clings to him, refuses to part with him, and on one pretext or another accompanies her husband farther and farther on his way. At last, in a remote grove, Thorney feels a dog rub against his leg. Instantly his mind is made up; he draws his knife, tells Susan of his adulterous marriage and its sordid motive, and stabs her to death. Then he wounds himself and, with the dog's assistance, binds himself to a tree so that it will appear that the couple has been set upon by footpads. In this condition he is found by Old Thorney and Old Carter. Frank will only describe his assailants, professing to be bound by oath from revealing who they are, but from what he says the two fathers immediately suspect Warbeck and Somerton, Susan's disappointed suitor and his friend. Hence, as they watch a morris dance at Sir Arthur Clarington's house, these young men are arrested for murder.

Act IV

Their grievances mounting against Mother Sawyer, Old Banks and other countrymen conduct a witch-hunt. "Our cattle fall, our wives fall, our daughters fall, and maidservants fall, and we ourselves shall not be able to stand," they reason, "if this beast be suffered to graze amongst us." Hence, they set fire to a handful of thatch from the old crone's hovel, to see if the witch will come running, as popular belief says. Sure enough, Mother Sawyer appears to fight back at her tormentors. She finds an unexpectedly sensible defender, however, in a justice of the peace, who calls ridiculous all of the villagers' so-called proofs of the old woman's guilt. He clears away the crowd except Sir Arthur Clarington and himself, tries to calm Mother Sawyer, and asks her a few questions. She defends herself ably, if defiantly, and in reply to Sir Arthur's accusations, she includes in the category "witch," all painted lascivious beauties of princes' courts, citizens' wives who waste in one year what it takes twenty to win, scolds on whose tongues a whirlwind sits to blow a man out of himself, men of law who build up clients' hopes with honeyed promises, and—certain proof to Sir Arthur that the woman has supernatural knowledge—all men who with gold tempt honest maidens to lose their honor. Sir Arthur dares no longer hold conference with her, and, warning Mother Sawyer to mend her life, he and the justice leave her alone.

But when they are gone, the impenitent old woman calls her familiar spirit Tom, hears his report of his sport among the clowns, and sets him on her old enemy Ann Ratcliffe, who "for a little soap licked by [her] sow, struck and almost had lamed it." Ann Ratcliffe runs mad and beats out her brains. Finally, when Old Banks and his followers again attack her, Mother Sawyer is able to rout them with the aid of her dog.

Meanwhile, in Old Carter's house, Katherine is tenderly nursing her brother-in-law, Frank Thorney, and heaping imprecations upon Warbeck and Somerton for their supposed murder of her sister. Jane, the servant, brings in a chicken, and, searching for a knife with which to cut Frank a piece, Katherine picks up his coat. As she goes through the pockets, Mother Sawyer's dog appears, dancing and shrugging his shoulders as if in joy, and Katherine discovers the bloody dagger that had killed her sister. She goes to fetch her father, and while she is out of the room, the ghost of Susan appears to Frank, and Winnifride returns still dressed as a page. To test his new suspicions, Old Carter brings in Susan's coffin; her wounds bleed afresh in the presence of her murderer, and the old man sends for officers to arrest Frank Thorney.

Act V

The unhappy story is quickly brought to conclusion. Tricked even by her familiar spirit, who turns white to deceive and torment her, Mother Sawyer at last is seized by Old Banks, Ratcliffe, and her other enemies, and carried off to Tyburn for execution. She is accused as an instrument of mischief and the agent of the devil which caused Frank Thorney to kill his wife and Ann Ratcliffe to kill herself, as well as the perpetrator of lesser evils. Mother Sawyer repents her wickedness, and goes to her death bidding "all take heed how they believe the Devil; at last he'll cheat you." Young Thorney also mounts the scaffold with a contrite heart; Warbeck and Somerton are freed and the latter is betrothed to Katherine; Sir Arthur is censured for his errors and ordered by the bench to pay Winnifride a thousand marks; and Old Carter welcomes her to his home.

JOHN FORD
(1586–c. 1639)

BIOGRAPHY.   John Ford was a Devonshire man, educated at Exeter College, Oxford, which he entered in March of 1601, and the Middle Temple, to which he was admitted in November of 1602. Little else is known about him, except that he wrote occasional poetry from 1606 on, that his dramatic career began about 1612, that his major work was done after 1621 when he began his collaboration with Webster, Rowley, and Dekker; and that after 1624 he worked alone and just dropped out of sight. He was still writing for the stage in 1638, but his death-date is unknown.

CRITICAL COMMENT.   Because of his interest in a problem, Ford is considered by some the most modern of the early dramatists. His unaided work is dominated by a single theme, that the marriage of true minds is the only marriage worthy of the name, and he frequently studies such a spiritual union when it runs counter to accepted ethical convention. Most of his plays treat stories of forbidden love, and in the modern psychological manner present estimable people in the clutches of sin or some other genuine moral dilemma which can only end in tragedy.

'Tis Pity She's a Whore is a serious treatment of the tragic theme of incest, which, far from condoning such a repulsive sin, treats it with rare understanding and restraint, and with not the least trace of lubricity. Two attractive characters, "gloriously fair, even in [their] infamy," are simply caught in a consuming passion, and the result is inevitable. The tragedy of the brother and the sister is especially poignant when seen against a background of craft, folly, laxness, and intrigue; there is so much more to them than to anyone else in the play.

The Broken Heart is a study of a triangle in which true lovers are separated by a forced marriage of the lady to an unsuitable mate, the lover's persistent claim to her love, the virtuous girl's resolute though heartbreaking denial of that claim, and the disappointed lover's revenge upon the brother who has been the cause of the wrong.

In Perkin Warbeck the playwright turned his hand to a kind of drama that had "been of late so out of fashion, so unfollowed," that he felt called upon to apologize for the revival. Perkin Warbeck is a chronicle play, but the legend is treated in such a manner that the authenticity of Perkin's claims are left problematical. Ford's transformation of the sorry imposter of his sources into a self-assured and sympathetic figure is a psychological triumph. "The custom, sure, of being styled a king hath fastened in [Perkin's] thought that he is such."

SOURCES.   For 'Tis Pity no source is known, and the same is true for The Broken Heart. But some lines in the Prologue to the latter play encourage the belief that the story was founded on fact:

> What may be here thought fiction, when Time's youth
> Wanted some riper years was known a truth.

Suggestion has been made that it is based upon the Sir Philip Sidney—Penelope Devereux—Lord Rich triangle (see Stuart P. Sherman, "Stella and The Broken Heart," PMLA, 1909, and the Introduction to his edition of the play in the Belles Lettres Series). But if so, the catastrophe is the author's own invention. The materials for Perkin Warbeck are derived from Francis Bacon's History *of the Reign of Henry the Seventh* (1622) and Thomas Gainsford's *True and Wonderful History of Perkin Warbeck* (1618).

BIBLIOGRAPHY

Collected Works:

The Dramatic Works of John Ford, edited by W. Gifford and revised by A. H. Bullen, 3 volumes, 1895.

John Forde's Dramatic Works, edited by Willy Bang and Henry de Vocht, Materialen zur Kunde des älteren englischen Dramas, 1908, 1927.

The Best Plays of John Ford, edited by Havelock Ellis, Mermaid Series, 1888.

Monographs:

M. Joan Sargeaunt, *John Ford*, Oxford, 1935.

G. F. Sensabaugh, *The Tragic Muse of John Ford*, Stanford University Press, 1945.

'Tis Pity She's a Whore:

Early edition: 1633.

Modern edition: ed. Stuart P. Sherman (Belles Lettres Series, 1915).

The Broken Heart:

Early edition: 1633.

Modern editions: ed. O. Smeaton (TD, 1906), Stuart P. Sherman (Belles Lettres Series, 1915).

Perkin Warbeck:

Early edition: 1634.

Modern edition: ed. Mildred C. Struble (1926).

'TIS PITY SHE'S A WHORE
(1625–1633)

DRAMATIS PERSONAE

ANNABELLA, a lady of Parma, daughter of Florio. "View well her face, and in that little round you may observe a world of variety; for color, lips; for sweet perfumes, her breath; for jewels, eyes; for threads of purest gold, hair; for delicious choice of flowers, cheeks; wonder in every portion of that form. Hear her but speak, and you will swear the spheres make music to the citizens in Heaven. . . . Hadst thou been virtuous, fair wicked woman, not the matchless joys of life itself had made [one] wish to live with any saint but thee! . . .

> *Of one so young, so rich in Nature's store,*
> *Who could not say, 'Tis Pity She's a Whore."*

GIOVANNI, her brother, "that miracle of wit, . . . once . . . esteemed a wonder of [his] age throughout Bononia. . . . [Now,] he is sold to death, and the Devil

shall not ransom him. . . . The love of [his sister] and the view of [her] immortal beauty have untuned all harmony both of [his] rest and life. . . . O, that
it were not in religion sin to make our love a god, and worship it! . . . 'Tis not,
I know, [his] lust, but 'tis [his] fate that leads [him] on. . . . O Giovanni, thou
hast had the spoil of thine own virtues! . . . Would thou hadst been less subject
to those stars that luckless reigned at [thy] nativity!"

FLORIO, father of Giovanni and Annabella, and a citizen of Parma. "As for worldly
fortune, [he is, he] thank[s his] stars, blessed with enough."

GRIMALDI, "a Roman and a soldier, near allied unto the Duke of
Montferrato, one attending on the nuncio of the Pope that
now resides in Parma, by which means he hopes to get the
love of Annabella. . . . He is no common man, but nobly
born, of princes' blood; . . . though he might serve if there
were no more men, yet he's not the man I would choose,"

SORANZO; "he is wise, and what is more, rich; and what is more
than that, kind; and what is more than all this, a nobleman.
. . . Then he is bountiful; besides, he is handsome, and, by
my troth, I think, wholesome—and that's news in a gallant
of three-and-twenty! Liberal, that I know; loving, that you
know; and a man sure, else he could never ha' purchased such
a good name with Hippolita . . . in her husband's lifetime."
Though perjured with Hippolita, Soranzo has loved Annabella
"long and loved [her] truly, and not hope of what [she has],
but what [she is], hath drawn [him] on,"

} rivals for the hand
of Signior Florio's
daughter.

RICHARDETTO, married to Hippolita and disguised as "a learned doctor lately come
from Padua, much skilled in physic."

HIPPOLITA, "Mistress She-Devil, . . . [his] wretched wife, [who] . . . hath paid
too soon the forfeit of her modesty and life." She was the mistress of Soranzo.
("Foolish woman, thou art now like a firebrand that hath kindled others and burnt
thyself.")

PHILOTIS, niece to Richardetto, "a very modest, well-behaved young maid." ("There
was a wench would have done a man's heart good to have looked on her.")

SIGNIOR DONADO, "the rich magnifico" of Parma and friend of Florio.

BERGETTO, nephew of Donado, and "his white-boy. . . . Here's another of your
ciphers to fill up the number. O, brave old ape in a silken coat!" Too stupid to
win Annabella, he falls in love with Philotis. ("Was ever the like ass seen?")

BONAVENTURA, "a grave friar, once tutor to" Giovanni and now his confessor. "That's
a blessed man, a man made up of holiness. . . . Proud of [his] tutelage, [he]
chose rather to leave [his] books than part with Giovanni. . . . But the fruits of
all [his] hopes are lost in [him], as [he is] in [him]self."

VASQUES, trusty servant to Soranzo, "by birth a Spaniard, brought forth [his] country
in [his] youth by Lord Soranzo's father whom whilst he lived [he] served
faithfully."

PUTANA, tutoress and guardian to Annabella.

POGGIO, servant to Bergetto.

A Cardinal, "the Pope's reverend nuncio," protector of Grimaldi.

A Masque of Ladies, "in white robes with garlands of willows," who dance at the
wedding of Annabella and Soranzo.

Banditti hired by Soranzo.

Officers, Servants, and Attendants.

Setting: Parma at some time during the Renaissance period.

> *"Never yet*
> *Incest and murder have so strangely met."*

Act I

Giovanni, the brilliant son of Signior Florio of Parma, has confessed to Friar Bonaventura, his former tutor at the University of Bologna, that he is infatuated with the matchless beauty of his own sister Annabella and overwhelmed by a fatal passion for her. The holy friar admonishes his pupil not to leave the schools of knowledge to converse with lust and death, for death waits on his lust, and begs him to pray earnestly that he may be freed from this leprosy that rots his soul.

The beautiful sister, Annabella, has several suitors—Grimaldi, a Roman and a "poor shadow of a soldier"; Soranzo, a rich young Parmese nobleman; and Bergetto, a simpleton, the nephew of a doting uncle, Donado. Of the three, Soranzo is the most desirable, even if he has been carrying on a flirtation with the lusty Hippolita, wife of Richardetto of Parma. Soranzo is handsome, and young, and bountiful. But in the eyes of Annabella, no one compares with her brother Giovanni. One day, seeing that unhappy young man walking with downcast eyes, beating his breast and drowned in tears, the girl tries to comfort him, and at last wrings from him a confession of his long suppressed infatuation. Melodramatically, Giovanni offers her his dagger that she may strike his guilty bosom and end his sinful life, but instead Annabella confesses her own love for him. On their knees the lovers exchange vows, rings, and a kiss.

Act II

Soon the rivalry among Annabella's suitors becomes acute. Soranzo is so much in love that he neglects Hippolita, and the jilted mistress comes to his rooms to reproach him with perjury and her shame. Encouraged by Soranzo's promises of marriage should she become a widow, Hippolita has counselled her husband Richardetto to make a voyage to Leghorn to bring home an orphaned niece; and on the way, it is reported, he has died. Now, for love of Annabella Soranzo has repudiated his vows, and the scorned woman plots revenge for his breach of promise. She makes overtures to Vasques, Soranzo's servant, for assistance in carrying it out. Unknown to both of the lovers, however, Richardetto has not died, but with his niece Philotis he has returned to Parma in the disguise of a learned physician so that he may keep an eye on his wife and be revenged upon her paramour. Grimaldi, in his turn, also plots against Soranzo, joining forces with the new physician, who finds him a ready agent for his revenge, and promises to supply poison for his rapier. Bergetto, the third lover, is soon eliminated as a contender. He cannot woo for himself; his uncle must speak for him, and Annabella graciously but emphatically suggests that he find someone more worthy of his choice, for she has no intention of becoming his wife. The uncle Donado is deeply disappointed, but Bergetto readily transfers his affections to Philotis, the physician's niece, who is a very modest, well-behaved young maid, and more attainable.

Meanwhile, in spite of the repeated entreaties of the friar, Giovanni and Annabella continue to meet. The holy man's counsel that the girl be married, Giovanni indignantly refuses to accept: "that's to damn her; that's to prove her greedy variety of lust."

Act III

At last it is necessary for Annabella to marry one of her suitors, and Soranzo is chosen, the formal betrothal to take place immediately at Friar Bonaventura's cell. Richardetto, the attending physician, however, informs Grimaldi of the plan and supplies him with the promised poison for their revenge. At the same time, Philotis, his niece, informs Richardetto of the plan of her suitor Bergetto to be married that very night, lest the match be opposed by his uncle. Hence, it happens that in the dark Grimaldi mistakes Bergetto for Soranzo on the way to the friar's cell, and kills the unfortunate fellow.

The betrothal of Annabella and Soranzo goes forward without immediate mishap. To the friar the girl makes full confession of her sins, repents sincerely with bitter tears, and receives absolution. The wedding is to take place two days hence. But Hippolita resolves to prevent it by revenging herself upon her lover Soranzo.

Act IV

At the wedding feast all drink to the happiness of the bride and groom, except Giovanni, whose unwillingness to do so passes almost unnoticed, because of a masque of ladies all in white who dance with garlands of willows. They are led by Hippolita, whose unmasking creates a sensation. She comes as a friend, she insists, asks for a cup of wine to confirm it, and Vasques, whom she thought her accomplice, proves his worth to his master by giving her a poisoned cup. Cursing

Soranzo and his marriage, Hippolita dies. In the presence of this double misfortune, Richardetto the husband then advises his niece Philotis to return to Cremona and to become a nun.

Soon after the wedding Soranzo discovers his wife's condition, and in his rage learns that it was not for love she chose him but for honor. Though threatened with death, she refuses to name her lover. But the clever and hypocritical Vasques extracts the truth from Putana, Annabella's maid and confidante, whom he immediately turns over for torture to banditti in his employ.

Act V

With the intention in a sensational manner of wreaking his vengeance upon the guilty brother and sister, Soranzo prepares a sumptuous birthday feast to which he invites not only Florio, their father, but all of the magnificoes of the city. But through a letter which Annabella has written with her blood and dropped from her window at the friar's feet, Giovanni is warned of Soranzo's intentions. Knowing that it is a plot to bring about his ruin, Giovanni nevertheless boldly resolves to attend. He has a last meeting with Annabella before the feast, however, and to save her fame as well as to forestall Soranzo's vengeance, he stabs her to death. With Annabella's heart upon his dagger, Giovanni enters the banquet hall, tells what he has done, fights with Soranzo and kills him, and dies at last at the hands of the banditti Vasques has hired for murder. Florio, the old father, dies of a broken heart, and Vasques, the villain, is banished.

THE BROKEN HEART

A TRAGEDY

(1625-1633)

DRAMATIS PERSONAE

(The Speakers' Names Fitted to Their Qualities)

AMYCLAS [*a name common to the kings of Laconia*], King of Sparta, and father of Calantha.

CALANTHA [*Flower of Beauty*], "the princess, the king's daughter, sole heir of Sparta," a girl of "beauty, virtue, sweetness, and singular perfections"; later, betrothed to Ithocles. Hers is the "Broken Heart."

NEARCHUS [*Young Prince*], Prince of Argos, suitor for the hand of Calantha, and grandchild to Amyclas' aunt.

ITHOCLES [*Honor of Loveliness*], son of Thrasus [*Fierceness*] and brother of Penthea; in love with Calantha. "Fair spring of manhood, . . . proud of youth, and prouder in his power, . . . [he] brings to [Sparta's] gates triumphs and peace upon his conquering sword. . . . Blunt and rough-spoken, vouchsafing not the fustian of civility, which less rash spirits style good manners, . . . [he is] a friend firm and unalterable, . . . but a brother more cruel than the grave. . . . [He] did the noble Orgilus much injury, but grieved Penthea more,"

PENTHEA [*Complaint*], only daughter of Thrasus, sister of Ithocles, wife of Bassanes, and once betrothed of Orgilus, "a miserable creature, . . . ruined by those tyrants, a cruel brother and a desperate dotage, . . . [and] a ravished wife widowed by lawless marriage. . . . Much old in griefs, in years [she is] a child,"

} "two branches of one stock, . . . brought up twins together, yet have lived at distance like two strangers."

BASSANES [*Vexation*], a jealous nobleman, aged husband of Penthea; "delights to him are troublesome. . . . What can you look for from an old, foolish, peevish, doting man but craziness of age?"

ORGILUS [*Angry*], son of Crotolon, brother of Euphranea, and once betrothed to Penthea; "he's an honest, very honest gentleman; a man of single meaning." He assumes the disguise of a student APLOTES [*Simplicity*], "a mushroom on whom the dew of heaven drops now and then."

EUPHRANEA [*Joy*], a maid of honor, daughter of Crotolon, sister of Orgilus, and, later, wife of Prophilus.

PROPHILUS [*Dear*], friend of Ithocles, "a deserving and a hopeful youth," and suitor for the hand of Euphranea.

CROTOLON [*Noise*], a councilor of state, "bold and bitter," and the father of Orgilus and Euphranea.

ARMOSTES [*an Appeaser*], another councilor and uncle of Ithocles and Penthea.

TECNICUS [*Artist*], a philosopher, a "reverend oracle" and man of wisdom.

AMELUS [*Trusty*], friend of Nearchus.

PHULAS [*Watchful*], servant of Bassanes.

GRAUSIS [*Old Beldam*], an old lady, overseer of Penthea.

HEMOPHIL, "the hardy" [*Glutton*],
"Most potent" GRONEAS [*Tavern Haunter*],
who "lie[s] beyond all modesty," } two courtiers.

CHRISTALLA [*Crystal*], later betrothed to Amelus; "she'll prove a constant wife,"
PHILEMA [*a Kiss*], later dedicated to Vesta's temple, } maids of honor.

Courtiers, Officers, Pallbearers, and Attendants.

Setting: Sparta about the eighth century B.C.

> "O, royal maid, would thou hadst missed this part;
> Yet 'twas a brave one."

Act I

Orgilus, a young gentleman of Sparta, asks leave of his father Crotolon to study for a time in Athens. At first Crotolon is reluctant to let his son go, until he hears the true reason for his journey. Some years previously there raged between the families headed by Crotolon and the now-dead Thrasus a feud which the present king Amyclas ended by reconciling the leaders and by betrothing Thrasus' only daughter, Penthea, to Crotolon's only son, Orgilus. But before the marriage could take place, Thrasus died, and Ithocles, his proud son, nursed closely the memory of former discontent to glory in revenge. Partly by cunning and partly by threats, he set aside the engagement of his virtuous sister to his enemy, ignored the fact that she and Orgilus were in love, and forced the girl to marry Bassanes, an old nobleman who is rich enough, but who is insanely jealous. "All eyes who gaze upon that shrine of beauty, he doth resolve, do homage to the miracle; someone, he is assured, may now or then, if opportunity but sort, prevail. So much, out of a self-unworthiness, his fears transport him—not that he finds cause in her obedience, but his own distrust." As a former suitor of Penthea, Orgilus is the husband's chief suspect, and for this reason the young man now prefers a voluntary exile in studious Athens to life in Sparta— his absence will relieve the cares of jealous Bassanes, free Penthea from a hell on earth, and help the lover himself forget what he has lost. When Crotolon hears these reasons, he gives Orgilus free consent to go. But as the young man takes leave of his sister Euphranea, he makes her swear never to marry any man, however worthy he may be, until she has not only her father's, but also her brother's, leave.

About the same time, Ithocles, Penthea's cruel brother, returns to Sparta in triumph after his conquest of Messene to receive upon his temples from the Princess Calantha a provincial chaplet in honor of his victory. In his train are many courtiers, including Hemophil, Groneas, and especially Prophilus, a gentleman of much desert, all of whom return with alacrity to the occupations of peace, including love-making.

Meanwhile, instead of traveling to Athens as he had said, Orgilus has disguised himself as Aplotes, a simple scholar, and become the pupil of the great philosopher Tecnicus. Thus transformed he thinks he may without suspicion keep an eye upon both "Penthea's usage and Euphranea's faith." One day, while enjoying the privilege accorded Tecnicus' pupils of walking in the palace gardens, Aplotes sees Euphranea in amorous conversation with Prophilus, the close friend of his enemy Ithocles, overhears their love-making, and, protected by his scholar's gown, agrees, for books, not money, safely and secretly to convey such letters as each shall send the other.

Act II

Bassanes' jealousy of Penthea is even worse than Orgilus has reported it. Prompted by a selfish love which is monstrous, but pretending that Penthea may be queen of what delights she fancies best, the old dotard keeps his lady a virtual prisoner in his house and sets two of his servants, Phulas and Grausis, to watch over her. Naturally, Penthea is oversad, indifferent to every interest, and in poor health. Naturally, too, because of what has occurred, Penthea has not immediately called upon her brother after his return to Sparta. But now she hears from Prophilus that Ithocles is somewhat altered recently, and that he is sad, silent, and slack in following his customary recreations. And when she receives from Ithocles himself a pressing invitation for her to come to see him, Penthea goes to court to visit her brother. The young warrior is called away, however, by the king, who is receiving the Prince of Argos, suitor for his daughter, Calantha, and Ithocles bids Penthea meet him alone an hour hence in the palace garden; he has a secret to communicate to her. Old Bassanes is suspicious of even this meeting of brother and sister.

As she waits for Ithocles in the garden, however, Penthea encounters the scholar Aplotes, who discloses his real identity to her, reminds her that their trothplight still makes her his, and demands to possess his wife. But to the virtuous Penthea the past is dead. Bidding Orgilus resume his scholar's gown and step back some distance from her, the unhappy lady acknowledges her love for him, begs him not to try to see her again, urges him to marry, and vows, even were she widowed, never to be his wedded wife—her true love "abhors to think that Orgilus deserved no better favors than a second bed." As they part, Orgilus resolves to act and not talk any more; he sighs Penthea's name, and looks "not like the ruins of his youth, but like the ruins of those ruins." Penthea is sent for by her brother, who has become suddenly ill.

Meanwhile, the love of Euphranea and Prophilus has resulted in a proposal of marriage which lacks only the approval of Orgilus to be confirmed. The betrothal also has the support of Ithocles, who thinks of it as a devout and hearty union between his own family and that of Crotolon, as if his own blood, and not only that of his friend, had interest in it. But Crotolon boldly presses home the old injury: "Had this sincerity been real once, my Orgilus had not been now unwived, nor your lost sister buried in a bridebed." Nevertheless, the old man gives his consent and writes to Athens for his son's return to Sparta.

Act III

In his interview with Penthea, whom he really loves, Ithocles reveals that he has been deeply moved by these reproaches and by the obvious unhappiness which his thoughtless cruelty has caused. Believing that his illness is serious, Ithocles begs his sister's pardon for what is past, and then reveals to her his secret. He too is in love—with Calantha, the princess, sole heir of Sparta! Such presumption, of course, is treasonable, but ambition has no part in Ithocles' motives, only love. As yet, Calantha knows nothing of it, nor does Prophilus, his nearest friend. Unable to refrain, in supposition, from asking Ithocles how he would feel if he should be contracted to Calantha and her father capriciously snatched her from his arms against her will and forced her on the Prince of Argos, Penthea, nevertheless, is reconciled with her brother and promises to assist him as best she can. Ithocles' contrition is cut short, however, by an exhibition of the insane jealousy to which his thoughtlessness has subjected his sister. Bassanes, poniard in hand, interrupts their interview, suspicious of incest, and has to be restrained from violence. But even this folly the long-suffering Penthea bears patiently.

In due time Orgilus, having taken leave of Tecnicus, puts in his appearance at court, where he enjoys unexpected cordiality from Ithocles, and where, with no apparent malice, he confirms his sister's betrothal to Prophilus. Meanwhile, Nearchus, Prince of Argos, receives Amyclas' permission to pay court to his daughter Calantha. And, finding an opportunity to be alone with the princess, Penthea skillfully fulfills her promise to Ithocles. Having gained Calantha's sympathy by allusion to the melancholy life from which only Death can free her, Penthea asks Calantha to be executrix of her will. Weeping, the princess consents. Penthea has only three jewels to bequeath: her youth, which she would leave to "virgin wives, such as abuse not wedlock by freedom of desires"; her fame, by scandal yet untouched, which she bequeaths "to Memory, and Time's old daughter, Truth"; and, more precious than the other two, her brother, which she bequeaths "in holiest rites of love . . . to great Calantha, Sparta's heir." To the earnest pleading which accompanies this bequest, Calantha appears deaf, and she gives Penthea no answer. But, clearly, the princess is moved by this revelation of Ithocles' love for her.

Act IV

However much Ithocles' new friendship for Orgilus may cause misgivings for both Crotolon and Armostes, it is clear that Penthea's reconciliation with her brother and her pleading for him have borne fruit. One day as Nearchus playfully tries to take a ring from Calantha's finger when Ithocles is by, the princess removes the jewel and with a witticism tosses it to Ithocles. As a result, jealous hatred breaks out between the Prince of Argos and the Spartan favorite, in which Ithocles' "tongue is not [his] friend," and in which Orgilus, like most peacemakers, draws the fire of the most impassioned side. It is then that Tecnicus, who is on his way to the king with a Delphian oracle which he has deciphered, gives each of the young men something to think about. To Ithocles he says, weeping:

> *When youth is ripe, and age from time doth part,*
> *The lifeless trunk shall wed the broken heart.*

With Orgilus he leaves this dark sentence:

> *Let craft with courtesy awhile confer;*
> *Revenge proves its own executioner.*

Neither prophecy is understood.

Sudden illness of the king has produced grave concern about the future, and the oracle Tecnicus has deciphered is promptly opened:

> *The plot in which the vine takes root*
> *Begins to dry from head to foot;*
> *The stock soon withering, want of sap*
> *Doth cause to quail [i.e., die] the budding grape;*
> *But from the neighboring elm a dew*
> *Shall drop, and feed the plot anew.*

This is the oracle; the philosopher's exposition is equally brief:

> *The plot is Sparta; the dried vine the king;*
> *The quailing grape his daughter; but the thing*
> *Of most importance, not to be revealed,*
> *Is a near prince, the elm—the rest concealed.*

The court can only await the fulfillment of the prophecy.

Meanwhile, events move rapidly. Penthea's anguish is more than she can bear, and she goes mad. Euphranea and Prophilus are married. Nearchus, who suspects Calantha's preference for Ithocles, is reconciled with his rival. At his daughter's request, King Amyclas betrothes Calantha to Ithocles. As Orgilus and Ithocles discuss this turn of fortune, their minds filled with thoughts of an earlier engagement that should have bound them together in perpetual amity, they hear from Penthea's lodging the strains of sad music which suddenly stop. The girl is dead. As the cruel brother and the disappointed suitor sit beside the body of the wronged Penthea, Ithocles is suddenly caught by a mechanical contrivance, prepared beforehand by the unforgiving, treacherous Orgilus, and held fast. Craft has with courtesy a while conferred, and revenge follows. Orgilus stabs Ithocles to death.

Act V

Dancing at the wedding of Euphranea and Prophilus the Princess Calantha receives in succession the news of her father's death, Penthea's death, and Ithocles' murder. All of these reports she receives with a most stoical spirit. But she is more deeply moved than she reveals. As successor to the crown, her first act is one of justice; she sentences Orgilus, the confessed murderer, to death, the method to be determined by Orgilus and the assembled court to be the spectators of his end. Orgilus chooses to bleed to death, and to open a vein in his own arm, becoming his own executioner, and thus fulfilling the last part of Tecnicus' prophecy. Then in a temple, before an altar covered with white and in the presence of the body of Ithocles, Calantha, dressed in white, performs her last rites. She fulfills the oracle by naming Nearchus King of Sparta, Armostes viceroy in Argos, Crotolon ruler of Messene, and Bassanes Sparta's marshal. She bestows her waiting woman Christalla on Amelus, friend of Nearchus, and commends Philema unto Vesta's temple. She confers upon Prophilus all of the honors and titles which had once belonged to Ithocles. And then, placing her mother's wedding ring upon the finger of the corpse, she marries Ithocles indeed. But as she presses a kiss upon the cold lips of her husband, and sad music plays, Calantha's heart breaks. Thus is Tecnicus' prophecy to Ithocles fulfilled: "the lifeless trunk [has] wed the broken heart."

THE CHRONICLE HISTORY OF

PERKIN WARBECK

A STRANGE TRUTH

(1629–1634)

DRAMATIS PERSONAE

PERKIN WARBECK, "the Christian world's strange wonder, . . . an ornament of Nature, fine and polished, a handsome youth indeed, . . . [who is] styled . . . 'the fair white rose of England,' . . . [and claims to be] King Richard IV, . . . [and] sole heir to the great throne of old Plantagenets. . . . Concealed I know not where this fourteen years, . . . this dukeling mushroom, . . . the new revived York, [says he is] Edward [IV's] second son murdered long since i' th' Tower, [but he is really] an obscure peasant, by the rage of Hell loosed from his chains to set great kings at strife." ("Was ever so much impudence in forgery? The custom, sure, of being styled a king hath fastened in his thought that he is such,") } imposters and pretenders to the English throne, the "idols of Yorkish malice."

LAMBERT SIMNEL, his "predecessor in a dangerous uproar, . . . [who also] leaped to catch the moon." Now in King Henry's service, Lambert has been "preferred by an officious care of duty from the scullery to a falc'ner." Once he personated Edward, Earl of Warwick and son of George, Duke of Clarence, claimant to the throne,

STEPHEN FRION, a "practiced politician, . . . sometimes secretary in the French tongue unto [King Henry], but Perkin's tutor now, . . . a subtle villain, . . . French both in heart and actions. . . . [A] pestilent adder, he will hiss out poison as dang'rous as infectious,"

JOHN A WATER, "sometimes Mayor of Cork,"

HERON, "a broken mercer,"

SKETON, "a tailor,"

ASTLEY, "a scrivener,"

} Warbeck's followers. "Whate'er these list to treat of, Perkin must hearken to."

LADY KATHERINE GORDON, "in the full spring of youth and fresh in beauty." Daughter of the Earl of Huntley, "she's the king's kinswoman, placed near the crown, a princess of the blood"; is married to Perkin Warbeck; and becomes the "unequaled pattern of a matchless wife. . . . Here lives majesty in league with love. . . . Such another treasure the earth is bankrout of."

JANE DOUGLAS, Lady Katherine's maid, "the willing follower of all misfortunes."

HENRY VII, King of England; "a prince composed of sweetness, . . . he is wise as he is gentle."

SIR WILLIAM STANLEY, Henry VII's "chamberlain, [his] counselor, the love, the pleasure of [his] court, [his] bosom friend, the charge and the controlment of [his] person, the keys and secrets of [his] treasury, . . . [but accused and convicted as] both in his counsel and his purse the chief assistant to the feigned Duke of York. . . . [His] heart [seems] figured on [his] tongue."

Giles, BARON DAUBENEY, or DAWBNEY, later named Lord Chamberlain, as successor of Sir William Stanley,

The EARL OF OXFORD,

Howard, EARL OF SURREY,

} loyal supporters of King Henry VII.

SIR ROBERT CLIFFORD, accuser of Sir William Stanley. "A state informer's character [is] more ugly stamped on a noble name than on a base."

RICHARD FOX, Bishop of Durham; "he's nimble in his industry, and mounting."

URSWICK, chaplain to King Henry VII.

DON PEDRO AYALA, or HIALAS, a Spanish agent and "a Castilian born. King Ferdinand, with wise Queen Isabel, his royal consort, write [him] a man of worthy trust and candor."

JAMES IV, King of Scotland; "young and forward, . . . 'a studies to be wise betimes."

Alexander Gordon, EARL OF HUNTLEY, "a plain subject, nor more nor less"; father of Katherine Gordon, he "doted on every hair that grew to trim her head."

LORD DALIELL, suitor for the hand of Katherine Gordon; later, the "rare, unexampled pattern of a friend. . . . Young in years, . . . [but] old in honors, . . . [he is] a noble lad, a handsome, descended from an honorable ancestry, . . . a spark of mettle! 'A has a brave fire in him."

The EARL OF CRAWFORD,

The COUNTESS OF CRAWFORD,

} attendants at the Scottish court.

MARCHMOUNT, a Scottish herald.

A Constable, a Sheriff, an Executioner, another Herald, a Post, Officers, Soldiers, Guard, Masquers, Noblemen, Ladies, Servingmen, Mob, and Attendants.

Setting: England and Scotland, 1495–99.

"The threats of majesty, the strength of passion,
Hopes of an empire, change of fortunes—all."

Act I

After ninety years of civil war in which there were sacrificed "ten English kings and princes, threescore great dukes and earls, a thousand lords and valiant knights, two hundred fifty thousand of English subjects," peace, it seemed, had come at last to England, and "this blood-shrunk commonwealth" been given "a new soul, new birth," in the person of King Henry VII. But the new sovereign is still haunted and pursued by the "ghosts of York." "Fresh coals of division" have been fanned into flame by Margaret of Burgundy, sister to the tyrant Richard of Gloucester, who with "some shreds, some useless remnant of the house of York," has recently supported two pretenders to the English throne. These are Lambert Simnel, who is said to be Edward, son of George, Duke of Clarence, and Perkin Warbeck, who is said to be Richard, younger son of Edward IV, thought murdered in the Tower by his uncle, Richard III. Lambert Simnel's claims, though supported by some powerful English and Irish nobles, soon came to naught, and for some time now the pretender himself has been in the service of King Henry, "preferred by an officious care of duty from the scullery to a falc'ner." But the star of Perkin Warbeck, the younger, is in the ascendancy. Styled "the fair white rose of England," Warbeck claims to be King Richard IV, has gained support in Ireland and France, and, having failed in one attempt to land in England, is now planning another. Attending Warbeck are Stephen Frion, "a subtle villain, . . . French both in heart and actions," who was once secretary in the French tongue to King Henry and is now turned traitor; Heron, a mercer; John a Water, once Mayor of Cork; Sketon, a tailor; Astley, a scrivener —"never had counterfeit such a confuséd rabble of lost bankrouts for counselors. . . . Whate'er these list to treat of, Perkin must hearken to." They have urged him "to fly to Scotland to young James the Fourth, and sue for aid to him."

Many of these circumstances are made known to King Henry by Sir Robert Clifford, once in the services of the "sorceress of Burgundy," but now imprisoned in the Tower, and prevailed upon by promises of mercy to reveal to the king what he knows of Warbeck's plots and the names of his English supporters. Clifford mentions several, including some churchmen—John Ratcliffe, Lord Fitzwater; Sir Simon Mountford; Sir Thomas Thwaites; Worsley, Dean of St. Paul's; and others— and then he hesitates to name one more—Sir William Stanley, King Henry's Lord Chamberlain and bosom friend, the knight who rescued

him on Bosworth Field from Richard's bloody sword and snatched from
that tyrant's head the kingly crown and placed it on the Tudor's. Sir
William Stanley, Clifford charges, both in his counsel and his purse is
the chief assistant to the feigned Duke of York. The revelation is truly
staggering to the king, who orders Stanley confined to his room under
guard. Hard upon the news of this treason comes word that ten thousand Cornish, grudging to pay King Henry's subsidies and led by a
blacksmith and a lawyer, are marching on London, gathering head as
they advance.

Meanwhile in Scotland, Lord Daliell, a handsome young nobleman
descended "from Adam Mure, . . . whose daughter was the mother
to him who first begot the race of Jameses," comes to woo Katherine
Gordon, daughter of the Earl of Huntley, and a princess of the royal
blood. Although he must overcome the objections of the lady's father
and does gain his support, young Daliell's suit does not thrive; fair
Katherine is glad to have him merely as a friend. Their interview is
interrupted by word that the secretary of the Duke of York has arrived at court, and rumors that Perkin Warbeck himself is following
close at hand. There's "bustling for majesty."

Act II

When Perkin Warbeck arrives at the Scottish court, his reception by
the king is extraordinary, although some of the court ladies cannot
refrain from remarking about the pretender and his followers that
"they are disguiséd princes, brought up . . . to honest trades." When
Warbeck tells his story and presents his claims, King James is impressed
by the young man's bearing and his princely language. He offers the
pretender his support in these words: "Be whate'er thou art, thou
never shalt repent that thou hast put thy cause and person into my
protection"—words which Perkin Warbeck is to remember ruefully
later. Even those who had scoffed before now are touched as if his
cause were theirs.

Before long, "this dukeling mushroom" charms both king and
court, wooing "the ladies as if his strength of language chained attention by power of prerogative." He is especially attentive to Katherine
Gordon, and, in spite of her father's strong objections, King James
bestows his kinswoman in marriage on Perkin Warbeck—"an union
this way settles possession in a monarchy established rightly." But old
Huntley refuses his blessing to his daughter. Thus far, however, the pretender's tide runs smoothly with but few adverse winds.

Meanwhile, in England, Sir William Stanley has been tried, condemned, and, despite King Henry's known tendency to mercy, sent to

the block. Lord Dawbney is appointed chamberlain, and Clifford the informer is banished from court and confined to London. The Cornish rebels have reached Winchester. Against them the king sends an army under Oxford and Dawbney, and to secure the border against invasion he dispatches the warlike Bishop of Durham to Norham. Against possible aggression by "the death-daring Scots," he bids Surrey raise an army. "War must breed peace; such is the fate of kings."

Act III

In his campaigns, King Henry is very successful. The Cornish rebels do indeed advance as far as Kent, but disappointed of expected aid from the Kentish, they are defeated, and the ringleaders of the commotion—Audley, Flammock, and Joseph—taken prisoner. Mercifully, the king permits such as have escaped thus far to steal back to their country without pursuit. The king keeps his army intact, however, until he hears the news from Scotland, where there are enemies more dangerous than those at home. But the king, in secret, has a political charm "that shall loose the witchcraft wherewith young King James is bound, and free it at [his] pleasure without bloodshed."

At his court in Westminster is Pedro Ayala, or Hialas, a Spaniard, emissary from King Ferdinand and Queen Isabel of Aragon. These sovereigns have just achieved success against the Moors, and with an eye on future amity, have sent Hialas to England and to Scotland to make peace between the neighbor kingdoms. King Henry receives Hialas graciously and rewards him bountifully for there is talk that if King Henry can be sure of his subjects, such a wild runagate as Perkin Warbeck might soon be caged, and that a marriage between Katherine, daughter of Ferdinand and Isabella, and Arthur, Prince of Wales, might be arranged on certain conditions. The king sends letters instantly to Bishop Fox of Durham. "King Ferdinand is not so much a fox but that a cunning huntsman may in time fall on the scent."

Meanwhile, in Scotland, the Earl of Huntley disowns his daughter Katherine because of her marriage to Perkin Warbeck; an expedition is fitted out; and the young pretender is proclaimed King of England. It remains to be seen how the English stand affected to his title.

That question is soon answered when the Scottish force lays siege to Norham Castle. Its defender, Bishop Fox, denounces Warbeck as an imposter and a vagabond, begs King James to consider how he breaks the peace with a neighbor king who courts his amity, and bids him, while there is time, to shake off the viper that now gnaws his entrails. James is deeply affected, not so much by the bishop's denunciation or by Warbeck's retaliatory rhetoric, as by the fact that not one nobleman, not a petty burgess of some town; no, not a villager has appeared to join the pretender's faction. It is apparent that Perkin Warbeck's fortunes are changing.

Especially is this clear when word comes that King Henry has in open field defeated the rebels who supported Warbeck, that Howard, Earl of Surrey, with strong backing is on his way to raise the siege, that Brooke is admiral at sea, and that Dawbney follows with a second army. In vain does Warbeck insist that these forces come to side with him. As a final gesture, however, King James sends to the general Surrey a challenge to single combat, brushing aside Warbeck's request that he take the quarrel on him.

Act IV

Near Ayton Castle on the border, when the opposing armies meet it is even more apparent that Perkin Warbeck is the pathetic dupe and pawn of intriguers less honest and more cunning than he is. The Scottish king grows frosty and wayward, especially since the Spanish agent has had private conferences with him. Warbeck is no longer called to council, and it is clear that King Henry's "policies stir with too many engines." The English have been everywhere successful in battle; Cundrestine, Hedonhall, Edington, Fulden, and Ayton—all have yielded and been demolished. King James's challenge to Surrey, therefore, is neither accepted nor declined. It is evaded and smothered in diplomacy, for to the English these gay flourishes, the bad weather, the cost of the campaign, and the lack of success—all are an indication that the Scots are tired of the war. Hence, Bishop Fox of Durham returns to the Scottish camp with the herald who brought the challenge, and soon King Henry scores another diplomatic victory. France, Spain, and Germany have joined in a league of friendship with England. Nothing is lacking for peace throughout Christendom but amity between the British monarchs, James and Henry. The King of Spain favors marriage of his daughter Katherine to Arthur, Prince of Wales, an alliance satisfactory to France. King James is a bachelor, and King Henry has a daughter, Princess Margaret. "I need not urge what honor, what felicity can follow on such affinity betwixt two Christian kings inleagued by ties of blood." The only condition is that James withdraw his protection from Perkin Warbeck and banish him from his kingdom. "A league with Ferdinand? A marriage with English Margaret? A free release from restitution for the late affronts? Cessation from hostility? And all for Warbeck, not delivered, but dismissed?" The Scottish king could not wish for better; "the Tudor hath been cunning in his plots."

Hence, Perkin Warbeck is sacrificed, and his sun is setting. Accompanied by his loving wife, Katherine, and the faithful Daliell, he sets out for Cornwall, where, rumor has it, the inhabitants expect him daily. Meanwhile, in England, to the surprise of his generals, the foxy King Henry orders his armies to peaceful Salisbury in the southwest. He has had letters from the North.

Act V

In Cornwall a few yeomen with bow and sword—some four thousand strong—do join the ill-fated pretender, but at Exeter they are dispersed by the Earl of Devonshire. Warbeck, himself, marches to Taunton, where he is met by Dawbney, and his army. But the night before the forces are to join battle, Warbeck flees, and the English are again victorious without bloodshed. At St. Michael's Mount, Katherine, her maid Jane, and Daliell are taken prisoners by the Earl of Oxford, and later, from sanctuary at Bewley, near Southampton, the fugitive Warbeck and his followers are apprehended. King Henry treats his captives with courtesy and consideration. He even tolerates Warbeck's rhetoric—"O, let him range. The player's on the stage still; 'tis his part; 'a does but act." But it is apparent that being treated like a king has convinced Warbeck that he is one, and it is necessary to teach him another language—in the Tower.

Even King Henry's patience comes to an end, however. Doomed by jury to the gallows, having escaped from the Tower twice, and having inveigled to his support his fellow prisoner, Edward, Earl of Warwick, whose head must pay the price, Perkin Warbeck is imprisoned in the stocks and pursued by a mob. But he still may have the king's mercy if he will but confess his parentage. Yet, he is stubborn to the end, even when Lambert Simnel, his predecessor in a dangerous Yorkist uproar, reveals that Perkin is "Osbeck's son of Tournay, a loose runagate, a landloper" and that his "father was a Jew, turned Christian merely to repair his miseries." Throughout, Perkin's wife remains constant to him. "Be what these people term thee," she says, "I am certain thou art my husband. . . . 'Tis injustice for any earthly power to divide us." At last, still maintaining his royal descent and bidding the onlookers see the termination of the glorious line of fourteen Plantagenet kings, Perkin Warbeck is led off to execution.

JAMES SHIRLEY
(1596–1666)

BIOGRAPHY. "The last of the Elizabethans," James Shirley wrote wholly in the reign of Charles I. Born in 1596, he was the son of a London merchant, was educated at the Merchant Tailors' School and at both Oxford and Cambridge. After his graduation he was ordained, and for a time served as both parish priest and schoolmaster in or near St. Albans. Probably he became a convert to Roman Catholicism; certainly he gave up his living about 1624, entered Gray's Inn, and about the time of the death of Fletcher "set up a play-maker" to become one of the most prolific authors for the stage. At the closing of the theatres he was the leading dramatist of the day for comedy, tragi-comedy, and tragedy, being equally proficient in all three forms. For a time he attended his patron, the Duke of Newcastle, during the Civil Wars, and then returned to schoolteaching. In 1647 he edited the first collected edition of Beaumont and Fletcher. Alone among the major dramatists Shirley survived until after the Restoration, and died in 1666 from exposure during the Great Fire. He was buried in St. Giles-in-the-Fields.

CRITICAL COMMENT. In the main, Shirley belongs to the school of Fletcher, and even more than his master he looks forward to the comedy of the Restoration. Like his successors, he wrote almost exclusively for the limited audience of the court. *The Lady of Pleasure* is a typical Shirley comedy, and a play like this reveals clearly how comedies of manners in the Restoration mode were already in the making before the closing of the theatres in 1642. The play is satirical, the dialogue is witty, the plot is one of intrigue in the lower levels of fashionable society. The theme is conversion from folly and libertinism, and the characters, of which there is a variety, tend to be well-defined types. Moreover, they are like the people of almost any comedy of manners, and specifically Sir Thomas Bornwell and his calculating lady Aretina anticipate Sir Peter and Lady Teazle in Sheridan's *The School for Scandal* (1777). In structure the play presents a brilliant contrast between a life of extravagance and licentiousness on the one hand, and one of moderate liberality and innocent gaiety on the other. Just as in the main plot a lady addicted to worldly pleasure is cured of her folly by a husband who pretends to follow a similar road to ruin, so in the subplot a noble roué slips into license and is brought again to a course of honor by the wit and the charm of a virtuous woman. Celestina, the rich and lovely widow, is a good example of Shirley's favorite character type, "the witty fair one," gay, frank, fond of men, but respectable.

The Cardinal, a thrilling tragedy, Shirley thought "the best of my flock," but it has many conventional elements. In essence it is a play of blood and revenge, consisting of three main variations on the theme: (*a*) the revenge of a discarded suitor upon his successful rival; (*b*) the revenge of a wife upon the murderer of her husband; and (*c*) the revenge of a ruthless Machiavellian churchman upon a lady who has defied his power and disprized his kinsman. *The Duchess of Malfi* is the play's closest prototype, but its central figure lacks the tragic strength and stature of Webster's heroine. To some extent *The Cardinal* had added interest for contemporary audiences because of Richelieu in France.

SOURCES. No literary sources for either *The Lady of Pleasure* or *The Cardinal* are known.

BIBLIOGRAPHY

Collected Works:

The *Dramatic Works and Poems of James Shirley*, edited by W. Gifford and Alexander Dyce, 6 volumes, 1833.

The Best Plays of James Shirley, edited by Edmund Gosse, Mermaid Series, 1888.

Monographs:

R. S. Forsythe, *Shirley's Plays in Their Relation to the Elizabethan Drama,* 1914.

A. H. Nason, *James Shirley: Dramatist,* 1915.

H. T. Parlin, *Shirley's Comedy of London Life,* University of Texas Bulletin, 1914.

The Lady of Pleasure:

Early edition: 1637.

The Cardinal:

Early edition: 1653 [in *Six New Plays*].

THE LADY OF PLEASURE

A COMEDY

(1635)

DRAMATIS PERSONAE

SIR THOMAS BORNWELL, who, to please his wife, "against [his] own opinion [has] quitted the country, . . . [and] changed a calm and retired life for this wild town, composed of noise and charge. . . . [Sir Thomas has] to such a height fulfilled her humor, all application's [i.e., all pleading with her to be reasonable is] dangerous." ("He has good parts, they say, but cannot help his lady's bias.")

ARETINA, his wife, come to town for pleasure, the fashionably extravagant "lady that so revels in the Strand. . . . A gamester, too."

CELESTINA, Lady Bellamour, a young widow that "has mourned out her year . . . for the honest knight that had compassion of her youth and died so timely. . . . My conversation ne'er knew so elegant and brave a soul, . . . so spirited, so courtly, speaks the languages, sings, dances, plays o' the lute to admiration, is fair and paints not, games too, keeps a table, and talks most witty satire. . . . [She's] not in love, and men shall never make [her] heart lean with sighing, nor with tears draw on [her] eyes the infamy of spectacles. . . . [But] no widow left wealthy can be thoroughly warm in mourning."

A Lord, kinsman to Aretina. "Since the fair Bella Maria died, [his] blood is cold, nor is there beauty enough surviving to heighten [him] to wantonness. . . . 'Tis time he were reduced to the old sport. One lord like him more would undo the court."

Master Alexander Kickshaw, "the gentleman with his own head of hair,"

Master John Littleworth, "the gallant that still danceth in the street, and wears a gross of ribbon in his hat; that carries oringado in his pockets, and sugarplums to sweeten his discourse, that studies compliment, defies all wit in black [i.e., in print], and censures plays that are not bawdy,"

"wits of the town, . . . whose jeers are all authentic. The taverns and the ordinaries are made academies where [they] come, and all [their] sins and surfeits made the time's example. [Their] very nods can quell a theatre; no speech or poem good without [their] seal; [they] can protect scurrility, and publish; by [their] authority believed, no rapture ought to have honest meaning."

Master Frederick, Lady Bornwell's nephew, "but lately come from the university, where they completely corrupted him. . . . [His] tutor gives [him] a handsome character . . . and is sorry [his] aunt's pleasure commands [him] from [his] studies. . . . [But, alas, his] clothes smell o' the lamp." ("I fear he's spoiled forever! He did name Logic, and may, for aught I know, be gone so far [as] to understand it.")

Sir William Scentlove, "an arrant epicure as this day lives, born to a pretty wit, a knight, but no gentleman. . . . There's one would be a client, . . . but in his guiltiness of little land, his expectation is not so valiant as it might be. He wears rich clothes and feeds with noblemen."

Master Haircut, a barber, "very gallant, and much courted by gentlemen of quality, . . . more than a trim, gay man; he has some great office, sure, by his confident behavior. . . . He is the sweetest of all men that visit [Celestina]." ("He is lost to goodness does not honor him.")

Lady Isabella Novice,
Mariana Novice, her sister, } kinswomen of Celestina's; "they partly are [her] pupils."

Madam Decoy, a procuress, who "does the trade an honor, credit to the profession. . . . [She has] done offices, and not a few of the nobility but have done feats within [her] house, which is convenient for situation and artful chambers and pretty pictures to provoke the fancy." ("I hope you make a difference between a lady that does honorable offices and one they call a bawd.")

Steward to the Lady Aretina; he "has some pretty notions, too, in moral mischief."

Steward to the Lady Celestina.

A Gentlewoman attending the Lady Celestina.

Secretary to the Lord.

Servants.

Setting: The Strand, London, in the seventeenth century.

> *"Give me the town wits, that deliver jests*
> *Clean from the bow, that whistle in the air,*
> *And cleave the pin at twelvescore!"*

Act I

Against his better judgment Sir Thomas Bornwell has sold his estates in the country and moved to London, changing "a calm and retired life for this wild town, composed of noise and charge"—all in order that his wife, Aretina, may enjoy the pleasures of the city. Now the lady follows all the ways of extravagance, buys gaudy furniture and pictures by this Italian master and that Dutchman, gives expensive banquets and suppers, keeps her coach and postilion, and dresses in rich satins, prodigal embroideries, plush, and cloth of silver. What is worse, she has taken to gaming, but as yet has acquired no skill to be a winner. She looks "not through the subtlety of cards and mysteries of dice"; she makes "play not a pastime but a tyranny," and wastes her husband's estate by it. So far her diversions are innocent if costly, her husband thinks, but Sir Thomas is at his wit's end to know where these ways will lead.

When callers begin to arrive, it is clear that Lady Bornwell has attracted a following in the world of fashion, and that Sir Thomas' misgivings have some foundation. There is Madam Decoy—just passing, but making bold to tender her respects. There is Master Alexander Kickshaw, whom the lady commended for his horsemanship in Hyde Park the other day. There is Master John Littleworth, who minces in his gait, studies compliment, and has a pretty reputation as a wit and a critic. They discuss a young widow, named Celestina, Lady Bellamour, who is so spirited, so courtly, so accomplished in languages, dancing, and music, and who is "fair and paints not, games too, keeps a table, and talks most witty satire. . . . She is full of jewels," adds Master Kickshaw, "but I am most taken with the bravery of her mind."

Sir Thomas knows that news of this rival troubles his wife and also that it will cost him something. Pretending to see the folly of thrift, the honest man corrects his censures, bids his wife follow her inclinations, and promises to be converted to pleasure himself. While "the outlandish man of art [i.e., a foreign artist] is copying out [his wife's] countenance," he gives directions to his steward for new extravagances. But his real purpose is to dance and play and spend as fast as Lady Bornwell does, and thus to frighten her into thrift.

In another house in the Strand, Celestina also interviews her steward and overrules all his caution that she live more nearly within her means. After a year of mourning she is "resolved to pay for some delight; [her] estate will bear it," and she can rein it shorter when she pleases. She, too, has callers—Master Haircut, who is obviously a gentleman and a sweet courtier; and Lady Novice and her sister, two of Celestina's kinswomen, who are partly her pupils in the art of living fashionably.

Act II

Lady Bornwell's social ambitions receive an unexpected and an undeserved setback in the arrival of Master Frederick, her favorite nephew, whom she has summoned from the university. Indeed, Aretina almost faints when she sees him. The young man is clad in black satin, "as if he were keeping Lent"; such costume is the vogue at the university, to be sure, but it is coming home from college thus that makes it dishonorable. What a pity Frederick was not sent to France! He might by this time have invented fashions for us and been a benefit to the kingdom. Then, when the young scholar speaks about his studies—Latin and Greek and Logic—Aretina calls for strong waters: "I fear he's spoiled forever! He did name Logic, and may, for aught I know, be gone so far [as] to understand it." There is, however, some hope for the boy. Aretina commends him to the breeding of Master Alexander Kickshaw and Master Littleworth, who are to help him "cast his academic skin, . . . make [him] a fine gentleman, and translate [him] out of [his] learned language . . . into the present Goth and Vandal, which is French." Advised by the steward to take a course of riot to content his friends, young Frederick repairs to the wine cellar to "commence in all the arts of London," and to make up for lost time.

Meanwhile, Celestina in turn is instructing her inexperienced kinswomen, Isabella and Mariana Novice, in the art of enjoying freedom and yet avoiding censure. "You see me merry," she boasts, "full of song and dancing, pleasant in language, apt to all delights that crown a public meeting; but you cannot accuse me of being prodigal of my favors to any of my guests. I do not summon by any wink a gentleman to follow me to my withdrawing chamber; I hear all their pleas in court. . . . Some ladies are so expensive in their graces . . . and so prodigal, that in a little time they have nothing but the naked sin left to reward their servants [i.e., lovers], whereas a thrift in our rewards will keep men long in their devotion, and preserve ourselves in stock, to encourage those that honor us."

This doctrine Celestina puts into effect with one suitor after another—Master Haircut, "the sweetest of all men" who visit her; Sir William Scentlove, who wears rich clothes but has little land; and Sir Thomas

Bornwell, who, though a stranger, has come to get acquainted with a neighbor and to invite Lady Bellamour to his house.

Act III

Meanwhile, Madam Decoy, the procuress, has sized up Aretina as virtuous but of "a very appliable nature," and calls on a lord, the distant kinsman of Aretina, to offer her services. At first the young man, who is still mourning for the fair Bella Maria, sends the old bawd packing. Then he reconsiders, calls the woman back, and dictates a letter for her to carry to Aretina. The letter warns his relative that her honor is in danger and that, should she fall from virtue, Madam Decoy would not blush to be a bawd. As he dictates his note, Sir William Scentlove and Master Kickshaw call to take this indifferent, constant man to visit the matchless Celestina. " 'Tis time he were reduced to the old sport. One lord like him more would undo the court."

The effect of the lord's letter upon the foolish Aretina is just the opposite of what he had intended. The lord has done Lady Bornwell a courtesy in disclosing Decoy's nature; here is a woman Aretina can trust, and she determines to employ her. Accordingly, Aretina whispers instructions to the bawd, mentioning no name, but insisting that the lover she has chosen shall not have the least knowledge of her name and person. Decoy is delighted.

By now, Master Littleworth and Master Kicksnaw have arrived, as well as Sir Thomas, with Celestina and her kinswomen. Lady Bornwell is instantly jealous of her rival, not so much because Sir Thomas is so attentive to her, but rather because Celestina's beauty outshines her own. Sir Thomas' attentions to the lady merely justify what Aretina has already done; "what would make other ladies pale with jealousy, gives but a license to my wand'rings." But she must also have revenge. Hence, she calls Littleworth and Kickshaw aside for instruction. They have reputations as wits and satirists; they must exercise their talents upon Celestina, seem to let all spring naturally from their own freedom, and talk her into humbleness or anger—Aretina doesn't care which. She will give them the signal to begin.

Celestina, however, is equal to all occasions. The preliminary introductions are conducted in fashionable French, in which language Celestina is accomplished. They are interrupted by young Frederick, intoxicated and completely out of hand; Celestina puts him in his place by calling him "little gentleman." When at last Aretina gives her avengers the nod to begin, the lady is only puzzled by the affront, rallies, and gives back remarks as caustic as she receives. But it is Sir Thomas who perceives that the attack is a conspiracy; he rescues Celestina from these "silken vermin," this "brace of horseleeches," these "pilchards." When Celestina has finished her tongue-lashing and leaves on the arm of Sir Thomas, the two men about town are not so triumphant as they pretend. Master Kickshaw, however, receives consolation in the form of a jewel and a letter, brought in by a servant. "'Tis some great lady, questionless, that has taken notice, and would satisfy her appetite." He agrees to obey the summons of his unknown admirer.

Act IV

Two men lead Master Kickshaw blindfold to a dark room in Madam Decoy's house. There, disguised as a beldam, Decoy meets him, tells him that she sent the jewel and the letter, and promises him better entertainment anon. To all appearances the hag has no teeth, one strong sneeze upon her "would make her quarters fall away; one kick would blow her up like gunpowder, and loose all her limbs. . . . Her phlegm would quench a furnace, and her breath would damp a musket bullet." Master Kickshaw has misgivings, but accepts the old woman's reassurances and a purse, and accompanies her to a chamber of love.

Soon, under the tutelage of Master Littleworth, young Frederick makes astonishing progress. A French tailor has transformed him into a perfect gentleman; he wears his clothes with a difference; his posture has improved; and Littleworth may converse with him now and preserve his credit. Frederick is ready for his fencing, his singing, his dancing, his riding, and his French masters, and other constant attendants upon a fine gentleman. Aretina is delighted, and Frederick grateful to his tutor's good discipline. The steward "has some pretty notions, too, in moral mischief," and when the elated Master Kickshaw arrives the three young men set out to put some of their knowledge into practice—to "outroar the Thames, and shake the bridge." Obviously, Master Kickshaw does not identify Aretina with his lady of the evening before, and she would be worse than mad to be her own betrayer.

Astonished at finding Aretina alone, Sir Thomas tries to make her jealous by acknowledging that it was his wife who disenchanted him from a dull husband to an active lover and that Celestina is a spell to keep off old age. But Aretina does not rise to the lure; she honestly commends her rival's excellencies and admits that Celestina is "a piece so angelically moving, I should think frailty excused to dote upon her form, and almost virtue to be wicked with her." Poor Sir Thomas is more puzzled than ever.

Meanwhile, introduced by Sir William Scentlove, the lord visits Celestina, who has by now imparted to her kinswomen, the Novices, all her knowledge of fashionable behavior, and is pleased to give them a demonstration. Celestina makes trial of the lord, but before he can make advances, she recalls him to virtue by a disconcerting report of his reputation for honor, and an appeal to his constancy to Bella Maria. He withdraws impressed by Celestina's charm and beauty.

Act V

From a servant Aretina hears that Sir Thomas is losing heavily at dice, that five hundred pounds are lost already, and five hundred more borrowed, and that now he has sent home for five hundred additional. Before the lady can grasp the significance of this prodigality, Sir Thomas himself comes home, treats the whole matter with extreme gaiety, speaks lightly of a diamond necklace he has ordered for Celestina, and describes the elaborate dinner party he is giving on the morrow. In vain does Aretina try to be casual about everything by mentioning the ball and the rich banquet she has arranged, especially when Sir Thomas mentions in passing that he has summed up his estate and finds that they have enough money left to last another month. He'd rather be lord of a month of pleasures than be years consuming what they have in foolish temperance, live in obscurity, and enjoy no fame for fashionable extravagance. When all is spent, Sir Thomas says he will join the army overseas, sleep in a muddy trench, earn four shillings a week, and if wounded badly enough, get a pension. As for his lady—no doubt she will do well enough. She has friends, and if her poverty and their pride cannot agree, she need have no trouble in finding a trade to live by; there are customers.

The appearance of Madam Decoy at this moment is ominous. So is that of Master Kickshaw and Master Frederick a minute later. The young men are tipsy; Littleworth has fallen into the Thames and turns up later. Left alone with Master Kickshaw, Aretina relies upon the sack he has drunk to make him talkative. She is not mistaken. Master Kickshaw grows boastful of the rich clothes he expects to have and the choice dishes that will grace his tables. Yesterday, to be sure, he was no such monarch. It is no fortunate hand at dice that has so lifted him up, but there are other games than dice. He places into Aretina's hands the jewelry and the purse he received from the dear friend who has promised to meet him again. Then he becomes confidential; it's a secret, but she is an "old witch, a strange, ill-favored hag, that for [his] company last night has wrought this cure upon [his] fortune. . . . 'Twas a she-devil, . . . a most insatiate abominable devil; . . . 'twas a hell-cat." Kickshaw's superstition is too much; when he is gone Aretina looks in the mirror: " 'Tis a false glass; sure I am more deformed. What have I done? My soul is miserable."

The problems of the Bornwells and their friends are quickly resolved. The lord who sent Aretina the warning letter comes to call, and Sir Thomas brings home Celestina. While Sir Thomas leaves the room with his repentant lady, the lord on second view of Celestina turns renegade and makes honorable love to her. Aretina Bornwell has come to her senses, promising to devote her life to virtue. Sir Thomas confesses that his prodigality was pretended merely to frighten his wife, and that they have wealth enough, if they use it nobly. The Bornwells will return to the country, and Frederick will be sent back to college. Decoy is dismissed, and may be converted. Master Kickshaw, come to borrow money because his Proserpine has broken her word and not met him today, is urged to repent his foolish life and find some other way to thrive at court than that of gigolo.

THE CARDINAL

A TRAGEDY

(1641)

DRAMATIS PERSONAE

The CARDINAL, "whom 'tis not wisdom to incense. . . . He governs all, . . . sits at helm of state, . . . [and] holds intelligence with every bird i' th' air. . . . When men of gifts and sacred function once decline from virtue, their ill deeds transcend example. . . . How came you by that cloven foot?"

DON COLUMBO, the Cardinal's nephew, "a gallant gentleman, . . . the darling of the war, whom victory hath often courted, . . . [and] the last of his great family. . . . He is a soldier, a rough-hewn man, and may show well at distance. His talk will fright a lady; War and grim-faced Honor are his mistresses; he raves to hear a lute; Love meant him not his priest. . . . His rage flows like a torrent, when he meets with opposition. Leave to wrastle with him, and his hot blood retreats into a calm, and then he chides his passion."

The DUCHESS ROSAURA, betrothed to Don Columbo, but in love with Count d'Alvarez, "divorced from her by the King's power. . . . She has a sweet and noble nature . . . that commends Alvarez; Hymen cannot tie a knot of two more equal hearts and blood."

COUNT D'ALVAREZ, in love with the duchess. "He's young and active, and . . . a gentleman of handsome composition."

DON HERNANDO, a colonel and "a man of a brave soul, . . . the less his safety."

The KING OF NAVARRE, a weak but honorable sovereign, eclipsed in power by the Cardinal; "none have more need of perspectives than kings."

VALERIA, a modest, noble lady.
CELINDA, "she that would be thought to have been Columbo's } ladies of the court. mistress; . . . she has not an honorable fame,"

PLACENTIA, a lady that waits upon the duchess.

ANTONIO, secretary to the duchess, "a staid and prudent gentleman; . . . I do suspect this fellow would be nibbling."

SIGNIOR ANTONELLI, the Cardinal's servant, one of his spawns.

ALPHONSO, a captain.

PEDRO, JAQUES, and others who prepare wedding theatricals.

A Surgeon, a Guard, a Gentleman-usher, Lords, Colonels, Captains, Officers, Soldiers, Torchbearers, Servants, and Attendants.

Setting: Navarre and the frontier of Aragon, at some unspecified time.

"You should be a reverend churchman."

Act I

In Navarre the Duchess Rosaura, virgin-widow of the young Duke Mendoza who was lost at sea, is to be married to Don Columbo, the great Cardinal's nephew. Columbo is a soldier, "a rough-hewn man, . . . [whose] talk will fright a lady; War and grim-faced Honor are his mistresses, . . . [and] Love meant him not his priest." But he has admirers. In spite of the betrothal, the duchess really loves the young Count d'Alvarez, a very different type of man, whose face, to some, has "too much of woman in 't," whose hair is black and curly, and who is "young and active, and composed most sweetly." Their engagement has been broken by order of the King on advice of the Cardinal, who is the power behind the throne, and who wishes his nephew Columbo, as the last of his great family, to add luster to their name by alliance to the duchess' fortune.

War breaks out with Aragon, of which, it is hinted, the Cardinal is not innocent as to cause, and Don Columbo is chosen general of the troops and ordered to leave for the front immediately. Hence, the wedding is postponed until he shall return, and, pretending concern for his safety, the duchess takes leave of her betrothed. But no sooner has he gone, than the lady sends for Count d'Alvarez. The lovers renew their vows, and Alvarez promises to marry her, should Columbo be killed in the war or should he for some reason—no matter what—give up his claim to the duchess and leave her free to choose another husband.

Act II

Columbo is an able general, but "his rage flows like a torrent when he meets with opposition," and he is oftentimes quick-tempered and hasty in his assignment of motives to those who disagree with him. At a council of war, called to consider the best means of taking a coveted town over the possession of which the enemy is jubilant, Columbo dislikes the advice of Colonel Hernando that they simply wait a while, and riot and overconfidence on the part of the Aragonese will spare them the effort of an attack. The general unjustly accuses the colonel of cowardice or treason—he may take his choice—and earns an enemy. Hernando promptly resigns his commission, and Columbo calls for ink and paper to write out his letter of release. The general's temper, therefore, is not of the best when he receives a letter from the duchess, and his disposition is not improved by the contents. Rosaura asks that he resign all interest in her love or person, leaving him no choice in honor but to agree to her request. To return to Navarre is impossible, as the lady must know; there is no opportunity to learn the cause of the request; and there is no other means of replying except by letter. In a rage Don Columbo draws a pistol on the innocent secretary who brought the duchess' letter, changes his tone as he professes to believe it a device to hasten his return from duty—love has a thousand arts—and writes an answer that the lady doesn't expect and that will put her soul to a noble test. Without reference to her letter he releases Rosaura completely and leaves her to her own choice.

When Don Columbo's release reaches the duchess, she hastens with it to the King, who has just been receiving Don Hernando and promising to reconcile him and his general. Rosaura asks that she be re-engaged to Count d'Alvarez. The court agrees that the request is only justice under the circumstances, and the King grants her plea. But the subtle Cardinal is both puzzled and incensed that Columbo should thus forsake his lady, and the subsequent interview between the churchman and the duchess bodes only evil for the reunited lovers.

Act III

Preparations for the marriage of the duchess and Count d'Alvarez progress rapidly, and word comes that Don Columbo has given the enemy a great defeat and is returning home. He arrives just as wedding theatricals are about to be produced, and he substitutes for the play which has been rehearsed a masque in which he and his followers are the participants. During the performance the masquers beckon to the bridegroom, as if desirous of speaking to him. Alvarez goes out, and when the masquers bring him back, he is dead. Columbo removes his disguise and admits the crime; but when the duchess demands justice on the murderer, the weak King vacillates. Don Columbo accuses the duchess of trying to destroy his reputation, and of using his love as a stalking-horse while she caught her curléd favorite Alvarez, and he produces Rosaura's letter against her. The Cardinal charges the lady

with cunning, and the King accuses her of being the cause of her own
sorrows and her lover of being an accessory. Before he is through the
King blames himself as a lateral agent in poor Alvarez' death. Moreover,
there is something else to charge Columbo with than murder. The blow
was struck in the presence of the King. Columbo's victory and merits
may balance murder, but the contempt of majesty transcends the King's
power to pardon. Hence, when Columbo is sent to prison it is for
frightening the King, and not for killing his rival. The duchess is in
despair, and the Cardinal well pleased.

Act IV

Within a few days, Don Columbo is at large and graced more than
ever. He has not been *pardoned;* that word would be prejudicial to his
fame. The murder is simply forgotten as if it had been a dream, and
the general is courted as the preserver of his country. He finds a mistress
in the compliant Celinda, and one day he forces his way in to speak to
the Duchess Rosaura. It is in no contrite or humble spirit that he comes;
it is rather to tell her what remains of his revenge. She may live, he
condescendingly promises her, but if she ever again presumes to marry
he will kill the bridegroom at the altar and quench all the smiling
tapers in his blood.

But Colonel Hernando's hatred for both the general and his Cardinal-
uncle continues to smolder, and his affection for Alvarez and the
duchess is great. Hence, with little urging Hernando undertakes the
revenge, first upon Columbo and afterward upon the Cardinal. In
reward, although Columbo has vowed to kill the man who aspires to
be Alvarez' successor, the duchess promises to accept Hernando, should
she ever entertain a thought of love hereafter. As he leaves, the avenger
passes the Cardinal, who is on his way to see the duchess and with
flattery and cozenry reconcile her to what has occurred.

Shortly after, Don Hernando and Columbo with their seconds fight
a duel in a lonely spot outside the city, and Columbo and both of the
seconds are killed. The first step in the revenge has been successfully
taken, and there is no one left to reveal the name of Columbo's slayer.

Act V

Columbo's death is the cause of much grief to King and Cardinal,
and Don Hernando's absence from the court has caused suspicion to
fall upon him. For the missing colonel the Cardinal has spread his nets.
The Lady Celinda seeks to stop tongues that wag about her relations
with the dead general by securing the Cardinal's protection, and to
gain her ends makes over to the churchman her entire estate. She finds a

father for Columbo's child in Antonio, the duchess' secretary. As for that most oppressed lady, Rosaura, even before Columbo's death she has been mad—her distraction being a stratagem she assumed for protection and for greater freedom in her plots. "It makes what act [she does] . . . appear no crime, but [her] defense." But her opportunities for further intrigues are circumscribed; the King has appointed the Cardinal her guardian, and she is "a lamb given up to a tiger."

Once the duchess is within the Cardinal's talons, his plans for revenge form apace. It is too cheap a satisfaction for Columbo's death to kill her by soft charm or force. He will rape her first, then poison her, and let the world believe that she has been her own destroyer. But Don Hernando returns in disguise, visits the duchess to renew his pledge, and hides behind an arras in her room when she receives the Cardinal and has supper with him. As the wicked churchman tries to embrace Rosaura, Hernando stabs him and then takes his own life. After such care to perfect his revenge, however, the Cardinal has no intention of being "thus banded out o' th' world by a woman's plot." He believes he is mortally wounded, and to the King and the courtiers who rush in he confesses his evil life—specifically mentioning the poisoned food he says he has just given the duchess. As one last act of mercy the old hypocrite offers some powder in an ivory box as an antidote. Mixed with wine this drug, he says, is a sovereign remedy which he has been carrying with him because of a prophecy that he should die by poison. To confirm his penitence the churchman even drinks from the bowl before he offers it to the duchess. But when she has drunk, the old fox gloats over his revenge, which has at last overtaken Rosaura. She has feigned madness to give more freedom to her plots for revenge and has succeeded. The Cardinal, too, has been capable of stratagems. The ivory box contained no antidote; it was filled with deadly poison. Thus, by what seemed a pious gesture the cunning Cardinal also achieved his end. The prophecy concerning his own death was his own prediction "to abuse your faith. . . . I have wracked all my own to try your charities," he gasps at last. "The mist is risen, and there's none to steer my wand'ring bark."

••••——◆——••••

WILLIAM DAVENANT
(1606–1668)

BIOGRAPHY. The alleged godson of Shakespeare whose vanity encouraged the rumor that he was actually the natural son of the poet, William Davenant was born into a vintner's family at Oxford in 1606. He entered Lincoln College in 1621, but in the next year on the death of his father left the university to enter the services of Frances, Duchess of Richmond, and later Fulke Greville, Lord Brooke. Davenant began to write plays early, composed masques for the court, and in 1638 became Jonson's successor to the laureateship. He was involved in the troubles leading up to the Civil War, fled to France, returned in 1642, was knighted the next year at the siege of Gloucester, and again fled to France—like other Royalists—after the defeat at Marston Moor. In 1650 he set out on a mission to America for Queen Henrietta Maria, but was captured in the Channel by a Parliamentary ship, imprisoned first at Cowes Castle, Isle of Wight, and later in the Tower. While there he wrote part of his epic *Gondibert,* under constant fear, as he said, of being "interrupted by so great an experiment as dying," under the axe of Cromwell's executioner. In 1656 he gave an entertainment at Rutland House with "declamations and music after the manner of the ancients"—a thinly veiled attempt to restore the drama to the stage, and in the same year produced *The Siege of Rhodes,* often called the first English opera. At the Restoration in 1660 Davenant became one of two patentees commissioned to reopen the theatres; Davenant headed the Duke of York's Company and Killigrew the King's Company. Davenant died in 1668.

CRITICAL COMMENT. *Love and Honor,* licensed in 1634, is significant for two reasons: it harks back to the romance of Beaumont and Fletcher and forward to the heroic play, a dramatic type which enjoyed its vogue in the Restoration Period. Like the old tragi-comedy, the heroic play was highly romantic and improbable, full of surprises and tragic emotion, but resolved happily. As in the heroic play, the predominant interest in *Love and Honor* is a contest between love on the one hand and a generous self-sacrifice on the other. The three men who are the lovers of one heroine all stand for love and are prepared to make any sacrifice for it, even to braving the displeasure of the Duke. The two women throughout are actuated by ethically higher motives. Evandra is willing to sacrifice herself because she alone is the object of the Duke's revenge and will permit no other to take her place. Melora tries to palm herself off as the princess out of sheer devotion to her lady. At the close of Act III Evandra forces her lover Leonell to choose honor rather than love, even though the choice involves her probable death. Only when both girls are condemned, and the hero can meet the claims of both love and honor by proving himself to be the object of the Duke's revenge, does the play end.

   Love and Honor may lack something of the heroic sentiment of the Restoration drama; its characters are not animated by the almost supernatural nobility of the persons of a true heroic drama, and there is no conflict in the breast of either hero or heroine between love and duty. But the play at least looks forward to the Restoration type.

   On October 21, 1661, *Love and Honor* opened the new playhouse in Dorset Gardens, "richly clothed, the King giving Mr. Betterton his coronation suit, in which he acted the part of Prince Alvaro; the Duke of York giving Mr. Harris his, who did Prince Prospero; and my Lord of Oxford gave Mr. Joseph Price his, who did Leonell, the Duke of Parma's son." Under the circumstances it is not surprising to learn that the play had a great run, and "produced to the company great gain and estimation from the town."

SOURCE. No source is known for the plot.

BIBLIOGRAPHY

Collected Works: *The Dramatic Works of Sir William Davenant,* edited by J. Maidmont and W. H. Logan, 5 volumes, 1872–74.

Monographs:

    Alfred Harbage, *Sir William Davenant* (1935).
    A. H. Nethercot, *Sir William Davenant* (1939).

Early editions: 1649; 1673 [in the collected edition of Davenant's works].

Modern edition: ed. J. W. Tupper (Belles Lettres Series, 1909).

ℒOVE ᴀND HONOR
(1634)

DRAMATIS PERSONAE

ALVARO, Prince of Savoy and son of the old Duke, "a prince renown'd and precious for [his] faith and courtesy." He is in love with Evandra, though his "years a little have o'ergrown [his] youth."

LEONELL, a valiant young knight, later known to be "the Duke of Parma's son, heir to his fortune and his fame." He is in love with Evandra.

PROSPERO, a valiant young count who "hath a great and daring heart, . . . [but a] minion of the war, whom Fortune, not success from virtue sprung, hath lifted [into eminence]. . . . I think he dares meet the Devil in duel, and give him two flashes of lightning odds; but he wants that they call learning, sir; Prince Alvaro is (as they say) a philosophy man. . . . This Prospero is a Turk when's whinyard's drawn, and shines in's eyes, . . . [but he is] averse to arts and written labors of the wise." He is also in love with Evandra.

VASCO, a colonel in the Duke of Savoy's armies and captor of the old Widow. He is "as cruel as a constable that's wak'd with a quarrel out of his first sleep. . . . By this hand, a Brownist [i.e., a strict Puritan] is more amorous; a notch'd prentice a very Aretine in comparison of thee."

ALTESTO, "a very lark in the morning, . . . [and] a very owl . . . at night,"   officers and soldiers in
FRIVOLO, "a coxcomb, beyond all redemption of wit,"   the Duke of Savoy's armies.
TRISTAN,

EVANDRA, "the beauteous heir of Milan, . . . the pride of Italy, in whom the graces met to rectify themselves"; prisoner of Prospero. "Was this a subject fit to bear the pride and insolent calamity of war?" ("A virgin's heart, I know, is sooner strok'd than check'd into a kind surrender of her breast.")

MELORA, sister to Leonell, prisoner of Altesto and later known to be the daughter of the Duke of Parma; "a girl in a bongrace thus high may ravish me."

A Widow, prisoner of Vasco, a "beldam [who took] order with her maidenhead ten years ere [he] was born." Indeed, she is "so old she might have given Hercules suck. . . . She's very deaf; . . . she hath no teeth fit for a dry banquet, and dancing she is past, unless with crutches in an antimasque." ("She's rich; I knew her husband. He thriv'd much by a monopoly he had of dead women's hair; all Milan talk'd of it.")

Lelia, prisoner to Tristan and maid-in-waiting to the old Widow; "this wench has been villainously ill bred." ("I knew her mother, too; she's wondrous rich in pewter, small wine casks, and spits. . . . She kept a thatch'd nunnery in my quarter.")

The Duke of Savoy, a stern old man "whose nature is severe and mortal to [the Duke of Milan's] blood, . . . a prince that rather loves to be thought cruel than to break his vow."

His Brother, taken prisoner by Milan ten years before,⎱ disguised as ambassadors.
The Duke of Milan,   ⎰

Caladine, an old councilor to the Duke of Savoy.

A Boy who sings a serenade to the Widow.

Musicians, Soldiers, and Servants.

Setting: Savoy; Turin and the country near it at some unspecified time.

"Some easy wit, but much more cruelty."

Act I

In a war between Milan and Savoy, the latter principality is victorious, and the Princess Evandra of Milan, together with her best guard and champion, Leonell, is captured by Count Prospero. This valiant soldier, however, is something of a social upstart and a boor, who is learned enough in the discipline of war, but somewhat "averse to arts and written labors of the wise," and unlearned in philosophy and the noble deeds of gentle knights. Hence, his friend and ineffective tutor in the social graces, Alvaro, Prince of Savoy, who is "a philosophy man," reproves him for being no more "pitiful than to have led a virgin into harsh captivity," and even threatens him with death for this "recreant act," for

A choleric bear or hungry panther would
Have us'd her with more soft remorse.

Further reasons for Alvaro's outburst are that he himself is in love with Evandra and that the old Duke of Savoy, his father, has vowed to put to death any member of the house of Milan who falls into his hands. This brutal vow was prompted years before by the supposed murder of the Duke's brother at the hands of the Milanese. It is too late to call back the fair prisoner who has already been sent on to Turin; hence, to save Evandra from the old Duke's rage, Prospero promises to make what amends he can for his social error by concealing the girl in a cave in his garden.

Act II

Soon it is proclaimed in Turin that all female prisoners taken in the war shall have free liberty to return to Milan, at the end of a year, without ransom being paid. Hence, the conquerors who took captives of noble birth and rich dowry will have only a brief opportunity to win their prisoners in marriage. The Savoyard officers resolve to do their best. Altesto has taken prisoner the fair Melora; Tristan has taken Lelia; and Vasco, an old colonel, is the captor of a decrepit, rich widow, "so old she might have given Hercules suck." In contrast with the heroic main action, the absurd, coarse subplot treats of Vasco's wooing and wedding of this creature.

Meanwhile, in spite of Prospero's pretence that the Princess Evandra has been stolen away from his custody, the angry Duke has ordered diligent search to be made for her and has placed a guard at all of the gates of the city to prevent her escape. Reconciled with Alvaro for his "uncomely valor," Prospero and his friend visit the prisoner in her cave, and together they obtain the forgiveness of Evandra herself. So gracious, indeed, is the princess that it is not surprising to learn that Prospero as well as Alvaro has fallen in love with her.

Act III

Love leads Count Prospero to make other reparations. He has already renounced in Colonel Vasco's favor his claims to the ransom of Leonell, the princess' bodyguard; now Prospero pays the sum himself, so that the knight may attend his lady. He has also ransomed Melora, Leonell's sister, so that the maid of honor may take her mistress' place in the cave and Evandra make her escape in disguise. Meanwhile, suspicious of deceit, and thwarted in his search for Evandra, the cruel Duke threatens death in turn to Prospero and to Alvaro, his own heir, unless the object of his revenge be delivered to him.

It is in Prospero's garden that a complicated conflict of love and honor is fought out. Unknown to Prospero, Leonell is also in love with the princess; and when he discovers the fact, Prospero's selfish love prompts him to challenge his rival to a duel. Leonell gladly accepts the opportunity to redeem the honor he lost in his earlier defeat at Prospero's hands. Then Alvaro comes to take his last farewell of his beloved Evandra, nobly commending her to Prospero, and charging him by all the care that bred in him from youth a sense of honor that he keep Evandra safe till happier days conspire to give her liberty. Alvaro will endure the wrath of his revengeful father. By a stratagem, Evandra locks this quixotic princeling in her cave until she can devise a plan of saving him. First she turns to Prospero. Selfish love and honor barely struggle in his breast; forgetting all about false Leonell, Prospero instantly expresses his wish to tempt the fury of the Duke in the hope that when the tyrant has quenched the thirst of his revenge on one, he will relent and forgive both the prince and the princess. It will be enough for him if Evandra should strew flowers on his grave. By another stratagem the princess also locks Prospero in the cave. Rather than have "these mighty spirits lay so vast an obligation on [her] sex, and leave eternal blushes on [her] soul," Evandra determines with her maid to give herself up. She calls back Leonell and makes him swear to obey "with real faith and punctual circumstance" whatever she requests of him. Bound by the injunctions of both his beloved and his sister, Leonell is left the custodian of Evandra's prisoners, while the two girls depart to appease the angry Duke. Poor Leonell!

> *What [has he] promis'd in the rashness of*
> *[His] dull and inconsiderate love? . . .*
> *. . . That simply by a forward and*
> *Unskillful duty can consent the queen*
> *And lady of [his] life should be a sacrifice*
> *To hinder others' deaths! This sure is such*
> *A great example of a female fortitude*
> *As must undo all men.*

Act IV

Melora the maid of honor is also capable of honorable stratagem; by such means she hopes to forestall her mistress' surrender to the Duke and to set Evandra and Alvaro free. Eventually, however, Evandra discovers Melora's plan and determines to equal her maid of honor in devotion. Both girls appear before the Duke, each insisting that she is Evandra, and each trying to outplead the other and satisfy the royal revenge. Unmoved by such rare heroism, and regardless of the murmuring of his court, the Duke solves the riddle in the simplest way by ordering both women executed next morning.

Meanwhile Leonell has released Alvaro and Prospero and told them everything that has occurred. As might be expected, Prospero cannot understand why Leonell has felt bound by the oath Evandra exacted from him, and the two quarrel again. Alvaro, however, "grows solemn with his grief; . . . his mourning gives his sorrows life and length, but not the guiltless cause a remedy." Hence, when Prospero and Leonell draw to fight, this philosopher separates them with a stern rebuke. All three have loved Evandra and loved sincerely; let them

> *Shew this truth in love's philosophy,*
> *That as one object equally allures*
> *Th'ambition of our hope, so we not interchange*
> *Malignant thoughts; but sev'ral lovers, like*
> *Strange rivers that to the same ocean trace,*
> *Do when their torrents meet, curl and embrace.*

Thus, the trio resolves to "see this dismal tragedy" on the morrow, and when

> *The fatal stroke is given, swell up our sad*
> *And injur'd hearts until they break.*

Act V

Accordingly, the lovers take formal farewell of the matchless ladies, who, as Alvaro says, are now in their heroic behavior indistinguishable in beauty and in virtue. The tragedy, however, is averted. At the last moment before the axe is to fall, Leonell, the perfect knight, has his opportunity of making his gesture to save the princess and his sister. He reveals himself as Prince of Parma, a near ally to the house of Milan, confesses that his father took the Duke's brother prisoner, and so draws upon himself the wrath of the cruel Duke. The ladies are unbound, and Leonell is borne to the block. But ambassadors have arrived from Milan, one of whom reveals himself as none other than the Duke of Milan, and the other as the missing brother of Savoy, whose supposed murder ten years before had justified the Duke's cruel vow. Hence, there is no need for an execution at all. Prince Leonell is united to Princess Evandra. Prince Alvaro marries Princess Melora, to whom five years before while in disguise in Milan he had promised marriage if ever their houses' enmity should end. For valiant Prospero it is possible at this time to provide no fitting bride; he'll to the wars "and fight to win you a perpetual peace."

RICHARD BROME

(?–1652)

BIOGRAPHY.   Richard Brome "playmaker," as he preferred to call himself, is first heard of in the Induction to *Bartholomew Fair* as the author's "man," and later in some verses prefixed to *The Northern Lass* (1632) Jonson addresses him as "my old faithful servant." Probably Brome once served as Jonson's amanuensis for a time. He was certainly a hard-working playwright, composing busily for the King's Men, the Queen's Men, and Beeston's boys until the closing of the theatres. Only four of Brome's plays were published during his lifetime, and several are lost. He died in 1652.

CRITICAL COMMENT. Samuel Pepys thought *A Jovial Crew* "the most innocent play that ever I saw," when he attended a revival of it in 1661. It is a gay play, illustrative of the curious mixture of realism and romance which is characteristic of Richard Brome, and its scenes are filled with humor characters that are almost like some in Dickens. In 1731, when the popularity of *The Beggar's Opera* was at its height, *A Jovial Crew* was made into a musical and held the stage intermittently until the time of Charles Lamb.

SOURCE. No source is known for the plot.

BIBLIOGRAPHY

Collected Works: *The Dramatic Works of Richard Brome,* edited by R. H. Shepherd, 3 volumes, Pearson Reprints, 1873.

Monograph: C. E. Andrews, *Richard Brome: A Study of His Life and Works,* New Haven, 1913.

Early editions: 1652; 1661; 1684.

A JOVIAL CREW

OR THE MERRY BEGGARS

(1641)

DRAMATIS PERSONAE

SQUIRE OLDRENTS, "an ancient gentleman, and a great housekeeper, and prayed for by all the poor in the country. He keeps a guest house for all beggars far and near, costs him a hundred a year, at least; and is as well beloved among the rich." But of late the squire has grown "so pensive . . . that he makes [his daughters] even sick of his sadness," and all because a fortuneteller has predicted that his children will prove beggars. "Do you not live free, out of law or grieving any man? Are you not the only rich man lives unenvied? . . . Did ever any servant or hireling, neighbor, kindred, curse you, or wish one minute shortened of your life? . . . Do they not teach their children . . . pray for you morn and evening, and in their graces too as duly as for King and Realm? . . . Cannot these sounds conjure that evil spirit of fear out of you? . . . Shall Squire Oldrents' daughters wear old rents in their garments, . . . because a fortuneteller told you so?"

HEARTY, friend of Squire Oldrents and uncle to Martin; "a decayed gentleman, lives most upon his own mirth and [Oldrents'] means. . . . He is the finest companion of all. He does so hold [his friend] up with stories and songs and catches and t'other cup of sack, and such tricks and jigs, you would admire. . . . Would I had your merry heart!"

RACHEL, the elder,
MERIEL, a year younger,
> Oldrents' two daughters, that "have liberty enough, or may take what they please. . . . They were his house doves. . . . At defiance . . . with reputation and the dignity due to [their] father's house," they become a "brace of the handsomest beggar-brachs that ever graced a ditch or a hedge-side. . . . They were born laughing, I think."

VINCENT,
HILLIARD,
> two young gentlemen who are suitors to Oldrents' daughters, "having had their growing loves up from [their] childhoods, and the old squire's good will before all men." They also turn beggars to please the girls.

SPRINGLOVE, benevolent steward to Squire Oldrents "so young in years, . . . so ripe in goodness." In the spring he feels an "inborn strong desire for liberty" and joins the beggars. " 'Tis the season of the year that calls him; what moves her notes provokes [his] disposition by a more absolute power of Nature than philosophy can render an account for. . . . Can there no means be found to preserve life in thee, but wandering, like a vagabond?"

RANDAL, a groom, servant to Oldrents, "the youngest of half a score in the house." He passes "through many offices of the house; . . . [he is] the running baily of it." But he has a poor opinion of his own honesty. As Springlove's deputy he is entrusted with a sum of money; he had "not had it so many minutes as [he had] been in several minds about it, and most of them dishonest."

A Chaplain,
An Usher, who has served "these twenty years, sir,"
A Butler, who has "never lost the value of a silver spoon, nor ever broke a glass,"
A Cook, "the oldest cook, and the ancientest house, and best for housekeeping, in this county, or the next,"
> Servants to Oldrents, all greybeards and fellows of calculating courtesy.

JUSTICE CLACK, guardian of Amie, and "an instrument [of the law]—nay, I may say, a pillar thereof. . . . [He has] taken a hundred examinations, . . . of felons and other offenders, out of their very countenances, and wrote 'em down verbatim, to what they would have said. . . . It has served to hang some of 'em and whip the rest. . . . He must talk all. His clack must only go. . . . Nay, if we both speak together, how shall we hear one another?"

AMIE, Justice Clack's niece. Betrothed to Master Talboy, she elopes with Martin, the clerk, but falls in love with Springlove. "Such young wenches will have their own ways in their own loves, what matches soever their guardians make for 'em."

MARTIN, nephew to Hearty and "wages-fellow" to Justice Clack. He stole away the justice's ward, Amie, with her own consent, but "his mind, more clownish than his habit, depraved by covetousness and cowardice, forced [her] into a way of misery, to take relief from beggars. . . . And, then, to offer to marry [her] under a hedge, . . . without book or ring, by the chaplain of the beggars' regiment, . . . only to save charges!"

MASTER TALBOY, "bridegroom that should ha' been"; betrothed of Amie, from whom she "would have fled with any, and without a guide. . . . But that she should respect a poor base fellow, a clerk at the most, and a servingman at best, before [one] that [is] a rich man, at the worst, and a gentleman, at least, makes [him] —I know not what to say. . . . Give him more sack, to drown his suspirations."

MASTER SENTWELL,
Two other Gentlemen who search for the runaways,
> friends to Justice Clack.

OLIVER, Justice Clack's son.

The Patrico, or priest of the beggars, "that solemn old fellow that neither speaks of himself nor anybody for him. . . . He is a prophet. See how he holds up his prognosticating nose. . . . A cunning man and a fortuneteller; 'tis thought he was a great clerk before his decay. . . . He has more soul than a born beggar in him."

His Autem-mort, or wife.

SCRIBBLE, "our hedge muse-monger here, . . . a decayed poet, . . . and begs as well as the best of us. . . . Phoebus, we see, inspires as well the beggar as the poet laureate."

A Lawyer, who "should have wit and knavery too, . . . for he was an attorney, till he was pitched over the bar; and, from that fall, he was taken up a Knight o' the Post, and so he continued till he was degraded at the whipping-post."

A Soldier, "a Netherland soldier, till he ran away from his colors and was taken lame with lying in the fields, . . . after which, by a second retreat—indeed, running away—he scambled into his country, and so scaped the gallows, and then snapped up his living in the City by his wit in cheating, pimping, and such-like arts, till the cart and the pillory shewd him too publicly to the world."

A Courtier, who "begs on pleasure, I assure you, refusing great and constant means from able friends to make him a staid man; yet (the want of a leg notwithstanding) he must travel in this kind against all common reason, by the special policy of Providence. . . . His father, sir, was a courtier—a great court beggar."

A Constable, the Watch, Beggars, and Fiddlers.

Setting: England at some unspecified time.

> "Of fortunetellers, damsels, and their squires,
> Exposed to strange adventures, through the briars
> Of Love and Fate."

Act I

Oldrents, a well-to-do and kindly squire, has two great worries—the prediction of a fortuneteller that his daughters will prove beggars, and the instability of his steward Springlove, a partially reclaimed vagabond, who is seized each spring with the wanderlust and rejoins a band of beggars for the summer. In spite of the fact that he has four thousand pounds a year and has made ample provision for his girls, the first of these cares has greatly upset the old squire and thrown him into melancholy. In vain does his merry old friend Hearty point out to him that he is universally beloved, has the praises of the rich and the prayers of the poor for his generosity, and is possessed of friends enough who would not permit his daughters to be destitute, should the worst befall them. "Shall Squire Oldrents' daughters wear old rents in their garments, . . . because a fortuneteller told [him] so?" To the sensible Hearty the idea is too absurd.

Oldrents' second care is almost as great as the first. Next to his own children Springlove has been his prime concern. To help him lead a settled life Oldrents has made the honest fellow his steward; the young man's charity goes hand in hand with his master's, and his accounts are always meticulously kept. But each May, when the nightingale sings and the cuckoo calls, Springlove feels an irresistible urge toward an unfettered life. With Oldrents' connivance, Springlove provides winter quarters and entertainment for the beggars in Oldrents' barn. Now, as the season opens, Springlove presents his accounts to his master, leaves his responsibilities to Randal, his deputy, and takes the road with this "jovial crew, the only people whose happiness [he] admires."

> They dream of happiness that live in state;
> But they enjoy it that obey their fate.

Act II

Meanwhile, Rachel and Meriel, Oldrents' two daughters, have grown sick of their father's muddy spirit and weary of his melancholy house. They "cannot live but by laughing, and that aloud, and nobody sad within hearing." Although they have liberty enough, or may take what they please, they have seen the beggars in the barn, and grown envious of the absolute freedom, the mirth, and the ease of the vagabond's life. Hence, for a "spring-trick of youth," they propose to their sweethearts, Vincent and Hilliard, that for a simple trial of their loves, they join them in becoming "stark, arrant, downright, . . . statute beggars, . . . that observe no law, obey no governor, use no religion, but what they draw from their own ancient custom, or constitute themselves." Thus, in effect, voluntarily the girls fulfill the gypsy's prediction, and Springlove, whom they take into their confidence, can think of no surer way in which they can benefit their father than by thus ridding him of his fears. Accordingly, he gives the two couples all necessary instruction and present preferment into a ragged regiment of vagabonds.

At the same time, Squire Oldrents has so thoroughly entered into a covenant with his friend Hearty to be merry in spite of fortune and her riddle-maker, that he receives the news of his daughters' running away with perfect equanimity, decrees that his tenants shall live rent-free for a year and that his servants shall have their wages doubled, and attends a riotous entertainment provided by the beggars in his barn.

Act III

Begging, however, is neither so easy, so comfortable, nor so pleasant as these amateurs had expected it to be. Never did knights-errant in all adventures merit more of their ladies than do Vincent and Hilliard of theirs. They are famished and lousy, and after one romantic sleepless night of beggary, the young men are ready to give up. But they dare not let the girls know. In their turn, Rachel and Meriel—"Madam Few-clothes and my Lady Bonnyrag" in their tatters—have found out the difference "between a hard floor with a little straw and a down bed with a quilt upon't." And they dare not admit it to the young men. Moreover, life on the road exposes all four to unforeseen difficulties. Getting one's dinner by begging is not as simple as it seems. Instructed by Springlove, Vincent and Hilliard try it; but their efforts at the beggars' trade are ludicrous, their language is so formal, that "the high sheriff's son o' the shire could not have spoke better," and the results are pitiful. The prospects these novices approach become suspicious, and they are in danger of arrest. The girls fare even worse. They beg as high as the men, and being "a brace of the handsomest beggar-brachs that ever graced a ditch or a hedge-side," they are subjected to the amorous advances of gentlemen they meet on the road. Springlove is kept busy getting all of his protégés out of scrapes.

Soon the band is joined by a pair of runaway lovers for whom the whole countryside is searching; Amie, the niece of Justice Clack, has eloped with Martin, his clerk. But hardship, Martin's parsimony, and his excessive caution, have already caused their love to fade somewhat when they accept the assistance of the beggars. Springlove offers to help them to a curate who will marry them, but it is apparent that he is himself smitten by Amie.

Act IV

Among those searching for the elopers are Master Talboy, the bridegroom the justice would have forced his niece to marry, and Oliver, the justice's son. They call at Oldrents' house and are entertained hospitably by Oldrents' greybeard servants until their master's return. Talboy is an absurd weeper whose vanity, not his heart, has suffered a blow at Amie's flight. He professes not to care about his loss of her, but he cries nevertheless, and at last drowns his sorrows in sack.

Meanwhile, among the beggars, Amie has fallen completely out of love with Martin, whose mind is shown to be even more clownish than his habit, for he offers to marry her "under a hedge, . . . without book or ring, by the chaplain of the beggars' regiment, . . . only to save charges." Springlove has courted her like a gentleman, and she is ready to accept the assurance of Rachel and Meriel that Springlove is not what he seems and also to return his love. To some extent this turn of events is prompted by the marriage in the beggars' camp of a bride of four-score and a bachelor but seven years her senior. There is revelling and dancing, and the beggar-poet makes plans for a masque to honor the old couple on their wedding night. The theme is "Utopia with all her branches, . . . the Country, the City, the Court, and the Camp, epitomized and personated by a gentleman, a merchant, a courtier, and a soldier." The casting is interrupted by the arrival of officers seeking Amie, who has been betrayed by Martin, and the amateur beggars welcome the opportunity of returning to their homes.

Act V

Upon his return to the house of the "odd-ceited Justice Clack," with news of where Amie is to be found, Martin is forgiven on condition that the girl be returned home safely—and that in spite of the justice's rule to punish before he examines, so as "to have the law the surer o' [his] side." But only Talboy enjoys the news that Amie has fallen in love with one of the beggars. Before Justice Clack and his guests—Oldrents, Hearty, Oliver, Sentwell, Talboy, and the rest—the beggars perform their play variously titled "The Two Lost Daughters," "The Vagrant Steward," "The Old Squire and the Fortuneteller," "The Beggars' Prophecy," and "The Merry Beggars." The story is a familiar one to the whole audience. The beggar-lawyer plays Oldrents, a broken-down soldier plays Hearty, and Springlove, Rachel, Meriel, Vincent, and Hilliard, enact their own roles. Realizing that the purpose of the play is but to make peace with him, Squire Oldrents does not see it through, but forgives everyone forthwith. But he learns that the beggars' patrico once had a sister to whom Squire Oldrents made love, and that their son— identified by an Agnus Dei emblem—is none other than Springlove. Oldrents' sadness is completely shaken off. He gives his blessing to all his children; the engagements of all three are announced; he confers upon Springlove a thousand pounds a year to entertain his wife, and upon the patrico a competent annuity for life. Talboy may whine his eyes out and go without, but Hearty promises to find another wife for his nephew Martin.

INDEX OF CHARACTERS

This Index records only those characters which are specifically named, which have a part in the action of the play in which they appear, or which are in some other way distinguished. Characters merely referred to are not listed, nor are the hosts of "Ladies, Gentlemen, Officers, and Attendants." Page references are to the appropriate lists of *Dramatis Personae*, where the character is described.

A Fight with a Snail (Cf. *Thersites,* page 14)

From Guy Marchant's *Kalendier des Bergers,* 1500.

INDEX OF PLAYS AND PLAYWRIGHTS

The Murder of Arden of Feversham

From the ballad entitled: "The Complaint and Lamentation of Mistress Arden of Feversham."